SHOCKRO

*Major Problems in American Immigration
and Ethnic History*

D1016263

DISCARD

MAJOR PROBLEMS IN AMERICAN HISTORY SERIES

GENERAL EDITOR
THOMAS G. PATERSON

Major Problems
in American Immigration
and Ethnic History

DOCUMENTS AND ESSAYS
EDITED BY

JON GJERDE
UNIVERSITY OF CALIFORNIA, BERKELEY

HOUGHTON MIFFLIN COMPANY   BOSTON   NEW YORK

Editor-in-Chief: Jean L. Woy
Senior Associate Editor: Frances Gay
Associate Project Editor: Rebecca Bennett
Associate Production/Design Coordinator: Deborah Frydman
Marketing Manager: Sandra McGuire
Manufacturing Coordinator: Andrea Wagner

Cover Designer: Sarah Melhado
Cover Image: *Sailing for Liberty,* Chen Tsing-Fang, Lucia Gallery, New York City.
© SuperStock.

Credits: Prints on pp. 149–150 from Print Collection, Miriam and Ira D. Wallach Division of Art, Prints and Photographs. The New York Public Library Astor, Lenox and Tilden Foundations.

Copyright © 1998 by Houghton Mifflin Company. All rights reserved.

No part of this work may be reproduced or transmitted in any form or by any means, electronic or mechanical, including photocopying and recording, or by any information storage or retrieval system without the prior written permission of the copyright owner unless such copying is expressly permitted by federal copyright law. With the exception of nonprofit transcription in Braille, Houghton Mifflin is not authorized to grant permission for further uses of copyrighted selections reprinted in this text without the permission of their owners. Permission must be obtained from the individual copyright owners as identified herein. Address requests for permission to make copies of Houghton Mifflin material to College Permissions, Houghton Mifflin Company, 222 Berkeley Street, Boston, MA 02116-3764

Printed in the U.S.A.

Library of Congress Catalog Card Number: 97-72475

ISBN: 0-395-81532-0

23456789–DH–01 00 99 98

To my friend and mentor
Rudy Vecoli

JUL 2000

Contents

CHAPTER 11
Immigrant and Ethnic Life in Twentieth-Century America, 1924–1965
Page 343

CHAPTER 12
Immigrants and Ethnics Amid Depression and War, 1929–1965
Page 381

CHAPTER 13
Immigration and Ethnicity in the Post-Industrial World, 1965 to the Present
Page 415

CHAPTER 14
Immigration Transforms America, 1965 to the Present
Page 450

Preface

Questions of immigration and ethnicity, citizenship and race have long vexed American society. Scarcely a day passes without newspaper and television reports that highlight the benefits and costs of immigration, portray differences among ethnic and racial groups, sketch government policy options, or explore the meaning of citizenship in the United States. This book illustrates that despite their present urgency, these topics have deep roots in the past. The United States, and the British American colonies that preceded it, has always been a society marked by ethnic and racial diversity. For centuries, the nation and its residents have puzzled over questions of citizenship and belonging to the nation. And episodes of racial and ethnic intolerance continue to trouble America. Learning about the nation's rich ethnic and racial history as well as about its failures in addressing squarely the issues of immigration, ethnicity, race, and citizenship will aid us in understanding and untangling problems of the present day.

Immigration to the United States is an epic story. A rich literature depicts the lives of people belonging to the scores of nationalities that made, and continue to make, their way to the United States. *Major Problems in American Immigration and Ethnic History* gives voice to the many people who experienced the joys and heartaches of life in a new country. This book presents the experiences of immigrants and ethnics from a wide variety of cultural contexts that span the centuries of American development. Chapter 1 explores different approaches to the study of immigration and ethnic history. Then beginning with the interaction between native peoples and those moving to the Americas from Europe and Africa in the 1600s and 1700s (Chapters 2–3), this volume considers the nineteenth-century migration prior to American industrialization (Chapters 4–5), the period of massive industrial migration in the decades straddling the turn of the twentieth century (Chapters 6–10), and concludes with the wave of immigration in recent decades that has changed the ethnic profile of the nation (Chapters 11–14).

As the book moves forward chronologically, several issues are covered in each period: the background of the migration and the peopling of the United States (Chapters 2, 4, 6, 11, and 14); the formation and development of ethnic and racial communities (Chapters 2, 4, 7, 8, 11, and 14); and considerations of citizenship, antagonism toward immigrants, and conceptions of nationhood in this most ethnic nation (Chapters 3, 5, 9, 10, 12, and 13). By exploring common themes in diverse historical contexts, we can attempt to weave together the varieties of immigrant experiences with these broader issues of immigration and ethnicity that were crucial contributors to American history.

Like other volumes in this series, *Major Problems in American Immigration and Ethnic History* approaches its subject through both primary sources and the interpretations of scholars. Readers are invited to examine critical issues through diverse viewpoints and approaches. Chapter introductions and headnotes to the documents and essays sections introduce the problem or theme and suggest key questions. The documents reflect the temper of the times, convey the intensity of debate, and encourage students to develop their own perspectives and to evaluate the explanations of others. The essays reveal how scholars can read documents in multiple ways, examine different aspects of the same problems, and come to different conclusions about what happened. Each chapter ends with a bibliography to guide further investigation. The format of the books in this series enables students to appreciate the complexity not only of history itself but the *writing* of history and to see that people who lived in the past and the issues they confronted are still instructive for today's students as they become scholars and citizens.

I have accumulated many debts in working on this volume, and I would like to thank those who helped me. Erika Lee, who assisted in the completion of the volume, has been consistently helpful, cheerful, and right on the mark in making suggestions for selections and anthology structure. The staff at Houghton Mifflin— Jean Woy, Frances Gay, Susan Westendorf, Rebecca Bennett, and Diane Kraut— have been great. I also thank the series editor, Thomas G. Paterson, who initiated this project and worked with the Houghton Mifflin editors to shape the volume.

I am grateful to the following colleagues who shared syllabi and made vital suggestions: David Hollinger, James Kettner, Elaine Kim, and Alex Saragosa, at University of California at Berkeley; Rudolph Vecoli and Lee Bernstein at University of Minnesota; Henry B. Leonard and Robert P. Swierenga at Kent State University; Thomas Dublin at University of Binghamton; Reed Ueda at Tufts University; Roger Daniels at University of Cincinnati; Philip Gleason and Walter Nugent at University of Notre Dame; Randall Miller at St. Joseph's University; K. Scott Wong at Williams College; John Bodnar and Robert L. Payton at Indiana University; Lizabeth Cohen and Hasia Diner at New York University; Tyler Anbinder at George Washington University; Walter Kamphoefner at Texas A & M University; Moses Rischin at San Francisco State University; John Higham at Johns Hopkins University; Elliott Barkan at California State University at San Bernardino; Frederick Luebke at University of Nebraska; David Gerber at University of Buffalo; Donna R. Gabaccia at University of North Carolina, Charlotte; Kerby A. Miller at University of Missouri, Columbia; Lawrence H. Fuchs at Brandeis University; Marilyn B. Halter at Boston University; June Namias at University of Alaska, Anchorage; Victor Greene at University of Wisconsin at Milwaukee; Janet Worrall at University of Northern Colorado; William Van Vugt at Calvin College; Milton Cantor and Suzanne Model at University of Massachusetts at Amherst; Mark Wyman at Illinois State University; Alan Kraut at American University; Barbara M. Posadas at Northern Illinois University; Peter Kivisto at Augustana College; Lynn Dumenil at Occidental College; Raymond A. Mohl and Stanford M. Lyman at Florida Atlantic University; Marianne S. Wokeck at Indiana University–Purdue University at Indianapolis; Deborah Dash Moore at Vassar College; Frances Kraljic at Kingsborough Community College of City University of New York; Barbara Winslow at Medgar Evers College of the City University of New York; Joel Perlmann at Bard College; James Grossman at the Newberry Library; Sally M. Miller at University of the Pacific; Noah Pickus at Middlebury College; Marianne Sheldon at Mills College; Barry R. Chiswick and Melvin G. Holli at University of Illinois at Chicago; Leonard Dinnerstein at the University of Arizona; Brian Gratton at Arizona State University; Diane Vecchio at Furman University; N. Rader at Empire State College; Robert B. Grant at Framingham State College; Lloyd J. Graybar at Eastern Kentucky University; Robert D. Cross at University of Virginia; Joe W. Trotter at Carnegie Mellon University; James Allen at California State University at Northridge; Sucheng Chan at University of California at Santa Barbara; David Goldberg at Cleveland State University; Mark J. Miller at the Center for Migration Studies; Josh DeWind at the Social Science Research Council; Anita Olson Gustafson at North Park College; Robert Hueston at University of Scranton; and Charles T. Johnson at Western Michigan University.

The following reviewers provided detailed and extremely helpful written comments on draft tables of contents: Elliott R. Barkan, California State University at San Bernardino; Lawrence H. Fuchs, Brandeis University; Sally M. Miller, University of the Pacific; and K. Scott Wong, Williams College. And I would like to thank Eliott Ashkenazi, Keith P. Dyrud, Dolores Liptak, Stina L. Hirsch, Sarah Refo Mason, Barbara J. Rozek, Judith A. Simonsen, Pien Versteegh, and Jacqueline Conant Whipple.

J. G.

Approaches to American Immigration and Ethnic History

It has been observed time and again that the United States is a nation of nations. Unlike many peoples of the world, Americans beginning with British colonization lived in a polyglot society that was continually replenished by immigrants. For the first Americans—the indigenous peoples—this immigration was nothing less than a disaster that wreaked havoc on their societies. For the immigrants, the circumstances varied from the enslavement of Africans forced to leave their home to the free migration of others who celebrated the freedom and opportunity they perceived in the United States. If we agree that we are a nation of mainly immigrants and their descendants, however, we cannot leave it at that. For this fact just prompts many questions that we need to address. At the most basic level, we need to rethink American history. What does it mean to colonial history that the bulk of immigrants in the eighteenth century did not come from England or that people of English ancestry composed less than one-half of the population in 1790 shortly after the Constitution was drafted? How is our understanding of America's urban history, its political history, and its social history shaped when we consider that immense waves of immigration continually repeopled the nation? How can we decipher the periodic episodes of virulent anti-immigrant sentiments that coursed through American society and targeted, among other groups, Roman Catholics, Asian immigrants, and political radicals?

When we focus on the immigrants themselves, new questions arise. What was the immigrant experience like, and how did it change across the centuries? How did the experience vary for different ethnic and racial groups, and why? Why did the nation integrate the various waves of immigrants differently? What models of national integration did Americans use to understand the relationship between their country and the members of many ethnic groups?

This anthology will illustrate that there are no easy answers to these questions. Moreover, it will argue that although the United States was, for the most part, a nation of immigrants, there was no single immigrant experience. Rather, a variety of historical circumstances lay the groundwork for a diversity of immigrant profiles. Likewise, it will contend that there was no single model of national integration, but an assortment of understandings of how the United States should be configured that modulated over time according to historical events and processes. It is

*the task of the historian to explore and seek to understand this diversity that consti-
tutes the American experience.*

*Whereas the chapters that follow explore how immigration historically in-
formed and, in many ways, created the American nation, this introductory chapter
contains short selections that lay out the major problems of immigration and ethnic
history from a historiographical perspective.*

*As we puzzle over whether the best way to understand immigration should be
from the perspective of uprootedness or transplantation or whether the focus should
be on assimilation or ethnicity, we need to remain aware of the variety of experiences of immigration and ethnicity over nearly four centuries. For example, how
did the immigration experience differ for African slaves, Italian peasants, and recent Korean immigrants? How did the conceptions of nation change as the United
States grew from a fragile republic in the eighteenth century to a world power in
the twentieth? By grappling with these questions in a variety of contexts, we are
able to understand better the kaleidoscope of life in the United States.*

ESSAYS

Historians for some time have puzzled over the immigrant experience. Oscar Handlin,
a historian at Harvard University, argued in 1951 that the experience of immigration
was one of uprootedness and alienation. Torn from their peasant communities by the
inroads of capitalism, many immigrants were forced to move from their disintegrating
villages to a lonely city and an alienating industrial workplace. No longer belonging to
their village and, for the most part, never really able to belong to American society,
immigrants were lost, rootless, alienated. For more recent historians, such as John
Bodnar of Indiana University (1985), the operative metaphor of the immigrant experience is transplantation, rather than uprooting. To be sure, Bodnar argues from a Marxist perspective, immigrants were affected by a capitalist transformation; indeed, he
calls them "children of capitalism." But these immigrants to the United States were
not without agency. Rather, they used familiar institutions, such as the family and the
community, to seek a degree of control of their lives. Although they could not oversee
the direction of economic change, even as they were transplanted by the forces of capitalist development, they too transplanted institutions that aided them in fashioning a
life as best they could.

If historians have been interested in the immigrant experience, they have also
sought to understand how immigrants and their children were integrated into a nation
that was based on a multiplicity of ethnic experiences but searching for a common
identity. Historian John Higham of Johns Hopkins University (1981) addresses the
question of assimilation in the nineteenth century and observes that the localism that
characterized American society segmented the nation into ethnic groups that could coexist—in many cases, peacefully and, occasionally, not so peacefully—under the umbrella of an American nation. However, by the late nineteenth century, according to
Higham, this segmentation was breaking down as Americans sought to create a more
interdependent, more centralized society. It was then that assimilation of immigrants
and others became a significant problem.

In another approach, a group of scholars, including Kathleen Conzen of the University of Chicago, focuses on the presence of ethnic groups rather than on the process
of assimilation (1992). They suggest that ethnicity was a cultural construction continually reinvented to provide symbols to unify an evolving ethnic group. As immigrants
"created" ethnic groups and ethnicity, Americans as a whole participated in a similar

process of inventing a national identity. Although these two efforts were related to one another, they were nonetheless parallel processes. These historians contend that the invention of a national identity did not necessarily supersede the creation of separate ethnicities. In so doing, they have denied the centrality of the process of assimilation.

Immigration Portrayed As an Experience of Uprootedness

OSCAR HANDLIN

The immigrant movement started in the peasant heart of Europe. Ponderously balanced in a solid equilibrium for centuries, the old structure of an old society began to crumble at the opening of the modern era. One by one, rude shocks weakened the aged foundations until some climactic blow suddenly tumbled the whole into ruins. The mighty collapse left without homes millions of helpless, bewildered people. These were the army of emigrants.

The impact was so much the greater because there had earlier been an enormous stability in peasant society. A granite-like quality in the ancient ways of life had yielded only slowly to the forces of time. From the westernmost reaches of Europe, in Ireland, to Russia in the east, the peasant masses had maintained an imperturbable sameness; for fifteen centuries they were the backbone of a continent, unchanging while all about them radical changes again and again recast the civilization in which they lived.

Stability, the deep, cushiony ability to take blows, and yet to keep things as they were, came from the special place of these people on the land. The peasants were agriculturists; their livelihood sprang from the earth. Americans they met later would have called them "farmers," but that word had a different meaning in Europe. The bonds that held these men to their acres were not simply the personal ones of the husbandman who temporarily mixes his sweat with the soil. The ties were deeper, more intimate. For the peasant was part of a community and the community was held to the land as a whole.

Always, the start was the village. "I was born in such a village in such a parish"—so the peasant invariably began the account of himself. Thereby he indicated the importance of the village in his being; this was the fixed point by which he knew his position in the world and his relationship with all humanity.

The village was a place. It could be seen, it could be marked out in boundaries, pinned down on a map, described in all its physical attributes.

* * * *

Yet the village was still more. The aggregate of huts housed a community. Later, much later, and very far away, the Old Countrymen also had this in mind when they thought of the village. They spoke of relationships, of ties, of family, of kinship, of many rights and obligations. And these duties, privileges, connections,

From *The Uprooted* by Oscar Handlin. Copyright 1991 by Oscar Handlin; copyright © 1973 by Oscar Handlin. By permission of Little, Brown and Company.

links, had each their special flavor, somehow a unique value, a meaning in terms of the life of the whole.

They would say then, if they considered it in looking backward, that the village was so much of their lives because the village *was* a whole. There were no loose, disorderly ends; everything was knotted into a firm relationship with every other thing. And all things had meaning in terms of their relatedness to the whole community.

In their daily affairs, these people took account of the relationships among themselves through a reckoning of degrees of kinship. The villagers regarded themselves as a clan connected within itself by ties of blood, more or less remote. That they did so may have been in recollection of the fact that the village was anciently the form the nomadic tribe took when it settled down to a stable agricultural existence. Or it may have been a reflection of the extent of intermarriage in a place where contact with outsiders was rare. In any case, considerations of kinship had heavy weight in the village, [sic] were among the most important determinants of men's actions.

But the ties of blood that were knotted into all the relationships of communal life were not merely sentimental. They were also functional; they determined or reflected the role of individuals in the society.

No man, for instance, could live alone in the village. Marriage was the normal expected state of all but the physically deformed. If death deprived a person of his marriage partner, all the forces of community pressure came into play to supply a new helpmate. For it was right and proper that each should have his household, his place in a family.

The family, being functional, varied somewhat to suit the order of local conditions. But always the unit revolved about the husband and wife.

* * * *

The family was then the operating economic unit. In a sense that was always recognized and respected, the land on which it worked was its own. The head of the household, it was true, held and controlled it; legally, no doubt, he had certain powers to waste or dispose of it. But he was subject to an overwhelming moral compulsion to keep it intact, in trust for those who lived from it and for their descendants who would take a place upon it.

The family's land was rarely marked out in a well-defined plot. The house, the garden, and the barnyard with its buildings were its own, but the bulk of agricultural lands were enmeshed in a wide net of relationships that comprehended the whole community.

Once, it seems, the village had held and used all the land communally; until very recent times recognizable vestiges of that condition persisted. The pastures and meadows, the waste, the bogs and woodlands, existed for the use of all. It hardly mattered at first that the nobility or other interlopers asserted a claim to ownership. The peasants' rights to graze their cattle, to gather wood for building and peat for fire, in practice remained undisturbed. In some parts of Europe, even the arable lands rested in the hands of the whole village, redivided on occasions among its families according to their rights and condition.

Even where particular pieces of land were permanently held, it was rarely in such consolidated plots as the peasants might later see on American farms. A holding consisted rather of numerous tiny strips that patched the slopes of the countryside in a bewildering, variegated design. A Polish peasant, rich in land, could work his nine acres in forty different places. . . .

Many important aspects of agriculture, moreover, were altogether communal. The pastures were open to all villagers; in the common fields, the boys tended the cattle together or a hired herdsman had their oversight. Women, working in groups at the wearisome indoor tasks, spinning or plucking cabbage leaves, could turn chores into festive occasions, lighten their labors with sociable gossip. The men were accustomed to give aid to each other, to lend or exchange as an expression of solidarity. After all, folk must live with each other.

So the peasants held together, lived together, together drew the stuff of life from an unwilling earth. Simple neighborliness, mutual assistance, were obligations inherent in the conditions of things, obligations which none could shirk without fear of cutting himself off from the whole. And that was the community, that the village—the capacity to do these things together, the relationships that regulated all.

* * * *

Emigration was the end of peasant life in Europe; it was also the beginning of life in America. But what a way there was yet to go before the displaced would come to rest again, what a distance between the old homes and the new! Only the fact that these harried people could not pause to measure the gulf saved them from dismay at the dizzy width of it.

Perhaps it is fortunate that, going onward, their sights are fixed backward rather than forward. From the crossroad, the man, alone or with his wife and children, turns to look upon the place of his birth. Once fixed, completely settled, he is now a wanderer. Remorseless circumstances, events beyond his control, have brought him to this last familiar spot. Passing it by, he becomes a stranger.

Sometimes, the emigrants at that moment considered the nature of the forces that had uprooted them. All the new conditions had conspired to depress the peasants into a hopeless mass, to take away their distinguishing differences and to deprive them, to an ever-greater extent, of the capacity for making willful decisions. The pressure of the changing economy had steadily narrowed every person's range of choices. Year by year, there were fewer alternatives until the critical day when only a single choice remained to be made—to emigrate or to die. Those who had the will to make that final decision departed.

That man at the crossroads knew then that this was a mass movement. Scores of his fellows in the village, hundreds in other villages, were being swept along with him. Yet he moved alone. He went as an individual. Although entire communities were uprooted at the same time, although the whole life of the Old World had been communal, the act of migration was individual. The very fact that the peasants were leaving was a sign of the disintegration of the old village ways. What happened beyond the crossroads, each would determine by himself. It was immensely significant that the first step to the New World, despite all the hazards it involved, was the outcome of a desperate individual choice.

He who turned his back upon the village at the crossroads began a long journey that his mind would forever mark as its most momentous experience. The crossing immediately subjected the emigrant to a succession of shattering shocks and decisively conditioned the life of every man that survived it. This was the initial contact with life as it was to be. For many peasants it was the first time away from home, away from the safety of the circumscribed little villages in which they had passed all their years. Now they would learn to have dealings with people essentially different from themselves. Now they would collide with unaccustomed problems, learn to understand alien ways and alien languages, manage to survive in a grossly foreign environment.

* * * *

The crossing in all its phases was a harsh and brutal filter. On land in Europe, in the port of embarkation, on the ocean, in the port of arrival, and on land in America, it introduced a decisive range of selective factors that operated to let through only a few of those who left the Old World. In part these factors were physical; the hardier survived the dangers and the difficulties, the weaker and more dependent fell by the side. In part, however, these factors were more than physical, for they measured also the power of adaptation: only those who were capable of adjusting from peasant ways to the needs of new conditions and new challenges were able to absorb the successive shocks of migration.

For the crossing involved a startling reversal of roles, a radical shift in attitudes. The qualities that were desirable in the good peasant were not those conducive to success in the transition. Neighborliness, obedience, respect, and status were valueless among the masses that struggled for space on the way. They succeeded who put aside the old preconceptions, pushed in, and took care of themselves. This experience would certainly bring into question the validity of the old standards of conduct, of the old guides to action.

Perhaps that was the most luminous lesson of the crossing, that a totally new kind of life lay ahead. Therein was the significance of the unwillingness of the peasants to undertake the journey in the old traditional communal units. Despite the risks entailed, they preferred to act as individuals, each for himself. Somehow they had been convinced that the village way which had been inadequate to save them at home would certainly prove inadequate away from home.

Not that they derived much joy or comfort from the conviction. In any case they suffered. The separation itself had been hard. The peasants had been cut off from homes and villages, homes and villages which were not simply places, but communities in which was deeply enmeshed a whole pattern of life. They had left the familiar fields and hills, the cemetery in which their fathers rested, the church, the people, the animals, the trees they had known as the intimate context of their being.

Thus uprooted, they found themselves in a prolonged state of crisis—crisis in the sense that they were, and remained, unsettled. For weeks, and often for months, they were in suspense between the old and the new, literally in transit. Every adjustment was temporary and therefore in its nature bore the seeds of maladjustment, for the conditions to which the immigrants were adjusting were strange and ever changing.

As a result they reached their new homes exhausted—worn out physically by lack of rest, by poor food, by the constant strain of close, cramped quarters, worn out emotionally by the succession of new situations that had crowded in upon them. At the end was only the dead weariness of an excess of novel sensations.

Yet once arrived, the immigrants would not take time to recuperate. They would face instead the immediate, pressing necessity of finding a livelihood and of adjusting to conditions that were still more novel, unimaginably so. They would find then that the crossing had left its mark, had significantly affected their capacity to cope with the problems of the New World they faced.

* * * *

Loneliness, separation from the community of the village, and despair at the insignificance of their own human abilities, these were the elements that, in America, colored the peasants' view of their world. From the depths of a dark pessimism, they looked up at a frustrating universe ruled by haphazard, capricious forces. Without the capacity to control or influence these forces men could but rarely gratify their hopes or wills. Their most passionate desires were doomed to failure; their lives were those of the feeble little birds which hawks attack, which lose strength from want of food, and which, at last surrendering to the savage blasts of the careless elements, flutter unnoticed to the waiting earth.

Sadness was the tone of life, and death and disaster no strangers. Outsiders would not understand the familiarity with death who had not daily met it in the close quarters of the steerage; nor would they comprehend the riotous Paddy funerals who had no insight of the release death brought. The end of life was an end to hopeless striving, to ceaseless pain, and to the endless succession of disappointments. There was a leaden grief for the ones who went; yet the tomb was only the final parting in a long series of separations that had started back at the village crossroads.

In this world man can only be resigned. Illness takes a child away; from the shaft they bring a father's crippled body; sudden fire eats up a block of flimsy shanties, leaves half of each family living. There is no energy for prolonged mourning. Things are as they are and must remain so. Resist not but submit to fortune and seek safety by holding on.

In this world the notion of improvement is delusive. The best hope is that matters grow not worse. Therefore it is desirable to stand against change, to keep things as they are; the risks involved in change are incomparably more formidable than those involved in stability. There is not now less poverty, less misery, less torture, less pain than formerly. Indeed, today's evils, by their nearness, are far more oppressive than yesterday's which, after all, were somehow survived. Yesterday, by its distance, acquires a happy glow. The peasants look back (they remember they lived through yesterday; who knows if they will live through today?) and their fancy rejoices in the better days that have passed, when they were on the land and the land was fertile, and they were young and strong, and virtues were fresh. And it was better yet in their fathers' days, who were wiser and stronger than they. And it was best of all in the golden past of their distant progenitors who were every one a king and did great deeds. Alas, those days are gone, that they believed existed, and now there is only the bitter present.

In this world then, as in the Old Country, the safest way was to look back to tradition as a guide. Lacking confidence in the individual's capacity for independent inquiry, the peasants preferred to rely upon the tested knowledge of the past. It was difficult of course to apply village experience to life in America, to stretch the ancient aphorisms so they would fit new conditions. Yet that strain led not to a rejection of tradition but rather to an eager quest for a reliable interpreter. Significantly, the peasants sought to acknowledge an authority that would make that interpretation for them.

Their view of the American world led these immigrants to conservatism, and to the acceptance of tradition and authority. Those traits in turn shaped the immigrants' view of society, encouraged them to retain the peasants' regard for status and the divisions of rank. In these matters too striving was futile; it was wiser to keep each to his own station in the social order, to respect the rights of others and to exact the obligations due. For most of these people that course involved the acceptance of an inferior position. But was that not altogether realistic? The wind always blew in the face of the poor; and it was in the nature of society that some should have an abundance of possessions and others only the air they breathed.

* * * *

. . . Eagerly the immigrants continued to look back across the Atlantic in search of the satisfactions of fellowship. But the search was not rewarded. Having become Americans, they were no longer villagers. Though they might willingly assume the former obligations and recognize the former responsibilities, they could not recapture the former points of view or hold to the former judgments. They had seen too much, experienced too much to be again members of the community. It was a vain mission on which they continued to dispatch the letters; these people, once separated, would never belong again.

Their home now was a country in which they had not been born. Their place in society they had established for themselves through the hardships of crossing and settlement. The process had changed them, had altered the most intimate aspects of their lives. Every effort to cling to inherited ways of acting and thinking had led into a subtle adjustment by which those ways were given a new American form. No longer Europeans, could the immigrants then say that they belonged in America? The answer depended upon the conceptions held by other citizens of the United States of the character of the nation and of the role of the newcomers within it.

Immigration Portrayed As an Experience of Transplantation

JOHN BODNAR

Because capitalism attempted to regulate human resources as well as natural resources, it became the central force in shaping individual lives in industrial regions

From John Bodnar, *Transplanted: A History of Immigrants in Urban America,* copyright © 1985. Reprinted by permission of Indiana University Press.

and in agricultural areas to which they were linked. In one manner or another populations in these regions in the United States, Mexico, Asia, or Europe were forced to make decisions about how they would confront the imperatives of this new economic and social order. Some embraced the promise of the system wholeheartedly; some rejected it completely. Most struggled the best they could somewhere in between. Since these responses were shaped largely by the material condition and social position in which individuals found themselves and their relationship to existing resources and the means of production, they helped to divide society into divergent classes, cultures, and ideologies. These social fissures produced a dialectic which explained a good deal of the political, social, and economic tension of urban America. In the American city and industrial town, workers protested the level of pay and the pace of production. Sometimes, culture served as a basis for group life and the societal struggle for power, control, and wealth turned on ethnic or cultural terms. This explanation has probably been used by scholars of immigration more than any other. Preindustrial cultures were thought to survive the transition to capitalism and determine the behavior and thought of immigrant workers and merchants. Divergent cultures were even used to explain varying group patterns of behavior and attainment.

The thrust of contemporary American social history has probed beyond the realm of group dynamics, however, and has exposed the private and personal dimension of individuals facing the historical currents of capitalism, industrialization, and urbanization alone. Thus, recent scholarly inquiry has inundated readers with thousands of pieces of information on household life, work routines, mobility, childhood, and even female fertility which have enriched the texture of the historical portrait. This direction, however, has rightfully disturbed some scholars who have lamented the abandonment of coherent theories which can somehow hold all of this disparate information together. Furthermore, the focus on private history has assuredly diminished the stress of Marxist scholars on power relationships and class division and of consensus historians on progress and uplift. Private history, the pursuit of the particular, has clearly deserved the charge of being history with the politics left out. The converse was also true: Marxist and Progressive history both paid insufficient attention to the struggle and perceptions of individuals.

This study of American immigrants in the century after 1830 certainly cannot reconcile all the problems of new ways of thinking about the dimensions of social and political history and of reconciling the long-standing debates between advocates of a class-based history and a past explained by cultural imperatives. Political history and private history, however, need not remain apart nor continue to launch critiques at one another. Beyond ethnic cultures, narrow conceptions of class, and group dynamics lies another level of explanation which can at least be partially glimpsed from an analysis of the relationship between immigration and capitalism.

Immigrant adjustment to capitalism in America was ultimately a product of a dynamic between the expanding economic and cultural imperatives of capitalism and the life strategies of ordinary people. Historian Gabriel Kolko wrote that millions of immigrants in industrial America had neither the desire nor the capacity to relate to the social order of capitalism. But, as the preceding discussion suggested, this observation was far from accurate. Immigrant people by definition related to capitalism and its attendant social order in complex and often ingenious ways which have often been misunderstood. Generally, this process of understanding and adjusting was carried on in two broad categories. In reality two immigrant Americas existed. One consisted largely of workers with menial jobs. The other, a smaller component, held essentially positions which pursued personal gain and leadership. Immigrants did not enter a common mass called America but adapted to two separate but related worlds which might be termed broadly working class and middle class.

These two components were represented everywhere. Middle-class supporters of capitalism could be found among commercial farmers in Mexico, Sicily, or Hungary, entrepreneurs within immigrants groups, or industrialists in all American cities. They wielded relatively more power than most of their contemporaries, enjoyed extensive reinforcement from loyal supporters in political and public life including government officials, educators and even reformers and placed a high value on individual freedom, personal gain, political power, and an improved future. Below them, although far more numerous, stood millions of ordinary people whose perspective was considerably more circumscribed. They were not immune to the satisfaction to be derived from personal gain or political power but could not realistically indulge in such pursuits for too long a period of time. Their power to influence public affairs and their supporters in public institutions were minimal. Tied considerably more to the concerns of family and communal welfare, they focused daily activities, in the words of folklorist Henry Glassie, "in the place where people are in control of their own destinies." These public and private spheres were not totally separate and, indeed, were part of a common system, but one was substantially more expansive, confident, and less circumscribed than the other.

Somewhere in time and space all individuals meet the larger structural realities of their existence and construct a relationship upon a system of ideas, values, and behavior which collectively gives meaning to their world and provides a foundation upon which they can act and survive. Collectively their thought and action are manifestations of a consciousness, a mentality, and ultimately a culture. Immigrants, who were after all common men and women, could not completely understand what was taking place as capitalism entered their world. They were not fully aware of the sweeping political and economic decisions and transitions which were altering the nineteenth and twentieth centuries. In lieu of a comprehensive understanding of social and historical change, they fashioned their own explanations for what they could feel and sense. To give meaning to the realities and structures which now impinged upon them, they forged a culture, a constellation of behavioral and thought patterns which would offer them explanations, order, and a prescription for how to proceed with their lives. This culture was not a simple extension of their past, an embracement of the new order of capitalism, or simply an affirmation of a desire to become an American. It was nurtured not by any one reality such as their new status as workers but was produced from whatever resources were at hand: kinship networks, folklife, religion, socialism, unions. It was a product of both men and women, believers and non-believers, workers and entrepreneurs, leaders and followers. It was creative yet limited by available options. It drew from both a past and a present and continually confronted "the limits of what was possible." The demands of economic forces, social structures, political leaders, kin, and community were real and could not be ignored. Life paths and strategies were informed by knowledge from the past and estimates about the future but largely from the specific options of the present. Immigrants were free to choose but barely.

It must be made clear, however, that this culture of everyday life, while generated at the nexus of societal structures and subjective experience, was ultimately the product of a distinct inequality in the distribution of power and resources within the system of capitalism. It would be convenient to call this a culture of the working class but it was not tied that simply to the means of production or the workplace and was not simply the prerogative of laborers. It was also tied to traditional culture, although it was certainly not entirely ethnic or premodern. Its core was a fixation upon the needs of the family-household for both laborers and entrepreneurs and the proximate community. The relative lack of resources and of a comprehensive knowledge of vast social economic change forced immigrants (and probably ordinary people in other places) to focus an inordinate amount of their lives in two areas. First, they had to devise explanations of their status in terms intelligible to themselves by drawing on folk thought, religion, ancestry, and similar devices close at hand. Second, they had to devote nearly all their attention to that portion of their world in which they actually could exert some power and influence: the family household, the workplace, and the local neighborhood or community. They sought, in other words, a degree of meaning and control. Like peasants in the Pyrenees studied by Pierre Bourdieu, they forged a world view that allowed for safeguarding what was considered "essential" at all times. The alternative would have been a life completely out of their hands, entirely bewildering and completely orchestrated by industrialists, public institutions, and economic forces.

The thrust of almost all previous scholarship seeking to interpret the immigrant experience in urban America around considerations of ethnic culture or class has been much too narrow and has failed to make a crucial distinction between the content and foundation of immigrant mentalities. The content which drew from ethnic traditions and present realities seemed as much cultural as it was class-based. That is to say, the newcomers acted as workers but also remained tied to selected ethnic symbols and institutions which appeared to mute solely class concerns. But the basis for this preoccupation with familiar ways, as well as with working-class realities, was to be found in the placement of these ordinary people in the larger social structure of capitalism. Even traditional family and ethnic communities were a preoccupation ultimately not because they were familiar but because they represented somewhat manageable and understandable systems to people who possessed little control or understanding of the larger society. Because they possessed relatively less material and social influence, they were preoccupied with understanding and constructing life at very immediate levels. They did this in part because they were relatively powerless to affect the sweeping currents of their times but, ironically, in doing so they actually generated a degree of power and social control of their own and transcended a status as simply victims.

This pragmatic culture of everyday life accepted the world for what it was and what it was becoming and yet ceaselessly resisted the inevitable at numerous points of contact in the workplace, the classroom, the political hall, the church, and even at home. *Mentalité* for the immigrants was an amalgam of past and present, acceptance and resistance. Ordinary people could never live a life insulated from the actions of their social superiors, nor could they ever fully retreat from their present. Peasants responded to the whims of nobles, immigrants responded to the profit-seeking activities of commercial farmers or industrial capitalists. Since they could not control the direction of either elites or capital, they placed most of their priorities and focused most of their attention on the immediate, the attainable, the portion of their world in which they could exert some influence. This was true in "material life" and life under capitalism as well. By implication the culture of everyday life, shaped primarily by social status and unequal ownership of the means of production and informed by traditions and communal needs, always aspired to modest goals and was devoid of extremely radical or liberal impulses. The extent newcomers would go in either direction depended a great deal on the ability and impact of various leaders. And still ordinary people left their mark. Leaders constantly had to modify their ideology to effectively attract immigrant support. Peasants in the homelands could do little to dissuade the upper classes from promoting the spread of commercial agriculture. They did, however, force local elites to pay more for their farm labor by deciding to emigrate. Similarly, immigrants could not make decisions where to locate plants or invest large amounts of capital, but they could force industrialists to change personnel and wage policies by their transiency which stemmed from their private agendas. Some scholars might call this a form of class antagonism, but it also represented an effort to construct life strategies within available options.

Ultimately, then, the mentality and culture of most immigrants to urban America was a blend of past and present and centered on the immediate and the attainable. Institutions from the past such as the family-household were modified but retained; the actions of landed elites at home and industrial capitalists abroad forced them to confront a new market and social order which they accepted but somewhat on their own terms. They would move, several times, if they had to, and become wage laborers or even small entrepreneurs. They did so not because they were victimized by capitalism or embraced it but because they pursued the immediate goal of family-household welfare and industrial jobs which were very accessible. If they had the skills or capital, which some did, even a small business was not out of the question. Those that moved had eschewed any retreat into a fictitious peasant past or becoming large, commercial farmers, although many still dreamed of living on the land. Overall, however, for people in the middle, immigration made a great deal of sense. Barrington Moore, who has written about German workers in the early twentieth century, has suggested that they were consumed by practical issues, such as the possible inability of the breadwinner to earn a living. Secondary concerns did include injustice and unfair treatment at the workplace but basically their fears and hopes revolved around everyday life: getting enough to eat and having a home of one's own. They expressed hopes for a better future but were usually too busy making ends meet to do much about it. The pattern apparently transcended time and space.

Since capitalism was the central force which created these immigrants, it is still not possible to conclude they made an inevitable and smooth transition to a new way of life and a new culture. They were not one-dimensional beings rooted only to old ways of life or a new economy. They did not proceed simply from an ethnic world to a class world. Rather their consciousness and culture were continually grounded in several levels of status and culture prior to emigration and after arrival as well. It was tied simultaneously to the lower levels of tradition, household, and community as well as to the higher levels of capitalism, industrialization, and urbanization. Between the microscopic forces of daily life, often centering around ethnic communal and kinship ties, and the macroscopic world of economic change and urban growth stood the culture of everyday life. This was a culture not based exclusively on ethnicity, tradition, class, or progress. More precisely, it was a mediating culture which confronted all these factors. It was simultaneously turbulent and comforting: It looked forward and backward, although not very far in either direction. It could not hope to exert the influence on history that industrial capitalism did, but it was far from being simply reflexive. Depending on premigration experience and leadership in America, it could prepare the way for a transition to a working-class or a middle-class America but seldom did it lead to a complete embracement of any new order.

If the culture of everyday life dominated the lives of most American immigrants, it did not mean that all newcomers were alike. Even within similar ethnic aggregations, a preoccupation with the practical and the attainable did not create identical life strategies. Some manifested a sojourning orientation and planned to return home fortified in their ability to live off the land. Others came to stay and effectively exploited their skills and resources to establish careers and businesses in urban America. Still others never really made up their minds and simply worked from day to day. Divergent resources and orientations in the homeland, moreover, often led to varying rates of attainment and participation in the culture of capitalism; those who settled in higher social stations and were already further removed from "material life" prior to emigration began to move more purposefully toward the new culture of acquisitiveness and personal gain. The origins of inequality in urban America were not located solely in the industrial workplace, or the city, or even ethnic cultures. They were also rooted in the social structure of the homeland and immigrant stream. Such divisions, in fact, would fragment immigrant communities and insure that urban-ethnic enclaves and settlements would only exist temporarily. But fragmentation at the group level should not obscure the ties that most of the first generation had to the culture of everyday life and the need to take what was available and secure the welfare of those closest to them. Immigrants were generally part of the masses and the culture of the masses in the nineteenth and much of the twentieth century was not solely traditional, modern, or working class. It was a dynamic culture, constantly responding to changing needs and opportunities and grounded in a deep sense of pragmatism and mutual assistance. Fernand Braudel spoke of three levels of historic time: political, which was rapid and episodic; social, which was modulated by the slower pace of everyday life; geographical, where change was nearly imperceptible. Immigrants were closely preoccupied with social time and the realities of the immediate and the present, although the levels of time and culture were never completely separated.

The center of everyday life was to be found in the family-household and the proximate community. It was here that past values and present realities were reconciled, examined on an intelligible scale, evaluated, and mediated. No other institution rivaled the family-household in its ability to filter the macrocosm and microcosm of time and space. Kinship and the household, of course, are not necessarily identical concepts and family and work need not be inextricably linked. The truth of the matter, however, was that during the first century of American capitalism they inevitably were. The family-household mobilized resources and socialized people. Even though capitalism entered the peasant household in the homeland and caused a shift from subsistence to market production, the transition was essentially one of function and not form. The linking of individuals to a wage rather than a household economy did not inevitably lead to a decline of the family-household. In the first century of industrial capitalism, the family-household continued to remain effective because supporting institutions of capitalism such as the state, public education, and even federally regulated unions had not yet become strong enough to fully penetrate the confines of private space.

Because of the continued viability of the family-household, the small community or urban neighborhood, usually built upon congeries of such units, continued to function and the culture of everyday life persisted. But this did not mean that private space was immune from public ritual and activity. Repeatedly, albeit episodically, the culture of everyday life was punctuated by "political time," by the rhetoric and ambitions of competing leaders. A new society and a new economy presented opportunities for newcomers with particular skills or resources to pursue power and middle-class status, to forsake the ambiguity of the culture of everyday life for the single-minded culture of power, wealth, and personal gain. Among all groups, not just among Japanese or Jewish entrepreneurs, this process of middle-class formation and pursuit of individual power took place to one extent or another.

While leaders emerged within all immigrant communities, they did not all advocate ideas and values consistent with the new order of capitalism or with each other. Many successful entrepreneurs advocated rapid Americanization and individual achievement. These leaders, such as Carl Schurz, A. P. Giannini, and Peter Rovnianek, were usually reinforced by the larger society which supported them and shared their faith. American political parties actually subsidized part of the ethnic press and further attempted to violate the boundaries of everyday life. Opposed to these accommodations, however, were those who exhibited a stronger defense of tradition and communal values. They included clerics and fraternal leaders, were usually less tied to the new economy than [were] politicians and entrepreneurs, and while not opposed to Americanization, were skeptical of rapid change, growing secularism, and the dangers inherent in a pluralistic society which threatened their elevated status. Irish Catholic prelates, for instance, could allow for Americanization but not accept public education in a society dominated by other cultures and religions. Advocates of religious authority and homeland causes, while often bitterly divided, were both ultimately defenders of the "everyday culture" in which they usually held prominent positions. Because they were tied closer to the culture of the masses, they generally exerted a stronger influence than leaders attached to external cultures such as trade unionists, socialists, educational reformers, or national political figures.

For leaders to be effective at any time and able to mobilize support for their activities they continually faced the need to establish their authority and bind the dominant and the subordinate through mutual obligations. In new circumstances the competition for this authority could be intense. The presence of vocal clerics, nationalists, fraternalists, socialists, trade unionists, and politicians underscored

just how great the competition was. Since these potential leaders usually lacked resources for direct coercion, they inevitably generated ideologies revolving around
words and symbols which were designed to appeal to the broadest possible numbers. It was the free market for leadership that produced the rich web of rhetoric
which pervaded immigrant communities. Religion, socialism, ethnic nationalism,
Americanization, unionism, and vocationalism were only a few of the ideological
manifestations of competing leaders who sought followers and who offered pre-
scriptions for living within the new order of industrial capitalism.

But not all leaders or elites were equally effective. Ideology cannot be reduced
to simple strategies advanced by the prominent to further their own interests nor
does it simply flow from the top to the bottom of society. The rhetoric and symbols
of leaders were most effective when they reflected to some extent the feeling and
thought of ordinary people themselves. Educational reformers, socialists, some political figures, and even trade unionists often failed to realize this fully. Those that
did, such as unionists who recruited ethnic organizers or editors who championed
the cause of the homeland, were much more successful in mobilizing portions of
the immigrant population. The Irish Land League, the rise of Catholic schools, the
quest for German-language instruction, the rise of the United Mine Workers, and
the cause of Russian Jews even in the 1890s illustrate how private issues could effectively enter public space. Religion, the homeland, and labor matters were probably the most debated issues. These matters concerned key elements of the past
and present and of everyday culture; religion and labor especially had deep implications for a well-ordered family-household.

Immigrants not only influenced their leaders in an episodic fashion but resisted intervention into the only world they could control on an ongoing basis even
while adjusting to a new economic order. They were not simply duped by a hege-
monic culture. Neither the prominent within their groups nor the owners of the
means of production were beyond their influence. Immigrant laymen fought to
maintain control of churches, Italians practiced rituals in defiance of clerical authority, religious and ethnic schools were established to resist the culture of outsiders, laborers controlled production, left jobs they did not like and struck spontaneously in colorful, communal fashion if it suited their purposes. They never tired
of assisting friends and relatives to find jobs and probably had as much as managers to do with shaping the informal system of employment recruitment which
dominated American industry during the century before World War II. Leaders
who urged newcomers to support extended schooling or various political parties
usually made little headway unless they addressed the issues relating to the family-
household and community that newcomers felt strongest about: homeownership,
jobs, neighborhood services, steady work, and traditional beliefs.

Immigrants lived in scattered urban-ethnic enclaves which were heavily working class. But these settlements were neither structurally nor ideologically monolithic. Newcomers were tied to no single reality. The workplace, the church, the
host society, the neighborhood, the political boss, and even the homeland all competed for their mind and bodies. On a larger level, industrial capitalism could not
be stopped. But on the level of everyday life, where ordinary people could inject
themselves into the dynamic of history, immigrants acquiesced, resisted, hoped,
despaired, and ultimately fashioned a life the best they could. Transplanted by

forces beyond their control, they were indeed children of capitalism. But like children everywhere they were more than simply replicas of their parents; independence and stubborn resistance explained their lives as much as [did]˙their lineage. Their lives were not entirely of their own making, but they made sure that they had something to say about it.

The Problem of Assimilation in the United States

JOHN HIGHAM

To speak of assimilation as a problem in nineteenth-century America is, in an important sense, to indulge in anachronism. That is because nineteenth-century Americans seemed for the most part curiously undaunted by, and generally insensitive to, the numerous and sometimes tragic divisions in their society along racial and ethnic lines. Leaving aside some significant exceptions, the boundaries between groups with different origins and distinct cultures caused little concern. Assimilation was either taken for granted or viewed as inconceivable. For European peoples it was thought to be the natural, almost inevitable outcome of life in America. For other races assimilation was believed to be largely unattainable and therefore not a source of concern. Only at the end of the century did ethnic mixing arouse a sustained and urgent sense of danger. Only then did large numbers of white Americans come to fear that assimilation was *not* occurring among major European groups and that it was going too far among other minorities, notably blacks, Orientals, and Jews.

This acute consciousness of assimilation as a problem marked a great crisis in ethnic relations. Extending from the 1890s to the 1920s, the crisis persisted until a new ethnic pattern came into being. The objects of this paper are, first, to describe the ethnocultural system of the nineteenth century in a way that may help us to understand more fully the ensuing crisis, and second, to glimpse within that crisis the origins of a new system of ethnic relations that has unfolded in subsequent decades.

Before considering assimilation as a newly perceived problem at the end of the nineteenth century, it will be necessary to give some account of assimilation as a process in earlier decades. Here we may note in passing that the blending, merging, and incorporation of peoples has occurred on many levels in the United States, not just on the level of nation-building that historians and politicians ordinarily have in mind when they speak of assimilation. Surely the most impressive instances of assimilation in American history are to be found in the formation of racial or national minorities from more particularistic antecedents. The African slaves imported into the English colonies in the late seventeenth and eighteenth centuries were a medley of peoples, differing widely in appearance, traditions, and language. In their own minds they belonged to distinct tribes, not to a race. Their English masters threw them together quite indiscriminately, however, and gave them a single, inclusive name: Negroes. Accordingly, the plantations of the colo-

Reprinted by permission of Transaction Publishers. "Integrating America: The Problem of Assimilation in the Nineteenth Century" by John Higham, *Journal of American Ethnic History*, Fall 1981. Copyright © 1981 by Transaction Periodicals; all rights reserved.

nial South functioned as a remarkable melting pot, in which distinctions between Mandigoes, Iboes, Angolans, and other African peoples were largely obliterated. Partly because the English ascribed a common identity to them, and partly because certain common themes in west African cultures facilitated their amalgamation in spite of disparate languages and customs, the Afro-Americans gradually became a single people in spite of enormous differences in their circumstances and their exposure to Anglo-American influences.

Although the slaves present the most striking example, a similar process of assimilation entered into the making of major European ethnic groups as well. Most of the peasants and villagers who came to the United States in the nineteenth century brought with them very little sense of having belonged to a nation. At first they thought of themselves as the people of a particular local area—a village or at most a province. They were not Germans but Wurttembergers, Saxons, and Westphalians; not Italians but Neapolitans, Sicilians, Calabrians, and Genoese; not Chinese, but members of particular districts and clans. Speedily in most cases, slowly in a few, these localized attachments were submerged within the wider identities we know today: identities that demonstrate both the special bond a common language provides and the special respect Americans have accorded to the principle of nationality as a basis of social identification.

When we turn from this very successful, intermediate level of assimilation, which Victor Greene has called "ethnicization," and consider the higher level on which an overarching American consciousness has formed, we find a more confusing and complicated situation. An enormous amount of inter-ethnic assimilation did in fact occur in the experience of individuals. Even while the emerging ethnic groups of nineteenth-century America were crystallizing, each of them was losing highly mobile families who cast off the old ways and the old identity, became in speech and manners indistinguishable from the native white population, and gradually faded into it. In the South, for example, many German Jews in the nineteenth century were so fully accepted into the white society that their descendants ceased to be Jewish. Meanwhile, in the North, miscegenation and mobility made possible a continual, silent passing of light-skinned Negroes across the color line. According to a Negro physician in 1844, at least six of his former classmates at the New York African Free School were then living as whites.

Even more important, entire ethnic groups lost much of their distinctiveness in the course of time. In upper New York State the asperities between the old Dutch settlers and incoming Yankees from New England gradually softened. By the 1820s the descendants of the French Huguenots in New Rochelle and elsewhere retained little more than their names to mark their origin. By the end of the nineteenth century the Irish Catholics, though still keenly distrusted in New England, were elsewhere sufficiently accepted and well established so that comic magazines no longer felt free to portray them as drunken louts with the faces of gorillas. In the twentieth century the crumbling of the great German-American community is the most familiar and spectacular case of collective assimilation. In some degree a multi-ethnic melting pot indubitably *has* worked—but so imperfectly, so inconsistently, so incompletely! It worked, but it did not prevail. Whereas virtually all of the local or tribal identities that the people of this country brought with them from other lands have been obliterated, every one of the racial and national groupings that was created in America has stubbornly persisted. It is not an outright failure of assimilation that needs to be understood in comprehending nineteenth-century America, but rather the peculiar contradictions the process of assimilation displayed.

The most obvious of these contradictions was between theory and reality. The theory of assimilation, as formulated by Hector St. Jean de Crèvecoeur in the Revolutionary era, seemed to allow for no exceptions. "Here individuals of all nations are melted into a new race of men," this wandering Frenchman declared. The Revolutionary belief that America offered a new start for mankind acquired, from Christian and classical sources, rich millennial overtones. Listen, for example, to Herman Melville's musings as he watched German emigrants boarding ships for America:

> We are not a nation, so much as a world. . . . Our ancestry is lost in the Universal paternity; and Caesar and Alfred, St. Paul and Luther, and Homer and Shakespeare are as much ours as Washington, who is as much the world's as our own. We are the heirs of all time, and with all nations we divide our inheritance. On this Western Hemisphere all tribes and peoples are forming into one federated whole; and there is a future which shall see the estranged children of Adam restored as to the old hearthstone in Eden.

More prosaically, Oliver Wendell Holmes described his compatriots as "the Romans of the modern world—the great assimilating people." This was not enough for George Bancroft, the first great historian of the United States, who declared: "Our country stands . . . as the realisation of the unity of the [human] race."

In actuality, of course, white Americans had no intention of translating a national myth into a literal command. Even the most radical abolitionists shrank from the accusation that they were promoting an amalgamation of races. Yet some kinds of assimilation did bridge the chasm between blacks and whites; and the relations of both blacks and whites with other minorities varied enormously. What needs to be explained is not a simple opposition between theory and practice but rather a baffling mix of inconsistencies.

✱ ✱ ✱ ✱

. . . the glaring contrasts we find in nineteenth-century America owe their salience to a distinctive combination in American culture of jealous localism and universalistic beliefs.

By localism I mean both a condition and an attitude. I mean a condition of decentralization, enabling towns and other local districts to be largely autonomous communities. I mean also a reinforcing attitude that such autonomy is the key to liberty. The settlements from which the United States emerged shared nothing more than an animus against remote, consolidated power. Scattered over 1,300 miles of the Atlantic coast, the English colonies in the eighteenth century were separated from one another to a degree hard to imagine today. Few people travelled from one province to another. Little news passed between them. Most colonists also felt remote from their own provincial capitals. While colonial assemblies continually chipped away at the power of royal governors and London officials, within each colony districts that were relatively distant from the centers of trade felt a similar distrust for the more cosmopolitan towns. In every colony the revolutionary impulse sprang from a profound suspicion of consolidated power. No wonder it took well over a decade before the patriots of 1776 could bring themselves to create a national government, and then only with great difficulty and reluctance.

Once established, the new government merely stabilized and perpetuated the traditional dispersal of power. As late as 1831, to serve a population of thirteen million people who were spreading rapidly over a territory of 1,750,000 square miles, the United States government employed just 11,491 civilians. Only 666 of them resided in the raw little capital on the banks of the Potomac. The rest were scattered across the country and beyond—a few in customs houses and embassies while nearly all the others operated the tiny post offices of which contemporary genre painters have given us many charming glimpses. It would not be unfair to say that the United States government in the nineteenth century consisted during peacetime mostly of post offices, and to conclude with Robert Wiebe that America was "a society without a core."

The point was made more colorfully by Henry James:

> No State, in the European sense of the word, and indeed barely a specific national name. No sovereign, no court, no personal loyalty, no aristocracy, no church, no clergy, no army, no diplomatic service, no country gentlemen, no palaces, no castles, nor manors, nor old country houses, nor parsonages, nor thatched cottages, nor ivied ruins; no cathedrals, nor abbeys, nor little Norman churches; no great universities nor public schools—no Oxford, nor Eton, nor Harrow; no literature, no novels, no museums, no pictures, no political society . . .

By putting first among America's shortcomings the absence of a state "in the European sense of the word," James's litany suggests that this was the most embracing of the symbols of legitimacy, the most fundamental of the structures of authority, that he missed. A society lacking that kind of state might have to do without all of the rest. Such was the situation of the American republic. Very scantily endowed with the outward trappings of power and social connection, it had almost no visible means of instilling allegiance. There was a flag and a Capitol, but no capital city in a European sense. Even the Capitol building was, at the time of the Civil War, still undergoing major alterations. The flag was not yet fully defined. The only really imposing memorial in the country, the Washington Monument, was not completed until 1885.

Nevertheless, this almost disembodied state lived as an idea—resonant, compelling, and universally espoused. The Americans depended on an ideology—a set of abstract principles—to hold their country together. Although nationalism everywhere in the nineteenth century acquired an ideological thrust, it seems unlikely that any other country defined itself so preeminently as a community of belief, a nation gathered around a creed. Americans who lived or travelled in Europe sometimes regretted the relative abstractness of American patriotism. To Nathaniel Hawthorne it seemed "as cold and hard . . . as the steel spring that puts in motion a powerful machinery," and he contrasted it with the human warmth and rich concreteness of an Englishman's sense of nationality. Yet the nonspecific and therefore universal aspect of American nationalism served a loose-knit, heterogeneous society well. A national ideology enabled Americans to do without—and even told them why they did not need—the unitary state, the imposing monuments, and the dense social fabric that James observed in Europe.

We are now in a position to understand how the localization of power in nineteenth-century America allowed innumerable separations to flourish within a matrix of national unity. First, decentralization encouraged ethnic groups to act differently in different contexts. As a result none of them—neither the powerful nor the weak—could present a united front against the rest of society. The dominant segment of the population was of course severely handicapped, in defining an exclusive identity or maintaining an exclusive preeminence, by the absence of a centralized state and its accouterments. Who were these Anglo-Americans, to call them by a name that always sounded slightly foreign or presumptuous? There was little to mark them as anything but a miscellany of regional and local types—southerners and northerners, easterners and westerners, rural and urban folk—all intensely conscious of their differences from one another. Similarly, ethnic minorities in the United States could not close ranks in stubborn resistance to assimilation because they did not, as in Europe, confront a centralized state controlled by others. At most, ethnic groups might hope to gain preponderance in particular localities; when that happened, decentralized power came easily into their hands. The system worked for them, and elicited their allegiance.

Secondly, decentralization fostered a scattering of population. This enabled local ethnic clusters to keep a certain distance from one another, particularly where economic competition could be acute. For a homogeneous people to have sprung from America's diversities, extensive interaction would have been required *between* the subordinate groups in addition to the contacts each might have with the dominant majority. It is true that minorities could not escape some involvement with one another, but the attention historians have given to spectacular incidents of conflict like the New York Draft Riots of 1863 has made us overlook the great extent to which ethnic groups in the nineteenth century kept out of one another's way. Moving west, European immigrants avoided areas where blacks were concentrated. At the same time the presence of huge immigrant populations in northern cities discouraged the northward migration of blacks. The principle of mutual avoidance also influenced the distribution of German and Irish immigrants, the former settling in the Middle West and the latter in the Northeast. Where large concentrations of both groups materialized, as in Detroit and Milwaukee, they clustered in widely separated divisions of the city. Thus, in a decentralized society mutual avoidance checked *both* conflict *and* assimilation.

The conditions that limited conflict between ethnic groups while promoting differences within each group were admirably suited to an ideological definition of America as a whole. A single canopy of beliefs made an otherwise loose-knit society of dissociated towns and neighborhoods comprehensible. Violations of the ideological norms could usually be understood as pragmatic adjustments to local realities rather than fundamental contradictions. Public schools could segregate minorities or preserve their cultures, depending on the particular ethnic accommodation in each locality, while all of them taught the same promises of the American ideology.

* * * *

. . . nineteenth-century Americans developed no consistent theory of how they should behave. The decentralization of society and the disjunction of values and traditions made every alternative feasible and no one policy authoritative. Issues could not crystallize; discontents could not converge. The ethnic crises of the 1850s present a major exception, but still a partial one. In all essential respects the antebellum pattern survived until the 1890s. Then a general and prolonged upheaval in ethnic relations, lasting from the nineties into the 1920s, marked the breakdown of that pattern and the beginning of a new social order.

The clearest indication of a fundamental change at the end of the nineteenth century was the interlinking of racial and religious tensions that had formerly been discrete. During the 1850s, for example, the Know-Nothing movement had been unable to formulate a national program. In the North Know-Nothings focussed almost exclusively on foreign Catholics as the subversive element in American society. Southerners, living in dread of slave conspiracies and of abolitionists, were completely unresponsive to the Catholic issue. Californians, preoccupied with the problem of the Chinese, cared nothing about the phobias of the South or the fears of the Northeast; and the indifference was reciprocated. In contrast, the ethnic hostilities that developed around the beginning of the twentieth century acquired a more generalized character. One fed into another. Southern whites became aroused for the first time about Catholics, Jews, and immigrants. Midwesterners and Far Westerners started to think of themselves as defenders of an America beleaguered on all sides. A sweeping rejection of all outsiders—of everyone who deviated from a conservative, Protestant, northern European pattern—gave a new, comprehensively ethnocentric meaning to the term "prejudice."

What was happening? In brief, the conditions that had sustained the intricate segmentation of the nineteenth century no longer prevailed. The local community lost much of its cherished autonomy, leaving Americans feeling increasingly vulnerable to the intrusion of outsiders. At the same time that the separateness of groups and localities diminished, the wall of separation between opposing values in American minds gave way as well.

The first of these two changes, the shift away from localism, is the more obvious and familiar. Recent interpretations of the political, economic, and cultural turmoil of the 1890s have highlighted, as the critical change in American life at that time, a new awareness of interdependence. Under the inroads of industrialism, bureaucracy, and specialized knowledge, the self-sufficiency of the "island communities" was irretrievably passing. As national organizations crisscrossed an increasingly crowded terrain, more and more of the American people became integrated into economic networks and status hierarchies that drastically reduced the significance of the local arena. On the international level also the world contracted alarmingly, and the entanglements of interdependence multiplied. Wherever one looked, the state was becoming a palpable reality. All this could be enormously stimulating to Americans who were ready and eager to move outward into a larger, less provincial milieu. It could also be very threatening. Either way, a consciousness of racial, national, and ethnic differences dramatically intensified.

The tightening mesh of interdependence goes far to explain why the internal disjunctions within nineteenth-century culture also broke down. The willingness of Americans to live with a divided heritage and an ambiguous national identity declined. A demand for consistency and sincerity—for an end to lies, deception and hypocrisy—swept through the tangled underbrush of American opinion in the first two decades of the twentieth century. Baffled by the obscure, complex forces that filled the modern world, millions of Americans cried out for light in dark places, for simplicity and wholeness, and finally for purification of the entire society. This was one of the meanings of Progressivism.

The Invention of Ethnicity in the United States

KATHLEEN NEILS CONZEN, DAVID A. GERBER, EWA MORAWSKA,
GEORGE E. POZZETTA, AND RUDOLPH J. VECOLI

Since the United States has received recurring waves of mass immigration, a persistent theme of American history has been that of the incorporation of the foreign born into the body politic and social fabric of the country. The dominant interpretation both in American historiography and nationalist ideology had been one of rapid and easy assimilation. Various theories which predicted this outcome, i.e., Anglo-conformity and the Melting Pot, shaped the underlying assumptions of several generations of historians and social scientists.

Historical studies in the United States over the past two decades have called these assumptions into question. Scholars have increasingly emphasized the determined resistance with which immigrants often opposed Americanization and their strenuous efforts at language and cultural maintenance. They no longer portray immigrants as moving in a straight-line manner from old-world cultures to becoming Americans. At the same time recent studies agree that the immigrants' "traditional" cultures did not remain unchanged. Rather immigration historians have become increasingly interested in the processes of cultural and social change whereby immigrants ceased to be "foreigners" and yet did not become "One Hundred Per Cent Americans." From immigrants they are said to have become *ethnic Americans* of one kind or another.

Ethnicity has therefore become a key concept in the analysis of this process of immigrant adaptation. Classical social theories as applied to the study of immigrant populations as well as indigenous peoples had predicted the inevitable crumbling of "traditional" communities and cultures before the forces of modernization. However, from the 1960s on, the rise of ethnic movements in the United States and throughout the world have demonstrated an unexpected persistence and vitality of ethnicity as a source of group identity and solidarity. These phenomena stimulated an enormous amount of research and writing on the nature of ethnicity as a form of human collectivity.

Although there are many definitions of ethnicity, several have dominated discussions of immigrant adaptation. One, stemming from the writings of anthropologists Clifford Geertz and Harold Isaacs, has emphasized its primordial character, originating in the "basic group identity" of human beings. In this view, persons

Reprinted by permission of Transaction Publishers. "The Invention of Ethnicity: A Perspective from the USA" by Kathleen Neils Conzen, David A. Gerber, Ewa Morawska, George E. Pozzetta, and Rudolph Vecoli, Journal of American Ethnic History, Fall 1992. Copyright © 1984. Reprinted by permission of The Johns Hopkins University Press.

have an essential need for "belonging" which is satisfied by groups based on shared ancestry and culture. For some commentators, like Michael Novak, such primordial ethnicity continued to influence powerfully the descendants of the immigrants even unto the third and fourth generations. Others, like sociologist Herbert Gans, have dismissed the vestiges of immigrant cultures as "symbolic ethnicity," doomed to fade away before the irresistible forces of assimilation.

A different conception of ethnicity, initially proposed by Nathan Glazer and Daniel Moynihan, deemphasizes the cultural component and defines ethnic groups as interest groups. In this view, ethnicity serves as a means of mobilizing a certain population behind issues relating to its socioeconomic position in the larger society. Given the uneven distribution of power, prestige, and wealth among the constituent groups in polyethnic societies and the ensuing competition for scarce goods, people, so the argument goes, can be organized more effectively on the basis of ethnicity than of social class. Leadership and ideologies play important roles in this scenario of "emergent ethnicity." While "primordial ethnicity" both generates its own dynamic and is an end in itself, "interest group ethnicity" is instrumental and situational.

The authors of this essay propose to explore a recently formulated conceptualization: "the invention of ethnicity." With Werner Sollors, we do not view ethnicity as primordial (ancient, unchanging, inherent in a group's blood, soul, or misty past), but we differ from him in our understanding of ethnicity as a cultural construction accomplished over historical time. In our view, ethnicity is not a "collective fiction," but rather a process of construction or invention which incorporates, adapts, and amplifies preexisting communal solidarities, cultural attributes, and historical memories. That is, it is grounded in real life context and social experience.

Ethnic groups in modern settings are constantly recreating themselves, and ethnicity is continuously being reinvented in response to changing realities both within the group and the host society. Ethnic group boundaries, for example, must be repeatedly renegotiated, while expressive symbols of ethnicity (ethnic traditions) must be repeatedly reinterpreted. By historicizing the phenomenon, the concept of invention allows for the appearance, metamorphosis, disappearance, and reappearance of ethnicities. This essay will seek to illustrate the processes which we believe account for periods of florescence and decline, for continuities and innovations, for phases of saliency and quiescence, in the histories of particular ethnic groups.

The invention of ethnicity furthermore suggests an active participation by the immigrants in defining their group identities and solidarities. The renegotiation of its "traditions" by the immigrant group presumes a collective awareness and active decision-making as opposed to the passive, unconscious individualism of the assimilation model. In inventing its ethnicity, the group sought to determine the terms, modes, and outcomes of its accommodation to "others." We conceive of this as a process of negotiation not only between immigrant group and dominant culture, but among various immigrant groups as well. One of the virtues of this research strategy is that it focuses upon *relationships* among specific immigrant groups and between them and the dominant ethnoculture, in this case, the Anglo American. These interactions, which could be competitive, cooperative, or conflictual, and perhaps a combination of all three, are seen as essential components of the process of ethnic group formation and definition.

Immigrant groups themselves were by no means homogeneous; they were divided by varying combinations of regional origin, dialect, class, politics, and religion. Internal debates and struggles over the nature of the group's emerging ethnicity were inevitable. One of the purposes of invented traditions was to provide symbols and slogans which could unify the group despite such differences. The symbolic umbrella of the ethnic culture had to be broad and flexible enough to serve several, often contradictory, purposes: provide the basis for solidarity among the potential members of the group; mobilize the group to defend its cultural values and to advance its claims to power, status, and resources; and, at the same time, defuse the hostility of the mainstream ethnoculture by depicting the compatibility of the sidestream ethnoculture (to use Joshua Fishman's term) with American principles and ideals. On the level of individual psychology, the invention of ethnicity sought to reconcile the duality of the "foreignness" and the "Americanness" which the immigrants and their children experienced in their everyday lives.

The concept of the invention of ethnicity also helps us to understand how immigration transformed the larger American society, engendering a new pluralistic social order. Once ethnicity had been established as a category in American social thought, each contingent of newcomers had to negotiate its particular place within that social order. Anglo Americans had to assimilate these distinctive groups into their conception of the history and future of "their" country, and to prescribe appropriate social and cultural arrangements. Inevitably all Americans, native born and immigrant, were involved in a continual renegotiation of identities. Further, a process of syncretism occurred by which much of ethnic cultures was incorporated into changing definitions of what was American and what it meant to be an American. Without corresponding to either the Anglo-conformity or Melting Pot models of assimilation, the interaction of mainstream ethnoculture and sidestream ethnoculture wrought major changes in both . . .

The Dual Construction of Ethnicity in Nineteenth-Century America

If immigrants were engaged in a continuous process of ethnic invention, so too was American society at large—and in a dual sense. At the onset of mass immigration to the United States in the second quarter of the nineteenth century, Americans themselves were engaged in a self-conscious project of inventing a national identity, and in the process found themselves also inventing the category of ethnicity—"nationality" was the term they actually used—to account for the culturally distinctive groups in their midst. These two inventions were closely intertwined with one another and indeed with the invention of particular immigrant ethnicities in ways that historians have only recently begun to uncover.

As long as historians regarded ethnic groups as "real" social groupings, it was easy to assume that once Americans became aware of their presence, they necessarily recognized them as ethnic groups. The only problematic issue was whether a given group would be evaluated positively or negatively. Thus the conventional narrative has Americans becoming aware of immigrants by the 1830s, and coming to think of Irish and Germans, in particular, as forming groups and exhibiting particular kinds of behavior. To some Americans, their behavior posed a sufficient threat to the political order that they voiced demands for immigrant exclusion from political participation for an extended period of time. Over time, as negative assessments of immigrants increased and grounds for criticism multiplied, Americans resorted to programs of forced Americanization and the immigration restriction acts of the 1920s. Historians long interpreted such nativist lack of confidence in the assimilative power of America as pathological and ethnocentric. But at the same time, efforts to cultivate an appreciation of the benefits to America of distinctive immigrant groups intensified, and a new positive valuation of a pluralist society began to gain headway.

But this conventional narrative raises questions. Only some immigrants were perceived and judged as what would come to be called ethnic groups. English immigrants, for example, often exhibited distinctive behaviors, yet generally were not placed within this category. Their foreignness was not problematic in the same way as that of immigrants of other European origins, hence it was not "seen"; the English had no ethnicity in American eyes. More importantly, why did Americans start seeing ethnicity when they had not done so before? Certainly, cultural differences and relatively closed immigrant communities were a common feature of the eighteenth-century landscape in many parts of the new nation. People were aware of the differences, some even worried over their political implications. But most had confidence in either the universality of human reason or the transforming power of free political institutions to make immigrants into Americans. When John Quincy Adams warned his German correspondent in 1819 that he would have to shed his European skin if he came to America, Adams was not imposing a demand so much as stating what he perceived to be a fact: immigrants themselves might never completely lose the traces of their origins, but like it or not, their children would become completely American in values and behavior. The immigrants themselves, despite any cultural differences, would be expected to exercise the rights and duties of citizens, no more and no less.

When fifteen years later, someone like Samuel F. B. Morse could argue that the Republic would be endangered if immigrants with certain kinds of cultural characteristics exercised the franchise, a very different way of thinking began to appear. It may be enough to say that for the first time large enough groups of culturally alien immigrants were concentrated in particular places to permit Americans to perceive them as threatening. But the point is that the threat was perceived, first in religioethnic, then increasingly in purely ethnic, terms. Why not, for example, in class terms? Ethnic differences had long been present; now they were being seen and coded as salient in a way that they previously were not. What had changed was not only the visibility of persons bearing the signs of immigrant origin, but also the ways in which Americans were viewing themselves and their society.

American nationality in the immediate post-Revolutionary period was defined largely in ideological terms. An American was someone who abjured foreign loyalties and volitionally subscribed to the basic tenets of republican self-government. While nationality so defined rested on assumptions of a general uniformity of values as well as conditions, there was no constitutional effort to defend against the consequences of cultural heterogeneity. The Revolutionary generation faced two fundamental problems of self identity: the need to differentiate themselves from Britain and the need to draw together states whose populations had very different cultural traditions and national origins. Nationality defined as culture and descent would have served neither purpose well.

The self-conscious campaigns to promote patriotic symbols and loyalties in the first decades of national existence soon began to toy with notions of special peoplehood based on descent. The need to define whiteness, Indianness, and blackness lent new weight to such classifications, and Americans were not isolated from the currents of romantic nationalism flowing from Napoleonic and post-Napoleonic Europe. At the same time, a polity experiencing rapid economic growth and social differentiation under conditions of virtually universal adult white male suffrage no longer seemed to function in quite the deferential fashion its founders had intended. Evangelical religion held out the promise of individual reform, internalized checks on disorder, and ultimate social perfection. These were the "mores" whose significance Alexis de Tocqueville noted for the functioning of the American system. But if Americans had to rest their faith in the republic on the culture of its people, what happened if that culture changed, or diversified? Anglo-Saxon descent alone offered a secure grounding for a national identity, or so it began to seem to many Americans.

Immigrants helped confirm this ethnic way of thinking by demonstrating that American republican institutions and environment could not be relied upon to change behavior automatically, and at the same time, as they began defining themselves in ethnic terms, Americans came to see others in the same light. Dale Knobel has traced, for example, how Americans began viewing the Irish in ethnic terms by the 1850s once they began regarding character as the product of nature rather than nurture. It was not only the obvious presence of culturally alien immigrants that provoked a new ethnic way of categorizing people. It was also the availability of those categories themselves, and the resolution they permitted—through symbolic exclusion—to peculiarly American dilemmas.

But immigrants were not merely passive victims in the process of inventing ethnicity as a category by which Americans could be classified. Ethnicization—in the sense of evoking a symbolically constructed sense of peoplehood vis-a-vis outsiders—had already proved its worth in regions like Ireland and Germany as a weapon in resisting an occupying power. It was, for many immigrants, not a new weapon that had to be invented, but a familiar one that could be wielded under new circumstances. It is a truism of immigration historiography that the masses of immigrants brought no sense of nationality to America with them, only local identities and allegiances. This may indeed have been true in a day-to-day sense. But it was not only the leaders who had memories of nationalist calls upon their loyalties. In various German states, for example, the nationalism evoked by the process of redemption from Napoleon was cultivated in schools, in public pageantry, in military service, and was equally embedded in the liberal oppositional culture of voluntary associations. It constituted an attitude, a vocabulary, and a set of invented traditions that could be drawn upon if similar need for solidarity again arose. Nowhere is its pervasiveness more evident, for example, than when Carl Schurz, in attempting to defend a vision of an America where ethnic differences would not count, still found himself listing the special contributions that different groups could make.

Thus the invention of ethnicity as a status category within American society occurred in a complex dialogue between American imposition of ethnic categories and immigrant rallying of ethnic identities. On the one hand were immigrants who, like Schurz in some of his moods, attempted to reject ethnicity altogether as an appropriate social category for the United States. Such people argued that it simply should not count. In a formal, legal sense they were largely successful throughout the nineteenth century. But these arguments did not halt perceptions of ethnic difference, nor the social consequences of such perceptions. So the battle was also fought on another front, one that involved accepting ethnicity as a legitimate category of difference, and then attempting to shift its weighting, either for an individual group or for ethnicity in general, from negative to positive. Certainly immigrants were tempted to play the game of arguing that someone else's ethnicity might be undesirable, but that theirs should be tolerated, even cultivated, for the sake of the positive contributions that it had to make. But immigrant spokesmen tended to realize that successful arguments for particular contributions presupposed agreement that American society was open to contributions, and thus led quickly to the more general case for ethnic difference itself as a positive social good.

Historiography has tended to see this argument erupting into the public discourse only in the early twentieth century. But it is clear that it begins to emerge as soon as ethnicity itself is invented, that its ramifications are worked out mainly within the ethnic communities themselves, but that countless political debates in place after place throughout the century kept the issue before the public and played a real role in the gradual shift of weighting that ultimately occurred. The positive assessment of pluralism was not a Progressive gift to the hapless immigrant; it was a position that countless immigrant spokesmen had elaborated and championed throughout the course of the nineteenth century.

Central to the immigrants' argument was their vision of America itself. Thus early Irish and German spokesmen adopted a literal version of republicanism, arguing that unlike other nations, America was held together by political allegiance alone. The wish to be free, the allegiance to the institutions of a free nation, made one American. Consequently cultural differences were irrelevant to the nation; immigrants could cultivate them or not as they wished, the nation's integrity would remain. But for many middle-class Germans, in particular, this position soon became insufficient. Their own sense of national self-worth, among other things, demanded for them a more explicit place in the scheme of American nationhood. By mid-century, therefore, many were expounding an explicitly melting-pot notion of America (the literal term "melting pot"—*Schmelztiegel*—gained currency among them by that time). America, they argued, may already be a political state, but its nationhood—its peoplehood—was yet unfinished. Thus each immigrant group could contribute its own special qualities to this peoplehood, indeed had a duty to do so. It followed that in order to perform this duty, a group had to protect, cultivate, and promote its qualities long enough to enable them to be absorbed. By the latter part of the century, their vision of a truly pluralist nation, in which American peoplehood was defined by its continuing diversity, was growing, but it was also losing intellectual rigor as it took on the quality of a Canute attempting to stem the tide; it became more and more the assertion of a positive ideal as the commitment or ability of group members to preserve ethnic culture and identity appeared to wane.

Such theorizing, of course, tended to be overwhelmed by more specific issues when it came to the assertion or defense of ethnicity in the course of political debate. But here, where specific flashpoints provoked German assertion of ethnic identity and solidarity—not only on issues like temperance, Sunday closing, and school language, where ethnic issues were directly at stake, but also arising from differing conceptions of the proper role of government in society or appropriate standards of civic morality—the demonstrated numbers and periodic unanimity of German voters itself constituted a powerful argument for the actual existence of ethnicity in the American public sphere. And as both sides learned almost unthinkingly to debate such issues in ethnic terms, the legitimacy of ethnicity as a political factor, in a way never fully articulated in earlier American political thinking, took firm hold; ethnic "interests" joined class, occupational, and sectional interests in the array of American political divisions, and the groundwork for viewing America as a pluralist society was laid.

FURTHER READING

Thomas Archdeacon, *Becoming American: An Ethnic History* (1983).

Dag Blanck and Peter Kivisto, eds., *American Immigrants and Their Generations* (1989).

John Bodnar, *The Transplanted: A History of Immigrants in Urban America* (1985).

Kathleen Neils Conzen, "Immigrants, Immigrant Neighborhoods, and Ethnic Identity: Historical Issues," *Journal of American History* (1979), 603–15.

Kathleen Neils Conzen, et al., "The Invention of Ethnicity: A Perspective from the USA," *Journal of American Ethnic History* (1992).

Roger Daniels, *Coming to America: A History of Immigration and Ethnicity in America* (1991).

Leonard Dinnerstein, et al., *Natives and Strangers: Blacks, Indians, and Immigrants in America* (rev. 1990).

Milton Gordon, *Assimilation in American Life* (1964).

Andrew Greeley, *Why Can't They Be Like Us* (1971).

Oscar Handlin, *The Uprooted* (2nd ed, 1973).

Marcus Lee Hansen, *The Immigrant in American History* (1940).

John Higham, "Current Trends in the Study of Ethnicity in the United States," *Journal of American Ethnic History* (1982), 5–15.

Maldwyn Jones, *American Immigration* (1960).

Russell A. Kazal, "Revisiting Assimilation: The Rise, Fall, and Reappraisal of a Concept in American Ethnic History," *American Historical Review* (1995), 437–71.

Stanley Lieberson and Mary C. Waters, *From Many Strands: Ethnic and Racial Groups in Contemporary America* (1988).

Maxine Seller, *To Seek America: A History of Ethnic Life in the United States* (rev. 1988).

Werner Sollors, *Beyond Ethnicity: Consent and Descent in American Culture* (1986).

Werner Sollors, ed., *The Invention of Ethnicity* (1989).

Philip Taylor, *The Distant Mirror: European Emigration to the USA* (1971).

Stephan Thernstrom, ed., *Harvard Encyclopedia of American Ethnic Groups* (1980).

Frank Thistlethwaite, "Migration from Europe Overseas in the Nineteenth and Twentieth Centuries," reprinted in Rudolph J. Vecoli and Suzanne M. Sinke, eds., *A Century of European Migrations, 1830–1930* (1991).

Rudolph J. Vecoli, "Ethnicity: A Neglected Dimension of American History," *The States of American History,* ed. by Herbert Bass (1970).

Rudolph J. Vecoli, "*Contadini* in Chicago: A Critique of *The Uprooted*," *Journal of American History* (1964).

Carl Wittke, *We Who Built America* (1939).

Virginia Yans-McLaughlin, *Immigration Reconsidered: History, Sociology, and Politics* (1990).

Olivier Zunz, "American History and the Changing Meaning of Assimilation," *Journal of American Ethnic History* (1985), 53–72.

CHAPTER
2

Strangers in the Realm: Migrants to British Colonial North America, 1609–1785

The formation of the British American colonies was predicated on a migration that would people newly claimed tracts of land. To Native Americans, it was, as historian Russell Menard points out, an invasion; to the European colonists, it was settlement; to slaves, it was forced migration followed by coerced labor. The result, according to historian Philip Morgan, was a society framed by a mingling of strangers in the British imperial realm. It is true that the earliest efforts at colonization were an English affair. Beginning in the late sixteenth century, groups of English people endeavored to plant colonies on American shores. Arriving with hopes of entrepreneurial gain or the freedom to practice their own religions, migrants had formed permanent settlements by the early seventeenth century in what would become Virginia and New England. If all the immigrants left an England undergoing immense change, their conditions of migration differed from the experience of those who arrived as indentured servants to propertied gentry.

What began as an English enterprise, however, soon was transformed into a society with a population diverse in its origins. Native Americans, whose numbers were greatly depleted by disease and war, nonetheless continued to oppose colonial incursions onto their land. As early as 1619, the first Africans arrived in Virginia and soon their status—and the status of those who followed them from Africa—was locked into a condition of perpetual slavery. By the mid-seventeenth century, the British empire had absorbed a group of colonies on the Atlantic seaboard that had been founded as Dutch and Swedish enterprises. And the migration from Europe itself expanded to include a wide variety of Europeans of non-English background. The migration to the colonies was especially remarkable in the eighteenth century. As late as 1700, only about 250,000 white and black people resided in the British colonies. In the next seventy-five years, an estimated half-million people would arrive, the vast majority of whom were not English. Rather, according to historian Aaron Fogleman, nearly half were of African birth, one-fifth were from Ireland, and one-seventh were German-speaking people from what is today Ger-

many, Switzerland, and France. Far fewer than one in ten of the immigrants were English. What is now the United States was a society of immigrants before it was a nation.

If the origins of migrants were diverse, so were their conditions of life. The statuses of immigrants varied greatly—unfreedom, semifreedom, and autonomy. Many Europeans arrived as indentured servants or "redemptioners" that required them to labor a period of time (in effect, to pay off their passage to the colonies) for propertied gentry who aspired to greater wealth in the empire. Others were lured to the colonies with promises of freedom to practice their own religions or of better conditions of life, which they often realized. For most Africans, the migration was a forced journey that typically ended in slave communities in the rapidly growing southern colonies. In sum, the British American colonial empire was an atypical society for many reasons that were linked to migration. Composed of people of diverse origins, it was a place celebrated by some for its great freedoms and cursed by others for its brutal slavery.

 D O C U M E N T S

As the following documents reveal, migrants to the British American colonies arrived in dissimilar circumstances and for a variety of reasons. The first two documents illustrate the different contexts of the journey to the colonies. Olaudah Equiano, in a rare 1757 narrative of a slave, describes the terror of enslavement in Africa, the journey to the West Indies, the bewilderment of slavery, as well as its cruelties. Gottlieb Mittelberger, in a work dating from 1750, shows that immigration from Germany was difficult as well, especially regarding what he calls the "commerce in human beings" known as the redemptioner migration. The second pair of documents illustrate how labor was defined by condition and race. William Moraley (1743), himself an indentured servant, and Peter Kalm (1750) depict the condition of slaves, indentured servants, and free laborers, and they both observe how race had become inextricably tied to status of freedom or slavery. The final three documents, however, show how immigrants also saw the possibilities of the colonies. A government official in northern Ireland, in a letter penned in 1728, bemoans the "evils" of migration as the residents from this region flee its oppressions. Benjamin Franklin (in 1794) illustrates how opportunity exists for laborers to gain a competence. And, in 1736, a land speculator writes to his agent in Europe in the hopes of attracting immigrants to develop his vast tracts of rich land.

Olaudah Equiano, an African, Recounts the Horror of Enslavement, 1757

. . . One day, when all our people were gone out to their works as usual, and only I and my dear sister were left to mind the house, two men and a woman got over our walls, and seized us both, and they stopped our mouths, and ran off with us into the nearest wood. Here they tied our hands, and continued to carry us as far

From Olaudah Equiano, *The Life of Olaudah Equiano*, 1789.

as they could, till night came on, when we reached a small house, where the robbers halted for refreshment, and spent the night. We were then unbound, but were unable to take any food; and, being quite overpowered by fatigue and grief, our only relief was some sleep, which allayed our misfortune for a short time. The next morning we left the house, and continued travelling all the day. . . . When we went to rest the following night they offered us some victuals; but we refused it; and the only comfort we had was in being in one another's arms all that night, and bathing each other with our tears. But alas! we were soon deprived of even the small comfort of weeping together. The next day proved a day of greater sorrow than I had yet experienced; for my sister and I were then separated, while we lay clasped in each other's arms. It was in vain that we besought them not to part us; she was torn from me, and immediately carried away, while I was left in a state of distraction not to be described. I cried and grieved continually; and for several days I did not eat any thing but what they forced into my mouth.

* * * *

The first object which saluted my eyes when I arrived on the coast was the sea, and a slave ship, which was then riding at anchor, and waiting for its cargo. These filled me with astonishment, which was soon converted into terror when I was carried on board. . . . I was now persuaded that I had gotten into a world of bad spirits, and that they were going to kill me. Their complexions too differing so much from ours, their long hair, and the language they spoke, (which was very different from any I had ever heard) united to confirm me in this belief. . . . When I looked round the ship too and saw a large furnace of copper boiling, and a multitude of black people of every description chained together, every one of their countenances expressing dejection and sorrow, I no longer doubted of my fate; and, quite overpowered with horror and anguish, I fell motionless on the deck and fainted. When I recovered a little I found some black people about me, who I believed were some of those who brought me on board, and had been receiving their pay; they talked to me in order to cheer me, but all in vain. I asked them if we were not to be eaten by those white men with horrible looks, red faces, and loose hair. They told me I was not; . . . Soon after this the blacks who brought me on board went off, and left me abandoned to despair. I now saw myself deprived of all chance of returning to my native country, or even the least glimpse of hope of gaining the shore, which I now considered as friendly; and I even wished for my former slavery in preference to my present situation, which was filled with horrors of every kind, still heightened by my ignorance of what I was to undergo. I was not long suffered to indulge my grief; I was soon put down under the decks, and there I received such a salutation in my nostrils as I had never experienced in my life: so that, with the loathsomeness of the stench, and crying together, I became so sick and low that I was not able to eat, nor had I the least desire to taste any thing. I now wished for the last friend, death, to relieve me; but soon, to my grief, two of the white men offered me eatables; and, on my refusing to eat, one of them held me fast by the hands, and laid me across I think the windlass, and tied my feet, while the other flogged me severely. I had never experienced any thing of this kind before; and although, not being used to the water, I naturally feared that element the first time I saw it, yet nevertheless, could I have got over the nettings, I would have jumped over the side, but I could not; and, besides, the crew used to watch us very closely who were not chained down to the decks, lest we should leap into the water: and I have seen some of these poor African prisoners most severely cut for attempting to do so, and hourly whipped for not eating. This indeed was often the case with myself. In a little time after, amongst the poor chained men, I found some of my own nation, which in a small degree gave ease to my mind. I inquired of these what was to be done with us; they gave me to understand we were to be carried to these white people's country to work for them. I then was a little revived, and thought, if it were no worse than working, my situation was not so desperate: but still I feared I should be put to death, the white people looked and acted, as I thought, in so savage a manner; for I had never seen among any people such instances of brutal cruelty; and this not only shewn towards us blacks, but also to some of the whites themselves. One white man in particular I saw, when we were permitted to be on deck, flogged so unmercifully with a large rope near the foremast that he died in consequence of it; and they tossed him over the side as they would have done a brute. This made me fear these people the more; and I expected nothing less than to be treated in the same manner. I could not help expressing my fears and apprehensions to some of my countrymen: I asked them if these people had no country, but lived in this hollow place (the ship): they told me they did not, but came from a distant one. "Then," said I, "how comes it in all our country we never heard of them?" They told me because they lived so very far off. I then asked where were their women? had they any like themselves? I was told they had "and why," said I, "do we not see them?" they answered, because they were left behind. I asked how the vessel could go? they told me they could not tell; but that there were cloths put upon the masts by the help of the ropes I saw, and then the vessel went on and the white men had some spell or magic they put in the water when they liked in order to stop the vessel. I was exceedingly amazed at this account, and really thought they were spirits. I therefore wished much to be from amongst them, for I expected they would sacrifice me: but my wishes were vain. . . .

. . . At last we came in sight of the island of Barbadoes, at which the whites on board gave a great shout, and made many signs of joy to us. We did not know what to think of this; but as the vessel drew nearer we plainly saw the harbour, and other ships of different kinds and sizes; and we soon anchored amongst them off Bridge Town. Many merchants and planters now came on board, though it was in the evening. They put us in separate parcels, and examined us attentively. They also made us jump, and pointed to the land, signifying we were to go there. We thought by this we should be eaten by these ugly men as they appeared to us; and, when soon after we were all put down under the deck again, there was much dread and trembling among us, and nothing but bitter cries to be heard all the night from these apprehensions, insomuch that at last the white people got some old slaves from the land to pacify us. They told us we were not to be eaten, but to work, and were soon to go on land, where we should see many of our country people. This report eased us much; and sure enough, soon after we were landed, there came to us Africans of all languages. We were conducted immediately to the merchant's yard, where we were all pent up together like so many sheep in a fold, without regard to sex or age. As every object was new to me every thing I saw filled me with surprise. What struck me first was that the houses were built with stories, and in every other respect different from those in Africa: but I was still more astonished on see-ing people on horseback. I did not know what this could mean; and indeed I thought these people were full of nothing but magical arts. . . . We were not many days in the merchant's custody before we were sold after their usual manner, which is this:—On a signal given (as the beat of a drum), the buyers rush at once into the yard where the slaves are confined, and make choice of that parcel they like best. The noise and clamour with which this is attended, and the eagerness visible in the countenances of the buyers, serve not a little to increase the apprehensions of the terrified Africans, who may well be supposed to consider them as the ministers of that destruction to which they think themselves devoted. In this manner, without scruple, are relations and friends separated, most of them never to see each other again. I remember in the vessel in which I was brought over, in the men's apart-ment, there were several brothers, who, in the sale, were sold in different lots; and it was very moving on this occasion to see and hear their cries at parting.

While I was thus employed by my master I was often a witness to cruelties of every kind, which were exercised on my unhappy fellow slaves. I used frequently to have different cargoes of new negroes in my care for sale; and it was almost a constant practice with our clerks, and other whites, to commit violent depredations on the chastity of the female slaves; and these I was, though with reluctance, obliged to submit to at all times, being unable to help them. When we have had some of these slaves on board my master's vessels to carry them to other islands, or to America, I have known our mates to commit these acts most shamefully, to the disgrace, not of Christians only, but of men. I have even known them gratify their brutal passion with females not ten years old; . . . And yet in Montserrat I have seen a negro man staked to the ground, and cut most shockingly, and then his ears cut off bit by bit, because he had been connected with a white woman who was a common prostitute: as if it were no crime in the whites to rob an innocent African girl of her virtue; but most heinous in a black man only to gratify a passion of na-ture, where the temptation was offered by one of a different colour, though the most abandoned woman of her species. Another negro man was half hanged, and then burnt, for attempting to poison a cruel overseer. Thus by repeated cruelties are the wretched first urged to despair, and then murdered, because they still retain so much of human nature about them as to wish to put an end to their misery, and re-taliate on their tyrants! . . .

Gottlieb Mittelberger, a German, Describes the Difficulties of Immigration, 1750

When the ships have weighed anchor for the last time, usually off Cowes in Old England, then both the long sea voyage and misery begin in earnest. For from there the ships often take eight, nine, ten, or twelve weeks sailing to Philadelphia, if the

From Gottlieb Mittelberger, *Reise nach Pennsylvania [Journey to Pennsylvania]*, 1756.

wind is unfavorable. But even given the most favorable winds, the voyage takes seven weeks.

During the journey the ship is full of pitiful signs of distress—smells, fumes, horrors, vomiting, various kinds of sea sickness, fever, dysentery, headaches, heat, constipation, boils, scurvy, cancer, mouth-rot, and similar afflictions, all of them caused by the age and the highly-salted state of the food, especially of the meat, as well as by the very bad and filthy water, which brings about the miserable destruction and death of many. Add to all that shortage of food, hunger, thirst, frost, heat, dampness, fear, misery, vexation, and lamentation as well as other troubles. Thus, for example, there are so many lice, especially on the sick people, that they have to be scraped off the bodies. All this misery reaches its climax when in addition to everything else one must also suffer through two to three days and nights of storm, with everyone convinced that the ship with all aboard is bound to sink. In such misery all the people on board pray and cry pitifully together.

In the course of such a storm the sea begins to surge and rage so that the waves often seem to rise up like high mountains, sometimes sweeping over the ship; and one thinks that he is going to sink along with the ship. All the while the ship, tossed by storm and waves, moves constantly from one side to the other, so that nobody aboard can either walk, sit, or lie down and the tightly packed people on their cots, the sick as well as the healthy, are thrown every which way. One can easily imagine that these hardships necessarily affect many people so severely that they cannot survive them.

Among those who are in good health impatience sometimes grows so great and bitter that one person begins to curse the other, or himself and the day of his birth, and people sometimes come close to murdering one another. Misery and malice are readily associated, so that people begin to cheat and steal from one another. And then one always blames the other for having undertaken the voyage. Often the children cry out against their parents, husbands against wives and wives against husbands, brothers against their sisters, friends and acquaintances against one another.

But most of all they cry out against the thieves of human beings! Many groan and exclaim: "Oh! If only I were back at home, even lying in my pig-sty!" Or they call out: "Ah, dear God, if I only once again had a piece of good bread or a good fresh drop of water." Many people whimper, sigh, and cry out pitifully for home. Most of them become homesick at the thought that many hundreds of people must necessarily perish, die, and be thrown into the ocean in such misery. . . . In a word, groaning, crying, and lamentation go on aboard day and night; so that even the hearts of the most hardened, hearing all this, begin to bleed.

When at last after the long and difficult voyage the ships finally approach land, when one gets to see the headlands for the sight of which the people on board had longed so passionately, then everyone crawls from below to the deck, in order to look at the land from afar. And people cry for joy, pray, and sing praises and thanks to God. The glimpse of land revives the passengers, especially those who are half-dead of illness. Their spirits, however weak they had become, leap up, triumph, and rejoice within them. Such people are now willing to bear all ills patiently, if only they can disembark soon and step on land. But, alas, alas!

When the ships finally arrive in Philadelphia after the long voyage only those are let off who can pay their sea freight or can give good security. The others, who lack the money to pay, have to remain on board until they are purchased and until their purchasers can thus pry them loose from the ship. In this whole process the sick are the worst off, for the healthy are preferred and are more readily paid for. The miserable people who are ill must often still remain at sea and in sight of the city for another two or three weeks—which in many cases means death. Yet many of them, were they able to pay their debts and to leave the ships at once, might escape with their lives.

* * * *

This is how the commerce in human beings on board ship takes place. Every day Englishmen, Dutchmen, and High Germans come from Philadelphia and other places, some of them very far away, sometime twenty or thirty or forty hours' journey, and go on board the newly arrived vessel that has brought people from Europe and offers them for sale. From among the healthy they pick out those suitable for the purposes for which they require them. Then they negotiate with them as to the length of the period for which they will go into service in order to pay off their passage, the whole amount of which they generally still owe. When an agreement has been reached, adult persons by written contract bind themselves to serve for three, four, five, or six years, according to their health and age. The very young, between the ages of ten and fifteen, have to serve until they are twenty-one, however.

Many parents in order to pay their fares in this way and get off the ship must barter and sell their children as if they were cattle. Since the fathers and mothers often do not know where or to what masters their children are to be sent, it frequently happens that after leaving the vessel, parents and children do not see each other for years on end, or even for the rest of their lives.

* * * *

It often happens that whole families—husband, wife, and children—being sold to different purchasers, become separated, especially when they cannot pay any part of the passage money. When either the husband or the wife has died at sea, having come more than halfway, then the surviving spouse must pay not only his or her fare, but must also pay for or serve out the fare of the deceased.

* * * *

No one in this country can run away from a master who has treated him harshly and get far. For there are regulations and laws that ensure that runaways are certainly and quickly recaptured. Those who arrest or return a fugitive get a good reward. For every day that someone who runs away is absent from his master he must as a punishment do service an extra week, for every week an extra month, and for every month a half year. But if the master does not want to take back the recaptured runaway, he is entitled to sell him to someone else for the period of as many years as he would still have had to serve.

William Moraley, an Indentured Servant, Explains the Condition of Labor in Pennsylvania, 1743

Almost every inhabitant, in the Country, have a Plantation, some two or more; there being no Land lett as in *England,* where Gentlemen live on the Labour of the Farmer, to whom he grants a short Lease, which expiring, he is either raised in his Rent, or discharged his Farm. Here they improve their Lands themselves, with the Assistance both of bought Servants and Negroes.

* * * *

At the first Peopling [of] these Colonies, there was a Necessity of employing a great Number of Hands, for the clearing the Land, being over-grown with Wood for some Hundred of Miles; to which Intent, the first Settlers not being sufficient of themselves to improve those Lands, were not only obliged to purchase a great Number of *English* Servants to assist them, to whom they granted great Immunities, and at the Expiration of their Servitude, Land was given to encourage them to continue there; but were likewise obliged to purchase Multitudes of Negro Slaves from *Africa,* by which Means they are become the richest Farmers in the World, paying no Rent, nor giving Wages either to purchased Servants or Negro Slaves; so that instead of finding the Planter Rack-rented, as the *English* Farmer, you will taste of their Liberality, they living in Affluence and Plenty.

The Condition of the Negroes is very bad, by reason of the Severity of the Laws, there being no Laws made in Favour of these unhap[p]y Wretches: For the least Trespass, they undergo the severest Punishment; but their Masters make them some amends, by suffering them to marry, which makes them easier, and often prevents their running away. The Consequence of their marrying is this, all their Posterity are Slaves without Redemption; and it is in vain to attempt an Escape, tho' they often endeavour it; for the Laws against them are so severe, that being caught after running away, they are unmercifully whipped; and if they die under the Discipline, their Masters suffer no Punishment, there being no Law against murdering them. So if one Man kills another's Slave, he is only obliged to pay his Value to the Master, besides Damages that may accrue for the Loss of him in his Business.

The Masters generally allow them a Piece of Ground, with Materials for improving it. The Time of working for themselves, is *Sundays,* when they raise on their own Account divers Sort of Corn and Grain, and sell it in the Markets. They buy with the Money Cloaths for themselves and Wives; as for the Children, they belong to the Wives Master, who bring them up; so the Negro need fear no Expense, his Business being to get them for his Master's use, who is as tender of them as his own Children. On *Sundays* in the evening they converse with their Wives, and drink Rum, or Bumbo, and smoak Tobacco, and the next Morning return to their Master's Labour.

As found in Susan E. Klepp and Billy G. Smith (eds.), *The Infortunate: The Voyage and Adventures of William Moraley, an Indentured Servant,* (University Park, PA: Pennsylvania State University Press, 1992).

They are seldom made free, for fear of being burthensome to the Provinces, there being a Law, that no Master shall manumise them, unless he gives Security they shall not be thrown upon the Province, by settling Land on them for their Support.

Their Marriages are diverting; for when the Day is appointed for the Solemnization, Notice is given to all the Negroes and their Wives to be ready. The Masters of the new Couple provide handsomely for the Entertainment of the Company. The Inhabitants generally grace the Nuptials with their Presence, when all Sorts of the best Provisions are to be met with. They chuse some *Englishman* to read the Marriage Ceremony out of the Common Prayer Book; after which they sing and dance and drink till they get drunk. Then a Negro goes about the Company and collects Money for the Use of the Person who marry'd them, which is laid out in a Handkerchief, and presented to him.

This is the only free Day they have, except Sundays, throughout the whole Course of their Lives, for then they banish from them all Thoughts of the Wretchedness of their Condition. The Day being over, they return to their Slavery. I have often heard them say, they did not think God made them Slaves, any more than other Men, and wondered that Christians, especially *Englishmen,* should use them so barbarously. But there is a Necessity of using them hardly, being of an obdurate, stubborn Disposition; and when they have it in their Power to rebel, are extremely cruel.

The Condition of bought Servants is very hard, notwithstanding their indentures are made in *England,* wherein it is expressly stipulated, that they shall have, at their Arrival, all the Necessaries specified in those Indentures, to be given 'em by their future Masters, such as Clothes, Meat, and Drink; yet upon Complaint made to a Magistrate against the Master for Nonperformance, the Master is generally heard before the Servant, and it is ten to one if he does not get his Licks for his Pains, as I have experienced upon the like Occasion, to my Cost.

If they endeavor to escape, which is next to impossible, there being a Reward for taking up any Person who travels without a Pass, which is extended all over the *British* Colonies, their Masters immediately issue out a Reward for the apprehending them, from Thirty Shillings to Five Pound, as they think proper, and this generally brings them back again. Printed and Written Advertisements are also set up against the Trees and publick Places in the Town, besides those in the Newspapers. Notwithstanding these Difficulties, they are perpetually running away, but seldom escape; for a hot Pursuit being made, brings them back, when a Justice settles the Expences, and the Servant is oblig'd to serve a longer time.

Peter Kalm, a Traveler, Observes the Variety of Labor in the Colonies, 1750

Servants. The servants which are employed in the English-American colonies are either free persons or slaves, and the former, again, are of two different classes.

As found in Adolph B. Benson (ed.), *Peter Kalm's Travels in North America,* volume I, (New York: Wilson-Erickson Inc., 1937).

1. Those who are entirely free serve by the year. They are not only allowed to leave their service at the expiration of their year, but may leave it at any time when they do not agree with their masters. However, in that case they are in danger of losing their wages, which are very considerable. A man servant who has some ability gets between sixteen and twenty pounds in Pennsylvania currency, but those in the country do not get so much. A maidservant gets eight or ten pounds a year. These servants have their food besides their wages, but they must buy their own clothes, and whatever they get of these as gifts they must thank their master's generosity for.

Indenture. 2. The second kind of free servants consists of such persons as annually come from Germany, England and other countries, in order to settle here. These newcomers are very numerous every year: there are old and young of both sexes. Some of them have fled from oppression, under which they have labored. Others have been driven from their country by religious persecution, but most of them are poor and have not money enough to pay their passage, which is between six and eight pounds sterling for each person. Therefore, they agree with the captain that they will suffer themselves to be sold for a few years on their arrival. In that case the person who buys them pays the freight for them; but frequently very old people come over who cannot pay their passage, they therefore sell their children for several years, so that they serve both for themselves and for their parents. There are likewise some who pay part of their passage, and they are sold only for a short time. From these circumstances it appears that the price on the poor foreigners who come over to North America varies considerably, and that some of them have to serve longer than others. When their time has expired, they get a new suit of clothes from their master and some other things. He is likewise obliged to feed and clothe them during the years of their servitude. Many of the Germans who come hither bring money enough with them to pay their passage, but prefer to be sold, hoping that during their servitude they may get a knowledge of the language and character of the country and the life, that they may the better be able to consider what they shall do when they have gotten their liberty. Such servants are preferable to all others, because they are not so expensive. To buy a negro or black slave requires too much money at one time; and men or maids who get yearly wages are likewise too costly. But this kind of servant may be gotten for half the money, and even for less; for they commonly pay fourteen pounds, Pennsylvania currency, for a person who is to serve four years, and so on in proportion. Their wages therefore are not above three pounds Pennsylvania currency per annum. These servants are, after the English, called *servingar* by the Swedes. When a person has bought such a servant for a certain number of years, and has an intention to sell him again, he is at liberty to do so, but is obliged, at the expiration of the term of servitude, to provide the usual suit of clothes for the servant, unless he has made that part of the bargain with the purchaser. The English and Irish commonly sell themselves for four years, but the Germans frequently agree with the captain before they set out, to pay him a certain sum of money, for a certain number of persons. As soon as they arrive in America they go about and try to get a man who will pay the passage for them. In return they give according to their circumstances, one or several of their children to serve a certain number of years. At last they make their bargain with the highest bidder.

3. The *negroes* or blacks constitute the third kind. They are in a manner slaves; for when a negro is once bought, he is the purchaser's servant as long as he lives, unless he gives him to another, or sets him free. However, it is not in the power of the master to kill his negro for a fault, but he must leave it to the magistrates to proceed according to the laws. Formerly the negroes were brought over from Africa, and bought by almost everyone who could afford it, the Quakers alone being an exception. But these are no longer so particular and now they have as many negroes as other people. However, many people cannot conquer the idea of its being contrary to the laws of Christianity to keep slaves. There are likewise several free negroes in town, who have been lucky enough to get a very zealous Quaker for their master, and who gave them their liberty after they had faithfully served him for a time.

At present they seldom bring over any negroes to the English colonies, for those which were formerly brought thither have multiplied rapidly. In regard to their marriage they proceed as follows: in case you have not only male but likewise female negroes, they may intermarry, and then the children are all your slaves. But if you possess a male negro only and he has an inclination to marry a female belonging to a different master, you do not hinder your negro in so delicate a point, but it is of no advantage to you, for the children belong to the master of the female. It is therefore practically advantageous to have negro women. A man who kills his negro is, legally, punishable by death, but there is no instance here of a white man ever having been executed for this crime. A few years ago it happened that a master killed his slave. His friends and even the magistrates secretly advised him to make his escape, as otherwise they could not avoid taking him prisoner, and then he would be condemned to die according to the laws of the country, without any hopes of being saved. This leniency was granted toward him, that the negroes might not have the satisfaction of seeing a master executed for killing his slave. This would lead them to all sorts of dangerous designs against their masters, and to value themselves too much.

Hugh Boulter Recounts the Discontent in Ireland That Resulted in Emigration, 1728

Dublin, November 23, 1728

To the Duke of Newcastle:

My Lord:—I am very sorry I am obliged to give your grace so melancholy an account of the state of this kingdom as I shall in this letter, but I thought it my duty to let his Majesty know our present condition in the north. For we have had three bad harvests together there, which has made oatmeal, which is their great subsistence, much dearer than ordinary. And as our farmers here are very poor and obliged as soon as they have their corn to sell it for ready money to pay their rents, it is much more in the power of those who have a little money to engross corn here and make advantage of its scarceness than in England.

As found in David Hawke, *U.S. Colonial History: Readings and Documents* (New York: Macmillan, 1966).

We have had for several years some agents from the colonies in America and several masters of ships that have gone about the country and deluded the people with stories of great plenty, and estates to be had for going for, in those parts of the world. And they have been the better able to seduce people by reason of the necessities of the poor of late.

The people that go from here make great complaints of the oppressions they suffer here, not from the government, but from their fellow subjects, of one kind or another, as well as of the dearness of provisions, and they say these oppressions are one reason of their going.

But whatever occasions their going, it is certain that above 4,200 men, women, and children have been shipped off from hence for the West Indies [i.e., North America] within three years, and of these, above 3,100 last summer. Of these, possibly one in ten may be a man of substance, and may do well enough abroad; but the case of the rest is deplorable. The rest either hire themselves to those of substance for passage, or contract with the masters of ships for four years' servitude when they come thither; or, if they make a shift to pay for their passage, will be under the necessity of selling themselves for servants when they come there.

The whole north is in a ferment at present, and people every day engaging one another to go next year to the West Indies. The humor has spread like a contagious distemper, and the people will hardly hear anybody that tries to cure them of their madness. The worst is that it affects only Protestants and reigns chiefly in the north, which is the seat of our linen manufacture.

This unsettled state puts almost a stop to trade and the more so as several who were in good credit before have taken up parcels of goods and disposed of them, and are gone off with the money, so that there is no trade there but for ready money.

We have had it much in consideration how to put some stop to this growing evil. We think by some old laws we can hinder money being carried abroad, and stop all but merchants that have not a license, from going out of the kingdom.

By this post we have sent my lord lieutenant the representation of the gentlemen of the north and the opinion of our lawyers what can be done by law to hinder people going abroad; but these are matters we shall do nothing in without directions from his Majesty. But whatever may be done by law, I feel it may be dangerous forcibly to hinder a number of needy people from quitting us.

Benjamin Franklin Advises Those Who Might Move to America, 1784

The truth is that though there are in that country few people so miserable as the poor of Europe, there are also very few that in Europe would be called rich; it is rather a general happy mediocrity that prevails. There are few great proprietors of the soil, and few tenants; most people cultivate their own lands or follow some handicraft or merchandise; very few rich enough to live idly upon their rents or

As found in David Hawke, *U.S. Colonial History: Readings and Documents* (New York: Macmillan, 1966).

incomes or to pay the highest prices given in Europe for painting, statues, architecture, and the other works of art that are more curious than useful. . . .

. . . It cannot be worth any man's while, who has a means of living at home, to expatriate himself in hopes of obtaining a profitable civil office in America; and, as to military offices, they are at an end with the war, the armies being disbanded. Much less is it advisable for a person to go thither who has no other quality to recommend him but his birth. In Europe it has indeed its value; but it is a commodity that cannot be carried to a worse market than that of America, where people do not inquire concerning a stranger, *What is he?* but *What can he do?* If he has any useful art, he is welcome; and if he exercises it, and behaves well, he will be respected by all that know him; but a mere man of quality, who, on that account, wants to live upon the public by some office or salary will be despised and disregarded. The husbandman is in honor there, and even the mechanic, because their employments are useful. The people have a saying that God Almighty is himself a mechanic, the greatest in the universe; and he is respected and admired more for the variety, ingenuity, and utility of his handiworks, than for the antiquity of his family. They are pleased with the observation of a Negro, and frequently mention it, that *Boccarora* (meaning the white man) *make de black man workee, make de horse workee, make de ox workee, make ebery ting workee, only de hog. He, de hog, no workee; he eat, he drink, he walk about, he go to sleep when he please, he live like a gempleman.* According to these opinions of the Americans, one of them would think himself more obligated to a genealogist who could prove for him that his ancestors and relations for ten generations had been plowmen, smiths, carpenters, turners, weavers, tanners, or even shoemakers, and consequently that they were useful members of society, than if he could only prove that they were gentlemen, doing nothing of value, but living idly on the labor of others, mere *fruges consumere nati* ["born merely to eat up the corn"], and otherwise *good for nothing,* till by their death their estates, like the carcass of the Negro's gentleman-hog, come to be *cut up.*

With regard to encouragements for strangers from government, they are really only what are derived from good laws and liberty. Strangers are welcome, because there is room enough for them all, and therefore the old inhabitants are not jealous of them; the laws protect them sufficiently, so that they have no need of the patronage of great men; and every one will enjoy securely the profits of his industry But, if he does not bring a fortune with him, he must work and be industrious to live. One or two years' residence gives him all the rights of a citizen; but the government does not, at present, whatever it may have done in former times, hire people to become settlers by paying their passages, giving land, Negroes, utensils, stock, or any other kind of emolument whatsoever. In short, America is the land of labor, and by no means what the English call *Lubberland* [imaginary land of plenty], and the French *Pays de Cocagne* [land of milk and honey], where the streets are said to be paved with half-peck loaves, the houses tiled with pancakes, and where the fowls fly about ready roasted, crying, *Come eat me!*

Who then are the kind of persons to whom an emigration to America may be advantageous? And what are the advantages they may reasonably expect? . . .

There is a continual demand for more artisans of all the necessary and useful kinds to supply those cultivators of the earth with houses and with furniture and utensils of the grosser sorts, which cannot so well be brought from Europe. Tolerably good workmen in any of those mechanic arts are sure to find employ and to be well paid for their work, there being no restraints preventing strangers from exercising any art they understand, nor any permission necessary. If they are poor, they begin first as servants or journeymen; and if they are sober, industrious, and frugal, they soon become masters, establish themselves in business, marry, raise families, and become respectable citizens.

Also, persons of moderate fortune and capital, who, having a number of children to provide for, are desirous of bringing them up to industry and to secure estates for their posterity, have opportunities of doing it in America, which Europe does not afford. There they may be taught and practice profitable mechanic arts, without incurring disgrace on that account, but, on the contrary, acquiring respect by such abilities. There, small capitals laid out in land, which daily become more valuable by the increase of people, afford a solid prospect of ample fortune thereafter for those children. . . .

The almost general mediocrity of fortune that prevails in America obliging its people to follow some business for subsistence, those vices that arise usually from idleness are in a great measure prevented. Industry and constant employment are great preservatives of the morals and virtue of a nation. Hence, bad examples to youth are more rare in America, which must be a comfortable consideration to parents. To this may be truly added that serious religion, under its various denominations, is not only tolerated, but respected and practiced. Atheism is unknown there; infidelity rare and secret; so that persons may live to a great age in that country without having their piety shocked by meeting with either an atheist or an infidel. And the Divine Being seems to have manifested his approbation of the mutual forbearance and kindness with which the different sects treat each other, by the remarkable prosperity with which He has been pleased to favor the whole country.

William Byrd II, a Land Speculator, Promotes Immigration, 1736

Letter of William Byrd II to Mr. Ochs, His Swiss Correspondent

Virginia, July 1736

If you will send over one hundred families to be here by the first day of May next, I will make a present to them of ten Thousand Acres of land lying on or under the South branch of Roanoke. Besides the 10,000 acres of land I propose to give to ye first Colony, I have much more Joining to that, which I propose to sell at the price of £3 pounds current money, per hundred acres. And if it should lye much in your way to help me to Customers for it, I should be obliged to you. If I should fail in my Intention, of planting a Swiss Colony, in this delightful part of the World (which are the People of the Earth I wou'd choose to have) I must then seat my land with Scots-Irish, who crowd from Pennsylvania in such numbers, that there is no Room for them. We have already a pretty many of them settled on the River Gerando, which neither the Clymate nor Soil is comparable to the Lands upon the Roanoke River. After I have so often repeated to you the good opinion we have of

Source: "Letters of the Byrd Family," *Virginia Magazine of History and Biography*, XXXVI, 353, 361–362. Reprinted by permission of the Virginia Historical Society.

the Switzers, you will not question any good Offices, I shall be able to do them. Especially when they shall come recommended from my old Friend.

Letter of William Byrd II to Dr. Zwiffler, His German Correspondent

Virginia, December 20, 1736

Sir,

. . . I chuse rather to have a Colony of Germans to settle that Frontier. I have a fine Tract of Land on the South Branch of Roanoke River, which I discovered when I ran the Line between this Colony & North Carolina, & have since pur-chased it of His Majesty. It contains in all 105,000 acres, besides the River, which runs thro the Length of it, & includes a large quantity of good Land within Roanoke, on both sides, so that no Land, can be better watered. It lyes in a mild & temperate Clymate, about 36½° where the Winters, are moderate and short, so that there will not be much trouble to maintain the Cattle. The woods are full of Buffalo's, Deer, & Wild Turkeys, & the Rivers abound with Fish and Wild Fowl. It lyes 40 miles below the Mountains, & is a very level Road from thence to water carrage. It is within the Government of Virginia, under the King, where Liberty & Property is enjoyed, in perfection & the impartial administration of Justices hinders the Poor from every kind of Oppression from the Rich, & the Great. There is not the least danger from the Indians, or any other Enimy, & all we know of War is from Hearsay. The quitrents we pay to the King, are no more than Two Shillings for every Hundred acres, & our Assembly hath made all Forreign Protestants, that will come, & inhabit this Land free from all other taxes, for the Space of Ten years, reckoning from the year 1738. And Last winter the Parliament of England, past an Act, to naturalize all strangers that shall live seven years in any of the British Plantations, so that Expence will be saved. The happiness of this Government, appears in nothing more than in its haveing Gold & Silver enough to Supply its occasions, without the vexation of Paper mony. The People too are hospitable to Strangers, nor is there that Envy, and aversion to them, that I have observed in other Places. Besides all these Recommendations of my Land, there is the cheapness of it, which makes it convenient to poor People. If any Person or Number of People will purchase 20,000 acres in one Tract, they shall have it for Three Pounds the Hundred, of this Currancy. Who so ever will purchase under that Quantity, & above 10,000 acres, shall have it for Four Pounds the Hundred of our mony. But if they will buy under that quantity, & buy only smaller Tracts, they must pay five Pounds, the Hundred of our mony, Because of the Trouble of laying off such small quantitys. They will be at no charge about the deeds of Conveyance, because I have had printed a great number, and unless they will have them recorded, when there will be a small Fee to the Clerk.

⚅ *E S S A Y S*

In the past, the histories of colonial America and of immigration to America have not been linked very well. Traditionally, historians have considered the era of immigration to have begun when the United States became an independent nation. Recently, historians have made considerable efforts to connect the two histories. In the first selection, T. H. Breen, a historian at Northwestern University, reflects upon what he considers the "creative adaptations" made by the variety of peoples who arrived in the British American colonies. As migrants of a variety of cultural pasts met a large and diverse Native American population, they worked together to create communities based on race and circumstance. Equally important, "charter groups"—those who were earliest in the migration process—had an advantage over later arrivals who didn't have the same economic and cultural opportunities. Nonetheless, red, white, and black people, early and later arrivals, together forged a "creole" society. In the second essay, published in 1991, historian Russell R. Menard of the University of Minnesota, building on Breen's essay, broadens his purview of immigration to observe its consequences from a series of perspectives. He considers the effects of the immigration—or invasion—on Native American populations, the number and origins of the migrants, and the results of the ethnic diversity in the colonies. Significantly, he argues that, as the colonies matured, they were characterized by less ethnic diversity than earlier—even though the number of immigrants was larger later in the period. As a "creole" culture was created in the colonies and as racial identities hardened, Menard believes that color—redness, whiteness, and blackness—superseded identities based on premigration pasts.

Creative Adaptations: Peoples and Cultures

T. H. BREEN

The tale of the peopling of the New World is one of human creativity. Colonization of the Caribbean islands and the North American mainland brought thousands of men and women into contact who ordinarily would have had nothing to do with each other. Whether migrants arrived as slaves or freemen, as religious visionaries or crass opportunists, they were forced to adjust not only to unfamiliar environments but also to a host of strangers, persons of different races, cultures, and backgrounds.

These challenges were staggering. Within the constraints of the peculiar circumstances in which they found themselves, blacks and whites learned to live with each other as well as with native Americans. However cruelly some exploited others, however much they resented each other's presence, in their development these three groups became intricately intertwined. How men and women chose to interact, therefore, how much they preserved of their original cultures, how much they borrowed from the strangers are topics of considerable importance, for their decisions made three centuries ago still powerfully affect the character of modern society.

This creative process [of forming a culture through exchanges among existing cultures] generated different results depending upon the social, economic, and environmental situations in which early Americans found themselves. The New World produced a kaleidoscope of human encounters. To suggest that Africans and Indians possessed the same voice in shaping cultural "conversations" as did

From T. H. Breen, "Creative Adaptations: People and Cultures," in Jack P. Greene and J. R. Pole (eds.), *Colonial British America*. Copyright © 1984. Reprinted by permission of The Johns Hopkins University Press.

Europeans would be absurd. Whites clearly enjoyed substantial advantages in such interracial exchanges. But it would be equally mistaken to claim that either blacks or native Americans—or the poorer whites for that matter—were overwhelmed by the dominant white cultures. Within obvious limits, these people also adapted traditional folkways to meet changing conditions, dropping some practices, acquiring new ones, and modifying others. The problem for the historian of colonial cultures, therefore, is to define with precision the constraints upon choice: What actually determined the character of specific conversations?

* * * *

After examining how in particular situations these elements more or less affected the character of interaction between strangers of diverse backgrounds and different races, I maintain that it is still possible to discern certain long-term trends in early American cultural and racial relations. In many English colonies the seventeenth century was a time of openness, of experimentation, of sorting out ideas. Race was important in negotiating social identities, but it was by no means the chief determinant. People formed niches in which they created fluid, often unique patterns of interaction. But during the eighteenth century—and the timing of course varied from community to community—race became more obtrusive in shaping human relations. To understand how this change came about, we must first consider constraints upon adaptation.

Cultural Conversations: Constraints

Background before contact.   Colonization in the New World brought men and women of diverse backgrounds together for the first time. These people did not greet each other as representatives of monolithic racial groups—as blacks, reds, or whites. Ethnic and class divisions, some of them deeply rooted in the history of a particular Old World community, cut across migrant populations. "Those peoples called Indians by Europeans were divided into hundreds of tribes and thousands of societies," observes Robert F. Berkhofer. "Even who was a member of a tribe at any one time and what a tribe was, changed greatly over time." Both immigrants and native Americans were products of dynamic, often locally oriented societies that were changing when the New World was discovered and would have continued to change even if it had remained unknown for centuries. The backgrounds of these peoples before initial contact affected the ways they adapted not only to each other but also to strangers of a different race.

Relatively little is known about the Indians of eastern North America and the Caribbean during the precontact period. Recent archaeological investigations suggest, however, that native American cultures were both dynamic and diverse. Tribal customs changed considerably over time in response not only to other tribes but also to environmental demands. The once accepted notion that the first major alteration in Indian cultures occurred only after the arrival of the white man turns out to have been an error based upon ethnocentrism. The native American population of these regions actually was divided into scores of self-contained tribal groups and bands—best described as ethnic groups—that spoke languages virtually unintelligible to members of other tribes, sometimes even to those living in close proximity. . . .

The cultures of "precontact" Africa were less unified than that of seventeenth-century Europe. Only recently, however, have anthropologists and historians come to appreciate fully the diversity and complexity of West African societies. It is still common to read of a general African heritage, a single background allegedly providing slaves with a set of shared meanings and beliefs once they reached the New World. But as anthropologists Sidney Mintz and Richard Price argue, "Enslaved Africans . . . were drawn from different parts of the African continent, from numerous tribal and linguistic groups, and from different societies in any region." Black men and women were transported to America as members of specific tribes—as Ibos, Yorubas, or Ashantis but not simply as Africans. Indeed, historians accustomed to thinking of European migrants in terms of national origin often overlook African ethnicity, overestimating perhaps the difficulty of obtaining evidence for the heterogeneity of African culture.

African ethnicity is not a modern invention. Colonial planters who purchased slaves recognized distinctions between various West African peoples, and in South Carolina and the Caribbean islands whites sought blacks from specific tribes thought to be particularly docile or strong. Even if the planters had not made such demands, however, the slave population in the English colonies—at least in the earliest years of settlement—would have reflected a wide range of geographic and cultural backgrounds. . . . Such diversity meant that the Africans themselves were often strangers to each other's customs and languages, and if a single African background developed at all, it came into being on board slave ships or plantations, where West Africans were compelled to cooperate in order to survive.

Colonial American historians seldom describe England on the eve of colonization as a "precontact" culture. The reasons for their reluctance are clear. Elizabethan society seems politically sophisticated, economically expansive, and, by the standards of the seventeenth century, technologically well developed. For the purposes of this essay, however, it is salutary to consider another perspective: to conceive of the earliest migrants as coming not from a well-integrated culture but from localized subcultures scattered throughout the kingdom. English people shared assumptions about the meaning of daily events—just as the eastern woodland Indians or West Africans did—but the lost world of the Anglo-Americans was generally a specific rural area. According to Peter Clark and Paul Slack, the England of 1700 was "still very much a rural nation." Whether a colonist came from Kent or Norfolk, East Anglia or the West Country, therefore, should be a matter of considerable importance for anyone interested in cultural interaction in the New World.

* * * *

Perceptions and prejudices.   Men and women involved in the colonization of North America generally regarded themselves as superior to the representatives of other groups with whom they came into contact. Such flattering self-perceptions developed long before anyone thought of moving to the New World. When Africans, Europeans, and Indians encountered individuals of unfamiliar races and cultures, they attempted to incorporate them into established intellectual frameworks, and it is not surprising that differences were often interpreted as evidence of inferiority. Early modern English writers left a particularly detailed record of how they viewed blacks and Indians, not to mention the Irish. Historians drawing upon this material concluded that ethnocentric biases pervaded the white colonists' world view. Only recently have scholars become aware that members of other cultures could be just as ethnocentric in their outlook as were the English. To the extent that these ideas and prejudices shaped the ways that persons of different race and culture actually interacted in the New World, they obstructed open, creative adaptation, especially by people of dependent status.

* * * *

Whites were not alone in their prejudice. West Africans possessed an image of the white man that was extremely unflattering. Blacks seem to have associated the color white, at least on human beings, with a number of negative attributes, including evil. In one magnificent Danish account compiled in the mid-eighteenth century, it was reported that an African ruler thought "all Europeans looked like ugly sea monsters." He ordered an embarrassed Danish bookkeeper to strip so that he could definitively discover if this was so. After examining the naked Dane, the African exclaimed, "You are really a human being, but as white as the devil." . . . [W]hile Indians were eager to obtain manufactured goods, they maintained a critical, even derogatory, stance towards the whites and their cultures. The northern tribes, for example, regarded Europeans as ugly—too hairy for their tastes. In fact, Jaenen reports that "on a wide range of points of contact . . . the Amerindian evaluation of French culture and civilization was often as unflattering as was the low regard of Frenchmen for Amerindian culture." . . .

* * * *

. . . Sociologists have found no direct connection between stereotypical notions about other groups and actual discrimination. "It is quite possible," observes George Fredrickson, "for an individual to have a generalized notion about members of another race or nationality that bears almost no relation to how he actually behaves when confronted with them." In other words, if we are to understand the creative choices that people made in the New World, we must pay close attention not only to what they said and wrote but also to what they did. Whatever racial images may have inhabited the "white mind," Englishmen certainly did not treat blacks and Indians the same way throughout the empire.

Ideas that people held concerning members of other groups are best regarded as loose, even inchoate bundles of opinion. These perceptions tended to be ambivalent, and it usually required a major event such as war or rebellion to trigger outbursts of hatred. In themselves, however, popular attitudes about race and culture did not determine the character of human interaction in the English colonies.

Motives for colonization.   English men and women moved to the New World for many different reasons, not the least of which was escape from personal misadventures. However, by concentrating narrowly upon economic and religious incentives for transfer, we can argue plausibly that the further north the colonists settled, the less obsessed they were with immediate material gain. As historians constantly reiterate, Puritans journeyed to New England for more than the reformation of the Church of England, but religious purity was certainly a matter of considerable importance in establishing a "city on a hill." By the same token, some English people undoubtedly thought they were doing the Lord's work in Virginia. The major preoccupation of these settlers, however, was making money—a great deal of it very quickly. As Edmund S. Morgan has pointed out, the Chesapeake colony in the early seventeenth century took on the characteristics of a "boom town," a place where powerful persons were none too particular about the means they used to gain their ends.

These scrambling, greedy tobacco planters look almost saintly when compared with the individuals who crossed the "line" into a Caribbean world of cutthroats and adventurers. "The expectations the English brought with them," writes Richard Dunn, "and the physical conditions they encountered in the islands produced a hectic mode of life that had no counterpart at home or elsewhere in English experience." In these tropical societies organized religion failed to make much impact upon the colonists' avariciousness. Sugar producers could not possibly have comprehended the communal controls over private gain that bound New Englanders together in small covenanted villages.

How much the expectations of early white leaders affected relations between persons of different races and cultures is difficult to ascertain. Unquestionably, for people of dependent status, life in the southern and island colonies was less pleasant than it would have been in Pennsylvania or Massachusetts Bay. Adventurers who demanded quick returns on investment eagerly exploited anyone's labor, whether they were black, white, or Indian. The ambition to become rich in the New World may have transformed planters into cruel and insensitive masters. But however much we recoil at their behavior, we should not confuse exploitation with racism. In early Virginia and Barbados—two well-recorded societies—the Irish, Africans, and native Americans were at equal disadvantage. In these colonies class rather than race may have been the bond that united workers, and the willingness of the poor whites and blacks to cooperate, to run away together, and in some cases to join in rebellion grew out of a shared experience of poverty and oppression.

Timing of transfer.   In shaping cultural patterns, the earliest migrants, English and African, enjoyed great advantage over later arrivals. The first colonists established rules for interaction, decided what customs would be carried to the New World, and determined the terms under which newcomers would be incorporated into their societies. According to John Porter, the founders should be regarded as "charter" groups. Porter explains that "the first ethnic group to come into a previously unpopulated territory, as the effective possessor, has the most to say. This group becomes the charter group of the society, and among the many privileges and prerogatives which it retains are decisions about what other groups are to be let in and what they will be permitted to do." A double challenge confronted men and women relocated at a later date. They had not only to adjust to an unfamiliar environment but also to accommodate themselves to the people already living there, to members of their own race as well as to other colonists. Timing of transfer, therefore, functioned as an important constraint upon cultural adaptation.

* * * *

Timing was a factor of profound importance in shaping distinct Afro-American cultures. Tensions between black Creoles and newly arrived Africans affected not only the development of specific slave communities but also the ways black people interacted with whites. The fullest evidence comes from the Caribbean islands, especially from Barbados and Jamaica, but similar frictions seem to have occurred in all English possessions south of New England, beginning with the landing of the first African slaves in the early seventeenth century. Frightened and ill, often separated from family and members of their own ethnic groups, these men and women found themselves thrown together with black strangers on ships and later on plantations. Since they spoke different languages, even casual conversation was difficult.

But as Sidney Mintz and Richard Price have argued so provocatively, these early blacks successfully created new cultures that were part African and part American. They transferred some customs familiar to blacks throughout West Africa. The slaves also negotiated compromises, invented new rules and languages, and learned how to deal with whites; in short, they crafted complex social orders in the face of great personal deprivation. The rich oral culture that flourished on plantations transformed these ad hoc measures into viable traditions. Older men and women, particularly obeah men and women, believed to possess special medical or spiritual powers, passed on the decisions of the founders to children born in America. Obviously it took many years and much suffering to establish genuine, stable creole cultures, but they did eventually spring up throughout the Caribbean and southern mainland colonies.

These developments sometimes aggravated hardships experienced by African-born slaves. Creoles established rules for their incorporation into Afro-American plantation communities which often seemed arbitrary to men and women fresh from West Africa. These "outlandish Negroes," "salt-water Negroes," or "Guiney-birds"—as they were called by Creole and whites—could barely comprehend the mechanisms that had deprived them of their freedom, much less the customs that governed exchanges between Afro-Americans. Adjustments generated tensions, even hostilities. Consider, for example, the pain of young Olaudah Equiano, who arrived in the Chesapeake region in 1757. This twelve-year-old slave declared, "I was now exceedingly miserable, and thought myself worse off than any . . . of my companions; for they could talk to each other, but I had no person to speak to that I could understand. In this state I was constantly grieving and pining, and wishing for death." In time most Africans in Equiano's position accepted the conventions of Afro-American culture, just as so many European migrants came to terms with Anglo-American culture. Newcomers, whatever their color, did not experience the possibility of creating a new culture. For them, interacting in strange situations required them to break the code—often under great pressure and quite quickly—of creole culture.

* * * *

From Charter to Creole: Shifting Contexts of Cultural Interaction

The movement of so many men and women to America—Africans as well as Europeans—changed Old World cultures in ways that even the participants only vaguely understood. However determined various ethnic groups may have been to recreate familiar patterns of life within the constraints of a new environment, none succeeded in doing so. Traditional values and beliefs were transformed, and out of this process emerged new cultural realities, mosaics in which one could identify certain elements of a former experience but which also contained pieces that were wholly original.

The process began during the earliest period of transfer, and despite local peculiarities, general patterns emerged. Seventeenth-century migrants were involved in two different kinds of cultural interaction. The first brought men and women of the same race together under conditions that most likely would not have occurred in the Old World. East Anglians were forced to deal with West Country and Kentish migrants, Ibos with Akan. Strangers had to sort themselves out, making compromises about institutional structure and rituals connected with the life cycle. These encounters produced *charter* societies, small, often isolated groupings of people scattered over an immense territory from Barbados to Massachusetts Bay. As we have already noted, the members of charter communities set the rules for the incorporation of later arrivals. One either conformed or moved on. In fact, the influence of the initial immigrants—the timing varied from region to region—was disproportionate to their actual numbers. The second form of encounter, the meeting of representatives of different races, took place among various charter settlers and particular native Americans. During the earliest years of colonization, therefore, men and women learned to live with each other in specific local contexts, and it was not until the eighteenth century that new commercial, demographic, and religious factors significantly changed patterns of cultural interaction.

The creation of Anglo-American cultures began the moment men and women departed from mostly rural areas that time out of mind had provided them and their forefathers with a compelling source of personal identity. These people—especially those who journeyed to New England—planned to reproduce the life they had known in Yorkshire or Kent, Suffolk or Sussex. But almost despite themselves, they became social innovators in America. . . .

. . . In small agricultural communities they effected compromises on sensitive issues, and persons who could not tolerate these arrangements moved on, forming their own charter societies in remote corners of New England. The territory was large enough to accommodate a range of solutions to common social problems. Other founders—William Penn, Lord Baltimore, the earl of Shaftesbury—enjoyed similar charter privileges, and while their economic plans came to nothing, they established legal procedures, institutional forms, and local traditions that in no small way determined how later immigrants would be incorporated into these societies. Virginia was no exception. Even though the founders died by the hundreds, they exercised surprising influence over later generations. After all, the early adventurers made enduring decisions about how to treat Indians and blacks, about the cultivation of staple crops, and about the shape of local government. Strictly speaking, English people who moved to America in the seventeenth century did not become Anglo-Americans. Rather, they joined insulated subcultures, where they were transformed willy-nilly into Anglo-New Englanders, Anglo-Pennsylvanians, Anglo-Barbadians, or Anglo-Virginians. Each was strikingly different from the others. As one historian explains, the Caribbean planters were "as different from their fellows on the mainland as the English were from the Portuguese."

West Africans transported to the New World as slaves also created wholly new cultures. They did so out of fragments—customs taken from one tribe, terms borrowed from another—and within a relatively short time transformed these shards of African experience into scores of separate Afro-American cultures. Slavery placed severe limits on this process. These people were not, however, passive victims. Much like the English migrants who oppressed them, Africans worked with whatever cultural materials they found at hand.

The formation of Afro-American cultures was initially a local process, an interaction among men and women on a single plantation or within a small area. Indeed, some historians argue that the story begins with the mingling of different African ethnic groups aboard slave ships bound for the New World. Whatever the case may have been, once they landed, black migrants attempted to "recreate" familiar customs. During this exciting period of reinvention, probably the most important encounters took place, not between black slaves and white masters, but between Africans of various ethnic backgrounds.

The obstacles to the creation of new cultures were formidable. Individuals spoke different languages; what one person took for granted was often alien to other slaves. Tribal rivalries reappeared in the New World. But by negotiating compromises, by making creative adaptations within hostile physical and social environments, African slaves formed genuine charter societies. . . .

In the early stages of colonization flexibility characterized relations between Afro-Americans and Anglo-Americans. Whatever general ideas the whites may have entertained about black inferiority, they seldom treated blacks as mere chattel. To be sure, patterns of race relations differed from colony to colony, but in none, not even in the staple colonies, did white masters draw boundaries solely upon the basis of color.

During the seventeenth century at least, the range of conversations between whites and blacks was immense. The Afro-American's conversion to Christianity, his ability to speak English, and his personal ingenuity figured into local cultural negotiations. The result was that some blacks became slaves, others servants, and a few successful planters who purchased dependent laborers of their own. . . .

Assessment of the full range of early white-Indian relations raises quite different interpretative problems. For one thing, native Americans suffered horribly from disease. As we have already observed, even before the establishment of permanent English colonies explorers introduced devastating illness, and many Indians who had never seen an English settler experienced terrible demographic reverses. This meant that some bands living along the Atlantic coast were at a great disadvantage in dealing with the colonists; for them the threads of traditional culture were coming unraveled. Initial contact, therefore, did not involve a confrontation between two monolithic racial groups. Rather, members of particular tribes, some weakened by sickness, encountered representatives of specific Anglo-American charter societies.

Creole societies. During the first half of the eighteenth century the peoples of America experienced a cultural transformation as great as that associated with the original transfer. Local "charter" societies began to merge into larger, racially defined "creole" societies. As they did so, patterns of cultural interaction changed profoundly. Many elements contributed to this cultural redefinition, but undoubtedly the most critical was the extraordinary expansion of the Anglo-American and Afro-American populations. Growth heightened cultural density. As these racial groups achieved the ability to maintain and then to expand their numbers through natural reproduction, a process that effected more frequent interaction among native-born adults, racial boundaries became more rigid. Especially in the southern colonies, earlier forms of cultural exchange—open, contingent negotiations based on a range of personal attributes—gave way to an ascriptive system in which people sorted themselves out according to the color of their skins. In fact, one could well argue that white racial prejudice—even racism—owes more to social, economic, and political developments that took place long after initial colonization than it does to general Old World notions about race and color.

During this period, Anglo-Americans increasingly became conscious of a shared cultural identity, a common set of values and beliefs connecting them to English men and women living in other localities. . . .

The forces bringing about greater homogenization in Anglo-American cultures cannot be treated in detail here. A few, however, should be mentioned. First, English rulers centralized administration and standardized legal procedures. If nothing else, the language of commerce, government, and law became less provincial than it had been during the seventeenth century. Second, the long imperial wars against France provided scattered English colonists with a common enemy, a foil that inevitably reinforced their Englishness even as they remained Virginians, Pennsylvanians, or New Englanders. Third, the religious revivals of mid-century, especially George Whitefield's phenomenally successful American tours, broke down local cultural boundaries. In Pennsylvania, for example, evangelical religion actually strengthened main-line Protestant denominations and thereby incorporated persons dispersed over a large area into larger institutional structures. "As the Reformed and Lutheran churches gained strength," John B. Frantz points out, "the fluidity which had characterized religion among the Germans gave way to solidity based on distinctive doctrines and practices."

Fourth, the eighteenth century saw a tremendous increase in commerce not only between the various colonies and the mother country but also among the colonies themselves. . . .

One final element stimulated the development of an expanded cultural core. White Americans of this period were caught up in a consumer revolution of unprecedented dimensions. English ships flooded colonial markets with manufactured goods of all sorts. . . .

The development of an expanded cultural core meant that white newcomers, migrants from the Old World, were no longer incorporated into distinct subcultures, as they had been in the seventeenth century. Rather, these men and women found themselves confronted with two quite different choices. They could move immediately to the frontier, as did many Ulster Scots, and attempt to create "charter" societies of their own. Such enterprises rarely succeeded for long: with each passing year, it became more difficult to establish separate cultural enclaves, ethnic or religious sanctuaries sealed off from the influence of the Anglo-American world. Bernard Bailyn tells of Scottish migrants who located in Vermont, at that time one of the more isolated areas of colonial America. These people—a not atypical group—rapidly lost their ethnic distinctiveness. "Before the revolutionary war was over," Bailyn claims, "the settlers in that remote spot, once part of a distinctive cultural concentration, had dispersed, lost their identity as Scots, and had become simply a collection of rural New Englanders with families and friends in Scotland."

The new immigrants could also embrace the dominant culture, learning English, changing diet, and altering dress. Certainly, many so-called Pennsylvania Dutch favored assimilation over separation. As Stephanie Wolf explains in her study of Germantown, these people undercommunicated cultural differences that might have frightened or angered their Anglo-American neighbors. In 1702, for example, one German advised his countrymen, "Do not stand upon your head, but take advice from the experience of others. In the mean time one need not act hastily, but await with patience the Divine dispensation, until one learns fully how to establish oneself according to the custom of the country." Jon Butler finds a similar pattern among the Huguenots: within a single generation they had shed all attributes—except perhaps their names—that might have set them apart from the dominant English culture.

The changing contexts of eighteenth-century life affected Afro-Americans both positively and negatively. Without doubt, the expansion of staple agriculture, now firmly tied to a world market, brought great misery to the entire slave population. . . .

But the planters' economic success transformed Afro-American cultures in ways that no one could have foreseen. In the mainland colonies the black population not only increased but also became much healthier. Men and women who would have died in the seventeenth century now lived, bore children, and formed extensive contacts with relatives living on neighboring plantations. Gradually, larger creole cultures began to replace isolated charter societies. The general process was analogous to that which the Anglo-Americans had experienced. . . . [B]y the middle of the eighteenth century we can legitimately speak of regional Afro-American cultures each of which was bound by well-defined rules of kinship, shared rituals and customs, and creole languages. . . .

The development of larger configurations based primarily upon skin color altered patterns of race relations throughout colonial America. The boundaries between the two groups were more rigidly drawn, in formal legal codes as well as in everyday practice, than they had been in the seventeenth century. With good reason, white colonists worried that black people would rise up and destroy their masters. Whenever rebellions—or threats of rebellion—occurred, the reaction by the white community was swift and terrible. As Willie Lee Rose observes, the Stono revolt of 1739 provoked the South Carolina legislature to enact "a general 'Negro Act' lumping free blacks and slaves into one category, and prescribing speedy second-class justice for both. . . . South Carolina was on the way to an unenviable reputation as the mainland colony with the harshest slave code." Certainly, English colonists did not attempt to romanticize the slave experience as southern writers did in the early nineteenth century. . . .

Relations between whites and Indians also changed dramatically during the course of the eighteenth century. As native Americans were either destroyed or driven from traditional lands, they ceased to be important in the lives of most colonial Americans. The early settlers had been forced to deal with local native Americans. . . . But by the time of the American Revolution, it is doubtful that many farmers living along the Atlantic coast had ever seen an Indian. . . .

* * * *

By the middle of the eighteenth century, but probably not before, one could reasonably describe American cultures in terms of color: red, white, and black. The openness of the seventeenth-century colonial frontier had spawned a number of promising experiments in cultural exchange. The charter groups gave way in the eighteenth century to larger, self-contained creole societies that were deeply suspicious of one another. It is tragic that poorer whites did not comprehend that they shared a common oppression with the blacks and Indians. With each passing decade throughout the English empire, their whiteness increasingly blinded them to the most daring, most creative forms of cultural adaptation.

Outcome of the Repeopling of British North America on Native Americans, Africans, and Europeans

RUSSELL R. MENARD

. . . With a few notable exceptions, historians of the American immigrant experience have ignored the preindustrial age, confining their comments to obligatory and cursory introductions as they hurry to get to the truly important issues. And despite some promising recent developments, immigration has failed to emerge as a central theme among colonialists, who have instead organized their field around other questions.

This division is artificial and unfortunate, for immigration historians and colonialists ought to have much in common. Certainly the main themes of immigration history as they emerge from scholarship on the nineteenth and twentieth centuries are also key issues in the colonial period. Immigration and opportunity,

From "Migration, Ethnicity, and the Rise of an Atlantic Economy: The Repeopling of British America, 1600–1790," in Vecoli and Sinke, *A Century of European Migrations, 1830–1930,* copyright © 1991. Reprinted by permission of the University of Illinois Press.

assimilation and ethnicity, oppression and resistance, community-building and the construction of a national identity were as central to the colonial era as to the industrial age. Certainly, too, there is continuity in process as well as theme. The great transatlantic migrations of the industrial era—one of the major transforming events of world history—originated in the movements of the early modern age. Indeed, from some perspectives these are not two migrations but a single stream; at the very least the second will not be fully understood without knowledge of the first. Colonialists and immigration historians have much to learn from each other. And they have a grand opportunity. If they work together they can elaborate a consistent vision of the American experience that spans more than four centuries and keeps the role of migrants in building a world economy at its center.

This (chapter) is a plea for such a collaboration. It surveys the colonial period from an immigrationist perspective, asking what we know, what we need to find out, and how we can best get from here to there. Along the way, I will sketch out the shape of the field and point to some key continuities between the colonial period and the national history of the United States. . . .

Native Americans

From the perspective of America's aboriginal inhabitants, the great transatlantic movement of the early modern age was not a migration but an invasion, and the process was not one of populating a wilderness but of re-peopling a once densely settled land. For Indians, the central consequences of that invasion were conquest and demographic disaster. Estimates of the native population of the Americas on the eve of the invasion show wild variation, from the just over eight million suggested by A. L. Kroeber in the 1930s to the more than a hundred million advanced by Woodrow Borah, Henry Dobyns, and others during the 1960s. Although it is unlikely that a universally accepted figure will ever be developed, William Deneven's estimate of fifty-seven million, cautiously offered with a range of 25 percent (forty-three to seventy-two million), reflects current opinion and probably captures the range of possibilities. That range is large, but it is nevertheless a robust result, sufficient to establish that the European invasion of America initiated a holocaust, one of the great demographic catastrophes of human history. By the middle of the seventeenth century there were fewer than ten million, and perhaps only five million, Indians left in the Americas. And, in contrast to the European and Asian experience with massive decline, where recovery was fairly quick, "the Indian population of America recovered only slowly, partially, and in highly modified form."

Additional perspective is provided by the North American experience. The best estimates suggest a population of 4.5 million for North America in 1500, although some argue for a much higher total. In 1770, on the eve of Independence, some 1.8 million whites and fewer than a half million blacks lived in British North America. We do not know how many Indians remained at that date, but it is clear that their numbers had fallen considerably. In all probability there were fewer people in North America in 1770, more than a century and a half after the settlement at Jamestown, than there had been at the beginning of the English invasion. That observation alone should be sufficient to destroy the myth of Europeans transforming an American wilderness into a garden.

It ought to be but it is not, and the myth persists. . . . We have largely failed to assimilate the Native American experience into a comprehensive American history. That assimilation will be difficult, but one strategy emerges from the collaboration between immigration historians and colonialists advocated here. The unifying threads are the fabrication of ethnicity and the persistence of distinct cultures within a pluralistic society despite hostility and oppression. This is not to argue that American Indians can be understood as just another national group. The conditions they faced were extreme, while their aboriginal status, tribal structure, and segregation from white society set them apart from European immigrants. Still, one way of understanding the Indian struggle with their English conquerors is to trace their transformation from independent tribal peoples into America's first ethnic groups.

How Many Immigrants?

. . . Given birth and death rates and the size of colonial populations, net migration can be calculated as a residual, as that portion of the change in population size not attributable to the difference between births and deaths. H. A. Gemery, David Galenson, and Robert Fogel and his collaborators have offered such estimates. Table 2.1 builds on their work to construct a series of net migration estimates for the years 1620 to 1780. These are net figures, it must be emphasized, for the method is unable to account for return migrants or for those who left for other regions in the Americas. As such, they should be read as absolute minimums: the true volume of transatlantic migration must have been a good deal higher.

At least six hundred thousand people, these estimates indicate, crossed the Atlantic between 1620 and 1780 to the British colonies that became the United States. By the standards of the industrial age, that seems a minor movement, barely more than the average annual migration of Europeans overseas in the century following 1820. . . . If we approach the numbers in colonial terms and compare the migration to the base population, it is more impressive. In 1730, for example, there were roughly 650,000 people in the colonies, exclusive of Native Americans: the nearly 150,000 immigrants who arrived between 1720 and 1740 were thus more than 20 percent of the base population, clearly sufficient to profoundly shape all aspects of life. In American history, the colonial period, not the industrial era, was the age of the immigrants.

Those six hundred thousand immigrants were not evenly distributed by region, race, or time. One can divide the colonial period into two broad eras, with a turning point or hinge in the late seventeenth century. The first, from 1620 to 1680, witnessed a steady growth of the migrant stream, although there were always sharp, short-term fluctuations obscured by the high level of aggregation employed in Table 2.1. The migrants were overwhelmingly white, indeed, almost exclusively English, the great majority going to New England and the Chesapeake colonies of Maryland and Virginia. The 1680s and 1690s were marked by both a decline in volume and the beginnings of a new pattern. Thereafter, New England ceased to be a major destination: more often than not it registered a net loss to migration in the eighteenth century. Two more recently settled regions, the mid-Atlantic colonies and the Lower South, emerged as major centers of migration. And, perhaps most

Table 2.1 Estimated Net Migration to British America, 1620–1780*

DATE	NEW ENGLAND			MIDDLE COLONIES			UPPER SOUTH			LOWER SOUTH			TOTAL		
	E	A	T	E	A	T	E	A	T	E	A	T	E	A	T
1620–39	11	0	11	1	0	1	10	0	10	0	0	0	22	0	22
1640–59	8	0	8	1	0	1	25	1	26	0	0	0	34	1	35
1660–79	10	0	10	5	0	5	44	5	49	1	0	1	60	5	65
1680–99	−19	1	−18	20	1	21	32	11	43	3	3	6	36	16	52
1700–1719	15	1	16	8	4	12	7	22	29	3	11	14	33	38	71
1720–39	3	1	4	40	−1	39	19	49	68	8	29	37	70	78	148
1740–59	−25	−1	−26	48	1	49	−1	56	55	13	13	26	35	69	104
1760–79	−27	−5	−32	11	−5	6	39	32	71	45	18	63	68	40	108
Totals													358	247	605

*All numbers in thousands. E = Europeans; A = Africans; T = Total.

Sources: Estimates follow the procedures described in Henry A. Gemery, "Emigration from the British Isles to the New World, 1630–1700: Inferences from Colonial Populations," *Research in Economic History* 5 (1980): 179–231, and David Galenson, *White Servitude in Colonial America: An Economic Analysis* (Cambridge, 1981), 212–18. However, I used estimates of population (and occasionally of vital rates) based on material discussed in John J. McCusker and Russell R. Menard, *The Economy of British America, 1607–1789* (Chapel Hill, 1985). New England includes New Hampshire, Massachusetts, Connecticut, and Rhode Island. Middle colonies include New York, New Jersey, Pennsylvania, and Delaware. The Upper South includes Maryland, Virginia, and North Carolina. The Lower South includes South Carolina and Georgia.

important, blacks came to dominate the migrant stream, outnumbering whites in most years from 1700 to 1760. In the eighteenth century, America was as much an extension of Africa as of Europe.

This last fact points directly to the profound Eurocentrism of immigration history as practiced in the United States. One of the grand opportunities missed by historians of international migration who ignore the colonial era is the chance to explore the African-American experience in their terms. As with Indians, this is not to suggest that blacks can be viewed as simply another ethnic group. Slavery and racism clearly set them apart. But they did struggle against oppression in a hostile environment to forge a new African-American identity out of their common Old World heritage and their shared New World experience. A comprehensive American history must include that process.

The Diversification of the Migrant Stream

The temporal pattern revealed in Table 2.1 suggests a considerable diversification of the migrant stream in the eighteenth century. Clearly, migrants became progressively darker. And a simple division by race obscures the full extent of that diversity. Fortunately, we have, in a surname analysis of the 1790 census originally conducted more than fifty years ago, a rough guide to just how diverse the migrant stream was in the late colonial period.

* * * *

Several historians have offered revisions of the estimates. Table 2.2 amalgamates and summarizes their results. . . .

Perhaps the most striking aspect of these data is the diversity they reveal: from its beginning, the United States was an ethnic mosaic. People of English background were by far the largest group, but they constituted less than half the total and only 60 percent of the whites, a fact that raises questions about the persistent tendency of colonialists to portray early America as a simple extension of England. Blacks were the next largest group, nearly 20 percent of the whole, although that category conceals a variety of cultural backgrounds. The remainder of the population came from Britain's Celtic fringe and from Western Europe, especially the Rhine Valley. It must be stressed that Native Americans do not appear in these estimates: their presence adds further variety to a highly diverse population.

The data also describe sharp regional variation. New England was clearly the most homogeneous area, its population overwhelmingly white, its whites largely English. The mid-Atlantic states were also largely white, but hardly homogeneous, as large concentrations of German, Dutch, and Scots-Irish settlers combined to outnumber the English and produce a truly polygot population. The South too was diverse, but in a different way. There the striking facts were the substantial black population, nearly 40 percent of the total in 1790, and the ethnic variety among whites due in large part to the heavy Celtic presence. We need to be careful in generalizing about the South, however, for the category obscures a major difference between plantation districts, where slaves were often a large majority and most whites were English, and the mixed-farming regions of the

Table 2.2 Composition of the U.S. Population in 1790 (in %)

	EUROPEAN	AFRICAN	ENGLISH	WELSH	SCOTS-IRISH	SCOTS	IRISH	GERMAN	FRENCH
New England	98	2	82	3	6	3	3	—	1
Mid-Atlantic states	94	6	38	3	11	5	5	30	2
Upper South	64	36	36	4	8	4	5	5	2
Lower South	58	42	29	4	10	5	5	3	2
Kentucky and Tennessee	85	15	45	4	15	7	7	6	1
United States	81	19	48	4	9	3	5	10	2

Sources: American Council of Learned Societies, "Report of the Committee on Linguistic and National Stocks in the United States," American Historical Association, *Annual Report for the Year 1931* (Washington, D.C., 1932), 1:122; Forrest McDonald and Ellen Shapiro McDonald, "The Ethnic Origins of the American People, 1790," *William and Mary Quarterly*, 3d ser., 37 (1980): 198; Thomas L. Purvis, "The European Ancestry of the United States Population, 1790," *William and Mary Quarterly* 41 (1984): 98.

German includes some people of Dutch and Swedish background. New England includes Vermont, New Hampshire, Massachusetts, Connecticut, and Rhode Island. The Mid-Atlantic states include New York, Pennsylvania, New Jersey, and Delaware. The Upper South includes Maryland, Virginia, and North Carolina. The Lower South includes South Carolina and Georgia. Native American peoples not included because they were not included in the 1790 federal census.

backcountry, where blacks were few and whites more often of Celtic or German background.

The Sources of Ethnic Diversity

Accounting for the ethnic and racial diversity of the American population and for the particular regional pattern it describes is no easy task. That variety reflected reproductive differences as well as the interaction of numerous migrations, themselves the product of countless individual choices made in three continents over two centuries. Research suggests that we can make some progress in sorting out the complexity by distinguishing between types of migrants and processes of recruitment. The bulk of people who moved to the colonies came either as workers recruited through a transatlantic labor market or as settlers recruited by land speculators.

The largest group of migrants, perhaps three-quarters of the total, came as workers, usually single, predominantly male, and generally young, in their late teens and early twenties, recruited through a transatlantic labor market developed during the first phase of England's invasion of North America. Initially, most of these migrants were English—indeed, at first the majority came from London and its immediate hinterland—who arrived as indentured servants in a movement that extended and complemented patterns of labor mobility within England. Over time, however, the English-American migrant stream proved inadequate to the needs of colonial employers. When it did so they turned to other areas to recruit workers, first within Great Britain, later on the European continent and in Africa, in the process changing the composition of the migrant group.

We can get some sense of why the migrant stream became increasingly diverse and a better appreciation of the extent of the change by a close look at the Chesapeake colonies of Maryland and Virginia. Documentation for that region is relatively full, and it has been the subject of intense study by social historians. Further, sitting at the center of the demographic spectrum that was British America, the tobacco coast reveals the full range of possibilities in the composition of colonial populations.

In the 1630s, when the English at last established permanent, secure colonies in North America, migrants to the Chesapeake were a homogenous lot. They were overwhelmingly young, single, English males in their late teens and early twenties, usually with some prior work experience and often sons of yeomen and artisans who arrived as indentured servants. By the end of the century the migrants were more diverse. The most obvious and striking change was the growth of slavery. By the 1690s, blacks were a majority among new arrivals. There were also significant shifts in the composition of white immigrants. The majority were still servants, but the migration stream now included a greater proportion of women, of young boys in their early to middle teens, and of the children of the very poor. And they came from different parts of Great Britain. In the 1630s, the majority of servants to the Chesapeake were from London and the home counties. By the 1690s, the recruiting net was cast more widely and captured large numbers from the southwest and north of England as well as from the Celtic fringe, particularly from the Welsh counties near Bristol and Liverpool and from Ireland.

The greater diversity of the migrant stream was triggered by changes in the supply of indentured servants. The number of servants delivered to Maryland and Virginia rose steadily from the 1630s to the 1660s. The supply leveled out in the mid-1660s, or at least grew at a slower rate, before registering a sharp decline in the 1680s, a decline that persisted into the eighteenth century. Demand for workers continued to grow, however, producing a severe labor shortage for planters.

... Why did the number of English immigrants to the Chesapeake increase rapidly during the first half of the seventeenth century, level out or grow much more slowly in the 1660s and 1670s, and then decline after 1680? Two processes seem of central importance: changes in the size of the potential migrant group and changes in the relative attractiveness of the several destinations available to English men and women on the move. Although neither can be measured precisely, it is clear that during the seventeenth century both changed in ways that tended first to increase and then to reduce the number of servants willing to try their luck in tobacco.

The number of potential emigrants in seventeenth-century England was a function of total population, an assertion that must be qualified by a recognition that migration was highly age, sex, and probably class specific and that the propensity to migrate varied with time. Nevertheless, changes in the rate of population growth provide a rough index to changes in the size of the potential migrant group. Despite disagreements over the absolute size of total population and the rate and sources of change, it is clear that the pattern of growth within England changed sharply near the middle decades of the seventeenth century. The most reliable estimates describe an average annual growth rate of 0.4 to 0.5 percent for roughly two centuries, beginning from a base of 2.5 million in the mid-fifteenth century and reaching 5.5 million in 1650. England's population declined slowly over the next forty years to about five million, its level during the 1620s, and then began to grow again, slowly at first, more rapidly toward the middle decades of the eighteenth century. If movement to the Chesapeake were a function of the size of the population alone, one would expect the rate of immigration to increase during the first half of the seventeenth century and then decline.

Other processes reinforced the impact of changes in the number of potential migrants, tending first to increase and later to reduce the attractiveness of the Chesapeake relative to other destinations. In part, this was a function of changing prospects at home. During the sixteenth and early seventeenth centuries, real wages in England fell as a growing number of workers competed for employment. Falling wages lowered the opportunity costs of migration and made movement to the colonies more attractive. Relieved of the pressure of a rapidly growing population, wages rose across the last half of the seventeenth century. Higher wages increased the opportunity cost to migration and worked both to reduce the size of the migrating population and, for those who still chose to move, to increase the attractiveness of destinations within England.

The course of opportunity for ex-servants in Maryland and Virginia helped shape the pattern of migration. The likelihood that a young man who completed servitude along the Bay would achieve a comfortable position in society was high to about 1660 and then began to decline, a decline that became especially sharp after 1680 when former servants often left the region in search of better prospects elsewhere. The chances for success along the tobacco coast were initially a substantial encouragement to prospective migrants, but the size of that inducement fell as the seventeenth century progressed.

Perhaps more important than the course of opportunity within the Chesapeake colonies was the changing attractiveness of the tobacco coast relative to other colonial regions. During the 1630s, poor English men and women who decided to cross the Atlantic could choose among three destinations, but in the 1640s sugar and disease gave the West Indies a bad reputation, while the failure of New England to find a profitable export prevented the growth of a lively demand for servants. These developments narrowed the options and focused the greatest part of the English transatlantic migratory stream on the tobacco coast. After 1680, the opening up of Pennsylvania and the Carolinas ended this near monopoly and diverted migrants away from the Chesapeake colonies. In short, changes in the size of the British-American migration stream and in the share of all migrants attracted to Virginia and Maryland worked first to increase and then to reduce the number of servants bound for the tobacco coast.

Planters and merchants were not passive in the face of these changes. Indeed, recruiting agents were a critical link in the process and could, by varying the intensity of their efforts, shape both the volume and direction of migration. During the seventeenth century their efforts were usually successful in the short run, and, as a consequence, the supply of new servants proved highly sensitive to short-term shifts in planter demand. Over the long haul, shifts in the composition of the servant group suggest some more permanent adjustment in recruiting practices as merchants cast their net more widely in the search for migrants.

In the middle decades of the seventeenth century, recruiters apparently focused on young men in their late teens and early twenties from the middling ranks of English families with some job skills and work experience. After 1660, however, as their numbers dwindled and their opportunities at home increased, few such men moved to Virginia and Maryland. Recruiters tried to meet the shortfall by drawing more heavily on other groups within Britain's population—Irish, women, convicts, homeless orphans, and the laboring poor. Despite these efforts it proved impossible to overcome the powerful secular processes—a stagnant English population and the increasing pull of other destinations—tending to diminish the ability of tobacco planters to attract willing workers. During the last decades of the seventeenth century merchants were unable to meet the growing demand for indentured labor without driving the cost of servants beyond what planters were willing to pay. The result was a major change in the composition of the Chesapeake work force as merchants tapped new sources of servants and planters turned increasingly to African slaves as their principle source of labor.

Work by H. A. Gemery and Jan Hogendorn suggests a way of generalizing this narrative of migration to the Chesapeake, of constructing a model that illuminates the movement of workers to the Americas as a whole. Their key insight concerns the differences in supply between African slaves and all other sources of labor available to colonial employers. The developers of British America had several options in recruiting and organizing a work force. They could draw on free workers and servants from England, Ireland, Wales, and the European continent, on Native Americans from the vast North American interior, and on colonial-born youths not yet established in households of their own. All of those workers moved in small, localized markets characterized by sharp, unpredictable shifts in volume and price. However, as long as demand for labor in a particular region remained low, one of those sources was adequate to meet the need for workers. Thus New England, where the failure to develop a major staple export meant a sluggish economy and relatively low levels of labor productivity, found enough workers in its own sons and daughters, thereby retaining its ethnic homogeneity.

Regions where demand for labor was higher, however, quickly ran into difficulty if they relied on a single source. The prices of workers in those small, localized markets rose sharply, pressed against profit margins, and set off a scramble by merchants who often exhibited considerable ingenuity in developing new sources of labor. Thus in the middle colonies, where a lively agricultural export sector and linked commercial development created a more expansive economy and higher levels of worker productivity, there emerged a complex and rapidly changing labor market that lay behind the ethnic diversity of that population. A different pattern emerged in the southern colonies. Those regions experimented with work forces drawn from a variety of sources early in the development of each area, but high productivity and increasing demand quickly exhausted those small and localized supplies and drove planters toward slaves, Africans trapped in a much wider net, commodities in a stable, large-scale, international labor market that made them the victims of choice in the rapidly expanding plantation colonies of European America.

While an analysis of labor markets along the lines suggested by Gemery and Hogendorn explains much of the diversity of the American population, it cannot account for it all. A substantial portion of the white migration, particularly during the eighteenth century, was not caught up in the labor markets that brought servants and slaves to British America. These were free migrants who moved in family groups, often, as Bernard Bailyn has described them, "sizeable families of some small substance, hit by rent increases that threatened their future security, resentful of personal services they were still required to perform," and, I would add, occasionally pursuing a utopian vision of religious freedom and community. Most, Bailyn continues, were "eager for a fresh start as landowners or at least tenants of independent status capable of expressing their energies in expansive ways." Few were rich, but they were able to scrape together enough money to pay their passage, "buy or rent a stake in the land, equip themselves for the work that lay ahead, and tide themselves over the lean period before the first crops could be produced.

Unfortunately, we cannot describe this migration with the precision possible in the case of workers caught up in the Atlantic labor market. It is clear, however, that land speculators, those much-maligned creatures of the American frontier, played a key role in the process. In efforts to develop their often vast holdings, speculators—perhaps it would be more accurate to call them estate developers— disseminated information, organized passage, provided creative financing, and offered a range of services, all at easy terms. Colonists from Britain and the European continent took up their offers, thus helping to create the ethnic complexity of early America.

Accommodating Ethnic Diversity

It is possible to describe the diversity of the people of early America with precision and to provide a systematic account of the migrations that produced the complex ethnic mosaic of 1790. Moving beyond those issues to the other major themes of immigration history is more difficult. The problem is not an absence of work on such questions by colonialists.

* * * *

. . . The difficulty lies rather in the complexity of the subject and in the absence of compelling, comprehensive generalizations.

Without pretending that it captures the full complexity of the matter, I offer this as an integrating hypothesis: in certain critical respects, the people of British America exhibited more homogeneity—or, more precisely, less ethnic diversity—in 1776 than they had earlier in the colonial period. By exploring this proposition we can make some progress toward constructing a history of British America from an immigrationist perspective.

Timothy Breen suggests that the question of ethnic identity can be approached through a focus on the cultural interactions characteristic of early America. During the seventeenth century, he notes, those interactions fell into two broad categories, both of them fluid, diverse, and complex, marked by the "creative adaptation" of participants to new, unstable, rapidly changing circumstances. One type brought people of the same race or nation but from different localities together under conditions of relative equality in ways rare in the Old World outside of Europe's major metropolitan capitals. Thus, "East Anglians were forced to deal with West Country and Kentish migrants, Ibos with Akan. Strangers had to sort themselves out, making compromises about institutional structure and rituals connected with the life cycle." While the sorting process went on, Old World identities at first persisted in an almost bewildering diversity. Eventually, however, and by means that remain obscure, those migrants—and, more completely, their descendents—coalesced into creole cultures, what can be called "charter communities" that "set the rules for the incorporation of later arrivals."

The second type of interaction involved people of different races: red, white, and black. Although it would be a gross exaggeration to claim that such encounters occurred among individuals or groups wielding equal power, those initial meetings were fluid, diverse, and flexible, and circumstances often made it "possible for individuals to negotiate social status on the basis of various attributes, only one of which was race." Again, however, there was a coalescence—perhaps hardening is the better word—of racial ideologies, and racial identities as structured, hierarchical, castelike relationships based on color overwhelmed the more fluid interactions of the early settlements.

Despite the gradual development of creole societies and racial identities, British America exhibited a remarkable cultural diversity in the early decades of the eighteenth century. Much of that diversity rested in the local, parochial character of colonial settlements. The charter societies and the relationships among whites, blacks, and Native Americans were elaborated in different ways and with unique outcomes in each of the major regions—New England, the middle colonies, the Chesapeake, and the low country—regions relatively isolated from one another, each integrated into a larger Atlantic world more through contacts with England than by relations with other colonies. And even within those regions, pockets of ethnic diversity persisted for the still-developing creole cultures—the charter societies built by the early European and African settlers—had not yet overwhelmed or absorbed the customs, loyalties, and identities of more recent migrants.

Although the migrant stream became more varied as the Revolution approached, British North America exhibited progressively less cultural diversity. Two related processes account for the paradox. The first is what John Murrin has called the "Anglicization" of British America, a "general standardization of procedures, tastes, and assumptions" as white colonials in each of the major regions developed a heightened sense of cultural identity and a common set of values and institutions that linked them to settlers in the other areas while gradually eroding the parochial, localized cultures of the seventeenth century. Anglicization had several roots: the creation of a centralized administrative bureaucracy, of standardized legal procedures, and of common institutional structures to govern the empire; the frequent imperial wars against Spain and France which helped forge a common consciousness; the religious revivals that crossed cultural boundaries; the growth of coast-wise trade which improved communications and linked colonial merchants and planters into a commercial network; an increase in migration between the major regions; the rapid economic growth and rising incomes which tied white Americans into a common consumer culture based on English manufactures; and, after 1763, the growing storm of protest against the encroachments of the British Empire which began the slow process of forging a national identity. These processes worked together rather than at cross-purposes to undermine local cultures and regional identities, leaving, as Jack Greene put it, "the separate colonies far more alike than they had ever been at any earlier time."

The second process promoting homogeneity was the continued elaboration of creole cultures established earlier in the colonial period. Africans and Europeans who arrived in British America during the eighteenth century encountered an increasingly structured, articulated social system and powerful incentives and pressures to embrace the dominant culture, to become Anglo Americans or African Americans quickly and with little resistance. Those who moved to the periphery of settlement sometimes maintained separate cultural identities, but most groups—the Scots of Vermont, the Pennsylvania Dutch of Germantown, the Huguenots, the Africans in the Chesapeake—quickly lost their distinctiveness, retaining only their names (and for blacks not even those) as reminders that they had once been separate peoples.

It will not do to exaggerate. Pockets of ethnic identity persisted in America through the late eighteenth and early nineteenth centuries. And the young United

States was a pluralistic society. It was, however, a pluralism based on color, a multicultural society of reds, whites, and blacks in which race rather than Old World origins proved the primary determinant of ethnic identity.

FURTHER READING

David Grayson Allen, *In English Ways: The Movement of Societies and the Transferal of English Local Law and Custom to Massachusetts Bay in the Seventeenth Century* (1981).
Thomas Archdeacon, *New York City, 1664–1710: Conquest and Change* (1976).
Bernard Bailyn, *The Peopling of British North America* (1986).
Bernard Bailyn and Philip D. Morgan, eds., *Strangers within the Realm: Cultural Margins of the First British Empire* (1991).
Bernard Bailyn and Barbara DeWolfe, *Voyagers to the West: A Passage in the Peopling of America on the Eve of the Revolution* (1986).
Randall H. Balmer, *A Perfect Babel of Confusion: Dutch Religion and English Culture in the Middle Colonies* (1989).
Patricia U. Bonomi, *Under the Cope of Heaven: Religion, Society, and Politics in Colonial America* (1986).
Jon Butler, *The Huguenots in America: A Refugee People in a New World Society* (1983).
David Cressy, *Coming Over: Migration and Communication Between England and New England in the 17th Century* (1987).
Philip Curtin, *Africa Remembered: Narratives by West Africans from the Era of the Slave Trade* (1967).
Philip Curtin, *The Atlantic Slave Trade: A Census* (1969).
Richard Dunn, *Sugar and Slaves: The Rise of the Planter Class in the English West Indies, 1624–1713* (1972).
Roger Ekirch, *Bound for America: The Transportation of British Convicts to the Colonies, 1718–1775* (1987).
David Hackett Fischer, *Albion's Seed: Four British Folkways in America* (1989).
Aaron Spencer Fogleman, *Hopeful Journeys: German Immigration, Settlement, and Political Culture, 1717–1775* (1996).
David Galenson, *White Servitude in Colonial America: An Economic Analysis* (1981).
Marcus Lee Hansen, *The Atlantic Migration, 1607–1860: A History of the Continuing Settlement of the United States* (1941).
James Horn, *Adapting to a New World: English Society in the Seventeenth-Century Chesapeake* (1994).
Ned Landsman, *Scotland and Its First American Colony, 1683–1765* (1985).
James G. Leyburn, *The Scotch-Irish: A Social History* (1962).
James T. Lemon, *'The Best Poor Man's Country': A Geographical Study of Early Southeastern Pennsylvania* (1972).
John J. McCusker and Russell R. Menard, *The Economy of British America, 1607–1789* (1985).
Sidney Mintz, *Sweetness and Power: The Place of Sugar in Modern History* (1985).
Edmund Morgan, *American Slavery, American Freedom: The Ordeal of Colonial America* (1976).
A. G. Roeber, *Palatines, Liberty, and Property: German Lutherans in Colonial America* (1993).
Sharon V. Salinger, *'To Serve Well and Faithfully': Labor and Indentured Servants in Pennsylvania, 1682–1880* (1987).

Sally Schwartz, *'A Mixed Multitude': The Struggle for Toleration in Colonial Pennsylvania* (1987).

Mechal Sobel, *The World They Made Together: Black and White Values in Eighteenth Century Virginia* (1988).

John van der Zee, *Bound Over: Indentured Servitude and American Conscience* (1985).

Stephanie G. Wolf, *Urban Village: Population, Community, and Family Structure in Germantown, Pennsylvania, 1683–1800* (1976).

Peter Wood, *Black Majority: Negroes in Colonial South Carolina from 1670 through the Stono Rebellion* (1974).

CHAPTER
3

Nation and Citizenship in the Age of Revolution, 1750–1800

In the era of the American Revolution, residents of the former British American colonies pondered how an American citizen was to be created. For some, the question was a theoretical one. Although some residents of the colonies feared the migration of non-English colonists, the perception that the colonies were "the best poor man's country in the world" led many others to see the colonies as a locale fundamentally superior to England—and Europe. These sentiments were perhaps best expressed by Hector St. Jean de Crèvecoeur, who celebrated the "great American asylum" where immigrants could profit from economic opportunity and political independence. In this asylum, a new people was created as immigrants of diverse backgrounds threw off the vestiges of their past and were "melted into a new race of men."

When the United States became an independent nation, however, the question was no longer theoretical. Americans who created the United States had to grapple simultaneously with loyalty to nation, citizenship, and the naturalization of citizens. The ways in which they dealt with these issues created critical precedents for future policies. As they fought a war, American leaders hoped to keep a diverse lot of people on the side of the fledgling new nation. Support for the American cause varied across ethnic and racial groups in the United States. Nonetheless, representatives from a variety of groups, from Germans living in Pennsylvania to African Americans in New England, used the rhetoric of the Revolution to voice support for independence and to petition, in the case of slaves, for freedom.

Despite this spirit of innovation emblematic of the creation of a republican form of government, not all Americans were treated equally. Because Americans created a republic, the consent of the governed was central. And because the United States already was a nation mainly of immigrants from diverse pasts, the problem of naturalization of future immigrants had to be addressed. It is true that colonial assemblies had already contemplated the issue of naturalization before the American Revolution, but only after independence was the United States as a nation forced to develop a policy regarding who could become a citizen, who could be naturalized, and even who could immigrate. The Naturalization Act of 1790 charted out the way in which an immigrant became a citizen. Also importantly, it provided citizenship for "free, white" people who had lived in the United States for a period of only two *years. Whereas the length of residence was subsequently increased to five years, the distinction between "free, white" people, who could attain citizenship, and "non-free, non-white" people, who could not, endured for eighty years. The United States thus had effectively color-coded citizenship rights. A flurry of legislation in 1798 considered the dangers of aliens as the new nation appeared to be careening toward war again. Although these acts illustrated a fear of the alien, the relatively simple route to citizenship for white immigrants was maintained. These early acts were central in framing the structures of citizenship. "White" people were given relatively simple terms for transferring allegiance to the United States, whereas naturalization was an impossibility for nonwhite people. One wonders if the new race of people imagined by Crèvecoeur was meant only to include people of European ancestry.*

DOCUMENTS

Shortly before the United States became a nation, an immense immigration was transforming the American population. For some colonists, this fact was a source of concern. Most notable, perhaps, is the argument made by Benjamin Franklin, found in the first document, as part of his analysis of population growth in the colonies. Because natural population growth in the colonies was so rapid, Franklin (1755) believes that people from England, rather than from, say, Africa or Germany, could populate the colonies for the benefit of Britain and the British colonies. Likewise, Daniel Dulany (1758) points to the discrimination faced by aliens that leads him to protest the actions by the Maryland general assembly in 1758. Others were more optimistic about the colonies' diversity, as illustrated in the next two documents. Patrick M'Robert (1774) and Crèvecoeur (1782) each celebrate the possibilities for what M'Robert called "people of small fortunes." For Crèvecoeur, it means that a new people would be forged in America. The next two documents show how the era of the American Revolution was a time of optimism for many people. German journalists in Philadelphia (1776) remembered how, as serfs in Europe, they were "little better than black slaves," whereas the United States allowed them liberty. African Americans (1774–1777) next use the rhetoric of the Revolution to petition for their freedom. Unfortunately, for the petitioners, their appeals were not heard by the new American Congress, as shown by the final documents. Although the Alien Act of 1798 gave the president great power to expel aliens from the country, the earlier Naturalization Act of 1790 differentiated between "white" and "non-white" people in enabling immigrants to become naturalized citizens.

Benjamin Franklin Opposes the Migration of Non-English into the Colonies, 1755

. . . 5. *Europe* is generally full settled with husbandmen, manufacturers, &c. and therefore cannot now much increase in People: *America* is chiefly occupied by Indians, who subsist mostly by hunting. But as the hunter, of all men, requires the greatest quantity of land from whence to draw his subsistence, (the husbandman subsisting on much less, the gardener on still less, and the manufacturer requiring least of all), the *Europeans* found *America* as fully settled as it well could be by

As found in Benjamin Franklin, *Observations Concerning the Increase of Mankind, Peopling of Countries, &c.* (Tarrytown, NY: William Abbatt, 1918).

hunters; yet these having large Tracts, were easily prevail'd on to part with portions of territory to the new comers, who did not much interfere with the natives in hunting, and furnish'd them with many things they wanted.

6. Land being thus plenty in *America,* and so cheap as that a labouring man that understands Husbandry, can in a short time save money enough to purchase a piece of new Land sufficient for a plantation, whereon he may subsist a family; such are not afraid to marry; for if they even look far enough forward to consider how their children when grown up are to be provided for, they see that more Land is to be had at rates equally easy, all circumstances considered.

7. Hence Marriages in *America* are more general, and more generally early, than in *Europe*. And if it is reckoned there, that there is but one marriage per annum among one hundred persons, perhaps we may here reckon two; and if in *Europe* they have but four Births to a marriage (many of their marriages being late) we may here reckon eight, of which if one half grow up, and our marriages are made, reckoning one with another at twenty years of age our people must at least be doubled every twenty years.

8. But not withstanding this increase, so vast is the Territory of *North America,* that it will require many ages to settle it fully; and till it is fully settled, labour will never be cheap here, where no man continues long a labourer for others, but gets a Plantation of his own, no man continues long a journeyman to a trade, but goes among those new settlers and sets up for himself, &c. Hence labour is no cheaper now in *Pennsylvania,* than it was thirty years ago, tho' so many thousand labouring people have been imported.

9. The danger therefore of these Colonies interfering with their Mother Country in trades that depend on labour, Manufacturers, &c. is too remote to require the attention of *Great Britain*.

. . . 12. 'Tis an ill-grounded opinion that by the labour of slaves, *America* may possibly vie in cheapness of manufactures with *Britain*. The labour of slaves can never be so cheap here as the labour of working men is in *Britain*. Any one may compute it. Interest of money is in the Colonies from six to ten per Cent. Slaves one with another cost thirty £. Sterling per head. Reckon then the interest of the first purchase of a slave, the Insurance or risque on his life, his cloathing and diet, expenses in his sickness and loss of time, loss by his neglect of business. (Neglect is natural to the man who is not to be benefited by his own care or diligence), Expence of a Driver to keep him at work, and his pilfering from time to time, almost every slave being *by Nature* a thief, and compare the whole amount with the wages of a manufacturer of iron or wool in *England*, you will see that labour is much cheaper there than it ever can be by negroes here. Why then will *Americans* purchase slaves? Because slaves may be kept as long as a man pleases, or has occasion for their labour; while hired men are continually leaving their master (often in the midst of his business,) and setting up for themselves.

13. As the increase of people depends on the encouragement of marriages, the following things must diminish a Nation, *viz.* . . .

* * * *

. . . The Introduction of slaves. The negroes brought into the *English* Sugar *Islands* have greatly diminished the whites there; the poor are by this means depriv'd of employment, while a few families acquire vast Estates, which they spend on foreign luxuries, and educating their children in the habit of those luxuries, the same Income is needed for the support of one that might have maintain'd one hundred. The Whites who have slaves, not labouring, are enfeebled, and therefore not so generally prolific; the slaves being work'd too hard, and ill fed, their constitutions are broken, and the deaths among them are more than the births; so that a continual supply is needed from *Africa.* The Northern Colonies having few slaves increase in Whites. Slaves also pejorate[1] the Families that use them; the white children become proud, disgusted with labour, and being educated in idleness, are rendered unfit to get a Living by industry.

* * * *

21. . . . Nor is it necessary to bring in foreigners to fill up any occasional vacancy in a country; for such vacancy (if the Laws are good) will soon be filled by natural generation. Who can now find the vacancy made in *Sweden, France* or other warlike nations, by the Plague of heroism forty Years ago; in *France* by the expulsion of the Protestants; in *England* by the settlement of her Colonies; or in *Guinea,* by one hundred years' exportation of slaves, that has blacken'd half *America?* The thinness of inhabitants in *Spain* is owing to national pride and idleness, and other causes, rather than to the expulsion of the *Moors,* or to the making of new settlements.

* * * *

22. . . . there are suppos'd to be now upwards of One Million *English* Souls in *North America,* (tho' 'tis thought scarce 80,000 have been brought over sea) and yet perhaps there is not one the fewer in *Britain,* but rather many more, on Account of the employment the Colonies afford to manufacturers at home. This million doubling, suppose but once in twenty-five years, will in another century be more than the people of *England,* and the greatest Number of *Englishmen* will be on this side the water. What an accession of Power to the *British* empire by the Sea as well as Land!

* * * *

23. In fine, A nation well regulated is like a Polypus; take away a limb, its place is soon supply'd; cut it in two, and each deficient part shall speedily grow out of the part remaining. Thus if you have room and subsistence enough, as you may by dividing make ten Polypes out of one, you may of one make ten nations, equally populous and powerful; or rather, increase a nation ten fold in numbers and strength.

And since detachments of *English* from *Britain* sent to *America,* will have their places at home so soon supply'd and increase so largely here; why should the *Palatine Boors* be suffered to swarm into our settlements, and by herding together establish their languages and manners to the exclusion of ours? Why should *Pennsylvania,* founded by the *English,* become a colony of *Aliens,* who will shortly be so numerous as to Germanize us instead of our Anglifying them, and will never adopt our language or customs, any more than they can acquire our complexion?

---

[1]Depreciate, or degrade.

24. Which leads me to add one remark: That the number of purely white people in the world is proportionably very small. All *Africa* is black or tawny. *Asia* chiefly tawny. *America* (exclusive of the new comers) wholly so. And in *Europe,* the *Spaniards, Italians, French, Russians* and *Swedes* are generally of what we call a swarthy complexion; as are the *Germans* also, the *Saxons* only excepted, who with the *English* make the principal body of white people on the face of the earth. I could wish their numbers were increased. And while we are, as I may call it, *scouring* our planet, by clearing *America* of woods, and so making this side of our globe reflect a brighter light to the eyes of inhabitants in *Mars* or *Venus,* why should we in the sight of superior beings, darken its people? why increase the sons of *Africa,* by planting them in *America,* where we have so fair an opportunity, by excluding all blacks and tawneys, of increasing the lovely white and red? But perhaps I am partial to the complexion of my Country, for such kind of partiality is natural to Mankind.

Daniel Dulany, a Jurist, Defends the Rights of Aliens in Maryland, 1758

The question being put, whether the Bill sent up from the Lower House entituled "an Act for the Security of purchasers and others Claiming by or from protestant Aliens" should pass and determined in the negative: To that negative I Dissent and desire that my Dissent with the following reasons for it may be entered.

1. Because Aliens who have settled in this Province, and by their Labour Industry & Frugality improved a Wilderness into regular Fruitful and well stocked Plantations, were invited hither by Proclamations Translated into the German Language and Carefully Dispersed in Germany; and the Faith of this Government, which ought to be religiously observed, hath been in the most solemn and explicit Terms engaged to them that they should be secure and protected in the enjoyment of their property.

3. Because the Rights of Aliens acquired upon the most meritorious Considerations were to be destroyed [*sic*] impeached or brought into Hazards for the delusive Prospect of a temporary Increase of his Lordships Revenues, and many Hundred Families of usefull industrious and well affected Subjects would be effectually Banished and others under their Circumstances Certainly prevented by Such a flagrant Violation of the Rules of good Faith and Justice from Settling here, to the real Diminution of his Lordships Revenue, the disgrace of his Government and the Impoverishment of his Province.

4. Because such a Bill (it having been the Subject of Deliberation and publick Debate) is now become Absolutely necessary to quiet the minds of the Alien Inhabitants who might be intimidated into a surrender of their Rights upon the Issuing of Escheat Warrants from their Ignorance of our Laws and Constitution, a Consciousness of

As found in Stephen Botein, *Early American Law and Society* (New York: Knopf, 1983).

their Inability to manage Law suits with the Same Advantage that others can, or a dread of Power; . . . .

6. Because such Bills have passed into Laws in the other Colonies, Particularly in New York, Pensilvania [*sic*] and Virginia, and the want of such a provision here will deprive this province of the Benefit accruing to the other Colonies from their better Policy in this Article, for the Situation and Circumstances of the Inhabitants of this Country (except a few Mechanicks) are such that they cant Subsist without the Allowance of Some portion of real Property, and Aliens are not Naturalized by "the Act of Parliament for naturalizing of Foreign Protestants" till after a residence in the Plantations for a Term of Years. . . .

7. Because the Miscarriage of the Bill in this House may set greedy men upon Disturbing the Possessions of Aliens from an Expectation of the Countenance of the Government, and should any of these Alien Inhabitants be hereafter naturalized (which depends upon the Probable Contingency of their Living the Time required by the Statute), after being Stripped of their Possessions for want of knowledge or ability or a defect of Spirit to defend their Rights, they might recover their Lands against Escheat Patentees from the Legal Operation of their Naturalization, and great oppression Confusion and multiplicity of Law Suites and other Inconveniencies may ensue.

9. Lastly, because the suggestion is as groundless as the apprehension is Chimerical, that if this Bill were passed into a Law some expressions artificially inserted in it may possibly introduce rule of Determination in the Courts of Law tending to invalidate his Lordships General Right in the matter of Escheats, and if there were Really such expressions they ought to be pointed out and corrected & not Assigned as a reason for rejecting the whole Bill. The Composition of the Bill is so Concise and plain, and the subject Matter of it so Confined and Simple, that the Dread of any Intent Design in the Framers of it Seems to be rather the effect of an excessive Diffidence than a prudent Caution.

Patrick M'Robert Defends Immigration, 1774

The misrepresentations and contradictory accounts received from that western world [America], since the spirit of emigration prevailed in North Britain, may perhaps apologize for publishing this Tour. For, while one represented the case of the emigrants as a state of perfect felicity, as if they had entered into elysium upon their setting foot on the American shore; another described it to be the most deplorable, as if when they crossed the Atlantic, they had plunged themselves into labyrinths of endless misery. These are only the relations of party and prejudice, and are exaggerated on both sides. For, as in this life, we need not expect uninterrupted prosperity in America more than in Europe, neither are they who

From "Patrick M'Roberts Tour Through Part of the North Provinces of America," 1774.

have emigrated wretched to any degree like what has been represented. On the contrary, the writer of these Letters will venture to affirm, that it was the best country in the world for people of small fortunes; or in other words, the best poor man's country, before these unhappy disputes arose. It takes a good while however, to get established on an agreeable footing even in this country; the difficulties to encounter in America are many: in the first place, a long sea voyage, there every thing is strange; you have all to seek, and as it were, to begin the world anew; to acquire acquaintances; to struggle hard for a character, &c. These require courage and resolution in the adventurer, and with a little share of these is easily overcome by young people, or by those who have emigrated from hardships at home; for men in this particular are like trees, they do not answer so well after a certain age for transplantation, nor do they do so well from a good soil as from a bad.

J. Hector St. John de Crèvecoeur Celebrates the Possibilities of America for Its Immigrants, 1782

I wish I could be acquainted with the feelings and thoughts which must agitate the heart and present themselves to the mind of an enlightened Englishman when he first lands on this continent. He must greatly rejoice that he lived at a time to see this fair country discovered and settled; he must necessarily feel a share of national pride when he views the chain of settlements which embellish these extended shores. When he says to himself, "This is the work of my countrymen, who, when convulsed by factions, afflicted by a variety of miseries and wants, restless and impatient, took refuge here. They brought along with them their national genius, to which they principally owe what liberty they enjoy and what substance they possess." Here he sees the industry of his native country displayed in a new manner and traces in their [*sic*] works the embryos of all the arts, sciences, and ingenuity which flourish in Europe. Here he beholds fair cities, substantial villages, extensive fields, an immense country filled with decent houses, good roads, orchards, meadows, and bridges where an hundred years ago all was wild, woody, and uncultivated! What a train of pleasing ideas this fair spectacle must suggest; it is a prospect which must inspire a good citizen with the most heart-felt pleasure. The difficulty consists in the manner of viewing so extensive a scene. He is arrived on a new continent; a modern society offers itself to his contemplation, different from what he had hitherto seen. It is not composed, as in Europe, of great lords who possess everything and of a herd of people who have nothing. Here are no aristocratical families, no courts, no kings, no bishops, no ecclesiastical dominion, no invisible power giving to a few a very visible one, no great manufactures employing thousands, no great refinements of luxury. The rich and the poor are not so far removed from each other as they are in Europe. Some few towns excepted, we

From J. Hector St. John de Crévecoeur, "What Is an American?" *Letters from an American Farmer,* 1782.

are all tillers of the earth, from Nova Scotia to West Florida. We are a people of cultivators scattered over an immense territory, communicating with each other by means of good roads and navigable rivers, united by the silken bands of mild government, all respecting the laws without dreading their power, because they are equitable. We are all animated with the spirit of an industry which is unfettered and unrestrained, because each person works for himself. If he travels through our rural districts, he views not the hostile castle and the haughty mansion, contrasted with the clay-built hut and miserable cabin, where cattle and men help to keep each other warm and dwell in meanness, smoke, and indigence. A pleasing uniformity of decent competence appears throughout our habitations.

* * * *

The next wish of this traveller will be to know whence came all these people. They are a mixture of English, Scotch, Irish, French, Dutch, Germans, and Swedes. From this promiscuous breed, that race now called Americans have arisen. . . .

In this great American asylum, the poor of Europe have by some means met together, and in consequence of various causes; to what purpose should they ask one another what countrymen they are? Alas, two thirds of them had no country. Can a wretch who wanders about, who works and starves, whose life is a continual scene of sore affliction or pinching penury—can that man call England or any other kingdom his country? A country that had no bread for him, whose fields procured him no harvest, who met with nothing but the frowns of the rich, the severity of the laws, with jails and punishments, who owned not a single foot of the extensive surface of this planet? No! Urged by a variety of motives, here they came.

* * * *

What, then, is the American, this new man? He is neither an European nor the descendant of an European; hence that strange mixture of blood, which you will find in no other country. I could point out to you a family whose grandfather was an Englishman, whose wife was Dutch, whose son married a French woman, and whose present four sons have now four wives of different nations. *He* is an American, who, leaving behind him all his ancient prejudices and manners, receives new ones from the new mode of life he has embraced, the new government he obeys, and the new rank he holds. He becomes an American by being received in the broad lap of our great Alma Mater. Here individuals of all nations are melted into a new race of men, whose labours and posterity will one day cause great changes in the world. Americans are the western pilgrims who are carrying along with them that great mass of arts, sciences, vigour, and industry which began long since in the East; they will finish the great circle. The Americans were once scattered all over Europe; here they are incorporated into one of the finest systems of population which has ever appeared, and which will hereafter become distinct by the power of the different climates they inhabit. The American ought therefore to love this country much better than that wherein either he or his forefathers were born. Here the rewards of his industry follow with equal steps the progress of his labour; his labour is founded on the basis of nature, self-interest; can it want a stronger allurement? Wives and children, who before in vain demanded of him a morsel of bread, now, fat and frolicsome, gladly help their father to clear those fields whence exuberant crops are to arise to feed and to clothe them all, without any part being claimed, either by a despotic prince, a rich abbot, or a mighty lord. Here religion demands but little of him: a small voluntary salary to the minister and gratitude to God; can he refuse these? The American is a new man, who sets upon new principles; he must therefore entertain new ideas and form new opinions. From involuntary idleness, servile dependence, penury, and useless labor, he has passed to toils of a very different nature, rewarded by ample subsistence. This is an American.

* * * *

An European, when he first arrives, seems limited in his intentions, as well as in his views; but he very suddenly alters his scale; two hundred miles formerly appeared a very great distance, it is now but a trifle; he no sooner breathes our air than he forms schemes and embarks in designs he never would have thought of in his own country. There the plenitude of society confines many useful ideas and often extinguishes the most laudable schemes, which here ripen into maturity. Thus Europeans become Americans.

But how is this accomplished in that crowd of low, indigent people who flock here every year from all parts of Europe? I will tell you; they no sooner arrive than they immediately feel the good effects of that plenty of provisions we possess. . . .

* * * *

. . . He is encouraged, he has gained friends; he is advised and directed; he feels bold, he purchases some land; he gives all the money he has brought over, as well as what he has earned, and trusts to the God of harvests for the discharge of the rest. His good name procures him credit. He is now possessed of the deed, conveying to him and his posterity the fee simple and absolute property of two hundred acres of land, situated on such a river. What an epocha in this man's life! He is become a freeholder, from perhaps a German boor. He is now an American, a Pennsylvanian, an English subject. He is naturalized; his name is enrolled with those of the other citizens of the province. . . . From nothing to start into being; from a servant to the rank of a master; from being the slave of some despotic prince, to become a free man, invested with lands to which every municipal blessing is annexed! What a change indeed! It is in consequence of that change that he becomes an American. This great metamorphosis has a double effect: it extinguishes all his European prejudices, he forgets that mechanism of subordination, that servility of disposition which poverty had taught him; and sometimes he is apt to forget it too much, often passing from one extreme to the other. . . . Ye poor Europeans—ye who sweat and work for the great; ye who are obliged to give so many sheaves to the church, so many to your lords, so many to your government, and have hardly any left for yourselves; ye who are held in less estimation than favourite hunters or useless lap-dogs; ye who only breathe the air of nature because it cannot be withholden from you—it is here that ye can conceive the possibility of those feelings I have been describing; it is here the laws of naturalization invite every one to partake of our great labours and felicity, to till unrented, untaxed lands!

The German Press in Philadelphia Defends the War for Independence, 1776

—Remember—and remind your families—, you came to America, suffering many hardships, in order to escape servitude and enjoy liberty.

—Remember, in Germany serfs ['leibeigene'] may not marry without the consent of their master, . . . they are regarded as little better than black slaves on West Indian islands. . . .

—Remember the forced labor ['Frondienst'] which subjects, especially peasants, must in some places still perform for their overlords. . . .

—Remember the almost unbearable taxes with which the princes burden their subjects. . . .

—Remember, how in many places a farmer is not permitted to shoot the deer which devastates his freshly sown fields. . . .

—Remember, how in times of war soldiers drive the citizen and farmer almost out of his house, occupy his best rooms and his beds, and make the owner himself sleep on straw or on a bench.

—Remember that the administration of Britain and its Parliament intends to treat Americans the same way, or worse.

African Americans Petition for Their Freedom, 1774–1777

To his Excellency Thomas Gage Esq Captain General and Governor in Chief in and over this Province. To the Honourable his Majestys Council and the Honourable House of Representatives in General Court assembled may 25 177— —

The Petition of a Grate Number of Blackes of this Province who by divine permission are held in a state of Slavery within the bowels of a free and christian Country
    Humbly Shewing
    That your Petitioners apprehind we have in common with all other men a naturel right to our freedoms without Being depriv'd of them by our fellow men as we are a freeborn Pepel and have never forfeited this Blessing by aney compact or agreement whatever. But we were unjustly dragged by the cruel hand of power from our dearest frinds and sum of us stolen from the bosoms of our tender Parents and from a Populous Pleasant and plentiful country and Brought hither to be made slaves for Life in a Christian land. Thus are we deprived of every thing that hath a tendency to make life even tolerable, the endearing ties of husband and wife we are strangers to for we are no longer man and wife then our masters or mestreses

As found in Bernard Bailyn and John B. Hench (eds.), *The Press and the American Revolution*, (Boston: Northeastern University Press, 1981).

As found in Donald McQuade et al., *The Harper American Literature*, volume 1, second edition (New York: HarperCollins, 1990).

thinkes proper marred or onmarred. Our children are also taken from us by force and sent maney miles from us wear we seldom or ever see them again there to be made slaves of for Life which sumtimes is vere short by Reson of Being dragged from their mothers Breest [*sic*] Thus our Lives are imbittered to us on these accounts By our deplorable situation we are rendered incapable of shewing our obedience to Almighty God how can a slave perform the duties of a husband to a wife or parent to his child How can a husband leave master and work and cleave to his wife How can the wife submit themselves to there husbands in all things. How can the child obey thear parents in all things. There is a grat number of us sencear [sincere]. . . members of the Church of Christ how can the master and the slave be said to fulfil that command Live in love let Brotherly Love contuner and abound Beare yea onenothers Bordenes How can the master be said to Beare my Borden when he Beares me down whith the Have [heavy] chanes of slavery and operson [oppression] against my will and how can we fulfill our parte of duty to him whilst in this condition and as we cannot searve our God as we ought whilst in this situation Nither can we reap an equal benefet from the laws of the Land which doth not justify but condemns Slavery or if there had bin aney Law to hold us in Bondege we are Humbely of the Opinion ther never was aney to inslave our children for life when Born in a free Countrey. We therfor Bage your Excellency and Honours will give this its deu weight and consideration and that you will accordingly cause an act of the legislative to be pessed that we may obtain our Natural right our freedoms and our children be set at lebety [liberty] at the yeare of Twenty one for whoues sekes more petequeley your Petitioners is in Duty ever to Pray.

> To the Honorable Counsel & House of [Representa]tives for the State of Massachusitte Bay in General Court assembled, Jan. 13, 1777.

The petition of A Great Number of Blackes detained in a State of slavery in the Bowels of a free & Christian Country Humbly shuwith that your Petitioners apprehend that thay have in Common with all other men a Natural and Unaliable Right to that freedom which the Grat Parent of the Unavers hath Bestowed equalley on all menkind and which they have Never forfuted by any Compact or agreement whatever—but thay wher Unjustly Dragged by the hand of cruel Power from their Derest friends and sum of them Even torn from the Embraces of their tender Parents—from A popolous Pleasant and plentiful contry and in violation of Laws of Nature and off Nations and in defiance of all the tender feelings of humanity Brough[t] hear Either to Be sold Like Beast of Burthen & Like them Condemnd to Slavery for Life—Among A People Profesing the mild Religion of Jesus A people Not Insensible of the Secrets of Rationable Being Nor without spirit to Resent the unjust endeavours of others to Reduce them to a state of Bondage and Subjection your honouer Need not to be informed that A Life of Slavery Like that of your petioners Deprived of Every social privilege of Every thing Requiset to Render Life Tolable is far worse then Nonexistance.

[In imitat]ion of the Lawdable Example of the Good People of these States your petiononers have Long and Patiently waited the Evnt of petition after petition By them presented to the Legislative Body of this state and cannot but with Grief Reflect that their Sucess hath ben but too similar they Cannot but express their Astonishment that It has Never Bin Consirdered that Every Principle from which

Amarica has Acted in the Cours of their unhappy Deficultes with Great Briton Pleads Stronger than A thousand arguments in favowrs of your petioners they therfor humble Beseech your honours to give this peti[ti]on its due weight & consideration and cause an act of the Legislatur to be past Wherby they may Be Restored to the Enjoyments of that which is the Naturel Right of all men—and their Children who wher Born in this Land of Liberty may not be heald as Slaves after they arive at the age of Twenty one years so may the Inhabitance of thes Stats No longer chargeable with the inconsistancey of acting themselves the part which they condem and oppose in others Be prospered in their present Glorious struggle for Liberty and have those Blessing to them, &c.

Congress Establishes Its Initial Policy on Naturalization, 1790

An Act to establish an uniform Rule of Naturalization.

SECTION 1. *Be it enacted by the Senate and House of Representatives of the United States of America in Congress assembled,* That any alien, being a free white person, who shall have resided within the limits and under the jurisdiction of the United States for the term of two years, may be admitted to become a citizen thereof, on application to any common law court of record, in any one of the states wherein he shall have resided for the term of one year at least, and making proof to the satisfaction of such court, that he is a person of good character, and taking the oath or affirmation prescribed by law, to support the constitution of the United States, which oath or affirmation such court shall administer; and the clerk of such court shall record such application, and the proceedings thereon; and thereupon such person shall be considered as a citizen of the United States. And the children of such persons so naturalized, dwelling within the United States, being under the age of twenty-one years at the time of such naturalization, shall also be considered as citizens of the United States. And the children of citizens of the United States, that may be born beyond sea, or out of the limits of the United States, shall be considered as natural born citizens: *Provided,* That the right of citizenship shall not descend to persons whose fathers have never been resident in the United States: *Provided also,* That no person heretofore proscribed by any state, shall be admitted a citizen as aforesaid, except by an act of the legislature of the state in which such person was proscribed.

APPROVED, March 26, 1790.

From The Naturalization Act of 1790. United States Statutes, vol. 1, p. 103 (First Congress, Session II).

Congress Restricts the Rights of Aliens, 1798

An Act Concerning Aliens.

SECTION 1. *Be it enacted by the Senate and House of Representatives of the United States of America in Congress assembled,* That it shall be lawful for the President of the United States at any time during the continuance of this act, to *order* all such *aliens* as he shall judge dangerous to the peace and safety of the United States, or shall have reasonable grounds to suspect are concerned in any treasonable or secret machinations against the government thereof, to depart out of the territory of the United States, within such time as shall be expressed in such order, which order shall be served on such alien by delivering him a copy thereof, or leaving the same at his usual abode, and returned to the office of the Secretary of State, by the marshal or other person to whom the same shall be directed. And in case any alien, so ordered to depart, shall be found at large within the United States after the time limited in such order for his departure, and not having obtained a *license* from the President to reside therein, or having obtained such *license* shall not have conformed thereto, every such alien shall, on conviction thereof, be imprisoned for a term not exceeding three years, and shall never after be admitted to become a citizen of the United States. *Provided always, and be it further enacted,* that if any alien so ordered to depart shall prove to the satisfaction of the President, by evidence to be taken before such person or persons as the President shall direct, who are for that purpose hereby authorized to administer oaths, that no injury or danger to the United States will arise from suffering such alien to reside therein, the President may grant a *license* to such alien to remain within the United States for such time as he shall judge proper, and at such place as he may designate.

SEC. 2. *And be it further enacted,* That it shall be lawful for the President of the United States, whenever he may deem it necessary for the public safety, to order to be removed out of the territory thereof, any alien who may or shall be in prison in pursuance of this act; and to cause to be arrested and sent out of the United States such of those aliens as shall have been ordered to depart therefrom and shall not have obtained a license as aforesaid, in all cases where, in the opinion of the President, the public safety requires a speedy removal. And if any alien so removed or sent out of the United States by the President shall voluntarily return thereto, unless by permission of the President of the United States, such alien on conviction thereof, shall be imprisoned so long as, in the opinion of the President, the public safety may require.

From The Alien Act of 1798. United States Statutes, vol. 1, pp. 570–571 (Fifth Congress, Session II).

The definition of citizenship and naturalization and the creation of national identity were questions that Americans were forced to address when they created the United States. As historian James H. Kettner of University of California at Berkeley argues (1978), the concept of American citizenship had deep roots in English tradition. Despite this foundation, however, events in the United States forced Americans to reevaluate the nature of citizenship. During the era of the American Revolution, Kettner contends, Americans began to see the tie between citizens and their nation as a volitional contract, rather than a perpetual and natural condition. These new patterns of citizenship were seriously tested, Kettner observes, in the late 1790s, when national security was linked to the presence of aliens as the United States nearly went to war with France. Arthur Mann, formerly of the University of Chicago, considers (1979) the issue of national identity in relation to the diversity of the non-native American population at the time of the American Revolution. Importantly, Mann argues that the diversity of the United States was critical in creating an American identity based on ideological forms. Because the United States was not a nation in the traditional sense, its people had to create novel forms in conceiving the new nation, its people, and citizenship.

The Creation of Citizenship in the British American Colonies and Early United States

JAMES H. KETTNER

The concept of American citizenship that achieved full legal form and force in the mid-nineteenth century grew from English roots. It was the product of a development that stretched over three hundred years, a development in which the circumstances of life in the New World shaped and transformed the quasi-medieval ideas of seventeenth-century English jurists about membership, community, and allegiance. The process of change was gradual, and those who participated in it did not fully perceive its patterns or direction. Nevertheless, as Americans first experienced, then sought to articulate the meaning of, their transformation from subjects to citizens, they made piecemeal changes and partial modifications of English ideas that developed, step-by-step, into a new concept of citizenship.

Americans inherited a complex set of ideas about the sources and character of "subjectship." These ideas were rooted deep in the English past, but not until the early seventeenth century were they integrated into a coherent doctrine. The basic theory of subjectship was coeval with the beginnings of American colonization and was the product of the period that formed the bridge between the eras historians have categorized as "medieval" and "modern." Conflicting concepts of community characterized those two eras. The medieval notion of "allegiance" reflected the

From *The Development of American Citizenship, 1608–1870* by James H. Kettner. Copyright © 1978 by the University of North Carolina Press. Published for the Institute of Early American History and Culture. Used by permission of the publisher.

feudal sense that personal bonds between man and lord were the primary ligaments of the body politic; the modern notion of "nationality" assumed a legal tie binding individuals to a territorial state and rendering them subject to its jurisdiction. The "community of allegiance" was in essence personal, the "national state" primarily territorial.

Historians have discovered elements of the modern doctrine of nationality as far back as the fourteenth century, particularly in connection with practices of naturalization, but such notions clearly were planted and nourished in an intellectual context dominated by medieval ideas of personal subjection and by a wide variety of statuses. Indeed, despite the early emergence of some elements of "nationality," English law long continued to stress the personal nature of the subject-king relationship and the gradation of ranks characteristic of an older social and political order.

Early English law had no fixed concept of subjectship or of nationality as a status; no consistent and fundamental distinction divided subject and alien. Rather there were levels and ranks of persons with varying rights and privileges—or conversely with different disabilities—that defined a broad spectrum and hierarchy of possible individual statuses. The notion of a primary distinction between member and non-member emerged slowly, in response to specific issues of landholding, taxation, and access to the king's courts. Before the Tudor period there appears to have been no firm sense of a fixed "national" status identified with a more or less specific complex of rights from which "non-nationals" were excluded. Naturalization—in the modern sense of a grant of status with an accompanying package of rights—was preceded by, and for a time coexisted with, the practice of removing disabilities and bestowing privileges piecemeal. Medieval English law posited a continuum of ranks and rights, but did not create distinctly separate categories of subject and alien.

By the seventeenth century the line dividing subject and alien was well marked; yet traces of the older ideas remained. English subjectship still comprised a variety of ranks and relationships. Jurists distinguished between natural-born subjects, naturalized subjects, and "denizens," all of whom were members of the community in some sense, although there were important differences in the nature of the ties that bound them as subjects and in the rights that they could claim. The general category of aliens, too, embodied separate classes of persons—perpetual aliens, alien friends, and alien enemies—whose respective legal positions varied in detail. Procedures for adopting outsiders into the community had become standardized, even though the rationale behind the processes of admission would not receive an articulate theoretical justification until the mid-seventeenth century.

* * * *

. . . It was not until Sir Edward Coke's influential opinion in *Calvin's Case* (1608) that a theory of allegiance and subjectship was fully articulated.

Coke's explication of the nature of membership and community may be seen as the first of four distinct phases in the development of the concept of citizenship. Written in response to the controversies surrounding the accession of James I, Coke's decision in *Calvin's Case* dominated English law for several centuries. The central conclusion of this decision was that subjectship involved a personal relationship with the king, a relationship rooted in the laws of nature and hence perpetual and immutable. The conceptual analogue of the subject-king relationship was the natural bond between parent and child. Although England's law envisioned various types of subjectship, ranging from the natural status of the native-born to the legally acquired status of the naturalized alien, all varieties of membership mirrored permanent hierarchical principles of the natural order. Once a man became a subject—by birth or otherwise—he remained a subject forever, owing a lasting obedience to his natural superior the king.

Coke's quasi-medieval assumption that social and governmental organization grew out of natural principles of hierarchy and subordination preceded, and eventually conflicted with, newly emerging concepts of society and government as the product of individual consent and contract. . . . Coke's authoritative interpretation of subjectship remained embedded in the law, where it continued to exert a profound influence. By the mid-eighteenth century English concepts of subjectship and community consequently encompassed a central ambiguity: on the one hand, society and government had come to be seen as resting on individual consent and compact; on the other, the legal status and obligations of the individual remained natural, perpetual, and immutable. . . .

The second stage in the development of American theories about citizenship occurred across the Atlantic, where colonial attitudes slowly diverged from those of Coke and his English successors. Circumstances in the New World led men to attenuate and modify these concepts of natural allegiance. Change was most apparent in the naturalization policies that quickly became a common feature of colonial governments. The concerns involved in the incorporation of aliens into colonial societies were preeminently practical, and little attention was paid to doctrinal consistency. There was at this time no attempt to rethink the traditional theory of membership from initial premise to ultimate conclusion. Americans continued to value their status as subjects and to affirm their allegiance to the king, but they also moved toward a new understanding of the ties that bind individuals to the community.

In the mid-seventeenth century when English judges turned their attention to the process of naturalization, they took as their starting point Coke's analysis of natural subjectship. Working from this theoretical base, the judges concluded that the essential purpose of naturalization was to make the alien legally the "same" as a native Englishman. Although in fact the adopted member's rights might remain somewhat less extensive than those of born subjects, in law his allegiance, though acquired by a legal process, must be considered to share the attributes that Coke had described; that is, it must be deemed natural, personal, and perpetual.

In the colonies this pattern of thinking was reversed. Americans first came to see the allegiance of adopted members as reflecting the character of the naturalization process. This legal procedure involved a form of contract between an alien who chose a new allegiance and a community that consented to adopt him as a subject, and the colonists began to view the allegiance that resulted as volitional and contractual. Should this consensual allegiance be limited to adopted subjects only? The need to attract settlers produced generous naturalization policies that promised aliens virtually the same rights as Englishmen. Despite some resistance from imperial authorities, the distinctions between the various categories of subjects—still quite real in the mother country—began to soften and blur. Naturalized subjects seemed in fact to share the same status as natives; thus their allegiance ought to be the same. Significantly, the colonists took the model of the naturalized subject as their starting point, and they ultimately concluded that all allegiance ought to be considered the result of a contract resting on consent.

A third phase in the development of an American concept of citizenship occurred when the Revolution impelled the colonists to articulate in theoretical form this new concept of allegiance. Amidst the conflict and confusion that marked the imperial controversy of the 1760s, the War of Independence, and the long search for new forms of republican government, Americans sought to define principles of membership that adequately encompassed their ideals of individual liberty and community security. In large part they built upon the notion inherent in the process of naturalization that the tie between the individual and the community was contractual and volitional, not natural and perpetual. This idea shaped their response to the claims of Parliament and the king, legitimized their withdrawal from the British empire, controlled their reaction to the loyalists, and underwrote their creation of independent governments.

The Revolution created the status of "American citizen" and produced an expression of the general principles that ought to govern membership in a free society: republican citizenship ought to rest on consent; it ought to be uniform and without invidious gradations; and it ought to confer equal rights. But if general principles were clear, particular questions about the source, character, and effects of citizenship remained open well into the nineteenth century.

In the fourth and final phase of conceptual development, Americans sought to work out the implications of their ideas in the context of a federal republic based on the principles of popular sovereignty. Logic often led to conclusions that were unanticipated and, to many, unacceptable. The newly emergent principles of citizenship clashed with deep-seated prejudices, including the traditional exclusion of Indians and Negroes, to produce confusion and contention. Ultimately, the attempt to arrive at a consistent doctrine of citizenship would be settled neither in the Congress nor in the courts, but on the battlefields of the Civil War.

Suspicion of the foreign-born and a belief that citizenship conferred political rights combined to shape the development of a federal naturalization policy in the 1790s. The story of the successive acts of 1790, 1795, and 1798 is a familiar one. The emergence and intensification of partisan divisions, occasioned in large part by events in Europe following the French Revolution, heightened sensitivity to the political alignments of the foreign-born and led to an increasingly harsh and restrictionist naturalization policy under the Federalist administrations of Washington and Adams.

The first federal naturalization act of 1790 was fairly liberal. Any "free white person" who resided for two years within the United States and for at least one year in the state where he sought admission, proving his "good character" and taking an oath to "support the constitution of the United States," was to be "considered as a citizen of the United States." Children under twenty-one dwelling within the United States were to be included in the parent's naturalization, and foreign-born children of citizens were themselves to be deemed natural-born citizens, provided that "the right of citizenship shall not descend to persons whose fathers have never been resident in the United States."   •

＊ ＊ ＊ ＊

Debate shifted to the proper residence requirement for naturalization. Thomas Hartley of Pennsylvania thought that the "terms of citizenship are made too cheap in some parts of the Union," and he wanted to delay admission long enough to insure the immigrant's "knowledge of the candidates" and "firm attachment to the Government." Michael Stone of Maryland also favored a term of residence long enough to guarantee "first, that he should have an opportunity of knowing the circumstances of our Government, and in consequence thereof, shall have admitted the truth of the principles we hold. Second, that he shall have acquired a taste for this kind of Government."

Virginia's John Page advocated a liberal policy. "Bigotry and superstition, or a deep-rooted prejudice against the Government, laws, religion, or manners of neighboring nations," he argued, had a weight in Europe that should not influence policy here. Americans would "be inconsistent with ourselves, if, after boasting of having opened an asylum for the oppressed of all nations, and established a Government which is the admiration of the world, we make the terms of admission to the full enjoyment of that asylum so hard as is now proposed." Page found a staunch ally in the Senate, William Maclay of Pennsylvania, who also thought the proposed two-year residence requirement "illiberal and void of philanthropy." Maclay saw in it a poorly disguised thrust by jealous and xenophobic New Englanders against the liberal and prosperity-producing admission policy of Pennsylvania:

> We Pennsylvanians act as if we believed that God made of one blood all families of the earth; but the Eastern people seem to think that he made none but New England folks. It is strange that men born and educated under republican forms of government should be so contracted on the subject of general philanthropy. . . . They really have the worst characters of any people who offer themselves for citizens. Yet these are the men who affect the greatest fear of being contaminated with foreign manners, customs, or vices.

In the end, Congress did include a two-year residence requirement in its first uniform rule of naturalization. Aliens seeking admission were thus obliged to spend at least that much time assimilating the habits and values of republican life before the federal government would confer upon them the status granting a constitutional right to the privileges and immunities of citizenship. This did not mean that aliens were in all cases without rights in the first two years of settlement, for the states were free to grant immigrants whatever privileges they wished within their own respective jurisdictions. The debates of 1790 specifically suggested that states could make their own regulations concerning the detailed rights of aliens and citizens, and many legislatures eased traditional alien disabilities by passing general or special acts permitting foreign immigrants to acquire and hold real property prior to their naturalization.

＊ ＊ ＊ ＊

This interpretation posed a serious threat to the belief that existing naturalization requirements were already too liberal, an opinion widely shared in Congress by the mid-1790s. The European crisis touched off by the French Revolution flared into war after 1792, and refugees fled the scenes of military conflict and rebellion. The neutral United States attracted "disenchanted Englishmen, aristocratic Frenchmen, German Pietists fleeing forced military service, French planters escaping from West Indian uprisings led by Toussaint l'Ouverture, and Irishmen in flight from British repression." The massive influx of foreign immigrants might have increased fears of alien intermeddling in politics in any case; however, the large number of refugees with passionate political beliefs made all newcomers doubly suspect.

In light of these circumstances, both Federalists and Jeffersonian Republicans could agree on the desirability of tightening the government's naturalization policy. From the outset, Theodore Sedgwick of Massachusetts was dubious of the "rash theory, that the subjects of all Governments, Despotic, Monarchical, and Aristocratical, are, as soon as they set foot on American ground, qualified to participate in administering the sovereignty of our country." The current crisis in Europe, he thought, provided a particularly inauspicious time to admit aliens indiscriminately: "A war, the most cruel and dreadful which has been known for centuries, was now raging in all those countries from which emigrants were to be expected. The most fierce and unrelenting passions were engaged in a conflict, which shook to their foundations all the ancient political structures in Europe." Sedgwick could not conceive that "men, who, actuated by such passions, had fought on grounds so opposite, almost equally distant from the happy mean that we had chosen, would here mingle in social affections with each other, or with us." Therefore, he favored restrictions that would check the number of immigrants and improve their political character.

The new naturalization act was approved January 29, 1795, increasing the period of residence from two to five years and requiring the applicant to declare publicly his intent to become a citizen three years before admission. The potential citizen had to swear that he had completed the required residence, that he renounced and abjured his former allegiance, and that he would support the Constitution of the United States. Immigrants who had "borne any hereditary title, or been of the orders of nobility" were required to renounce that status, and all had to satisfy the court of admission that they had behaved as men of good moral character, were attached to the principles of the Constitution, and were "well disposed to the good order and happiness of the same." Aliens were to be naturalized on these conditions "and not otherwise"—a provision effectively ending admission under separate state laws.

✻ ✻ ✻ ✻

The naturalization law and the Alien and Sedition acts passed by the Fifth Congress were clearly Federalist measures, designed both to increase national security at a time when war with France seemed imminent and to strike at an alleged source of Jeffersonian Republican strength. "No acts ever passed by Congress had ever been so clearly the work of one party; no laws had ever been so unanimously opposed by the other party." The law of 1795 was amended to require a residence of fourteen years before the applicant could be admitted and a declaration of intent to become a citizen five years before admission. On the motion of Albert Gallatin (and not without considerable reluctance on the part of some extremists) a one-year grace period was allowed for aliens already resident in the country to qualify under the terms of the old law of 1795. Special provisions were made for the central recording of all declarations and naturalizations, for the registration of all alien immigrants, and for the punishment of all persons who failed to comply with the registry provisions. Enemy aliens were barred from naturalization while their native country was at war with the United States.

* * * *

Jefferson's election in 1800 was quickly followed by a repeal of the obnoxious Naturalization Act of 1798. A new law approved April 14, 1802, reinstated the general requirements established in 1795: residence of five years with a declaration of intent three years before admission; oaths or declarations abjuring titles and foreign allegiance and swearing attachment to the principles of the Constitution; and satisfactory proof of good character and behavior. The act included provisions for the registration of all immigrants, and alien enemies were still barred from naturalization.

The Naturalization Act of 1802 was the last major piece of legislation on this subject during the nineteenth century. A number of minor revisions were introduced before the Civil War, but these merely altered or clarified details of evidence, certification, and the like without changing the basic nature of the admission procedure. At the heart of the naturalization process remained the idea that a prolonged term of residence was the surest way of guaranteeing an alien's attachment to the country and adoption of its ways. The declaration of intent gave notice to the public at large that the alien was committed to becoming a fellow citizen, and it served to focus closer attention on his behavior; but above all, continued residence "gave the knowledge and feeling, and gave the opportunity, for the intercourse that amalgamated the aliens with us, and gave them a common interest. It was the surest standard by which to test the desire for citizenship; it was action, and not declaration; it was fact and not theory."

By the beginning of the nineteenth century Americans had begun to address some of the problems involved in the creation of a new concept of citizenship. Old bonds of personal allegiance that had once united men in a common subjectship under the British king had been replaced by new contractual terms by which civil and political rights in the community were to be exchanged for support for republican principles, adherence to the Constitution, and responsible and virtuous behavior under enlightened forms of self-government.

The idea that citizenship must be complete in itself—that it was an undifferentiated status—was challenged by some who retained the traditional view that membership was appropriately divided by ranks and orders. But the majority resisted the notion that only those born under the principles of self-government could become citizens. Fears for the nation's security in the face of both external and internal threats produced a sometimes harsh and ultimately cautious naturalization policy, but they were not strong enough to override the sense that citizenship should ultimately depend not on some magical result of birth alone, but on belief, will, consent, and choice. Thus the legislators were most concerned with insuring a candidate's sincere commitment to the basic values and principles of the Republic. Once this commitment was shown, the naturalized alien had the right to claim virtually all the privileges of full membership.

The Creation of American Identity in the Late Eighteenth Century

ARTHUR MANN

Who Were Our Romulus and Remus?

To the founders of the Republic, the American Revolution was a transforming experience. It brought about a separation from the parent country, the creation of a unique and independent polity, and a conviction among Americans that they were a special breed of men. Looking back on those radical changes, Thomas Jefferson, just elected President of the United States, exclaimed: "We can no longer say there is nothing new under the sun. For this whole chapter in the history of man is new."

Jefferson was typical of his contemporaries. No more than he did they foresee in the 1760s that the quarrel with England over taxes would end a quarter-century later with the drafting and the adoption of the Constitution. The result was an extraordinarily self-conscious nationalism. "Before the establishment of the American States," Jefferson wrote in 1801, "nothing was known to history but the man of the old world."

The words are clear, but the meaning behind them is puzzling. The Revolutionary generation founded a nation-state without the then traditional prerequisites for nationhood. Americans did not occupy a territory "naturally" their own. They did not look back on a long history whose beginnings shaded off into legend. They did not share an ancient folklore in the oral or written tradition. They did not belong to the same church. Above all, the Americans did not descend from a common stock.

Alexis de Tocqueville had such considerations in mind when he remarked that the United States lacked the roots of an instinctive patriotism. "Picture to yourself . . . if you can, a society," he wrote to a European friend, unlike any society in the Old World. The Americans were not held together by such emotional ties as ancient memories, ancient habits, ancient prejudices, ancient heroes, an ancient dynasty, an ancient faith, or ancient attachments to place. And picture, too, Tocqueville added, "a society formed from all the nations of the world."

From Arthur Mann, *The One and Many: Reflections on the American Identity*, copyright © 1979. Reprinted by permission of the University of Illinois Press.

The assumption that eighteenth-century America was ethnically homogeneous is false. The English were, of course, the largest stock. They were also the most influential, and it would be hard to overstate the importance, then or now, of the English language, of English law, of English religious ideas, and of English political ideals and institutions. All the same, the English were not—nor were they destined to be—the parent stock of the American people as a whole.

Since this is a statistical matter, statistics are in order. Of the 3,929,000 inhabitants enumerated in the first census of 1790, the English and their descendants constituted just under half the population. The next largest group—from Africa—accounted for close to 20 percent. Almost a third or so consisted of persons of Scotch-Irish, German, Scottish, French, Irish, Swiss, Spanish, Dutch, and still other origins.

The same stocks were represented in the 250,000 inhabitants of the British colonies in 1700, and it would therefore seem that the population had been pluralist as early as the seventeenth century. It was not, because of a lopsided proportion of groups to each other. Except for scattered ethnic pockets (eighteen different languages were spoken in seventeenth-century New York City), the British settlements in 1700, stretching in a thin, broken line along the Atlantic seaboard, were almost wholly English in birth or derivation.

Things changed in the decades after the Treaty of Utrecht of 1713. With France and Britain no longer at war in the New World, a huge migration set in from Europe. Concurrently, an extraordinary increase took place in the importation of African slaves. Even the best colonial statistics are extrapolations from a variety of sources, but it is safe to say that, between 1700 and 1775, at least two and a half times as many people came to America as the 250,000 who had lived there in 1700. More significantly still, although the English were among the newcomers, they were outnumbered by the combined arrivals from Ireland, Germany, Scotland, Wales, France, Switzerland, and Africa. By the time of the Revolution, "the English homogeneity of the colonies had been decisively broken."

But the resulting heterogeneity varied from one part of the colonies to another. New England's population, relatively unaffected by the eighteenth-century migrations from continental Europe, non-English Britain, and Africa, remained the most English into the Revolutionary period. The most multiethnic areas were Pennsylvania, the Carolinas, and the 600-mile-long southern backcountry. New York fell between the two extremes, although its principal city was well on the way toward becoming the major symbol of New World cosmopolitanism. With tragic consequences for the future, in the eastern parts of the South a population took shape that was not mixed but dual—English and African.

The inner life of the eighteenth-century mosaic has received much less attention from historians than its geographical contours. Then as now, though, religious pluralism accompanied ethnic pluralism. Immigrant groups transplanted their churches, challenging the religious hegemony that the English had enjoyed in the seventeenth century. By 1775, as a result of the shift in the sources of immigration, the number of non-English houses of worship was equal to those in the Anglican and Congregational denominations.

In 1776 a committee appointed by the Continental Congress proposed that the Great Seal include a symbol for the major lands from which the American people had originated. New Englanders might think that "God . . . made none but New England folks," wrote a Pennsylvanian, but it was common knowledge that a Maryland signer of the Declaration descended from an old Irish family; that most of Pennsylvania's general officers in the War of Independence were foreigners; that three Continental Congress presidents bore French Huguenot names; that a major architect of the Constitution had been born in Scotland; that Hamilton's successor as Secretary of the Treasury had immigrated to America from Switzerland. Even that great Virginian of universal principles, Thomas Jefferson, thought it of some importance to point out, at the beginning of his autobiography, that he was Welsh on his father's side. Despite an English preponderance, the founders were a mixed lot, and knew it.

* * * *

[Some] other leaders of the Revolutionary generation made careful, even invidious distinctions among northern Europeans in America. Alarmed by the huge German influx in Pennsylvania, Benjamin Franklin scorned the newcomers as "the most ignorant Stupid Sort of their own Nation" and warned his fellow English that the Germans "will soon . . . out number us." Charles Lee, equally disturbed by the mixed but heavily Ulsterized back settlements in Virginia, referred contemptuously to that frontier as a "Mac-ocracy" in which the reigning group was "a banditti of low Scotch-Irish whose names usually begin with Mac." Sentiments like Franklin's and Lee's were by no means unusual before the Revolution.

But as independence approached, ethnic diversity was celebrated for making America unique. Of some four hundred pamphlets published in the decade and a half leading up to the Revolution, Tom Paine's *Common Sense* (1776) was the most widely read and the most influential. In it Paine asserted: "Europe, and not England, is the parent country of America." A few years later, in a work also admired, J. Hector St. John de Crèvecoeur, a naturalized New Yorker, gave praise to "that strange mixture of blood, which you will find in no other country." Neither Paine nor Crèvecoeur traced the mixture to the homogenizing genetic source in northern Europe. "This new world hath been the asylum for the persecuted lovers of civil and religious liberty from"—Paine italicized his point—"*every part* of Europe."

* * * *

All this means that when the Americans founded a nation-state and proclaimed their common peoplehood, they could not claim a common ethnic descent. Their past had denied to them, and to their posterity as well, that kind of nationalizing cement. "For who was our father and our mother?" Herman Melville asked in 1849, after listing the different stocks that had formed the American people and were still forming it. "Or can we point to any Romulus and Remus for our founders?" The New York writer summed up an enduring fact in the American experience when he remarked: "Our ancestry is lost in the universal paternity."

But if that was so, what, then, was American about the Americans?

The American as Idealized Citizen

The founders' answer was ideological. Crèvecoeur himself, although opposed to independence, described the American as "a new man, who acts upon new principles . . . new ideas . . . new opinions." Revolutionary leaders made the same point in one way or another. In a long and tendentious work published in 1792, Joel Barlow argued that what Americans think is what Americans are. An ideological answer was the only sort possible to the then youngest country in the Western world. The Americans could not claim an ancestral land, a long history, an old folklore, a common church, or the same progenitors.

Recognizing that their countrymen were not a nation in the then traditional sense, the founders used the word "people" when they referred to Americans in their collectivity. In the Declaration of Independence, Jefferson justified the necessity "for one People to dissolve the Political Bands which have connected them with another." Similarly, the Preamble to the Constitution reads: "WE THE PEOPLE of the United States . . ." A quarter-century later, in a retrospective look at the origins of the Revolution, John Adams traced them to "the Minds of the People."

Is it possible, too, that the eighteenth-century architects of the United States preferred the word people to nation because nation was too static in its connotation for their purpose? A nation was then regarded as the sum, and therefore as the custodian and the captive, of its parochial past. The people, in contrast, were unfettered and dynamic, endowed with the power to choose and to change, to break the crust of custom if need be and to shape the future. A nation *was* history; the people *made* history.

Such attributes of will were essential to the Revolutionary mind. What we think, Joel Barlow said, is what we are—and dare to become. The people chose, in 1776, "to assume among the Power of the Earth . . . [a] separate and equal Station." Six years later Tom Paine informed a French correspondent: "We are now really another people." In 1787–88, at still another turning point, the people decided to "form a more perfect Union," by ordaining and establishing a new constitution.

In addition to will, the people were invested with rights, deriving from God, Nature, or Law. The Declaration stated that, by right, the American people ought to be independent. As for the Constitution, it actually contained a *Bill of Rights*. Together with other sections of the national charter, it defined and enumerated the rights and privileges and liberties and immunities that belonged to the people. Their supreme right was the right of sovereign power.

What, then, was an American? To the eighteenth-century founders, an American was a bundle of rights, freely chosen.

Fully to document how the national identity came to be expressed in that way would require telling the intellectual history of the American Revolution from the 1760s through the 1780s. Happily, historians have already shown how the developments leading up to independence resulted in "a radical idealization and conceptualization of the previous century and a half of American experience"; and that the Constitution consolidated, through law, the ideological consensus that had evolved in the struggle against England. More plainly, the Americans discovered what kind of people they were by having to say in what kind of society they believed.

The process of self-definition went on for close to thirty years. At critical points in the Revolution there was a need to convince public opinion, at home as well as abroad, of the legitimacy of the movement. The founders were learned men and drew on arguments from varied sources—biblical, classical, legal, Whiggish. Above all, they expressed themselves in the language of the eighteenth-century

Enlightenment, proclaiming that the American people had been born free and meant to stay free through institutions of their own making.

Because of that kind of thinking, historians have remarked that, when compared to the French and Russian Revolutions, the American Revolution was "conservative." The insight is valid. The Americans did not start out to overthrow a reactionary regime, as did the French and the Russians, but to hold on to liberties they had long enjoyed in the then freest empire in the world. Indeed, from the beginning of the imperial crisis with the parent country in 1763 until the final rupture thirteen years later, the colonists were confident of devising a formula to safeguard their rights as Englishmen.

But if seen in another light—as the first successful anticolonial movement in modern history—the American Revolution wrought its own kind of radical transformation. It broke the century-and-a-half-old hyphen in the Anglo-American identity, thereby releasing the full force of American nationalism. Thenceforth the Americans asserted, unambiguously and without qualification, that they constituted a new, distinct, indivisible nationality. Neither America nor the world has been the same since that root change in self-awareness.

Like everyone else who has ever claimed to be liberated from an old identity, the founders equated the past with folly, and themselves and their country with all that was good in the present and likely to be good in the future. The Great Seal of the United States, adopted in 1782, declared that America's independence had inaugurated "a new order of the ages" (NOVUS ORDO SECLORUM). Even more epoch-making than the war, in the minds of the Revolutionary generation, was the making of the Constitution. One of its principal drafters, James Wilson, exclaimed that nothing like the American compact had been put together in the "six thousand years since the creation of the world."

Had the Revolutionary leaders been ignorant men given to extravagant flights of speech, their rhetoric could be dismissed as the enthusiasm of Yahoos. But they were a learned lot, and also sober, hardheaded, and legal-minded. At a time when few persons went to college, more than half the delegates to the Constitutional Convention were college men. Wilson himself, trained in the classics and a lawyer by profession, attended three Scottish universities. He and his contemporaries prided themselves on their knowledge of history, especially the history of politics and government extending back to ancient times.

No, it was not due to ignorance—on the contrary, it was because they claimed to know the past through careful study—that the founders were certain that the United States was "without example in the world." When Jefferson said that America was "new under the sun," he also said that until the creation of the American Republic "nothing was known to history but the man of the old world." The us-them image contained in those words—the antithesis between the New and the Old Worlds—was fundamental to the national self-image. Americans were what Europeans were not and had never been.

Revolutionary spokesmen were tireless in pointing out why that was so. Unlike Europe, which the founders homogenized into a bundle of evils, America stood for liberty, opportunity, religious toleration, balanced and representative government, equality before the law, and a better tomorrow for everyone. Above all, this side of the Atlantic defied the conventional wisdom that no nation could survive without the historic props of king, aristocracy, and established clergy. A republican people were themselves a sufficient source of authority.

Therein lay the heart of a transformed nationality. "A citizen of the *United States*," wrote David Ramsay in 1789, "means a member of this new nation." Formerly subjects of the British monarch, the Americans changed status through the republic they created. The effect, Ramsay went on to say, was radical to the extreme. "Subjects look up to a master, but citizens are so far equal, that none have hereditary rights superior to others."

The doctrine of citizen-rule legitimized both the War of Independence and the foundations of the American state. It denied the principle, in which even Whigs believed, that the sovereign power resided in the throne. More profoundly, in the name "of reason and philosophy," it rejected the whole hierarchical view of mankind. The "political condition of citizens is more exalted than that of noblemen," explained Ramsay. "Dukes and earls are the creatures of kings, and may be made by them at pleasure: but citizens possess in their own right original sovereignty."

The polarity that the founders saw between America and Europe was reinforced from two sources: an inherited sense of mission and contemporary foreign opinion of the Revolution.

In the previous century of colonization, settlers had also described the New and Old Worlds in terms of opposites. More than that, the Puritans set out for New England with the conviction that God had chosen them to regenerate, by example, Europe's false and dying forms of Christianity. The Reformation-derived sense of mission continued into the 1700s. Jonathan Edwards, who believed that the Second Coming was at hand and would take place on this side of the Atlantic, wrote that God had designated America as "the glorious renovator of the world."

But the eighteenth century was a secularizing century, and Edwards's more earthbound contemporaries gave the inherited messianic complex a special twist. John Adams, who a generation or so earlier would have become a minister instead of a lawyer, put it this way in 1765: "I always consider the settlement of America with Reverence and Wonder—as the Opening of a grand scene and Design in Providence for the Illumination of the Ignorant and Emancipation of the slavish Part of Mankind all over the Earth." Salvation for men like Adams took on a this-worldly meaning.

After independence and the adoption of the Constitution, Revolutionary leaders were even more assertive about their country's redemptive power. If the American nation-state fulfilled the universal principles of the Enlightenment, then the American way was valid for all human beings. "A just and solid republican government maintained here," declared President Jefferson, "will be a standing monument and example for the aim and imitation of the people of other countries."

That national self-regard was reflected with mirror-like accuracy in liberal opinion abroad. "A great revolution has happened," wrote a British Whig, "—a revolution made, not by chopping and changing of power in any of the existing states, but by the appearance of a new state, of a new species, in a new part of the globe." More flattering still, in France and then in Ireland, Norway, Sweden, Belgium, and Latin America, reformers and revolutionaries undertook, in varying degrees, to remake their countries according to the American model. To the far-flung parties of the Enlightenment, the United States was a beacon of freedom for still unliberated societies.

Such praise ratified the national identity that the Revolutionary generation had articulated for their infant republic. Declaring themselves to be the freest society known to history, the Americans heard from foreign admirers that they were indeed so. Seldom have a people received as good a press as did the Americans in the eighteenth century. Forced by their Revolution to define their better selves, they expressed their specialness in terms that appealed to humanitarian opinion the world around.

FURTHER READING

Benedict Anderson, *Imagined Communities: Reflections on the Origins and Spread of Nationalism* (rev. 1991).

Yehoshua Arieli, *Individualism and Nationalism in American Ideology* (1964).

Richard D. Brown, *The Strength of a People: The Idea of an Informed Citizenry in America, 1650–1870* (1996).

Philip Gleason, "American Identity and Americanization," in Thernstrom, *Harvard Encyclopedia of American Ethnic Groups* (1980), 31–58.

Jack P. Greene, *Pursuits of Happiness: The Social Development of Early Modern British Colonies and the Formation of American Culture* (1988).

Samuel P. Huntington, *American Politics: The Promise of Disharmony* (1981)

Hans Kohn, *American Nationalism: An Interpretative Essay* (1957).

James H. Kettner, *The Development of American Citizenship, 1608–1870* (1978).

Seymour Martin Lipset, *The First New Nation: The United States in Historical and Comparative Perspective* (1963).

Arthur Mann, *The One and the Many: Reflections on American Identity* (1979).

Richard L. Merritt, *Symbols of American Community, 1735–1775* (1966).

John C. Miller, *Crisis in Freedom: The Alien and Sedition Acts* (1951).

Paul Nagel, *This Sacred Trust: American Nationality, 1798–1898* (1971).

William H. Nelson, *The American Tory* (1961).

Benjamin T. Spencer, *The Quest for Nationality: An American Literary Campaign* (1957).

Reed Ueda, "Naturalization and Citizenship," in Thernstrom, *Harvard Encyclopedia of American Ethnic Groups* (1980).

CHAPTER
4

European Migration and the
Radical Attempt to Conserve,
1830–1880

Beginning in the 1830s, a resurgence in immigration began that would redefine the American population. Whereas fewer than 150,000 immigrants arrived in the 1820s, the numbers surged to over a half million immigrants in the 1830s, nearly two million in the 1840s, and over two and one-half million immigrants in the 1850s. With a population of just over 23 million in 1850, the United States sustained an immigration equivalent to over one-tenth of the total population in the ensuing decade. If the numbers of immigrants swelled, their origins remained similar throughout the period: Ireland and the German states were the homelands of roughly two-thirds of the immigrants between 1830 and 1860. Immigration would slow during the Civil War, but another five million immigrants would arrive in the two decades prior to 1880, principally from Germany, Ireland, the United Kingdom, and Scandinavia. Although immigrants would also arrive in this era from new destinations, such as China (see Chapter 6), the European immigration stemmed mainly from perceptions of increasing economic opportunity in the United States and growing population and economic change that resulted in an immense settler migration in Europe. Whether they moved to the vast agricultural regions of the Middle West or to the rapidly growing cities on the eastern seaboard, most of the European immigrants were leaving home for good and arriving in the United States to stay.

If most of the immigrants' origins were European and most of them intended to remain in the United States, the motivations of these immigrants varied. Many of them were leaving Europe as part of what historian Mack Walker has described, in writing about the German immigration, as a radical attempt to conserve. Immigrants came to America, Walker argues, "less to build something new than to regain and conserve something old," so that they "were conservatives, who acted radically in order to preserve." In sum, according to Walker, they "journeyed to *another world to keep their homes." In building communities and transplanting ties to kinship, many immigrants hoped to retain their old patterns of life under more auspicious economic circumstances. Yet this model of immigration did not encompass the entire migration: Other immigrant streams resulted from crises. The most poignant example was the massive emigration from Ireland following the potato famine in the 1840s. As many of the Irish starved and as many more were pushed off the land, thousands found their way to the United States where, historian Kerby Miller argues, they considered immigration an exile that was a consequence of British colonialism in Ireland.*

Whether the immigration was a radical attempt to conserve or an exile, many European immigrants extolled the virtues of American society and government, and they marveled at American opportunity. To be sure, some were disappointed with life in the United States. But many of them wrote home of the "freedoms" that distinguished life in the United States from life at home. They often urged family and friends to join them in America. When examining this migration, we ought to consider the variety of experiences of immigrants—ranging from a radical attempt to conserve to a virtual exile. And, given these dissimilar contexts of immigrant life, we should explore whether the radical attempt to conserve could succeed. Could immigrants who wanted to do so continue to conserve their traditions? Or were the purported freedoms a force that inexorably changed their communities?

 D O C U M E N T S

These documents illustrate European immigrants' lives in city and countryside in the mid-nineteenth-century United States. The first document, by Gottfried Duden (1827), is among the earliest examples of promotional literature written by a nineteenth-century German immigrant. Writing from Missouri, Duden writes of the "fairy-tale world" of the United States, considers the possibility of creating a German state in the western United States, and rues the slavelike status of German servants at the same time that he calculates how immigrants could use African American slaves to build their farms. The next two documents highlight the varied background of the emigrants from Europe. Svein Nilsson (1868) shows how "American fever" diffused the mountain valleys of Norway in the 1830s and how the ethnic communities in Wisconsin varied, whereas as Robert Whyte (1847) explains the ways in which emigration from Ireland was coupled with the capriciousness of the potato harvest and the greed of the landlords. In the fourth document, James Burn describes the Irish and German working communities in New York City in 1850. The fifth document (1841–1848) is a newspaper report and a series of letters written by Swedish women and men who marvel at the political and economic differences between their country of birth and the United States. The next document is another series of letters, these written by a German immigrant to her family in Germany (1850–1857). The letters illustrate how her early optimism is tempered so that, by 1857, she writes of her "misfortune" in the United States. The final document (1866–1883), relying on the experience of Swedish immigrants, graphically portrays how immigrants often moved in a "chain migration" pattern so that neighbors in Europe often became neighbors in the United States.

Gottfried Duden, a German, Assesses the Possibilities for Immigrants to Missouri, 1827

Many times I have said to myself and to my traveling companion (whom I shall leave behind in the most fortunate situation): People in Europe will not and cannot believe how easy and how pleasant it can be to live in this country. It sounds too strange, too fabulous. Believing in similar places on this earth has too long been consigned to the fairy-tale world. The inhabitants of the Mississippi area, on the other hand, consider the reports of need in Europe exaggerated. The citizens of the state of Missouri, together with their slaves, doubt so much that there are so many white people in Europe who with the greatest exertion can enjoy scarcely as much meat in an entire year as is here thrown to the dogs in a few weeks. They cannot believe that some families would even starve or freeze to death in winter without the charity of others; they are accustomed to attribute such statements to the intention and desire to praise and flatter America. However, sometimes one hears a person say: "Yes, yes, my grandfather told us that life was very hard there."

And yet I must advise against moving here by oneself and without careful consideration. Success depends completely on the way emigration is carried out; and without special preparation or adequate guidance, everyone will be exposed to chance more than he might expect. If a person has successfully survived the first two years, he is safe. But that is a difficult condition to meet. The initial effects of the new climate, the lack of domestic stability and service, attacks of homesickness—all these general causes hardly require the inevitable minor nuisances to produce disturbances in the healthiest body, which, even if they do not endanger life, usually decrease one's means considerably and cause one to lose the courage to use properly what remains.

If a small city were founded with the intention of serving the American Germans as a center of culture, one would soon see a rejuvenated Germania arise and the European Germans would then have a second country here, such as the British have. If only a live interest for such a project would develop in Germany! No plan of the present day can be more promising to the individual and to the whole than such a plan for the founding of a city as the center of German culture in western North America, and especially in the areas west of the Mississippi. It would immediately make the new continent a home for the Germans and would add to all the direct gifts of nature that which must always proceed from human beings themselves. No one should fear that any political obstacle or envy of the Americans would oppose it. German immigrants are generally welcome here, and as soon as they have set foot on the new continent, they are considered equals of the citizens (aside from political rights, which are dependent on a residence of five years and in

Selection from Gottfried Duden, *Bericht über eine Reise nach den westlichen Staaten Nordamerikas . . . [Report on a Journey to the Western States of North America and a Stay of Several Years Along the Missouri]*, 1829.

the beginning are more of a hindrance than a help). I have already told you that in the state of Missouri even a foreigner can acquire landed property. . . . How many men there are in Germany who have funds amounting to four to six thousand *Thaler* without any other prospect than to use them for living expenses! But this sum is more than abundant to provide a happy life for an entire family on the banks of the Missouri, even if eight hundred to a thousand *Thaler* should be spent for traveling expenses, provided that they did not lack guidance. Such a financial status is very common in Germany among persons who are forced by what is called propriety and decorum to make expenditures that, without providing pleasure for the present, veil the future with anxiety. With the above-mentioned sum the immigrant can buy two adult slaves (one male and one female), which cost about twelve hundred Prussian *Thaler,* and establish himself in such a manner that he can live more happily and, especially in regard to the future lot of numerous descendants, with many less worries than if he possessed six times that amount in Germany. . . . A quarter of a mile from me there lives a farmer by the name of Jacob Haun. Seven years ago he began to establish a homestead. Because he possessed scarcely a hundred *Thaler,* he at first lived on state property and there tried to earn enough for the purchase of 160 *Morgen.* Then he continued to farm on his own property after the usual fashion and prospered, so that in seven years, without any assistance, he acquired a fortune of three thousand *Thaler.* Meanwhile his wife bore him five children, and now his household annually consumes over twelve hundred pounds of pork, an oxen weighing five to six hundred pounds, and several dozen roosters and hens. Also, at least ten to twelve deer are killed and a large number of turkeys. (No powder is used for partridges; it is left to the children to catch them in traps.) Who would believe that so much meat could be consumed in one household of two adults and five children, of whom the oldest is scarcely six years old? Some, of course, is contributed to hospitality. But most of it is due to the extravagant use of an article of food that is almost cheaper here than the most common vegetables in Germany.

. . . Finally, I scarcely like to mention the lot of those unfortunate ones who become slaves in return for the payment of traveling expenses. Only a galley slave will find his lot improved in this situation. They are called redemptioners here, and perhaps also white slaves. Their fate is far worse than that of the Negro slaves, and it is incomprehensible to me that some German publications can pass over this so lightly. The health of the Negro is, after all, to the owner's advantage. Negroes are acclimatized; most of them call America their home and have never known freedom. The poor Europeans who think they have purchased the land of their desires by the hardships endured during the journey across the sea are enslaved for five, seven, and more years for a sum that any vigorous day laborer earns within six months. The wife is separated from the husband, the children from their parents, perhaps never to see each other again. Just because so little is expected of such workers during the first years, their term of service is extended so much. But let no one believe that these first years will be years of play. They are indeed the most oppressive ones. That individuals survive and later become rich does not alter the general prospect. Ten perish miserably, while scarcely one prospers.

Svein Nilsson Chronicles Norwegian American
Immigration to Wisconsin, 1868

In the mountain districts in those days the strangest stories were told about America and the dangers of a trip across the ocean. Some of the mountain people had heard that skippers often sold emigrants as slaves to the Turks; others maintained that the ocean swarmed with horrible monsters capable of devouring a whole ship—cargo and all. But according to some accounts, an even worse fate awaited those who were not swallowed by sea-beasts or crushed between towering icebergs. In America, so the stories went, the natives commonly captured white men and ate them on festive occasions to the glory of their gods. These and similar tales circulated in the mountain valleys and many of the inhabitants crossed themselves in sheer amazement at the reckless daring of the emigrants.

In spite of all the solemn warnings, the emigrants clung to their decision. To realize the dream of departing for America in those days must surely have required great willpower. America was but little known in Norway thirty years ago, and even short trips were seldom undertaken in the mountain areas. It seems that scarcity of tillable soil and shortage of profitable employment were the factors which caused the emigrants from these regions to shoulder the knapsack. One of them, John Nelson, now a respected, prosperous farmer . . ., has spoken about these matters: "I was my father's oldest son and as such was entitled to inherit [a] farm, which was held to be one of the best in the community; but it was encumbered with a debt of fourteen hundred dollars. I worked at home until I was twenty-five years old and consequently was unable to save any money. It was obvious that I would assure myself a hopeless future by taking charge of the farm with its heavy indebtedness, buying out my brothers and sisters in such a fashion that they suffered no injustice, and, finally, providing a pension for my father. I noticed with apprehension how one farm after another fell into the hands of the sheriff or other moneylenders. This increased my fear of getting involved with any kind of farming. But I got married and had to make some provision for the future. Then it occurred to me that it would be best to leave for America. I was strengthened in this resolve by letters from Norwegian settlers in Illinois, and the idea ripened into firm determination when I read a book written by a Norwegian immigrant who had spent some time in the United States. What I have just said explains what brought me to leave my native land, and I presume that the other members of our party were led to their decisions by similar reasoning."

. . . At that time people looked at this undertaking with suspicion and pity. The emigrants were considered foolish daredevils; it was even hinted that they acted upon the inspiration of the Evil One himself who thus sought to lead them to destruction. No one had any inkling at the time that with their journey these farmers from Tinn were shattering the wall of custom which made people lie at home in poverty rather than seek work and food elsewhere. Despite all the horror stories

Selection from Svein Nilsson's articles in *Billed-Magazin*, 1868–1870.

and the loud talk about the sinfulness of leaving the spot where one was born, the America fever gradually spread in wide circles; and, during the following years, every spring saw large groups of emigrants . . . trudging through the valley . . . toward the sea.

* * * *

I wish to add some observations made by one of our countrymen living in the settlement. He says: "The stolidity and slowness which characterize the Norwegians disappear in America. The determination and energy of the American people seem to electrify the newcomer. He soon notices that the saying 'help yourself' is not mere play with words but a slogan to be followed in all the vicissitudes of life. Necessity compels him to become more enterprising; the force of example strengthens and stimulates him; old prejudices vanish; energy awakens; dejection gives place to buoyancy; he tackles one or another worthwhile job; if the first or second attempt does not succeed, he turns to something else, because here work is respected and all legitimate pursuits, except the sale of liquor, are looked upon as honorable. As a result, many who back home might have become a public burden here become useful citizens. All class barriers are broken down. No one asks about birth or family connections. A good character and sobriety are everywhere the best recommendations. The well-informed man is respected, but he is also required to give proof of his ability through the spoken or written word or some useful activity. Emphasis is placed on the practical aspects of life; theories are taken into account only in so far as their utility is demonstrable.

"Formerly I believed that it was the rich and the official classes who impoverished the common man in Norway. I discovered long ago that this idea was wrong. . . . If respect for manual labor could be enhanced back home and things done with more energy and initiative, then Norway would provide her people with their daily bread just as well as any other land. In this country the ambitious young man tries to discover early what type of activity will bring him the best salary; he tackles any kind of work within his range of abilities which promises a good income.

"At home, on the other hand, the knack of living on society like a parasite seems to have been elevated to a science; and the man who does not need 'to struggle for existence' is regarded as fortunate. A bit of schooling, instead of acting as a spur to greater industry, is regarded as a license to lead a life of ease, free from all manual work. This attitude tends to depress and demoralize the laboring class, which, as a consequence, performs its work grudgingly, becomes listless and dispirited, gives up the hope of a brighter future, and looks with envious eyes at the higher classes. The phrase 'only a working man or a peasant from the country' expresses the arrogant attitude taken toward all manual labor. So great is the power of custom that even sensible people often sincerely pity the man who is forced by circumstances to earn his livelihood by the labor of his hands. . . . Here in America it happens quite frequently that the man who sat behind a desk yesterday is seen out in the field today; the man who recently stood behind the counter in a store can later labor with a spade in his hands; even officers of justice are often seen in a shop, and it does not occur to anyone that these men are to be pitied, nor do they themselves feel that they have been wronged by fate.

* * * *

. . . In general the Germans and Scandinavians who have come here from Europe seem to have acquired economic independence more easily than the Yankees from the eastern states. The hard work and thrift of the former lead to progress; unless some misfortune strikes them, their hopes for wealth and independence are realized. The latter, on the contrary, make many demands on life: the wife wants to live in style, while the husband's ideas of a decent existence often lead to expenses which do not correspond to their income. "They are anxious to fly before they have sprouted wings," a local Norwegian said recently, "and unless they have considerable capital to start with, they often fail at farming and suffer complete economic collapse."

Even though at present emigration and immigration in these regions about balance, the population is steadily increasing as a result of strong inner growth. "The Scandinavians in this country distinguish themselves by great fertility," say the Yankees, and a comparison between the birth rates in Norwegian and American families undeniably serves to corroborate this statement. But the Germans and certainly the Irish do not take a back seat to anyone in this respect. Consequently, Americans of the older generation admit that "the future belongs to the European immigrants of the present century." Already the Yankees of unmixed race constitute a decided minority in many areas.

Our countrymen who first settled on Koshkonong belonged to the industrious and thrifty people still found in Norway's mountain valleys. Accustomed to privation and physical exertion in their native land, they were peculiarly suited to tackle the frontier and clear the way for later groups of immigrants. When these fathers of emigration tell about happenings of past days and their own experiences in this country we must admire the courage which defied all dangers and the endurance which has transformed a wilderness into flourishing fields. The difference between past and present is so great that only through a bold flight of fancy can we possibly visualize the change which has taken place. And when we consider that all this has transpired within three decades we can well understand why America has been called "the land of wonders."

Robert Whyte Explains the Irish Migration Following the Potato Famine, 1847

Emigration has for a long time been considered by British political economists the most effective means of alleviating the grievous ills under which the Irish peasantry labour. It is not our province to enquire into its expediency; but viewing the subject with the single eye of common sense it is difficult to see the necessity of

---

As found in James J. Mangan (ed.), *Robert Whyte's 1847 Famine Ship Diary: The Journey of an Irish Coffin Ship* (Mercier Press).

expatriating the superfluous population of a country wherein hundreds of thousands of acres of land susceptible of the highest culture, lie waste, whose mines teeming with wealth remain unworked and which is bordered by more than 2,000 miles of sea coast whose banks swarm with ling, cod, mackerel, etc, while salt-fish is largely imported from Scotland.

Many years previous to legislators taking up the matter, emigration from Ireland existed—and that of a class of persons which could be badly spared from the already impoverished island, consisting as it did of small but substantial farmers who, perceiving but a gloomy prospect before them, sold off their land and, turning their capital into cash, availed themselves of the opportunities that existed to find comfort and independence by settling in America.

The majority of these adventurers being successful in their undertakings, they induced their relatives and friends to follow them and thus a strong tide of emigrants whose number gradually increased each season, set toward the West.

This progressive and natural system of emigration, however, gave place within the last few years to a violent rush of famished, reckless human beings, flying from their native land to seek food in a distant and unknown country.

The cause of this sudden change is easily ascertained. Everyone is familiar with the wretched lot of the Irish peasantry: obliged to work for a miserable pittance, their chief reliance was upon the crop of potatoes grown by each family in the little patch of ground attached to their hut—a poor dependence indeed, not only as regards the inferiority of the potato as the sole diet of a people, but from the great uncertainty always attending its propagation. The consequences of even a partial failure—an event of common occurrence—were, therefore, of the most serious nature.

In the year 1822, the deficiency was so general that the price quadrupled and the peasantry of the south and west were reduced to actual starvation. To alleviate the distress, a committee was formed in London and subcommittees throughout England, and such was the benevolence of individuals that large funds were in a short time at their disposal. By the end of the year, subscriptions had been raised in Great Britain amounting to £350,000 to which parliament added a grant of £150,000, making altogether £500,000—a large sum, but how inadequate to meet the wants of some three or four millions of starving people!

This serious warning it should be supposed would have opened the eyes of the country to the necessity of having something else as a resource under similar emergency, but a plentiful season lulled them into forgetfulness of what they had suffered, and apathy concerning the future.

So abundant was the produce of the seasons 1842 and 1843 that the poorest beggar refused potatoes and they were commonly used to manure the land.

However, the blight of the crop of 1845 and the total destruction of that of 1846 brought the country to the lowest ebb, and famine with its attendant, disease, stalked through the land.

Charity stretched forth her hand from far and near, America giving liberally of her abundance. But all that could be done fell far short of the wants of the dying sufferers. The government stepped forward and advanced funds for the establishment of public works; this was attended with much advantage and mitigated a great deal of distress but unfortunately all the money had to be returned in the shape of onerous taxation upon the landowners.

The gentry became seriously alarmed and some of them, perceiving that the evil was likely to increase year after year, took into their consideration what would be the surest method of terminating it.

At length it was discovered that the best plan would be to get completely rid of those who were so heavy a burden upon them by shipping them to America; at the same time publishing to the world as an act of brotherly love and kindness, a deed of crafty, calculating selfishness: for the expense of transporting each individual was less than the cost of one year's support in a workhouse.

It required but little argument to induce the prostrated people to accede to their landlords' proposal by quitting their poverty-stricken country for 'a land flowing with milk and honey'—poor creatures, they thought that any change would be for the better. They had nothing to risk, everything to gain. 'Ah! Sir,' said a fellow passenger to me after bewailing the folly that tempted him to plunge his family into aggravated misfortune, 'we thought we couldn't be worse off than we war but now to our sorrow we know the differ for sure supposin' we were dyin' of starvation or if sickness overtuk us, we had a chance of a doctor and if he could do no good for our bodies sure the priest could for our souls and then we'd be buried along wid our own people, in the ould churchyard, with the green sod over us, instead of dying like rotten sheep thrown into a pit, and the minit the breath is out of our bodies flung into the sea to be eaten up by them horrid sharks.'

It cannot excite the least surprise that these wretched beings should carry with them the seeds of that plague from which they were flying and it was but natural that these seeds should rapidly germinate in the hot-bed holds of ships crammed almost to suffocation with their distempered bodies. In short, nothing was wanted to encourage the speedy development of the direst disease and misery but—alas!—everything that could check their spread was absent.

My heart sickens when I think upon the fatal scenes of the awfully tragic drama enacted upon the wide stage of the Atlantic Ocean in the floating lazar houses that were wafted upon its bosom during the never-to-be-forgotten year 1847.

Without a precedent in history, may God grant that this account of it may descend to posterity without a parallel.

* * * *

James Burn Describes Irish and German Immigrants in New York City, 1850

Though society in New York is made up of almost every nationality on the face of the earth, the Irish and German elements are by far the most predominant. "Schenck" and "Shaughnessy" represent the plodding Teuton and the impulsive Celt, over the portals of lager-beer saloons and whisky stores, in all the leading

Selection from James D. Burn, "Three Years Among the Working-Classes in the United States," 1865.

thoroughfares, from the back slums in the vicinity of the wharves to the pave on the Broadway, where Republican "big bugocracy" sports its jewels, silks and drapery. America may be looked upon as a sort of promised land for the children of ould Ireland. After coming here, if they do not get milk and honey in abundance, they are able, at all events, to exchange their national "male of potatoes" for plenty of good substantial food; their mud cabins and clay floors with fires on the hearth, for clean, comfortable dwellings with warm stoves and "bits of carpits on their flures." It is worthy of note how the more prudent and industrious class of Irishmen succeed in the different walks of life, when they are favoured with a fair field for the exercise of their genius and industry. In New York there is scarcely a situation of honour or distinction, from the chief magistrate down to the police, that is not filled by a descendant of some Irishman who lived in savage hatred of England beyond the pale! The mere labouring Irish, like those of the same class at home, may be seen engaged in all the humbler occupations from shouldering the hod to rag-gathering, but in whatever business they may be employed, they have a decided advantage over their compeers in the old country—as they are sure to be remunerated in such a way as enables them to live comfortably, so far at the least as food and clothing are concerned. One of the principal trading branches of business in which Irishmen are generally successful, is that of the liquor store line, a trade which the Irish and Germans may be said to divide between them. As the body is composed of a large number of members, its influence in a political point of view is a matter of no small importance during elections, whether for municipal authorities, state officers, or presidents.

The rapid transformation effected both in the manners and personal appearance of the young members of the Celtic family after arriving in this country, even for a short time, if located in any of the large cities, is well worthy of notice. Instead of the indolent deportment, careless manner, and slouching gait, which characterized him at home, the young Hibernian receives the genteel inspiration of fashion, and speedily has himself tailored into external respectability; he learns to walk with his head erect, and assumes an air in keeping with his altered condition. That crouching servility and fawning sycophancy to people above his own grade, which made him a slave in all but the fetters, is cast aside, and he dons the character of a free citizen of the United States. Still, whatever change time or circumstances may effect in improving the social condition of Irishmen, . . . the idiosyncracies of their race cling to them as broad distinguishing features from all the other members of the human family. It is not wonderful that the Irish peasant at home, should contract indolent and careless habits. As a cotter or small landholder, his tenure is uncertain, his means of living precarious, and when he has an opportunity of plying his industry, the miserable remuneration he receives is not sufficient for his limited wants. Generally speaking, there is much shrewdness and common sense in his character as well as a fund of ready wit: these traits, however, are frequently mingled with the traditions of his country, by which the wrongs of centuries are kept fresh upon his memory, and as he broods over the past, he carefully nurses feelings which bode no good to those he esteems his oppressors.

* * * *

The improved condition of Irishmen in America does not make them forget the soil made sacred to them by the graves of their fathers and the memories of their early loves and youthful aspirations, when they knew no other land. The records of the money-order office will form a lasting memorial of the industry, prudence, filial duty, and affection of thousands of the sons and daughters of the Green Isle, who have nobly aided their relations to escape from the bondage of poverty, and unite their fortunes and affections in their new homes.

Much of the development of the great natural resources of America during the last forty years is no doubt owing to the energy and industry of the Irish and German settlers. These two races of the human family are vastly different from each other in nearly all the aspects and phases of their social characters. The German is plodding, frugal, and cautious; he is quiet, too, and seldom commits himself by noisy demonstrations. In his adopted country he enjoys both social and political liberty, and is proud of the dignity his citizenship confers; these advantages were denied to him in his fatherland, and he uses them in his new home with becoming discretion. The Tutonic [sic] family is largely wedded to the soil in all the agricultural districts, from the eastern seaboard to the far west. Many, however, are engaged in commercial pursuits, and a goodly number ply their industry in various branches of skilled labour.

I find there are two reasons that induce large numbers of the German people to leave their homes—the conscription is the first, and the low standard of wages the second. When the unskilled labourer arrives in America he finds himself placed on a level with the citizen who has passed a probation in learning a trade, and by becoming a citizen he is enabled to enjoy those social, religious, and political privileges which were denied him in his own country.

Those emigrants who come to the country in early life very soon become Americans in feeling, manners, and habits, but as a general rule it is very different with men who are advanced in years. Their thoughts, modes and habits have been fixed, they cannot, therefore, reconcile themselves to the new order of things without doing violence to their feelings. Young people on coming to America, if at all willing to labour, find two of the principal objects of their ambition in abundance; these are food and clothing, and what is more they find themselves on a level with those classes in society they were wont to look up to in their own country. People in years do not "live by bread alone," and they only value clothing for the comfort it gives the body, the quiet pleasures and enjoyments resulting from a friendly intercourse with kindred spirits is to them as rain is to the parched earth. It may be that the members of upper grades of society in America mingle with each other in friendly intercourse, in which the warmth of the heart and the purity of thought are not subdued by conventionalities, and if so, it is well, but from what I have seen and felt, down below all is cold, unnatural, and formal. It is a fact that numbers of people in humble positions in this country, after having made a little money, become starched with foolish pride; they are not contented to enjoy the goods the gods have sent them in a rational manner; they must assume the airs of gentility, in the doing of which they make fools of themselves.

Swedish Women and Men Observe the "Freedom" and Opportunity in America, 1841–1848

[A letter from Gustaf Unonius]

Milwaukee, Wisconsin, 13 October 1841

The soil here is the most fertile and wonderful that can be found and usually consists of rich black mold. Hunting and fishing will provide some food in the beginning, but they must by pursued sparingly, otherwise time which could more profitably be spent in cultivating the soil is wasted. I beg the emigrant to consider all these factors carefully and closely calculate his assets before he starts out. . . . he will have to suffer much in the beginning, limit himself considerably, and sacrifice much of what he was accustomed to in Europe. . . . I caution against all exaggerated hopes and golden air castles; cold reality will otherwise lame your arm and crush your courage; both must be fresh and active.

As far as we are concerned, we do not regret our undertaking. We are living a free and independent life in one of the most beautiful valleys the world can offer; and from the experiences of others we see that in a few years we can have a better livelihood and enjoy comforts that we must now deny ourselves. If we should be overcome by a longing for the fatherland (and this seems unlikely), we could sell our farm which in eight years will certainly bring ten or twelve dollars per acre. . . . But I believe that I will be satisfied in America.

I am partial to a republican form of government, and I have realized my youthful dream of social equality. Others may say what they will, but there are many attractive things about it. It is no disgrace to work here. Both the gentleman and the day laborer work. No epithets of degradation are applied to men of humble toil; only those whose conduct merits it are looked down upon. . . . Liberty is still stronger in my affections than the bright silver dollar that bears her image. . . .

Pine Lake, Wisconsin, 25 January 1842

. . . I admit that I am no friend of the big city of New York. The shopkeeper's spirit is too prevalent, but to judge the American national character from that is incorrect. I have found the Americans entirely different. We live in an industrial era and it is true that the American is a better representative of that than any other nationality. Despite this fact, there is something kindly in his speculation for profit and wealth, and I find more to admire in his manner than in that of the European leaders. The merchant here is withal patriotic; in calculating his own gain he usually includes a share for his country. . . . the universities and other educational institutions, homes for the poor, and other institutions of value to society are dependent on and supported by the American merchants. Canals, railroads, etc., are all financed by companies composed of a few individuals whose collective fortunes serve the public for its common benefit and profit. One must, therefore, overlook an avariciousness which sometimes goes to extremes.

Selection from H. Arnold Barton, *Letters from the Promised Land: Swedes in America, 1840–1914.*

It is true that the American is a braggart; his love for his country is a predilection; the experience he has had with European culture and institutions often leads him to censure them and in considering the advantages of his own country to pass over the good things which the Old World still retains. We find him to be a proud egotist, a quarrelsome patriot, and, if I may say so, an intolerable fellow citizen. Instead of the jealousy that prevails among other nationalities, he has these faults, if faults they be. During the struggles which rend and agitate the countries of the Old World he sees in the progress of his peaceful fatherland the results of liberty and equality which he considers impossible to obtain under any other conditions. Even though I do not wish to blame him for this, yet I do not deny that his resulting self-satisfaction expresses itself in a highly ridiculous fashion in trivial matters. . . .

✻ ✻ ✻ ✻

[From a report printed in a Småland newspaper in 1846]

The desire to emigrate to America continues to increase in the Kisa area and has evidently spread to neighboring regions. A beggar girl from Kisa, who went up to the plain region to carry on her activity, is said to have described America in much more attractive colors than Joshua's returning spies described the Promised Land for the children of Israel. "In America," she is supposed to have said, "the pigs go and eat themselves full on raisins and almonds, which everywhere grow wild, and when the pigs are thirsty, they drink from the ditches, where nothing but wine flows." Naturally, the simple peasantry must draw the conclusion that it is far better to be a pig in America than a human being in Sweden. The desire to emigrate overwhelms them and the governor's officials get no sleep at night from preparing emigrant passes. More than a hundred of these are supposed to have been issued.

[A letter from Christina Källström in 1848]

. . . I have sent word several times . . . that if someone intends to come over here . . . , they would be much better off here than in Sweden. Until they learned the language they could not get more than four dollars a week plus food and gifts, but as soon as they got more used to things they could surely get more; women do not have to do any other work here but wash clothes and cups and keep the house tidied up and at some places also cook food. And here people live well, there is nothing but wheat bread. There is no need to tell about conditions, for word has surely spread through various letters that have been sent from here. . . . It is up to Providence whether we shall ever meet again in this earthly life, but let us then meet in a better world. . . . If anyone should possibly want to come over and they could get some help with money for the journey, they could quickly repay it here. Oh! How happy I would be if I had with me my boys and girls who stayed behind in Sweden; I could dance with joy to my grave and be sure that they would soon earn enough here to assure themselves of a carefree old age. Many greetings to you all. God be with you. So wishes your loving sister.

A German American Family Changes Its Assessment of American Life, 1850–1883

Anna Maria Schano, née Klinger

[New York, probably mid-1850]

[Beginning of letter missing] I've saved up to now in the time we've been married some 40 dollars in cash, not counting my clothes. Dear parents and brothers and sisters, I certainly don't want to tell you what to do, do what you want, for some like it here and some don't, but the only ones who don't like it here had it good in Germany, but I also think you would like it here since you never had anything good in Germany. I'm certainly glad not to be over there, and only those who don't want to work don't like it here, since in America you have to work if you want to amount to anything, you mustn't feel ashamed, that's just how you amount to something, and so I want to tell you again to do what you want, since it can seem too trying on the journey and in America as well, and then you heap the most bitter reproaches on those who talked you into coming, since it all depends on whether you have good luck, just like in Germany. Dear parents, you wrote me that Daniel wants to come to America and doesn't have any money, that is certainly a problem. Now I want to give you my opinion, I've often thought about what could be done, I thought 1st if he could borrow the money over there, then when he has saved enough over here then he could send it back over, like a lot of people do, and secondly, I thought we would like to pay for him to come over, but right now we can't since it costs 28 dollars a person and I also want to tell you since my husband wrote to you, the money we want to send you, whether you want to use it to have one or two come over here or if you want to spend it on yourselves, you just have to let us know so we have an idea how much you still need, and you'll have to see to it that you have some more money, too, since we can't pay it all. . . . Dear parents and brothers and sisters, if one of you comes over here and comes to stay with us we will certainly take care of you, since we are now well known, and you needn't be so afraid of America, when you come to America, just imagine you were moving to Stuttgart, that's how many Germans you can see here.

And as far as the Americans are concerned, whites and blacks, they won't harm you, since the blacks are very happy when you don't do anything to them, the only thing is the problem with the language. It's not as easy to learn as you think, even now I don't know much, and there are many people here who don't even learn it in 6 to 8 years, but if you start off working for Americans then you can learn in one year as much as in 10 years living with Germans. Dear parents and brothers and sisters, I'd like to be with you, you will surely be pleased to get the picture of us, to see me again, and I would also be so happy to see you again. In my dreams

From Walter Kamphoefner, et al., *News From the Land of Freedom: German Immigrants Write Home.*
Copyright © 1991. Reprinted by permission of Verlag C. H. Beck.

I've often been with you and also in my old job in Germany, but when I woke up, it wasn't true, but still I am happy in any case that I am in America.

* * * *

[New York, probably 1851]

You probably never thought I would be a washerwoman, but in America you needn't be ashamed if you work, in America if you don't work and don't save and so on, you don't have anything either. . . .

. . . You also wanted to know about Barbara, she is fine, she is so pleased and so happy that she is in America, she's never once wished to be back in Germany she is working for some French people, she likes it fine, she's paid back the money for her passage and if you saw her, you'd be quite surprised, she goes for a walk with us every Sunday, you'd see no difference in the way she's dressed. Dear parents and brothers and sisters, if you wish to come here to us then write us right away so you can come over this fall so you'll still have some food.

* * * *

[Albany, December 22, 1856]

. . . Now, I want to explain, since we certainly know his situation, so first of all, if he comes here he won't be able to depend on his trade, and second, if he runs around as a day laborer or farmhand his prospects aren't good, either, and third, if he leaves his family over there, then he won't have any peace of mind either, because you can't earn money quite so fast as you may think, all sorts of things can happen, first of all you can get sick, second you may not earn anything, then it's easy to get into debt instead of sending money to Germany to feed your family or bring them over here, you just can't imagine it, and you don't believe it, either, that a person can have a hard time here at the start, but when someone's been here longer, then he can do well, if he is lucky, in a short time he can save as much of a fortune as in Germany, now I've told you the truth.

* * * *

[Albany, February 18, 1883]

. . . I have suffered much turmoil and misfortune since I have been in America, but the dear Lord has always helped me back on my feet. I put my trust in God and hope he continues to do so until I die and in eternity. My first husband has been dead now for 22 years, we had one child, a son, we were married for 11 years, then my son died 4 years ago and went on ahead of me. He was 26 years old, had been married for one year and left behind his mother, wife and a child, a son named after my husband's grandfather, his name is Frantz Karl Schanno, he'll be 5 years old on May 28th, that is the only grandchild descended from me and my husband, my only relative and joy as long as we are still alive.

A Graphic Portrayal of a Chain Migration from Sweden, 1866–1883

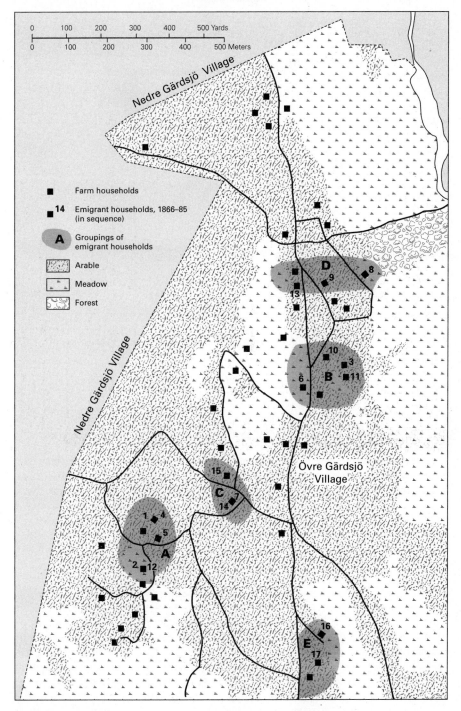

Figure 4.1   Emigrant Households in Övre Gärdsjö Village, 1866–83

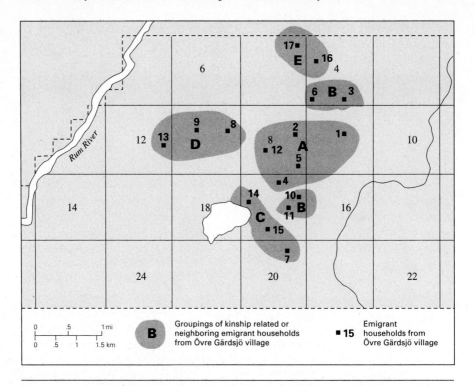

Figure 4.2   Immigrant Households from Övre Gärdsjö Village in Midsection of Athens Township, ca. 1885

ESSAYS

These two essays illustrate the very different reasons for emigration from Europe that created very different ethnic communities in the United States. Historian Kerby A. Miller from the University of Missouri uses the concept of the "American wake" to illustrate the perception that emigration from Ireland was an exile. Like traditional wakes, at which a recently deceased person was mourned, the American wake symbolized the "death" of an immigrant who was, in effect, forced to depart for the United States. In an inextricable combination of nationalism, alienation, and guilt, nineteenth-century Irish immigrants saw themselves as forced to leave their island because of the unfair practices of the British government and large landholders. Because they felt that they were not leaving Ireland voluntarily, they could argue that they were not forsaking country and kin on purpose. Rather, they were exiled, a fact that foretold that, for most, emigration would be an unhappy experience. Kathleen Conzen, a historian at the University of Chicago, provides us with a different story. In exploring the experiences of German Catholic immigrants in a rural settlement in Minnesota from mid- to late-nineteenth century, Conzen illustrates how immigrants could replant communities in the United States and maintain the habits and beliefs that they had carried with them from Europe. As immigrants "made their own America," they distinguished themselves from their American-born neighbors in the ways that they farmed, worshipped, and built their families. This exemplary example of a radical attempt to conserve differs in a variety of ways from the Irish exile illustrated by the "American wake."

Irish Immigrants Who Perceive America as Exile

KERBY A. MILLER

. . . Irish-American homesickness, alienation, and nationalism were rooted ultimately in a traditional Irish Catholic worldview which predisposed Irish emigrants to perceive or at least justify themselves not as voluntary, ambitious emigrants but as involuntary, nonresponsible "exiles," compelled to leave home by forces beyond individual control, particularly by British and landlord oppression. In premodern times Gaelic culture's secular, religious, and linguistic aspects expressed or reinforced a worldview which deemphasized and even condemned individualistic and innovative actions such as emigration. Although Gaelic Ireland withered from the blasts of conquest and change, not only did certain real continuities remain to justify the retention of archaic attitudes and behavior patterns but in fact those institutions—family, church, and nationalism—which dominated modern Catholic Ireland strove to perpetuate old outlooks which both minimized the demoralizing impacts of change and cemented communal loyalties in the face of internal conflicts and external enemies. Thus, tradition and expediency merged, and emigration remained forced banishment—demanding political redress and the emigrants' continued fealty to sorrowing Mother Ireland.

All these themes, attitudes, and social pressures were epitomized by the emigrants' leave-taking ceremonies, commonly known as "American wakes." Archaic in origin yet adapted to modern exigencies, the American wakes both reflected and reinforced traditional communal attitudes toward emigration. Indeed, these rituals seemed almost purposely designed to obscure the often mundane or ambiguous realities of emigration, to project communal sorrow and anger on the traditional English foe, to impress deep feelings of grief, guilt, and duty on the departing emigrants, and to send them forth as unhappy but faithful and vengeful "exiles"— their final, heartrending moments at home burned indelibly into their memories, easily recalled by parents' letters, old songs, or the appeals of Irish-American nationalists.

The American wake seems to have been a peculiarly Irish custom, unknown in Britain or continental Europe. Most extant evidence of the practice dates from the post-Famine decades, but Asenath Nicholson witnessed an American wake in County Kilkenny in 1844, and similar ceremonies—called living wakes—were common in late-eighteenth- and early-nineteenth-century Ulster, where they were held by Presbyterians as well as by Catholics. Nevertheless, the American wake

From *Immigrants and Exiles: Ireland and the Irish Exodus to North America* by Kerby A. Miller. Copyright © 1988 by Oxford University Press, Inc. Used by permission of Oxford University Press, Inc.

seems to have been primarily a Catholic peasant custom carried on most persistently and in its original forms in areas which were still, or in recent memory, Irish-speaking. Thus, by the late nineteenth and early twentieth centuries, American wakes were most common in west Munster, Connaught, and west and mid-Ulster, while in the midlands and eastern counties the custom had either become disused or lost many of its traditional features. In short, like its model—the wake for the dead—the American wake was a product of Gaelic culture, and both customs eventually disappeared with the routinization of emigration and the westward advance of Anglicization. However, as late as 1901, American wakes were still common throughout most of Catholic Ireland, and one newspaper lamented that the entire island had become "one vast 'American wake.'" The name given the custom differed from area to area. Although the term "American wake" was most common, peasants in the Golden Vale called the ceremony a "live wake," while in east Ulster it was a "convoy." In Connaught Irish-speakers referred to "the farewell supper" or "feast of departure," those in Donegal to the "American bottle night" or "bottle drink." In especially Anglicized counties with long experience of emigration, such as Meath and Wexford, the leave-taking occasion was called the "parting spree," indicating the attrition of its once-tragic connotations.

Nevertheless, despite regional variations of nomenclature, save in east Leinster the custom remained substantially similar throughout the island, and its most common name—the American wake—best reflected its character and tone. Of course, in traditional wakes for the dead, the relatives and neighbors of the deceased sat through the night and watched the corpse until burial. Among Catholic peasants the custom was a seemingly incongruous mixture of sorrow and hilarity, with prayers for the dead and the mournful keening of old women alternating with drinking, dancing, and mirthful games. Although real deaths did not occasion American wakes, the choice of name was significant since Catholic countrymen at least initially regarded emigration as death's equivalent, a final breaking of earthly ties. Such attitudes were rooted deep in Irish folklore, for example, in voyage tales which symbolized death or banishment and in popular beliefs which equated going west with earthly dissolution. In the mists of the west Atlantic, in the direction of America, lay the mythical isles which ancient traditions held to be abodes of the dead. Westward travelers, even peasants who added west rooms to their cottages, were believed fated for early demise; likewise, west rooms in farmhouses were traditionally reserved for aged parents who had relinquished control of farms to sons and daughters-in-law. More concretely, in emigration's early decades, when money was scarce, travel slow and perilous, illiteracy widespread and mail service highly uncertain, and destinations only vaguely perceived, the departure for North America of a relative or neighbor represented as final a parting as a descent into the grave. Indeed, given the high mortality rates which afflicted Irish emigrants in both colonial Virginia and early-twentieth-century New York City, associating emigration and death was not illogical, as churchmen warned and as peasants' own observations of consumptive "returned Yanks" seemed to verify, ironically corroborating ancient tales of *Tír na nÓg*, the mythical western Land of the Young, whence no traveler returned except to wither and die. In addition, for the politically minded the American wake seemed a proper commemoration of a process that was bleeding Ireland of its young men and women. As the Irish-Irelander

Robert Lynd observed in 1909, it was "not without significance that so funereal a name should be given to the emigration ceremonies, for the Irish emigrant is not the personification of national adventure, but of something that has the appearance of national doom." Given such traditions and attitudes, it was not unnatural for Irish countrymen to hold wakes for departing emigrants. Even in the late nineteenth century, traditional countrymen "made very little difference between going to America and going to the grave," and as one elderly informant remembered, when you left home, "[i]t was as if you were going out to be buried."

The American wakes resembled the traditional deathwatches in their outward characteristics as well as in their symbolic significance. Both were held to gather together relatives and neighbors to honor the "departed," to share and assuage the grief of the bereaved, and to express at once communal sorrow and a reaffirmation of communal continuity in the face of potentially demoralizing disruptions. The American wakes usually took place in the home of the prospective emigrant and generally lasted from nightfall until early morning of the next day, when the "Yankee"—as he or she was called in west Munster—made the final departure. During the week preceding the American wake, the intending emigrant visited relatives and neighbors to bid them personal farewells and invite them to attend. Priests seem to have been rarely or only briefly present at these affairs (perhaps because traditional wakes generally were clerically proscribed occasions of sin), but by the late nineteenth century it was customary for the "Yankee" to make confession and take communion on the Sunday before departing, and also to pay an obligatory visit to the parish priest's house, there receiving his blessing, presents of prayer books, scapulars, and holy pictures and medals, "as well as much excellent advice and warnings as to the dangers to faith and morals to be met with by those who leave the Catholic atmosphere of holy Ireland." Through these rituals churchmen both sanctioned and, they hoped, retained some control over a process which they opposed but could not halt. Meanwhile, the women of the emigrant's house were busy baking, cooking, and cleaning in preparation for the American wake. Unless times were very bad or the community exceptionally poor, either the emigrant's parents or the guests supplied liberal amounts of food and refreshments, including large quantities of whiskey or, later, porter and stout. While their elders sat around the hearth, the young folk danced to the music of fiddles, flutes, pipes, or melodeons. Between dances the guests cried, sang songs, told stories, and drank away the night.

Thus, like their more gruesome counterparts, the American wakes combined elements of gaiety and grief, but all the evidence indicates that the latter emotion predominated. This was particularly true in the earliest American wakes, held in areas which had witnessed little previous emigration and in traditional or Irish-speaking districts generally. Dancing and singing were often absent at such early wakes, and the participants passed the night with sighs and somber conversation, in an atmosphere laden with gloom and foreboding. Frequently, as in real wakes, the emigrant's mother or another old woman raised a keen over the "dead" one. These were long, sorrowful elegies which alternately praised the emigrant's virtues and descanted upon the sufferings which his or her loss would inflict on parents and community. Indeed, both the traditional keens for the dead and these stylized lamentations over emigration often bitterly reproached their subjects, thus projecting parental and communal responsibility and guilt upon the "departed." "Why did you leave us? had you not every comfort that heart could wish? were you not beloved by your parents and friends?" sang a keener for the dead in 1817: sentiments replicated later in the century by an emigrant's mother in Kilkenny— "O mavoureen, and why do ye break the heart of her who raired ye? Was there no turf in the bog, no praties in the pit, that ye leave the hairth of yer poor ould mother?"—and still later by another in Connemara— "Is there anything so pitiful as a son and a mother / Straying continually from each other? I who reared him without pain or shame / And provided food and good clean sauce for him. . . . Isn't it little my painful disease affects him / And the many sorrows that go through my heart?" . . . .

* * * *

Regardless of the emigrant's ambitions or the real roles parents may have played in obliging departure, the effects of such laments, delivered in shrill, piercing wails, were irresistible and devastating. Before long, "with tears rolling down worn cheeks and feeble old men tearing their gray hair," a chorus of wailing women and weeping men, including the emigrant, joined the old keener in her despair. No wonder that participants in such starkly primitive American wakes described them as "harrowing affairs" displaying "naked grief" and "elemental emotions." No wonder, either, that participants, especially the emigrants themselves, would seek to relieve the tensions of such occasions by making elaborate promises to return or send remittances and by excusing their actions as involuntary, nonresponsible "exile."

* * * *

Perhaps the most telling indicators of the spirit prevalent in the American wakes were the songs which the participants sang. These were a mixture of folk compositions, broadside ballads, and—increasingly by the late nineteenth century—songs published in popular periodicals such as *The Nation's Penny Readings* or in cheap collections like *The Harp of Tara Song Book*. The later published ballads were almost invariably nationalistic, interpreting emigration in political terms, but in fact it is often difficult, if not impossible, to distinguish "genuine" folk compositions from commercial productions, so similar were their themes and so frequently did authors of both kinds of songs borrow images and phrases from each other and from the earlier formal-song traditions. To be sure, the great majority of the emigrants' ballads were unoriginal, clumsily worded and rhymed, and replete with mawkish sentimentality. However, their sheer number and immense popularity on both sides of the Atlantic (many songs current in late-nineteenth-century Ireland had been composed in America) indicate that they both reflected and reinforced conventional Irish perceptions of emigration, and were so deemed highly appropriate to express communal sentiments at the American wakes.

That such sentiments were nevertheless not entirely unambiguous is demonstrated by a significant minority of songs which conceptualized emigration in other than political or negative terms. For example, several ballads portrayed emigration unhappily but realistically depicted its usually mundane causes. Thus, the author of "The Emigrant's Farewell to Donegal" lamented, "My father [held only] five acres of land / it was not enough to support us all, / Which banished me from my native land, / to old Ireland dear I bid farewell." A few songs went further and blamed emigration on parental decisions regarding inheritances and marriage prospects: "How cruel it was of my parents to send me / Away o'er the dark rolling waves of the sea," cried "Barney, the Lad from Kildare," now alone, "out of work, and without a red penny" on the cold streets of urban America. In addition, a number of ballads actually celebrated emigration as a blessed release from poverty or oppression, and predicted that the emigrants would enjoy prosperity and liberty in "The Glorious and Free United States of America." "If you labour in America," promised that song's composer, "In riches you will roll, / There's neither tithes nor taxes there / Nor rent to press you down; / It's a glorious fine free country, / To welcome every man, / So sail off to America, / As soon as e'er you can." Some songs were positively joyful, portraying emigration as an exciting adventure best undertaken by footloose "playboys" such as "The Rambling Irishman," "The Wild Irish Boy," and the author of "Muirsheen Durkin," who declared he was "sick and tired of working" and so was "off to California, where instead of diggin' praties / I'll be diggin' lumps of gold." Likewise, "The Irishman now going to America" told the rollicking story of an Irish canal laborer who fought and wooed his way into the heart and purse of an American widow with $2,000 and a well-stocked farm. That song's composer, like many others, urged his listeners to reject Irish poverty and follow his example. More extreme was the atypical ballad "The Green Fields of America," whose unsentimental author declared, "[It's] little I'd care where my bones should be buried," and cursed those so supine as to remain willingly in Ireland.

Songs which described emigration and America positively seem to have been most common in the late eighteenth and early nineteenth centuries, and most popular then and later in Anglicized districts whose relatively advantaged inhabitants had had long and generally favorable experiences with emigration. For example, most of the emigrants' ballads sung in Counties Meath and Wexford around 1900 were optimistic, promising opportunity and even "independence" in a still-idealized America. Coinciding as they did with the Great Famine's horrors, the 1848 California gold strikes at least temporarily reinvigorated the old image of America as a land of easy riches; even in traditional Kerry, songs promising freedom and happiness in the United States (especially to the unmarried) were popular in the late nineteenth and early twentieth centuries. Such songs certainly served useful purposes, for as rhymed renditions of the *caisleán óir* myth they assuaged many of the fears and tensions surrounding emigration. However, theirs remained a *minority* viewpoint, especially in the post-Famine period, when emigration became at once more intensely politicized and most prevalent in hitherto-traditional or Irish-speaking districts. Moreover, despite their undoubted popularity such songs were generally inappropriate at American wakes, for those occasions were designed not to celebrate departures but to lament them, not to extol the emigrant as an ambitious or carefree individual but rather to impress upon him or her the full burden of a communal opinion which demanded grief, duty, and self-abnegation as the price of departure. Thus, although a number of songs praised the "Land of Liberty" as a refuge, usually this was in the context of politicized exile from a beloved Ireland rather than a simple eulogy of America's abstract attractions. More typical was a composition entitled "My woe be to Columbus who first found out the way," and even in the early nineteenth century the majority of emigration ballads were profoundly melancholic. Indeed, one elderly woman later recalled, "All the songs that ever I heard about going away to America were sad. . . ."

Taken together, the great majority of ballads sung at American wakes represented a stylized dialogue between the emigrants and those who remained in Ireland—a dialogue which fully and dramatically expressed the central elements of the traditional Irish worldview in its conventional applications to the emigration experience. For example, among the saddest and most popular songs were those which, like the traditional keens, reproached and reminded the emigrants how lonely and miserable their parents would be after their departure. "Where are our darling children gone," asked one song heard in County Kerry; "Will they nevermore return, / . . . To their fathers and their mothers, / They have left in misery?" Replete with parents' self-pity, songs of this genre seemed intended to inspire guilt in departing children:

> God keep all the mothers who rear up a child,
> And also the father who labors and toils.
> Trying to support them he works night and day,
> And when they are reared up, they then go away.

These ballads scarcely reflected an accurate picture of emigration's practical causes or of Irish family relationships, but, given their childhood training, neither ambitious nor resentful emigrants could help feeling remorse and guilt for leaving home when they heard such songs. However, the emigrants' tears shed in response were not sufficient recompense for their communal apostasy—"ye go to sarve yourselves, and why do ye bawl about the thing that's yer own choosin'," exclaimed one reproachful father—and other songs composed from the parents' perspective made clear the continued obligations which the emigrants were enjoined to fulfill. "Good-bye Johnny dear," sang one apocryphal mother, "when you are far away,

> Don't forget your poor old mother,
>   Far across the sea,
> Write a letter now and then,
>   And send me all you can,
> But don't forget where'er you roam,
>   that you are an Irishman.

Similarly, related songs warned of the dire consequences of *not* sending remittances home. Thus, in "The Three Leaved Shamrock" a young Irishwoman begs a traveler to carry a tragic message to her brother in the United States—their aged mother has been evicted:

> Tell him since he went away how bitter was her lot,
> And the landlord came one winter's night and turned
>   us from our cot.
> Our troubles they were many and our friends they
>   were but few,
> And brother dear our mother used to ofttimes talk of you,

> Saying darling son come back again, she often
>   used to say,
> 'Till at last one day she sickened, aye, and soon
>   was laid away,
> Her grave I watered with my tears, it's where these
>   flowers grew,
> This is all I've got now and them I send to you.

"Imagine," exclaimed an old woman from Donegal, "if you were going away the next morning and hear a song like that: wouldn't it put you out of your mind with longing!"

The natural counterparts to such ballads were the many songs which dramatized the emigrants' own sorrow for leaving and predicted their unhappiness in North America. Of course, the fact that many young Irishmen and -women left home eagerly, if often naïvely, contradicted the ballads' messages, but the songs accurately reflected young emigrants' frequent regrets and self-pity for their lost childhood as well as the reactions of those who stayed behind and projected their own loneliness on their children overseas. Even more important, such songs allowed the emigrants to exorcise guilt and responsibility for breaking familial and communal ties, because their dominant theme was that all Irish emigrants were really griefstricken and involuntary "exiles," compelled to leave home against their will. For example, many ballads—such as this original composition by a west Ulster emigrant—described the "exile's" feelings at the moment of departure:

> Gazing back through Barnes Gap on my own dear native hills
> I thought no shame (Oh! who could blame?) 'twas there I cried my fill,
> My parents kind ran in my mind, my friends and comrades all,
> My heart did ache, I thought 'twould break in leaving Donegal.

Most songs of this genre emphasized that "Poor Pat *Must* Emigrate," that young Irishmen and -women were all, in the words of one emigrant composer, "*forced* to rove abroad far from the Shamrock shore, / And leave the land which gave me birth, and her whom I adore." However, as might be expected, only rarely did they attribute causation to "cruel parents," Catholic "land-grabbers" or employers, or even to abstract poverty and natural disasters, but instead they almost invariably projected responsibility on Catholic Ireland's historic oppressors, thus portraying the emigrants as "exiles" for faith and country, as victims of landlord or British/Protestant tyranny. Highly politicized emigration ballads were most common in the late nineteenth century, when they reflected the Land League's and home rulers' efforts to propagandize and mobilize the countryside. For example, a popular Land League ballad sung at contemporary American wakes declared defiantly, "We want no emigration / Or coercion of our nation," while "Home Rule and Freedom" described the emigrants as "driven away from the home of their childhood." Likewise, in another "New National Ballad" of the period, the singer laments, "From my cabin I'm evicted and alas compelled to go, / And leave this sainted island where the green shamrocks grow." However, "exile" was hardly a novel theme in Irish popular literature: the Gaelic poetry of the sixteenth and seventeenth centuries; the *aisling* verses and traditional keens of the eighteenth century; and the ubiquitous broadside ballads of the pre-Famine decades—all blamed

Catholic Ireland's sorrows and discontinuities on British oppression and depicted emigration as analogous to political banishment. In short, for emigrants compelled to self-exculpation, historical and literary traditions, cultural and psychological predisposition, contemporary expedience, and continued communal conflicts with landlords and British officialdom merged to perpetuate in song the image of emigration as forced "exile."

Moreover, although some late-eighteenth- and early-nineteenth-century emigration/exile ballads promised the emigrants happiness in the "land of plenty and sweet liberty," the majority of songs heard at American wakes prophesied only poverty and homesickness in the "land of the stranger," where the Irish would wander "lonely . . . in sorrow and fear, / Not a hand that can sooth, nor a smile that can cheer." Thus, "The Irish Labourer" and "The Honest Irish Lad" foretold unemployment and prejudice in America, while "The Irish Emigrant's Lament" expressed the anguish of traditional personalities adrift in an alien and ruthlessly competitive country: "They say I'm now in freedom's land, / Where all men masters be," cried that song's composer, "But were I in my winding-sheet / There's none to care for me." In part, these dire predictions accurately reflected the harsh and uncertain conditions of Irish-American life, especially at midcentury. However, their prevalence in song at the American wakes indicated the strength of conventional outlooks, which persisted throughout the period whether corroborated by or conflicting with the realities to be encountered overseas. Logically, if emigration was reluctant and sorrowful "exile," then the Irish going to America should not —indeed, could not—find happiness there, separated as they would be from their ancestral homes and beloved country. If truly "Exiles in Erin" (*An Díbirteac Ó Éirinn*), then they could never be content abroad. As the author of "Song of an Exile" declared, although "cold," "senseless," ambitious emigrants might forget "the loved isle of sorrow," "the heart of the patriot—though seas roll between them— / Forgets not the smiles of his once happy home": thus,

> Time may roll o'er me its circles uncheering,
>   Columbia's proud forests around me shall wave,
> But the exile shall never forget thee, loved *Eire*
>   Till, unmourned, he sleep in a far, foreign grave.

In effect, by declaring in verse that their lives in America, as well as their departures from Ireland, were or would be unhappy—riven with inconsolable homesickness—the emigrants further satisfied the demands of the exile convention and effectively deflected both communal and self-accusations of selfish and nontraditional behavior. In addition, many ballads sung at American wakes specifically promised parents not only that the emigrants would never forget them "In the land I'm going to" but also that they would fulfill their duties to those left behind. Thus, the composer of "Farewell to Ireland" swore to "write to all relations" and "send my savings home to keep / My mother, dear, alive." Indeed, by the late nineteenth century American remittances had become so customary and obligatory that a number of emigration ballads were written in the form of letters from cheerfully self-sacrificing emigrants who thus provided the participants at American wakes with models for future emulation. "Dear Mother, I take up my pen to write you these few lines," sang one composition,

> Hoping to find you well, and close on better times,
> I send home a ten-pound note [!] to my brothers Mick and Joe,
> And that's all I can afford till the champions grow. . . .

At least equally gratifying both to apprehensive emigrants and to loved ones at home were those songs which in a sense completed the "exile" cycle by predicting that someday the homesick emigrant would "Once . . . more return to my dear native home, / And from that old farm ne'er again will I roam." Finally, not a few ballads sung on both sides of the Atlantic promised not only that the emigrants would remit money and, if possible, return to their parents but also that they would always remember and someday wreak vengeance on those deemed responsible for their country's sufferings and their own unhappy "exile." Thus, the composer of "Evicted" demanded that Irish-Americans never forget "the homeless ones tonight who lie on Irish soil,

> Where British red-coats ruthlessly their sacred homes despoil
> Where mothers, bent and worn with age, are turned abroad to die,
> While from a thousand breaking hearts, there comes this wailing cry:
>
> Torn from the home that has shelter'd us, home of our joys and tears,
> Thrust from the hearth where the laugh and songs gladden'd us many years,
> Homeless we wander tonight, under the moonlit sky.
> England may break the Irish heart, but its spirit will never die.

In short, despite the dancing and drinking, these sad and angry ballads expressed the essence of the American wake experience. As one elderly returned emigrant recalled, "On the night of the Bottle Drink . . . you would think that they were trying to see who could sing the oldest and saddest songs . . . and if you were going away yourself and hear them it would break your heart." Inspiring profuse weeping and bitter lamentations, the ballads helped make the American wake an occasion the emigrants would never forget, filling them with memories associated with intense sorrow and regret—memories easily evoked whenever they gathered in America to sing and hear the old songs from home.

When at last dawn broke, the emotionally draining American wake itself came to an end, but the poignant rituals surrounding the final parting continued until the last terrible moment. Among Catholic emigrants the parish priest again appeared to sanction and sacralize the event, often sprinkling holy water on the heads of the departing while invoking God's and the church's reluctant blessing on their enterprise. Then came the emigrant's last look around his old house and, perhaps, his last farewell before he started on foot or by horse cart to meet the stagecoach or the train which would carry him to Queenstown or some other port. At such moments "[t]he last embraces were terrible to see; but worse were the kissings and the claspings of the hands during the long minutes that remained." When Maura O'Sullivan left her mother's cottage, the old women of the village raised a last mournful keen: "Oh, musha, Maura, how shall I live after you when the long winter's night will be here and you not coming to the door nor your laughter to be heard!" Their testimony indicates that even the most stoic of emigrants were shaken by these last good-byes. For example, James Greene recalled, "The parting

Shake hands . . . brought tears to my eye & an ache to my heart," and years later an elderly Ulster-American remembered, "The last thing I saw was Father, Mother, and the children standing at the gate. I never saw them again. . . ." "I took my seat [in] the Jaunting car," wrote another; "the whip was applied, and amidst the waving of hats and handkerchiefs I took a last and lingering look at that little town where I spent some of my happiest days."

However, in many districts it was customary for parents and friends to prolong the agony as much as possible by accompanying or "convoying" the emigrant for a certain distance from home. One historian argues that the "convoys" were intended to "cheer" the emigrants, but contemporary descriptions indicate that usually the practice was anything but cheerful. Peig Sayers remembered that when her neighbors left west Kerry, at first some people in the convoy were "crying and others were laughing," but "[b]y the time we moved up the Well Road one would think that it was a funeral procession." In 1863 the *Nation* reported, "Every other night a wailing cry passes over the roads of the country from the friends of the emigrants conveying them to the different railway stations, and lamenting their departure. . . . It is melancholy to hear this mournful lament before daybreak in the silent country." Sometimes relatives and friends would walk only a short distance with the emigrant, perhaps to some traditional and appropriate landmark such as "the Rock of the Weeping of Tears" in west Clare. There the emigrant and his "mourners" would take their last sight of one another and say their last good-byes; it was a "sorrowful sight, for parted they were from that day forward as surely as if they were buried in a grave." However, if the railroad station was near, the peasant Irish had no compunctions about enacting their last scenes of grief among strangers. Such leave-takings were especially tumultuous and traumatic:

> A deafening wail resounds as the station-bell gives the signal of starting. . . . [G]ray-haired peasants so clutch and cling to the departing child at this last moment that only the utmost force of three or four friends could tear them asunder. The porters have to use some violence before the train moves off, the crowd so presses against door and window. When at length it moves away, amidst a scene of passionate grief, hundreds run along the fields beside the line to catch yet another glimpse of the friends they shall see no more.

Nevertheless, at last the final break with home had come, and the emigrants were now on their way to North America.

"The final break with home"? Not really, save in a physical sense, for the significance of the American wake and, indeed, of the entire Irish leave-taking ritual was that it both reflected and reemphasized in an extremely forceful fashion all of the conventional Irish attitudes toward life in general and toward emigration in particular. For most young Irishmen and -women leaving home was in some respects a traumatic initiation into adulthood, because emigration literally expelled them from the confines of childhoods passed in largely parochial and still-traditional societies. However, the parting ceremonies reinforced old patterns in such a dramatic manner that they ensured that all but the most "cold" and "senseless" emigrants carried away burning memories and burdensome emotional obligations—that despite their physical departure, they would not break totally away from the values and behavior demanded by tradition and by parents, priests, and nationalist politicians. In a very tangible sense, these heartwrenching scenes and songs constituted the emigrants' final overt exposure in Ireland to the values and symbolism of a traditional worldview which "explained" and justified emigration only in terms of involuntary "exile." Perhaps revealing were the promises which many emigrants, under the stress of these moments, gave to return someday to Ireland, convincing those who remained behind that "[n]early every Irish person that went to America had the intention of coming back . . . and settling down at home." Of course, such promises were unrealistic and rarely fulfilled. However, the fact that they were made, remembered, and cherished and that their failure was regretted on both sides of the Atlantic served to keep Irish-Americans emotionally oriented to their childhood homes. Furthermore, even if they enjoyed material prosperity in the New World, their guilt about promises unfulfilled reinforced internalized obligations to ensure that most emigrants would send remittances and that at least occasionally they would still regard or portray themselves as involuntary "exiles." "For God's sake and for ours," begged one harassed emigrant of his parents at home, "endeavor to shake off your sorrow and do not leave us to accuse ourselves of bringing down your grey hairs with sorrow to the grave by leaving you when we should have stayed by you. Our intentions were good and still continue—and, if God prosper our endeavors, we will soon be able to assist and cheer you." Finally, the same guilt, refracted through the stark memories of the American wakes, provided fertile ground for the appeals of Irish-American nationalists that the emigrants "do something" for Mother Ireland. Images of their mothers' tears, their fathers' graves, their parents' hypothetical sufferings from poverty, English oppression, or their children's alleged "ingratitude": all these were the nationalists' stock-in-trade, just as they had been the prevalent themes of the songs sung at the moment when the emigrants had been most vulnerable. Freeing Ireland, declared one orator, "is a debt we owe to nature and nature's God, and until it is discharged, all who call themselves Irishmen . . . cannot be at peace"—and, he might have added, would not be left at peace.

German Catholic Immigrants Who Make Their Own America

KATHLEEN NEILS CONZEN

In 1950 a prominent New York journalist, Samuel Lubell, bounced his way over the unpaved roads of central Minnesota's Stearns County to the isolated rural parish of St. Martin, in a quest for the roots of a distinctive conservative voting behavior that he identified with farm areas of German and particularly Catholic background. St. Martin's Benedictine pastor, Father Cyril Ortmann, who extended the

From Kathleen Neils Conzen, *Making Their Own America: Assimilation Theory and the German Peasant Pioneer*. Copyright © 1990. Material has been renamed and abridged and is reprinted by permission of Berg Publishers, Oxford, UK.

visitor his full cooperation, felt betrayed when Lubell's initial findings appeared the following year in *Harper's Magazine*. In a few trenchant paragraphs, the journalist sketched a picture of a community dominated by its autocratic priest, one where many farmers still spoke German with greater ease than English, where many refused electrification because the old ways were best, where a father's word was law and children's ambitions extended no farther than farming or a religious vocation, and where both priest and people were bitterly anti-Communist but fatalistically reliant upon prayer alone as the resolution to the world's problems. Father Cyril, who recognized derision when he saw it, finally found his opportunity to reply when he came to write the centennial history of his parish a few years later. Lubell, he observed, had failed to appreciate the worth of a rural way of life that Virgil had praised two millennia earlier. "Political analysts might well probe here for genuine reaction to political issues, and honest grass roots temper characterized by a tenacious adherence to the tenets of a democratic Republic, resting on sound premises." Those "sound premises," Father Cyril made clear, arose from the conjunction of Catholicism, German ethnicity, and farming. "Future students of history might well marvel some day at the stamina and integrity displayed by the descendants of this ethnic group along the Sauk Valley, and come to realize that the impelling force stems from deep religious conviction translated into the unostentatious but practical every day way of Christian living."

How and why the German Catholic peasants who settled the valley of the Sauk beginning in 1854 created and conserved the way of life that gave Lubell such pause and Father Cyril so much satisfaction form the subject of this [selection]. Despite their radically differing judgments on the value of this distinctive way of life, these two protagonists were in essential agreement upon its existence, its religious and ethnic roots, and its enduring significance for personal and political decision making. The phenomenon that they recognized forty years ago remains evident today: a significant segment of American rural life still rests upon communities and cultures that German immigrants like those of the Sauk created.

In Stearns County itself, the outward signs of this heritage are legible in the overwhelming preponderance of German names in the phone directory, in the steeples of the thirty parish churches in which German was once spoken, even in the rhythms and intonations of local speech and in the ubiquity and ambience of village saloons. Less tangible evidence of local distinctiveness can be read in everything from the area's aggressive anti-abortion movement to the fiscal caution of its governmental bodies, the high persistence rates of its conservative farmers, the unusually large size of its families, and the traces of traditional legalism, clericalism, and devotionalism that still mark its spirituality. Nor is Stearns County the only area in the United States where even the casual visitor can perceive the traces of this distinctive patterning. Midwestern rural German Catholic islands as widely separated as DuBois County in southern Indiana, Effingham County in central Illinois, Fond du Lac County in eastern Wisconsin, and Osage County in central Missouri, to name only four among many, still bear its visible stamp. Similar cultural persistence marks many German Protestant farming areas. While there is widespread agreement among scholars that the urban German communities of the era of mass immigration have long since disappeared, at least some of their rural counterparts clearly remain, defined not only by homogeneity of descent within the community but by common values focused on the bond between family and farm that social scientists are able to attribute only to ethnic and religious origins.

✳ ✳ ✳ ✳

. . . the course of local history during the first generation was particularly favorable to the development of an isolated, inward-looking, and autonomous immigrant settlement region, one able to impose its own view on its world. The frontier was indeed a source of opportunity to the Germans of the Sauk, the opportunity to develop along their own trajectory. A southern Minnesota cavalryman stationed in the region in 1864 captured the sense of discomfort and alienation that it evoked from Anglo-Americans when he wrote: "One would imagine while passing along the road that he was traveling in Mexico. Every four of five miles there are great crosses erected with Latin inscriptions on the bar. I may be counted wild in my remarks," he concluded, "but the next internal struggle will be a war upon the Catholics."

His prophecy happily proved false, but he was correct in sensing that the German pioneers of the Sauk were constructing a local order profoundly at odds with the standard American rural model of that place and time. At Maine Prairie and Eden Valley on their southern flank and on the Winnebago Prairie to the north, Yankees from northern New England and Ohio were busily reproducing the societies they had left behind. Using their own or borrowed capital, they pushed to put their full acreages into rapid production, hired laborers—often German—to help work their land, gave their wives and daughters the comforts of a bourgeois lifestyle, tried to send their sons to college or set them up in town businesses, founded debating clubs, literary societies, and farm improvement associations, fought the railroads over shipping rates, and as the wheat frontier passed, cashed in on the capital gains of their land and retired to town on the proceeds. Kin and community played central roles in the lives of these Yankee farmers; their migration chains tended to be even clearer and more direct than those of their German neighbors. But their resources were increasingly marshaled for individualistic, speculative ends.

Not so the Germans. If that cavalryman could have read the inscriptions—which were in German, not Latin—on those fourteen-foot high mission crosses that dotted the Sauk Valley landscape throughout the nineteenth and twentieth centuries, he could have decoded one of the central values of the transplanted culture: "Blessed is he who perseveres to the end." Endurance, perseverance—in its religious meaning of persistence in grace, this was a prime virtue stressed by nineteenth-century Catholicism. But it also summarizes a dominant attitude in many areas of Sauk Valley immigrant life. Endurance, not success, was the good to be sought. Few Stearns County Germans left anything even implicitly formulating what they took to be the meanings that structured their lives and their communities, nor how they altered with time. But a little 1930 history of the town of Millerville, written in a curious combination of German and English by an elderly storekeeper deeply disturbed by recent changes in his community, provides revealing insight into the enduring values held dear by at least one product of the local culture.

The poem with which Karl Matthias Klein begins his history, entitled "Der deutsche Engel," summarizes his basic theme: the immigrants, trusting in God, drove out evil as they cleared the wilderness, their farms becoming refuges and themselves "Herr auf dieser Au." They had to work hard, but were able to provide for the German language and the church and could take joy in celebration; now it is the task of the younger generation to preserve these gains. But Klein worries whether they are up to it: "O you dear new world, faithless consequence of my choice! Every culture has its thorns, don't lose faith in your destiny." His chronological listing of the main events in the community's history gives a sense of what was considered noteworthy: the homesteading of new farms and the introduction of new farm machinery; the development of local businesses; the hardships of early settlers; the founding of the parish, new church buildings, and changes in forms of worship; major religious celebrations; quarrels with the priests and nuns; bankruptcies, lawsuits, adulteries, and public violence; the World War (fought because "ever since the time the Germans wore the Catholic Roman Crown, the world hated them," when "our boys . . . were dragged over to France, after war was made on Good Friday"); departures to other colonies; and prohibition. Missing was any political narrative, any pantheon of local heroes, or any celebration of economic progress and improved living standards—business events generally entered the story only as markers of community autonomy or parables of falls from grace. Included within his perceptual community were the local "Polanders" who usually knew German and "were in perfect harmony with out religion"; marginal members were the Irish who shared the community's religion and German Lutherans who shared its tongue; anathema were the Swedes whose "push" had to be "averted" and the English—Anglo-Americans—who had to be bought out, not because they were hated but "as neither had a heart for our religion or language, they were not desirable in our colony."

Equally revealing were the qualities for which he praised or disparaged his fellow townsmen. Men were valued for their farming ability, their willingness to work hard, their hunting skills, their moderate drinking, their strength, and their support of the church; business speculation, pride, and heavy drinking that led to fighting or neglect of the farm earned his disapprobation. His highest praise was reserved for "der fromme Peter": "Pious Peter . . . He was a good practicing soul; helped the priest at church services; was pious, honorable, just, and moderate in drinking . . . a true reader of German Catholic newspapers . . . a model for this parish." Much less praiseworthy was a local public official because "in politics he pretended to be the whole government; in religion he was the buck of the congregation, not coming up to his ordinary duties, and causing much discord and fear with his government authority, his pride." Women entered his narrative only when they operated farms on their own or had exceptional reputations for strength, working ability, or piety, like the woman who "seconded the common prayer, sounding her Amen after the others, singly." A central part of a family's history was the worth of its farm and the details of its inheritance, as well as its ancestry, the date of its arrival in the community, and any exceptional gifts it had made to the church. His particular quarrel with the modern world was linked with the disappearance of the German language and the presence of a pastor who had pushed the parish deeply into debt with his building program. He found immoral both the debt and the pride that led to it and could interpret the priest's reaction to his disapproval only as personal spite. His disapproval of the automobile may have grown out of resentment for the loss of trade it meant for his store, but it also summarizes the prime sins in the mind of his community: "It is true there was drunkenness [in the past], but this drunkenness of liquor was not so bad in all, as the drunkenness of the automobile, with its squander, lewedness, falsehood, ignorance, and pride, dispersion."

The habits and beliefs of most Stearns County Germans, unlike those of Klein, must be read largely through their actions. But taken together, they suggest a similar picture of an unusually coherent culture nurtured by the cohesion and isolation of the founding generation, defended by German dominance of the full range of local institutions, and slowly and organically modified under the influence of new opportunities, constraints, and ideas. Its prime initial concerns seem to have been the perpetuation of the intertwined unit of the family and the farm and, inseparable from it, the salvation of the souls of its members. The farm, after all, insured the dedication of time and resources that religious practice required, while religion provided the farm and its family with protection from God's seasonal wrath, moral and educational support for the perpetuation of its life-style, the main source of status roles and communal festivity, and the grace that led to heaven.

The very act of emigration suggested that traditional peasant horizons had already expanded, and most had some exposure to a more risk-taking, profit-oriented economy before settling in the shelter of the Sauk. Yet the structure of the settlement process itself has suggested that their coming was a partial rejection of that kind of economy—not that they would refuse its profits, but that they preferred to avoid its risks, or better, that in seeking to attain other goals as well, they by and large denied themselves much exposure to the chance for large-scale profits. Unlike their Yankee neighbors, for example, they were unwilling to engage in any practice to restrict fertility other than postponement of the average age of marriage by about five years as land became scarcer and more valuable toward the end of the century. The average completed family had five children throughout the period, and among the stable families who remained in the area for at least two generations, families of eight or even twelve or more children were not uncommon. By 1940, German fertility was still higher than it was in nearby Yankee areas sixty-five years earlier, and today Stearns County's rural farm fertility is exceeded only by that of two heavily Amish counties among all counties in the twelve-state midwestern area. The county's German Catholics were long unwilling to make much investment in education beyond the minimum necessary for literacy and religious training, since this would only encourage children to leave farming; instead, adolescents of both sexes universally worked, if not for their parents, then for other farmers or at town jobs, returning their wages to the family coffer. Debt was a necessary evil, undertaken periodically for the sake of the farm but not as a risk for the sake of potential gain. To avoid debt, many farms were cleared slowly and laboriously, two or three acres a year, by the hand labor of all family members over the lifetime of the first generation, while Yankees tended to bring their entire arable into production as quickly as possible; and where Yankees gave high priority to the replacement of log cabins with comfortable frame dwellings, many Germans remained in their small cabins—fourteen by twenty feet was a large dwelling—until the prosperous eighties. While they had no principled objection to machinery, conservative investment strategies kept many still threshing with oxen or even flails through the 1870s.

German farms in Stearns County were family farms in the fullest sense of the term, owned by the farmer, worked by family labor, used to provide an equal start in life for each child, and retained in the family so that the next generation could begin the process anew. Nowhere is this familial focus more evident than in the norms governing the transmission of the farm from one generation to the next. Both the scholarly literature and Stearns County examples suggest that by the last third of the nineteenth century dominant nonethnic midwestern practice dictated that farms either be sold outright at time of retirement or be retained and rented out until the farmer's death, possibly to one of his children but possibly not, and then sold at auction—again, one of the children might be the successful bidder—and the proceeds divided among the heirs according to the provisions of the will or intestacy law. But a rather different pattern prevailed among the farmers of St. Martin, for example, first settled by Eifelers in 1857. Here, the usual practice, as in the homeland, was for farmers to turn the ownership of the land over to their children at the time of retirement, with the children then supporting parental retirement either through bonds of maintenance or, more frequently, through below-market mortgage payments using income derived from the farm. Nonfarming male heirs received their shares in cash, daughters often in stock, tools, and furniture at the time of marriage. But American circumstances also encouraged major differences. Though there is some evidence that farmers initially thought in terms of subdividing their usual 160-acre initial claims among their heirs, they quickly realized both the need for larger farms and the possibility of using family labor while sons and daughters were growing up to accumulate the funds to provide each son with a farm of his own when he reached marriageable age. This strategy depended on the willingness of the growing children to subordinate their individual interests to those of the family strategy and on the willingness of the farmer to forego landowner status during his retirement. Essentially the same system was still in operation in the mid-twentieth century; its success helps explain the Germans' ability to maintain their commitment to farming.

The family system placed special demands on its women. It probably gave them greater say in the family's financial affairs than was common among Yankee women, as well as differing kinds of spiritual responsibilities, but it also subjected them to much harder physical labor, constant childbearing, and little time for affectionate child rearing or bourgeois homemaking, while denying them any public sphere outside the church. Where one Yankee diarist's wife in Maine Prairie spent her days supervising housework and gardening, shopping, visiting neighbors, attending Grange sociables, and collecting donations for good causes, Margaretha Kulzer worked side by side with her husband clearing their land with a grub hoe and axe. She dug roots, hoed, plowed, lifted and rolled logs, tended the cows, picked berries, built furniture, managed the money, joined her husband in the saloon for a glass of beer, and even after they achieved some prosperity, cooked for his hotel guests so that they could accumulate money to set up their children in life. Memoirists suggest that while the love between mothers and children could be strong and deep, such activities left mothers little time for affectionate child rearing; the vocabulary with which a child was addressed within the home might never exceed five hundred words, and most moral and religious instruction—beyond sharply enforced behavioral prohibitions—was left to the school, the pulpit, and the confessional. Marriages ended in divorce for German women only when physical danger within marriage became intolerable and the lesser remedy—legally binding their husbands to refrain from injuring them—failed to provide protection; they almost never sued on the grounds of adultery or desertion, which were most common among Yankee women in the county.

Their family roles likewise governed women's public activity. They played a far more active role in the process of estate devolution than did non-German women, as patterns of testation demonstrate, and while their husbands donated the money to build the churches, it was usually they who made the financial contributions for the Masses and prayers that they believed would release their loved ones from purgatory. German wives might join their husbands in saloons, at card games, and at dances and festivals. But their only organizations were church-based societies; teaching school was regarded as inappropriate; and township records make it clear that very few women dared vote in the first years that suffrage was open to them. Yet they were far more apt to appear in court as litigants in non-debt cases than their Yankee sisters. In particular, they sued one another for assault and defamation of character, and they sued their seducers for rape and bastardy, suggesting their acceptance of another family duty, the defense of family honor. Yankees maintained their honor and the purity of their women by silence; Germans forced public exposure, resolution, and reaffirmation of place in a community whose status system, in the absence of incentives for large-scale profit making, was linked as much to personal qualities and family honor as to achievement and wealth.

The men's world was equally governed by such considerations. Their main sphere of activity outside the farm and the church was the saloon, where business was conducted, politics debated, reputations discussed, and honor challenged and defended. Through the turn of the century, Germans were far more prone than their Yankee neighbors to be indicted for crimes against persons than crimes against property, a statistic that reflects not only their exaggerated respect for property rights but their propensity to engage in violence when honor was challenged, both under the influence of drink and in the property line confrontations that were a major feature of daily life. These kinds of fights were almost unknown among Americans, who also did not sue for slander nearly as often as the Germans.

The church was central to the defense of this familial rather than individualistic nexus and provided one of the main motives for its construction. The church warned against the dangers of worldly ambition and urged the necessity of strong families; its rituals marked the major stages of the family life cycle and its teaching mission helped embed the values of the culture in the next generation. Moreover, the Sauk Valley farmers' Catholicism helped to contribute to their sense of being an island in a hostile Protestant sea, to be left only at great risk. The church also provided valley settlements with an educated leadership and mediators with the outside world. But their religion should not be thought of as a set of beliefs and demands imposed upon them by the heavy hand of clerical authority. Through the 1880s, there was a perennial shortage of priests, and most priests were young, often unfamiliar with America, overworked—several parishes frequently had to share one priest—and frequently moved; three years was an exceptionally long pastoral tenure throughout this period. This meant that the formation of parishes, the construction of churches, the manner in which religious education was provided, and even the dominant elements of worship were heavily influenced by lay leadership and demand, and unpopular pastors were easily removed by parish pressure. Thus, for example, it was largely lay demand that reestablished in the parishes of the Sauk the rich annual round of processions and pilgrimages that punctuated parish life in Germany, and only in the late 1880s and early 1890s did the more private and individualistic modes of worship favored by the American church begin to gain some ground.

That time period was a critical turning point in many areas of the local culture. The settlement phase was over, the older farms were finally coming into full production, and the wheat frontier was passing. Many of the Yankees left with it, but for Germans the shift to dairying, newly feasible with improved rail transportation to urban markets, made eminent sense. It was a way of effectively utilizing their surplus family labor after the clearing period, and they were culturally prepared to accept the home-bound never-ending round of labor that care for a dairy herd entailed. It tied them even more securely to their farms and communities while giving them a steadier source of income than they had thus far enjoyed. With the end of the hunger years and the prospect of a satisfying retirement in store for many of the pioneers, the horizons of life widened and standards of living improved. Better roads and the change from oxen to horses made farmfolk much more mobile, and ever more ramified networks of kin, business, and social ties broke down local isolation and drew the communities of the Sauk together. The coming of age of the second generation, without personal memories of the old country and with somewhat greater English facility than their parents, encouraged increased if still cautious contact with the outside world. And the church itself managed to impose its formal structure more securely on the parishes as the numbers and acculturation of the priests increased, their tenures lengthened, and the secular clergy pried all but a dozen of the parishes away from the Benedictines. Processions and pilgrimages faded, more individualized novenas and sodalities grew, parents stopped naming their children after godparents and turned instead to highly idiosyncratic, elegant-sounding saints' names, and the numbers of religious vocations mounted rapidly.

But if local life was changing in a somewhat more individualistic, progress-oriented direction by the turn of the century, the changes remained governed by the meanings of the prevailing culture, thanks largely to the extent of its embeddedness in local institutions. Scholars often insist almost without examination that the church was the only Old World formal institution that could survive transplantation. Yet in Stearns County, even if the physical container of German village life was not reconstructed, many of its basic elements found their practical counterparts in the conditions of the frontier. In the context of the weak governmental reach of the nineteenth century, the lay-dominated church itself extended its reach into many areas of secular life, coordinating defense during the Indian uprising and relief work during periods of grasshopper plague or epidemics and by the end of the century moving into the provision of bowling alleys, dance halls, and baseball fields to keep the young under its guiding hand. The same leaders who sat on the parish boards of trustees tended to dominate township government, with its responsibility for tax assessment, poor relief, road construction, and control of the open range—the public land where cattle ran at will. They also controlled the local public school boards, a control that permitted them to develop a system of tax-supported Catholic schools taught by seminary-trained lay Catholic men hired with the pastor's approval, who taught in German, let Catholic doctrine permeate their instruction, and directed the church choir and played the organ. They defended these schools equally against a series of legal challenges by local Protestants and against clerical efforts to create parochial schools staffed by nuns.

German Catholic dominance of the local institutions that influenced their lives included the courts. The system of justice of the peace courts for the resolution of minor crimes and lawsuits and for the initial hearing of major charges guaranteed that local justice would be dispensed within the community by its own members acting according to their own norms. And if cases were remanded or appealed to the county district court, Germans were generally able to control both grand and petit juries. Thus it was virtually impossible until Prohibition to get any conviction on violation of liquor laws, no matter how solid the evidence, unless community sentiment turned against the violator for other reasons. Most other areas of county government also passed into German hands by the early 1870s, so that within reason their norms governed taxing and spending policy. It is a cliché of immigration history that Germans lacked both political interest and ability, but in Stearns County, at least, this was not the case: local government was immediately recognized as an instrument for community construction and defense and was quickly mastered and put to use. Only in the mid-1870s was a local German weekly newspaper able to establish itself, but thereafter the Germans also had a formal communication medium of their own separate from the pulpit and the gossip of the saloon. Economic life too came under their purview; one of the earliest successful group efforts was the establishment of monthly cattle and horse markets on the German model in the two largest towns of the county. They developed what was essentially a separate system of banking and mortgage lending and by the 1890s found in the cooperative creamery movement their most effective base for economic defense.

They could not, of course, protect themselves completely either from the shifting economic realities of American commercial farming or from the growing intervention of activist state and federal governments, which they looked upon with suspicion as reservoirs of alien values from the outset. But, through one device or another, they protected their peculiar school system until the post-World War II era of consolidation. Nor, despite state law and church insistence, did English take over as the sole medium of instruction until that same time period. During World War I they proved not as resistant to patriotic pressure as German communities elsewhere nor as victimized by oppression, thanks to their control of local government; township governments bought Liberty Bonds to meet local quotas for their residents, local officials turned a blind eye to state directives, and the only citizens who had any interest in forcing the issue were small-town German merchants who saw in an alliance with state anti-German fanatics a chance of breaking the hold of St. Cloud leaders on county politics and trade. Federal officials met similar indifference during Prohibition, when Stearns County became notorious for both the number of its stills and the quality of its "Minnesota 13" moonshine. Though raids by treasury agents were common and numerous local residents spent a term in a federal penitentiary, such "sitters" lost little community status, and speakeasies and blind pigs proliferated. The main permanent loser was the quality of local beer.

Life would continue to change, but change would continue to be assimilated through the local culture produced and reproduced without sharp break in the behavior and institutions of the Sauk.

FURTHER READINGS

Carol Coburn, *Life at Four Corners: Religion, Gender, and Education in a German-Lutheran Community, 1868–1945* (1992).

Kathleen N. Conzen, *Immigrant Milwaukee: 1836–1860* (1976).

Jay Dolan, *The Immigrant Church: New York's Irish and German Catholics, 1815–1865* (1975).

Charlotte Erickson, *Invisible Immigrants: The Adaptation of English and Scottish Immigrants in Nineteenth-Century America* (1972).

Robert Ernst, *Immigrant Life in New York City, 1825–1863* (1949).

David Gerber, *The Making of an American Pluralism, Buffalo, New York 1825–1860* (1989).

Jon Gjerde, *From Peasants to Farmers: The Migration from Balestrand, Norway to the Upper Middle West* (1985).

Jon Gjerde, *The Minds of the West: The Ethnocultural Evolution in the Rural Middle West, 1830–1917* (1997).

Clyde Griffen and Sally Griffen, *Natives and Newcomers: The Ordering of Opportunity in Nineteenth Century America* (1978).

Oscar Handlin, *Boston's Immigrants, 1790–1865: A Study of Acculturation* (1941).

Walter D. Kamphoefner, *Transplanted Westfalians: Chain Migration from Germany to a Rural Midwestern Community* (1987).

Royden K. Loewen, *Family, Church, and Market: A Mennonite Community in the Old and the New Worlds, 1850–1930* (1993).

Frederick C. Luebke, *Germans in the New World: Essays in the History of Immigration* (1990).

D. Aidan McQuillan, *Prevailing over Time: Ethnic Adjustment on the Kansas Prairies, 1875–1925* (1990).

Kerby Miller, *Emigrants and Exiles: Ireland and the Irish Exodus to North America* (1985).

Stanley Nadel, *Little Germany: Ethnicity, Religion, and Class in New York City, 1845–1880* (1990).

Robert C. Ostergren, *A Community Transplanted: The Trans-Atlantic Experiences of a Swedish Immigrant Settlement in the Upper Middle West, 1835–1915* (1988).

Jane Pedersen, *Between Memory and Reality: Family and Community in Rural Wisconsin, 1870–1970* (1992).

David Roediger, *The Wages of Whiteness: Race and the Making of the American Working Class* (1991).

Harald Runblom and Hans Norman, eds. *From Sweden to America: A History of the Migration* (1976).

Robert Swierenga, ed., *The Dutch in America: Immigration, Settlement and Cultural Change* (1985).

Stephan Thernstrom, *Poverty and Progress: Social Mobility in Nineteenth Century America* (1964).

Mack Walker, *Germany and the Emigration, 1816–1885* (1964).

Mark Wyman, *Immigrants in the Valley: Irish, Germans, and Americans in the Upper Mississippi Country, 1830–1860* (1984).

Nativism and Becoming American at Midcentury, 1830–1860

The vast immigration during the thirty years before the Civil War elicited concerns among American-born that the immigrants' presence would change the United States in most harmful ways. Many native-born Americans feared that their fragile republic might be undermined by immigrants who did not understand and perhaps did not agree with American republicanism. These misgivings were based on the belief that a republic needed a citizenry that was not so heterogeneous as a nation of immigrants would create. They were made all the more worse by assertions that the immigrants were ill-equipped to be citizens, because of poverty, inexperience with republican institutions, or adherence to the Roman Catholic Church. Eventually, such anxiety persuaded many Americans to join nativist organizations to protest the immigrant threat. The most notable movement was a political one: The American Party, also known as the "Know Nothing Party," became a tremendous political force in the 1850s that vied for control of the national political arena.

Antebellum nativist expressions tell us much about the importance of immigration to the United States and about the state of mind of many Americans in the mid-nineteenth century. The magnitude of immigration did indeed transform the population of the United States. Immigrant enclaves in the cities and vast settlements of European groups in the agricultural Middle West changed the complexion of human geography. Greater supplies of available laborers, economic historians have since discovered, resulted in lower wages for working people of the United States and certainly exacerbated the tensions in the cities. The sweeping rural settlements summoned fears that immigration might be so large that the Europeans would control the West, a region considered by many to hold the key of destiny for the young American republic.

Given these fears, many nativist expressions focused not only on the magnitude of the immigration, but on the backgrounds of the immigrants themselves. Among the most significant aspect of the nativists' arguments was a suspicion of the Roman Catholic Church and its immigrant members. Anti-Catholicism had a long tradition in the United States, but it burst forth in the decades following the 1830s. It was then that writers expressed fears about the designs of the church on the republic. Because they argued that Roman Catholics could not be independent of the church, they claimed that Catholics could not perform the duties of citizenship.

Some feared that the Pope, in league with other alleged regressive forces, sought to undermine the American republic because he was concerned about republican influences in Europe. Still others were strangely fascinated by the celibate lives of the clergy and wrote lurid—and wildly popular—descriptions of the purported life among priests and nuns.

Anti-Catholic and anti-immigrant sentiments coalesced in the 1850s when the Know Nothing Party attempted to forge a national coalition of voters to oppose continued immigration. Solidly backed in certain sections of the nation, particularly in the northeastern states, the Know Nothings carried their political campaign to the presidential elections of 1852 and 1856. While nativists were protesting immigration, however, others were searching for ways to integrate immigrants into society and some, such as Walt Whitman, were celebrating the diversity that characterized the United States.

D O C U M E N T S

The following documents portray the variety of concerns voiced by American-born whites with regard to the immense immigration in the mid-nineteenth century. The first three selections were written in the mid-1830s shortly after immigration from the Catholic countries of Europe began to swell. In the first document, Lyman Beecher, influential clergyman and father of Harriet Beecher Stowe, shows his fear about the growing immigration particularly as it was moving into the West. Next, Samuel F. B. Morse, inventor of the telegraph, enumerates his perceptions of how "foreign interference" will threaten the American republic and its "liberties." And Maria Monk recounts in lurid detail the purported life of nuns in nineteenth-century convents. Only *Uncle Tom's Cabin,* written by Stowe, sold more copies than this book in the nineteenth century. Note how all three of these early documents show their concern in a variety of ways about the impact of Roman Catholicism. The next three documents illustrate the maturation of political nativism in the mid-1850s. Frederick Saunders argues again that the Republic is threatened by immigrants, especially Catholic ones. Thomas R. Whitney is even more explicit: for him "Romanism is diametrically opposed to Republicanism" in the freedoms and intelligence of its adherents. The *Know Nothing Almanac* provides a history of the Know Nothing movement in the United States. Political cartoons, as well as written words, explored the meaning of immigrants, as depicted in the seventh selection. Not all American-born people, however, supported these nativist beliefs. Among the best examples is the final selection: Walt Whitman's paean to the diversity of the United States.

Lyman Beecher Warns About Immigrants Flooding into the American West, 1835

This danger from [the] uneducated mind is augmenting daily by the rapid influx of foreign emigrants, unacquainted with our institutions, unaccustomed to self-government, inaccessible to education, and easily accessible to prepossession, and inveterate credulity, and intrigue, and easily embodied and wielded by sinister de-

---

Selection from Lyman Beecher, *A Plea for the West,* 1835.

sign. In the beginning this eruption of revolutionary Europe was not anticipated, and we opened our doors wide to the influx and naturalization of foreigners. But it is becoming a terrific inundation; it has increased upon our native population from five to thirty-seven per cent, and is every year advancing. It seeks, of course, to settle down upon the unoccupied territory of the West, and may at no distant day equal, and even outnumber the native population. What is to be done to educate the millions which in twenty years Europe will pour out upon us?

But what if this emigration, self-moved and slow in the beginning, is now rolling its broad tide at the bidding of the powers of Europe hostile to free institutions, and associated in holy alliance to arrest and put them down? Is this a vain fear? Are not the continental powers alarmed at the march of liberal opinions, and associated to put them down? and are they not, with the sickness of hope deferred, waiting for our downfall? It is the light of our republican prosperity, gleaming in upon their dark prison house, which is inspiring hope, and converting chains into arms. It is the power of mind, roused by our example from the sleep of ages and the apathy of despair, which is sending earthquake under the foundations of their thrones; and they have no hope of rest and primeval darkness, but by the extinction of our light. By fleets and armies they cannot do it. But do they, therefore, sleep on their heaving earth and tottering thrones? Has Metternich yet to form an acquaintance with history? Does he dream that there is but one way to overturn republics, and that by the sword? Has he yet to learn how Philip, by dividing her councils, conquered Greece? and how, by intestine divisions, Rome fell?

It is the testimony of American travelers, that the territorial, civil and ecclesiastical statistics of our country, and the action and bearing of political causes upon our institutions, are more familiar at Rome and Vienna, than with us; and that tracts and maps are in circulation, explanatory of the capacious West, and pointing out the most fertile soils and most favored locations, and inviting to emigration. These means of a stimulated expatriation are corroborated by the copious and rapidly increasing correspondence of those who have already arrived, and the increasing facilities of transportation.

The simple fact, that the clergy of the Catholic denomination could wield in mass the suffrage of their confiding people, could not fail, in the competition of ambition and party spirit, to occasion immediately an eager competition for their votes, placing them at once in the attitude of the most favored sect; securing the remission of duties on imported church property, and copious appropriations of land for the endowment of their institutions; shielding them from animadversion by the sensitiveness of parties on account of their political ends; and turning against their opponents, and in favor of Catholics, the patronage and the tremendous influence of the administration, whose ascendancy and continuance might, in closely contested elections, be thought to depend on Catholic suffrage.

Nor is this all—the secular patronage at the disposal of an associated body of men, who under the influence of their priesthood may be induced to act as one, for those who favor and against those who oppose them, would enable them to touch far and wide the spring of action through our cities and through the nation. How many presses might they influence by their promised patronage or threatened withdrawment? How many mechanics, merchants, lawyers, physicians, in any political crisis, might they reach and render timid, and temporizing, and prudent, not to say sturdy eulogists of Catholics, lest they should lose the patronage of a sect, who alone can wield a patronage to favor or to punish those who favor or obstruct their views. And if while they are few and feeble, compared with the whole nation, their consolidated action gives them such various and extended influence, how will its power extend and become omnipresent and resistless as emigration shall quadruple their numbers and action on the political and business men of the nation?

No government is more complex and difficult of preservation than a republic, and in no political associations do little adverse causes produce more disastrous results. Of all influences, none is more pernicious than a corps of men acting systematically and perseveringly for its own ends upon a community unapprized of their doings, and undisciplined to meet and counteract them. A tenth part of the suffrage of the nation, thus condensed and wielded by the Catholic powers of Europe, might decide our elections, perplex our policy, inflame and divide the nation, break the bond of our union, and throw down our free institutions. The voice of history also warns us, that no sinister influence has ever intruded itself into politics, so virulent and disastrous as that of an ambitious ecclesiastical influence, or which demands, now and always, keener vigilance or a more active resistance.

But before I proceed, to prevent misapprehension, I would say that I have no fear of the Catholics, considered simply as a religious denomination, and unallied to the church and state establishments of the European governments hostile to republican institutions.

Let the Catholics mingle with us as Americans, and come with their children under the full action of our common schools and republican institutions, and the various powers of assimilation, and we are prepared cheerfully to abide the consequences. If in these circumstances the protestant religion cannot stand before the Catholic, let it go down, and we will sound no alarm, and ask no aid, and make no complaint. It is no ecclesiastical quarrel to which we would call the attention of the American nation.

Samuel F. B. Morse Enumerates the "Dangers" of the Roman Catholic Immigrant, 1835

I have set forth in a very brief and imperfect manner the evil, the great and increasing evil, that threatens our free institutions from *foreign interference.* Have I not shown that there is real cause for alarm? Let me recapitulate the facts in the case, and see if any one of them can be denied; and if not, I submit it to the calm decision of every American, whether he can still sleep in fancied security, while incendiaries are at work; and whether he is ready quietly to surrender his liberty, civil and religious, into the hands of foreign powers.

Selection from Samuel F. B. Morse, *Imminent Dangers to the Free Institutions of the United States through Foreign Immigration and the Present States of the Naturalization Laws,* 1835.

1. It is a fact, that in this age the subject of civil and religious liberty agitates in the most intense manner the various European governments.

2. It is a fact, that the influence of American free institutions in subverting European despotic institutions is greater now than it has ever been, from the fact of the greater maturity, and long-tried character, of the American form of government.

3. It is a fact, that Popery is opposed in its very nature to Democratic Republicanism; and it is, therefore, as a political system, as well as religious, opposed to civil and religious liberty, and consequently to our form of government.

4. It is a fact, that this truth, respecting the intrinsic character of Popery, has lately been clearly and demonstratively proved in public lectures, by one of the Austrian Cabinet, a devoted Roman Catholic, and with the evident design (as subsequent events show) of exciting the Austrian government to a great enterprise in support of absolute power.

5. It is a fact, that this Member of the Austrian Cabinet, in his lectures, designated and proscribed this country by name, as the *"great nursery of destructive principles; as the Revolutionary school for France and the rest of Europe,"* whose contagious example of Democratic liberty had given, and would still give, trouble to the rest of the world, unless the evil were abated.

6. It is a fact, that very shortly after the delivery of these lectures, a Society was organized in the Austrian capital, called the St. Leopold Foundation, for the purpose "of promoting the greater activity of Catholic Missions in America."

7. It is a fact, that this Society is under the patronage of the Emperor of Austria,—has its central direction at Vienna,—is under the supervision of Prince Metternich,—that it is an extensive combination, embodying the civil, as well as ecclesiastical *officers,* not only of the *whole Austrian Empire,* but of the neighbouring Despotic States,—that it is actively at work, collecting moneys, and sending agents to this country, to carry into effect its designs.

8. It is a fact, that the agents of these foreign despots, are, for the most part, *Jesuits.*

9. It is a fact, that the effects of this society are already apparent in the otherwise unaccountable increase of Roman Catholic cathedrals, churches, colleges, convents, nunneries, &c., in every part of the country; in the sudden increase of Catholic emigration; in the increased clanishness of the Roman Catholics, and the boldness with which their leaders are experimenting on the character of the American people.

10. It is a fact, that an unaccountable disposition to riotous conduct has manifested itself within a few years, when exciting topics are publicly discussed, wholly at variance with the former peaceful, deliberative character of our people.

11. It is a fact, that a species of police, unknown to our laws, has repeatedly been put in requisition to keep the peace among a certain class of foreigners, who are Roman Catholics, viz., Priest-police.

12. It is a fact, that Roman Catholic Priests have interfered to influence our elections.

13. It is a fact, that politicians on both sides have propitiated these priests, to obtain the votes of their people.

14. It is a fact, that numerous Societies of Roman Catholics, particularly among the Irish foreigners, are organized in various parts of the country, under various names, and ostensibly for certain benevolent objects; that these societies are

united together by correspondence, all which may be innocent and praiseworthy, but viewed in connexion with the recent aspect of affairs, are at least suspicious.

15. It is a fact, that an attempt has been made to organize a military corps of Irishmen in New York, to be called the O'Connel Guards; thus commencing a military organization of foreigners.

16. It is a fact, that the greater part of the foreigners in our population is composed of Roman Catholics.

Facts like these, I have enumerated might be multiplied, but these are the most important, and quite sufficient to make every American settle the question with himself, whether there is, or is not, danger to the country from the present state of our Naturalization Laws. I have stated what I believe to be facts. If they are *not* facts, they will easily be disproved, and I most sincerely hope they will be disproved. If they are facts, and my inferences from them are wrong, I can be shown where I have erred, and an inference more rational, and more probable, involving less, or perhaps no, danger to the country, can be deduced from them, which deduction, when I see it, I will most cheerfully accept, as a full explanation of these most suspicious doings of Foreign Powers.

I have spoken in these numbers freely of a particular religious sect, the Roman Catholics, because from the nature of the case it was unavoidable; because the foreign political conspiracy is identified with that creed. With the *religious tenets* properly so called, of the Roman Catholic, I have not meddled. If foreign powers, hostile to the principles of this government, have combined to spread any religious creed, no matter of what denomination, that creed does by that very act become a subject of political interest to all citizens, and must and will be thoroughly scrutinized. We are compelled to examine it. We have no choice about it. If instead of combining to spread with the greatest activity the Catholic Religion throughout our country, the Monarchs of Europe had united to spread Presbyterianism, or Methodism, I presume, there are few who would not see at once the propriety and the necessity of looking most narrowly at the political bearings of the peculiar principles of these Sects, or of any other Protestant Sects; and members of any Protestant Sects too, would be the last to complain of the examination. I know not why the Roman Catholics in this land of scrutiny are to plead exclusive exemption from the same trial.

Maria Monk, a Supposed Escaped Nun, Recounts the Perils of the Convent, 1835

After taking the vows, I proceeded to a small apartment behind the altar, accompanied by four nuns, where was a coffin prepared, with my nun name engraven upon it:

"SAINT EUSTACE."

My companions lifted it by four handles attached to it, while I threw off my dress, and put on that of a nun of Sœur Bourgeoise; and then we all returned to the chapel. I proceeded first, and was followed by the four nuns; the Bishop naming

Selection from Maria Monk, *Awful Disclosures of the Hotel Dieu Nunnery of Montreal,* 1836.

a number of worldly pleasures in rapid succession, in reply to which I as rapidly repeated—"Je renonce, je renonce, je renonce"—[I renounce, I renounce, I renounce].

The coffin was then placed in front of the altar, and I advanced to lay myself in it. This coffin was to be deposited, after the ceremony, in an outhouse, to be preserved until my death, when it was to receive my corpse. There were reflections which I naturally made at that time, but I stepped in, extended myself, and lay still. A pillow had been placed at the head of the coffin, to support my head in a comfortable position. A large, thick black cloth was then spread over me, and the chanting of Latin hymns immediately commenced. My thoughts were not the most pleasing during this time I lay in that situation. The pall, or Drap Mortel, as the cloth is called, had a strong smell of incense, which was always disagreeable to me, and then proved almost suffocating. I recollected also a story I had heard of a novice, who, in taking the veil, lay down in her coffin like me, and was covered in the same manner, but on the removal of the covering was found dead.

When I was uncovered, I rose, stepped out of my coffin, and kneeled. The Bishop then addressed these words to the Superior, "Take care and keep pure and spotless this young virgin, whom Christ has consecrated to himself this day." After which the music commenced, and here the whole was finished. I then proceeded from the chapel, and returned to the Superior's room, followed by the other nuns, who walked two by two, in their customary manner, with their hands folded on their breasts, and their eyes cast down upon the floor. The nun who was to be my companion in future, then walked at the end of the procession. On reaching the Superior's door, they all left me, and I entered alone, and found her with the Bishop and two priests.

The Superior now informed me, that having taken the black veil, it only remained that I should swear the three oaths customary on becoming a nun; and that some explanations would be necessary from her. I was now, she told me, to have access to every part of the edifice, even to the cellar, where two of the sisters were imprisoned for causes which she did not mention. I must be informed, that one of my great duties was, to obey the priests in all things; and this I soon learnt, to my utter astonishment and horror, was to live in the practice of criminal intercourse with them. I expressed some of the feelings which this announcement excited in me, which came upon me like a flash of lightning but the only effect was to set her arguing with me, in favour of the crime, representing it as a virtue acceptable to God, and honourable to me. The priests, she said, were not situated like other men, being forbidden to marry; while they lived secluded, laborious, and self-denying lives for our salvation. They might, indeed, be considered our saviours, as without their services we could not obtain the pardon of sin, and must go to hell. Now, it was our solemn duty, on withdrawing from the world, to consecrate our lives to religion, to practice every species of self-denial. We could not become too humble, nor mortify our feelings too far; this was to be done by opposing them, and acting contrary to them; and what she proposed was, therefore, pleasing in the sight of God. I now felt how foolish I had been to place myself in the power of such persons as were around me.

From what she said I could draw no other conclusion, but that I was required to act like the most abandoned of beings, and that all my future associates were habitually guilty of the most heinous and detestable crimes. When I repeated my expressions of surprise and horror, she told me that such feelings were very common at first, and that many other nuns had expressed themselves as I did, who had long since changed their minds. She even said, that on her entrance into the nunnery, she had felt like me.

Doubts, she declared, were among our greatest enemies. They would lead us to question every point of duty, and induce us to waver at every step. They arose only from remaining imperfection, and were always evidence of sin. Our only way was to dismiss them immediately, repent, and confess them. They were deadly sins, and would condemn us to hell, if we should die without confessing them. Priests, she insisted, could not sin. It was a thing impossible. Every thing that they did, and wished, was of course right. She hoped I would see the reasonableness and duty of the oaths I was to take, and be faithful to them.

She gave me another piece of information which excited other feelings in me, scarcely less dreadful. Infants were sometimes born in the convent: but they were always baptized and immediately strangled! This secured their everlasting happiness; for the baptism purified them from all sinfulness, and being sent out of the world before they had time to do any thing wrong, they were at once admitted into heaven. How happy, she exclaimed, are those who secure immortal happiness to such little beings! Their little souls would thank those who kill their bodies, if they had it in their power!

Into what a place and among what society had I been admitted! How differently did a Convent now appear from what I had supposed it to be! The holy women I had always fancied the nuns to be, the venerable Lady Superior, what were they? And the priests of the Seminary adjoining, some of whom indeed I had had reason to think were base and profligate men, what were they all? I now learnt they were often admitted into the nunnery, and allowed to indulge in the greatest crimes, which they and others called virtues.

Frederick Saunders, a Nativist, Considers the Dangers of Immigration to the Republic, 1856

In a republic the power is in the hands of the whole people, for the entire land is theirs. For convenience in legislation they appoint men to represent their interests, hence the representative is the servant of the represented. This is obvious: no man can represent the interests of others unless delegated so to do; this power *conferred* necessarily subjects him to the will of those who bestow the office. Hence no man has a *right* to office, which it may be in the power of others to refuse.

Representatives having to be chosen, there arises a momentous question— What gives the right to vote? We have shown that where the right to property belongs to all, power is universal; therefore, suffrage must be universal. But we must

---

Selection from Frederick Saunders and T. B. Thorpe, *The Progress and Prospects of America*, 1855.

define this, in regard to men who have not a *born-right* in the country, but simply one of tolerance or permission.

... Demagogues enunciate a monstrous proposition in asserting this republic to be one of composite races. It is not. The Republic of the United States is Anglo-Saxon in all its bearings: other peoples may arrive, but they must be gradually absorbed, and, in process of time, become amalgamated with, and lost among, the predominant race. Ethnology and history both assert this fact, and the senseless opponents of it are merely perpetuating the evils of *caste,* in pandering to the prejudices of various nationalities. It is the province and duty of the patriot to discountenance such endeavors.

... The foreign voters, who are proved to be *ignorant* and in every way *incompetent,* are admitted to the enjoyment of the electoral franchise.

We, who never knew what a blind and passive obedience to law is, can form no adequate idea of the recklessness and delirium which seize hold of so many foreign immigrants the moment they put foot upon our shores. We admit that some of them are men of intellectual culture, while it will not be denied that too many are persons of the most degraded character, and destitute even of the most meager attainments. The ignorance, however, from which Americans experience the greatest cause for distrust, is that which relates to the nature and spirit of republican institutions. These they do not seem either able or inclined to comprehend. They scout all ideas of obedience, because they claim that here they are free. Liberty and lawlessness are with them one and the same thing. Hitherto, they have never borne any intelligent relation to the existence or execution of law, but have occupied the places of unreflecting persons, accustomed, in passive silence, to bear the burdens with which they were weighed down. Coming to a country like America, and hearing the most exaggerated and extravagant stories of its ample freedom for all men, without a thought of their responsibility to the nation sustaining the fabric of this glorious freedom, they conclude that here the field of license lies open, and that any sort of restraint is powerless and illegal against unbounded indulgence.

The danger to be apprehended from carelessness in this particular, has been foreseen by our best men. The following extract from the writings of Thomas Jefferson, one of the wisest and most farseeing of the great men who have influenced the politics of our country, fully sustains the views here taken of the essential significance of naturalization laws, and of the dangers to our country, from laxity in making or administering them. He says: "But are there no inconveniences to be thrown into the scale against the advantages expected from a multiplication of numbers by the importation of foreigners? It is for the happiness of those united in society to harmonize as much as possible in matters, which they must of necessity transact together. Civil government being the sole object of forming societies, its administration must be conducted by common consent. Every species of government has its specific principles. Ours, perhaps, are more peculiar than those of any other in the universe. It is a composition of the freest principles in the English

Constitution, with others derived from natural reason. To these nothing can be more opposed than the maxims of absolute monarchies. Yet from such we are to expect the greatest number of emigrants. They will bring with them the principles of the governments they leave, imbibed in their early youth; or, if able to throw them off, it will be in exchange for an unbounded licentiousness, passing, as is usual, from one extreme to the other. It would be a miracle were they to stop precisely at the point of temperate liberty. These principles, with their language, they will transmit to their children. In proportion to their numbers, they will share with us the legislation. They will infuse into it their spirit, warp and bias its directions, and render it a heterogeneous, incoherent, distracted mass."

Have not these predictions been fulfilled? Have we not already amongst us an Irish nationality, a German nationality, a French nationality, a Dutch nationality, an Italian nationality? Has not our legislation already been "warped and biased" by their influence? Have they not already, to a great extent, "infused their spirit" into it, and are they not trying to make the infusion stronger?

* * * *

The prospect of future immigration, however, demands some consideration. There seems to be no reason why the exodus from Europe to America should not yet grow and continue. Even if the remainder of the Irish population should stay at home, there are millions and millions on the Continent who will complete the yearly number of immigrants. So far as material interests are concerned, greater and greater inducements are offered by the increasing wealth, enlarged capacity, and demand for labor within our own country. We have abundance of room and of riches. Such inducements have already operated upon so many of the overcrowded and poverty-stricken European nations, that it is quite certain that they will continue to operate. And on the other side of the Atlantic there are not wanting impulses to co-operate with the attractions here. The future of the European nations is stormy and dark. Revolutionary principles are seething under the apparently smooth surface of her political aspect, and before long, despotism, anarchy, and liberty will be struggling together; wars and rebellions exert their disorganizing and unhappy influence, and increasing crowds will flee from the home misery to the foreign peace upon our territory. Europe then, crowded with people, oppressed with poverty, containing much sterile land, and doomed to the horrors of complicated and obstinate wars, will long send vast and vaster yearly bands to share our free peace, our rich and boundless lands, and our quiet wealth. We shall, apparently, also continue to receive the refuse of almshouses, and the felon garbage of prisons, shipped hither wholesale by European governments and societies.

During the periods of ten years, from 1810 to 1850, the successive totals of immigration have arisen from one hundred and fourteen thousand to two hundred and four thousand seven hundred and eighty thousand, and lastly, one million four hundred and forty thousand. Within the ten years now passing, viz., from 1850 to 1860, all the facts and probabilities indicate that we shall receive four millions of European immigrants of the poorest, and most worthless class of the population. What the increase will be beyond that time, we have no means of estimating. But this number is sufficient to show the vast and increasing importance of the movement, and the certainty of the speedy operation of such a mass of humanity upon our own people in some way, either for good or evil.

. . . an ominous change in the demeanor of our foreign beneficiaries has appeared. They seem to be steadily seeking to overthrow our own institutions, whenever those institutions happen to conflict with the prejudices or hatreds engendered in their own minds in the darkness of their native despotisms. The wise Sabbath laws which are so general in our commonwealths, are a living evidence of the intimate connection of Christianity with their fundamental policy. That connection is the very basis of their strength and durability. But a band of atheistical Germans, thinking that in this country there is no need, even outwardly, either to fear God or to regard man, get together and call upon the government to abrogate all laws enforcing the observance of the Christian Sabbath.

We see, then, that the United States offer the field for the fair trial of this great experiment of man. The experiment is,—to learn whether men are of more worth than things; and if autocracies, and monarchies, and all tyrannies,—disguise them as you may,—are not violent usurpations of the very laws of existence. Upon our fortunes rests the destiny of the world. Our success and our example are making all peoples restive; our moral strength is more powerful than fleets, more dreaded by tyrants than unnumbered men in arms. We are to conquer, but not by the sword. We are to subjugate, but not by violence. All nations are to come under the sway of our principles, but never are they to pass under any yoke. All is to be freedom and light, and the eye is to see as clearly as at the noonday. Whatever is done, will be done in the direction of a single purpose: and that is, the *emancipation of our race.* We are not working for mere wealth; nor position; nor social consideration; but while laboring for all these, we are insensibly helping on the great cause, and solving the grand problem of a world's freedom.

America—not even yet thinly populated—is the battle-field where the contest is waged between the armies of freedom and tyranny. Every sign points to this imposing fact. Here the last great onset must be made by the phalanxes of darkness, bigotry, illiberality, and bondages of all descriptions; and, under God, if Americans are but true to themselves and their principles, here will occur a glorious victory for freedom and truth—a victory having the regeneration of man for its object, and the happiness of the universe for its result.

Europe is now a seething caldron. The great game of the kings, carried on so long with impunity, at last appears to be completely blocked. The rulers are at a stand. Events have mastered ambitious men; and the extended laws of cause and effect, running silently through a course of centuries, at length seem about to vindicate their supreme authority. Politics is now another name for confusion. Ministers study and scheme how they may extricate their royal masters from their dilemma, and give over their efforts with exclamations of mortification and despair. The rulers grasp their sceptres more firmly, fearing that it cannot be long ere they must give them up forever. Cabinets have grown timid, and dare not assert with former boldness the policy of their several courts. There is a manifest want of confidence everywhere. Armies are called into service, till there are scarcely any men left to recruit them. The treasuries are depleted by enormous drafts, and bankruptcy and ruin threaten nations that but yesterday were prolific in resources.

But in the midst of this inextricable confusion, certain signs are beginning to betoken the increasing interest which foreign countries take in our national welfare. We see, from time to time, symptoms of a more decided leaning to republicanism. Here and there sturdy words are spoken—at the right time and in the right place—in our behalf. The spirit and principles of our government find admiring friends where it was least to be expected. Our institutions are criticised and commented on in an appreciative temper, and without that rancor and prejudice which was once so certain to be excited, by the mere mention of our name.

It is too important a truth for any of us to overlook, that the American Republic is the home of Liberty, and the final hope of the world. Through the efficacy of her example and her teachings, must redemption finally come. We hold the treasure in our own keeping; we are the trustees of a possession that is to enrich mankind. On our soil dwells that living spirit, which is, in time, to overthrow error, tear away the deceits of usurpation, deprive tyranny of its power, and everywhere animate the human soul with the belief that freedom was coeval with its birth.

Thomas Whitney, an Anti-Catholic, Compares "Romanism" and "Republicanism," 1856

Here are two *isms* that deserve the consideration of all men of all parties, but they are not the isms of *the* day, nor of *a* day—they are for all time. They are vital principles, venerable, pervading . . . .

But we set out to show that Romanism is diametrically opposed to Republicanism, this being the *third* feature of this subject which I deem it necessary to review. It would seem almost unnecessary to add a word to what has been already written, in order to show that the Romish Church, in its whole character and spirit, is hostile to the character and spirit of our free institutions. The simple fact that one is an *absolute* government, and the other a *popular* government, establishes the antipodal. These are the extremes of social organism, and when extremes meet, decomposition of one or the other must ensue, unless the repulsive power is sufficient in the one or the other to prevent an actual contact.

Selection from Thomas R. Whitney, *A Defence of the American Policy,* 1856.

American Republicanism cultivates intelligence among the people. Romanism suppresses intelligence.

American Republicanism recognizes and secures to all men the right of trial by jury. Romanism adjudicates in the sombre dungeon of the inquisition, or through the will of a single prelate, who may be at once the accuser, the judge, and the executioner.

American Republicanism ensures the freedom of the press, and the right of free speech. Romanism silences, or else muzzles the press and forbids discussion; it puts a bridle on the lips of its subjects, as we do on the lips of our state-prison convicts.

American Republicanism secures to its citizens the right of suffrage in the choice of their rulers, with the power to impeach and remove. Romanism chooses its executive officer or sovereign, by a vote of the college of cardinals; that sovereign holds his authority, which is absolute, for life, and the cardinals are appointed by him. The people have no voice.

American Republicanism secures the full liberty of conscience to all its people, and to the stranger within its gates. Romanism pronounces liberty of conscience to be a wicked heresy.

American Republicanism permits every human creature to read and study the Word of God. Romanism forbids it. In a word, American Republicanism is FREEDOM; Romanism is *slavery.*

* * * *

We could very well afford to set aside the secular and political features of the Romish Church, and still it would remain, in its religious character alone, the antagonist of American Republicanism. Throughout its whole construction, there is not a single element in sympathy with our free, energetic, and soul-inspiring institutions. The hierarchy in the United States, *professes* attachment to the government, and her children from the Emerald Isle (made desolate and repulsive through priestcraft), avail themselves of the liberty *we* give to them, and weave the harp of oppressed, downtrodden Erin, in the folds of the unsullied ensign of American Liberty. What a mockery of their own vassalage! What a contrast! The relic of national degradation blended with the emblem of national glory and might!

But the hierarchy admires our institutions only for the facilities which they afford for the propagation of its power in the land. It will rear the stripes and stars on the topmost spire of its houses of worship during the ceremony of consecration. It will wave them over the heads of its listless votaries, and command them to fight under them and for them. It will struggle to maintain the name and the insignia of the Republic, but *the institutions of civil and religious liberty* cannot exist where the hierarchy presides. It matters little to the papacy, what form of government ostensibly prevails, or what colors are on the national bunting. The Austrian eagle, or the stars and stripes are the same to it, and the latter, even though shorn of its prestige, and its genius, and compelled to blazon to the world its own infamy, would float as gracefully from the turrets of a papal palace as over the capitol of a free people.

Like all other monarchical and despotical governments, the papacy demands a *hereditary* allegiance. The child born of papal parents is a papal subject at its birth, in whatever clime or country it is born. This is in accordance with the claim set up, that "the Pope is prince of all nations." It partakes in nothing of a religious character, but is a part of that system of regal authority, employed by monarchists, which stands, in its very nature, opposed to republicanism. Nothing can be more incompatible than the two systems are in this respect. In the one, the individual is held to be a free agent, social and religious; in the other, the individual possesses not freedom either of conscience or allegiance, and when, after the conviction which age and reason afford, he revolts against the unnatural authority, he is proscribed as an apostate, a renegade and a heretic.

But there is another peculiarity of contrast between the two forms of government, which stands forth a tangible and visible embodiment, a living evidence of the incompatibility of the two systems, one with the other.

American Republicanism is the parent of progress; it encourages the development of human energy, and gives free play to the faculties. It expands the intellect, invigorates the soul, and elevates the standard of the individual man. It builds locomotives, erects manufactories, disembowels the earth, causing her to yield up her treasures to the uses of man. It encourages commerce, and sends its smoking steamships to the far ends of the earth. It strikes out into the wilderness, talks with the savage without enslaving his soul, and develops the resources of the earth. Romanism gives to the red man a cross and a rosary; American Republicanism places in his hands a Bible and a hoe. It builds a school-house for his children, and teaches him that sowing and reaping are more manly and more profitable than hunting and fishing. American Republicanism cultivates the sciences, arts and literature, as well as the soil, and puts in every bosom the heart and impulses of a *man.* It is honest, ingenuous, and courageous. It pays its debts, speaks its mind, keeps a clear conscience, and looks the world in the face without quailing or winking. How is it with Romanism?

Romanism is the open foe of progress. It stifles the energies of its subjects, stultifies the intellect, and wraps the soul in a mantle of superstitions, prostrating all self-respect in the individual. It makes no advances towards civilization, and if it encourages art, it is only for the purpose of multiplying its own weapons against human freedom. It gives no incentive to industry, and by claiming to itself supreme sovereignty, neutralizes every sentiment of patriotism and nationality—it is cosmopolitan. Romanism denies the necessity of literature beyond what is required as an instrument of control over the souls and bodies of mankind. It is selfish, dishonest, double-dealing, and cowardly. Instead of openly combating the opinions and intelligence of the human race, and striving manfully, and by frank, overt means, to convert men to its own dogmas, it moves mysteriously, skulkingly, in dark corners, and by covert and insidious courses, and false pretences, Jesuitically seeks to entrap rather than to convert or convince.

Where Romanism prevails, there is stagnation and public lethargy. Where American Republicanism prevails, there is industry, intelligence, energy, and public prosperity.

The Know Nothings, "The American Party," Defend Their Political Movement, 1855

The American Party can date its existence as far back as the day and hour when the "one idea" of deliverance from foreign influence, rule, and dictation, first found birth in the head and heart of a true patriot. When first the idea of a distinctive nationality was broached by a native of this country, *then* the American party had its beginning; and from such beginnings have many nations sprung—many whose national individualities are as strongly defined as are the English, the French, or the Scotch. Let those who scoff at, and laugh to scorn the idea of an American nationality, remember how few of the modern nations can claim a consanguineous connection with the aborigines of the territories they inhabit. If it is desirable that a beginning should be made, that a foundation for a nationality should be laid, we cannot commence the work too soon,—but if this country is to be a thing without a name, or, having a name—*America*—signifying nothing; if this territory is to be considered by the nations of the world as a common property, to be claimed by anything bearing the human form, however beastly, degraded and vile,—then let us understand it, and govern ourselves accordingly. But let us see if it has not from our beginning, as a nation, been a prominent principle with our best men that native hearts and native heads should govern the hand. American or native legislation was adopted while the country was yet in its infancy—as the records will show; and the older we have grown, the more determination have the people, and the purer public men, manifested in their efforts to secure an American nationality. WASHINGTON proclaimed those principles embodied in the ideas of the present American party, and were the father of his country now living, he, too, would come in for a share of the abuse and vilification poured out from the husky throats of the besotted party hacks, upon those who have resolved on having a country which they can call their own.

Revolutions never go backward. For many years the American Party has continued to struggle for the preservation of American institutions. It has been again and again defeated—yet never has defeat caused its advocates, for a moment, to despair, or to surrender one iota of principle. So far from this, each successive defeat, whilst it has demonstrated the necessity, has also inspired the firmness to demand such further remedial measures as in the altered circumstances of the case appeared to be required.

Revolutions in public sentiment are necessarily of slow development, yet they are ever onward. The American party in its first movement claimed only a guarantee for the purity of the ballot-box. That guarantee was resisted by all the political demagogues of the old parties, and the Native American party, as if in scorn of the baseness that could tamely surrender the palladium of our Republican Government to the scum of Europe, advanced another principle, more distasteful still to the trading politicians, who at present control the policy of our government—a

Selection from *Know Nothing Almanac and True Americans' Manual for 1855* (New York: DeWitt & Davenport, 1855).

requirement of twenty-one years residence before a foreigner should be permitted to thrust their unhallowed hands into the ark of our political covenant. Then the party demanded a capitation tax, that should restrain the most worthless and vicious of foreign emigrants from debarking on our shores. That, too, encountered the bitter hostility of the money-making politicians of one school, and the office-seeking and spoils-devouring cormorants of the other. Still the American Party, undismayed by the hostility it encountered, and undaunted by the reverses which befel it, moved forward, and demanded a capitation tax to an amount that should virtually check the unprecedented current of emigration, which, if not soon arrested and turned back to its source, must inevitably lead to that abasement of the people, which such an infusion must certainly produce. It was a glorious step, which, in after times,—when the whirlwind of passion has subsided,—will be remembered with gratitude by every American, in whose bosom the love of country is stronger than the love of money, and the lust of office. It is a position which no sophistry can undermine, and that will not be abandoned, cost what it may to maintain it. It is the first blow of the axe at the root of the deadly *upas,* whose pestilential influence cramps the genius of our government, and filches their birthright from the native sons of the soil. Revolutions are still onward. The sublime idea of *deliverance from foreign influence,* which first prompted an exclusion of the hordes of Europe from the elective franchise until they had resided twenty-one years in the country, now counsels still another and a bolder measure—a partition of the public domain among the *native born,* male and female, in quantities of 160 acres to each, to the end that it may not be seized by the swarms of aliens, who are hastening to secure possession of our heritage. The American mechanics and working men, with their wives and children, require *something* to fall back upon when they are ousted from their employments by the terrible competition of pauper laborers from the Old World. Then let the public lands be appropriated to the use of those Americans who are compelled to give way to pauper prices, and retire from their various callings in the cities before the onward march of foreign labor. Give the Americans some kind of protection against European competition in the home marts of industry, or else apportion out to them the public domain, on which they may build permanent homes at once, and abandon the cities for ever to the foreign hordes now pouring in upon us in a continuous stream.

Revolutions never go backward. The Americans now demand inalienable homesteads for all time—never to be driven therefrom. They require at the hands of the American Government, homes on their own soil—their portion of their birthright to the land of their forefathers.

Portrayals of Immigrants in Political Cartoons of the Era

Nativists blamed drunken immigrants for election-day violence. Here, a whiskey-drinking Irish immigrant and a beer-drinking German immigrant steal a ballot box while their compatriots riot at the polls.

A priest, an Irish immigrant, and the Democratic Party.

Thomas Nast's portrayal of the Pope viewing America, 1870.

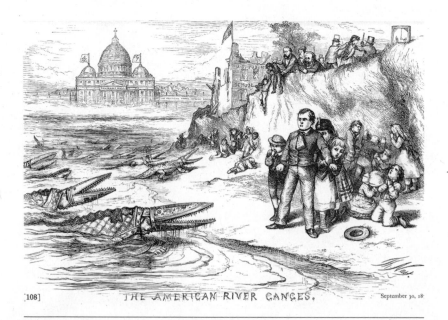

Thomas Nast's cartoon where bishops are like alligators.

Walt Whitman Celebrates the Diversity in the United States, 1855

America does not repel the past or what it has produced under its forms or amid other politics or the idea of casts or the old religions . . . accepts the lesson with calmness . . . is not so impatient as has been supposed that the slough still sticks to opinions and manners and literature while the life which served its requirements has passed into the new life of the new forms . . . perceives that the corpse is slowly borne from the eating and sleeping rooms of the house . . . perceives that it waits a little while in the door . . . that it was fittest for its days . . . that its action has descended to the stalwart and wellshaped heir who approaches . . . and that he shall be fittest for his days.

The Americans of all nations at any time upon the earth have probably the fullest poetical nature. The United States themselves are essentially the greatest poem. In the history of the earth hitherto the largest and most stirring appear tame and orderly to their ampler largeness and stir. Here at last is something in the do-ings of man that corresponds with the broadcast doings of the day and night. Here is not merely a nation but a teeming nation of nations. Here is action untied from strings necessarily blind to particulars and details magnificently moving in vast masses. Here is the hospitality which forever indicates heroes. . . .

The American poets are to enclose old and new for America is the race of races. Of them a bard is to be commensurate with a people. To him the other conti-nents arrive as contributions . . . he gives them reception for their sake and his own sake. His spirit responds to his country's spirit. . . .

ESSAYS

These two essays explore the relationships between ethnic identity and citizenship, and nativist expressions about immigrants and citizenship in the mid-nineteenth cen-tury. Writing in 1992, Tyler Anbinder, a historian at George Washington University, lays out the six basic tenets of the ideology of the Know Nothing Party. He illustrates how followers of this major political movement coupled Protestantism with what they considered the foundation of American society. Because the Know Nothings associ-ated individualism, egalitarianism, and republican citizenship with Protestantism, they could thus attack the Catholicism of the immigrant both as an individual failing and as part of a larger threat to American society and polity. Historian Dale Knobel, of South-western University in Texas, complements Anbinder's essay in showing the relation-ship between common perceptions of American citizenship and Irish immigration (1986). Because of the volitional nature of citizenship, many Americans believed that American citizens were "made" rather than "born." As a result, they argued that it would be difficult for immigrants from Ireland to be made into Americans because of their past experiences in Ireland. Knobel grapples with the changing ideas of charac-ter, whether people were born with character traits or whether they developed them, and how these issues of "character" were embedded in the debate about making immi-grants into citizens.

From Walt Whitman, "Preface," *Leaves of Grass.*

The Ideology of the Know Nothing Party

TYLER ANBINDER

At the heart of the Know Nothing ideology lay six basic tenets. First, and most important, Know Nothings believed that Protestantism defined American society. Protestantism encouraged the individualism that flourished in America, said Know Nothings, because it allowed each Christian to interpret the Bible personally and to pray as he or she saw fit. Know Nothings also pointed with pride to the democratic aspects of Protestant Christianity. In most denominations, congregations chose their own ministers, and if churchgoers disapproved of him, they could select a new one. Protestants also believed that their method of devotion was the most egalitarian. Even without attending church, the humblest person might attain saintly standing through study of the Bible and private prayer. Know Nothings insisted that American reverence for democracy and freedom evolved from these Protestant religious practices: "The freedom we enjoy, the liberty of conscience, the freedom of religious faith and worship, the sanctity of civil, religious, social, and personal rights, are but the normal results of the enlightened liberalism of the Protestant faith."

Second, Know Nothings maintained that Catholicism was not compatible with the basic values Americans cherished most. While Protestantism was democratic, Know Nothings saw Catholicism as autocratic, because the pope directed all its adherents through his bishops and priests. As one Know Nothing newspaper described the hierarchy, "the Pope utters his wish to his Bishops, the Bishops bear it to their Priests, the Priest[s] direct the members of the church, and they all obey, because the Pope has a right to rule them, *they are his subjects. . . .*" Unlike Protestantism, Catholicism was also believed to restrain freedom of thought. Protestants contended that the notes in the annotated Douay Bible (the version Catholics read) and the fact that Catholics were discouraged from reading the Bible in private prevented them from freely interpreting the Scriptures. Catholicism also inhibited the individual autonomy that flourished under Protestantism, said Know Nothings, because priests interceded between the worshipper and God in almost every aspect of devotion. Catholicism also seemed to impose too many rituals, symbols, and images between God and the congregation :

> These vestments, and crossings, and genuflexions, . . . this swinging of censers and sprinkling of holy water, this tinkling of bells, this odour of incense, this glare of lighted candles at noonday . . . tend to divert the mind from the essence of religion, to satisfy it with forms, to substitute frivolous and superstitious observances in the place of moral and religious duties.

The Catholic emphasis on miracles, the apparent worship of saints and the Virgin instead of God, absolution, and transubstantiation further persuaded Protestants that Catholicism was based on mysticism and ignorance, while Protestantism represented reason and progress. Because American institutions were rooted in

From *Nativism and Slavery: The Northern Know Nothings and the Politics of the 1850s* by Tyler G. Anbinder. Copyright © 1994 by Tyler G. Anbinder. Used by permission of Oxford University Press, Inc.

Protestant values, Know Nothings concluded that "a Romanist is by necessity a foe to the very principles we embody in our laws, a foe to all we hold most dear."

Third, Know Nothings insisted that although few "Papists" lived in the United States, Catholics had attained political power disproportionate to their numbers. According to nativists, priests usually determined how Catholics voted, which gave a few Catholic leaders the power to decide elections. When not following the instructions of their prelates, Catholics purportedly "sold" their votes to the highest bidder, usually in return for patronage. Know Nothings also believed that immigrants gained excessive political power through extensive fraudulent voting and through the instigation of election-day violence that discouraged native-born citizens from going to the polls. Know Nothings concluded that such practices would become the norm if America continued "to receive a class of voters who have no Sabbath, and no Bible; and who are not really Americans, but only residents in America." In fact, Know Nothings believed that Catholic immigrants threatened America's bold experiment in republicanism:

> The cornerstone of our Republic is political, mental and social liberty, and in direct antagonism with these principles, stands Romanism. It denies the liberty of free inquiry, the liberty of speech, and thus saps the fountain of freedom. . . . There can be no republicanism where Catholicism bears sway.

These conditions made it imperative that native-born citizens counteract the growing political influence exerted by Catholic immigrants.

Antipathy for political parties and professional politicians formed the next facet of Know Nothing ideology. Nativists condemned politicians because they believed that conniving ones helped immigrants and Catholics acquire undue political power. Know Nothings charged that unscrupulous demagogues, concerned only with gaining office, sold their influence to immigrants in return for the newcomers' votes. But the Know Nothing critique of politicians went beyond their involvement with immigrants. Unlike the Founding Fathers, modern politicians lacked the commitment to "virtue" and "the public good" necessary for the operation of a successful republic. Elected officials placed party welfare before that of the nation, resulting in the passage of unpopular laws such as the Kansas-Nebraska Act. "The *national* interest is never considered by your real '*party man*,'" explained one Know Nothing leader. "His own success or that of his cabal, as a means for their own advancement in place or in fortune," motivated the new breed of politician. Only when voters removed professional politicians from office and reduced the influence of political parties would Americans manage to re-establish responsible government.

Finally, most northern Know Nothings believed in legal limitations on both the extension of slavery and liquor consumption. Know Nothings did not display the unanimity of opinion on these issues that one finds amongst Know Nothings concerning the threats posed by Catholicism and corrupt politicians. Yet a vast majority of northern Know Nothings believed that the spread of slavery should be curbed and the sale of liquor curtailed. The Know Nothings' commitment to these issues derived from their devotion to Protestant values, as American ministers regularly condemned "rum, Romanism, and slavery" as the three evils cursing the nation. Most northern Know Nothings saw the increasing political power of liquor traffickers and slaveholders as a natural outgrowth of the declining influence of Protestantism in America and considered opposition to these evils to be an integral part of their agenda.

Know Nothings proposed a number of remedies to combat the problems they identified. First, because the existing five-year probationary period before naturalization purportedly provided insufficient time for immigrants to assimilate, they suggested that the newcomers wait twenty-one years before attaining the privilege of voting. Second, Know Nothings urged voters to select only native-born citizens for office and to elect only those who would not appoint immigrants to patronage positions. Only those born and raised in America, they felt, understood the complexities of operating a republican government. While arguing that immigration laws also required modification to prevent the importation of paupers and criminals, Know Nothings never actually sought restrictions or quotas on the flow of immigration. Instead, they hoped to delay or mitigate the political influence of the newcomers. Only in this manner did Know Nothings believe that good government could be guaranteed and Protestant values preserved.

Know Nothings traced most of the problems facing their communities to the increasing number of immigrants arriving in the United States. While other Americans believed that the recent flood of newcomers would provide cheap labor and help populate the vast expanse of unsettled territory, Know Nothings saw only danger in the demographic trends. Most troubling to nativists was the belief that the immigrants of the "Great Migration" resisted assimilation. Whereas earlier immigrants had quickly adopted American customs, Know Nothings believed that those arriving in the 1850s were "determined that neither themselves nor their children shall ever conform to American manners, American sentiments, or the spirit of American Institutions." Because of the way "foreigners banded together" in resistance to assimilation, New York had become "much more a foreign than an American city," and Know Nothings believed that other American towns would soon suffer the same fate. In order to arrest this trend, Know Nothings wanted to mix immigrants "up in the American crucible and get them to adopt our ideas." New York Know Nothing Daniel Ullmann agreed that "where races dwell together on the same soil and do not assimilate, they can never form one great people—one great nationality." America, continued Ullmann, must "mold and absorb" the "castes, races, and nationalities" accumulating in the United States "into one great homogeneous American race," or else internal divisions would destroy the nation.

Know Nothings also believed that immigrants threatened the nation's well-being because of their propensity to commit crime. A Massachusetts newspaper reported that forty of forty-one persons arrested in Charlestown in one week had been born abroad. Noting that immigrants were ten times more likely to be arrested than native-born citizens, a Know Nothing paper in Albany concluded that "immigration" represented "the chief source of crime in this country." Violent crime had reached epidemic proportions in all major cities, reported the Harrisburg *Herald,* and "if these disgraceful outrages are looked into . . . it will be found that [the perpetrators] are FOREIGNERS, in nine cases out of ten." Catholic immigrants were especially prone to commit crime because when they went to confessional, the priest absolved them of guilt. "They are thus duped and incited to the committal of new and perhaps worse crimes," explained the Cleveland *Express,* "because they know no matter what the deed, they will be forgiven." Know Nothings also felt that the patronage preference given by politicians to immigrants contributed to the increasing crime rates. In the nineteenth century, politicians appointed police officers to their posts, and Know Nothings believed that immigrants received an unfair share of these positions. Police departments, they claimed, were "corrupt in proportion to the number of foreigners of which they are composed." Statistics from nearly every major city indicated that immigrants perpetrated crimes far out of proportion to their numbers, and, according to nativists, only when immigrants had been removed from police forces would American cities once again become safe.

According to Know Nothings, increasing pauperism also resulted from immigration. Nativists pointed to statistics such as those from Buffalo—where 1,436 of 1,558 paupers had been born abroad—to show that America imported most of its almshouse residents. Know Nothings believed this resulted in part from the fact that "the character of our foreign immigration, and especially the Irish portion of it, has entirely changed." Earlier immigrants displayed industriousness and frugality, but many recent newcomers were simply "too lazy to work." Know Nothings thought that most pauperism (and much crime as well) resulted from the European practice of "dumping" destitute citizens and convicts in America. "From the 'refuge of the oppressed,' we have come to be the great Botany Bay of the world," claimed one nativist journal. European governments deported paupers so that "the burden of their support might be placed on the American people," and Know Nothing newspapers printed dozens of circulars and letters purporting to document the frequency of the practice. Know Nothings particularly resented the number of Catholics who became public charges, for while "the fat sleek priests . . . build splendid cathedrals and churches, . . . we poor, good-natured Americans are taking care of their criminals and paupers."

Know Nothings also blamed immigrants for declines in the income and status of American workingmen. "Our native-born citizens hate to work by the side of an Irishman," reported a nativist journal, because they feel degraded "and dishonored by the contact. . . . It is the same feeling which makes it impossible for a respectable white man to labor by the side of slaves in the South." A Know Nothing council in Trenton likewise insisted that Americans should not have to work for the "foreign starvation wages" that immigrants accepted. Because immigrants had "been accustomed to live in poverty" in Europe, they continued to accept low pay when they got to America, and native-born workers realized that this drove down their wages. Even though many workers might not have yet noticed the effect of immigrant competition, Know Nothings insisted that "the enormous influx of foreigners will in the end prove ruinous to American workingmen, by REDUCING THE WAGES OF LABOR to a standard that will drive them from the farms and workshops altogether, or reduce them to a condition worse than that of Negro slavery."

Know Nothings worried not only about America's economic prosperity, but about the country's military preparedness as well. They felt that if the United States fought a war against Germans or a Catholic nation, the presence of so many immigrants would threaten the nation's security. Nativists particularly condemned the frequency with which immigrants formed militia units composed entirely of those born abroad. Military companies served a primarily social function in antebellum America, and because immigrants tended to socialize amongst themselves, immigrant militia units became a popular form of recreation for the newcomers. But Know Nothings opposed the creation of these companies. "To organize these amongst us," asserted Ohio Know Nothing president Thomas Spooner, "with foreign names and foreign insignia, is an insult to the hospitality we have extended to those who compose them." The fact that many German militia companies displayed not the Stars and Stripes but the red "revolutionary flag of Europe, is a taunt too bold not to be REBUKED AND REFORMED." Military companies composed of Irish Catholic immigrants posed an even greater threat, warned Know Nothings. These groups would never respond to the needs of the United States, but instead "rally at the call of the Bishop and the Priest. They are the *soldiers of the Church of Rome,* bound to defend its interests at whatever peril, and *not* the citizens of Boston. . . ." Now that these immigrants lived in the United States, reasoned the New York *Express,* it was "their duty to amalgamate with, and become part of us,—in our American regiments."

Although Know Nothings blamed some of the nation's problems on the overall increase in immigration, they concentrated their attacks on Catholic immigrants. "We are not now contending against foreigners, but against the principles of Roman Catholicism and its devotees," announced the Cleveland Know Nothing organ. As the Cincinnati *Times* explained it, "Romanism is the head and front" of Know Nothingism, while the proscription of all immigrants, known as "Native Americanism," was "secondary and contingent." Nativists justified this double standard on the grounds that "Protestant foreigners . . . appear to be open to reason, and act in accordance with their convictions," while Catholic immigrants were thought to be hostile to American values."

* * * *

Know Nothings believed that the new Catholic assertiveness carried grave implications for the future of American Protestantism. With Catholic immigrants pouring into the country, they would eventually outnumber Protestants. Once they gained hegemony, nativists reasoned, their purported intolerance would lead them to ban Protestantism altogether. According to Massachusetts Know Nothing Anson Burlingame, the Bishop of St. Louis had promised that " 'America will soon be Catholic, and then religious liberty will cease to exist.' " Other nativists agreed that Catholics "crushed out every feature and semblance of civil and religious liberty" in the countries they controlled. Such conditions existed in Catholic nations, concluded the Harrisburg *Herald,* because the "bigoted minions of the Pope know no toleration, nor will they allow any if they can help it." Know Nothings also believed that if given the opportunity, Catholics would outlaw all Bibles, not just the Protestant version. They asserted that many Catholic nations banned Bibles, burned them if they were found, and imprisoned those who read them. "Give Popery sway," Know Nothings concluded from this evidence, "and there will be no Bible."

Know Nothings claimed that if Catholics gained control of America, other liberties would suffer. "Romanism allows no freedom of thought," asserted the Hartford *Courant,* calling it "the most degrading despotism of which the world is cognizant." The Boston *Bee* agreed, stating that "Romanism . . . seeks to destroy all individual liberty, all private judgment, all power on the part of man to think or to act for himself. . . ." To prove the point, Know Nothing congressman Thomas R. Whitney quoted an encyclical written by the current pope, Pius IX, that called "liberty of conscience . . . absurd and dangerous" and "liberty of the press" a "great . . . horror." Efforts to suppress Protestant street preachers proved that Catholics had already begun "restraining the conscience, restraining thought, restraining all that makes up and characterizes and . . . gives beauty to the American name and nation."

Following a traditional theme of anti-Catholicism, Know Nothings also accused priests of sexual licentiousness. Richard Hofstadter noted that "anti-Catholicism has always been the pornography of the Puritan," and the popularity of Maria Monk's convent "revelations" demonstrates that the Protestant obsession with sexual impropriety by the priesthood preceded the Know Nothings by many years. The notion that convents provided the setting for illicit sex was so prevalent that customers commonly referred to nineteenth-century brothels as "nunneries."

While Know Nothing journals did not describe convent life in the sordid detail provided in convent exposés, their language left no doubt as to what they imagined went on within their walls. "Convents are the very hot-beds of lust and debauchery," reported one Know Nothing journal, while another described how they were "impregnated with vice and crime." Priests in convents exercised the most "shocking licentiousness and most unmitigated despotism over the hearts, minds, and persons of the nuns." Know Nothings asserted that the priests' authority allowed them to cover up their convent indiscretions by condemning their victims to a life of cloistered silence.

Despite the array of evils that Know Nothings identified in the Catholic religion, Know Nothings claimed that their movement would not have been necessary had Catholics not attempted to gain control of American politics and thereby impose their views upon the rest of America. "Our opposition is not to the [Catholic] Church," insisted an Ohio Know Nothing leader, ". . . but to its grasping for political power." A New York newspaper agreed that "what Americans are battling in Catholicism is not the religion of Jesus, . . . but a political Roman Jesuitism, whose aim is, and ever has been, to grasp temporal with spiritual power. . . ." Know Nothings opposed Catholicism "as a political institution" and promised not to interfere with Catholic religious practices. They sought instead "to destroy their political influence."

Catholics insisted that they sought no greater influence over American politics than any other religious group. But Know Nothings responded that "the systematic interference of the Church of Rome, *as an ecclesiastical organization,* . . . in the political controversies of this republic" set Catholicism apart from any other sect. Know Nothings asserted that ever since the time of Constantine, there had been "a *political* stripe along the whole length of Romanism." While Protestant ministers confined their activities to spiritual matters, Know Nothings found that "the Roman Hierarchy is the most gigantic political association on earth. . . . Its purpose [is] the government of mankind."

According to Know Nothings, proof of the political designs of Catholicism could be found in the actions of the popes. Know Nothings reminded Americans that "the Pope himself has been an active agent in political quarrels, intrigues, and wars of Europe," attacking sovereign nations, ordering assassinations, and dethroning kings in order to carry out his political designs. "Roman Pontiffs ever since the institution of Popedom" had attempted not only "to subjugate civil rulers—and not only to connect church and state, but to invest the priesthood with the civil magistracy." When Philadelphia congressman Joseph Chandler (a convert to Catholicism) responded that popes no longer exercised political power as they had in the past, Know Nothing newspapers reprinted articles from Catholic newspapers insisting that Chandler was wrong, and that the pope did still possess the power to depose sovereigns. Nativists pointed to recent events in Sardinia, for example, where the pope had declared null and void a law regulating Catholic Church property and threatened to put the island under interdict unless the statute was repealed. Know Nothings also listed recent incidents in Piedmont, Spain, England, France, Holland, Germany, and Ireland to prove that the pope had not lost his enthusiasm for interfering in political affairs.

Many Americans could not imagine how the pope could influence American politics. But Know Nothings believed that the visit of Papal Nuncio Gaetano Bedini as well as Catholic attempts to remove the Bible from the public schools, split school funds, change church property laws, and create Catholic political tickets marked the beginning of Catholicism's political assault upon the United States. While Irish immigrants often insisted that a certain percentage of an electoral ticket be made up of Catholics, Know Nothings asserted that Presbyterians or Episcopalians never made such demands for their denominations. According to one Know Nothing, Bishop John Purcell of Cincinnati had bragged to Democratic leaders that he controlled the votes of 6,200 Catholics and had produced a list of names to prove it. It was this concentration of power in the hands of a few leaders (and ultimately the pope himself) that made Catholic influence in American politics so potentially dangerous.

In addition, while Protestant immigrants were divided between the Whig and Democratic parties, Know Nothings believed that Catholics always voted in an unbroken bloc for Democratic candidates. "There is no other denomination in the United States which moves in a solid body in elections," grumbled one Know Nothing journal. Another agreed that "their vote is almost always a unit." This uniformity at the polls proved to Know Nothings that Catholics did not choose their candidates, but rather "receive[d] their instructions and their tickets from the Priests, and vote[d] accordingly." Skeptics might argue that there were too few Catholics in America to alter election results, but Know Nothings contended that "in a government where the opposing parties are so nearly balanced as in this country, a slight addition to either side may determine the preponderance." Although the Catholic population was small, Know Nothings insisted that bloc voting gave them power to sway elections that exceeded their nominal strength.

According to Know Nothings, Irish-Catholic immigrants augmented the political power that bloc voting gave them by committing a preponderance of the voting fraud in America as well. Look at any American city, nativists said, and accounts of illegal immigrant voting could be found:

> At the Seventh Ward, Irishmen were seen after having voted, to fall into the ranks and work their way up to the window and vote again, while around the polls stood a wild, excited mob of a thousand Celts, threatening death to all who oppose them. Hundreds who were challenged and rejected at the wards on the South side, swarmed over to their countrymen on the north side, and there deposited their ballots. A great many swore in their votes who were unnaturalized, and when the Bible was held to them, grasping it, they kissed their thumbs instead of the holy book, and by this dodge eased their tender consciences.

The concluding sentence alludes to the fact that immigrants were not required to produce naturalization papers in order to vote. Voting laws required that they merely swear at the polls that they had been naturalized. Know Nothings insisted that the ability to receive absolution at the confessional made all such oaths nonbinding on Catholics and encouraged them to continue their fraudulent voting. Nativists also asserted that the hiring of immigrant "blacklegs and bullies" as poll watchers made it easier for newcomers to vote illegally, since immigrants were likely to ignore the crimes of their countrymen.

* * * *

Know Nothings admitted that the country needed immigrants, and consequently they never proposed restricting the flow of newcomers as a means to preserve the homogeneity they valued. Instead, they sought to assimilate future immigrants more thoroughly and mitigate their political influence by modifying the naturalization laws that transformed immigrants into voting citizens. Naturalization laws required that in order to become American citizens, immigrants had to live in the United States for five years, and then swear before a judge that they disavowed all allegiance to their former home. Nativists found this naturalization procedure deficient for a number of reasons. Most important, they believed that immigrants could not be sufficiently "Americanized" in five years. "Foreigners are made . . . 'American citizens' altogether too rapidly," said the Boston *Know Nothing.* "Raw, verdant, outlandish fellows, fresh from the emigrant ship, with no more comprehension of the duties of a citizen; no more knowledge of our government; no more fitness to act the great character of a Republican than a Chinese automaton, are daily, by the thousands, metamorphosed into the stature and privileges of full American citizenship." Others complained that the naturalization process had become too perfunctory. An immigrant might spend his or her entire probationary period in a prison or poor-house, and still at the end of five years gain all the rights and privileges of "honest" natives. Know Nothings suggested that the waiting period before naturalization be increased to twenty-one years, since native Americans waited that long (from the day of their birth) before gaining the full rights of citizenship. Nativists argued that a twenty-one-year wait would allow immigrants to become fully assimilated and learn the responsibilities and rights "peculiar to our people, our country, and our republicanism." Massachusetts governor Henry J. Gardner summed up Know Nothing opinion on the subject best, asserting that Americans must "nationalize before we naturalize."

The Relationship Between the Portrayal of Irish Americans and Citizenship at Midcentury

DALE KNOBEL

Alexis de Tocqueville, the famed observer of early antebellum America, thought it easy to distinguish between American patriotism and European. In the Old World, love of country was "instinctive," a birthright refined by "a taste for ancient customs and a reverence for traditions of the past." But in the United States, it was a product of personal experience and calculated self-interest, of participation in shared political life.

In making this distinction, Tocqueville underscored the two meanings of the word which the French and English languages alike render as "nation." On the one hand, nation refers to a people or descent group. On the other, it describes a political unit, a state. According to Tocqueville, European nationality was of the first type, American of the second. In contrast to the "historical" national peoples of the Old World, what made the Americans a nation at all was the republican polity, its laws, and the shared rights and benefits citizens derived from it. In America, no real nation existed prior to the state. In the words of a modern student of American nationality, Yehoshua Arieli, "National identity was not a natural fact but an ideological structure." Citizenship, not membership in what might be denominated a "Volk," was the basis for inclusion in the nation. Loyalty to nation was one and the same with loyalty to Constitution. This decidedly anti-romantic construction of nationality, which placed little stock in blood or hoary tradition, was extraordinarily consequential for the early republic. It made possible a self-limited popular sovereignty in which individual and minority rights could be protected by law against majority will; after all, the nation—having no existence before the state—could scarcely claim primacy for itself over the statutory framework that gave the state life. At the same time, it offered encouragement to anyone who would give authority to individual conscience over social convention; and ultimately it could be used as a rationale for secession and the dissolution of the nation-state. The state was, after all, a temporal convenience, not the will of an historical "people" in any organic sense.

From Dale Knobel, excerpts of Chapter 2, "The Sin of the Irishman is Ignorance—The Cure is Liberty" from *Paddy and the Republic: Ethnicity and Nationality in Antebellum America* © 1986 by Dale T. Knobel, Wesleyan University Press by permission of University Press of New England.

Historians disagree over the intentions that lay behind such a construction of American nationality—whether they were only the product of a desire to differentiate New World nationality from Old (especially English) and in so doing legitimize the revolt of the thirteen colonies, or whether they reflected an effort to sever Americans from ethnocultural obligation to England, or, on the contrary, were a palpable necessity to differentiate American from Englishman in order to create a nation out of a colonial population already substantially non-English. Historians agree that this conception of nationality rendered citizenship, as James Kettner puts it, "contractual, volitional, and legal rather than natural and immutable." By education and predilection, the founding fathers found such citizenship as natural for a republic as they found it hazardous. Arthur M. Schlesinger, Jr., reminded scholars during the Bicentennial era that the first generation of Americans was convinced of the improbability of their experiment in self-government and of the absence of any exceptional qualities innate to the American people that might allow them to pull it off more easily than their precursors in Florence, Athens, or Rome. History and theory alike persuaded them of the cyclical mortality of states and the special vulnerability of republics to corruption. European contemporaries reminded them of the hopelessness of their venture in ways they did not appreciate but could not ignore. The latent Calvinism of their culture suggested that judgment fell on the just as well as the unjust and warned them against reliance upon a manifest destiny (that would come later). If there was any hope for the republic it was in environment—in the happy circumstances of geography and demography or in the incentives for popular virtue and intelligence that prudent men could create.

The implications were at once that while citizenship was volitional the republic could ill afford to accept every volunteer and that there was nothing outside of nurture that rendered a man suitable or unsuitable for republican citizenship. Evidence of this outlook showed up in the form of the earliest federal naturalization acts, those of 1790, 1795, and 1802 (the politically charged act of 1798 was exceptional). All required a period of residence before admission as a citizen during which the probationer could discharge the effects of a prior environment and take on those of the new. A Maryland congressman argued in the debates on the 1795 act that such a probation was demanded of immigrants so that "prejudices which the aliens had imbibed under the Government from whence they came might be effaced, and that they might, by communication and observance of our laws and government, have just ideas of our Constitution and the excellence of its institutions before they were admitted to the rights of a citizen." Moreover, they might come to feel a part of society, share the interests of their neighbors, and take on local habits. The act of 1802 reinforced this thrust by calling for a declaration of intent to naturalize three years before finalization which would both ensure continuous residence and focus community scrutiny upon an applicant's character.

To the first generations of republic citizens, then, the American was made, not born. The beneficent influences of nature in North America which permitted— *encouraged,* they would have it—material and intellectual independence, the mutual familiarity and obligation occasioned by being born into the midst of a national community, or the assimilation of republican ideas, interests, and ways through acclimation prior to naturalization—these were what made the American.

These were the hallmarks of nationality. Notably, they did not include blood membership in a Volk, in other words, ethnicity. (That the act of 1790 made *race* a qualification for naturalization, few contemporaries would have found contradictory.)

The way in which Americans viewed themselves went a long way toward conditioning the way in which they viewed others. That their nation did not have, officially, a specifically ethnic basis by no means made the early antebellum Americans that Tocqueville reported upon insensitive to ethnicity; it simply placed a certain construction upon it. Ethnicity denoted environment of origin and the institutionalization of environment in character. Republican theory held that character was critical to citizenship, hence to nationality. Any tendency to scrutinize character was a stimulus to examine ethnicity. This is exactly what stood out about the early antebellum word image of the United States' principal ethnic minority—the Irish. The Irish were clearly treated in language as a distinctive ethnic category, associated with particular environmental influences and a certain resultant character matrix. This stereotype did not suggest that character was fixed and changeless. But it did imply that some conscious effort was necessary to dispel the associations of ethnicity. And it suggested that the environment of Ireland was particularly ill-suited for the generation of republican character.

* * * *

"The Irish in general are quick of apprehension, active, brave, and hospitable, but passionate, ignorant, vain and superstitious," wrote American textbook author Jesse Olney in a widely-circulated school geography, first published in 1828. Intermixture of praise and censure like this was entirely typical of Anglo-Americans' conversation about the stock for the United States' fastest-growing immigrant minority during the early antebellum period. So was the concentration of words upon "character," upon the capacity of the Irish for intelligence, morality, and social amicability. These not only turned up when Anglo-Americans like Olney were specifically groping for words to capture the essence of the Irish but also made a pattern in incidental references to Irish men and women, individually and generically, preserved for us in many forms of print. In this they were precedented by English stereotypes. But, as noted, unlike the ambivalence that seemed to characterize the verbal portrait of the Irish among genteel Englishmen during the first part of the nineteenth century, the summary assessment implicit in the American idiom was unmistakably pejorative. The less admirable attributes of the Irish fully checked their better qualities. Goodrich explained to readers of his popular "family library" that there was simply no question that the "improvident restlessness" of Irish character "about canceled out the patriotism," its chief merit. Likewise, wrote Francis Bowen for the *North American Review,* "in the same degree in which they are originally warm and social, they become morose and gloomy." Virtue and vice, wit, and blunder, good-temper and ill coexisted in this word portraiture but vice, blunder, and bad-humor usually prevailed.

It is scarcely surprising that the words that came to Anglo-American lips (and pens) when "conversation" turned to the Irish directed attention to "character" rather than to conduct, condition, or physical appearance. For "character" was central to Anglo-Americans' perception of themselves and had been since the Revolution. Though the English descent of a substantial majority was undeniable, after their departure from the British empire most citizens of the fledgling United States were far more interested in authenticating themselves as "Americans" than in identifying with an inherited ethnicity. But what was distinctively "American" about this people if not its Englishness? The United States possessed an untried political philosophy, infant governmental institutions, brief traditions, a potentially fluid social order, and—even at the time of the Revolution—something less than cultural homogeneity.

The problem of giving meaning to "American" seemed particularly acute when it was agreed upon both sides of the Atlantic that every durable nation-state required some uniformity, either of experience or inheritance. It was impossible to predict anything of a nation's future without some sustained history, or, barring that, widely-shared human character attributes to support a forecast. During the early nineteenth century, Americans were still suffering the barbs of Europeans on this matter. Michael Chevalier, a visitor to the United States during the presidency of Martin Van Buren, tweaked his hosts by describing their country as "a body not yet in a state of consistency; it has no definable character, no fixed destination, it is incapable of anything great." As much as they resented these taunts, Americans were inclined to agree that they had some merit and offered similar self-criticism. Displaying typical concern, an antebellum correspondent of the *Southern Literary Messenger* said that "every people should have a *national character;* that is, the people of the nation should have some particular trait of character common to all, and, at the same time, differing from other nations." Americans were especially concerned with forecasting their nation's future for the simple reason that, as the *Western Monthly Magazine*'s James Hall put it, "every previous attempt to maintain a free government upon a large scale had failed." Furthermore, no one—certainly not the founding fathers—suspected that a republic could be dropped among just any people and survive. Despite their elaborate scheme of institutional checks and balances, none of the nation's architects—not even James Madison, the chief advocate of safety in diversity—anticipated that self-government would work among any but a united people. "It is for the happiness of those united in society to harmonize as much as possible in matters they must of necessity transact together. Civil government being the sole object of forming societies, its administration must be conducted by common consent," Jefferson had written in his wartime *Notes on the State of Virginia*. Common "character," it was widely understood among both first generation United States citizens and third, could offer both unity and predictability.

Besides, republican ideology seemed to demand that a self-governing citizenry display particular character traits. "We live under republican institutions," editor Hall wrote in an article titled "On the Formation of National Character," "where the whole power of the government is in the hands of the people, where every act of sovereignty is but an emanation of the public will." This was both the genius and the pitfall of republican government. What was the danger? Hall's successor at the helm of the Cincinnati magazine, Joseph Reese Fry, supplied the answer: "Ignorance is the poison of a republic and no citizens are really desirable save those who are well informed. . . . Republics always tend strongly to radicalism—they always have their demagogues who excite the passions and prejudices of the ignorant, that they may mislead them for their own advantage. . . . One man of bad moral character, no matter how ingenious he may be, will do more injury to a country than a thousand spinning jennies will do good." Virtue and intelligence—sound character—that was the sustenance of the American state. This is hardly a revelation. Gordon Wood and Bernard Bailyn, among others, have written extensively upon the opinions of the founding fathers in this regard. To serve as the working principle of a society, liberty required more self-discipline and restraint, more selflessness and community spirit than the inhabitants of European monarchies—where the state provided heavy-handed discipline—customarily were called upon to display. Without benevolence, the product of sound moral nurture, and intelligence, the consequence of education, popular self-government—even of the kind restricted to white male property-holders that characterized the early American republic—would not work. Thus the writings of the founding fathers are rife with insistent calls for virtue and intelligence in the people. "This virtue; morality and religion; is the armor, my friend, and this alone, that renders us invincible," Patrick Henry counseled a correspondent in the last year of his life. Less confident in religion, perhaps, as a guardian of morality, Thomas Jefferson recommended education. The important truths, he wrote George Ticknor in 1817, are "that knowledge is power, that knowledge is safety, that knowledge is happiness."

What is significant here is not that "virtue" and "intelligence" were well-represented in the rhetoric of first generation republicans but that they were sustained in the vocabularies of the second and the third. In fact, they became cultural dogma. "To borrow a cant phrase of the day," historian William Hickling Prescott wrote in 1841, "we shall be true to our *mission*—the most momentous ever intrusted to a nation; that there is sufficient intelligence and moral principle in the people . . . to choose the right rulers." We can, in fact, find this verbiage just about anywhere in early antebellum culture; we do not need to limit our attention to intellectuals—to semi-official keepers of patriotic rhetoric—like Prescott. When voters of Washington County, New York petitioned the United States House of Representatives in 1838, they prefaced their memorial: "Experience has proved the weakness of all human institutions under the attacks of corrupt principles, and has made the fact evident that the material of their strength lies in the intelligence, sound principles, and good morals of the people." It even seemed that the republic not only needed to sustain intelligence and good morals to survive but also owed its origins to these very commodities. "Governments are not formed but grow," declared New England essayist Frederick Henry Hedge in 1838; they "have their origin with the character and habits of the people governed." The republican form of American government was a direct outgrowth of the character and habits of Americans of the Revolutionary generation. But, as Thomas Paine had warned those very rebels in *Common Sense,* virtue was neither hereditary nor perpetual. The sustenance of sound character demanded the people's constant attention. In the 1820s, 1830s, and 1840s, the survival of the nation still seemed to hinge upon virtue and intelligence—upon good character, that is. An authentic American was one who demonstrated the moral and intellectual character requisite to participate in the American experiment in popular sovereignty.

Did native-born Americans or Anglo-Americans generally have a monopoly upon good character? Contemporaries doubted it. When the question of what constituted American nationality came up at the Anti-Masonic party national convention in 1830, the key speakers roundly denounced the proposition that Americanness naturally attached to those "born within certain boundaries." Rather, nationality was a matter of "inner strength or character," of "heart." To a considerable extent, then, American nationality was volitional. One proved one was a genuine American by loyalty, of course, to the laws and government of the United States. But, more fundamentally, one assumed nationality by guarding one's virtue and cultivating one's intelligence. Character was assumed to be a product of nurture rather than nature. "We owe all this prosperity, under Providence, to the intelligence that planted, to the intelligence that maintains, our republican institutions. We owe it to education," offered the *Western Monthly Magazine.* "The virtue of the people has heretofore saved our country; and if we would perpetuate its freedom, we must cherish religion, cultivate sound morals, and disseminate knowledge." Virtue was not inborn but was something to "cultivate." Intelligence did not run in the blood but was the product of "education." In part, then, the attainment of appropriate republican character required some activity, some nurture. But it was also popularly assumed that virtue and intelligence had become habitual among the American people and to some extent were absorbed by socialization. "As the flavor of the grape depends greatly on the soil by which it is nourished," Cincinnati physician-essayist Daniel Drake enthused, "so the temperament of individuals is modified by the intellectual 'aliment' in which their minds subsist in childhood and youth." The American "aliment" was regarded as especially conducive to character development. American liberty "frees the spirit, improves the condition, and raises the character," preached an enraptured patriot in 1835.

What did all of this have to do with the perception of European immigrants— particularly the Irish—by those who accounted themselves truly "American"? It meant, of course, that newcomers would be primarily scrutinized for their character. What were their moral values, their intellectual capacities, their amicability in social relations? Since Americans regarded themselves as having certain attainments in these respects, they would focus their attention upon them in others. Would the moral and intellectual fiber of the foreign-born be suspect? Of course it would, since to a great degree morality and intelligence were understood to be products of environment. And the American environment was deemed peculiar. "What can he know of these [the "sympathies," "feelings," and "ways of thinking which form the idiosyncrasy of the nation"] , who has never been warmed by the same sun, lingered among the same scenes, listened to the same tales in childhood, been pledged to the same interests in manhood by which these fancies are nourished; the loves, the hates, the hopes, the fears that go to form national character?" asked the historian Prescott. National character—*uniform* national character—involved virtue and intelligence and was heavily dependent upon environment. In nationality, blood availed little but birth and nurture much. Thus in the early years of the republic even English immigrants would be suspect. We remember how quickly Anglo-Americans were to manipulate the United States' naturalization laws to exclude the French and their alleged confederates from citizenship during the 1790s, but we forget the alacrity with which such laws were turned against newcomers from England at the time of the War of 1812. If even English character was subject to scrutiny—and rejection—how predictable was the close Anglo-American inspection of the Irish. And how predictable it was too that treatment of the Irish in language was especially a treatment of Irish "character."

* * * *

But the Irish in America were also—paradoxically—heirs to aspersions Anglo-Americans cast upon Great Britain. This, of course, is one of the things that made early antebellum characterizations of the Irish somewhat different from contemporaneous British ones. Anglo-Americans saw the seed of Irish character deficiencies not just in continental infection but in the effects of British rule. Surveying recent books about Ireland and the Irish, the *North American Review* of July 1840 declared that the general view was that those leaving the island for the United States overwhelmingly seemed to be the "worn down, servile victims of licentiousness and poverty." They were products—in their moral, intellectual, and social character alike—of their condition. That condition was created largely by others. "The Irish peasantry," wrote W. C. Willard and E. Woodbridge in what may have been the most influential American school geography of the mid-nineteenth century, "are in the most wretched ignorance and poverty. They are degraded by the oppression of the landlords; and their stewards or 'middlemen.' " Combined with the absence of "free and tolerant laws," noted another contemporary textbook writer, such oppression inevitably "discourages the spirit of industry." The consequences of these conditions, as this author suggested, were deemed to be as much spiritual as material. In an age which linked material success directly to character, what was really important was the impact that condition had upon the mental and moral faculties. For the Irish, that condition was held by many to be characteristically British. In a popular exercise book in elocution, American children read:

> By the fruits of it I will judge your system. What has it done for Ireland? New Zealand is emerging—Otaheite [Tahiti] is emerging—Ireland is not emerging—she is still veiled in darkness—her children safe under no law, live in the very shadow of death. . . . How is the wealth of Ireland proved? Is it by the naked, idle, suffering savages who are slumbering on the mud floors of their cabins?

Bad government was a principal source of that environment which enfeebled the Irish character. Worse, the fruits of British maladministration in Ireland seemed to be gathered to an alarming extent in America. "We are persuaded that there is nothing which has operated, and is operating, so unfavorably upon the peace and prosperity of the Union, as the irruption of these hordes of vicious and ignorant vassals from Great Britain and Ireland, who pour in upon us like the Goths upon Rome," shrilled the usually temperate editors of the *New England Magazine* late in 1834, combining the traditional English representation of the Irish as "wild" barbarians with an unambiguous declaration that the distinctive Irish character ought to be considered the responsibility of Britain itself. Once again, the immediate consequences of Britain's benighted governance were treated as moral and intellectual. They were "viciousness" and "ignorance." These, of course, might well have social and political ramifications, but they were derivative of flawed character, not ideology.

What made this imputed character seem worse, however, was a perception that American society was ill-equipped to tame it. An open society emphasizing voluntary deference rather than rank and privilege, self-restraint rather than discipline, America was susceptible to ruin from vices which blossomed under the conditions of liberty. "What is to become of a poor, wretched population, ignorant in the extreme, naturally passionate, very mistaken in their views of American freedom, thousands of them too superstitious to seek wisdom from their neighbors, and almost always under the influence of strong drink?" a correspondent enquired in a letter to the *New York Morning Herald.* The question was rhetorical; the writer anticipated that most Anglo-Americans would respond with the same answer. The newcomers would mistake freedom for license; they would become, in the words of a New York City magistrate, "mischievous strangers." The repressions and frustrations they faced in their homeland were genuine, but the consequences were all too likely to be realized in America. "Foreigners," a Philadelphia judge charged the jury in the trial of an Irish-American during 1844, "used at home to a military police, taught by long oppression to regard all laws as tyranny and all officers of the law as enemies, and feeling none of the American interest in self-government, are a constant element of disorder." The immigrants' failings were of a moral kind and these were bound to be a source of apprehension in a nation which had learned to "trust the execution of the laws to the voluntary obedience of the offender or the casual support of the citizen." A United States House of Representatives report on immigration issued a few years earlier stated the case this way: "The character of our free institutions was not adapted for such citizens; nor did the framers of those institutions contemplate the nature and mental character of the bulk of those who have since blotted our country."

If the Irish in America were problematic enough when left to their own devices, they were intolerably burdensome to the republic when they fell into the hands of designing and unscrupulous Americans. The rude and unlettered Irish immigrant, it was often predicted, would all too easily become a tool of unethical and overcompetitive native politicians and their supporters, turning American politics into a contest of sheer numbers rather than principles. "Look at the New York *Courier* and *Enquirer*," charged newspaperman (and future abolitionist martyr) Elijah Lovejoy in an 1835 editorial for his *St. Louis Observer.* "Two or three years ago it was the champion of the Irishmen; it would not suffer a word to be used in derogation of them or their priests. And why? Simply because it was then attached to that party to which most of these ignorant foreigners belonged. . . . And though we believe it is now on the right side, so far as Popery is concerned, yet have we any confidence in such a coadjutor?" Servile, uneducated, unaccustomed to self-government or the rule of law itself, prone to take liberty as an excuse of cast off inhibition, the Irish in America were a substantial danger to a self-governing republic which welcomed all to citizenship. Criticism of the Irish on this score, however, was again not precisely criticism of their political ideology or practices. It was criticism of the moral and intellectual aptitudes which made them unsafe repositories for political privilege.

No wonder, then, that the specifically political characteristics of the Irish were so infrequently a part of early antebellum conversation. Political character was merely symptomatic of a disease of a moral or intellectual nature. Might this also explain the relative infrequency of treatments of the religious character of the Irish in everyday American discourse, that is, the explicit identification of Irish and Catholic? The evidence suggests so. In 1835 a Cincinnati magazine editor, commenting on sectarian violence that had lately rocked the city, noted that even the most intemperate Protestant zealots seemed not to object directly to Irish Catholics' "religious tenets, but [to] their moral character." Irish Romanism was no more than a natural blight upon minds cramped by poverty, ill-education, and bad government. "No man, in his senses, ever believed fully and fairly, the [Roman Catholic] doctrine of transubstantiation," wrote a Protestant minister in the mid-1830s. "Let us not be misunderstood; there have, doubtless, been many men who *thought* they believed it, but owing to the prejudice of education, their minds, in this point, were dark, and saw things that were not as they thought they were. So often do we see individuals inflicted with mental imbecility on some particular subject." Such was the plight, he thought, of the Irish. But the implication was that once freed from the yoke of British tyranny and priestly domination and accorded a proper republican public school education, even the Irish could be rendered receptive to the truths of Protestant faith.

All of this is testimony to the fact that the early antebellum stereotype of the Irish was environmental. The Irish were a distinctive people, but their distinctiveness derived from nurture rather than nature. Poverty, oppression, misgovernment all set the conditions for life in Ireland. These affected not only lifestyle and outlook, but, more important, character. The Irish took to drink and emotional excess to escape their misery. They confused liberty with license from reaction to tyranny. They were misled by Catholicism because their minds were contracted by ill-education and dependence. At the same time these conditions might bring out the best in the Irish character: joviality, neighborliness, goodheartedness, and loyalty. Shared trials encouraged such personality traits. These would not be dominant, however, and would at best share time with the less attractive qualities. And that in itself would take a toll on Irish character. It would render the Irish—in the popular Anglo-American perception—unpredictable, mercurial, moody, vacillating between selflessness and selfishness. But this character was not understood by Anglo-Americans to be innate. Wrote Timothy Dwight, cleric and educator, of his observations of the Irish in New England: "The evils which I have specified are not, however, derived from the native character of these people. . . . Give them the same advantages which are enjoyed by others, and they will stand upon a level with any of their neighbors." If the Irish were products of condition, why, change the condition, and the Irish would be changed.

FURTHER READING

Tyler Anbinder, *Nativism and Slavery: The Know Nothings and the Politics of the 1850s* (1992).

David Bennett, *The Party of Fear: From Nativist Movements to the New Right in American History* (1988).

Ray Allen Billington, *The Protestant Crusade 1800–1860: A Study in the Origins of American Nativism* (1938).

Ray Allen Billington, *Nativism in the United States, 1800–1844* (1974).

David Brion Davis, "Some Themes of Counter-Subversion: An Analysis of Anti-Masonic, Anti-Catholic, and Anti-Mormon Literature," *Mississippi Valley Historical Review* (1960–61).

Michael Feldberg, *The Philadelphia Riots of 1844: A Study in Ethnic Conflict* (1975).

Jenny Franchot, *Roads to Rome: The Antebellum Protestant Encounter with Catholicism* (1994).

William E. Gienapp, *The Origins of the Republican Party, 1852–1856* (1987).

Michael F. Holt, "The Politics of Impatience: The Origins of Know Nothingism," *Journal of American History* (1973), 309–31.

Michael F. Holt, *The Political Crisis of the 1850s* (1978).

Robert Francis Hueston, *The Catholic Press and Nativism, 1840–1860* (1976).

Dale T. Knobel, *Paddy and the Republic: Ethnicity and Nationality in Antebellum America* (1986).

Dale T. Knobel, *America for the Americans: The Nativist Movement in the United States* (1996).

Vincent P. Lannie, *Public Money and Parochial Education: Bishop Hughes, Governor Seward, and the New York School Controversy* (1968).

Ira M. Leonard, *American Nativism, 1830–1860* (1971).

Stephen E. Maizlish, "The Meaning of Nativism and the Crisis of the Union: The Know-Nothing Movement in the Antebellum North," in Maizlish, *Essays on American Antebellum Politics: 1840–1860* (1982), 166–98.

Evangeline Thomas, *Nativism in the Old Northwest, 1850–1860* (1936).

CHAPTER
6

Emigration and Return: Migration Patterns in the Industrial Age, 1850–1920

A new pattern of international migration, one often associated with industrial employment and improved transportation, characterized the immigration of the late nineteenth and early twentieth centuries. Many immigrants moved to the United States with the hope that they could eventually return home with greater resources. The pioneers of this strategy were Chinese immigrants who arrived in California, or "gold mountain," as they called the United States, as early as 1850. As a part of a Chinese diaspora that emanated from coastal regions of the provinces of Guangdong and Fujian, the Chinese migration to the United States was only one segment of a large Chinese migration to a variety of destinations throughout southeast Asia, Australia, and beyond. The some 300,000 Chinese immigrants who arrived in the United States were overwhelmingly male, and their community was molded by a merchant class that was a central force in organizing work and life for the laboring immigrants. Many Chinese immigrants indeed intended to return home to family members; nonetheless, their reception in the United States became increasingly hostile in the late nineteenth century. A series of laws passed to restrict the immigration of Chinese laborers raised the legal hurdles for immigrants in China. After the passage of the Chinese Exclusion Act in 1882, many immigrants faced detention or rejection when they attempted to migrate to "gold mountain."

The Chinese immigrant blazed a path that was followed by industrial immigrants from Europe, Latin America and other nations of Asia who were not subject to immigration exclusion, like Chinese people, at least in the short term. Often labeled "birds of passage," these immigrants moved to industrial occupations and to higher wages in hopes of returning home with the capital that would enable them to live more comfortably, to purchase homes, perhaps even land. Moving from agrarian, oftentimes peasant, economies, these immigrants tended to work in immense factories and live in huge cities. The immigration in this era was immense:

170

About 18.4 million legal immigrants came to the United States between 1880 and 1920. And the origins of this wave of immigrants were shifting compared to those of earlier periods. Between 1890 and 1920, immigrants from Italy, Russia, and the Austro-Hungarian empire constituted well over half the immigrant total. In the first decade of this century, they made up nearly two-thirds of the 8.8 million immigrants to the United States. Moreover, the stirrings of an immense migration from Mexico, a movement which began in the late nineteenth century, mushroomed in the decade following the Mexican Revolution in 1910.

Despite a common hope to return home, some immigrants of this period intended to remain. The best example is the Jewish migration from eastern Europe and Russia, as Jews fled anti-Semitic persecution that was especially virulent between 1882 and 1907. And many of the immigrants, from Asia, Europe, and Mexico alike, who expected to return when they left their homeland eventually remained in the United States to build ethnic communities and neighborhoods.

Students of this industrial migration, then, are challenged to understand the strategies of a return migration and its effects on those who remained at home and those who migrated to the United States. What impact did these migration patterns—from Europe, Asia, and Latin America—have on the immigrant community and family that, in many cases, stretched across the Atlantic and Pacific Oceans or across the Mexican border? How did the idea of America animate the peasant communities of Europe, Asia, and Latin America, and how did their intentions of returning home influence life in the United States?

 D O C U M E N T S

These documents illustrate the motivations and strategies of industrial immigrants between 1882 and 1924 from a variety of perspectives. The story of Lee Chew (1882), which illustrates the early Chinese immigration to the United States, is the first document. Notice how Lee Chew's desire to move to the United States is fostered by the return to China of a man who left in poverty and came back with "unlimited wealth" and how his migration is financed by his father. Observe, as well, his protests against the prejudices aimed at Chinese immigrants. The next two documents explore the roots of emigration in eastern Europe. A series of reminiscences by eastern European immigrants (1915–1923) recalls the poverty of life in the Old Country and, again, illustrates the influence of returned immigrants who encouraged migration—a migration that was often predicated on a return home with wealth. Another eastern European immigrant (1909), however, remembers how his uncritical awe of America was undermined by the return of a Slovenian immigrant broken by work in the United States. Mary Antin (1912), in the next document, illustrates how the emigration of Jews from Russia and eastern Europe was fueled by virulent anti-Semitism and by the hope that the United States offered a better life. She gives us a romantic view of what America, the "promised land," meant. Many Mexican immigrants in the twentieth century also expressed the desire to return home, sentiments confirmed in a selection of ballads (1924) written by such immigrants. Whereas migration and return remained a common strategy into the twentieth century, legal constraints made it increasingly difficult for certain groups. Perhaps the best example is the detention of Chinese on Angel Island in San Francisco Bay beginning in 1910. A series of poems (1910–1940) carved into the walls by immigrants detained at Angel Island expresses the injustice of detention, but also the people's hopes to return home to family in China.

Lee Chew, a Chinese Immigrant, Describes Life in the United States and Denounces Anti-Chinese Prejudice, 1882

When I was ten years of age I worked on my father's farm, digging, hoeing, manuring, gathering and carrying the crop. We had no horses, as nobody under the rank of an official is allowed to have a horse in China, and horses do not work on farms there, which is the reason why the roads there are so bad. The people cannot use roads as they are used here, and so they do not make them.

I worked on my father's farm till I was about sixteen years of age, when a man of our tribe came back from America and took ground as large as four city blocks and made a paradise of it. He put a large stone wall around and led some streams through and built a palace and summer house and about twenty other structures, with beautiful bridges over the streams and walks and roads. Trees and flowers, singing birds, water fowl and curious animals were within the walls.

The man had gone away from our village a poor boy. Now he returned with unlimited wealth, which he had obtained in the country of the American wizards. After many amazing adventures he had become a merchant in a city called Mott Street, so it was said.

When his palace and grounds were completed he gave a dinner to all the people who assembled to be his guests. One hundred pigs roasted whole were served on the tables, with chickens, ducks, geese and such an abundance of dainties that our villagers even now lick their fingers when they think of it. He had the best actors from Hong Kong performing, and every musician for miles around was playing and singing. At night the blaze of the lanterns could be seen for many miles.

Having made his wealth among the barbarians this man had faithfully returned to pour it out among his tribesmen, and he is living in our village now very happy, and a pillar of strength to the poor.

The wealth of this man filled my mind with the idea that I, too, would like to go to the country of the wizards and gain some of their wealth, and after a long time my father consented, and gave me his blessing, and my mother took leave of me with tears, while my grandfather laid his hand upon my head and told me to remember and live up to the admonitions of the Sages, to avoid gambling, bad women and men of evil minds, and so to govern my conduct that when I died my ancestors might rejoice to welcome me as a guest on high.

My father gave me $100, and I went to Hong Kong with five other boys from our place and we got steerage passage on a steamer, paying $50 each. Everything was new to me. All my life I had been used to sleeping on a board bed with a wooden pillow, and I found the steamer's bunk very uncomfortable, because it was so soft. The food was different from that which I had been used to, and I did not like it at all. I was afraid of the stews, for the thought of what they might be made of by the wicked wizards of the ship made me ill. Of the great power of these people I saw many signs. The engines that moved the ship were wonderful monsters, strong enough to lift mountains. When I got to San Francisco, which was before the passage of the Exclusion act, I was half starved, because I was

As found in David M. Katzman and William M. Tuttle, Jr. (eds.), *Plain Folk: The Life Stories of Undistinguished Americans* (Chicago: University of Illinois Press, 1982).

afraid to eat the provisions of the barbarians, but a few days' living in the Chinese quarter made me happy again. A man got me work as a house servant in an American family, and my start was the same as that of almost all the Chinese in this country.

The Chinese laundryman does not learn his trade in China; there are no laundries in China. The women there do the washing in tubs and have no washboards or flat irons. All the Chinese laundrymen here were taught in the first place by American women just as I was taught.

When I went to work for that American family I could not speak a word of English, and I did not know anything about housework. The family consisted of husband, wife, and two children. They were very good to me and paid me $3.50 a week, of which I could save $3.

I did not know how to do anything, and I did not understand what the lady said to me, but she showed me how to cook, wash, iron, sweep, dust, make beds, wash dishes, clean windows, paint and brass, polish the knives and forks, etc., by doing the things herself and then overseeing my efforts to imitate her. She would take my hands and show them how to do things. She and her husband and children laughed at me a great deal, but it was all good natured. I was not confined to the house in the way servants are confined here, but when my work was done in the morning I was allowed to go out till lunch time. People in California are more generous than they are here.

✳ ✳ ✳ ✳

. . . Men of other nationalities who are jealous of the Chinese, because he is a more faithful worker than one of their people, have raised such a great outcry about Chinese cheap labor that they have shut him out of working on farms or in factories or building railroads or making streets or digging sewers. He cannot practice any trade, and his opportunities to do business are limited to his own countrymen. So he opens a laundry when he quits domestic service.

The treatment of the Chinese in this country is all wrong and mean. It is persisted in merely because China is not a fighting nation. The Americans would not dare to treat Germans, English, Italians or even Japanese as they treat the Chinese, because if they did there would be a war.

There is no reason for the prejudice against the Chinese. The cheap labor cry was always a falsehood. Their labor was never cheap, and is not cheap now. It has always commanded the highest market price. But the trouble is that the Chinese are such excellent and faithful workers that bosses will have no others when they can get them. If you look at men working on the street you will find an overseer for every four or five of them. That watching is not necessary for Chinese. They work as well when left to themselves as they do when some one is looking at them.

It was the jealousy of laboring men of other nationalities—especially the Irish—that raised all the outcry against the Chinese. No one would hire an Irishman, German, Englishman or Italian when he could get a Chinese, because our countrymen are so much more honest, industrious, steady, sober and painstaking. Chinese were persecuted, not for their vices, but for their virtues. There never was any honesty in the pretended fear of leprosy or in the cheap labor scare, and the persecution continues still, because Americans make a mere practice of loving justice. They are all for money making, and they want to be on the strongest side always. They treat you as a friend while you are prosperous, but if you have a misfortune they don't know you. There is nothing substantial in their friendship.

* * * *

Irish fill the almshouses and prisons and orphan asylums, Italians are among the most dangerous of men, Jews are unclean and ignorant. Yet they are all let in, while Chinese, who are sober, or duly law abiding, clean, educated and industrious, are shut out. There are few Chinamen in jails and none in the poor houses. There are no Chinese tramps or drunkards. Many Chinese here have become sincere Christians, in spite of the persecution which they have to endure from their heathen countrymen. More than half the Chinese in this country would become citizens if allowed to do so, and would be patriotic Americans. But how can they make this country their home as matters now are! They are not allowed to bring wives here from China, and if they marry American women there is a great outcry.

Immigrants Recall Their Life in Eastern Europe and Their Emigration, 1915–1923

John Lukasavicius

We owned a small tract of land of about five acres in the village and the whole family—my mother, elder brother, and younger sister—all worked the land. My father left for America when I was four years old and used to send us money once in a while so that we managed to get along. He was working in a mine in Pennsylvania.

Until we children grew up so that we were able to help on the land, our mother did most of the farm work with the help of neighbors. When I was about six years old, I started to help by herding the few pigs and other animals we had. Our house was like the rest of those in the village, a log cabin with a thatched roof, dirt floor, one room with a clay stove built in one corner. My brother and I used to sleep outdoors or in the barn when the weather was warm. We only slept in the house in the winter. All summer we worked hard, from dawn to dusk, raising food for ourselves and the animals. With my father sending money occasionally we were able to use that to pay taxes with and were able to keep our food instead of selling part of it in the market.

Most of our meals were black rye bread, soup from vegetables we raised, and milk and cheese. On holidays we had better meals, roast goose or duck, vegetables with sour cream, and perhaps a loaf of wheat bread bought from a baker in the neighboring town. Our clothes were almost all homemade, though my father sent us some from America. He sent me a woolen overcoat, my brother a suit and shoes, and my mother and sister each a velvet dress. We only wore those clothes to church on Sundays and holidays. . . .

My mother was the boss in our house and we all obeyed her orders. If we disobeyed she would give us a good beating. As we grew older my brother and I worked the land and she helped with my sister, when they weren't busy in the house. The only time we did anything different from working and sleeping was

From *From The Old Country: An Oral History of European Migration to America* by Bruce M. Stave and John F. Sutherland, with Aldo Salerno. Copyright © 1994 by Twayne Publishers. Reprinted by permission of the authors.

when there was a dance at one of the neighbors' houses or a wedding. I never paid much attention to my sister, and my brother was a moody fellow so we didn't do many things together outside of our work. . . .

Michael Daunis

The village I was born in had about 30 houses. My father owned a small farm of about 20 American acres. There were 10 people in my family, 3 boys and 5 girls besides my parents. Everybody in the family went to work on the land as soon as they were able to do something. We had to because our farm was small for such a large family. Most of the year we worked from dawn until dark. In winter we were not so busy because all the crops were harvested.

Our house was like the rest of them in the village. It was a log cabin with a thatched roof, two rooms and only one of them had a wooden floor. Our furniture was homemade and for light we had a kerosene lamp. Like the rest of the houses we had a clay stove in one corner of the kitchen. The floor was hard-packed dirt. My mother used to clean it by sweeping and then covering the dirt with white sand.

We raised everything we ate and wore. Most of the time we ate black rye bread and soup. Three times a week we had a little fat pork for meat. On holidays of course we ate a little better. Those were the only times that we had a goose or chicken for our own table. Any other time we killed animals it was for market, because the only time we had any money was when we sold some of the things we raised. Our clothes were made from cloth that my mother and sisters weaved from wool or flax we raised on the farm. I never wore any other clothes until I came to this country. . . .

A year before I came to this country, a cousin of mine had come here. He wrote once in a while and told of how he was earning a lot of money and how everybody in America lived like princes. Other people in the village had relatives here, too, and they used to talk over the letters that were sent. All the letters said how big wages were paid for easy work and how wonderful it was in America. I wrote my cousin and begged him to send me a ticket to America. I thought that I could come and work hard and get enough money to buy a big farm in Lithuania for myself. I didn't want to stay on my father's farm because I knew that when he died my older brother would own the farm and I would have to depend on his good will to make a living.

When my cousin sent me a ticket, everybody was happy at my good fortune. I left home two days after it came. I crossed the border with six other fellows who came from nearby villages and started my journey to America. I expected that when I came back in a few years I would be able to own the biggest farm in the village.

Maru Strokonos

When I get to be about 22, 23, I think all the time I come to America. Landlord's daughter come to America, then, two, three years come back to see family. Tell big stories about America. She had American clothes and nice things; she bring big blue teapot to mother. I listen to stories like baby listen to stories at bedtime, you know. I think I go to America too, have same things as she has.

My people do not like me to go when I tell them, so I play like fox and no say anything more about plans. Every time I go to market I keep little money for trip. Three, four years ago, then one market day I don't go back home. I walk long time, then farmer give me ride on hay wagon. Ride all night, fall asleep on soft hay. In morning farmer shake me awake and tell me I am in city. What city? I can't think of name now.

I go down to where trains are and I ask the man how much it cost to go to America. He laugh and say you can't ride train all the way to America. But he nice man, he put me on train and I finally get to town where I take boat. Where do I get boat? I think in Germany, maybe Berlin. I can't read or write, so I can't tell. I get to boatman after long time in town. When I told him I wanted to get boat for America, he ask for my money. Then he take some, put some in bag and give it back to me, and tell me I need this in America.

When boat sail I am downstairs in boat. Many, many people down there, very crowded. Everybody very sick. I am so sick I cry and cry, I think I die, then I wish I back on farm. On boat is a young farmer from near town I come from. I lonesome and he is nice to talk to.

After boat rock like cradle back and forth we stop at island. Doctor come in and see if anybody sick, then he let everybody out on island. We wait long time, then we get to America. I get scared when I see so many people and buildings. I walk along street and I come to a shop they have windows full of cakes and goodies like only rich in old country can have. I go into store, but I can't speak English so I point to man and then to cookies. He put them in paper bag and then I show him money and take one, two pieces. I am very, very lonely and I start to cry and it gets very dark but I don't know where to go. I walk along and then I feel a hand on my shoulder. It is a cop and I think I am going to be put in jail, but he take me to a house where the woman is a Lithuanian. I am so happy I kiss his hand, but he only laughs. The woman gets me a job in hotel doing work, but I don't know American way and I am very dumb; everybody laughs at me. I am very saddened; every night I cry.

One day when I leave the hotel I met Walter Stroknos who I met on boat. I am so happy to see someone I can talk to that I hate to see him leave. I come to America in summer and I marry him in fall. We live in New York for a while, then we come to here to farm. We work for people who own farm. It is so nice! People are nice. We live in shed where chickens live now. Old lady in house give us a bed and table and two chairs and a stove and mirror; she give us pans and dishes too. We very happy. After little Walter and Josie were come, old man die and old lady go to live with son. She sell farm to us for $300. Walter get money from man on paper—you know, he sign his name. After we move into big house, Albert and Mary and Vera and Peter were come.

Now Walter is not so nice and one day he throw stick of wood at me. It hit me and cut my head. He get doctor and he sew it up, then he tell him he send him to jail if he do it another time. I don't like my life no more. I wish I don't marry Walter. He work hard but he very mean, say bad things.

A Slovenian Recounts Varying Assessments of America Made by Returned Immigrants, 1909

As a boy of nine, and even younger, in my native village . . . I experienced a thrill every time one of the men of the little community returned from America.

Excerpts (pp. 3–6, 12–17, 19, 20) from *Laughing in the Jungle* by Louis Adamic. Copyright © 1932 by Louis Adamic. Copyright © renewed 1960 by Stella Adamic. Reprinted by permission of HarperCollins Publishers, Inc.

Five or six years before, as I heard people tell, the man had quietly left the village for the United States, a poor peasant clad in homespun, with a mustache under his nose and a bundle on his back; now, a clean-shaven *Amerikanec,* he sported a blue-serge suit, buttoned shoes very large in the toes and with india-rubber heels, a black derby, a shiny celluloid collar, and a loud necktie made even louder by a dazzling horseshoe pin, which, rumor had it, was made of gold, while his two suitcases of imitation leather, tied with straps, bulged with gifts from America for his relatives and friends in the village. In nine cases out of ten, he had left in economic desperation, on money borrowed from some relative in the United States; now there was talk in the village that he was worth anywhere from one to three thousand American dollars. And to my eyes he truly bore all the earmarks of affluence. Indeed, to say that he thrilled my boyish fancy is putting it mildly. With other boys in the village, I followed him around as he went visiting his relatives and friends and distributing presents, and hung onto his every word and gesture.

Then, on the first Sunday after his homecoming, if at all possible, I got within earshot of the nabob as he sat in the winehouse or under the linden in front of the winehouse in Blato, surrounded by village folk, ordering wine and *klobase*— Carniolan sausages—for all comers, paying for accordion-players, indulging in tall talk about America, its wealth and vastness, and his own experiences as a worker in the West Virginia or Kansas coal-mines or Pennsylvania rolling-mills, and comparing notes upon conditions in the United States with other local *Amerikanci* who had returned before him.

I remember that, listening to them, I played with the idea of going to America when I was but eight or nine.

My notion of the United States then, and for a few years after, was that it was a grand, amazing, somewhat fantastic place—the Golden Country—a sort of Paradise—the Land of Promise in more ways than one—huge beyond conception, thousands of miles across the ocean, untellably exciting, explosive, quite incomparable to the tiny, quiet, lovely Carniola; a place full of movement and turmoil, wherein things that were unimaginable and impossible in Blato happened daily as a matter of course.

In America one could make pots of money in a short time, acquire immense holdings, wear a white collar, and have polish on one's boots like a *gospod*—one of the gentry—and eat white bread, soup, and meat on weekdays as well as on Sundays, even if one were but an ordinary workman to begin with. In Blato no one ate white bread or soup and meat, except on Sundays and holidays, and very few then.

In America everything was possible. There even the common people were "citizens," not "subjects," as they were in Austria and in most other European countries. A citizen, or even a non-citizen foreigner, could walk up to the President of the United States and pump his hand. Indeed, that seemed to be a custom in America. There was a man in Blato, a former steel-worker in Pittsburgh, who claimed that upon an occasion he had shaken hands and exchanged words with

Theodore Roosevelt, to whom he familiarly referred as "Tedi"—which struck my mother very funny. To her it seemed as if some one had called the Pope of Rome or the Emperor of Austria by a nickname. But the man assured her, in my hearing, that in America everybody called the President merely "Tedi."

Mother laughed about this, off and on, for several days. And I laughed with her. She and I often laughed together.

* * * *

Late in the spring of 1909, four months before I was taken to school in Lublyana, and six or seven months after I had first announced my intention to go to America, there returned to Blato a man who had been in America for more than twenty years.

He was Peter Molek, brother of Francé Molek, a rather well-to-do peasant who was our nearest neighbor. Peter had no property in the village, and so he went to live in Francé's house. His brother had not heard from or of him for eight years. He had thought him dead. None of the returned *Amerikanci* had seen him in America. Then, of a sudden that spring, there came a letter from him that he was "coming home to die."

Peter Molek was an unusual *Amerikanec* to return to Blato.

At the supper table the day after his homecoming, I heard my parents discuss him. Father said that he remembered when Peter had gone to America. "He was one of the sturdiest and lustiest young men in this parish, even stronger and taller than Francé," who, although in his fifty-seventh year, was still a big and powerful man. "Now look at him!"—and Father shook his head.

Although not yet fifty, Peter Molek was a gaunt, bent, and broken man, hollow-eyed, bald, mostly skin and bone, with a bitter expression on his face; suffering from rheumatism and asthma—two diseases till then all but unknown in Blato. He was eight or nine years younger than Francé, but only a shadow of his brother.

"America is an evil place," said Mother, glancing at me concernedly, although I had not spoken of going to America again. "They say Peter came home almost penniless. I guess Francé will have to keep him till he dies."

Which, to me, was the most extraordinary aspect of Peter Molek. With my ideas about America, I could not understand how anyone, after spending twenty years in that country—in the midst of abundance—could return home in such a state. And it doubtless was true what people said about Peter Molek having no money. He brought no presents even for his closest relatives. He did not go to the winehouse, nor talk about his adventures in America with anyone. He kept, for the most part, to himself. All day long he sat in the sun on the bench in front of his brother's house. He read books and papers which evidently were American publications. He took slow walks in the fields. Sometimes he coughed for ten or twenty minutes at a spell.

Peter Molek's cough was a great sensation among the children in Blato. When the asthmatic spasm seized him, his face turned purple, his deep-sunken eyes bulged and looked wide and terror-stricken; and bending over, he held his chest in desperation. The first two or three weeks after his return, as soon as one of the boys heard him cough, there was much yelling in the village and, with the heartless, unthinking curiosity of youth, ten or a dozen husky, barefooted urchins came dashing from all sides to Molek's house, to watch the strange *Amerikanec* choke, and listen to the wheezing sound that issued from his tortured chest. When he emitted an especially long wheeze, the boys looked at one another in wonder and smiled.

In this respect I was no better than the other boys, until Mother forbade me to go near Peter Molek when he coughed. Then I watched him from the distance. Our house was only a couple of hundred yards from Molek's.

But occasionally, when he was not coughing, I walked by him. I wanted to talk with him, but could not work up enough courage to address him first.

One day he smiled faintly and said to me, "You are the neighbor's boy, aren't you?"

"Yes," I said. "My father remembers you when you went to America."

Peter Molek nodded his head. "That was a long time ago," he said.

"Why do you cough like you do all the time?" I asked.

Peter Molek did not answer for a while. He stared at me in a way that made me uneasy. Then he looked away and swung one of his large bony hands in a vague gesture. "America," he said. ". . . America."

I did not know what he meant.

"How old are you?" Peter Molek asked me.

"Ten," I said. "Soon I'll be eleven. I am going to city school in the fall."

Peter Molek smiled again and nodded his head. "You are *all right*." He said "all right" in English.

"I know what that means—'*all right*,'" I said, eagerly. "It means 'good' in the American language. I have often heard other men who came from America say '*all right*.' I also know other American words. '*Sure Mike!*' . . . '*Sonabitch*.' . . ." I was pleased with my knowledge.

Peter Molek peered at me from under his eyebrows. He seemed to want to touch me, but probably was afraid that I might draw away from him because he was a sick man. "You are *all right*," he said again.

I was delighted with his approval. . . .

Then I said, "Some day I am going to America."

Peter Molek looked at me, startled. He was about to say something, when another asthmatic spasm seized him. . . .

"This is what America did to me," said Peter Molek, after he had stopped coughing.

"What does this mean?" I said, pointing at the title of a book on the bench.

"*The Jungle*," said Peter Molek. "That means *dzhungla* in Slovenian."

I did not even know what *dzhungla* meant. The forests around Blato were neat, thinned-out, idyllic groves where one went to pick berries or gather mushrooms.

"A jungle," Peter Molek explained, "is a wild place, a great forest, all tangled up with vegetation, everything growing crisscross, almost impenetrable, mysterious and terrible, infested with beasts and snakes, and spiders bigger than my fist. . . . This is a book about the United States, although there are no jungles in the United States, so far as I know. But the whole of America is a jungle. This is a story about people like me—foreigners—who go there and are swallowed by the jungle. Understand?"

I nodded in the affirmative, but I did not really understand.

"America swallowed me," continued Peter Molek, "but she did not digest me." He smiled, as if to himself, a peculiar, mirthless smile.

Peter Molek went on: "America the jungle swallows many people who go there to work. She squeezes the strength out of them, unless they are wise or lucky enough to escape before it is too late; unless they work in the mills or the mines only a few years and save every cent they can and return home, or buy themselves a piece of land where land is still cheap."

* * * *

"But for some people America is not a bad place," said Peter Molek one day. "Many foreigners have greatly bettered themselves there, but these fortunate ones are few when compared with the multitude of immigrants who, I believe, would be better off had they remained in the old country. American industries use them, then cast them off."

"More people go to America all the time," I said. Lately I had read in a newspaper to which my father subscribed that four thousand more persons had emigrated from Carniola to the United States in 1908 than in 1907.

"Yes," said Peter Molek. "They go because each thinks that he will get the better of America and not America the better of him. They listen to the few who return home from the United States with two or three thousand dollars. They hear that some one else who stayed there has succeeded on a big scale. And they think they will do the same. America is the Land of Promise to them. She lures them over by the thousands and hundreds of thousands—people from many countries, not only from Carniola. She needs their hands even more than they need her dollars, and makes use of them. Once upon a time immigrants were called 'dung' in America; that was a good name for them. They were the fertilizer feeding the roots of America's present and future greatness. They are still 'dung.' The roots of America's greatness still feed on them. . . . Life in America is a scramble. More people are swept under than rise to riches."

Mary Antin, a Russian Woman, Encounters Anti-Semitic Violence and Flees Russia, 1912

The next year or so my father spent in a restless and fruitless search for a permanent position. My mother had another serious illness, and his own health remained precarious. What he earned did not more than half pay the bills in the end, though we were living very humbly now. . . .

Just at this time occurred one of the periodic anti-Semitic movements whereby government officials were wont to clear the forbidden cities of Jews, whom, in the intervals of slack administration of the law, they allowed to maintain an illegal residence in places outside the Pale, on payment of enormous bribes and at the cost of nameless risks and indignities.

It was a little before Passover that the cry of the hunted thrilled the Jewish world with the familiar fear. The wholesale expulsion of Jews from Moscow and its surrounding district at cruelly short notice was the name of this latest disaster. Where would the doom strike next? The Jews who lived illegally without the Pale turned their possessions into cash and slept in their clothes, ready for immediate flight. Those who lived in the comparative security of the Pale trembled for their

---

As found in Mary Antin, *The Promised Land,* second edition (Princeton, NJ: Princeton University Press, 1969).

brothers and sisters without, and opened wide their doors to afford the fugitives refuge. And hundreds of fugitives, preceded by a wail of distress, flocked into the open district, bringing their trouble where trouble was never absent, mingling their tears with the tears that never dried.

The open cities becoming thus suddenly crowded, every man's chance of making a living was diminished in proportion to the number of additional competitors. Hardship, acute distress, ruin for many: thus spread the disaster, ring beyond ring, from the stone thrown by a despotic official into the ever-full river of Jewish persecution.

Passover was celebrated in tears that year. In the story of the Exodus we would have read a chapter of current history, only for us there was no deliverer and no promised land.

But what said some of us at the end of the long service? Not "May we be next year in Jerusalem," but "Next year—in America!" So there was our promised land, and many faces were turned towards the West. And if the waters of the Atlantic did not part for them, the wanderers rode its bitter flood by a miracle as great as any the rod of Moses ever wrought.

My father was carried away by the westward movement, glad of his own deliverance, but sore at heart for us whom he left behind. It was the last chance for all of us. We were so far reduced in circumstances that he had to travel with borrowed money to a German port, whence he was forwarded to Boston, with a host of others, at the expense of an emigrant aid society.

I was about ten years old when my father emigrated. I was used to his going away from home, and "America" did not mean much more to me than "Kherson," or "Odessa," or any other names of distant places. I understood vaguely, from the gravity with which his plans were discussed, and from references to ships, societies, and other unfamiliar things, that this enterprise was different from previous ones; but my excitement and emotion on the morning of my father's departure were mainly vicarious.

I know the day when "America" as a world entirely unlike Polotzk lodged in my brain, to become the centre of all my dreams and speculations. Well I know the day. I was in bed, sharing the measles with some of the other children. Mother brought us a thick letter from father, written just before boarding the ship. The letter was full of excitement. There was something in it besides the description of travel, something besides the pictures of crowds of people, of foreign cities, of a ship ready to put out to sea. My father was travelling at the expense of a charitable organization, without means of his own, without plans, to a strange world where he had no friends; and yet he wrote with the confidence of a well-equipped soldier going into battle. The rhetoric is mine. Father simply wrote that the emigration committee was taking good care of everybody, that the weather was fine, and the ship comfortable. But I heard something, as we read the letter together in the darkened room, that was more than the words seemed to say. There was an elation, a hint of triumph, such as had never been in my father's letters before. I cannot tell how I knew it. I felt a stirring, a straining in my father's letter. It was there, even though my mother stumbled over strange words, even though she cried, as women will when somebody is going away. My father was inspired by a vision. He saw something—he promised us something. It was this "America." And "America" became my dream.

* * * *

I am sure I made as serious efforts as anybody to prepare myself for life in America on the lines indicated in my father's letters. In America, he wrote, it was no disgrace to work at a trade. Workmen and capitalists were equal. The employer addressed the employee as *you,* not, familiarly, as *thou.* The cobbler and the teacher had the same title, "Mister." And all the children, boys and girls, Jews and Gentiles, went to school! Education would be ours for the asking, and economic independence also, as soon as we were prepared. . . .

* * * *

. . . My father's letters warned us to prepare for the summons [to move to America], and we lived in a quiver of expectation.

Not that my father had grown suddenly rich. He was so far from rich that he was going to borrow every cent of the money for our third-class passage; but he had a business in view which he could carry on all the better for having the family with him; and, besides, we were borrowing right and left anyway, and to no definite purpose. With the children, he argued, every year in Russia was a year lost. They should be spending the precious years in school, in learning English, in becoming Americans. United in America, there were ten chances of our getting to our feet again to one chance in our scattered, aimless state.

So at last I was going to America! Really, really going, at last! The boundaries burst. The arch of heaven soared. A million suns shone out for every star. The winds rushed in from outer space, roaring in my ears, "America! America!"

Mexican Ballads Justify and Condemn Immigration, 1924

An Emigrant's Farewell

Good-bye, my beloved country,
Now I am going away;
I go to the United States,
Where I intend to work.
Good-bye, my beloved mother,
The Virgin of Guadalupe;
Good-bye, my beloved land,
My Mexican Republic!

I go sad and heavy-hearted
To suffer and endure;
My Mother Guadalupe,
Grant my safe return.

Mexico is my homeland
Where I was born a Mexican;
Give me your benediction
With your powerful hand.

From María Herrera-Sobek, *Northward Bound: The Mexican Experience in Ballad and Song,* copyright © 1993. Reprinted by permission of Indiana University Press.

I go to the United States
To seek to earn a living.
Good-bye, my beloved land;
I bear you in my heart!

For I am not to blame
That I leave my country thus;
The fault lies in the poverty,
Which keeps us all in want. . . .

The Northerners

The northerners have come
From the (U.S.) border
All are showing off
Thinking they are top dogs.

Because now they're wearing pants
They think they are dandies
They left barefooted
And now they show off their half boots.

They're also wearing a vest
With a false collar and a coat
Even if they wear frock coats
They are still lower-class dudes.

They go to the railroad stations
And ask the clerk
(To prove how learned they are),
Give me a "ticket," Mister.

Ask me for a ticket here
You are not in a foreign country
We speak Spanish here
Don't speak to me in dog language.

To tell the truth, it's really funny
Those recent arrivals,
Who think just because they're wearing a shirt
They are learned people.

Don't believe that because you travel
Back and forth to foreign cities
Your peasant background
Is going to disappear.

When they go up north
They tell their wives:
"In order to have enough money for my transportation
I am going to sell the house."

"Believe me, God will provide.
From the U.S. I will send you
Many a handful of money
So that you can spend it here."

If their wife is faithful
She suffers and waits,
But if she has few scruples
She cuckolds him.

How do you think they'll look
With those goat horns?
Just stop to think
If what I say is not the truth.

Chinese Immigrants Explain Their Migration and Lament Their Detention, 1910–1940

As a rule, a person is twenty before he starts making a living.
Family circumstances have forced me to experience wind and dust.[1]
The heartless months and years seem bent on defeating me.
It is a pity that time quickly ages one.

The gold and silver of America is very appealing.
Jabbing an awl into the thigh[2] in search of glory,
I embarked on the journey.
Not only are my one-thousand pieces of gold already depleted, but
My countenance is blackened. It is surely for the sake of the family.

For what reason must I sit in jail?
It is only because my country is weak and my family poor.
My parents wait at the door but there is no news.
My wife and child wrap themselves in quilt, sighing with loneliness.
Even if my petition is approved and I can enter the country,
When can I return to the Mountains of Tang[3] with a full load?
From ancient times, those who venture out usually become worthless.
How many people ever return from battles?

From *Island: Poetry and History of Chinese Immigrants on Angel Island, 1910–1940*, Him Mark Lai, Genny Lim, and Judy Yung. Copyright © 1991. Reprinted by permission of the University of Washington Press.

[1] I.e., the rigors of travel.

[2] Su Qin (?–317 B.C.), a scholar during the period of the Warring States (403–221 B.C.), was unsuccessful in gaining a post in the courts upon finishing his studies. Returning home, the contempt of his family drove him to study harder. To keep awake at night, he would hold an awl over a thigh so that as he became drowsy, his hand would drop, jabbing the awl into his flesh. Later, Su Qin became the prime minister to six states concurrently. The expression, thus, means to make a determined effort.

[3] A Cantonese colloquial term for China.

People from Doumen[4] are going to Daxidi,[5]
Having been in the wooden building for more than ten days.
From Daxidi, there are people returning to the Mountains of Tang.
How were they to know this would be such a callous city?
There are people returning and there are people leaving.
Having wasted over three-hundred silver dollars,
If I do not get to this city, I will be unhappy.
If I return home, my parents would be extremely grief-torn.
Unpaid interest would be piled one on top of another,
Not knowing when it would be repaid to the lender.

E S S A Y S

Immigration to America with the intent to return home profoundly affected both the homelands of the immigrants and the United States. Historian Dino Cinel, of the City University of New York, writing in 1982, explores the connections between American money and Italian land for immigrants from Italy in the period from 1870 to 1930. He argues that immigration to the United States was part of a strategy for achieving goals in Italy. Only about one-quarter of the Italian immigrants who emigrated said they were leaving Italy for good. Instead, these immigrants were leaving their country to make money and return home with greater material wealth. Sucheng Chan, of the University of California at Santa Barbara, illustrates how the Chinese immigration to the United States in the second half of the twentieth century was only part of a larger diaspora that had connected the coastal region of southern China to immigrant communities in many countries for centuries prior to 1850 (1986). Many of these immigrants were skilled miners who found their way to "gold mountain." This long-standing strategy of using migration to better the conditions of family members who remained at home, Chan argues, was made more urgent by the chaos in south China in the nineteenth century. It was also made more difficult, she concludes, by the hostility that Chinese immigrants encountered on the West Coast of the United States.

The Relationship Between American Money and Italian Land in Stimulating Return Migration

DINO CINEL

Even when undertaken under the most favorable of circumstances, emigration brings about major changes in the lives of individuals and groups. From the 1870's to the 1920's several million Italians opened themselves to such changes by leaving their villages for North or South America. Their decision to leave may be sur-

---

Reprinted from *From Italy to San Francisco: The Immigrant Experience* by Dino Cinel with the permission of the publishers. Stanford University Press. © 1982 by the Board of Trustees of the Leland Stanford Junior University.

[4]An area in the southwest of the Pearl River Delta, Doumen was formerly part of the Zhongshan district. Today, it forms a separate district.

[5]Tahiti? Identification of place is uncertain.

prising if we recall that those emigrants were the same people Coletti described as imbued with a transcendent resistance to change. What forces, we may ask, broke that resistance and drove them to cross the Atlantic? Or perhaps another hypothesis comes nearer to the mark: that emigration was not so drastic a change as it seems, after all, but only the continuation of trends already present among the Italians of the late nineteenth century.

Most immigration historians of the last two decades would agree with John Briggs in discarding the notion that immigrants "were Old World minds and souls who either clung irrationally and at an unreasonable cost to an irrelevant past, or who submitted passively to the powerful forces shaping their future." On the contrary, most accept that "immigrants were rational, confident, capable, and talented individuals who contributed to shaping their future rather than receiving their destinies wholly defined and packaged by others." Some historians have attempted to demonstrate the active role of the immigrants by pointing to patterns of continuity between the immigrants' lives in the Old World and the New. The emphasis, however, has been on the New World. Apart from the fact that the immigrants were poor, we learn little about how the social dynamics of the Old World shaped the immigrant experience.

To show continuity, moreover, it is not enough simply to document that certain Italian social institutions and patterns of living were similar in both Italy and America. This approach, in my opinion, uses marginal evidence to prove a central point. It seems obvious that any group of people forced to live in a strange land will seek security by trying to preserve some continuity with its past. But such efforts by immigrants to protect themselves were only palliatives masking the central fact that separation from the home country implied a basic break with it. To see a deeper continuity in the immigrants' lives we have to address this central question: was emigration only an apparent break with the past, despite the geographical distance between Italy and America? From this perspective, we will see that emigration was a strategy for achieving goals in Italy. It was an act in the larger drama of social change in late-nineteenth-century Italian society.

* * * *

The prolonged agricultural depression from the mid-1880's through the 1890's hit the peasants hard. In the late 1880's the prefetto of Genoa reported: "The cost of oil and other items is so high that people are forced to leave for overseas to avoid starvation." In the province of Cosenza the conditions were described as "extremely precarious," and those in Verbicaro as "alarming." Crops failed in 1889, 1890, and 1893 in most communes of the province; during the winter of 1893–94 the people of several communities survived by eating roots. In the spring of 1894 the prefetto wrote: "People are leaving in large numbers; they think they have no alternative, and they are unwilling to face another winter here. Poverty seems to have broken their will to fight. Their departure is like the flight of people who have nothing to lose by going."

In Palermo at the end of 1888 the prefetto cabled Rome: "Conditions were bad last year. I have only to add that this year they are worse, and that starvation is forcing the peasants to go, although most of them are reluctant to make that decision." The reports arriving in Rome from Palermo between 1888 and 1893 informed the government that wages were decreasing, foodstuffs were unavailable in a number of communes in the interior, and cholera epidemics were breaking out. The production of olive oil, a major commodity in the local economy, was falling off because of foreign competition and damage to the olive groves by an unknown disease. Fishing too was hurt by the depression. In 1895 the mayor of Santa Flavia reported: "The fishermen of this town are forced to leave. The basic reason is that they cannot sell their catch. There is simply no cash in the region, and commerce has come to a standstill."

The American Fever

Under these circumstances, it is no surprise that America became a household word. An American visitor to the south wrote: "There was constant talk of America on the trains, on the roads, and in towns. In a small southern town I saw a great throng of people. Upon inquiring, I was told that they had been to the station to say goodbye to 120 of their townsmen who had just left for America." Even in the most isolated communities, emigration to America was the topic of lively discussion. There were people who could name the President of the United States but not the King of Italy. In 1896 the prefetto of Palermo reported: "America seems to have an irresistible attraction for these people. Sicilians have traditionally been unwilling to leave the island, even to go to Italy. But America seems to be different. Or is it that they leave because they have no alternative, and anything is an improvement over their present condition in Sicily?"

Adolfo Rossi, the commissioner of emigration, asked the president of an agricultural society in the province of Cosenza why America had become so popular in just a few years. The president answered: "Life was impossible here. When the first pioneers came back with money and told the peasants that it was possible to make a living across the ocean, desperation turned into hope. Why shouldn't they go? Or more to the point, do these people have other alternatives? America has become a disease, but out of necessity." Letters from America and reports by returnees had a profound impact. The prefetto of Palermo, after visiting a ship about to leave for New Orleans, wrote: "There were over 300 people departing. As I talked to several of them, I realized that the most powerful arguments in favor of leaving had been the stories they heard from returnees and the fact that they had no alternatives left. It is either starvation or emigration." A peasant was reported to have said: "If America did not exist, we would have to invent it for the sake of our survival."

In addition to letters from America and stories told by returnees, the work of emigration agents was important in making emigration a mass movement even from remote villages. These agents, acting on behalf of Italian and foreign shipping companies and immigration agencies abroad, promoted the idea of emigration and also arranged for the departure of those who wanted to go. In the northern provinces emigration agents distributed pamphlets and made public appearances at local celebrations. In 1884 there were 34 agencies in the city of Genoa, employing several hundred agents throughout the province. The prefetto reported that promoters of emigration to California were active in Fontanabuona, Sestri Levante, and Lorsica. Apparently, there were fewer emigration agents in the province of Lucca.

The prefetto notified the Minister of the Interior that some were active in the southern communes of the province. But in the northern communes of Lucca the idea of emigration was mainly spread by word of mouth. The southern communes of Genoa province, such as Varese Ligure and Lignano, were only twenty miles north of the northernmost communes of Lucca, such as Giuncugnano, Sillano, and Minucciano.

In the southern provinces, where literacy was rarer and outsiders not readily accepted, emigration was promoted by other means. Large posters were put up; agents were more often local people than in the north; and local leaders were paid by the agents to provide lists of families in great poverty. The prefetto of Cosenza described how agents came to a celebration in Orsomarso, ten miles from Verbicaro: "Early in the morning, they erected a podium in the town square. From it, they addressed the people, offering explanations and especially dispelling doubts whenever peasants approached them and showed an interest in leaving."

The rapid increase in emigration in the 1870's and 1880's, along with the widespread poverty of Italian peasants, suggests that departing Italians had little time to make plans, that they were forced to leave by events beyond their control. The vigorous activity of the emigration agents, who sent Italians overseas according to the demands of the American markets, and the interests of the shipping companies, seems to support the idea that departing Italians were at the mercy of outside forces. On the surface, then, emigration seems a sudden, unplanned change, rather than a gradual and deliberate response to long-term social dynamics.

. . . It is possible, in a general way, to divide Italy into areas with low and high rates of emigration. The areas of low emigration were the Emilia-Romagna region, located south of the Po River and stretching from the Tyrrhenian Sea to the Adriatic, with the exception of the three provinces of Modena, Parma, and Piacenza; the central regions, like Tuscany, Marche, Umbria, and Lazio, with the exception of the province of Lucca; the Apulia region, located in the southeast; the Sicilian hinterland; and the island of Sardinia. The areas of high emigration were all the regions north of the Po; the three provinces of Modena, Parma, and Piacenza; the province of Lucca; except for Apulia, all the regions of the south, such as Abruzzi, Campania, Basilicata, and Calabria; and the coastal areas of Sicily. The four provinces of Genoa, Lucca, Cosenza, and Palermo all fall into this second category.

The evidence does not justify the conclusion that the regions of high emigration were poorer than those of low emigration. . . .

The Returnees

If neither poverty nor the other factors mentioned can explain the differing rates of emigration from Italy, where does the answer lie? A clue may be found in the rate of return migration. After 1901 Italians applying for a passport had to declare whether they intended to stay abroad indefinitely or to return. The names of those leaving for good were canceled from the communal population registers, the names of the others retained. On the average, less than 25 percent of the emigrants declared that they intended to stay abroad. In 1909, for instance, 22 percent of all emigrants were canceled from the communal registers. The percentage was even lower in previous years, and in both 1912 and 1913 only 19 percent of the emigrants were canceled. Of course, a declaration of intent is not a guarantee of what will happen, but it is a strong indication.

Emigrants who had thus been canceled from the communal registers, if they returned to Italy, could apply for reregistration. The number of those reregistering was high, especially compared with the number canceled. In the two years 1908–9, for instance, when 243,000 Italians were canceled, a total of 155,000 asked to be reregistered; that is, 64 reregistered for every 100 canceled. In 1912 there were 48 reregistrations per 100 cancellations. The following year the ratio was 39 per 100. To summarize, over 75 percent of the Italians who left declared their intention of returning; and every year, for every two emigrants who declared their intention to stay abroad permanently, one emigrant who had made the same declaration before departing reestablished his domicile in Italy after a residence of one or more years abroad.

✳ ✳ ✳

Was it nostalgia for Italy that brought immigrants back in such large numbers? [Robert] Foerster seems to support this idea. The Italian's affections, he wrote, "are warm and deep, attaching him to the family and the scenes of his childhood. When he breaks from these tugging intimacies, it is conditionally, not absolutely. He must live in them again, and he departs only that he may live in them more richly than before. Life abroad is strange and difficult for the unsheltered Italian, who tolerates it only for the promise of the return to Italy."

In reality, Italian emigrants were not the nostalgic people Foerster made them out to be. In Calabria in the early 1900's a large number of returnees were polled, including many contemplating emigration for a second or third time. Nostalgia was seldom mentioned as a reason to come back to Italy. Most returnees said their decision to return to Italy had been based on economic plans made before they had departed for the first time. Emigration and return, then, were not decisions Italians took lightly. The returnees were for the most part neither rejected by American society nor spurred by nostalgia. Rather they were individuals actively pursuing goals they had set before departing.

Americans noticed the phenomenon of return migration, and they did not look upon it with favor. Italian migrants in the United States, and in Europe too, were called "birds of passage." An American who studied several hundred Italian migrants wrote in 1913: "Many Italians come in the spring to work during the summer, when public works are undertaken, and return to Europe in the fall when the demand for labor diminishes. . . . In many cases immigrants have visited this country five, six, seven times, and cases of two, three, and four visits are common." An Italian traveler reported on what he deemed the American impression of temporary migrants: "They come in the spring to escape poverty in Italy, they compete with our workers and accept minimal wages, and when winter comes they leave like birds of passage."

The writer Giuseppe Giacosa, after crossing the Atlantic with a group of Italians en route to Texas, reported: "The children were in Italy with the grandparents because, it was understood, everybody intended to return. It was common everywhere in America." Many of the Italians in Cleveland "dreamed of returning to Italy one day to establish themselves as independent farmers or small businessmen." The Italian consuls in New York, Boston, and New Orleans all reported high return migration rates. Foerster wrote: "After 1870, for the first time, it became evident that, following a somewhat indeterminate state, many Italians repacked their chattels and went home again. No previous immigrants in this land of promise had done that." Immigrants of other nationalities did change their minds: for every 100 immigrants who entered the United States from 1908 to 1924, 38 were repatriated. But of all the larger groups of immigrants, the Italians showed a much greater tendency to return home.

✷ ✷ ✷ ✷

. . . northerners usually returned only after a long absence and did not necessarily settle in their original communities; and reemigration seems to have been less frequent in the north than in the south. In the south, emigration ordinarily lasted from three to five years; returnees settled in their original towns, and reemigration was common. The mayor of Santa Flavia wrote: "Emigrants usually return after three to four years. Those who cross the Atlantic every year are not exceptional. And most of those who come back cross the Atlantic again sooner or later." As the prefetto of Cosenza put it: "There are a few who stay in America more than five years. But reemigration is the rule."

Land Tenure, Emigration, and Militancy

Why did so many emigrate from the provinces of Lucca, Genoa, Cosenza, and Palermo, and so few from Forli, Florence, Lecce, and Syracuse—at least until the First World War? And why did so many emigrants return and then reemigrate? The answers to these questions are suggested by several statements dealing with two regions in the south.

A social scientist from Cosenza wrote in 1883:

> One of the main characteristics of the economy of the south, and especially of this province, is the supply of land. When feudal land tenure came to an end with the ordinances of 1810 and 1811, the Kingdom of the Two Sicilies began dividing public land among the peasants. But the division did not go very far. It was only after 1860 that the division of public land was actively promoted. There is still a long way to go, and peasants are excited about the possibility of becoming landowners; but very few can afford to buy. Moreover, even those who have the money are often forced to resell because of a lack of funds for necessary improvements or for paying the mortgage.

As Luigi Izzo noted, in a study of the Calabria region: "The supply of land exceeded the demand. Land was available for everyone, of course for a price." Ettore Blandini, the director of the agency for setting up homesteads in Cosenza, supervised the sale of 500 acres of land in the province in 1900. Once placed on the market, the land was sold within a month. Blandini later wrote that "90 percent of the land was purchased with money coming from the United States." Most buyers, he added, were either farmers who had never owned land or small landowners whose purpose in going to America had been to enlarge holdings too small to support a family. The sale of land, he concluded, came to an end in 1926 "as a result of the end of the free emigration to the United States and the consequent decline in savings arriving in the province from America."

In the province of Palermo, in contrast, the mayor of Santa Cristina wrote: "Some people migrated to America from this commune. But when they came back and realized that they could not buy land because it was not for sale, they left forever. Few followed them, since there is no hope of buying land when they return. Those who come back and want to stay invest their savings in a house; but there are only a few such people." The mayor of Piana dei Greci wrote: "Returnees are disappointed because they cannot convince landlords to sell them land. Unfortunately, there are no small properties in this town; this is a region of large estates. Frustrated in their hope of buying land, returnees leave forever. But since land is not for sale, only a few emigrate at all." And the prefetto of Palermo wrote: "Not many peasants leave from the hinterland, which is the area of large estates. Emigration and return migration from the coastal communities are intense; this is an area of small properties, and returnees ordinarily invest in land."

This seems to have been the general pattern in all Italy: emigration and return migration were much more frequent where land was for sale than where it was not. The land tenure system, then, is important to an understanding of emigration. In the late nineteenth century, two different systems of land tenure were present in Italy, with a virtually endless variety of regional adaptations. In one system, the large estate predominated and little buying and selling of land went on; in the other, small and medium-sized landholding predominated and there was an active market for land. These two systems of land tenure derived from the ways that feudalism had come to an end in different regions, and the differences between the systems increased as a result of the sale of land promoted by the new government of the united Italy.

The end of feudalism in Italy is a confused story because the laws abrogating feudalism in the various Italian states in the early nineteenth century were neither promulgated at the same time nor implemented in the same way. In general, the end of feudalism in Emilia-Romagna, Tuscany, Marche, Umbria, Lazio, Apulia, and the hinterland of Sicily and Sardinia did not bring about the subdivision of large holdings. Rather, it encouraged the transformation of the great landlords into owners and operators of estates. In those regions, as late as 1880, most land was worked by sharefarmers or gang laborers. Under the sharefarming system, every family received a relatively self-sufficient farm with a farmhouse. Small independent landholdings were rare in these regions and always threatened by large holdings. This system of land tenure, therefore, brought about a pyramidal social structure with a few large-scale entrepreneurs and a large class of sharefarmers and laborers.

In other parts of Italy, though the end of feudalism did not bring the subdivision of all large estates, it did lead to the creation of a large number of small and medium-sized holdings. The result was a process of buying and selling land that became irreversible. This occurred mainly in the regions north of the Po River; the provinces of Lucca, Piacenza, Parma, and Modena; the regions of Campania, Abruzzi, Basilicata, and Calabria; and the coastal area of Sicily. In these areas the predominant unit was the small farm, which was cultivated by the owner and his nuclear family household, rather than the extended family household that ordinarily served as the labor force on large estates. The mixture of small, medium, and large holdings in these areas prevented the formation of a clear-cut pyramidal hierarchy, and a more differentiated society developed, based on the intense buying and selling of land and the consequent competition among peasants. Contrary to common opinion, there were few large estates in regions of high emigration, such as Basilicata, Calabria, and Campania; this was pointed out as early as 1911 in the survey on conditions in the south, and later documented in studies of entrepreneurial activity in Italy.

The breakup of church, state, and communal land increased the differences between the regions of large estates and those of small and medium holdings. Church land was confiscated by a series of laws passed from 1862 to 1873. Land that had belonged to the former Italian states was put up for sale by the new national government, both to offset the national debt and to increase the number of small landholders. Communal land—that owned by the communes—had been used in feudal times to support the poor. Land from these three sources was divided into almost 300,000 parcels that were put up for sale between 1861 and 1899. Since there were fewer than half a million landowners in Italy in 1881, the availability of 300,000 additional small farms had a national impact. The Società Anonima, the agency supervising land distribution on behalf of the government, divided the land into very small tracts of two to four acres each, as the 1867 law required, in order to offer as many peasants as possible the chance to become landowners.

This goal of redistribution was not achieved everywhere. In the regions where small and medium properties were the rule, the sale of land increased the number of small holdings; but where large estates dominated, the sale increased the size of large estates. Although the letter and spirit of the law required that landholdings be sold to any propertyless peasant who could make a down payment, large landowners often bribed the officials supervising the sale or forced peasants who had bought land out of the market. Thus much of the newly distributed land was incorporated into large estates.

The two different systems of land tenure arising out of the end of feudalism and the sale of public land had important political effects on the peasantry. In regions where small and medium holdings prevailed, and thus where the buying and selling of land was intense, peasants found themselves competing to purchase available land; their main concern was how to generate the necessary cash. In the regions of large estates, the polarization between the few landowners and the many sharefarmers and laborers led to peasant militancy, inspired largely by Marxist socialism, syndicalism, and anarchism.

These differences help explain the phenomenon of emigration. In the regions of small properties, where there was land for sale and farmers were in competition, emigration became the way to generate cash to buy land. In the regions of large estates, with no land for sale, peasant militancy rather than emigration was seen as the solution. Militant farmers organized to obtain better contracts and working conditions, to prevent layoffs and lockouts, and most of all to increase their earnings. Only rarely did this militancy bring about land division, which was sometimes used by landowners or the government as a political strategy to defuse militancy.

Although most observers saw Italian emigration as simply the flight from poverty, a few perceptive students did not fail to notice the relationship between land tenure, emigration, and militancy. As early as 1863 Giovanni Massari and Stefano Castagnola, in a study of banditry in the south, pointed out that "where holdings are large and controlled by a few people, land is simply not available, even for those who can afford it, and unrest is high." In the province of Foggia, in the Apulia region, where a handful of families virtually owned the entire territory, at least 8,000 bandits kept the province in a state of permanent unrest. Twenty years later, analyzing the explosive situation in Sicily, the deputy Napoleone Colajanni observed: "I do not think that Sicily can be spared a rebellion by peasants. [A rebellion occurred only a few months later.] I am aware that in the hinterland of Sicily, where landholdings are large and most peasants are laborers, hatred has no limits and will lead to a revolution. A handful of landowners control the region, and small landholdings are not for sale." In 1890 Massimo Pestalozza held that the creation of small properties was the best way to defuse peasant militancy, since competition among peasants would eliminate mass unrest.

A survey by the Italian Association of Farmers in 1900 clearly showed a high incidence of unionism and strikes in Emilia-Romagna, Apulia, and the hinterland of Sicily, all areas of large estates and low emigration rates. At the same time, unionism and strikes were rare in Liguria, in the province of Lucca, in the Basilicata and Calabria regions, and along the coast of Sicily, all areas of small properties and high emigration rates; "in these areas," the study concluded, "emigration is a substitute for militancy." Within regions, too, this pattern could be seen. Ernesto Marenghi, an astute observer of Italian society, wrote of Calabria: "Emigration started in towns marked by small properties in the early 1880's. Soon it became a mass phenomenon. But in the areas of large estates—like Crotone—emigration started only after the turn of the century and involved only a few people." The province of Cosenza, for instance, had many small properties, and generally a high emigration rate; but from the few pockets of large estates in the province, the emigration rate was low.

Coletti, in a comprehensive study of Italian emigration, thus summarized the difference between a region of high emigration and the most militant region in Italy at the time: "In Calabria emigration occurs because land is available and the biggest problem is the lack of cash. In Emilia-Romagna the problem is sociopolitical; land is simply not available and peasants stay to bring about change." After visiting Calabria in 1907, Leonello De Nobili noted: "Peasant organizations are weak in these provinces. As we well know, unionism is strong in Apulia, Emilia-Romagna, and the hinterland of Sicily. Where peasants are organized, they refuse to leave." De Nobili was obviously sympathetic to the peasants who remained and fought; but he failed to take into account that they did not have the option of leaving and returning to purchase land in their own region. Their only solution was permanent emigration, and most peasants did not choose that course.

The four provinces of Genoa, Lucca, Cosenza, and, in part, Palermo, were all areas where there was land for sale, almost negligible peasant unionism, and a high rate of emigration; but they differed in the availability of land. Much more land was available in the south than in the north, which helps to explain why return migration was greater in the south than in the north, and why northern returnees stayed abroad a longer time than southerners.

The province of Genoa illustrates these tendencies. As early as 1861 the Chamber of Commerce of Genoa described the local agricultural economy as one of small properties and intense buying and selling of land. By seasonal migration to the Po Plains, many Genoese earned enough to purchase or enlarge small land-holdings. The commerce in land continued throughout the 1870's and 1880's, but the demand for land far exceeded the supply. Returnees could buy land only from small landowners who for one reason or another wanted, or were forced, to sell their property. But these sellers were few: even those who left for the New World generally refused to sell. Meanwhile, there was little land for sale by the government after the 1860's. Thus returnees to Genoa in the late nineteenth century had a hard time finding land to buy. This might explain why the Genoese emigrants stayed overseas longer than southerners: they were trying to save enough money so that they could either live on their savings or open a business in the rapidly growing Ligurian economy. For either of these purposes emigrants needed a larger sum of money than that needed to buy a few acres of land.

In Lucca in the late 1870's there was land for sale, but few had the money for a down payment. Nor were banks willing to assist peasants who wanted to become landowners. About a decade later, however, the prefetto of Lucca reported that the demand for small landholdings, stimulated by the arrival of American savings, far exceeded the supply. Many returnees, the report concluded, were leaving permanently because they were frustrated in their desire to buy land.

There seems to have been more land available in the two southern provinces than in the north. From 1860 to 1880, 3,700 families purchased a total of over 10,000 acres of land in the Calabria region, mostly with American savings. As we have seen, after 1860 the sale of public land was promoted in the south; and in Cosenza land was generally available to those who could afford the price. In Palermo the buying and selling of land along the coast was among the most intense in the nation, despite a complaint by the prefetto in 1891 that a sound system of credit was lacking.

Internal Migration as a Model

If Italians wanted land, one may ask, why did they not stay in America, where land was more plentiful and fertile than in Italy. Some did, of course, but to the great majority the idea had no appeal. According to Coletti, some emigration agents told peasants there was plenty of land across the ocean; but the negative reaction convinced the agents to drop the suggestion. "When peasants cross the ocean," Coletti wrote, "they have only one goal: to come back and buy land in Italy. A piece of land somewhere else, no matter how fertile and large, does not interest them. When they return, they buy land regardless of the price. It is like a ritual the peasants think they have to perform; only in one's native village, where one's ancestors lived and died, does owning land have meaning." A peasant in the province of Cosenza told an interviewer: "This is the only true land. We can live somewhere else for a while. But we can buy land only here." Adolfo Rossi, the Italian commissioner of emigration, described a conversation he had with Rosa Granata, a peasant woman from Calabria. She explained how her marriage had ended when her husband Rosario, who had gone to South America, asked her to sell the two acres the family owned and join him across the ocean. She had refused to go, concluding: "Land in America is not good enough. This is the only land we can buy. I will never go."

Coletti wrote at length about how the psychology of Italians made them reluctant to accept any change that would separate them from their communities. The peasants' world view was limited to the world they knew, around their villages. They would accept change only in order to cope with a temporary emergency such as a family problem. But any lasting solution had to be found at home. In Italy this attitude was not unique to peasants; Italian society at large resisted for years the idea of permanent emigration. The Italian Bureau of Statistics had two categories of emigration: temporary and permanent. By temporary, the bureau meant emigration for less than a year; by permanent, it meant emigration of several years' duration. There was no word to indicate the definitive departure for another country—in Italy the concept did not exist.

The Chinese Migration to the United States in the Context of the Larger Chinese Diaspora

SUCHENG CHAN

The Chinese who came to California in the second half of the nineteenth century were but one branch of a much larger emigrant stream. Their migration was roughly contemporaneous with the infamous "coolie trade" to Peru and Cuba (1847–74) and the movement of Chinese from 1852 onward to join the gold rush in Australia. These nineteenth-century migrations represented a new stage in the long history of Chinese emigration.

Emigration as an aspect of Chinese history has frequently been overlooked because historians and the Chinese themselves have tended to view China as an inward-looking agrarian society. Students of the overseas Chinese, however, have been quite aware of the fact that certain groups of Chinese have been among the world's great migratory peoples. As a matter of fact, Chinese have emigrated to so many parts of the world that it is possible to speak of a Chinese diaspora, of which Chinese emigration to the United States was but one small segment.

Seaborne Chinese migration was a continuation of the overland movement over many centuries of the Han Chinese people who expanded from the Yellow River valley of northern China southward to populate contiguous territory. One stream of migrants went in a southwesterly direction and settled in the area that became the provinces of Szechwan, Kweichou, and Yunnan, while a second, southeasterly movement of peoples brought what are now the provinces of Kwangsi,

From Sucheng Chan, *This Bittersweet Soil: The Chinese in California Agriculture, 1860–1910*. Copyright 1986 The Regents of the University of California Press. Reprinted by permission of the University of California Press and Sucheng Chan.

Kwangtung, and Fukien under Chinese jurisdiction. The latter came under firm Chinese control only during the T'ang dynasty (618–907); for that reason, people from southeastern China refer to themselves as T'ang-jen (T'ang people) rather than as Han-jen (Han people).

When one talks about pre–World War II Chinese emigration, one is really talking about the emigration of people from only five small regions in the two southeastern provinces of Fukien and Kwangtung and the island of Hainan. In the literature on the overseas Chinese, these major emigrant groups have usually been identified by the regional dialects they speak. Though there is only one script for written Chinese, there are many different Chinese dialects, some of which are so unintelligible to speakers of other dialects that they might almost be considered different languages. The dialect one speaks, therefore, often is the most important mark that separates an individual from members of other groups.

* * * *

Chinese emigration can be divided broadly into two historical phases according to which groups emigrated and what motivated them to go abroad. Before the nineteenth century, Hokkien and Teochiu emigrants predominated, whereas from the early nineteenth century onward, Cantonese were more prominent. Hakka and Hailam emigrants never matched the Hokkien, Teochiu, and Cantonese in numbers or in social significance. The earliest emigrants were religious pilgrims, merchants, and artisans, but as time passed, more and more laborers joined the emigrant stream. One group of emigrants who always stood out were those who went abroad to mine for precious metals. Beginning in the fifteenth century, when Chinese went to mine for tin in southern Thailand, aspiring miners have been an especially dynamic element among their fellow emigrants. The tin miners in southern Thailand and the ones who went later to Malaysia, as well as those who went to mine for gold in Borneo, were precursors of the large number of Chinese who joined the gold rushes in California, elsewhere in the United States, and in Australia, British Columbia, and Alaska in the nineteenth century.

Throughout the history of Chinese emigration, geography, trade patterns, shipping routes, chain migration, and European incursion each played a significant role in determining the pattern of overseas migration and settlement. Some of these factors served to "push" Chinese out of their native places, others served to "pull" them to particular locations abroad, while yet others provided the means that made emigration possible.

The geography of Fukien and Kwangtung provided certain natural conditions that created a propensity in the inhabitants of those provinces to emigrate. Both provinces were relatively isolated from the rest of China, being separated from central China by mountains penetrated only by a small number of passes. After Han Chinese settled this region, communication with central and north China was easier by sea than by land. Fukien, in particular, had little arable land, so the people there depended a great deal on fishing for sustenance. Plying junks along the coast to travel, fish, and trade allowed the residents of these two coastal provinces to develop an early expertise in seafaring—a factor that facilitated overseas migration.

Chinese imperial policy that confined maritime trade to a few large ports in the provinces of Chekiang, Fukien, and Kwang-tung also gave the people there the added advantage of gaining experience in dealing with foreigners, enabling them to overcome some of the psychological and social barriers posed by Chinese culture against departure from home. Furthermore, the pattern of trade at different ports in southeastern China helped to determine which groups went overseas in the largest numbers at particular points in time.

Chinese maritime trade, which began to flourish in the late eighth century, was initially handled largely by foreign merchants who operated out of enclaves set aside for them in the major ports, but in the heyday of that trade during the Northern Sung, Southern Sung, and Yuan Dynasties (979–1127, 1127–1279, and 1279–1368), Chinese shipbuilders and -owners as well as sailors and merchants in the lower Yangtze valley and along the southern coast played an increasingly prominent part in it. Chinese officials confined the bulk of the foreign trade to several large ports to facilitate the collection of anchorage fees and custom duties. In the late T'ang and the Northern Sung periods, the city of Canton handled the bulk of the trade, but beginning in the Southern Sung dynasty, ports in Fukien also became ascendant. By 1760, however, the Chinese government had restricted foreign commerce solely to Canton, and foreign merchants were allowed to deal only with Chinese merchants of the *cohong*.[1]

Since Canton had been most consistently accessible to outsiders, Chinese merchants in Canton had to compete with Arab, Indian, Malay, European, and other merchants. Frequently, merchandise shipped out of Canton was carried in foreign bottoms. In the Fukien ports, which were not always open to foreigners, on the other hand, Chinese shipowners, sailors, and merchants controlled every phase of foreign commerce, so much so that before the nineteenth century, trade carried on in Chinese junks—be it Chinese coastal or foreign trade—became a near monopoly of Fukien merchants. As a result, the Hokkien became the earliest group of Chinese to settle overseas in sizable numbers, particularly in the Philippines, Indonesia, the former Straits Settlements in Malaysia (Malacca, Penang, and Singapore), and southern Thailand.

Chinese junks of several hundred tons plied a number of trade routes: one went northward along the China coast and then eastward across to Japan; one followed a southwesterly direction, hugging the coast of Vietnam, Cambodia, Thailand, Malaya, and the east coast of Sumatra; a third proceeded across the South China Sea in a southeasterly direction to Manila, wound its way through the Philippine Islands to the Sulu archipelago at the southwestern tip, thence turned either southward to Borneo and Java or eastward to the Moluccas, the famed spice islands. Not surprisingly, these areas had some of the earliest Chinese overseas settlements.

Prior to the introduction of steamships, the monsoons dictated in which particular season trading junks could sail in what direction toward which destinations.

---

[1]*Cohong:* a small group of merchants, licensed individually, which together had rights to all legitimate foreign trade. Because imperial officials did not want to meet directly with foreigners, they issued orders and eventually conducted diplomacy through the cohong merchants. Begun in 1760, the cohong was ultimately abolished by treaty in 1842.

During the winter months, when the northeast monsoons blew across the South China Sea, junks left Chinese ports in January or February to sail southward to Southeast Asia. These junks returned during the southwest monsoon season, usually departing from Southeast Asian ports for China in August. Chinese traders therefore had an eight-month trading season away from home, but some stayed away more than a year, giving rise to a practice that came to be called "double wintering." The natural elements had a further effect on the destination of these Chinese ships because varying degrees of turbulence encountered in different parts of the South China Sea caused captains to favor certain locations over others. Where sojourning traders landed, more permanent settlers tended to follow.

When steamships were introduced by Western firms in the second half of the nineteenth century, transportation and trade patterns changed. Junks had preferred sheltered upriver ports, but steamers required deep-water harbors and different docking facilities. Hong Kong, Canton, Amoy, and Swatow became the most important ocean ports on the southeastern China coast in the nineteenth century. For the passengers, the introduction of steamers meant that a far larger number of persons could be carried in each ship, fares became lower, passage was safer and quicker, and more distant destinations across oceans—rather than seas—became accessible. More important, migration increased dramatically between ports connected by direct steamship service. Regularly scheduled, direct steamer service between Amoy and Manila, and Hong Kong and Singapore, was established in the 1860s, facilitating the movement of Hokkien and Cantonese not only to those locations but to points beyond in Indonesia, the Malay peninsula, and Burma. In 1882 direct steamship service was opened between Swatow and Bangkok, enabling a large number of Teochiu and a smaller number of Hakka (to whom Swatow was the most accessible port) to migrate to central Thailand. Emigrants from Hainan continued to sail in small junks from their island to points along the coast of Indochina and into the Gulf of Siam.

Once the initial migration patterns of the different regional groups had been established, the tendency of potential emigrants to go where they already had relatives or village mates created a chain migration that caused particular groups to cluster in certain localities and in a limited range of occupations. Old emigrants, known as "head guests," would return to their villages in China to recruit "new guests." Frequently, the old emigrants advanced the passage for the new emigrants, tying the latter to themselves through debt bondage, and made all arrangements for housing them on their arrival and finding employment for them. Common dialect and place of origin, therefore, not only became the main bases for associating with others overseas, but more often than not also helped to determine the emigrants' choice of occupation.

More than any of the above factors, the appearance of Europeans in Asia from the fifteenth century onward led to increased Chinese migration to Southeast Asia. In the early decades of the sixteenth century, the Portuguese set up trading posts stretching from the Iberian peninsula, around the coast of Africa, across the Indian Ocean to India, eastward to Southeast Asia, and on to China and Japan. The Spanish conquered the Philippines in the 1570s, and the Dutch showed up in the Indonesian archipelago soon afterward. After an initial effort to establish commercial hegemony in insular Southeast Asia, the British withdrew from the area to concentrate on building an empire in India, but they returned in force in the early nineteenth century to colonize Malaysia. The French colonial effort in Vietnam, Cambodia, and Laos was also a nineteenth-century phenomenon. European trading companies needed middlemen, and colonial settlements needed provisioners, craftsmen, and laborers. An increasing number of Chinese merchants, artisans, and workers came to earn a living in the newly established European colonies. European colonialism thus created powerful "pull" factors that lured Chinese in increasing numbers to different parts of Southeast Asia.

The presence or absence of European colonialists became a key factor in differentiating two different patterns of interaction between the Chinese and the Southeast Asian host societies. In the countries which were colonized by Europeans, the Chinese were treated with ambivalence because the colonial masters both needed and feared them. Consequently, the Chinese were alternately courted and persecuted. In Thailand—the only Southeast Asian country that was never colonized—on the other hand, the Chinese were accepted more easily, and many became well integrated into the host society.

Despite its long history, emigration was never something the central Chinese government approved of, much less promoted. In the 1640s, in the transition from the Ming to the Ch'ing dynasty, warfare and unstable social conditions led many to leave China from both Fukien and Kwangtung provinces. This outflow alarmed the Ch'ing government, which feared that Ming loyalists might foment anti-Ch'ing campaigns from overseas bases. Because of this worry, the Ch'ing government adopted the attitude of the Ming rulers (who had viewed Chinese emigrants as "deserters," "criminals," and "potential traitors") and codified it into law. Between 1656 and 1729, the Ch'ing officials promulgated a series of edicts that prohibited voyaging overseas on pain of death. Reflecting the Ch'ing government's vacillating attitude, these imperial edicts first requested foreign governments to repatriate all Chinese residing abroad so that they might be executed, then stipulated that amnesty would be provided to those who returned to their homeland within a given period, and still later announced that those who failed to return would be barred forever from reentry.

These prohibitory edicts notwithstanding, Chinese continued to go overseas to trade, work, and settle. In the middle of the nineteenth century, the forcible "opening" of China by European powers qualitatively changed the nature of Chinese emigration. Whereas in earlier centuries European activities served mainly to create the "pull" factors that lured Chinese overseas, in this new stage of Chinese international migrations, the actions of Europeans gave rise not only to the "pull" but also to the "push" factors. In addition, it was also Europeans who provided the means that enabled large numbers to sail to distant lands across not just seas but oceans.

Cantonese Emigration

In the century between the end of the Opium War in 1842 and the beginning of World War II, Chinese proceeded abroad to work and live in every continent on the earth. It has been estimated by Sing-wu Wang that in the last six decades of the nineteenth century, at least two and a half million Chinese went overseas. Asian international migrations of this period were an integral part of Western economic development and imperialist expansion. Chinese emigrants left to escape poverty in China, which resulted from insufficient land and overpopulation but was exacerbated by the political, economic, and social disruptions caused by Western activities. They went to the Americas, the West Indies, Hawaii, Australia, New Zealand, Southeast Asia, and even Africa to take advantage of the economic opportunities created by the colonial development of some of these areas and by the discovery of gold in others. Thus, "push" and "pull" factors—both of which were linked to the dynamic growth of Western capitalism—appeared simultaneously to create conditions that stimulated emigration. At the same time, Western ships, eagerly waiting in Asian ports to take large numbers of destitute peasants to faraway lands to work, served as the means that made emigration possible.

The Cantonese emigrants to America originated in a small region stretching over some two dozen districts in the Pearl River Delta or on its periphery in Kwangtung province. Eight of the twenty-two districts were numerically quite important in terms of sending emigrants to North America. . . .

* * * *

Though they were paid lower wages than white workers, Chinese immigrants were by no means the dregs of Chinese society. There is, unfortunately, no reliable information on the social origins of the Chinese emigrants of this period. It is not known what the relative distribution of peasants, laborers, artisans, merchants, or gentry among the emigrants was, and how the distribution varied for groups going to different destinations. There is little evidence that members of gentry families went abroad except for individuals sent to foreign countries for higher studies, but it is certain that among the first immigrants to California, a considerable number were merchants, because California newspapers reported their presence. . . .

Regardless of their class background, it is probable that family members left behind depended on those who went abroad to send sufficient money home that they might live, but this hope must have been tinged with realism, for centuries of experience with emigration must have acquainted Chinese villagers with the fact that while some lucky ones indeed might succeed economically in foreign lands, many others would face destitution or even death. It can be assumed that the members chosen to go abroad were among the strongest and bravest because their families knew that physical stamina, ingenuity, and the willingness and ability to provide mutual aid and protection to each other would determine how well the emigrants could cope with hostile treatment in alien lands.

* * * *

In the 1850s, California, the "Old Gold Mountain," and Australia, the "New Gold Mountain," were the most desired destinations even though they were farther away than the more familiar lands of Southeast Asia and passage was accordingly more expensive. Traveling abroad to mine for precious metals was, after all, nothing new, so it can be assumed that aspiring gold miners to California and Australia were an intrepid lot whose movement across the Pacific was based on rational calculations. Migration being a gamble and an investment, the possibility of finding gold made emigration to California and Australia the best bet available.

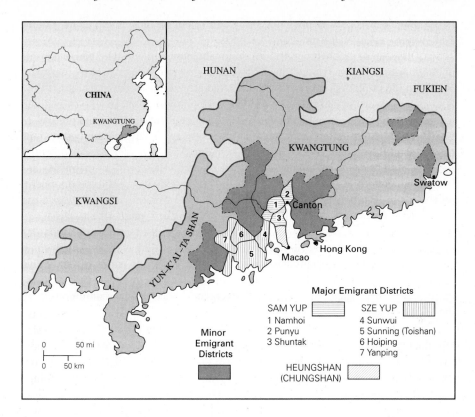

Map 6.1   Kwangtung Province: Emigrant Districts

Source: Thomas Chinn, Him Mark Lai, and Phillip Choy, *A History of the Chinese in California: A Syllabus* (San Francisco: Chinese Historical Society of America), 1969, p. 3.

At least, that was their expectation. What they did not know was that they would be the first large groups of Chinese to enter white men's countries. Though the lands of Southeast Asia they had long traveled to had been colonized by Europeans, those were colonies of trade and exploitation acquired for the sake of gaining access to desired tropical agricultural products and minerals. The number of Europeans who actually settled there was never large. In contrast, the United States, Canada, Australia, New Zealand, and southern Africa became colonies of settlement to which millions of Europeans emigrated. Chinese would be treated in these temperate countries quite differently from the way they had been received in the tropical colonies, where, despite sporadic persecution, they had been tolerated because they were needed as middlemen and artisans. In the latter, by dint of perseverance and hard work, it was possible for some of them to succeed economically, while more than a few even acquired considerable social standing. In the temperate countries of European settlement, however, Chinese—and other peoples of color—historically have been wanted only as cheap labor. Any attempt by them to rise above the status of laborer would be met with resistance and retaliation.

Persecution now came not from the ruling elite, as in pre-nineteenth-century colonial Southeast Asia, but from white workers.

As a matter of fact, Chinese immigration and opposition to it helped to consolidate the white labor movement in California and probably elsewhere too. In many Western industrializing countries, attempts were made to organize workers in the late nineteenth century in response to the growing power of those who owned and managed large industries and businesses. Although collective action did give white workers strength and a modicum of political power, the newly acquired power was always tenuous, so that white workers remained vigilant against the potential threat posed by cheaper and more exploitable and exploited foreign (mainly Asian) labor. Whenever they perceived an "invasion" of "alien" workers to be imminent, they rose up to repel it. Regardless of whether the Chinese who came to these countries were free or contract laborers, white workers indiscriminately called them coolies and argued that white societies were imperiled by the influx of hordes of people able to survive on very thin margins of subsistence. Politicians and some employers eventually also climbed on board the anti-Chinese bandwagon because racism overrode considerations of class interest. In the United States, Canada, Australia, and New Zealand, anti-Chinese movements ended Chinese immigration by the end of the nineteenth century.

Thus, the tragic irony of the Chinese experience in America lies in the fact that although the Chinese had come filled with hope and were imbued with a strong desire for economic success—desire fueled by the burden of being responsible for the survival of their extended families—many were never allowed to become much more than mudsills in white men's societies.

FURTHER READING

Josef J. Barton, *Peasants and Strangers: Italians, Rumanians, and Slovaks in an American City, 1890–1950* (1975).
John Bodnar, *The Transplanted: A History of Immigrants in Urban America* (1985).
John Briggs, *An Italian Passage: Immigrants to Three American Cities, 1890–1930* (1978).
John J. Bukowczyk, *And My Children Did Not Know Me: A History of Polish Americans* (1987).
Betty Boyd Caroli, *Italian Repatriation from the United States* (1974).
Sucheng Chan, *Asian Americans: An Interpretive History* (1990).
Sucheng Chan, *This Bittersweet Soil* (1986).
Lucie Cheng and Edna Bonacich, *Labor Immigration Under Capitalism: Asian Workers in the United States before World War II* (1984).
Dino Cinel, *From Italy to San Francisco: The Immigrant Experience* (1982).
Dino Cinel, *The National Integration of Italian Return Migration, 1870–1929* (1991).
Donna Gabaccia, *From Sicily to Elizabeth Street: Housing and Social Change Among Italian Immigrants, 1880–1930* (1983).
Donna Gabaccia, *Militants and Migrants: Rural Sicilians Become American Workers* (1988).
Caroline Golab, *Immigrant Destinations* (1977).
Victor Greene, *For God and Country: The Rise of Polish and Lithuanian Ethnic Consciousness in America* (1975).
Richard Griswold del Castillo, *The Los Angeles Barrio, 1850–1890* (1980).
John Higham, *Send These to Me: Jews and Other Immigrants in Urban America* (1975).

Irving Howe, *The World of Our Fathers* (1976).

Yuji Ichioka, *The Issei: The World of the First Generation Japanese Immigrants, 1885–1924* (1988).

Thomas Kessner, *The Golden Door: Italian and Jewish Immigrant Mobility in New York City, 1880–1915* (1977).

Alan Takeo Moriyama, *Imingaisha: Japanese Emigration Companies and Hawaii* (1985).

Gary R. Mormino and George E. Pozzetta, *The Immigrant World of Ybor City: Italians and Their Latin Neighbors, 1885–1985* (1987).

Robert Orsi, *The Madonna of 115th Street: Faith and Community in Italian Harlem 1880–1950* (1988).

Michael J. Piore, *Birds of Passage: Migrant Labor and Industrial Societies* (1979).

Moses Rischin, *The Promised City: New York's Jews, 1870–1914* (1970).

Theodore Saloutos, *The Greeks in the United States* (1964).

Ronald Sanders, *Shores of Refuge: A Hundred Years of Jewish Emigration* (1989).

Judith E. Smith, *Family Connections: A History of Italian and Jewish Immigrant Lives in Providence, Rhode Island, 1900–1940* (1985).

Ronald Takaki, *Strangers from a Different Shore: A History of Asian Americans* (1989).

Shin-Shan Henry Tsai, *The Chinese Experience in America* (1986).

Mark Wyman, *Round Trip to America: The Immigrants Return to Europe, 1880–1930* (1993).

Virginia Yans-McLaughlin, *Family and Community: Italian Immigrants in Buffalo, 1880–1930* (1977).

Industrial Immigrants in the City and in the Countryside, 1880–1920

The immigration of millions of people between 1880 and 1920 had a profound impact on the cities and countryside of the United States. Because most immigrants arrived to work in a variety of laboring jobs, they tended to work in low-paying jobs. As a result, they often lived in neighborhoods distinguished by common ethnic backgrounds but also identified with poverty. Observers in American society often viewed these developments with concern. They argued that immigrants were huddled in impermeable enclaves of privation and vice; they were troubled by the relationships between government corruption and the immigrant vote; and they often contended that immigrants' low pay adversely affected the wages of American labor.

Amid these concerns, immigrants adjusted to life in the United States and, in effect, became "ethnics." And as they did so, they accustomed themselves to American life and to the often bewildering changes accompanying industrial labor. Meanwhile, they formed a variety of institutions—from churches to fraternal organizations—and joined associations such as labor unions and political parties. These efforts were, in many ways, attempts to temper life in a very difficult environment. Membership in labor unions was aimed at improving working conditions in the field, the factory, or the mines. Insurance companies or burial societies, based on common national background, were commonsense attempts to plan for the uncertainties of life in dangerous work environments prior to a nationalized system of social welfare. Yet these new institutions also animated the ethnic community. Entertainment in the literature, newspapers, or theatre—often written or performed in the native tongue, provided immigrants and their children social channels to express the joys and heartaches of their lives in an alien, and occasionally hostile, world.

The role these institutions played in linking ethnic groups to larger society is ambiguous. On the one hand, the institutions helped to create an institutional framework that fostered the maintenance of ethnic group identification. Institutions such as fraternal organizations based on national identities nurtured the development of an ethnic leadership that was critical in established national ethnic identities in the United States. On the other hand, many of the institutions that immigrants and their children joined were necessarily not based on ethnicity. Churches, political parties, and labor unions often attempted to create memberships across the boundaries of nationality and native tongue. Whereas many among the leadership of the Roman Catholic Church in the late nineteenth century hoped to produce devoted church members and loyal Americans, so did the leadership of the union movement and political parties seek to form coalitions that spanned many ethnic identities.

D O C U M E N T S

The millions of immigrants who moved to live and work in America's burgeoning cities or to its expanding agricultural enterprises in the countryside influenced and were influenced by life in the United States. These documents explore the impact of immigrants on American politics, cultural life, and labor organization. They also show how immigrants created their own institutions. The first two documents report what the immigrants' lives were like in the eastern cities. Jacob Riis (1890), in *How the Other Half Lives,* his late nineteenth century work on immigrant tenement life in New York City, describes the lives of tenement dwellers. A report from *Harper's Weekly* around the same time (1895) recounts the difficult conditions of labor for sweatshop workers in the same city. The next four documents inquire into the immigrants' world. A politician (1905) explains the world of urban politics and proposes that Irish American politicians are the most honest people in the world. A contemporary explores the Yiddish print culture in New York City (1902), with particular reference to anarchist newspapers. Next, two Italian Americans remember the 1912 strike in Lawrence, Massachusetts, which was a bitter contest between labor and management that ultimately resulted in victory for the polyglot unionist forces. Then, three Chinese Americans recall the significance of ethnic institutions in San Francisco's Chinatown and in outlying Chinese settlements from 1877 to 1917. They show how Chinese pioneered such foodways as asparagus, crab, and abalone. They also describe mutual protection societies that were especially influential in urban Chinese settlements. Finally, in the last document, a sociologist (1910) explores how immigrants were grappling with acculturation and assimilation in the early twentieth-century United States.

Jacob Riis Describes the Impoverished Tenements of New York City, 1890

New York's wage-earners have no other place to live, more is the pity. They are truly poor for having no better homes; waxing poorer in purse as the exorbitant rents to which they are tied, as ever was serf to soil, keep rising. The wonder is that

As found in Jacob Riis, *How the Other Half Lives* (Williamstown, MA: Corner House, 1972).

they are not all corrupted, and speedily, by their surroundings. If, on the contrary, there be a steady working up, if not out of the slough, the fact is a powerful argument for the optimist's belief that the world is, after all, growing better, not worse, and would go far toward disarming apprehension, were it not for the steadier growth of the sediment of the slums and its constant menace. Such an impulse toward better things there certainly is. The German rag-picker of thirty years ago, quite as low in the scale as his Italian successor, is the thrifty tradesman or prosperous farmer of to-day.

The Italian scavenger of our time is fast graduating into exclusive control of the corner fruit-stands, while his black-eyed boy monopolizes the boot-blacking industry in which a few years ago he was an intruder. The Irish hod-carrier in the second generation has become a bricklayer, if not the Alderman of his ward, while the Chinese coolie is in almost exclusive possession of the laundry business. The reason is obvious. The poorest immigrant comes here with the purpose and ambition to better himself and, given half a chance, might be reasonably expected to make the most of it. To the false plea that he prefers the squalid homes in which his kind are housed there could be no better answer. The truth is, his half chance has too long been wanting, and for the bad result he has been unjustly blamed.

As emigration from east to west follows the latitude, so does the foreign influx in New York distribute itself along certain well-defined lines that waver and break only under the stronger pressure of a more gregarious race or the encroachments of inexorable business. A feeling of dependence upon mutual effort, natural to strangers in a strange land, unacquainted with its language and customs, sufficiently accounts for this.

The Irishman is the true cosmopolitan immigrant. All-pervading, he shares his lodging with perfect impartiality with the Italian, the Greek, and the "Dutchman," yielding only to sheer force of numbers, and objects equally to them all. A map of the city, colored to designate nationalities, would show more stripes than on the skin of a zebra, and more colors than any rainbow. The city on such a map would fall into two great halves, green for the Irish prevailing in the West Side tenement districts, and blue for the Germans on the East Side. But intermingled with these ground colors would be an odd variety of tints that would give the whole the appearance of an extraordinary crazy-quilt. From down in the Sixth Ward, upon the site of the old Collect Pond that in the days of the fathers drained the hills which are no more, the red of the Italian would be seen forcing its way northward along the line of Mulberry Street to the quarter of the French purple on Bleecker Street and South Fifth Avenue, to lose itself and reappear, after a lapse of miles, in the "Little Italy" of Harlem, east of Second Avenue. Dashes of red, sharply defined, would be seen strung through the Annexed District, northward to the city line. On the West Side the red would be seen overrunning the old Africa of Thompson Street, pushing the black of the negro rapidly uptown, against querulous but unavailing protests, occupying his home, his church, his trade and all, with merciless impartiality. There is a church in Mulberry Street that has stood for two generations as a sort of milestone of these migrations. Built originally for the worship of staid New Yorkers of the "old stock," it was engulfed by the colored tide, when the draft-riots drove the negroes out of reach of Cherry Street and the Five Points.

Within the past decade the advance wave of the Italian onset reached it, and to-day the arms of United Italy adorn its front. The negroes have made a stand at several points along Seventh and Eighth Avenues; but their main body, still pursued by the Italian foe, is on the march yet, and the black mark will be found overshadowing to-day many blocks on the East Side, with One Hundredth Street as the centre, where colonies of them have settled recently.

Hardly less aggressive than the Italian, the Russian and Polish Jew, having overrun the district between Rivington and Division Streets, east of the Bowery, to the point of suffocation, is filling the tenements of the old Seventh Ward to the river front, and disputing with the Italian every foot of available space in the back alleys of Mulberry Street. The two races, differing hopelessly in much, have this in common: they carry their slums with them wherever they go, if allowed to do it. Little Italy already rivals its parent, the "Bend," in foulness. Other nationalities that begin at the bottom make a fresh start when crowded up the ladder. Happily both are manageable, the one by rabbinical, the other by the civil law. Between the dull gray of the Jew, his favorite color, and the Italian red, would be seen squeezed in on the map a sharp streak of yellow, marking the narrow boundaries of China-town. Dovetailed in with the German population, the poor but thrifty Bohemian might be picked out by the sombre hue of his life as of his philosophy, struggling against heavy odds in the big human bee-hives of the East Side. Colonies of his people extend northward, with long lapses of space, from below the Cooper Insti-tute more than three miles. The Bohemian is the only foreigner with any consider-able representation in the city who counts no wealthy man of his race, none who has not to work hard for a living, or has got beyond the reach of the tenement.

A Portrait of Sweatshop Labor in New York City, 1895

Two years since it was my duty, as chairman of a Congressional committee, to in-vestigate the so-called "sweating system," New York being one of several cities visited. The "sweating system" is practically the process by which ready-made clothing is manufactured in tenement houses.

Conditions have radically changed during the last twenty-five years. Formerly the women of each household made up the greater part of its clothing, the rest being supplied by the local tailor, and made up on his premises. The "ready-made" busi-ness has developed new economies, especially in divisions of labor and the method of its employment. Middle-men have been given a place between the "manufac-turer" and the actual operative, processes have been cheapened, and labor degraded.

The materials are cut and "bunched" for each garment by the manufacturer. They are then distributed in large lots to special jobbers, known as "contractors," each a specialist in his line. For example, one makes coats, another cloaks, another pantaloons, while some make special grades or sizes. With this distribution the wholesaler washes his hands of the business, his ignorance of how and where his goods are actually made up being as ideal as intentional.

From John DeWitt Warner, "The 'Sweating System' in New York City," *Harper's Weekly,* February 9, 1895, 135–136.

Not far from one-half of the goods thus distributed are made up in the contractors' factories. As to the other half, the first contractor sublets the work to a "sweater," whose shop is generally one of the two larger rooms of a tenement flat, accommodating from six to fifteen or twenty "sweating" employés—men, women, and children. In the other large room of the flat are his living, sleeping, and cooking arrangements, overflowing into the workroom. Employés whom he boards, who eat at their work, and who sleep on the goods, frequently complete the intimate connection of home and shop. One-fourth of our ready-made and somewhat of our custom-made clothing are thus put together.

. . . But this is not the worst. Single families, inhabiting one or more rooms, generally having a family as subtenants, or a number of lodgers or boarders, subcontract work from the tenement "sweaters." . . . The homes of these home-workers include many of the most wretched in which human beings exist among us. The conditions of squalor and filth are frequently such as to make even inspection impossible, except by one hardened to the work, while the quarters in which this work is centred are those into which tend the most helpless of our population.

From the wholesale manufacturer, handling each year a product of millions, through the contractor to the "sweater," and on to the "home-worker," the steps are steadily downward—of decreasing responsibility, comfort, and compensation. The profit of each (except the wretch at the bottom) is "sweated" from the next below him.

The lot . . . of . . . "sweat-shop" workers is luxury compared to that of those engaged in tenement home work. The home-worker is generally a foreigner just arrived, and frequently a woman whose husband is dead, sick, or worthless, and whose children keep her at home. Of these tenement home workers there are more women than men, and children are as numerous as both. The work is carried on in the one, two, or three rooms occupied by the family, with its subtenants or boarders. No pretence is made of separating shop work from household affairs. The hours observed are those which endurance alone limits. Children are worked to death beside their parents. Contagious diseases are especially prevalent among these people; but even death disturbs from their occupation only the one or two necessary to dispose of the body.

A New York Politician Justifies the Urban Political Machine, 1905*

There's only one way to hold a district: you must study human nature and act accordin'. You can't study human nature in books. Books is a hindrance more

---

*These are talks given by George Washington Plunkitt, a machine politician in New York City, ostensibly from a bootblack stand at the New York County Courthouse. They were transcribed by William L. Riordan of the *New York Evening Post*. A transcription can be found in William L. Riordon, *Plunkitt of Tammany Hall* (New York: E. P. Dutton, 1963).

than anything else. If you have been to college, so much the worse for you. You'll have to unlearn all you learned before you can get right down to human nature, and unlearnin' takes a lot of time. Some men can never forget what they learned at college. Such men may get to be district leaders by a fluke, but they never last.

To learn real human nature you have to go among the people, see them and be seen. I know every man, woman, and child in the Fifteenth District, except them that's been born this summer—and I know some of them, too. I know what they like and what they don't like, what they are strong at and what they are weak in, and I reach them by approachin' at the right side.

For instance, here's how I gather in the young men. I hear of a young feller that's proud of his voice, thinks that he can sing fine. I ask him to come around to Washington Hall and join our Glee Club. He comes and sings, and he's a follower of Plunkitt for life. Another young feller gains a reputation as a baseball player in a vacant lot. I bring him into our baseball club. That fixes him. You'll find him workin' for my ticket at the polls next election day. Then there's the feller that likes rowin' on the river, the young feller that makes a name as a waltzer on his block, the young feller that's handy with his dukes— I rope them all in by givin' them opportunities to show themselves off. I don't trouble them with political arguments. I just study human nature and act accordin'.

Lincoln Steffens [the muckraker journalist who wrote *The Shame of the Cities*] made one good point in his book. He said he found that Philadelphia, ruled almost entirely by Americans, was more corrupt than New York, where the Irish do almost all the governin'. I could have told him that before he did any investigatin' if he had come to me. The Irish was born to rule, and they're the honestest people in the world. Show me the Irishman who would steal a roof off an almhouse! He don't exist. Of course, if an Irishman had the political pull and the roof was much worn, he might get the city authorities to put on a new one and get the contract for it himself, and buy the old roof at a bargain—but that's honest graft. It's goin' about the thing like a gentleman, and there's more money in it than in tearin' down an old roof and cartin' it to the junkman's—more money and no penal code.

One reason why the Irishman is more honest in politics than many Sons of the Revolution is that he is grateful to the country and the city that gave him protection and prosperity when he was driven by oppression from the Emerald Isle. Say, that sentence is fine, ain't it? I'm goin' to get some literary feller to work it over into poetry for next St. Patrick's Day dinner.

Yes, the Irishman is grateful. His one thought is to serve the city which gave him a home. He has this thought even before he lands in New York, for his friends here often have a good place in one of the city departments picked out for him while he is still in the old country. Is it any wonder that he has a tender spot in his heart for old New York when he is on its salary list the mornin' after he lands?

The Yiddish Press in New York City, 1902

Yiddish newspapers have, as compared with their contemporaries in the English language, the strong interest of great freedom of expression. They are controlled rather by passion than by capital. It is their joy to pounce on controlling wealth, and to take the side of the laborer against the employer. A large proportion of the articles are signed, a custom in striking contrast with that of the American newspaper; the prevalence of the unsigned article in the latter is held by the Yiddish journals to illustrate the employer's tendency to arrogate everything to himself, and to make the paper a mere organ of his own policy and opinions. The remark of one of the Jewish editors, that the "Yiddish newspaper's freedom of expression is limited by the Penal Code alone," has its relative truth. It is, of course, equally true that the new freedom of the Jews, who in Russia had no journal in the common Yiddish, runs in these New York papers into an emotional extreme, a license which is apt to distort the news and to give over the editorial pages to virulent party disputes.

Nevertheless, the Yiddish press, particularly the Socialistic branch of it, is an educative element of great value in the Ghetto. It has helped essentially to extend the intellectual horizon of the Jew beyond the boundaries of the Talmud, and has largely displaced the rabbi in the position of teacher of the people. Not only do these papers constitute a forum of discussion, but they publish frequent translations of the Russian, French, and German modern classics, and for the first time lay the news of the world before the poor Jewish people. An event of moment to the Jews, such as a riot in Russia, comes to New York in private letters, and is printed in the papers here often before the version "prepared" by the Russian Government appears in the Russian newspapers. Thus a Jew on the east side received a letter from his father in Russia asking why the reserves there had been called out, and the son's reply gave him the first information about the war in China.

The make-up of the Yiddish newspaper is in a general way similar to that of its American contemporary. The former is much smaller, however, containing only about as much reading matter as would fill six or eight columns of a "down-town" newspaper. The sporting department is entirely lacking, the Jew being utterly indifferent to exercise of any kind. They are all afternoon newspapers, and draw largely for the news upon the morning editions of the American papers. The staff is very limited, consisting of a few editors and, usually, only one reporter for the local news of the quarter. They give more space proportionately than any American paper to pure literature—chiefly translations, tho there are some stories founded on the life of the east side—and to scientific articles of popular character. The interesting feature of these newspapers, however, consists in their rivalries and their differences in principle. This can be presented most simply in a short sketch of their history.

As found in Hutchins Hapgood, *The Spirit of the Ghetto* (Cambridge, MA: Harvard University Press, 1967).

By far the most interesting of the papers which are not dailies are the two Anarchistic sheets, the *Freie Arbeiter-stimme,* a weekly, and the *Freie Gesellschaft,* a monthly.

Contrary to the general impression of the character of these people, in which bombs play a large part, the Anarchists of the Ghetto are a gentle and idealistic body of men. The abnormal activity of the Russian Jews in this country is expressed by the Socialists rather than the Anarchists. The latter are largely theorists and aim rather at the education of the people by a journalistic exploitation of their general principles than by a warlike attitude towards specific events of the time. Their attitude is not so partisan as that of the Socialists. They quarrel less among themselves, and are characterized by dreamy eyes and an unpractical scheme of things. They believe in non-resistance and the power of abstract right, and are trying to work out a peaceful revolution, maintaining that the violence often accompanying the movement in Europe is due to the fact that many Anarchists are passionate individuals who in their indignation do not live up to their essentially gentle principles. The Socialists aim at a more strictly centralized government, even than any one existing, since they desire the whole machinery of production and distribution to be in the hands of the community; the Anarchists desire no government whatever, believing that law works against the native dignity of the individual, and trusting to man's natural goodness to maintain order under free conditions. A man's own conscience only can punish him sufficiently, they think. The Socialists go in vividly for politics, while the Anarchists have nothing to do with them. The point on which these two parties agree is the common hatred of private property.

The weekly Anarchistic paper, the *Freie Arbeiter-stimme,* prints about 7,000 copies. Out of this circulation, with the assistance of balls, entertainments, and benefits at the theatres, the paper is able to exist. It pays a salary to only one man, the editor, S. Janowsky, who receives the sum of $13 a week. He is a little dark-haired man, with beautiful eyes, and soft, persuasive voice. He thinks that government is so corrupt that the Anarchists need do little to achieve their ends; that silent forces are at work which will bring about the great day of Anarchistic communism. In his newspaper he tries to educate the common people in the principles of anarchy. The aim is popular, and the more intelligent exploitation of the cause is left to the monthly. The *Freigesellschaft,* with the same principles as the *Freie Arbeiter-stimme,* has a higher literary and philosophical character. The editors and contributors are men of culture and education, and work without any pay. It is still gentler and more pacific in its character than the weekly, of whose comparatively contemporaneous and agitatory method if disapproves calmly; believing, as the editors of the monthly do, that a weekly paper cannot exist without giving the people something other than the ideally best. With reference to the ideally best, a number of serious, contemplative men gather in a basement opposite the Hebrew Institute, the headquarters of the monthly, and there talk about the subjects often discussed within its pages, such as Slavery and Freedom, Darwinism and Communism, Man and Government, the Purpose of Education, etc.,—any broad economic subject admitting of abstract treatment.

Two Italian Americans Recount the 1912 Lawrence, Massachusetts, Strike

[*Interviewer:*] What do you remember of the Lawrence Strike?

Philip: There was a strike in 1912; there was one in 1919; there was one in '22; there was one in '31; and there was one in '41.

Theresa: The worse one was 1912 and 1919.

Philip: Yes, 1912 was the worst. It hit a lot of people. Things were really tough. See, I was ten years old. I remember I had to read the paper for my father. I remember the bread lines. On Common Street they set up a place for the strikers. They used to give 'em a loaf of bread and some salt pork. That's what you had to have to eat. Things were pretty damn bad.

Theresa: . . . And that strike was in the winter months. It was terrible. The Polish were used to cold more than the people that came from southern Europe. Half of 'em weren't provided with warm clothes.

I was going to the first grade or second grade at the Walton School. I remember there were the cops there, with the bayonets. When you're a child if there is a soldier or a cop near you, you feel so safe, and they didn't do anything to anybody.

* * * *

Philip: I don't remember too much, only my older brother was very active. He was one of these guys they used to call, not comrade, socialists. He was a Wobbly. He was eleven years older than I was.

That 1912 strike, the Italians were pretty strong. They were really the spearheads of that strike, but every group—the Polish had their area meetings, the French had their meetings, and the Lithuanians. The Italians were picketing, and going to homes, "Don't go to work or you'll get your head bashed in."

Theresa: We were all with the strike. One of the things I remember—of course, this was with the later strike, 1919—they decided *not* to send the children to school so that [the company] would give in. I don't know what the purpose of that was. I wanted to go to school, but one morning my brother says that we should stay home and we didn't go. Right away the teachers knew *why.*

One of the incidents I remember very well was when my sister made a dress for me. The material was a khaki dress; it was on the same line as a uniform, only there was a skirt and there was a blouse with a belt. She had all these buttons of the IWW. They used to screw on. So she thought she'd use them, but not with the exposed part, with the IWW—with the other side, the brass.

When I was at school, everybody admired the dress. The teacher sent me from one room to another. "What a beautiful dress!" For some reason, things get unscrewed by themselves. One button unscrewed and the side with the IWW fell on the floor of the school. Somebody picked it up. I think it was the teacher in my room that got hold of it. She wanted to know "Who had that button! Where's the

From *First Generation: In the Words of Twentieth-Century American Immigrants.* Copyright 1992 by June Namias. Used with the permission of the author and the University of Illinois Press.

button!" She looked around. She has an idea she saw my brass button on my dress. "Where did you get this?"

I said, "I don't know. My sister made the dress and they were around so she used them."

That sort of made it bad. There was an embarrassment there all the time.

Philip: I remember some beatings in picket lines, 1919 strike. Some of them were scabs; the strikers were beatin' 'em. Some of the strike-breakers were with the cops. Oh yeah, there were clubbin's.

You know what I was makin' when I worked forty-eight hours? I started out after the strike, I'll never forget, $5.03.[1] But wages had got *better* when I got in. Because during the 1912 strike things got better.

Three Chinese Americans Recall Life and Labor in Their Ethnic Community, 1877–1917

Leland Chin

My father came over here in 1877, and when he first came in he worked in a hemp factory. You know, in those days it was slave labor, and besides, it was hard to get a job. And my father went around and peddled vegetables. In those days they carried two baskets over their shoulders, so he peddled vegetables for a while and then, later on, he learned to be a tailor, and he ran around and peddled ladies' wear. In those days, there were a lot of, you know what I mean, they had red lights and all that district, and my father was making all this ladies' wear to sell down around the red light district. Then later on he and a few cousins organized a little shop, and then from that shop, they kept growing, and grew until the business was destroyed by the earthquake. My father never had much education, but he picked up English pretty well. So in those days, if you could speak English it meant a lot to the community, to the individual, it's quite a qualification. Also, when you knew how to speak English, the community always asked you to be an interpreter, and then you had a chance to contact a lot of Caucasian friends. So that's how my father started business, and he would go down to the wholesalers and suppliers, and he did quite well at it. He made quite a little fortune.

Now Richmond in those days was nothin' but shrimp camps. There was a lot of shrimp in the bay, and at least thirty shrimp camps in Richmond. Sure, all Chinese! Everything was Chinese in those days. They started everything, you know. Oh, a lot of things in agriculture, in farming. When they started fishing shrimp, you know, they got all their nets from China. The Americans said, "Those Chinese are

[1]The dollar was worth $1.17 in real buying power in relation to $14.83 in 1989. Put differently, in 1912 a pound of bacon cost on average 24.4¢; a pound of butter, 37.4¢; a dozen eggs, 34.1¢; and five pounds of sugar, 31.5¢.

From *Longtime Californ'* by Victor G. Nee and Brett de Bary Nee. Copyright © 1972, 1973 by Victor G. and Brett de Bary Nee. Reprinted by permission of Pantheon Books, a division of Random House, Inc.

really able to do a lot of things we never thought of!" And then, Chinese were the first ones to get the abalone. In those days the Americans didn't even know what abalone was. They said, "Is *that* something to eat?" "It's so dirty!" But the Chinese people got the abalone. And the crab. Then later on, they knew how to get all the seaweed and dry it and make nice soup! Oh, there's so many things that the Chinese started! Asparagus, too! And they were laughing at the Chinese, "Why do you eat grass? That grass is for the horses!" But the Chinese knew that where that grass was coming up there was a little sprout coming up, and they thought, "That must be good!" you know, the green part, so they plucked it up in the middle and got it out, and it actually turned out to be asparagus!

Now we left Oakland and went up the Sacramento River and settled around there. My father went down and opened a store in Isleton to begin with. Not a ladies' wear because there's no such customer down there [laughs], but he opened a store to cater to the farmers. You know, candy for the children or whatever they needed. And then he had the foresight to say, "Well, if I pay three and a half for a dozen shirts, if I buy gross, it only costs us two and a half." And he said, "Well, why don't I spread out?" and then he opened a store in Walnut Grove. And then later on he opened another one in Locke. You know these old gentlemen were pretty wise [laughs], those days they had no schooling, but still, they figured on the cost.

* * * *

Lew Wah Get

I first heard about the Suey Sing Tong in 1917. All the gambling houses were prospering around that time. I decided that if I went to work in one, I might make a better living than by working as a cook. I knew that in Stockton, especially, there were lots of gambling houses. People used to say that the Chinatown there was just one street long, with the businesses on one side of the street, and nothing but gambling houses on the other. I learned that all these houses were owned by the Suey Sing Tong. So when I went to Stockton and became involved in one of the houses as a dealer, I also became a member of the tong.

If you wanted to join a tong, you had to have a friend who was already a member sponsor you. He had to swear to your good character, and even then the tong would investigate your name for one month before they let you in. This was the rule for everybody. You could be a cook, a waiter, work in a gambling house or do any kind of work, but you had to have a friend to sponsor you. And once you were a member, you were on your honor to follow all the rules. If you did, then the tong would protect you. If anyone threatened you, or interfered with your business, the tong would help you out. . . .

* * * *

Ching Wah Lee

One factor which bound the Chinese together in the early days was a certain loneliness. They felt that the people here were not too interested in them, except as curiosities, and then when the gold mines petered out and there was competition for jobs, there was actual antagonism toward the Chinese, especially among the laboring class. There were frequent anti-Chinese agitations and one leader known as "Sandlot Kearney" was famous for his speeches on street corners and sandlots saying that the Chinese must go. So in a negative way, this fear was a cementing factor, too. Because of the agitation, a lot of Chinese leaders, the cream of the crop, eventually did go back to China. The ones who remained felt almost deserted, and that was another factor which brought them together.

After this time Chinese began organizing their own societies for mutual protection. There were many hoodlums who would attack Chinese for no reason whatsoever, and that caused them to look back to China. Before the revolution of 1911, or at least before the turn of the century, the Chinese here still had great faith in the "mandarin system." They thought if only they could petition the mandarin or viceroy to petition the emperor for them, problems could be settled. But early in the 1900s, after the fire, they realized that the Manchu government was tottering and they were completely disillusioned with it. Then they began to look to the Chinese revolutionaries. The province we come from, Kwangtung Province, is rich with revolutionaries. One, Kang Yu Wei, was able to influence the emperor to start a series of reforms in education, modernization, and national defense, and so forth. By 1900, however, the new hero was Dr. Sun Yat-sen. The Chinese here raised a tremendous sum of money to help him, and there were street corner rallies in the evenings which would draw hundreds of people who contributed money generously. Towards the end, people were a bit disillusioned in Sun Yat-sen, too, because he failed to create a stabilized government.

Now this was all on the political side. On the religious side it was very interesting, because the early Chinese leaned toward gods which would protect them. One of the most popular was Kwang Kung, the god of literature and war. Bak Ti, the god of the north, was known in Chinese religious lore for doing away with ten thousand demons who were organized to fight him. Perhaps, since Chinese call many Caucasians "foreign devils," this played some part in the significance of Bak Ti. The third thing, strange to say, was the cult of Hou Yin, the monkey god. This was a small cult which grew out of the novel about a monk traveling to India with a pig and a monkey. The pig represented the greedy qualities of man, and the monkey, who was somewhat of a magical creature, represented his mischievous qualities. I think in this cult he was worshipped for the ability to cope with all kinds of unusual situations.

In the day to day life of the early Chinese-Americans there were many festivals and ritual observations which have disappeared today. The best remembered by anyone who is still alive now is probably the funeral procession. A substantial part of Chinatown's economy was even involved in this. There were two stores on Jackson Street, for instance, which dealt with funeral items. One, the Tai Yuen, is still there. It sold candles, incense, paper money to throw at demons during the funeral procession, and gold and silver paper bullion in the shape of ingots. They also sold colored paper garments to be burned at the cemetery and as offerings to the deceased. Selling these things supported one whole store. Then diagonally across the street, at 741 Jackson, was a store which produced figures which were used in the procession to accompany the deceased as servants. These were made of paper and rattan work, about a yard high, in the form of a jade girl and a golden boy.

* * * *

For years the Chinese couldn't be buried in, say, Masonic cemeteries or Jewish cemeteries, so they had their own. Anyway, before World War II it was the general custom for at least three-fourths of the Chinese to have their bones exhumed later and packed in tin cans, and sent back to their ancestral cemetery in China. It was purely sentimental, of course, like many Americans I know who write in their will that they want to be buried in Iowa or Nebraska or wherever they come from and it's something of the same situation, you see, because the early Chinese looked on the country here as rather hostile to them. They felt more comfortable if they knew their bones would be sent back to China.

A Sociologist Analyzes the Process of Assimilation Among Slavic Immigrants, 1910

. . . in the United States assimilation is not quite without signs of difficulty and apprehension and conflicting purposes—signs of dread and jealousy, on the part of Americans, of the alien influences brought in by the streams of newcomers, and, on the part of the immigrants, of jealousy of American influence and dread of Americanizing pressure.

A Polish View

One comes sometimes with a sense of shock to a realization of points of view strange to one's own. Take, for instance, a conversation that I once had with a Polish-American priest. I had said something about "Americans," that they were not apt to be interested in Polish history, or something of the sort. Instantly he was on fire.

"You mean English-Americans," he said. "You English constantly speak as if you were the only Americans, or more American than others. The History of the United States, published by Scribners, is written wholly from the English point of view, and that is very common. Even such a great paper as the Chicago *Tribune* is written by men who are just over from England, and who yet speak of foreigners when they mean any Americans but English. For instance, in a recent bank failure they said that many 'foreigners' would lose, referring to German-Americans and others who had been in the country for generations. A priest born in Baltimore of Italian parents, speaking English and Italian equally naturally, will see priests, new come from Ireland, promoted over him because he is a 'foreigner.' "

I remarked that if I went to Poland he would not consider me a Pole.

From Emily Green Balch, *Our Slavic Fellow Citizens* (New York: Charities Publication Committee, 1910).

"No, that is different," was his reply. "America was empty, open to all comers alike. There is no reason for the English to usurp the name of American. They should be called Yankees if anything. That is the name of English-Americans. There is no such thing as an American nation. Poles form a nation, but the United States is a country, under one government, inhabited by representatives of different nations. As to the future, I have, for my part, no idea what it will bring. I do not think that there will be amalgamation, one race composed of many. The Poles, Bohemians and so forth, remain such, generation after generation. Switzerland has been a republic for centuries, but never has brought her people to use one language. For myself, I do favor one language for the United States, *either English or some other,* to be used by every one, but there is no reason why people should not also have another language; that is an advantage, for it opens more avenues to Europe and elsewhere."

He was indignant at the requirement of the naturalization law of 1906, making a knowledge of English a condition of citizenship. . . . "What are Americans?"

America as Seen from Europe

In a composite people like the American, it is inevitable that the color of the whole should appear different to those who view it from different points. The Englishman is apt to think of the United States as literally a new England, a country inhabited in the main by two classes; on the one hand descendants of seventeenth century English colonists, and on the other newly arrived foreigners.

The continental European, on the contrary, is apt to suffer from the complementary illusion, and to believe that practically all Americans are recent European emigrants, mainly, or at least largely, from his own country. Frenchmen have insisted to me that a large proportion of the United States is French, and Germans often believe that it is mainly German, and that one could travel comfortably throughout the United States with a knowledge of German alone. This is very natural. A man sees his own country-people flocking to America, perhaps partly depopulating great tracts of the fatherland; he receives copies of newspapers in his own language printed in America; if he travels in America he is fêted and entertained everywhere by his own countrymen, and is shown America through their eyes. "I visited for two weeks in Cedar Rapids and never spoke anything but Bohemian," said a Prague friend to me. An Italian lady in Boston said, speaking in Italian, "You know in Boston one naturally gets so little chance to hear any English," much as Americans make the corresponding complaint in Paris and Berlin. On each side such exaggerated impressions are very hard to shake off.

The Second-Generation American

A thousand more items to show the separateness of the foreign life in our midst might be piled together, and in the end they would all be as nothing against the irresistible influence through which it comes about that the immigrants find themselves the parents of American children. They are surprised, they are proud, they are scandalized, they are stricken to the heart with regret,—whatever their emotions they are powerless. The change occurs in different ways among the educated and the uneducated, but it occurs in either case.

The prestige of America and the hatred of children for being different from their playmates is something the parents cannot stand against. The result is often grotesque. A graduate at one of our women's colleges, the daughter of cultivated Germans, told a friend: "My father made me learn German and always was wanting me to read it. I hated to have anything to do with it. It seemed to me something inferior. People in the West call a thing 'Dutch' as a term of scorn. It was not till I was in college that I realized what German literature and philosophy have meant in the world, and that to be a German is not a thing to be ashamed of." Less educated parents, or those using a language less important than German, have a still more difficult task to hold the next generation. "I ain't no Hun, I'm an American," expresses their reaction on the situation.

* * * *

Bad Example

. . . Unfortunately, . . . the immigrant generally begins at the bottom. His helplessness makes him sought for as prey by sharpers and grafters; it is all that the immigration officials can do to keep them off as he lands. As soon as he leaves the paternal care of Ellis Island they attack in force. Boarding-house runners, shady employment agents, sellers of shoddy wares, extortionate hack drivers and expressmen beset his way. One hears all sorts of stories of abuses from both Americans and Slavs—of bosses who take bribes to give employment or to assign good chambers in the mine, of ill usage at the hands of those who should be officers of justice, of arrests for the sake of fees, of unjust fines, of excessive costs paid rather than incur a greater expense. The litigiousness of the Slavs is exploited by "shyster" lawyers till the immigrants learn wisdom by experience. . . .

But it is not only direct ill-treatment that is a peril; the economic pressure and low standards of our lowest industrial strata are in themselves disastrous.

"*My people do not live in America, they live underneath America. America goes on over their heads.* America does not begin till a man is a workingman, till he is earning two dollars a day. A laborer cannot afford to be an American."

These words, which were said to me by one of the wisest Slav leaders that I have ever met, have rung in my mind during all the five years since he spoke them. Beginning at the bottom, "living not in America but underneath America," means living among the worst surroundings that the country has to show, worse, often, than the public would tolerate, except that "only foreigners" are affected. Yet to foreigners they are doubly injurious because, coming as they often do, with low home standards but susceptible, eager, and apt to take what they find as the American idea of what ought to be, they are likely to accept and adopt as "all right" whatever they tumble into.

Among the most significant arenas of immigrant life in this era was the workplace. Whether it was in the fields of industrial-agricultural operations or in the mills, mines, and factories of industrializing America, immigrants toiled in arduous, and occasionally bewildering, circumstances. These two essays depict different challenges of immigrant workers in two very different environments. Historian Herbert G. Gutman, formerly of the University of Rochester, analyzes, in a path-breaking essay, how immigrants in a variety of industrial contexts adjusted to regimens such as "clock time," and the dangers of the factory. Carrying traditions, customs, and beliefs from their homelands, these former peasants adapted, to and occasionally opposed, a world of rigid time and burdensome work discipline. Sociologist Tomàs Almaguer, from the University of Michigan, explores the world of agricultural labor from a racial and Marxist perspective. He investigates how two different racial groups—in this case, Japanese and Mexican farm workers—united in 1903 to form the Japanese-Mexican Labor Association, the first major union of agricultural workers in California. Almaguer analyzes the ways in which labor organization intersected, and occasionally conflicted, with ethnic and racial identifications. Less concerned than Gutman with the transition from peasant to industrial laborer, he considers the significance of racial difference in informing the workers' world.

Immigrants Adjust to Industrial Labor, "Clock Time," and Unionization in the Early Twentieth Century

HERBERT G. GUTMAN

The work ethic remains a central theme in the American experience, and to study this subject afresh means to re-examine much that has been assumed as given in the writing of American working-class and social history. Such study, moreover, casts new light on yet other aspects of the larger American experience that are usually not associated with the study of ordinary working men and women. Until quite recently, few historians questioned as fact the ease with which most past Americans affirmed the "Protestant" work ethic.

* * * *

. . . Just before the First World War the International Harvester Corporation, converted to "scientific management" and "welfare capitalism," prepared a brochure to teach its Polish common laborers the English language. "Lesson One," entitled "General," read:

> I hear the whistle. I must hurry.
> I hear the five minute whistle.
> It is time to go into the shop.
> I take my check from the gate board and hang it on the department board.

From Herbert Gutman, *Work, Culture, and Society in Industrializing America,* Random House. Copyright © 1976. Reprinted by permission.

I change my clothes and get ready to work.
The starting whistle blows.
I eat my lunch.
It is forbidden to eat until then.
The whistle blows at five minutes of starting time.
I get ready to go to work.
I work until the whistle blows to quit.
I leave my place nice and clean.
I put all my clothes in the locker.
I must go home.

This document illustrates a great deal. That it shows the debasement of the English language, a process closely related to the changing ethnic composition of the American working population and the social need for simplified English commands, is a subject for another study. Our immediate interest is in the relationship it implies between Americanization, factory work habits, and improved labor efficiency.

* * * *

. . . When significant numbers of Mexicans lived in Chicago and its industrial suburbs and labored in its railroad yards, packing houses, and steel mills (in 1926, 35 percent of Chicago Inland Steel's labor force had come from Mexico), "El Enganchado" ("The Hooked One"), a popular Spanish tune, celebrated the disappointments of immigrant factory workers:

I came under contract from Lorelia.
To earn dollars was my dream,
I bought shoes and I bought a hat
And even put on trousers.
For they told me that here the dollars
Were scattered about in heaps
That there were girls and theatres
And that here everything was fun.
And now I'm overwhelmed—
I am a shoemaker by trade
But here they say I'm a camel
And good only for pick and shovel.
What good is it to know my trade
If there are manufacturers by the score
And while I make two little shoes
They turn out more than a million?
Many Mexicans don't care to speak
The language their mothers taught them
And go about saying they are Spanish
And denying their country's flag . . .
My kids speak perfect English
And have no use for Spanish,
They call me "fadder" and don't work
And are crazy about the Charleston.
I am tired of all this nonsense
I'm going back to Michogan.

American society differed greatly in each of the periods when these documents were written. . . . A significant strand, however, tied these documents together. . . . a good deal is learned about recurrent tensions over work habits that shaped the national experience.

The traditional imperial boundaries (a function, perhaps, of the professional subdivision of labor) that have fixed the territory open to American labor historians for exploration have closed off to them the study of such important subjects as changing work habits and the culture of work. Neither the questions American labor historians usually ask nor the methods they use encourage such inquiry. With a few significant exceptions, for more than half a century American labor history has continued to reflect both the strengths and the weaknesses of the conceptual scheme sketched by its founding fathers, John R. Commons and others of the so-called Wisconsin school of labor history. Even their most severe critics, including the orthodox "Marxist" labor historians of the 1930s, 1940s, and 1950s and the few New Left historians who have devoted attention to American labor history, rarely questioned that conceptual framework.

The pages that follow . . . emphasize the frequent tension between different groups of men and women new to the machine and a changing American society.

Nevertheless the focus in these pages is on free white labor in quite different time periods: . . . After 1893 the United States ranked as a mature industrial society. . . . a recurrent tension also existed between native and immigrant men and women fresh to the factory and the demands imposed upon them by the regularities and disciplines of factory labor. That state of tension was regularly revitalized by the migration of diverse premodern native and foreign peoples into an industrializing or a fully industrialized society. The British economic historian Sidney Pollard has described well this process whereby "a society of peasants, craftsmen, and versatile labourers became a society of modern industrial workers." "There was more to overcome," Pollard writes of industrializing England,

> than the change of employment or the new rhythm of work: there was a whole new culture to be absorbed and an old one to be traduced and spurned, there were new surroundings, often in a different part of the country, new relations with employers, and new uncertainties of livelihood, new friends and neighbors, new marriage patterns and behavior patterns of children within the family and without.[1]

That same process occurred in the United States.

---

[1]Pollard, "The Adaptation of the Labour Force," in *Genesis of Modern Management,* 160–208. Striking evidence of the preindustrial character of most American manufacturing enterprises before 1840 is found in Allen Pred, "Manufacturing in the American Mercantile City, 1800–1840," *Annals of the American Association of Geographers,* 56 (1966), 307–25. See also Richard D. Brown, "Modernization and Modern Personality in Early America, 1600–1865: A Sketch of a Synthesis," *Journal of Interdisciplinary History,* 2 (1972), 201–28.

. . . primitive work rules for unskilled labor, fines, gang labor, and subcontracting were commonplace. In 1910 two-thirds of the workers in twenty-one major manufacturing and mining industries came from Eastern and Southern Europe or were native American blacks, and studies of these "new immigrants" record much evidence of preindustrial work habits among the men and women new to American industry. According to Moses Rischin, skilled immigrant Jews carried to New York City town and village employment patterns, such as the *landsmannschaft* economy and a preference for small shops as opposed to larger factories, that sparked frequent disorders but hindered stable trade unions until 1910. Specialization spurred anxiety: in Chicago Jewish glovemakers resisted the subdivision of labor even though it promised better wages. "You shrink from doing either kind of work itself, nine hours a day," said two observers of these immigrant women. "You cling to the variety . . . , the mental luxury of first, finger-sides, and then, five separate leather pieces, for relaxation, to play with! *Here* is a luxury worth fighting for!" American work rules also conflicted with religious imperatives. On the eighth day after the birth of a son, Orthodox Jews in Eastern Europe held a festival, "an occasion of much rejoicing." But the American work week had a different logic, and if the day fell during the week the celebration occurred the following Sunday. "The host . . . and his guests," David Blaustein remarked, "know it is not the right day," and "they fall to mourning over the conditions that will not permit them to observe the old custom." The occasion became "one for secret sadness rather than rejoicing." Radical Yiddish poets, like Morris Rosenfeld, the presser of men's clothing, measured in verse the psychic and social costs exacted by American industrial work rules:

> The Clock in the workshop,—it rests not a moment;
> It points on, and ticks on: eternity—time;
> Once someone told me the clock had a meaning,—
> In pointing and ticking had reason and rhyme. . . .
> At times, when I listen, I hear the clock plainly;—
> The reason of old—the old meaning—is gone!
> The maddening pendulum urges me forward
> To labor and still labor on.
> The tick of the clock is the boss in his anger.
> The face of the clock has the eyes of the foe.
> The clock—I shudder—Dost hear how it draws me?
> It calls me "Machine" and it cries [to] me "Sew"!

Slavic [non-Jewish] and Italian immigrants carried with them to industrial America subcultures quite different from that of village Jews, but their work habits were just as alien to the modern factory. Rudolph Vecoli has reconstructed Chicago's South Italian community to show that adult male seasonal construction gangs as contrasted to factory labor were one of many traditional customs adapted to the new environment, and in her study of South Italian peasant immigrants Phyllis H. Williams found among them men who never adjusted to factory labor. After "years" of "excellent" factory work, some "began . . . to have minor accidents" and others "suddenly give up and are found in their homes complaining of a vague indisposition with no apparent physical basis." Such labor worried early twentieth-century efficiency experts, and so did Slavic festivals, church holidays, and "pro-longed merriment." "Man," Adam Smith wisely observed, "is, of all sorts of lug-gage, the most difficult to be transported." That was just as true for these Slavic immigrants as for the early nineteenth-century native American factory workers. A Polish wedding in a Pennsylvania mining or mill town lasted between three and five days. Greek and Roman Catholics shared the same jobs but had different holy days, "an annoyance to many employers." The Greek Church had "more than eighty festivals in the year," and "the Slav religiously observes the days on which the saints are commemorated and invariably takes a holiday." A celebration of the American Day of Independence in Mahanoy City, Pennsylvania, caught the eye of a hostile observer. Men parading the streets drew a handcart with a barrel of lager in it. Over the barrel "stood a comrade, goblet in hand and crowned with a garland of laurel, singing some jargon." Another sat and played an accordion. At intervals, the men stopped to "drink the good beverage they celebrated in song." The witness called the entertainment "an imitation of the honor paid Bacchus which was one of the most joyous festivals of ancient Rome" and felt it proof of "a lower type of civilization." Great Lakes dock workers "believed that a vessel could not be un-loaded unless they had from four to five kegs of beer." (And in the early irregular strikes among male Jewish garment workers, employers negotiated with them out of doors and after each settlement "would roll out a keg of beer for the entertain-ment of the workers.") Contemporary betters could not comprehend such behavior. Worried over a three-day Slavic wedding frolic, a woman concluded: "You don't think they have souls, do you? No, they are beasts, and in their lust they'll perish." Another disturbed observer called drink "un-American, . . . a curse worse than the white plague." About that time, a young Italian boy lay ill in a hospital. The only English words he knew were "boots" and "hurry up."

* * * *

Aspirations and expectations interpret experience and thereby help shape be-havior. . . . Men as well as women who expect to spend only a few years as factory workers have little incentive to join unions. That was just as true of the immigrant male common laborers in the steel mills of the late nineteenth and early twentieth centuries (when multiplant oligopoly characterized the nation's most important manufacturing industry) as in the Lowell cotton mills nearly a century earlier. David Brody has explained much about the common laborers. In those years, the steel companies successfully divorced wages from productivity to allow the market to shape them. Between 1890 and 1910, efficiencies in plant organization cut labor costs by about a third. The great Carnegie Pittsburgh plants employed 14,359 com-mon laborers, 11,694 of them South and East Europeans. Most, peasant in origin, earned less than $12.50 a week (a family needed fifteen dollars for subsistence). A staggering accident rate damaged these and other men: nearly 25 percent of the re-cent immigrants employed at the Carnegie South Works were injured or killed each year between 1907 and 1910, 3,723 in all. But like the Lowell mill women, these men rarely protested in collective ways, and for good reason. They did not plan to stay in the steel mills long. Most had come to the United States as single men (or married men who had left their families behind) to work briefly in the mills, save some money, return home, and purchase farm land. Their private letters to European relatives indicated a realistic awareness of their working life . . .: "if I don't earn $1.50 a day, it would not be worth thinking about America"; "a golden land so long as there is work"; "here in America one must work for three horses"; "let him not risk coming, for he is too young"; "too weak for America." Men who wrote such letters and avoided injury often saved small amounts of money, and a significant number fulfilled their expectations and quit the factory and even the country. Forty-four South and East Europeans left the United States for every one hundred that arrived between 1908 and 1910. Not a steelworker, a young Italian boy living in Rochester, New York, summed up the expectations of many such immigrant men in a poem he wrote after studying English just three months:

> Nothing job, nothing job,
> I come back to Italy;
> Nothing job, nothing job,
> Adieu, land northerly. . . .
>
> Nothing job, nothing job,
> O! sweet sky of my Italy;
> Nothing job, nothing job,
> How cold in this country. . . .
>
> Nothing job, nothing job,
> I return to Italy;
> Comrades, laborers, good-bye;
> Adieu, land of "Fourth of July."

Immigrant expectations coincided for a time with the fiscal needs of industrial manufacturers. . . . When frequent recessions caused recurrent unemployment, immigrant expectations and behavior changed. What Brody calls peasant "group consciousness" and "communal loyalty" sustained bitter wildcat strikes after employment picked up. The tenacity of these immigrant strikers for higher wages amazed contemporaries, and brutal suppression often accompanied them (Cleveland, 1899; East Chicago, 1905; McKees Rock, 1909; Bethlehem, 1910; and Youngstown in 1915 where, after a policeman shot into a peaceful parade, a riot caused an estimated one million dollars in damages). The First World War and its aftermath blocked the traditional route of overseas outward mobility, and the consciousness of immigrant steelworkers changed. They sparked the 1919 steel strike. The steel mill had become a way of life for them and was no longer the means by which to reaffirm and even strengthen older peasant and village life-styles.

* * * *

. . . In Gilded Age America (and afterward in the Progressive Era despite the radical change in patterns of immigration), working-class and immigration history regularly intersected, and that intermingling made for powerful continuities. In 1880, . . . more than 70 of every 100 persons in San Francisco (78), St. Louis (78), Cleveland (80), New York (80), Detroit (84), Milwaukee (84), and Chicago (87) were immigrants or the children of immigrants, and the percentage was just as high in many smaller American industrial towns and cities. "Not every foreigner is a workingman," noticed the clergyman Samuel Lane Loomis in 1887, "but in the cities, at least, it may almost be said that every workingman is a foreigner." And until the 1890s most immigrants came from Northern and Western Europe, French- and English-speaking Canada, and China. In 1890, only 3 percent of the nation's foreign-born residents—290,000 of 9,200,000 immigrants—had been born in Eastern or Southern Europe. (It is a little recognized fact that most North and West European immigrants migrated to the United States after, not before, the American Civil War.) When so much else changed in the industrializing decades, tenacious traditions flourished among immigrants in ethnic subcultures that varied greatly among particular groups and according to the size, age, and location of different cities and industries. ("The Irish," Henry George insisted, "burn like chips, the English like logs.") Class and occupational distinctions within a particular ethnic group also made for different patterns of cultural adaptation, but powerful subcultures thrived among them all.

Immiserization and poverty cut deeply into these ethnic working-class worlds. In reconstructing their everyday texture there is no reason to neglect or idealize such suffering, but it is time to discard the notion that the large-scale uprooting and exploitative processes that accompanied industrialization caused little more than cultural breakdown and social anomie. Family, class, and ethnic ties did not dissolve easily. "Almost as a matter of definition," the sociologist Neil Smelzer has written, "we associate the factory system with the decline of the family and the onset of anonymity." Smelzer criticized such a view of early industrializing England, and it has just as little validity for nineteenth-century industrializing America. Family roles changed in important ways, and strain was widespread, but the immigrant working-class family held together. Examination of household composition in sixteen census enumeration districts in Paterson in 1880 makes that clear for this predominantly working-class immigrant city, and while research on other ethnic working-class communities will reveal significant variations, the overall patterns should not differ greatly. The Paterson immigrant (and native white) communities were predominantly working class, and most families among them were intact in their composition. For this population, at least (and without accounting for age and sex ratio differences between the ethnic groups), a greater percentage of immigrant than native white households included two parents. Ethnic and predominantly working-class communities in industrial towns like Paterson and in larger cities, too, built on these strained but hardly broken familial and kin ties. Migration to another country, life in the city, and labor in cost-conscious and ill-equipped factories and workshops tested but did not shatter what the anthropologist Clifford Geertz has described as primordial (as contrasted to civic) attachments, "the 'assumed' givens . . . of social existence: immediate contiguity and kin connections mainly, but beyond them, the givenness that stems from being born into a particular religious community, speaking a particular language, and following particular social patterns." Tough familial and kin ties made possible the transmission and adaptation of European working-class cultural patterns and beliefs to industrializing America. As late as 1888, residents in some Rhode Island mill villages figured their wages in British currency. . . . When his wife died in the late 1890s a significant ritual occurred during the funeral: some friends placed a chaff of wheat on her grave. Mythic beliefs also cemented ethnic and class solidarities. The Irish-American press, for example, gave Martin O'Brennan much space to argue that Celtic had been spoken in the Garden of Eden, and in Paterson Irish-born silk, cotton, and iron workers believed in the magical powers of that town's "Dublin Spring." An old resident remembered:

> There is a legend that an Irish fairy brought over the water in her apron from the Lakes of Killarney and planted it in the humble part of that town. . . . There were dozens of legends connected with the Dublin Spring and if a man drank from its precious depository . . . he could never leave Paterson [but] only under the fairy influence, and the wand of the nymph would be sure to bring him back again some time or other.

When a "fairy" appeared in Paterson in human form, some believed she walked the streets "as a tottering old woman begging with a cane." Here was a way to assure concern for the elderly and the disabled.

* * *

Ethnic ties with particular class dimensions sometimes stretched far beyond local boundaries and even revealed themselves in the behavior of the most successful practitioners of Gilded Age popular culture. In 1884, for example, the pugilist John L. Sullivan and the music-hall entertainers Harrigan and Hart promised support to striking Irish coal miners in the Ohio Hocking Valley. Local ties, however, counted for much more and had their roots inside and outside of the factory and workshop. Soon after Cyrus H. McCormick, then twenty-one, took over the management of his father's great Chicago iron machinery factory (which in the early 1880s employed twelve hundred men and boys), a petition signed by "Many Employees" reached his hands:

> It only pains us to relate to you . . . that a good many of our old hands is not here this season and if Mr. Evarts is kept another season a good many more will leave. . . . We pray for you . . . to remove this man. . . . We are treated as though we were dogs. . . . He has cut wages down so low they are living on nothing but bread. . . . We can't talk to him about wages if we do he will tell us to go out side the gate. . . . He discharged old John the other day he has been here seventeen years. . . . There is Mr. Church who left us last Saturday he went about and shook hands with every old hand in the shop . . . this brought tears to many mens eyes. He has been here nineteen years and has got along well with them all until he came to Mr. Evarts the present superintendent.

* * *

Quite diverse patterns of collective working-class behavior (some of them disorderly and even violent) accompanied the industrialization of the United States, and certain of them (especially those related to artisan culture and to peasant and village cultures still fresh to factory labor and to the machine) deserve brief attention. Characteristic European forms of "premodern" artisan and lower-class protest in the United States occurred . . . after (1893–1919) the years when the country "modernized." The continuing existence of such behavior followed from the changing composition of the working-class population. Asa Briggs's insistence that "to understand how people respond to industrial change it is important to examine what kind of people they were at the beginning of the process" and "to take account of continuities as well as new ways of thinking," poses in different words the subtle interplay between culture and society that is an essential factor in explaining lower-class behavior.

* * * *

. . . In 1902, and a few years before Upton Sinclair published *The Jungle,* orthodox New York City Jews, mostly women and led by a woman butcher, protested the rising price of kosher meat and the betrayal of a promised boycott of the Meat Trust by retail butchers. The complaint started on the Lower East Side and then spontaneously spread among Jews further uptown and even among Jews in Brooklyn, Newark, and Boston. The Lower East Side Jews demanded lower prices. Some called for a rabbi to fix for the entire New York Jewish community the price of meat, as in the East European *shtetl.* Others formed a cooperative retail outlet. But it is their behavior that reveals the most. The nation's financial metropolis saw angry immigrant women engage in seemingly archaic traditional protest. Outsiders could not understand its internal logic and order. These women did not loot. Like the 1837 demonstrators, they punished. Custom and tradition that reached far back in historical time gave a coherence to their rage. The disorders started on a Wednesday, stopped on Friday at sundown, and resumed the following evening. The women battered butcher shops but did not steal meat. Some carried pieces of meat "aloft on pointed sticks . . . like flags." Most poured kerosene on it in the streets or in other ways spoiled it. "Eat no meat while the Trust is taking meat from the bones of your women and children," said a Yiddish circular apparently decorated with a skull and crossbones. The New York police and *The New York Times* came down quite hard on these Jewish women. A "dangerous class . . . very ignorant," said *The Times,* explaining:

> They mostly speak a foreign language. They do not understand the duties or the rights of Americans. They have no inbred or acquired respect for law and order as the basis of the life of the society into which they have come. . . . The instant they take the law into their own hands . . . they should be handled in a way that they can understand and cannot forget. . . . Let the blows fall instantly and effectively.

* * * *

Symbolic secular and, especially, religious rituals and beliefs differed among Catholic and Jewish workers fresh to industrial America between 1894 and the First World War, but their function remained the same. Striking Jewish vestmakers finished a formal complaint by quoting the Law of Moses to prove that "our bosses who rob us and don't pay us regularly commit a sin and that the cause of our union is a just one." ("What do we come to America for?" these same men asked. "To bathe in tears and to see our wives and children rot in poverty?") An old Jewish ritual oath helped spark the shirtwaist strike of women workers in 1909 that laid the basis for the International Ladies Garment Workers Union. A strike vote resulted in the plea, "Do you mean faith? Will you take the old Jewish oath?" The audience responded in Yiddish: "If I turn traitor to the cause, I now pledge, may this hand wither and drop off at the wrist from the arm I now raise." (Incidentally, during this same strike a magistrate who advised troublesome Jewish women that "you are on strike against God" provoked Bernard Shaw's classic quip, "Delightful, medieval America always in the most intimate personal confidence of the Almighty.") Immigrant Catholic workers shared similar experiences with these immigrant Jews. A reporter noticed in 1910 at a meeting of striking Slavic steelworkers in Hammond, Indiana: "The lights of the hall were extinguished. A candle stuck into a bottle was placed on a platform. One by one the men came and kissed the ivory image on the cross, kneeling before it. They swore not to scab." Not all rituals were that pacific. That same year, Slavic miners in Avelia, Pennsylvania, a tiny patch on the West Virginia border, crucified George Rabish, a mine boss and an alleged labor spy. An amazed journalist felt their behavior "in the twentieth century . . . almost beyond belief":

> Rabish was dragged from his bed and driven out into the street amid the jeers of the merciless throng. . . . Several men set about fashioning a huge cross out of mine timbers. They even pressed a crown of thorns upon his temples. After they had nailed him to the cross, the final blasphemy was to dance and sing about the still living man.

That event was certainly unusual, but it was commonplace for time-honored religious symbols as well as American flags to be carried in the frequent parades of American workers. Western Pennsylvania Slavic and Italian coal miners in a bitter strike just east of Pittsburgh (eighteen of twenty thousand miners quit work for seventeen months when denied the right to join the United Mine Workers of America) in 1910 and 1911 carried such symbols. "These rural marches," said Paul Kellogg, "were in a way reminiscent of the old time agrarian uprisings which have marked English history." But theirs was the behavior of peasant and village Slavs and Italians fresh to modern industrial America, and it was just such tenacious peasant-worker protests that caused the head of the Pennsylvania State Police to say that he modeled his force on the Royal Irish Constabulary, not, he insisted, "as an anti-labor measure" but because "conditions in Pennsylvania resembled those in strife-torn Ireland." Peasant parades and rituals, religious oaths and food riots, and much else in the culture and behavior of early twentieth-century immigrant American factory workers were cultural anachronisms to this man and to others, including Theodore Roosevelt, William Jennings Bryan, Elbert Gary, and even Samuel Gompers, but participants found them natural and effective forms of self-assertion and self-protection.

* * * *

The native-born poet William Carlos Williams . . . lived near the city of Paterson and grasped its tragic but rich and deeply human interior textures far more incisively than temporary visitors such as Alexander Hamilton and William D. Haywood and illustrious native sons such as William Graham Sumner and Nicholas Murray Butler. The poet celebrated what gave life to a city in which men, women, and children made iron bars and locomotives and cotton and silk cloth:

It's the anarchy of poverty
delights me, the old
yellow wooden house indented
among the new brick tenements

Or a cast iron balcony
with panels showing oak branches
in full leaf. It fits
the dress of the children

reflecting every stage and
custom of necessity—
chimneys, roofs, fences of
wood and metal in an unfenced
age and enclosing next to
nothing at all: the old man
in a sweater and soft black
hat who sweeps the sidewalk—

his own ten feet of it—
in a wind that fitfully
turning his corner had
overwhelmed the entire city.

Karabin and Carlos Williams interpreted life and labor differently from the Chicago *Times* editor who in the centennial year (1876) boasted that Americans did not enquire "when looking at a piece of lace whether the woman who wove it is a saint or a courtesan."

The Interactions of Race and Class in Agricultural Labor

TOMÁS ALMAGUER

In February 1903 over 1,200 Mexican and Japanese farm workers organized the Japanese-Mexican Labor Association (JMLA) in the southern California community of Oxnard. The JMLA was the first major agricultural workers' union in the state comprised of different minority workers and the first to strike successfully against capitalist interests. In addition to being significant to labor history, the Oxnard strike also has sociological importance. The strike raises issues such as the historical interplay between class and racial stratification, the importance of these factors in labor organizing, and variations in Anglo-American racial attitudes at the time. Emerging as one of the many "boom towns" in California at the turn of the century, Oxnard owed its existence to the passage of the 1897 Dingley Tariff Bill, which imposed a heavy duty on imported sugar, and the introduction of the sugar beet industry to Ventura County. The construction of an immense sugar beet factory in Ventura County by Henry, James, and Robert Oxnard, prominent sugar refiners from New York, drew hundreds into the area and led to the founding of the

From Tomás Almaguer, *Racial Domination and Class Conflict in Capitalist Agriculture: The Oxnard Sugar Beet Workers' Strike of 1903*. Copyright © 1984 by Tamiment Institute. Reprinted by permission.

new community. The sugar beet factory quickly became a major processing center for the emerging U.S. sugar beet industry, refining nearly 200,000 tons of beets and employing 700 people by 1903.

The developing Ventura County sugar beet industry had an important social impact on the new community. One major repercussion was the racial segregation of Oxnard into clearly discernible white and non-white social worlds. The tremendous influx of numerous agricultural workers quickly led to the development of segregated minority enclaves on the east side of town. The Mexican section of Oxnard, referred to as "Sonoratown," was settled by Mexican workers who migrated into the area seeking employment. Arriving in the early 1900s, the Mexican population was viewed by the Anglo population with disdain. The local newspaper, for example, disparagingly reported on the Mexican community's odd "feasting," "game playing," and "peculiar customs." Mexicans were seen as "queer" people who could be tolerated so long as they kept to themselves.

Also segregated on the east side of town, adjacent to the Mexican colonia, was the "Chinatown" section of Oxnard. This segregated ethnic enclave was even more despised by the local Anglo population than "Sonoratown." Chinatown was described in the Oxnard *Courier* as consisting of numerous "measley, low, stinking and dirty huts with all kinds of pitfalls and dark alleys where murder can be committed in broad daylight without detection." Despite widespread anti-Oriental sentiment in the local community, the Asian population grew to an estimated 1,000 to 1,500 people in less than a decade after the founding of Oxnard.

Ventura County residents greatly disapproved of the impact that the minority population of Oxnard had on the social character of the county. Popular opinion blamed the minority population for all the detested vices (such as gambling, liquor, drugs, and prostitution) existing in Oxnard. One prominent Anglo pioneer described Oxnard at the time as a "very disreputable town," primarily inhabited by "riff raff" and "Mexicans." Corroborating this description, one visitor of Oxnard in 1901 described the community as a "characteristic boom town," with "many saloons" and numerous "Mexicans and others loitering around."

Thus, two very different social worlds emerged in Oxnard during its early years. On the east side of town were the Mexican and Chinese enclaves, whose presence contributed to Oxnard reputedly having a "damning influence on her neighbors." The Anglo residents on the west side of town, in contrast, were comprised of "upstanding" German and Irish farmers and several Jewish families. "While the east side of town was a rip-roaring slum," according to one local historian, "the west side was listening to lecture courses, hearing WCTU [Women's Christian Temperance Union] speakers, having gay times at the skating rink in the opera house, [and] putting on minstrel shows . . ."

Underlying the segregated social worlds existing in Oxnard was the organization of the community along distinct racial and class lines. Along the class axis there existed a small class of large-scale entrepreneurs (such as the Oxnard brothers and the major growers); an intermediate stratum of farmers and independent merchants operating small-scale concerns; and a large working class comprised of skilled and unskilled wage workers tied to the local agricultural economy.

The existence of a racial-class stratification system that was not completely symmetrical had important consequences on the contending forces involved in the 1903 Oxnard strike. While racial status and class position were closely related, there did exist some fluidity in the stratification system. The particular location of minority labor contractors in the local class structure played a key role in the 1903 strike

The development of the sugar beet industry in Ventura County led to a precipitous increase in the demand for seasonal farm laborers in Oxnard. Initially, sugar beet farmers in Oxnard relied upon Mexican and Chinese contracted laborers. The decline in the local Chinese population and the utilization of Mexicans in other sectors of agriculture, however, led to the recruitment of Japanese farm laborers to fill this labor shortage. Japanese farm laborers were first employed in the Oxnard sugar beet industry in 1899. By 1902 there were nine Japanese labor contractors meeting nearly all the seasonal need for farm laborers in the area.

In the spring of 1902, however, a number of prominent Jewish businessmen and bankers in Oxnard organized a new contracting company, the Western Agricultural Contracting Company (WACC). Among the first directors and principal organizers of the company were the presidents of the Bank of Oxnard and Bank of A. Levy, and two of the most important merchants in Oxnard. The major sugar refiner in the county, the American Beet Sugar Company, also played an instrumental role in supporting the formation of the WACC.

The initial purpose in forming the WACC was to provide local farmers with an alternative to the Japanese labor contractors in the area. . . .

Undermining the position of Japanese labor contractors and gaining control of approximately 90% of the contracting business by February 1903, the WACC forced all minority labor contractors to subcontract through their company or go out of business. . . .

Most of the Japanese farm laborers and labor contractors working in Oxnard were extremely dissatisfied with having to subcontract through the WACC. Mexican farm laborers in the area and the other numerous minority laborers recruited from other parts of the state also expressed displeasure with the new system. . . .

The grievances of these disgruntled workers provided the key impetus for forming a union comprised of Japanese and Mexican farm workers and contractors in Oxnard. At a subsequent meeting held on February 11, 1903, approximately 800 Japanese and Mexican workers organized the Japanese-Mexican Labor Association, electing as officers Kosaburo Baba (president), Y. Yamaguchi (secretary of the Japanese branch), and J. M. Lizarras (secretary of the Mexican branch). Among the charter members of the JMLA were approximately 500 Japanese and 200 Mexican workers. The decision to form this union and challenge the WACC marked the first time the two minority groups successfully joined forces to organize an agricultural workers' union in the state. This was no minor achievement, as the JMLA's membership had to overcome formidable cultural and linguistic barriers. At their meetings, for example, all discussions were carried-out in both Spanish and Japanese, with English serving as a common medium of communication.

The major purpose of the Japanese-Mexican Labor Association was to end the WACC's monopoly of the contract labor system in Oxnard. By eliminating the WACC's control, the JMLA sought to negotiate directly with local farmers and to secure better wages. Since the formation of the WACC, the prevailing rate of $5.00 to $6.00 per acre of beets thinned had been reduced to as low as $2.50 per acre. The new union wanted to return to the "old prices" paid for seasonal labor. By eliminating the WACC from the contracting business, the JMLA also sought to end the policy of enforced patronage. One of the WACC's company stores—the Japanese-American Mercantile Store—routinely overcharged for items by more than 60%. Japanese contracted laborers patronizing the store, for example, paid $1.20 for a $0.75 pair of work overalls.

In order to secure their demands the JMLA membership agreed to cease working through the WACC and their subcontractors. This decision was tantamount to call for a strike. In striking the JMLA threatened seriously the success of the local sugar beet crop because its profitability rested on the immediate completion of the thinning operation. This labor-intensive process required that workers carefully space beet seedlings and allow only the strongest beet plants to remain. Unlike the harvest, where timeliness was not as crucial, beet thinning required immediate attention in order to ensure a high-yield crop.

By the first week in March, the JMLA had successfully recruited a membership exceeding 1,200 workers or over 90% of the total beet workforce in the county. The JMLA's recruitment drive resulted in the WACC losing nearly all of the laborers it had formerly contracted. The growing strength of the JMLA greatly alarmed beet farmers in the area, for nothing like the new union had been organized in Ventura County or, for that matter, anywhere else in southern California.

One of the first public displays of the JMLA's strength was exhibited at a mass demonstration and parade held in Oxnard on March 6, 1903. Describing the event, the Oxnard *Courier* reported that "dusky skinned Japanese and Mexicans marched through the streets headed by one or two contractors and beet laborers four abreast and several hundred strong." Although impressed by their numbers, the *Courier* described the JMLA's membership as "a silent grim band of fellows, most of them young and belonging to the lower class of Japanese and Mexicans."

Immediately after its formation, the IALU began working in conjunction with the WACC to meet the pressing labor needs of local farmers. These efforts were, of course, seen by the JMLA as a strikebreaking tactic. Describing the ensuing tension, one county newspaper reported that: "Oxnard is up against labor turmoil, and bloodspots are gathering on the face of the moon as it hovers over the sugartown.

The Japanese-Mexican labor union has inspired an enmity and opposition that threatens to terminate in riot and bloodshed. . . ." This proved to be prophetic, as an outburst of violence occurred a few days after the IALU was organized.

Occurring on March 23, 1903 in the Chinatown section of Oxnard the violent confrontation was triggered when members of the JMLA attempted to place their union banner on a wagon loaded with IALU strikebreakers being taken to a ranch of a local farmer. The union's insignia consisted of a white banner with a red rising sun and pair of clasped hands. Superimposed over this insignia were the letters "J.M.L.A."

One newspaper described the ensuing confrontation in the following way: ". . . [A] fusillage of shots was fired from all directions. They seemed to come from every window and door in Chinatown. The streets were filled with people, and the wonder is that only five persons were shot." When the shooting subsided, two Mexican and two Japanese members of the JMLA lay wounded from the erupting gunfire. Manuel Ramirez was shot in the leg and two Japanese workers were struck, one in the arm and the other in the face. Another Mexican, Luis Vasquez was dead, shot in the back.

Responsibility for the violent confrontation was placed on the JMLA. The Los Angeles *Times,* for example, reported that "agitation-crazed striking Mexicans and Japanese" had attacked "independent workmen" and precipitated a "pitched battle" in which dozens had been wounded and "thousands gone wild." The *Times* charged that "loud-mouthed and lawless union agitators" had directly triggered the violence. More specifically, it was the "trouble-making" Mexican leadership of the JMLA that had inflamed the "ignorant peons" into action and that "most of the firing was done by Mexicans." Even the Japanese laborers, seen as being "inclined to be peaceable," were "excited by their leaders" and fell victim to their exhortations "a good deal like sheep."

In response to further strikebreaking efforts, the JMLA organized laborers being brought to Oxnard and succeeded in winning them over to the union's side. In doing so, the union stationed men at the nearby Montalvo railroad depot and met the newly recruited laborers as they arrived in the county. In one incident reported by the Ventura *Free Press,* a local rancher attempted to circumvent JMLA organizers by personally meeting incoming laborers and scurrying them off to his ranch. Before arriving at his ranch, however, the farmer was intercepted by a group of JMLA members who unloaded the strikebreakers and convinced them to join the union. In discussing the success of the JMLA in organizing potential strikebreakers, one county newspaper summarily noted that "by the time these men reached Oxnard they were on the side of the union and against the Western Agricultural Contracting Company."

The success of the JMLA in maintaining their strike led to a clearcut union victory. In the aftermath of the violent confrontation in Chinatown, representatives of local farmers, the WACC, and the JMLA met at the latter's headquarters in Oxnard to negotiate a strike settlement. . . .

* * * *

On March 30, 1903, the tumultuous Oxnard sugar beet worker's strike ended with the JMLA winning a major victory. The agreement reached included a provision forcing the WACC to cancel all existing contracts with local sugar beet growers. The only exception to this was the 1,800 acre Patterson ranch, which was owned by the same family that operated the American Beet Sugar Company. This ranch remained the only farm that the WACC would continue to provide labor. Thus, the final settlement meant that the WACC relinquished the right to provide labor to farmers owning over 5,000 acres of county farm land.

The success of the Oxnard Strike of 1903 raised a number of important issues for the labor movement. For years, trade unions were opposed to organizing minorities in industry and were even less interested in organizing agricultural workers. The JMLA's victory, however, forced the union movement to confront the issue of including agricultural workers in their ranks. It also forced white unions to clearly articulate their position on the organization of Japanese and Mexican workers.

The issue of admitting Mexicans and Japanese workers to the trade union movement became an important issue in both northern and southern California after the JMLA victory. In reporting local union discussion on whether or not to organize Asian workers in Oakland, the Oakland *Tribune,* for example, noted that the "recent strike of about 1,000 Japs and Mexicans at Oxnard against starvation wages and hard-treatment has brought the matter to the front."

The official attitude of organized labor toward the JMLA was, from the very beginning, mixed and often contradictory.

＊ ＊ ＊ ＊

While left elements in the trade union movement supported the JMLA, labor's principal organization—the AFL—was essentially hostile. Although the AFL convention of 1894 formally declared that "working people must unite to organize irrespective of creed, color, sex, nationality or politics," the reaction of the Federation leadership to the JMLA belied this stated purpose. Following the JMLA victory in March 1903, J. M. Lizarras—Secretary of the Mexican branch of the union—petitioned the AFL Executive Council for a charter making the JMLA the first agricultural laborers' union to be admitted into the AFL.

＊ ＊ ＊ ＊

For years after the Oxnard strike, AFL hostility towards organizing Japanese workers and farm laborers persisted. Not until 1910 did the AFL Executive Council attempt to organize farm workers as an element of the Federation. These efforts, however, accomplished very little. According to one authority, the AFL's activities after 1910 were explicitly "designed to favor white workers at the expense of Orientals." Finally, during the war years, the Federation's efforts to organize farm laborers were abandoned altogether.

Beyond its significance for labor history, the Oxnard sugar beet workers' strike also has sociological importance. The strike, for example, provides us with important clues into the nature of class and race relations in California at the turn of the century. As in other parts of the state, the capitalist economy emerging in Oxnard gave birth to a class structure in which racial divisions closely paralleled class divisions. The overrepresentation of Mexican and Japanese as contracted farm laborers and unskilled workers, and of Anglo-Americans as farmers and businessmen in Oxnard reveals the important convergence of racial and class stratification lines during this period. The class structure in Oxnard was not, however, a static one that approximated a caste system. Instead, a modicum of fluidity existed and some minorities successfully made inroads into the middle strata of the local class structure. . . .

* * * *

The experience of the JMLA with organized labor at the time also clearly reveals differences in the racial attitudes of Anglo-Americans. Mexicans and Japanese workers were not perceived as posing the same threat to the white working class. Differences between these two groups in racial and political-legal status, religion, language, and previous competition with white labor, shaped the way that the AFL reacted to the JMLA's petition for a Federation charter. Gompers' attitude toward the Japanese branch of the JMLA clearly illustrated that white racism at the time was not a monolithic structure that affected all minority groups in precisely the same way. Instead, important differences existed in the way Anglo Americans viewed and discriminated against different minority groups.

Anglo-American attitudes toward the Japanese were essentially an extension of their earlier view of the Chinese. Like the Chinese, the Japanese were seen as a direct threat to the jobs, wages, and working conditions of white labor. Furthermore, the non-white, alien status of the Japanese also contributed to their being seen as a threat to the preservation of the white race and American cultural standards and ideals.

Mexican workers, on the other hand, were not perceived at the time as posing the same threat to white labor. A number of factors account for this important difference. Foremost among these was the legal status of Mexicans as U.S. citizens and their racial status as a "white" population. The Treaty of Guadalupe Hidalgo in 1848 had extended all U.S. citizenship rights to Mexicans and socially defined them as "free white persons." Also important in mitigating Anglo racism toward Mexicans was the latters' perceived assimilability. Unlike Asians, who were viewed as uncivilized "pagan idolators," Mexicans were viewed as a Christian population possessing a culture that was not as completely foreign as that of the Asian groups. In addition, economic factors tempered anti-Mexican sentiment at this time. The late entry of Mexicans into the capitalist labor market in California resulted in their not openly competing with Anglo workers for jobs. Additionally, Mexicans were concentrated largely in the rural backwaters of southern California, away from the urban manufacturing centers where white working class opposition to minority laborers emerged first. Finally, the Mexican population was relatively small. There were, for example, fewer Mexicans than Japanese in California at the time of the Oxnard strike. All of these factors contributed directly to the existing differences in Anglo attitudes toward the Mexican and Japanese population.

The Oxnard strike vividly captured these differences in racial attitudes. Anglo reaction toward these two groups in Oxnard and Samuel Gompers reaction to the JMLA request for an AFL charter provide clear examples of this. In both cases, reaction to the Japanese was more vehement and hostile than that toward the

Mexican. Further Mexican immigration and direct competition with Anglos in later years would, however, lead to an anti-Mexican sentiment that was just as intensely racist as that against the Japanese in 1903. Thus, racism must be viewed in historical terms as a form of group domination that is shaped by the interaction of social, political, economic and demographic factors. It was the unique interplay of these factors in California at the turn of the century that accounts for the different reaction of Anglos to the Japanese and Mexican membership of the JMLA.

FURTHER READING

June Granatir Alexander, *The Immigrant Church and Community: Pittsburgh's Slovak Catholics and Lutherans, 1880–1915* (1987).

John M. Allswang, *A House for All Peoples: Ethnic Politics in Chicago, 1890–1936* (1971).

Paul Avirch, *Sacco and Vanzetti: the Anarchist Background* (1991).

James R. Barrett, *Work and Community in the Jungle: Chicago's Packinghouse Workers* (1987).

John Bodnar, *Immigration and Industrialization: Ethnicity in an American Mill Town* (1977).

David Brody, *Steelworkers in America: The Non-Union Era* (1960).

Jay P. Dolan, *The American Catholic Experience* (1985).

Melvyn Dubofsky, *We Shall Be All: A History of the Industrial Workers of the World* (1969).

David Emmons, *The Butte Irish: Class and Ethnicity in an American Mining Town, 1875–1925* (1989).

Steven Erie, *Rainbow's End: Irish Americans and the Dilemmas of Urban Machine Politics, 1840–1985* (1988).

Herbert Gans, *The Urban Villagers: Group and Class in the Life of Italian Americans* (1962).

Juan R. Garcia, *Mexicans in the Midwest, 1900–1932* (1996).

Gary Gerstle, *Working Class Americanism* (1990).

Victor Greene, *The Slavic Community on Strike: Immigrant Labor in Pennsylvania Anthracite* (1968).

Victor Greene, *American Immigrant Leaders, 1800–1910* (1987).

Herbert G. Gutman, *Work, Culture, and Society in Industrializing America* (1976).

Andrew Heinze, *Adapting to Abundance: Jewish Immigrants, Mass Consumption, and the Search for American Identity* (1990).

John Higham, ed., *Ethnic Leadership in America* (1978).

Thomas M. Henderson, *Tammany Hall and the New Immigrants — The Progressive Years* (1976).

Edward Kantowicz, *Polish-American Politics in Chicago* (1975).

Alan M. Kraut, *The Huddled Masses: The Immigrant in American Society, 1880–1921* (1982).

David Leviatin, *Followers of the Trail: Jewish Workingclass Radicals in America* (1989).

S. Frank Miyamoto, *Social Solidarity Among the Japanese in Seattle* (1984).

Ewa Morawska, *For Bread with Butter: The Life Worlds of East Central Europeans in Johnstown, Pennsylvania, 1890–1940* (1985).

Ewa Morawska, *Insecure Prosperity: Small Town Jews in Industrial America, 1890–1940* (1996).

Dominic A. Pacyga, *Polish Immigrants and Industrial Chicago: Workers on the South Side, 1880–1922* (1992).

Wayne Patterson, *The Korean Frontier in America: Immigration to Hawaii, 1896–1910* (1988).

Ronald Takaki, *Pau Hana: Plantation Life and Labor in Hawaii* (1983).
Louise Carroll Wade, *Chicago's Pride: The Stockyards and Packingtown* (1987).
David Ward, *Poverty, Ethnicity and the American City* (1989).
Jack Wertheimer, *The American Synagogue: A Sanctuary Transformed* (1987).
Olivier Zunz, *The Changing Face of Inequality: Urbanization, Industrial Development, and Immigrants in Detroit, 1880–1920* (1982).

Women and Children Immigrants Amid a Patriarchal World

The behavior within the family—the relationships between women and men, children and parents—is a useful subject to use in probing the differences between immigrant communities and that of broader American society. For example, how did the familial context of immigration change over the centuries? In what ways were immigrants' families different from those of the American-born? How did immigrant parents treat their children differently compared to native-born American parents? How did the lives of immigrant wives vary from those of their American-born counterparts? Commentators observed contrasts between immigrants and native-born as early as the eighteenth century. Gottlieb Mittelberger, among others, contemplated the differences between "English" and "German" women from an immigrant perspective. And American-born observers often connected the "advance" of American civilization to the "backwardness" of recent immigrants by using contrasts in the familial context. In the predominantly rural United States in the nineteenth century, one commonly used benchmark was the degree to which women labored in the fields in American farms. The fact that immigrant women toiled in field labor was often a source of pride among immigrants and a sign of the lack of enlightenment to the American-born.

As the United States underwent a period of urbanization and industrialization in the late nineteenth and early twentieth centuries, the comparisons endured, and their cultural significance became, if anything, even more pressing. Yet people continued to disagree on what the differences meant. On the one hand, sociologists in the early twentieth century examined with great care the immigrant family and its changes in the United States as it adapted to an urban, industrial world. They analyzed how a patriarchal, peasant family was transformed by the American environment and were often concerned about the social "disorganization" that ensued. Social reformers, such as Jane Addams, were disquieted about the inequalities of the immigrant family and worried about its consequences for women and children. They sought to effect change in what they often decried as an improper social environment. Immigrants also marveled at the differences between American women and their immigrant counterparts. They often focused on the materialism in American society and independence that "freedoms" of the United States created. Although they often agreed with social reformers that there were differences between

*the family in the homelands and the family in the United States, then, immi-
grants—and male immigrants in particular—often lamented the cultural change
that accompanied Americanization.*

*If observers paid particular attention to the family, that is not to say that all
immigrant women lived in families. Indeed, the fact that this was an era when
women could choose not to marry was connected to the concerns about the family's
decline. Yet it is also true that some women could not marry even if they wanted to
do so. Perhaps the best example of this condition was the plight of Chinese women
who had only a semifree status as prostitutes. Students of immigration thus are
challenged to try to understand the varieties of experience of immigrant women in
the United States at the same time that they must strive to comprehend the perceptions of change in the household that immigration engendered.*

 D O C U M E N T S

Americans in the early twentieth century were immensely interested in studying the immigrant family both as an institution and in terms of the relationships within it among
its members. The first three documents provide portrayals of the immigrant family in
the United States and the changes it underwent as its members adapted to American
life. Eminent sociologists W. I. Thomas and Florian Znaniecki (1918) explore how the
"familial solidarity" in the Polish peasant family is challenged by the individualism of
American life. Note how they portray women in the family as a force that assists the
process of individualization. Social worker Jane Addams (1910) depicts the "stern
bondage" in which children are held in the "peasant" households of immigrants. She illustrates, however, how people can be changed through civic instruction. Finally, another sociologist (1920–1930) describes patterns of marriage and child rearing in the
"patriarchal" family in New York City's Greenwich Village, which she associates with
Irish, eastern European Jews, and Germans. Immigrants themselves also were aware of
the differences between their families and those of the larger society, as the next three
documents illustrate. Three Italian American males claim that parental authority is less-
ened in the United States and describe how women's behavior is transformed. Next, in
a series of letters Swedish American women and men (1896–1914) write of the consequences of immigration in changing gender roles. Finally, a series of ballads written
by male Mexican immigrants (1924) decry the modifications of women in the United
States. Note the similarities between the representations of immigrant women made by
Italian, Swedish, and Mexican men. The last document illustrates the hardships of a
Chinese American woman (1898) who was trapped in a life as a prostitute.

Sociologists Describe the Disruption of Familial Solidarity
Resulting from Immigration, 1918

The [Polish peasant] family is thus a very complex group, with limits only
approximately determined and with very various kinds and degrees of relationship between its members. But the fundamental familial connection is one and

---

As found in William I. Thomas and Florian Znaniecki, "The Peasant Family," in *The Polish Peasant in
Europe and America.*

irreducible; it cannot be converted into any other type of group relationship nor reduced to a personal relation between otherwise isolated individuals. It may be
termed *familial solidarity,* and it manifests itself both in assistance rendered to, and
in control exerted over, any member of the group by any other member representing the group as a whole. . . .

The relation of husband and wife is controlled by both the united families, and
husband and wife are not individuals more or less closely connected according to their
personal sentiments, but group members connected absolutely in a single way. Therefore the marriage norm is not love, but "respect," as the relation which can be controlled and reinforced by the family, and which corresponds also exactly to the situation of the other party as member of a group and representing the dignity of that
group. The norm of respect from wife to husband includes obedience, fidelity, and
care for the husband's comfort and health; from husband to wife, good treatment, fidelity, and not letting the wife do hired work if it is not indispensable. In general, neither husband nor wife ought to do anything which could lower the social standing of
the other, since this would lead to a lowering of the social standing of the other's family. Affection is not explicitly included in the norm of respect, but is desirable. . . .

These general principles of control and of assistance within the narrower marriage group and within the larger family, and from any member to any member, are
reinforced not only by the opinion of the family itself but also by the opinion of the
community (village, commune, parish, and loose-acquaintance milieu) within
which the family lives. The reality of the familial ties once admitted, every member of the family evidently feels responsible for, and is held responsible for, the behavior and welfare of every other member, because, in peasant thinking, judgments
upon the group as a whole are constantly made on the basis of the behavior of
members of the family, and vice versa. On this account also an immediate nearness
is assumed between any two relatives, wherever [they are] found, which normally
leads to friendship.

. . . Generally speaking, the woman has the familial group-feelings much less
developed than the man and tends unconsciously to substitute for them, wherever
possible, personal feelings, adapted to the individuality of the family members.
She wants her husband more exclusively for herself and is often jealous of his family; she has less consideration for the importance of the familial group as a whole
and more sympathy with individual needs of its members; she often divides her
love among her children without regard for their value to the family; she chooses
her friends more under the influence of personal factors. But this is only a matter
of degree; the familial ideal is nowhere perfectly realized, and, on the other hand,
no woman is devoid of familial group feelings. Nevertheless, in the evolution of
the family these traits of the woman certainly exert a disintegrating influence, both
by helping to isolate smaller groups and by assisting family members in the process of individualization. . . .

The traditional form of the Polish peasant family can evidently subsist only in an agricultural community, settled at least for four or five generations in the same locality and admitting no important changes of class, religion, nationality, or profession. As soon as these changes appear, a disintegration is imminent. The marriage group or the individual enters into a community different from that in which the rest of the family lives, and sooner or later the old bonds must be weakened or broken. The last fifty years have brought many such social changes into the peasant life. Emigration into Polish cities, to America, and to Germany scatters the family. . . .

* * * *

. . . an adaptation relatively easy and successful—gives birth to a particular kind of individualization found among the bulk of young immigrants of both sexes in America and among many season-immigrants in Germany. The success of this adaptation—which should of course be measured by the standard of the immigrant, not of the country to which he comes—consists mainly in economic development and the growth of social influence. In both America and Germany this is due, in the first place, to the higher wages, but in democratic America the Polish social life gives the immigrant also a feeling of importance which in Polish communal life is the privilege of a few influential farmers. . . . Formerly the individual counted mainly as member of a family; now he counts by himself and still more than formerly. The family ceases to be necessary at all. It is not needed for assistance, because the individual gets on alone. It is not needed for the satisfaction of sociable tendencies, because these tendencies can be satisfied among friends and companions. A community of experience and a similarity of attitudes create a feeling of solidarity among the young generation as against the old generation, without regard to family connections. The social interests and the familial interests no longer coincide but cross each other. Externally this stage is easily observable in Polish colonies in America and in Polish districts which have an old emigration. Young people keep constantly together, apart from the old, and "good company" becomes the main attraction, inducing the isolated emigrant to join his group in America or return to it at home, but at the same time drawing the boy or the girl from the home to the street.

The familial feelings do not indeed disappear entirely; the change which the individual undergoes is not profound enough for this. But the character of their manifestation changes. There is no longer an attitude of dependence on the family group, and with the disappearance of this attitude the obligatory character of familial solidarity disappears also; but at the same time a new feeling of self-importance tends to manifest itself in an attitude of superiority with regard to other members of the group, and this superiority demands an active expression. . . .

. . . the unequal rate at which the process of individualization and the modification of traditional attitudes takes place in different family members leads often to disintegration of both the familial and the personal life. This is seen particularly in the relations of parents and children as it appears in emigration. . . .

. . . The children brought with the family or added to it in America do not acquire the traditional attitude of familial solidarity but rather the American individualistic ideals, while the parents remain unchanged, and there frequently results a complete and painful antagonism between children and parents. This has various expressions, but perhaps the most definite one is economic—the demand of the parents for all the earnings of the child, and eventually as complete an avoidance as possible of the parents by the child. The mutual hate, the hardness, unreasonableness, and brutality of the parents, the contempt and ridicule of the child—ridicule of the speech and old-country habits and views of the parents—become almost incredible. The parents, for example, resort to the juvenile court not as a means of reform but as an instrument of vengeance; they will swear away the character of their girl, call her a "whore" and a "thief," when there is not the slightest ground for it. It is the same situation we shall note elsewhere when the peasant is unable to adjust his difficulties with his neighbors by social means and resorts to the courts as a pure expression of enmity, and with a total disregard of right or wrong.

Jane Addams Renounces the Patriarchal Authority in Immigrant Households in Chicago, 1910

From our very first months at Hull-House we found it much easier to deal with the first generation of crowded city life than with the second or third, because it is more natural and cast in a simpler mold. The Italian and Bohemian peasants who live in Chicago still put on their bright holiday clothes on a Sunday and go to visit their cousins. They tramp along with at least a suggestion of having once walked over plowed fields and breathed country air. The second generation of city poor too often have no holiday clothes and consider their relations a "bad lot."

There are many examples of touching fidelity to immigrant parents on the part of their grown children; a young man who day after day attends ceremonies which no longer express his religious convictions and who makes his vain effort to interest his Russian Jewish father in social problems; a daughter who might earn much more money as a stenographer could she work from Monday morning till Saturday night, but who quietly and docilely makes neckties for low wages because she can thus abstain from work Saturdays to please her father; these young people, like poor Maggie Tulliver, through many painful experiences have reached the conclusion that pity, memory, and faithfulness are natural ties with paramount claims.

This faithfulness, however, is sometimes ruthlessly imposed upon by immigrant parents who, eager for money and accustomed to the patriarchal authority of peasant households, hold their children in a stern bondage which requires a surrender of all their wages and concedes no time or money for pleasures.

There are many convincing illustrations that this parental harshness often results in juvenile delinquency. A Polish boy of seventeen came to Hull-House one day to ask a contribution of fifty cents "towards a flower piece for the funeral of an

As found in Jane Addams, *Twenty Years at Hull House*, New American Library, a division of Penguin Books, USA, Inc.

old Hull-House club boy.' A few questions made it clear that the object was fictitious, whereupon the boy broke down and half-defiantly stated that he wanted to
buy two twenty-five cent tickets, one for his girl and one for himself, to a dance of
the Benevolent Social Twos; that he hadn't a penny of his own although he had
worked in a brass foundry for three years and had been advanced twice, because he
always had to give his pay envelope unopened to his father; "just look at the
clothes he buys me" was his concluding remark.

Perhaps the girls are held even more rigidly. In a recent investigation of two
hundred working girls it was found that only five per cent had the use of their own
money and that sixty-two per cent turned in all they earned, literally every penny,
to their mothers. It was through this little investigation that we first knew Marcella,
a pretty young German girl who helped her widowed mother year after year to care
for a large family of younger children. She was content for the most part although
her mother's old-country notions of dress gave her but an infinitesimal amount of
her own wages to spend on her clothes, and she was quite sophisticated as to
proper dressing because she sold silk in a neighborhood department store. Her
mother approved of the young man who was showing her various attentions and
agreed that Marcella should accept his invitation to a ball, but would allow her not
a penny toward a new gown to replace one impossibly plain and shabby. Marcella
spent a sleepless night and wept bitterly, although she well knew that the doctor's
bill for the children's scarlet fever was not yet paid. The next day as she was cutting off three yards of shining pink silk, the thought came to her that it would make
her a fine new waist to wear to the ball. She wistfully saw it wrapped in paper and
carelessly stuffed into the muff of the purchaser, when suddenly the parcel fell
upon the floor. No one was looking and quick as a flash the girl picked it up and
pushed it into her blouse. The theft was discovered by the relentless department
store detective who, for "the sake of the example," insisted upon taking the case
into court. The poor mother wept bitter tears over this downfall of her "frommes
Mädchen" and no one had the heart to tell her of her own blindness.

I know a Polish boy whose earnings were all given to his father who gruffly
refused all requests for pocket money. One Christmas his little sisters, having been
told by their mother that they were too poor to have any Christmas presents, appealed to the big brother as to one who was earning money of his own. Flattered by
the implication, but at the same time quite impecunious, the night before Christmas he nonchalantly walked through a neighboring department store and stole a
manicure set for one little sister and a string of beads for the other. He was caught
at the door by the house detective as one of those children whom each local department store arrests in the weeks before Christmas at the daily rate of eight to twenty.
The youngest of these offenders are seldom taken into court but are either sent
home with a warning or turned over to the officers of the Juvenile Protective Association. Most of these premature law breakers are in search of Americanized clothing and others are only looking for playthings. They are all distracted by the profu-
sion and variety of the display, and their moral sense is confused by the general air
of openhandedness.

* * * *

On the other hand, an Italian girl who has had lessons in cooking at the public school will help her mother to connect the entire family with American food and household habits. That the mother has never baked bread in Italy—only mixed it in her own house and then taken it out to the village oven—makes all the more valuable her daughter's understanding of the complicated cooking stove. . . . As a result of this teaching I recall a young girl who carefully explained to her Italian mother that the reason the babies in Italy were so healthy and the babies in Chicago were so sickly, was not, as her mother had firmly insisted, because her babies in Italy had goat's milk and her babies in America had cow's milk, but because the milk in Italy was clean and the milk in Chicago was dirty. She said that when you milked your own goat before the door you knew that the milk was clean, but when you bought milk from the grocery store after it had been carried for many miles in the country, you couldn't tell whether it was fit for the baby to drink until the men from the City Hall who had watched it all the way said that it was all right.

Thus through civic instruction in the public schools, the Italian woman slowly became urbanized in the sense in which the word was used by her own Latin ancestors, and thus the habits of her entire family were modified. The public schools in the immigrant colonies deserve all the praise as Americanizing agencies which can be bestowed upon them, and there is little doubt that the fast-changing curriculum in the direction of the vacation-school experiments will react more directly upon such households.

A Depiction of the Patriarchal Immigrant Household in Greenwich Village, 1920–1930

. . . the patriarchal [family type] . . . characterized . . . the Italian tradition, . . . The patriarchal form was closely adhered to by the Spanish, and certain of its elements were retained by Irish, Jews, and Germans. The large, close family was traditional to Irish and Jews, but the mother, so far from being completely subordinated to male domination, often came near to ruling the family themselves [*sic*], while masculine dominance was the chief patriarchal feature of the German form. . . .

With respect to each of the stages in the cycle of the family and each of its traditional functions, differences among the several types affected the social life of the locality.

Contacts and courtship leading to marriage were not supposed to be necessary in the patriarchal family because the arrangement of marriages was a responsibility of the parents. The conservative Italians and Spanish continued to regard such contacts as unnecessary and undesirable. The Italian girls, under the watchful eyes of parents and neighbors and living in congested quarters where they could hardly entertain men, could only meet men with the greatest difficulty, at work or secretly

Excerpts from *Greenwich Village 1920–1930* Copyright, 1935 by Caroline F. Ware. Copyright © renewed 1963 by Caroline F. Ware. Reprinted by permission of Houghton Mifflin Company. All rights reserved.

on the street corners. Courting had to go on at the movies, at dances, in the park, on the street, or occasionally in the dark entrance-ways of the near-by factory district—but a girl who valued her reputation must not be known to be willing to go on these streets at night, and even the tougher of the local boys hesitated to start a girl on the downward path by taking her there.

At the same time, the inability of their parents to arrange their marriages sent Italian girls hunting for men by hook or crook. Various places at which dances were held were rated according to the kind of crowd—i.e., the chances that one might have of finding a good match. In the summer time, beaches and uptown swimming pools were attractive for the same reason. One girl, who thought herself very superior to the neighborhood, gave the situation away in discussing the Sunday excursions which she and her girl friend made to a certain lake in the country. It was a long, hard trip, but they went there rather than to nearer places—'And you don't think we go there just for the swimming, do you? That's the place where you meet swell men,' and she launched into an account of the Packard car driven by the ones they had picked up the week before.

* * * *

Marriage itself, in the patriarchal institution, was a union of families rather than simply of individuals. In the Catholic view, it was an indissoluble sacrament. In the Italian tradition, it was governed by fate. The older women were almost completely dominated by a fatalistic attitude, and though those of the younger Italian girls who had taken on the romantic attitude regarded marriage in quite a different light, there were many who continued to feel that they were instruments of something beyond their control. Health clinics encountered this fatalistic attitude; it was apparent in the statements of the more conservative of the girls; it was registered in the eyes of the young brides whose pictures filled the windows of photographers' shops. The girls who faced the camera on their wedding day with that characteristic expression of impersonal and fearless resignation bore eloquent testimony to the persistence of the outlook on marriage which their mothers had had.

The foundation of romantic marriage, as none who attended the movies or read the mass magazines could fail to note, was love. It was a union of individuals, not of families, which might retain its sacramental character if the couple was Catholic or it might not. It was assumed to be permanent, but since it was supposed to be held together by love, infidelity was recognized as a cause for divorce by the non-Catholics, and even by some of the less observing Catholics. This was the form which marriage took for the old American and Irish young people. The Italian young men approved it verbally, but there were grounds for suspecting that some of the latter actually took the patriarchal relationship more for granted. It was becoming increasingly the ideal of the Italian girls—so much so that an Italian social worker, who was closer to the minds of her people than, probably, any other social worker in the community, was very much worried by the romantic attitude of the girls. 'They see the movies and read the love-story magazines and get their adolescent minds chock full of romantic notions, and they have nothing to take hold of.'

* * * *

The relation between husband and wife in the patriarchal family rested upon the complete subordination of the woman. Although many women actually ruled the house, the show of masculine authority was maintained. It was not an unusual sight to see an Italian father stand at the foot of the tenement steps and sharply order his wife and children to go up before him, arrogantly bringing up the rear himself.

* * * *

The ideal of the patriarchal family was as many children as possible. Among the older Italians large families were conspicuous, furnishing a large proportion of the children who played on the street and who attended settlements and other centers. They did not constitute so large a proportion of the local Italian families, however, as their prominence in public places would suggest.

* * * *

In the patriarchal family, all members, and especially the children, were subordinated to the family group. The relation between parent and child was one of absolute obedience on the latter's part and responsibility toward the group for support and cooperation. Children took it for granted that the support of their parents would be their responsibility. 'They sacrificed for us when we were little. It is only fair that we should support them in return.' In a patriarchal home, children had no 'rights,' only duties. Until the Italian home was broken by the impact of American institutions, this attitude remained, and nothing in the whole process of adaptation served more to cast the younger Italian adrift than the undermining of this assumption.

Three Italian Americans Analyze Changing Familial and Gender Patterns Among Immigrants, 1939

Unidentified Italian American, 1939

Now I know how these children are in this country; you can't tell them nothing because they mix with all kinds of people that are different from Italian people, so they learn not to respect the father and mother. In Italy the father and the mother—they have all the ideas made for the children, and the children have to do like they say, and that's the way how they learn right. In this country it's like you raise up the animals, to raise children. . . .

See, everything changes. The people now are more like the American people. Before, all the people come from the other side they used to be strict with the children just like myself; now what's the use. This is a different climate and the children they are growing different. Before, the children used to do all the things that the father says; now they do what they see and what they think is alright. Now you

From *From the Old Country: An Oral History of European Migration to America* by Bruce M. Stave and John F. Sutherland, with Aldo Salerno. Copyright © 1994 by Twayne Publishers. Reprinted by permission of the authors.

don't know the difference with the Italian boys and the boys from the other nationalities. For my part I don't care now; what's the use. But I think that the boys should not forget the country that we come from because it's not right to do this, because there is lots of things that is good from their Italian habits—that all the nationalities could learn.

Mr. Gerino, 1939

That time the Italian men they were more strict with the family and with the wife. The wife had to be in the house all the time, and she could only go with the husband when she had to go someplace. Now, the women they go to the show with the children and they go to anyplace when the church makes the good times and they have more liberty. The children they could go anyplace that they want; before, they had the orders that they have to stay near the house and they could not go far. Now the children they go to the clubs for the boys and the girls have their clubs too, and they meet all kinds of people. So these things we never had a long time before. When our children they grow up they will be Americans and you never know that they are Italians. . . .

Long time before, all the Italian people they had the children follow the ideas from the old-country style, but now you could see that all these things they don't mean nothing because all the Italian people born in this country they are not like the Italian people that come from Italy. When I was in Italy my father and mother they were the ones that tell me what their father and mother was doing and how I should follow the ideas that they had. The father in the family he was like the teacher, and everything he said we had to do. This was the way that everybody was brought up. When you try to do this thing in America you can't do it. Because the trouble here, you tell the children one thing and they do it for one day, then they go outside and they see the children that they have the different ideas because they are other nationality. Then they come home and they say that the other children they don't do the same things I want them to do.

Joseph Lazzaro, 1939

The girls in this country are just like Gypsies—they paint like Indians and smoke like men. That's a shame. If I knew that my daughter touched a cigarette I would have her out of the house forever. The girls here are like crazy; they do everything that a man does, and the bad thing is that the men like this. In Italy you never hear of this; they always stay home and always go to places where the respectable people go. . . .

I go to the moving picture about once a year. The pictures are bad because they show a lot of crazy things: women smoking; stories that can't be true, how a rich boy marries a rich woman. I think that this is bad for the young people. My children don't believe these moving pictures. Sometimes they have a good Italian show, and that's good because the Italian *romanzo* is good, and is true. Sometimes they have Italian propaganda pictures; these are pretty good but sometimes they have too much propaganda.

The Italian people believe that the woman's place is in the house. Where I come from, the women are told by their families before they are married that when they are married that they should not speak to any other man unless they know him to be a friend of the family. If the woman want to go to a church on Sunday, no man can go with her; if she is engaged, then it is alright that her men could take her, but with the permission of the parents. In Italy only one man goes with one girl; in America one girl knows 100 men before she is married. This is not right. The Italian system is good and it is right. In America, it's a shame. The girls here go to dance halls and meet all kinds of bums; in Italy the only place a girl goes to dance is at the fiesta with her people. This the right way. I think the people here should try to act like the Italian people. They could learn very much of the way to act like decent people.

Swedish Americans Write of the Consequences of Changing Gender Roles Among Immigrants in America, 1896–1914

* * * *

[George F. Erickson, September 1914]

. . . I have a girl I like a lot, but she has gone to Chicago where she is going to stay till next summer, so it is a bit sad, of course, but it can't be helped. Now you probably think I am head over heels in love, but that is certainly not the case. You said to me one time at home that I had too high thoughts about girls in general. But here in this country I don't have such high thoughts about the girls as I had at home, for the girls here in this country have another kind of upbringing, demand an awful lot of fuss and attention, and I don't respect that. So if I find a girl here who is different from the others I respect her, for there are not many of them. Now you understand that I am not so dumb but that I see quite clearly in this case. There are girls here who doll themselves up enough to frighten you. They would be better as scarecrows than anything else, so if you need any of those I can send you a boatload. . . .

* * * *

[Mrs. E. C., West Rulland. *Emigrated 1896*. From Kristianstads län.]

. . . Mother worked out for farmers for forty *öre* a day (when she worked in the rye fields, she got fifty *öre*), and in between she wove cotton material and sold it. Then my brothers went to America and sent her a little money now and then, about twenty *kronor* twice a year, and that helped enough so that she did not have to go to the commune for help.

* * * *

. . . then my brother's wife died here in America and then he sent tickets for me, my mother, and my sister. It was in 1896 in the fall that we left Sweden. . . .

As I said, we came here. Mother and Sister stayed with my brothers and I took service. At first it was hard and I did not understand what they said to me, but they were kind and after a while I understood more or less what they wanted. I got two

From H. Arnold Barton, *Letters From the Promised Land: Swedes in America.* Copyright © 1980. Reprinted by permission of University of Minnesota Press.

dollars a week at first, and then I got three dollars. Every Saturday I got my pay. I was free every evening after six o'clock and every Thursday afternoon to go out or to do my own work. And what work! At first I was ashamed to get paid for what little I did. I had to learn to cook as quickly as I could, then there was the washing and ironing every week, and the housecleaning. There was such a great difference in my eyes. I got time to rest and time to look after my clothes.

[M. M., North Dakota. Year of emigration not indicated. From Värm lands län.]

I am a woman, born in Värmland and belonged to the poor class. I had to go out and earn my bread already at the age of eight. Most of what I did was to look after children. Had to get up at four o'clock in the morning with the others. Seldom got anything to eat or drink before eight o'clock, for the coffee mixed with rye was thought dangerous to the health. I got rotten herring and potatoes, served out in small amounts so that I would not have the chance to eat myself sick. That was my usual fare. . . .

∗ ∗ ∗ ∗

Then one day, I was then in my seventeenth year, the hour of freedom struck. I got a ticket from my two brothers, who had managed to get to America, after living through a childhood like mine. I was soon ready to travel, my few possessions were packed in a bundle: my New Testament, which I had gotten from the pastor, a bad report card from school, one *krona* in money which two kind women gave me. Thus prepared, I set off with a light heart for the great land in the West. And I have never regretted that journey. Certainly I have had to work, but I was considered a human being even when I was poor. Have a good home here. Am not burdened with love for the fatherland so I have no wish ever to return to Sweden.

Mexican Ballads Ridicule Women's Changing Behavior, 1924

Modern-Day Girls

Today's young women
Do not think about housework;
They are all well-powdered
Even though they don't cook.
Who remembers the metate,
Washing dishes or ironing;
That would be unthinkable,
All they want is to have fun.
That is why Our Lord
Has seen fit to punish us;
It's all the women's fault,
Because they've shortened their dresses.

From Maria Herrera-Sobek, *Northward Bound: The Mexican Experience in Ballad and Song,* copyright © 1993. Reprinted by permission of Indiana University Press.

Modern-Day Girls

Young women today
Do not like work any more
They are always on the street
Cruising up and down.
Young women today
Do not want to do housework
As soon as the boyfriend comes
No one can find them.
The girls who follow fashion
Wear pants
And at home they don't cook
Not even a pot of beans.
Young women today
Love to go to the movies
They almost don't wear dresses
Only shorts and bikinis.
When they are fifteen years old
They want an expensive gift
They tell their fathers,
"Buy me a new car."
Young women today
When they are newly wed
They tell their husbands,
"Get me a servant."
Now I take my leave
'Cause I am dying from laughter
Pity the poor men
Who now iron their own shirts.

A Chinese American Woman Details Life as a Prostitute in America, 1898

Q.   How did you happen to come to the United States?

A.   When I was nineteen years old, the mistress No. 3 of a noted procurer, by the name of Gwan Lung, who lives in San Francisco, went back to Canton, where my mother happened to be living with me at that time, and gave me glowing accounts of life in California. She painted that life so beautifully that I was seized with an inclination to go there and try my fortune, Mother taking $200. Mexican and consenting to my going.

I arrived in this country, together with six other girls brought by this woman, on the 22nd of June, 1893. We all came on fraudulent certificates. . . .

Statement of Chun Ho, rescued slave girl, at Presbyterian Chinese rescue home, Miss Cameron, matron, to U.S. Commissioner of Immigration, Hart H. North, San Francisco, Cal., September, 17th, 1898. U.S. Immigration and Naturalization Service, National Archives, Washington, DC.

I was told to claim that I was a married woman; that my husband's name was a Mr. Tsoy, merchant in San Francisco. He was then said to have been a member of the firm of Gum Pun Kee, that was then on Sacramento St., to the best of my recollection. I was also told to claim that my parents were in San Francisco. I was told that if I stuck to these claims I could be landed, and I was landed.

When I was first landed I was taken to one of May Seen's houses that were kept by respectable families. They always do that first. From time to time parties came to May Seen's house to see me and to bargain with May Seen as to what price I should be sold at. At the end of two months after my arrival, a Chinaman by the name of Kwan Kay, a highbinder[1] and one who owned some of these houses, came with his woman, Shing Yee, and bought me for $1950. gold. They gave me a written promise that in four years I should be free. At the end of two years, after taking all my earnings in the meantime, they said I could be redeemed, if anyone would pay the sum of $2100.

I paid my first owners hardly less than $290. a month for the two years; then I was sold for $2100. to another highbinder by the name of Tsoy Lung Bo. I was in Tsoy Lung Bo's house for about a year when he wanted to take me into the country. I had to promise that I would go, but in the meantime I took steps to get into the Rescue Home, and before he was able to take me to the country the matron of the Rescue Home came with the police and had me rescued. That was about a year ago, and I am still in the home, but I understand Tsoy Lung Bo has ever since, from time to time, been demanding from me the amount he paid for me, threatening to kill me if I should not pay it before going home to China or leaving the mission. Highbinder after highbinder, through men in his employ or men who are members of his own clique, have been going backwards and forwards in the vicinity of the home, threatening me and saying it would be much better for me to return to this man; that if I valued life at all, to go right back, as the matron of the home could not always protect me.

I have an aunt living near the home and sometimes I have visited her, thinking they would not know, but they soon found out, and even threatened my aunt, saying that if she would persist in keeping me, if any harm came to her, they would not be responsible. These men stood on the street and called these things out to me at the windows.

Q. Tell us what kind of treatment you received during your stay in either one of these two places.

A. My owners were never satisfied, no matter how much money I made. When they were angered in any way, they would vent their anger upon me, which they would also do on the other girls. When they saw that the matrons of the different rescue

---

[1]Highbinder is a term used mostly by American-born people to refer to members of secret societies (or tongs) that controlled organized crime in Chinatown. In fact, highbinders constituted only a small percentage of Chinese tongs in America that were primarily fraternal organizations meant to unite members of minority families' clans against economic exploitation by large family clans.

homes were very much on the alert, they very often removed us from the houses of ill repute to family dwellings, when they wanted to punish us, so that anyone passing by could not hear our cries very well. Those who frequent those places say that they could not report any ill treatment; I was often punished in that way. The instruments used were wooden clubs and sometimes anything that they could lay their hands on, and one time I was threatened with a pistol held at me.

The work of removing myself and other girls from where we were to family places where we were punished, was done by members of the Highbinder Sociaties [*sic*]. That was a part of their work for which they receive pay.

E S S A Y S

These two essays illustrate a variety of women's relationships in the immigrant family in different contexts. The first essay, written by historian Hasia Diner of New York University, explores the nineteenth-century Irish American family with particular reference to the central role played by wives and mothers. Diner notes that Irish patterns, such as the tendency to marry late in life—or not at all—were carried by immigrants to the United States. But this behavior, she argues, was not simply a transplantation of custom. It was also a means that women used to cope with the strains and tensions— associated with poverty, domestic violence, and occasional desertion by their husbands—of life in America. Vicki L. Ruiz, a historian at Arizona State University, considers the changes that occurred among Mexican American daughters in the early twentieth century. She stresses how the diffusion of popular culture influenced Mexican American homes and how it created tension between parents and daughters. Ruiz explores how the appeal of American popular culture had to be balanced with the threats posed to the Mexican American community. She suggests that the adoption of new patterns of life did not undermine the Mexican identity.

Changes Between Women and Men in the Irish American Family

HASIA DINER

If it were possible to peek through the cracks of a quickly improvised shack of a mid-nineteenth-century Irish shanty town in a dilapidated section of New York or Boston or Philadelphia, huddled on the dirt floor would likely be a mother and her children, poor and desperate. The male "breadwinner" probably has died, a victim of an accident, or perhaps he has deserted his family, ashamed of his inability to find a job and incensed at his lack of authority within the domestic circle. Three or four decades later, the father still might not have returned as a constant family member, and the household might include a boarder or two, as the family eagerly seeks any extra sources of income to ensure upward movement for at least one of its large

From Hasia Diner, *Erin's Daughters in America,* copyright © 1983. Reprinted by permission of The Johns Hopkins University Press.

brood. Living close by that same family might also reside an unmarried aunt, a bachelor uncle, or a widowed grandmother, contributing to the survival of all.

Drawing aside the freshly washed fabric of the "lace curtain" that symbolized the arrival of the Irish into the realm of the middle class, one would note changes. In this two-parent household, the father holds down a white-collar job; a number of daughters in the family attend high school or normal school; the mother, who would not have dreamed of being employed after marriage, sets the tone of refined, civilized living which would announce to all the world—or at least the relevant part of it, the surrounding parish community—that this family had permanently liberated itself from shanty, tenement existence. A stable family was viewed as an important piece of evidence in that announcement.

Yet, no matter the relative economic class, certain features of the Irish family as it had evolved in post-Famine Ireland and was carried over as cultural baggage by the millions of young women and men persisted. In a survey of the nature of Irish family structure and the position of women within those families over the course of two generations, that is, the immigrating generation and the first crop of American-born Irish men and women, a pattern of remarkable stability appears. The propensity of the post-Famine Irish to view marriage as an economic arrangement that ought not be rushed into too young and too precipitously linked the Irish on both sides of the Atlantic. The striking number of Irish who somehow never married bore further testimony to the retention of cultural patterns despite a radical change in the nature of economic arrangements.

The importance of sibling relationships in adulthood also survived the transoceanic journey. As brothers and sisters provided the links of movement from Ireland to America, so too after settlement they succored one another and provided support in the cycle of crises of poverty and illness, desertion and widowhood, in the tortuously slow climb of the Irish from shanty to tenement to lace curtains. Furthermore, despite official dictates of the culture and teachings of the religion, women within their families continued to play roles far from subservient and passive in the United States, underscoring the strength and centrality of female family members. The economic assertiveness of women before marriage and the continued gender segmentation that defined the home as woman's turf and kingdom placed immigrant Irish women and their daughters in positions of strength and dominance within.

Certain major aspects of life, however, changed dramatically. The United States was not Ireland . . . The Irish family bent and stretched to accommodate itself, within the imperatives of the traditional value system, to confront new situations. A whole range of problems unknown in the Old World beset the Irish arrivals and forced family members to rethink certain roles and patterns. Widowhood became an even more common life experience for Irish women in the United States than it had been in Ireland and, coupled with male desertion in America, made the Irish female-headed household a strikingly common element of the social tableau.

Irish men generally experienced a decline in status and power within their families as a result of migration, pushing women—wives and mothers—into authoritative roles far greater than they had experienced in the countryside. The daughter in the Irish family no longer occupied the lowest rung of importance and respect, and the comparatively open range of economic options for young Irish women—in domestic work, in white-collar employment, and in the professions of nursing and school teaching—made her someone of note in her family and, by extension, in her community. These changes—the general augmentation of female family authority—importantly occurred without any active rejection by women or men of the dictates of traditional Irish cultural values which split the world in two—into a male and female sphere. These changes in real power within the household did not herald a rebellion in attitude or a revolution in ideals, but silently and thoroughly changed the way Irish women—and men—lived.

Studies of the Irish in New York, Boston, Milwaukee, Buffalo, Pittsburgh, Detroit, and elsewhere all documented the continuing tendency of the Irish to marry reluctantly. The rate of marriage among the Irish in the United States did outpace that in Ireland, since people no longer were bound to the single-inheritance system. The Irish in the United States, however, married less frequently than any other immigrant group, Catholic and non-Catholic alike. Nineteenth-century Irish-Americans hesitated to marry. In 1850, one Irish person in fifty in Boston married, as opposed to one German in twenty-seven. In New York in 1873, more than two decades after the Famine, only ten of every thousand Irish-Americans chose to marry, as opposed to forty-two per thousand of the German residents. . . . In short, the low rate of marriage, born of the economic necessities of rural Irish life, remained a common practice among the Irish people who had chosen to leave Ireland and who confronted an economy of a very different sort.

The continuity of peculiarly Irish family patterns can be seen not only in statistics on marriage rates but in data on ages of marriage. In most cultures, marriage for a young person heralded the emergence from youth to adulthood. Among the Irish the transition from childhood had occurred long before, and individuals married when they were well established as grown-up members of their community. Although the Irish in America married younger than did their brothers and sisters who remained at home, they married later than German, French-Canadian, or Italian immigrants or their children. . . .

The persistence of these Irish forms can be measured by looking at Irish-born men. . . . In [1880], among Irish-born men in Cohoes, New York, age 20 to 29, only 24 percent had married, as compared to 32.3 percent of the French-Canadians, 39.3 percent of the English-born, and 52.5 percent of the American natives. . . . In Lawrence in 1910, 71 percent of the Irish male mill hands 20 to 29 had not yet found a spouse, whereas 68 percent of the native-born whites, 63 percent of the Canadians, and 65 percent of the British found themselves similarly unattached. . . . Twenty-four percent of the sons of Ireland after age 45 still were single, as compared to only 3.8 percent of the American-born and none of the Canadians or British.

✷ ✷ ✷ ✷

Like their brothers, immigrant women from Ireland opted to marry much later than other American women—native-born and immigrant alike—and this pattern changed little during the final decades of the nineteenth century. In Buffalo, New York, Irish women who married Irish men between 1877 and 1882 averaged 31 years of age while their "young" men averaged 35 when they entered into the married state. In places like Cohoes, New York, a cotton textile town with a large number of mill jobs for women, Irish women vastly outnumbered Irish men. Only 8 percent of the Irish women age 20 to 29 found themselves married, and among those age 30 to 39, only 44.2 percent had found a life's partner. By contrast, 13 percent of English operatives in their twenties and 83.3 percent in their thirties were married. Just as marriage ages rose for male Irish residents of Lowell over the course of the last half of the nineteenth century, so too for Irish women. . . . Even where Irish women did not outnumber their fellow Irish men, as in San Francisco, Irish women still demonstrated a reluctance to marry.

Irish women passed on this tradition to their American-born daughters, testifying to the retention of the Irish ideals, and among second-generation Irish-American women the tendency to marry late persisted in force. Once again, Lawrence textile employees serve as good examples. In 1910, 97.7 percent of native-born women with Irish fathers were not married in their twenties, and 66.7 percent of those between the ages of 30 and 44 were still single. The female mill hands undoubtedly provide a skewed sample because most Irish women refused to work for wages after marriage.

Yet another index of the retention of Irish family forms emerges from the data on nonmarriage, that is, from those Irish men and women who chose never to marry. Once again, local statistics from Massachusetts, New York, Rhode Island, Pennsylvania, and New Jersey demonstrate that the Irish in the United States were behaving in the late nineteenth and early twentieth centuries somewhat like their kin who had not made the transoceanic journey. Among the young men and women who chose to leave Inis Beag, an Irish island community, 37.4 percent of the first generation never married. In Pittsburgh the Irish had the highest rate of nonmarried women of any white group in the female population. Among the Irish, twenty-three per thousand eschewed marriage as did only thirteen per thousand among the German and eleven per thousand among native-born in the two-and-a-half decades from 1865 until 1890.

Why did the Irish in industrial America continue to marry—or not to marry—in the fashion of the rural countryside of Ireland? This family pattern had grown out of the harrowing experience of the Famine, which convinced the agricultural Irish to mend their ways and eschew early marriage and land division with a vengeance. Why then should the Irish immigrants to industrial Buffalo, to urban New York, to metropolitan Pittsburgh, to cities like Chicago carry over this particular rural behavior? The commitment of the Irish to this form is particularly striking when one considers that it had become universal in Ireland only recently. Unlike the Irish commitment to Catholicism or the zeal of the Irish to shake off British rule, it did not have a centuries-old history rooted in the soil of Ireland's antiquity. For the young single migrants this marriage pattern was fairly new and sprang from the very immediate experiences of their own or their parents' lifetime. There certainly must have been something extremely appealing and meaningful to them in the family forms of post-Famine Ireland, that they depended so nearly on them to survive the migration, and that they flourished so well in the new urban, industrial clime. The appeal and the meaning must have struck a very responsive chord in the way Irish women viewed themselves and in the kinds of options they defined as important for their lives.

That the Irish in America chose to marry reluctantly and comparatively late in their lives indicates sharply the stability and continuity of cultural patterns among the migrants. It indicates that the economic motives for migration remained paramount. Irish women did not migrate primarily to find the husbands they could not find at home. Whereas their chances for meeting an eligible man and falling in love were certainly better in the United States than in Ireland, the opportunities for marriage to an Irish man were not favorable in the United States either.

Irish women across the last half of the nineteenth century continued to flock to Boston, Lowell, Chicago, New York, Lawrence, Buffalo, Providence, and Philadelphia, and in all of these cities Irish women continued to outnumber Irish men. These cities and mill towns did not offer large numbers of eligible bachelors. Instead they proffered jobs: factory jobs and millwork, domestic service and, later in the century, clerical and shop work. Probably the most rational thing for a young Irish woman to do if matrimony were indeed her primary goal would have been to immigrate temporarily to the United States, work here, probably as a domestic in order to incur the least expenses, and, after squirreling away her "fortune," return to Ireland and find herself an unmarried boy who could not quite afford a local girl with dowry. This certainly happened occasionally. The literature of late-nineteenth- and early twentieth-century small town Ireland alluded intermittently to the returned "Yank" woman who brought back her money, her stove—to the wonderment of the residents of the town—her newly acquired twang, and her memories of life in America.

Although Irish women brought over from Ireland a tradition, admittedly a relatively new one, of late marriage or nonmarriage, the tradition remained strong in America because it continued to make economic sense. . . . Upon marrying an Irish woman ended her life as a worker, as an earner of income. Although married Irish women worked for wage under situations of duress—when their husbands were incapacitated or when they deserted—Irish wives generally had among the lowest rates of employment. In Fall River at the turn of the century 30 percent of all French-Canadian wives held down factory jobs, as did 28 percent of the Portuguese, whereas only 12 percent of Irish wives found themselves on the assembly line. . . . A study of Irish women in Holyoke, Massachusetts, once again revealed that unlike women in other groups, "hers was the role of homemaker, and husband and children alike bent every effort to maintain her in it. In consequence the Irish family had a unity and dignity which neither poverty nor prosperity could destroy."

Furthermore, Irish families were unique in their aversion to homework. Eastern European Jews on New York's Lower East Side engaged in sweatshop labor at home, making garments, and Italians made buttons and artificial flowers in their apartments. Social workers, government investigators, and settlement house observers who studied the sweatshop syndrome almost never reported any such enterprise among Irish wives. . . . Irish widows were another story, and they often opted for homework as a way to care for their children and earn an income. These were the exceptions, however. Generally an Irish woman's earnings ended with marriage.

For Irish women, therefore, the large sums of money that they collected to send home as remittance to those family members holding down the farm in Ireland dried up upon marriage. When they were single Irish servant girls and mill workers they made a staggering contribution to the Irish economy in the form of these remittances, but all nineteenth-century observers agreed that when a girl changed her state to that of a married woman she no longer continued to underwrite the expense of her family back home. Given the tremendous loyalty of Irish children for parents and love for their siblings, this certainly constituted a sacrifice in order to marry.

Yet married Irish women abandoned their jobs with the same zeal and ardor with which they had rushed into them as single women. Traditional Irish culture stressed the centrality of the woman in her home with her husband and children as did the cultures of most other European immigrants. Yet Italian and French-Canadian women, who worked in fewer numbers than did the Irish before marriage, remained in the labor market more frequently afterward. The Catholic church frowned gravely upon such behavior and insistently thundered that a married woman belonged in the home and the only work of importance that she ought to engage in was motherhood. Irish women seem to have agreed with this position, in that they rarely sought work after they married and did not consciously limit the number of children they bore and raised. To the Irish the Church represented the single most important institution in their lives and probably the only source of real authority—authority to be adhered to with devotion. Not so for the Italians who, in the United States as well as in the *mezzogiorno,* had a much more ambivalent and less intimate relation with the Catholic church and its clergy.

Irish marriage quickly brought with it the burden of a growing and hungry family. This may have deterred Irish women and men from taking the plunge into matrimony. Marriage was synonymous with economic hardship and duress for unskilled workers. Importantly, many of the successful Irish political and business figures, young men who dedicated their lives to rising into the middle and upper classes, consciously chose money and power over marriage and family.

Marriage involved a profound change in one's economic status. Irish women by all possible measures made that change with deliberation and assessed the advantages and disadvantages of the polar states of singleness and matrimony. Lelia Hardin Bugg, a novelist of American-Irish life in the late nineteenth century, noted quite clearly the weighing and the calculations involved when she moralized in her sketches of *The People of Our Parish,* "the sensible woman realizes that any sort of work is a thousand times better than an unhappy marriage, and the unselfish one often chooses to earn a living rather than to be a burden on an overtaxed father or brother."

In a series of lessons for working Catholic girls, appearing first in 1868 and reissued in 1892, George Deshon spent a great deal of time painting the ideal Catholic marriage for his young female readers, and he advised that although "marriage is a state of life instituted by God Himself," young people should "not be too hasty in making a decision" as to their life's partner. The wrong choice, a poor decision, could have disastrous results. He asked:

> Who is that bloated, coarse-looking woman who has not apparently combed her hair for a week, with a lot of ragged children bawling and fighting and cursing around her in her miserable, dirty hovel? That was, a few years ago, a pretty, modest girl, who was innocent and light-hearted, earning an easy living in a quiet pleasant family, and attending to her duties regularly and with great delight in her soul.

Deshon, therefore, cautioned that women wait patiently for a partner, although he believed that the typical girl wanted "to settle herself in life by marriage. She may be happy enough, and well enough off, at the present, but she has to consider the future; her life in middle age and when she is old."

Equally romantic views of marriage abounded in late-nineteenth-century Irish-American literature penned by women as well as men and in the sermons and religious tracts of the Catholic church. Many of the Irish women who consciously chose the single state might have agreed with Elizabeth Gurley Flynn about this (but probably about nothing else) when she remembered her mother's hours of drudgery and labor, her parcel of children, and her inability to act on her own. As she recalled, "A domestic life and possibly a large family had no attraction for me. My mother's aversion to both had undoubtedly affected me profoundly. She was strong for her girls 'being somebody' and 'having a life of their own.'" The hesitancy of the Irish to marry grew out of the economic needs of the Famine. The economic needs of American life allowed Irish women and men to keep that tradition alive.

If Irish women upon marriage gave up their careers as servants, mill hands, shopgirls, and factory operatives, they did gain large numbers of children. . . .

Women of Irish extraction also married later than German women, for example, therefore commencing their childbearing years later, but for the Irish those years extended far longer than for others. . . . Studies of Irish family patterns . . . in Massachusetts, in Milwaukee, in Pittsburgh, in a number of Rhode Island towns, in New York City, in Buffalo, . . . all yielded very similar pictures. Importantly, Irish women were more likely to become widowed or deserted than Italian or German women. Irish husbands more likely would take a job on a railroad construction crew or a canal-building gang, which took them away from home, often for years at a stretch, limiting the opportunities for conception. The nonmarrying and late-marrying Irish women and widows therefore brought down the total of Irish births.

The kinds of families they formed bore a very close resemblance to the arrangements of social life in Ireland. Although changes occurred and the Irish-American birth rate dipped in the twentieth century in the United States, this occurred quite gradually, and second- or even third-generation Irish families did not differ radically from those of the immigrants, particularly in terms of family size.

While much of Irish-American family life preserved the functional element of the Old World, new realities added strains and tensions to the lives of women within their families. The family life among these immigrants and their children was ravaged by a whole range of problems—a high rate of domestic violence and discord, the frequent desertion of the male breadwinner, and a high rate of industrial accidents that created many a widow and orphan. Taken together, these forces produced a striking number of female-headed households. An Irish immigrant woman who chose in the 1860s or 1870s to marry a construction worker in Boston or Providence or a factory hand living in New York or Worcester ran a very high risk of having some day to be sole support for a house full of children, existing indeed on starvation's edge.

This certainly does not imply that *all* Irish families rocked and reeled under the strain of disorganization; that all Irish families as they settled in and sought to adjust to American life were the scenes of disarray and chaos. Clearly, families existed in which husband and wife, children, and other kin lived and worked together, earning enough money to propel the next generation into a somewhat more comfortable station. But since they did not add to the cases on the police docket or the charity files nor did their harmony and stability make material for newspaper vignettes, they have escaped into anonymity. . . .

Importantly, the Irish themselves, writers, clergy, publicists, and journalists, recognized the high incidence of violence in the Irish home. One of the most extensive activities of the Irish-founded Sisters of Mercy in American cities was to provide a place of refuge for battered Irish wives, who had no other place to escape the wrath of their husbands. Irish newspapers and those Irish leaders who defined the curse of the Irish man as drink and city life frequently pointed out the grisly details of wife-beating and even murder. . . . Although the typical journalistic-moralistic view stressed the violence of Irish husbands toward their wives, one sterling commentator of Irish-America, Mr. Dooley, placed the shoe on the other foot, and his narratives of life on Archey Road depicted Irish wives who rendered effective assault. Poor Malachi Duggan, for example, "won day he had a fallin' out with his wife, f'r the championship iv th' Duggan family," wrote the sardonic Finley Peter Dunne, creator of this immensely popular genre of Irish-American narrative,

> an' Malachai was winnin' when Mrs. Duggan she r-run him into a clothes closet and shtood ga-ard at th' dure like a sinthry. "Come out," says she, "an' fight" she says, "ye Limerick buthermilk" she says. She come fr'm Waterford an' her father was th' best man with a stick in Ireland till he passed away to his repose iv pnoomony iv th' lungs.

The Irish homes of Chicago, as portrayed by Dunne and described by Dooley, indeed provided an arena for physical violence with women in a position of strength. However accurate this assessment of female physical prowess may or may not have been, observers of all kinds stressed the extremely high level of tension in the Irish homes of urban America which sparked into domestic discord and ignited into violence with striking frequency.

Domestic violence was not unheard of in Ireland. It grew in part out of the Irish traditions of sex segregation and gender animosity. It underscored the basic tension in the culture between men and women, between husbands and wives. This tension surfaced in America as a major domestic problem in the Irish enclaves.

Other families might have coped with marital tension through the divorce court, but as devout Catholics the Irish could not consider divorce. A marriage made in heaven was forever. Official records of charity organizations, Catholic and non-Catholic, as well as social settlements indicate that the tone of male-female relations within the Irish families was indeed characterized by intense animosity. Settlement workers, usually women of native-born Protestant origin, did in fact often get a chance to observe the day-to-day workings of Irish domestic relations, and the notations of the representatives of the North Bennett Street Industrial School, for example, etched a portrait of deep hostility across gender lines within the family. Irish women confided to the settlement workers that they would not live with their husbands one more day and pleaded with the settlement workers to provide them with some shelter or assistance to free them of dependence on their husbands. Irish women appeared repeatedly as either deserted or deserting and their feeble attempts at reconciliation proved fruitless. While such reports weighed the evidence toward the deviant and problematic, emphasizing the intensity of conflict, stressing the most extreme cases of discord among the poor, the Irish themselves confirmed their essential accuracy. The generalized lack of interest that Irish men displayed toward women, the rigidly segregated world in which they functioned, and the disdain they demonstrated for interacting with women made the deviant patterns not so aberrant at all. Martin Lomasney, the leader of Boston Irish politics in the late nineteenth century, prided himself that he "never married, never had a romance, never attended a wedding"—a bit extreme perhaps in the degree of the sentiment, yet not out of line with the general tone of expression in the self-descriptions of Irish-American life. Although James Michael Curley did marry, at age thirty-two, he informed readers of his autobiography that "I had no time for girl friends," and when he and the new Mrs. Curley went on their honeymoon he "visited every town officer or city hall possible, picking up pointers from officials." His descriptions of the honeymoon mentioned his new bride only in passing, as he used the occasion to meet Irish-American political luminaries along the way. . . . When John Morrissey, a heavyweight champion of the 1870s, was seen dressed up in "swallowtail coat, patent leather boots, white kid gloves," a friend asked, " 'John, what's up now? Going to a wedding?' " " 'No,' " answered Morrissey, " 'not so bad as that.' "

Irish-American culture de-emphasized romance. Social realities created a pattern whereby marriage and the interaction between husband and wife was at best one of irritability and separate spheres and at worst one of tension and domestic violence. This grew out of the combined influence of old-world patterns, in which sex segregation and hostility measured even greater, and the influences of American economic conditions, whereby individuals married as adults, with women particularly having experienced any number of years as independent wage earners. Women in such marriages rarely submitted passively to the domination of their husbands, and the high level of female assertiveness within the home offered a direct challenge to their spouses' view that authority belonged to men. . . .

One way men responded to such patterns of domestic discord and eroded authority was to desert, to simply pick up and leave their wives and children to fend for themselves temporarily or permanently. How much of the desertion actually involved Irish men going off in search of work—on railroad gangs, on construction crews—is unclear, since official records were always spotty. Yet if women admitted to being deserted, they most likely were. . . .

With so many widows, with so many deserted wives, it was only natural that the Irish-American world contained a large number of female-headed households, families supported and controlled by women. By all accounts, statistical and literary, quantitative and qualitative, the female-directed family appeared often in Irish-America. Among the Irish in Philadelphia in 1870, for example, female-headed households appeared more often than among any other white group, although the black rate exceeded that of the Irish. Of the Irish families, 16.9 percent were headed by a woman, as opposed to 5.9 percent of the Germans and 14.3 percent of the native white Americans (a significant portion of whom were of Irish stock). In Buffalo in 1855, 18 percent of the Irish homes had a woman at their head. Ten years later the number had dropped to 14 percent, and then in 1875 it jumped back to 16 percent. . . . Boston's South End not only housed the city's largest Irish enclave but it also registered the highest percentage of female-headed households of any neighborhood of the Hub City.

Despite all sorts of problems, Irish women had a fierce determination to sustain their families and to ensure some degree of upward movement. In fact, Irish women exerted tremendous influence within their families. Families with fathers present could also have been described as mother-centered. The impact of these matricentered families on Irish-American social development shaped the American-born children of the immigrants strongly. The tradition of strong, assertive Irish women which had its roots in Ireland's rural economy became even more pronounced in America and its urban environment.

The status of father in the Irish family eroded after migration since the father no longer exerted the same degree of authority connected with the whole process of the transfer of land. Since sons in urban industrial America were not expected to take over their father's job on a construction crew or a factory assembly line, fathers generally lost the power that accompanied the role of passing on the skills and expertise that they had held in agricultural Ireland. As the male role weakened, the female one accumulated greater prestige and authority. From scattered autobiographies, from the fragmentary evidence of letter collections of Irish immigrants, one can see that Irish men endured a harder process of adjustment to life in America and demonstrated less emotional flexibility in learning to cope with their new home than did Irish women. Perhaps the tremendous advantages that Irish society accorded to men and the preferential treatment they received from their families made them yearn more for their home communities than did the young women, who in Ireland clearly occupied the lowest rank in the scale of prestige.

Since married life held out so many pitfalls, since being the wife of an Irish man in America during the mid-nineteenth to the early twentieth century held out so many possible tragedies, many Irish women reluctantly entered into blessed matrimony. Because they had immigrated to the United States in order to better their lot, to guide their own destinies, Irish women exchanged their roles as wage earner and income producer to that of wife and mother with a degree of circumspection. Given a long Irish tradition that called upon women to assert themselves, particularly in the home, and given the grim realities of life for the poor in urban America, Irish women, as wives and mothers, found themselves thrust into positions of power and authority. Significantly, the late age of marriage and the extended number of years spent in the labor force may have cushioned the shock and blunted the pain for the Irish wife who found herself pushed into central responsibility for her family, with few sources of support or solace.

Changes Between Daughters and Parents in the Mexican American Family

VICKI L. RUIZ

The Spanish-speaking population in the United States soared between 1910 and 1930 as over one million Mexicanos migrated northward. Pushed by the economic and political chaos generated by the Mexican Revolution and lured by jobs in U.S. agribusiness and industry, they settled into existing barrios and forged new communities both in the Southwest and the Midwest, in small towns and cities. For example, in 1900 only three thousand to five thousand Mexicans lived in Los Angeles, but by 1930 approximately one hundred fifty thousand persons of Mexican birth or heritage had settled into the city's expanding barrios. On a national level, by 1930 Mexicans, outnumbered only by Anglos and blacks, formed the "third largest 'racial' group."

Pioneering social scientists, particularly Manuel Gamio, Paul Taylor, and Emory Bogardus, examined the lives of these Mexican immigrants, but their materials on women are sprinkled here and there and at times are hidden in unpublished field notes. Among Chicano historians and writers, there appears a fascination with second-generation Mexican-American men, especially as *pachucos*.[1] The lifestyles and attitudes of their female counterparts have gone largely unnoticed, even though women may have experienced deeper generational tensions. "Walking in two worlds," they blended elements of Americanization with Mexican expectations and values. . . .

This study relies extensively on oral history. The memories of thirteen women serve as the basis for my reconstruction of adolescent aspirations and experiences (or dreams and routines). . . .

The women themselves are fairly homogeneous by nativity, class, residence, and family structure. With one exception, all are U.S. citizens by birth and attended southwestern schools. Ten of the interviewees were born between 1913

From David G. Gutiérrez (ed.), *Between Two Worlds,* copyright © 1993 The Regents of the University of California Press. Reprinted by permission of the University of California Press.

[1]A Mexican-American term used to describe young Chicano males.

and 1929. Although two came from families once considered middle class in Mexico, all can be considered working class in the United States. Their fathers' typical occupations included farm worker, day laborer, and busboy. Two women had fathers with skilled blue-collar jobs (butcher and surveyor), and two were the daughters of small family farmers. The informants usually characterized their mothers as homemakers, although several remembered that their mothers took seasonal jobs in area factories and fields. The mother of the youngest interviewee . . . supported her family through domestic labor and fortune-telling. Eleven grew up in urban barrios, ten in Los Angeles. Most families were nuclear rather than extended, although kin usually (but not always) resided nearby. Rich in detail, these interviews reveal the complex negotiations across generation and across culture.

* * * *

Americanization seemed to seep into the barrios from all directions—from schools, factories, and even their ethnic press. Parental responses to the Americanization of their children can be classified into two distinct categories: accommodation and resistance. These responses seem more rooted in class than in gender. In the sample of thirteen interviews and in my survey of early ethnographies, I can find no indication that intergenerational tension occurred more frequently among fathers and daughters than among mothers and daughters. While parents cannot be viewed as a monolithic group, certainly both took an active interest in the socialization of their children. Although resistance was the norm, some parents encouraged attempts at acculturation, and at times entire families took adult education courses in a concerted effort to become "good Americans." Paul Taylor argues that middle-class Mexicans desiring to dissociate themselves from their working-class neighbors had the most fervent aspirations for assimilation. Once in the United States, middle-class Mexicanos found themselves subject to ethnic prejudice that did not discriminate by class. Because of restrictive real estate covenants and segregated schools, these immigrants had lived in the barrios with people they considered inferiors. By passing as "Spanish," they cherished hopes of melting into the American social landscape. Sometimes mobility-minded parents sought to regulate their children's choice of friends and later marriage partners. "My folks never allowed us to go around with Mexicans," remembered Alicia Mendeola Shelit. "We went sneaking around, but my dad wouldn't allow it. We'd always be with whites." Interestingly, Shelit was married twice, both times to Anglos. As anthropologist Margarita Melville has concluded in her contemporary study of Mexican women immigrants, "aspirations for upward mobility" emerged as the most distinguishing factor in the process of acculturation. Of course, it would be unfair to characterize all middle-class Mexican immigrants as repudiating their mestizo identity. As one young woman cleverly remarked, "Listen, I may be a Mexican in a fur coat, but I'm still a Mexican."

Although enjoying the creature comforts afforded by life in the United States, Mexican immigrants retained their cultural traditions, and parents developed strategies to counteract the alarming acculturation of their young. Required to speak only English at school, Mexican youngsters were then instructed to speak only Spanish at home. Even when they permitted the use of English, parents took steps to ensure the retention of Spanish among their children. Rosa Guerrero fondly remembered sitting with her father and conjugating verbs in Spanish, "just for the love of it." Proximity to Mexico also played an important role in maintaining cultural ties. Growing up in El Paso, Texas, Guerrero crossed the border into Ciudad Juárez every weekend with her family in order to attend traditional recreational events, such as the bullfights. Her family, moreover, made yearly treks to visit relatives in central Mexico. Those who lived substantial distances from the border resisted assimilation by building ethnic pride through nostalgic stories of life in Mexico. As one San José woman related: "My mother never . . . tired of telling us stories of her native village in Guanajuato; she never let us children forget the things that her village was noted for, its handicrafts and arts, its songs and its stories. . . . She made it all sound so beautiful with her descriptions of the mountains, and the lakes, the old traditions, the happy people, and the dances and weddings and fiestas. From the time I was a small child I always wanted to go back to Mexico and see the village where my mother was born." While many youngsters relished the folk and family lore told by their parents or grandparents, others failed to appreciate their elders' efforts. "Grandmother Perez's stories about the witches and ghosts of Los Conejos get scant audience, in competition with Dick Tracy and Buck Rogers."

In bolstering cultural consciousness, parents found help through youth-oriented community organizations. Church, service, and political clubs reinforced ethnic awareness. Examples included the "Logia 'Juventud Latina' " of the Alianza Hispano Americana; the Mexican-American movement, initially sponsored by the Young Men's Christian Association; and the youth division of El Congreso de Pueblos que Hablan Español [Spanish-Speaking Peoples' Congress]. Bert Corona, a leading California civil rights advocate for over four decades, began his career of activisim as a leader in both the Mexican-American movement and the youth auxiliary of the Spanish-Speaking Peoples' Congress.

Interestingly, only two of the thirteen women mentioned Catholicism as an important early influence. The Catholic church played more of a social role; it organized youth clubs and dances, and it was the place for baptisms, marriages, and funerals. For others, Protestant churches offered a similar sense of community. Establishing small niches in Mexican barrios, Protestant missionaries envisioned themselves as the harbingers of salvation and Americanization. Yet some converts saw their churches as reaffirming traditional Mexican values. "I was beginning to think that the Baptist church was a little too Mexican. Too much restriction," remembered Rose Escheverria Mulligan. Indeed, this woman longed to join her Catholic peers who regularly attended church-sponsored dances. "I noticed they were having a good time." Whether gathering for a Baptist picnic or a Catholic dance, teenagers seemed more attracted to the social rather than the spiritual side of their religion. Certainly, more research is needed to assess the impact of Protestant social workers and missionaries on the attitudes of adolescent women. Mary Luna, for example, credited her love of reading to an Anglo educator who converted a small house in the barrio into a makeshift community center and library. The dual thrust of Americanization, education and consumerism, can be discerned in the following excerpt from Luna's oral history: "To this day I just love going to libraries. . . . There are two places that I can go in and get a real warm, happy feeling; that is, the library and Bullock's [department store] in the perfume and makeup department." Blending new behavior with traditional ideals, young women also had to balance family expectations with their own need for individual expression.

Within families, young women, perhaps more than their brothers, were expected to uphold certain standards. Indeed, Chicano social scientists have generally portrayed women as "the 'glue' that keeps the Chicano family together" and as the guardians of "traditional culture." Parents, therefore, often assumed what they perceived as their unquestionable prerogative to regulate the actions and attitudes of their adolescent daughters. Teenagers, on the other hand, did not always acquiesce in the boundaries set down for them by their elders. Intergenerational tension flared along several fronts.

Generally, the first area of disagreement between a teenager and her family would be over her personal appearance. During the 1920s, a woman's decision "to bob or not to bob" her hair assumed classic proportions in Mexican families. After considerable pleading, Belen Martínez Mason was permitted to cut her hair, though she soon regretted her decision. "Oh, I cried for a month." Differing opinions over fashions often caused ill feelings. One Mexican-American woman recalled that, when she was a young girl, her mother dressed her "like a nun" and she could wear "no makeup, no cream, no nothing" on her face. Swimsuits, bloomers, and short skirts also became sources of controversy. Some teenagers left home in one outfit and changed into another at school. Once María Fierro arrived home in her bloomers. Her father inquired, " 'Where have you been dressed like that, like a clown?' " "I told him the truth," Fierro explained. "He whipped me anyway. . . . So from then on whenever I went to the track meet, I used to change my bloomers so that he wouldn't see that I had gone again." The impact of flapper styles on the Mexican community was clearly expressed in the following verse, taken from a *corrido* appropriately entitled "Las Pelonas" (The Bobbed-Haired Girls):

> Red bandannas
> I detest,
> And now the flappers
> Use them for their dress.
> The girls of San Antonio
> Are lazy at the *metate*.
> They want to walk out bobbed-haired,
> With straw hats on.
> The harvesting is finished,
> So is the cotton;
> The flappers stroll out now
> For a good time.

With similar sarcasm, another popular ballad chastised Mexican women for applying makeup so heavily as to resemble a piñata.

Once again, bearing the banner of glamour and consumption, *La Opinión* featured sketches of the latest flapper fashions as well as cosmetic ads from both Latino and Anglo manufacturers. The most elaborate layouts were those of Max

Factor. Using celebrity testimonials, one advertisement encouraged women to "FOLLOW THE STARS" and purchase "Max Factor's Society Makeup." Factor, through an exclusive arrangement with *La Opinión,* went even further in courting the Mexican market by answering beauty questions from readers in a special column—"Secretos de Belleza" (Beauty Secrets).

The use of cosmetics, however, cannot be blamed entirely on Madison Avenue ad campaigns. The innumerable barrio beauty pageants—sponsored by *mutualistas,* patriotic societies, churches, the Mexican Chamber of Commerce, newspapers, and even progressive labor unions—encouraged young women to accentuate their physical attributes. Carefully chaperoned, many teenagers did participate in community contests from La Reina de Cinco de Mayo to Orange Queen. They modeled evening gowns, rode on parade floats, and sold raffle tickets. Carmen Bernal Escobar remembered one incident where, as a contestant, she had to sell raffle tickets. Every ticket she sold counted as a vote for her in the pageant. Naturally, the winner would be the woman who had accumulated the most votes. When her brother offered to buy twenty-five dollars' worth of votes (her mother would not think of letting her peddle the tickets at work or in the neighborhood), Escobar, on a pragmatic note, asked him to give her the money so that she could buy a coat she had spotted while window-shopping.

The commercialization of personal grooming made additional inroads into the Mexican community with the appearance of barrio beauty parlors. Working as a beautician conferred a certain degree of status, "a nice, clean job," in comparison to factory or domestic work. As one woman related: "I always wanted to be a beauty operator. I loved makeup; I loved to dress up and fix up. I used to set my sisters' hair. So I had that in the back of my mind for a long time, and my mom pushed the fact that she wanted me to have a profession—seeing that I wasn't thinking of getting married." Although further research is needed, one can speculate that neighborhood beauty shops reinforced women's networks and became places where they could relax, exchange *chisme* (gossip), and enjoy the company of other women.

Conforming to popular fashions and fads cannot be construed as a lack of ethnic or political consciousness. In 1937, Carey McWilliams spoke before an assembly of fifteen hundred walnut workers in Los Angeles and was "profoundly stirred" by this display of grass-roots labor militancy on the part of East European and Mexican women. In describing the meeting, he wrote, "And such extraordinary faces—particularly the old women. Some of the girls had been too frequently to the beauty shop, and were too gotten up—rather amusingly dressy." I would argue that dressing up for a union meeting could be interpreted as an affirmation of individual integrity. Although they worked under horrendous conditions (actually cracking walnuts with their fists), their collective action and personal appearance gave evidence that they did not surrender their self-esteem.

The most serious point of contention between an adolescent daughter and her parents, however, regarded her behavior toward young men. In both cities and rural towns, girls had to be closely chaperoned by a family member every time they attended a movie, a dance, or even church-related events. Recalling the supervisory role played by her "old maid" aunt, María Fierro laughingly explained, "She'd check on us all the time. I used to get so mad at her." Ruby Estrada recalled that in a small southern Arizona community, "all the mothers" escorted their daughters to the local dances. Even talking to male peers in broad daylight could be grounds for discipline. Adele Hernández Milligan, a resident of Los Angeles for over fifty years, elaborated: "I remember the first time that I walked home with a boy from school. Anyway, my mother saw me and she was mad. I must have been sixteen or seventeen. She slapped my face because I was walking home with a boy." Describing this familiar protectiveness, one social scientist aptly remarked that the "supervision of the Mexican parent is so strict as to be obnoxious."

Faced with this type of situation, young women had three options: they could accept the rules set down for them; they could rebel; or they could find ways to compromise or circumvent traditional standards. "I was *never* allowed to go out by myself in the evening; it just was not done." In rural communities, where restrictions were perhaps even more stringent, "nice" teenagers could not even swim with their male peers. "We were ladies and wouldn't go swimming out there with a bunch of boys." Yet many seemed to accept these limits with equanimity. "It wasn't devastating at all," reflected Ruby Estrada. "We took it in stride. We never thought of it as cruel or mean. . . . It was taken for granted that that's the way it was." In Sonora, Arizona, as in other small towns, relatives and neighbors kept close watch over adolescent women and quickly reported any suspected indiscretions. "They were always spying on you," Estrada remarked. Women in cities had a distinct advantage over their rural peers in that they could venture miles from their neighborhood into the anonymity of dance halls, amusement parks, and other forms of commercialized leisure. With carnival rides and the Cinderella Ballroom, the Nu-Pike amusement park of Long Beach proved a popular hangout for Mexican youth in Los Angeles. It was more difficult to abide by traditional norms when excitement loomed just on the other side of the streetcar line.

Some women openly rebelled. They moved out of their family homes and into apartments. Considering themselves freewheeling single women, they could go out with men unsupervised, as was the practice among their Anglo peers. "This terrible freedom in the United States," one Mexicana lamented. "I do not have to worry because I have no daughters, but the poor señoras with many girls, they worry." Those Mexican-American adolescents who did not wish to defy their parents openly would "sneak out" of the house in order to meet their dates or to attend dances with female friends. A more subtle form of rebellion was early marriage. By marrying at fifteen or sixteen, these women sought to escape parental supervision; yet it could be argued that many of these child brides exchanged one form of supervision for another, in addition to taking on the responsibilities of child rearing.

The third option sometimes involved quite a bit of creativity on the part of young women as they sought to circumvent traditional chaperonage. Alicia Mendeola Shelit recalled that one of her older brothers would always accompany her to dances, ostensibly as a chaperone. "But then my oldest brother would always have a blind date for me." Carmen Bernal Escobar was permitted to entertain her boyfriends at home, but only under the supervision of her brother or mother. The practice of "going out with the girls," though not accepted until the 1940s, was fairly common. Several Mexican-American women, often related, would escort one another to an event (such as a dance), socialize with the men in attendance, and then walk home together. In the sample of thirteen interviews, daughters negotiated their activities with their parents. Older siblings and extended kin appeared in the background as either chaperons or accomplices. Although un-wed teenage mothers were not unknown in the Los Angeles barrios, families ex-pected adolescent females to conform to strict standards of behavior. As can be ex-pected, many teenage girls knew little about sex other than what they picked up from friends, romance magazines, and the local theater. As Mary Luna remem-bered, "I thought that if somebody kissed you, you could get pregnant." In *Singing for My Echo,* New Mexico native Gregorita Rodriguez confided that on her wed-ding night she knelt down and said her rosary until her husband gently asked, "'Gregorita, *mi esposa,* are you afraid of me?'" At times this naïveté persisted be-yond the wedding. "It took four days for my husband to touch me," one woman re-vealed. "I slept with dress and all. We were both greenhorns, I guess."

Of course, some young women did lead more adventurous lives. A male inter-viewer employed by Mexican anthropologist Manuel Gamio recalled his "rela-tions" with a woman he met at a Los Angeles dance hall. Though born in Her-mosillo, Elisas "Elsie" Morales considered herself Spanish. She helped support her family by dancing with strangers. Although she lived at home and her mother and brother attempted to monitor her actions, she managed to meet the interviewer at a "hot pillow" hotel. To prevent pregnancy, she relied on contraceptive douches pro-vided by "an American doctor." Although Morales realized her mother would not approve of her behavior, she noted that "she [her mother] is from Mexico. . . . I am from there also but I was brought up in the United States, [so] we think about things differently." Just as Morales rationalized her actions as "American," the in-terviewer also regarded her as "American," though in a distinctly less favorable sense of the word. "She seemed very coarse to me. That is, she dealt with one in the American way." In his field notes, Paul Taylor recorded an incident in which a young woman had moved in with her Anglo boyfriend after he had convinced her that such living arrangements were common among Americans. Popular *corridos,* such as "El Enganchado" and "Las Pelonas," also touched on the theme of the cor-rupting influence of U.S. ways on Mexican women.

It is interesting to note that Anglo and Mexican communities held almost iden-tical preconceptions of each other's young female population. While Mexicans viewed Anglo women as morally loose, Latina actresses in Hollywood found themselves typecast as hot-blooded women of low repute. For example, Lupe Velez starred in such films as *Hot Pepper, Strictly Dynamite,* and *The Mexican Spitfire.*

The image of loose sexual mores as distinctly American probably reinforced parents' fears as they watched their daughters apply cosmetics and adopt the ap-parel advertised in fashion magazines. In other words, "If she dresses like a flap-per, will she then act like one?" Seeds of suspicion reaffirmed the penchant for tra-ditional supervision.

Tension between parents and daughters, however, did not always revolve around adolescent behavior. At times, teenagers questioned the lifestyles of their parents. "I used to tell my mother she was a regular maid," Alicia Shelit recalled. "They [the women] never had a voice. They had to have the house clean, the food ready for the men . . . and everything just so." As anthropologist Tuck observed: "Romantic literature, still more romantic movies, and the attitudes of American teachers and social workers have confirmed the Perez children in a belief that their parents do not 'love' each other; that, in particular, Lola Perez is a drudge and a slave for her husband."

However, I would argue that the impact of Americanization was most keenly felt at the level of personal aspiration. "We felt if we worked hard, proved ourselves, we could become professional people," asserted Rose Escheverria Mulligan. Braced with such idealism, Mexican Americans faced prejudice, segregation, and economic segmentation. Though they considered themselves Americans, others perceived them as less than desirable foreigners. During the late 1920s, the *Saturday Evening Post,* exemplifying the nativist spirit of the times, featured inflammatory characterizations of Mexicans in the United States. For instance, one article portrayed Mexican immigrants as an "illiterate, diseased, pauperized" people who bear children "with the reckless prodigality of rabbits." Racism was not limited to rhetoric; between 1931 and 1934, an estimated one-third of the Mexican population in the United States (over five hundred thousand people) were either deported or repatriated to Mexico, even though many were native U.S. citizens. Mexicans were the only immigrants targeted for removal. Proximity to the Mexican border, the physical distinctiveness of mestizos, and easily identifiable barrios influenced immigration and social welfare officials to focus their efforts solely on the Mexican people, people whom they viewed as foreign usurpers of American jobs and as unworthy burdens on relief rolls. From Los Angeles, California, to Gary, Indiana, Mexicans were either summarily deported by immigration agencies or persuaded to depart voluntarily by deplicitous social workers who greatly exaggerated the opportunities awaiting them south of the border. According to historian George Sánchez: "As many as seventy-five thousand Mexicans from southern California returned to Mexico by 1932. . . . The enormity of these figures, given the fact that California's Mexican population was in 1930 slightly over three hundred and sixty thousand . . . , indicates that almost every Mexican family in southern California confronted in one way or another the decision of returning or staying."

By 1935, the deportation and repatriation campaigns had diminished, but prejudice and segregation remained. Historian Albert Camarillo has demonstrated that in Los Angeles restrictive real estate covenants and segregated schools increased dramatically between 1920 and 1950. The proportion of Los Angeles-area municipalities with covenants prohibiting Mexicans and other minorities from purchasing residences in certain neighborhoods climbed from 20 percent in 1920 to 80 percent in 1946. Many restaurants, theaters, and public swimming pools discriminated against their Spanish-surnamed clientele. In southern California, for example, Mexicans could swim at the public plunges only one day out of the week (just before they drained the pool). Small-town merchants frequently refused to admit Spanish-speaking people to their places of business. "White Trade Only" signs served as bitter reminders of their second-class citizenship.

In 1933, a University of California study noted that Mexicans in southern California were among the most impoverished groups in the United States. Regardless of nativity, they were often dismissed as cheap, temporary labor and were paid "from 20 to 50 percent less per day for . . . performing the same jobs as other workers." This economic segmentation did not diminish by generation. Writing about San Bernardino, California, in the 1940s, Ruth Tuck offered the following illustration:

"There is a street . . . on which three families live side by side. The head of one family is a naturalized citizen, who arrived here eighteen years ago; the head of the second is an alien who came . . . in 1905; the head of the third is the descendant of people who came . . . in 1843. All of them, with their families, live in poor housing; earn approximately $150 a month as unskilled laborers; send their children to Mexican schools; and encounter the same sort of discriminatory practices."

Until World War II, Mexicans experienced restricted occupational mobility as few rose above the ranks of blue-collar labor. Scholars Mario García and Gilbert González have convincingly argued that the curricula in Mexican schools helped perpetuate this trend. Emphasis on vocational education served to funnel Mexican youth into the factories and building trades. In the abstract, education raised people's expectations, but in practice, particularly for men, it trained them for low-status, low-paying jobs. Employment choices were even more limited in rural areas. As miners or farmworkers, Mexicans usually resided in company settlements, where almost every aspect of their lives—from work schedules to wage rates to credit with local merchants—was regulated. In 1925, a newspaper editor in Greeley, Colorado, bluntly advocated "a caste system," even though, he alleged, such a system "will be worse upon us, the aristocracy, than upon the Mexicans in the serfdom." Both in urban and rural areas, ethnicity became not only a matter of personal choice and heritage but also an ascribed status imposed by external sources.

Considering these circumstances, it is no surprise that many teenagers developed a shining idealism as a type of psychological ballast. Some adolescents, such as the members of the Mexican-American movement, believed that education was the key to mobility, while others placed their faith in the application of Max Factor's bleaching cream. Whether they struggled to further their education or tried to lighten their skin color, Mexican Americans sought to protect themselves from the damaging effects of prejudice.

Despite economic and social stratification, many Mexicans believed that life in the United States offered hope and opportunity. "Here woman has come to have place like a human being," reflected Señora ———. More common perhaps was the impact of material assimilation, the purchase of an automobile, a sewing machine, and other accoutrements of U.S. consumer society. The accumulation of these goods signaled the realization of (or the potential for realizing) the American dream. As Margaret Clark has eloquently commented: "In Sal Si Puedes[1] [a San José barrio] where so many people are struggling to escape poverty and want, a 'luxury item' like a shiny new refrigerator may be the source of hope and encouragement—it may symbolize the first step toward the achievement of a better way of life." One of Clark's informants made the point more directly: "Nobody likes to be poor."

The World War II era ushered in a set of new options for Mexican women. In southern California, some joined unions in food-processing plants and negotiated higher wages and benefits. Still others obtained more lucrative employment in defense plants. As "Rosie the Riveters," they gained self-confidence and the requisite earning power to improve their standard of living. A single parent, Alicia Mende-

---

[1] *Sal Si Puedes* translates to "get out if you can."

ola Shelit purchased her first home as the result of her employment with Douglas Aircraft. The expansion of clerical jobs also provided Mexican-American women with additional opportunities. By 1950, 23.9 percent of Mexican women workers in the Southwest held lower white-collar positions as secretaries or sales clerks. They could finally apply the office skills they had acquired in high school or at storefront business colleges. Intermarriage with Anglos, although beyond the scope of this study, may have been perceived as a potential avenue for mobility.

Most of the thirteen interviewees continued in the labor force, combining wagework with household responsibilities. Only the oldest (Ruby Estrada of Arizona) and the youngest (Rosa Guerrero of Texas) achieved a solid, middle-class standard of living. While one cannot make a facile correlation, both women are the only informants who attained a college education. Six of the eleven California women took their places on the shop floor in the aerospace, electronics, apparel, and food-processing industries. Two became secretaries and one a sales clerk at Kmart. The remaining two were full-time homemakers. Seven of these eleven informants married Anglo or Jewish men; yet their economic status did not differ substantially from those who chose Mexican spouses. With varying degrees of financial security, the California women are now working-class retirees. Their lives do not exemplify rags-to-riches mobility but, rather, upward movement within the working class. Though painfully aware of prejudice and discrimination, people of their generation placed faith in themselves and in the system. In 1959, Margaret Clark asserted that the second-generation residents of Sal Si Puedes "dream and work toward the day when Mexican Americans will become fully integrated into American society at large." The desire to prove oneself appears as a running theme in twentieth-century Mexican-American history. I should hasten to add that, in the process, most people refused to shed their cultural heritage. "Fusion is what we want—the best of both ways."

In this essay, I have attempted to reconstruct the world of adolescent women, taking into account the broader cultural, political, and economic environment. I have given a sense of the contradictions in their lives—the lure of Hollywood and the threat of deportation. The discussion gives rise to an intriguing question. Can one equate the desire for material goods with the abandonment of Mexican values? I believe that the ideological impact of material acculturation has been overrated. For example, a young Mexican woman may have looked like a flapper as she boarded a streetcar on her way to work at a cannery; yet she went to work (at least in part) to help support her family, as part of her obligation as a daughter. The adoption of new cultural forms certainly frightened parents, but it did not itself undermine Mexican identity. The experiences of Mexican-American women coming of age between 1920 and 1950 reveal the blending of the old and the new, fashioning new expectations, making choices, and learning to live with those choices.

 F U R T H E R   R E A D I N G

Robert Alvarez, Jr., *Familia: Migration and Adaptation in Baja and Alta California, 1880–1975* (1987).
Charlotte Baum, et al., *The Jewish Woman in America* (1976).

Miriam Cohen, *Workshop to Office: Two Generations of Italian Women in New York City, 1900–1950* (1992).

Adelaida Del Castillo, *Between Borders: Essays on Mexicana/Chicana History* (1990).

Sarah Deutsch, *No Separate Refuge: Culture, Class, and Gender on an Anglo-Hispanic Frontier in the American Southwest, 1880–1940* (1987).

Michaela Di Leonàrdo, *The Varieties of Ethnic Experience: Kinship, Class, and Gender Among California Italian Americans* (1984).

Hasia Diner, *Erin's Daughters in America: Irish Immigrant Women in the 19th Century* (1983).

Elizabeth Ewen, *Immigrant Women in the Land of Dollars: Life and Culture on the Lower East Side, 1890–1925* (1985).

Donna Gabaccia, *From the Other Side: Women, Gender, and Immigrant Life in the US, 1820–1990* (1994).

Susan Glenn, *Daughters of the Shtetl* (1990).

Richard Griswold del Castillo, *La Familia: The Mexican-American Family in the Urban Southwest* (1984).

Tamara Hareven, *Family Time and Industrial Time: The Relationship Between Family and Work in a New England Industrial Community* (1982).

Akemi Kikumura, *Through Harsh Winters: The Life of a Japanese Immigrant Woman* (1981).

Elaine Kim, *With Silk Wings: Asian American Women at Work* (1982).

Louise Lamphere, *From Working Daughters to Working Mothers: Immigrant Women in a New England Industrial Community* (1987).

Valerie Matsumoto, *Farming the Home Place: A Japanese American Community in California, 1919–1982* (1993).

Margarita Melville, ed., *Twice a Minority: Mexican-American Women* (1979).

Magdalena Mora, and Adelaida Del Castillo, eds., *Mexican Women in the United States: Struggles Past and Present* (1980).

Evelyn Nakano Glenn, *Issei, Nisei, War Bride: Three Generations of Japanese American Women in Domestic Service* (1986).

Linda S. Pickle, *Contented Among Strangers: Rural German-Speaking Women and Their Families in the Nineteenth-Century Midwest* (1996).

Vicki Ruiz, *Cannery Women, Cannery Lives: Mexican Women and the California Food Processing Industry* (1987).

Maxine Seller, ed., *Immigrant Women* (1981).

Sydney Stahl Weinberg, *The World of Our Mothers: The Lives of Jewish Immigrant Women* (1988).

Virginia Yans-McLaughlin, *Family and Community: Italian Immigrants in Buffalo, 1880–1930* (1977).

Judy Yung, *Unbound Feet: A Social History of Chinese Women in San Francisco* (1995).

CHAPTER
9

Racialization of Immigrants,
1880–1930

Issues of immigration, citizenship, and race were intertwined as early as 1790 when naturalization was made possible only for "free, white" people. By the late nineteenth century, the questions had become, if anything, even more heated. Whereas immigrants of African descent could become naturalized as of 1870, an anti-Asian movement only a few years later focused especially on Chinese immigrants and worked to continue to deny them citizenship. Utilizing a series of stereotypes about Chinese immigrants and Chinese civilization, some Americans also voiced concerns that Chinese immigrants threatened the American government and American workers. By racializing Chinese immigrants, their American detractors argued that Chinese not only were too immature for citizenship, but that they were cheap, docile laborers who ultimately threatened the independence of American labor. As a result of their clamorings, the Chinese Exclusion Act was passed in 1882, which forbade the immigration of Chinese laborers to the United States. This act, the most significant in a series of anti-Asian legislation, is critical to the understanding of national immigration policy: It was the first piece of national legislation that specifically excluded a national group. As such, it was the opening salvo in a decades-long process that would lead to widespread restriction of immigration in the twentieth century.

Significantly, racial categorization extended beyond Asians and eventually even included immigrants defined by most as "white." Invigorated by scientific and pseudo-scientific research on genetics and race, observers began to focus on a new conceptualization of "races" of Europeans. They argued that the less distinguished "Mediterranean" race could be differentiated from the more sophisticated "Nordic" race by virtue of characteristics of body and skull. And they overlaid characteristics of behavior onto racial appearance. These developments were occurring precisely when immigrants from southern and eastern Europe, who were identified as "Mediterraneans," were replacing those from northwestern Europe, who were reputedly "Nordic." As a result, issues of immigration were connected to issues of "racial stock." Some Americans argued that the gene pool of the United States was diluted by the arrival of southeastern Europeans, who were now dubbed the "new" immigrants. They argued that the selection of

*immigration had changed: Whereas the earlier immigrants had been hardy pio-
neers, the "best" of their group, the new immigrants' passage was made simple
by improvements in transportation, so that the least able were now moving to the
United States. In a post-Darwinian era, when "natural selection" had become a
watchword, some Americans rued the fact that an "inferior" body of immigrants
was arriving on American shores. And because these distinctions often were
based on popular interpretations—and misinterpretations—of genetics, it appeared to many that these immigrants would not be transformed by life in the
United States. Rather, the United States would be transformed by them. These developments were powerful forces for increasingly strident calls for immigration
restriction, calls that came to fruition in the immigration restriction laws of 1921
and 1924.*

*Ironically, this continued evolution of racial thinking influenced questions of
who was and was not a "white" person. Whereas defining a "white" person once
had been seemingly intuitive, it now was less apparent because of the research on
genetics and what was purported to be the historical development of peoples. Who
was to say that an Indian or a Japanese was not "white"? A series of Supreme
Court rulings, in fact, grappled with the definition of "whiteness" while Congress
was drafting great "race-based" restriction legislation.*

DOCUMENTS

This collection of documents illustrates the progression of thinking regarding "race"
and immigration in late-nineteenth- and early-twentieth-century America. The first
two documents illustrate how Asians were racialized and portrayed as an unassimil-
able people. Writing in 1902, Samuel Gompers, leader of the American Federation of
Labor, distinguishes the white laborer from the Chinese worker, while stereotyping
African Americans and discounting Native Americans, and suggests that only one
group will emerge victorious on the West Coast. The Asiatic Exclusion League (1911)
echoes these claims, arguing that because of "mental and moral differences," Asians
can never be integrated or Americanized into the society of the United States. Asian
Americans protested against these characterizations, as illustrated by the next document. Fu Chi Hao (1907) writes how his view of the United States changed when he
saw the mistreatment and humiliation undergone by Chinese immigrants. The next
two documents show how issues of "race," widened to again include distinctions
among Europeans, albeit different from earlier distinctions. One (1915) argues that
the Nordic" race, which predominated earlier in immigration streams, was being
replaced by lesser, "Mediterranean" people. Furthermore, it contends that the former
American notion that the environment could transform people was a "pathetic" belief
that needed to be replaced with fears that any racial mixture would lower the "racial
stock" of Americans. The writer of the next document (1914) agrees that immigrants
in the early twentieth century were "subcommon" both in appearance and morality.
The racialized ideas and bias continued well into the century, as evidenced by U.S.
Congressman John Box's characterizations of Mexicans and Mexican Americans in
1928 as "peonized masses" whose immigration would further the "mongrelization" of
the nation's racial stock. The final document is the Supreme Court's 1923 ruling that
grapples with the meaning of "whiteness" and whether an Indian American was
"white."

Samuel Gompers Racializes Chinese
American Labor, 1908

... Beginning with the most menial avocations they [the Chinese] gradually invaded one industry after another, until they not merely took the places of our girls as domestics and cooks, the laundry from our poorer women and subsequently from the white steam laundries, but the places also of the men and boys, as boot and shoemakers, cigarmakers, bagmakers, miners, farm laborers, brickmakers, tailors, slippermakers and numerous other occupations. In the ladies' furnishing line they gained absolute control, displacing hundreds of our girls who would otherwise have found profitable employment. Whatever business or trade they entered was, and is yet, absolutely doomed for the white laborer, as competition is simply impossible. Not that the Chinese would not rather work for high wages than low, but in order to gain control he will work so cheaply as to bar all efforts of his competitor. But not only has the workingman and workingwoman gained this bitter experience, but certain manufacturers and merchants have been equally the sufferers. The Chinese laborer will work cheaper for a Chinese employer than he will for a white man, as has been invariably proven, and, as a rule, he boards with his Chinese employer. The Chinese merchant or manufacturer will undersell his white competitor, and if uninterrupted will finally gain possession of the entire field. Such is the history of the race wherever they have come in contact with other peoples. None can withstand their silent and irresistible flow, and their millions already populate and command the labor and trade of the islands and nations of the Pacific.

The cigar, boot and shoe, broom making, and pork industries were for many years entirely in the hands of the Chinese, depriving many thousands of Americans of their means of livelihood. As their power grew they became more independent, and in the pork industry they secured so strong a hold that no white butcher dared kill a hog for fear of incurring the displeasure of the Chinese. This state of affairs became so obnoxious and unbearable that the retail butchers could no longer submit, and with the assistance of the wholesale butchers and the citizens generally finally succeeded in wresting the monopoly from the hands of their Chinese competitors.

Asiatic Labor Degrades as Slave Labor Did.   For many years it has been impossible to get white persons to do the menial labor performed by Chinese and Japanese—**"It is Mongolian's labor and not fit for whites."** In the agricultural districts a species of help has been created, known as the blanket man. White

From Samuel Gompers and Herman Gutstadt *Meat vs. Rice: American Manhood Against Asiatic Coolieism: Which Shall Survive?* (San Francisco: Asiatic Exclusion League, 1908).

laborers seldom find permanent employment; the Mongolian is preferred. During harvest time the white man is forced to wander from ranch to ranch and find employment here and there for short periods of time, with the privilege of sleeping in the barns or haystacks. He is looked upon as a vagabond, unfit to associate with his employer or to eat from the same table with him. The negro slave of the South was housed and fed, but the white trash of California is placed beneath the Mongolian. The white domestic servant of today is expected to live in the room originally built for John, generally situated in the cellar, or attic, and void of all comforts, frequently unpainted or unpapered, containing only a bedstead and a chair. Anything was good enough for "John"[1] and the white girl must be satisfied as well. Is it any wonder that self respecting young women refuse to take service under such conditions? And what is true of agricultural laborers and domestics applies, equally, to all trades in which Mongolians are largely employed. Absolute servility (civility is not enough) is expected from those who take the place of "John" or "Togo" and it will take many years to obliterate these traces of inferiority and re-establish the proper relations of the employer and the employed.

* * * *

Have Asiatics Any Morals?

Sixty years' contact with the Chinese, twenty-five years' experience with the Japanese and two or three years' acquaintance with the Hindus should be sufficient to convince any ordinarily intelligent person that they have no standard of morals by which a Caucasian may judge them. A reference to the report previously quoted sheds considerable light upon the subject:

> It is a less difficult problem to ascertain the number of Chinese women and children in Chinatown than it is to give with accuracy the male population. First, because they are at present comparatively few in numbers; and second, because they can nearly always be found in the localities which they inhabit. This investigation has shown, however, that whatever may be the domestic family relations of the Chinese empire, here the relations of the sexes are chiefly so ordered as to provide for the gratification of the animal proclivities alone, with whatever result may chance to follow in the outcome of procreation. There are apparently few families living as such, with legitimate children. In most instances the wives are kept in a state of seclusion, carefully guarded and watched, as though 'eternal vigilance' on the part of their husbands 'is the price of their virtue.' Wherever there are families belonging to the better class of Chinese, the women are guarded and secluded in the most careful manner. Wherever the sex has been found in the pursuance of this investigation under other conditions, with some few exceptions, the rule seems to be that they are here in a state of concubinage merely to administer to the animal passions of the other sex, with such perpetuation of the race as may be a resultant consequence, or else to follow the admitted calling of the prostitute, generally of the low-

---

[1] "John" (or "John Chinaman") was a derogatory term used to refer to all Chinese men.

est possible grade, with all the wretchedness of life and consequence which the name implies. . . .

Though much more could be said upon each phase of this great and burning question we have tried to touch upon all of them sufficiently to enable our readers to obtain reliable information on a subject that is yet barely understood east of the Rocky Mountains. It must be clear to every thinking man and woman that while there is hardly a single reason for the admission of the Asiatics, there are hundreds of good and strong reasons for their absolute exclusion.

As a fitting close to this document we submit the remarks made by one of the greatest of American statesmen, Hon. James G. Blaine, February 14, 1879, when a bill for restriction of Chinese immigration was before the United States Senate. Mr. Blaine said:

"Either the Anglo-Saxon race will possess the Pacific slope or the Mongolians will possess it. You give them the start today, with the keen thrust of necessity behind them, and with the inducements to come, while we are filling up the other portions of the Continent, and it is inevitable, if not demonstrable, that they will occupy that space of the country between the Sierras and the Pacific.

"The immigrants that come to us from the Pacific isles, and from all parts of Europe, come here with the idea of the family as much engraven on their minds and hearts, and in customs and habits, as we ourselves have. The Asiatic can not go on with our population and make a homogeneous element.

"I am opposed to the Chinese coming here. I am opposed to making them citizens. I am unalterably opposed to making them voters. There is not a peasant cottage inhabited by a Chinaman. There is not a hearthstone, in the sense we understand it, of an American home, or an English home, or an Irish, or German, or French home. There is not a domestic fireside in that sense; and yet you say it is entirely safe to sit down and permit them to fill up our country, or any part of it.

"Treat them like Christians say those who favor their immigration; yet I believe the Christian testimony is that the conversion of Chinese on that basis is a fearful failure; and that the demoralization of the white race is much more rapid by reason of the contact than is the salvation of the Chinese race. You cannot work a man who must have beef and bread, alongside of a man who can live on rice. In all such conflicts, and in all such struggles, the result is not to bring up the man who lives on rice to the beef-and-bread standard, but it is to bring down the beef-and-bread man to the rice standard.

"Slave labor degraded free labor. It took out its respectability, and put an odious cast upon it. It throttled the prosperity of a fine and fair portion of the United States in the South; and this Chinese, which is worse than slave labor, will throttle and impair the prosperity of a still finer and fairer section of the Union on the Pacific coast.

"We have this day to choose whether we will have for the Pacific coast the civilization of Christ or the civilization of Confucius."

The Asiatic Exclusion League Argues That Asians Cannot Be Assimilated, 1911

A new race conflict threatens America, infinitely worse than the one we are now struggling with.

The Yellow Peril from Asia is the impending danger.

Can we afford to permit another vexatious race conflict to get a firm hold on this country?

Isn't the race question which we already have about as severe a strain of this kind as the nation can stagger under?

It is a calamity for a nation to be vexed with a race question which from its very nature will not and can not down. The nationality of our immigrants is of trifling importance provided they are of the white race, because in such case they, or at all events their children, become assimilated and indistinguishably blended with the mass of our population; but if they are of a different race with marked physical and perhaps mental characteristics which are perpetuated through successive generations and thus keep them a separate and distinct people with us but not of us, they become a source of trouble and of possible danger.

Conflict is inherent in the situation whenever and wherever two races so diverse that they do not readily amalgamate dwell in large numbers in the same community, for history proves that the invariable result is closely drawn social and other lines of distinction attended with jealousy and discord culminating in a contest for race supremacy. Therefore it is of the utmost importance for a nation, and especially in case of a republic, to have a homeogeneous population. Unfortunately that is impossible in this country because about half the population of our southern states is colored. And in saying this we intend no unkindly or disparaging reflection on the negroes. It would have been better for both races if the African had been permitted to work out its own destiny in its own way in the land of its origin. The race conflict which inevitably resulted from bringing the negroes to America has been a hardship and an injury to the whites as well as to them, beside being the cause of the great Civil War.

These Asiatic immigrants are an unmitigated nuisance in every community in which they have settled. The Chinese were the first orientals to enter by the Golden Gate and nearly forty years ago their presence in the Pacific coast states had produced conditions so demoralizing as to attract the attention of Congress and result in a law in 1882 excluding them from citizenship and practically prohibiting their further immigration. But this law is not sufficiently strict and has been continually and flagrantly evaded by those who have made big money by importing them illegally, so that they have largely increased in number in this country.

From "Proceedings of the Asiatic Exclusion League," July 1911.

Don't be deceived by any delusive hope that the yellow race can possibly become amalgamated with the white race in this country through intermarriage. The very thought is preposterous and revolting in view of their physical, mental and moral differences, and especially because of the prevailing oriental treatment of women as man's inferior, little better than his slave, even to the extent among the lower classes of the yellow race of buying their wives and selling their daughters into slavery for immoral purposes. . . .

* * * *

Nor in any true sense will they ever become Americanized. For profit or convenience a few do, and in course of time more of them may, adopt our style of dress, and even cut off their pigtails and outwardly affect other of our manners, but the essential characteristics which distinguish their mode of life, their ideals, religion, morals and aspirations individually and as a race they adhere to most tenaciously. Their case would be much more hopeful if they came mere savages, for then, like the negroes, they would adopt our civilization and our religion, and aspire to work out their destiny in harmony with ours.

But their ways are not as our ways and their gods are not as our God, and never will be. They bring with them a degraded civilization and a debased religion of their own ages older, and to their minds far superior to ours. We look to the future with hope for improvement and strive to uplift our people; they look to the past, believing that perfection was attained by their ancestors centuries before our civilization began and before Jesus brought us the divine message from the Father. They profane this Christian land by erecting here among us their pagan shrines, set up their idols and practice their shocking heathen religious ceremonies. . . .

* * * *

We must, as a nation, take immediate and vigorous measures to stop further Asiatic immigration, for what will be the fate of the nation when the white race is outnumbered by the negroes in the South and has to contend with the yellow men for supremacy in the North? And as their numbers increase the yellow men will overrun the South also and become a disturbing element there.

We need hardly mention the destructive effect of Chinese cheap labor in driving out white labor and ultimately monopolizing certain lines of industry and trade, as so much has been said and written on that subject. A Chinaman can live and save money on wages or profits that will not support a white man to say nothing of the white man's family.

We have spoken mostly about the Chinese as they largely outnumber the Japanese and Hindus in this country. But the Japanese are already settled in sufficient numbers in the Pacific coast states to be a nuisance and a menace and the Hindus have begun to come. The Japanese are even more objectionable than the Chinese because sharper [sic], and reputed to be more tricky and unscrupulous, while they are much more aggressive and warlike.

Because the Japanese are more advanced in modern arts and sciences than the Chinese does not make them the less objectionable immigrants, for their civilization, which in its essential quality is not to be measured by material progress, is still the yellow man's civilization, in which his paganism and his vice and immorality persist.

We have no law to prohibit or limit Japanese and Hindu immigration, nothing but an unwritten understanding that the Japanese government is to discourage its subjects from emigrating to the United States.

Fu Chi Hao, Chinese American, Reprimands Americans for Anti-Chinese Attitudes and Law, 1907

America has always been a very sweet and familiar name in my ears, because I have been told by my American friends that it is the only free country in the world, the refuge of the oppressed and the champion of the weak; so I have had a great affection for this country since my childhood days. I had an idea for a great many years that America was the best nation on the earth, and a good friend to China.

There is a close connection between America and China. The modern invention of steamboats brought these two nations nearer together. The great Pacific Ocean served as an indestructible tie. It is America that sent out her missionaries and merchants to China early in the nineteenth century, to instruct her people and help her to open the long-closed doors, and thus to get into contact with the new civilization of the twentieth century. We of China owe a great debt to America, especially during the Boxer uprising in 1900. It is largely due to America that China stands intact as she is today. Without America China might have been divided among the European nations seven years ago. Certainly America is China's best friend.

Don't be shocked if I tell you that, after six years of careful study and close observation, and after the personal treatment I have received from your country, my attitude toward America is totally changed. America is not so good a friend to China as I had mistakenly thought, because in no part of the earth are the Chinese so ill treated and humiliated as in America.

I hope I shall not be misunderstood. I have no hard feelings whatever against the American people. I can sincerely say that some of my best friends are Americans, and I have a great many sympathetic friends all over the country, but I do hate the misinterpretation of the Chinese exclusion law by your Government. The original idea of the law is lost. The officials on the Pacific Coast have made it their special business to find errors in the papers of every Chinese who came to this country, so as to send them back, whether they were laborers or not.

Pardon me if I give you a brief review of the personal treatment I received from America a few years ago. In the fall of 1901 a college-mate and myself were brought by an American missionary to this country, with the hope of getting an American college education which would enable us to take part in the uplifting of

From Fu Chi Hao, "My Reception in America," *The Outlook,* 80, 1907.

China in the near future. Glad indeed were we when the steamer Doric entered the Golden Gate on September 13, 1901. The peril of the water, the seasickness on the boat, were both ended. Christian America was reached at last. Our hearts were full of anticipation of the pleasure and the warm welcome we were going to receive from our Christian friends.

I was very much surprised to learn, after waiting several days on the steamer, that the passports which we had with us were not accepted by the American Government. There were several objections to the papers. In the first place, we ought to have got them, not from Li-Hung-Chang, the highest and most powerful official in North China at that time, but from his subordinate, the Customs Taotai, the Collector of the Port at Tientsin. In the second place, our papers were in the form of passports, while the law of this country requires certificates. The careless American consul at Tientsin had made still other mistakes and omissions in his English translation. We learned that we were denied the privilege of landing, and were to go back to China on the same steamer one week later.

I wish I could end the story with the deportation, but fortunately, or, if you please, unfortunately, our friends in this country did their best to have us stay. Letters and telegrams began to fly to the Chinese Minister and the Secretary of the Treasury Department in Washington. We were finally allowed to stay in the detention shed when the Doric left for China.

The detention shed is another name for a "Chinese jail." I have visited quite a few jails and State prisons in this country, but have never seen any place half so bad. It is situated at one end of the wharf, reached by a long, narrow stairway. The interior is about one hundred feet square. Oftentimes they put in as many as two hundred human beings. The whitewashed windows and the wire netting attached to them added to the misery. The air is impure, the place is crowded. No friends are allowed to come in and see the unfortunate suffering without special permission from the American authority. No letters are allowed either to be sent out or to come in. There are no tables, no chairs. We were treated like a group of animals, and we were fed on the floor. Kicking and swearing by the white man in charge was not a rare thing. I was not surprised when, one morning, a friend pointed out to me the place where a heartbroken Chinaman had hanged himself after four months' imprisonment in this dreadful dungeon, thus to end his agony and the shameful outrage.

A Racialized Description of Immigrants from Europe, 1915

The native American[1] has always found, and finds now, in the black men, willing followers who ask only to obey and to further the ideals and wishes of the master race, without trying to inject into the body politic their own views, whether racial, religious, or social. Negroes are never socialists or labor unionists, and as long as the dominant imposes its will on the servient race, and as long as they remain in the

---

From Madison Grant, *The Passing of the Great Race* (New York: Charles Scribner's Sons, 1916).

[1]By "native American" the author means native-born, white Americans.

same relation to the whites as in the past, the negroes will be a valuable element in the community, but once raised to social equality their influence will be destructive to themselves and to the whites. If the purity of the two races is to be maintained, they cannot continue to live side by side, and this is a problem from which there can be no escape.

The native American by the middle of the nineteenth century was rapidly becoming a distinct type. Derived from the Teutonic part of the British Isles, and being almost purely Nordic, he was on the point of developing physical peculiarities of his own, slightly variant from those of his English forefathers, and corresponding rather with the idealistic Elizabethan than with the materialistic Hanoverian Englishman. The Civil War, however, put a severe, perhaps fatal, check to the development and expansion of this splendid type, by destroying great numbers of the best breeding stock on both sides, and by breaking up the home ties of many more. If the war had not occurred these same men with their descendants would have populated the Western States instead of the racial nondescripts who are now flocking there.

The prosperity that followed the war attracted hordes of newcomers who were welcomed by the native Americans to operate factories, build railroads, and fill up the waste spaces—"developing the country" it was called.

These new immigrants were no longer exclusively members of the Nordic race as were the earlier ones who came of their own impulse to improve their social conditions. The transportation lines advertised America as a land flowing with milk and honey, and the European governments took the opportunity to unload upon careless, wealthy, and hospitable America the sweepings of their jails and asylums. The result was that the new immigration, while it still included many strong elements from the north of Europe, contained a large and increasing number of the weak, the broken, and the mentally crippled of all races drawn from the lowest stratum of the Mediterranean basin and the Balkans, together with hordes of the wretched, submerged populations of the Polish Ghettos.

With a pathetic and fatuous belief in the efficacy of American institutions and environment to reverse or obliterate immemorial hereditary tendencies, these newcomers were welcomed and given a share in our land and prosperity. The American taxed himself to sanitate and educate these poor helots, and as soon as they could speak English, encouraged them to enter into the political life, first of municipalities, and then of the nation.

The result is showing plainly in the rapid decline in the birth rate of native Americans because the poorer classes of Colonial stock, where they still exist, will not bring children into the world to compete in the labor market with the Slovak, the Italian, the Syrian, and the Jew. The native American is too proud to mix socially with them, and is gradually withdrawing from the scene, abandoning to these aliens the land which he conquered and developed. The man of the old stock is being crowded out of many country districts by these foreigners, just as he is to-day being literally driven off the streets of New York City by the swarms of Polish Jews. These immigrants adopt the language of the native American; they wear his clothes; they steal his name; and they are beginning to take his women, but they seldom adopt his religion or understand his ideals, and while he is being elbowed out of his own home the American looks calmly abroad and urges on others the suicidal ethics which are exterminating his own race.

As to what the future mixture will be it is evident that in large sections of the country the native American will entirely disappear. He will not intermarry with inferior races, and he cannot compete in the sweat shop and in the street trench with the newcomers. Large cities from the days of Rome, Alexandria, and Byzantium have always been gathering points of diverse races, but New York is becoming a *cloaca gentium* which will produce many amazing racial hybrids and some ethnic horrors that will be beyond the powers of future anthropologists to unravel.

One thing is certain: in any such mixture, the surviving traits will be determined by competition between the lowest and most primitive elements and the specialized traits of Nordic man; his stature, his light colored eyes, his fair skin and blond hair, his straight nose, and his splendid fighting and moral qualities, will have little part in the resultant mixture.

The "survival of the fittest" means the survival of the type best adapted to existing conditions of environment, to-day the tenement and factory, as in Colonial times they were the clearing of forests, fighting Indians, farming the fields, and sailing the Seven Seas. From the point of view of race it were better described as the "survival of the unfit."

A Sociologist Portrays the Racial Dimensions of Immigrants from Europe, 1914

. . . the conditions of settlement of this country caused those of uncommon energy and venturesomeness to outmultiply the rest of the population. Thus came into existence the pioneering breed; and this breed increased until it is safe to estimate that fully half of white Americans with native grandparents have one or more pioneers among their ancestors. Whatever valuable race traits distinguish the American people from the parent European stock are due to the efflorescence of this breed. Without it there would have been little in the performance of our people to arrest the attention of the world. Now we confront the melancholy spectacle of this pioneer breed being swamped and submerged by an overwhelming tide of latecomers from the old-world hive. . . . *Certainly never since the colonial era have the foreign-born and their children formed so large a proportion of the American people as at the present moment.* I scanned 368 persons as they passed me in Union Square, New York, at a time when the garment-workers of the Fifth Avenue lofts were returning to their homes. Only thirty-eight of these passers-by had the type of face one would find at a county fair in the West or South.

* * * *

From E. A. Ross, *The Old World in the New* (New York: The Century Co., 1914).

In this sense it is fair to say that the blood now being injected into the veins of our people is "sub-common." To one accustomed to the aspect of the normal American population, the Caliban type shows up with a frequency that is startling. Observe immigrants not as they come travel-wan up the gang-plank, nor as they issue toil-begrimed from pit's mouth or mill gate, but in their gatherings, washed, combed, and in their Sunday best. You are struck by the fact that from ten to twenty per cent. are hirsute, low-browed, big-faced persons of obviously low mentality. Not that they suggest evil. They simply look out of place in black clothes and stiff collar, since clearly they belong in skins, in wattled huts at the close of the Great Ice Age. These oxlike men are descendants of those *who always stayed behind.* Those in whom the soul burns with the dull, smoky flame of the pine-knot stuck to the soil, and are now thick in the sluiceways of immigration. Those in whom it burns with a clear, luminous flame have been attracted to the cities of the home land and, having prospects, have no motive to submit themselves to the hardships of the steerage.

To the practised eye, the physiognomy of certain groups unmistakably proclaims inferiority of type. I have seen gatherings of the foreign-born in which narrow and sloping foreheads were the rule. The shortness and smallness of the crania were very noticeable. There was much facial asymmetry. Among the women, beauty, aside from the fleeting, epidermal bloom of girlhood, was quite lacking. In every face there was something wrong—lips thick, mouth coarse, upper lip too long, cheek-bones too high, chin poorly formed, the bridge of the nose hollowed, the base of the nose tilted, or else the whole face prognathous. There were so many sugar-loaf heads, moon-faces, slit mouths, lantern-jaws, and goosebill noses that one might imagine a malicious jinn had amused himself by casting human beings in a set of skew-molds discarded by the Creator.

That the Mediterranean peoples are morally below the races of northern Europe is as certain as any social fact. Even when they were dirty, ferocious barbarians, these blonds were truthtellers. Be it pride or awkwardness or lack of imagination or fair-play sense, something has held them back from the nimble lying of the southern races. Immigration officials find that the different peoples are as day and night in point of veracity, and report vast trouble in extracting the truth from certain brunet nationalities.

Nothing less than verminous is the readiness of the southern Europeans to prey upon their fellows. Never were British or Scandinavian immigrants so bled by fellow-countrymen as are South Italian, Greek and Semitic immigrants. . . .

* * * *

The Northerners seem to surpass the southern Europeans in innate ethical endowment. Comparison of their behavior in marine disasters shows that discipline, sense of duty, presence of mind, and consideration for the weak are much more characteristic of northern Europeans. The southern Europeans, on the other hand, are apt, in their terror, to forget discipline, duty, women, children, everything but the saving of their own lives. In shipwreck it is the exceptional Northerner who forgets his duty, and the exceptional Southerner who is bound by it.

Congressman John Box Objects to Mexican Immigrants, 1928

The people of the United States have so definitely determined that immigration shall be rigidly held in check that many who would oppose this settled policy dare not openly attack it. The opposition declares itself in sympathy with the policy and then seeks to break down essential parts of the law and opposes any consistent completion of it making it serve the Nation's purpose to maintain its distinguishing character and institutions. Declaring that they do not believe that paupers and serfs and peons, the ignorant, the diseased, and the criminal of the world should pour by tens and hundreds of thousands into the United States as the decades pass, they nevertheless oppose the stopping of that very class from coming out of Mexico and the West Indies into the country at the rate of 75,000, more or less, per year.

Every reason which calls for the exclusion of the most wretched, ignorant, dirty, diseased, and degraded people of Europe or Asia demands that the illiterate, unclean, peonized masses moving this way from Mexico be stopped at the border. Few will seriously propose the repeal of the immigration laws during the present Congress, but the efforts of those who understand and support the spirit and purpose of these laws to complete them and make them more effective by the application of their quota provisions to Mexico and the West Indies, will be insidiously and strenuously opposed.

The admission of a large and increasing number of Mexican peons to engage in all kinds of work is at variance with the American purpose to protect the wages of its working people and maintain their standard of living. Mexican labor is not free; it is not well paid; its standard of living is low. The yearly admission of several scores of thousands from just across the Mexican border tends constantly to lower the wages and conditions of men and women of America who labor with their hands in industry, in transportation, and in agriculture. One who has been in Mexico or in Mexican sections of cities and towns of southwestern United States enough to make general observation needs no evidence or argument to convince him of the truth of the statement that Mexican peon labor is poorly paid and lives miserably in the midst of want, dirt, and disease.

In industry and transportation they displace great numbers of Americans who are left without employment and drift into poverty, even vagrancy, being

As found in speeches by John Box, *Congressional Record*, 1928, 1930.

unable to maintain families or to help sustain American communities. Volumes of data could be presented by way of support and illustration of this proposition. It is said that farmers need them. On the contrary, American farmers, including those of Texas and the Southwest, as a class do not need them or want them. I state the rule as of country-wide application, without denying that a small percentage of farmers want them, and that in some restricted regions this percentage is considerable. I doubt if a majority of the bona fide farmers of any State want or need them. I have given much attention to the question and am convinced that as a state-wide or nation-wide proposition they are not only not needed and not wanted, but the admission of great numbers of them to engage in agricultural work would be seriously hurtful to the interests of farmers, farm workers, and country communities. They take the places of white Americans in communities and often thereby destroy schools, churches, 285and all good community life.

American farmers are now burdened with a surplus of staple farm products which they can not sell profitably at home or abroad. That surplus weighs down the prices of the entire crop in both the domestic and foreign markets, until it threatens agriculture with financial ruin. Individual farmers, farm organizations, their Representatives in Congress, students of farm economics, bankers, and business men of the farming sections, all are striving to find a means of getting rid of this surplus of farm products, with its dead weight upon the price of farmers' crops. Congress is continually being urged to make appropriations to help carry the farmers' surplus, to levy taxes on farm products, to restrain overproduction, and otherwise to provide a method of getting rid of this oversupply of the farmers' leading crops. The President in his messages to Congress has repeatedly discussed this surplus and dealt with proposed remedies for it.

The importers of such Mexican laborers as go to farms at all want them to increase farm production, not by the labor of American farmers, for the sustenance of families and the support of American farm life, but by serf labor working mainly for absentee landlords on millions of acres of semiarid lands. Many of these lands have heretofore been profitably used for grazing cattle, sheep, and goats. Many of them are held by speculative owners.

A great part of these areas can not be cultivated until the Government has spent vast sums in reclaiming them. Their development when needed as homes for our people and in support of American communities is highly desirable. Their occupation and cultivation by serfs should not be encouraged. These lands and this mass of peon labor are to be exploited in the enlargement of America's surplus farm production, possibly to the increased profit of these speculative owners, but certainly to the great injury of America's present agricultural population, consisting of farmers, living and supporting themselves by their own labor and that of their families, on the farms of America.

The dreaded surplus, which already makes an abundant crop worse for farmers as a whole than a scant one, is to be made more dreadful by the importation of foreign labor working for lower wages and under harder conditions. The surplus which I have mentioned often hurts worse than a pest of locusts on the wheat crop or of boll weevil in the cotton fields.

While farmers, business interests in agricultural sections, Congress, and the President are deep in the consideration of the great problem presented by the farm surplus, and when presidential campaigns may turn on the condition and its consequences, labor importers are scheming and propagandizing for the purpose of bringing in armies of alien peons, claiming that they are needed on the farms, where they would only make the farm-surplus problem worse. If the Government tries to relieve this distress of the farmer caused by surplus production, shall it at the same time be de-Americanizing farms and farming communities and making the surplus and price situation worse by importing masses of serf laborers? Some think that agricultural prices can be sustained by a high tariff. Why have a tariff wall to keep out the products of pauper labor abroad and at the same time be bringing in armies of peons to increase the oversupply inside the tariff wall to the ruin of our own farmers?

Another purpose of the immigration laws is the protection of American racial stock from further degradation or change through mongrelization. The Mexican peon is a mixture of Mediterranean-blooded Spanish peasant with low-grade Indians who did not fight to extinction but submitted and multiplied as serfs. Into that was fused much negro slave blood. This blend of low-grade Spaniard, peonized Indian, and negro slave mixes with negroes, mulatoes, and other mongrels, and some sorry whites, already here. The prevention of such mongrelization and the degradation it causes is one of the purposes of our laws which the admission of these people will tend to defeat.

Every incoming race causes blood mixture, but if this were not true, a mixture of blocs of peoples of different races has a bad effect upon citizenship, creating more race conflicts and weakening national character. This is worse when the newcomers have different and lower social and political ideals. Mexico's Government has always been an expression of Mexican impulses and traditions. Rather, it is an exhibition of the lack of better traditions and the want of intelligence and stamina among the mass of its people. One purpose of our immigration laws is to prevent the lowering of the ideals and the average of our citizenship, the creation of race friction and the weakening of the Nation's powers of cohesion, resulting from the intermixing of differing races. The admission of 75,000 Mexican peons annually tends to the aggravation of this, another evil which the laws are designed to prevent or cure.

To keep out the illiterate and the diseased is another essential part of the Nation's immigration policy. The Mexican peons are illiterate and ignorant. Because of their unsanitary habits and living conditions and their vices they are especially subject to smallpox, venereal diseases, tuberculosis, and other dangerous contagions. Their admission is inconsistent with this phase of our policy.

The protection of American society against the importation of crime and pauperism is yet another object of these laws. Few, if any, other immigrants have brought us so large a proportion of criminals and paupers as have the Mexican peons.

Thind v. *United States:* The United States Supreme Court Clarifies the Meaning of "White," 1923

MR. JUSTICE SUTHERLAND delivered the opinion of the Court.

This cause is here upon a certificate from the Circuit Court of Appeals, requesting the instruction of this Court in respect of the following questions:

"1. Is a high caste Hindu of full Indian blood, born at Amrit Sar, Punjab, India, a white person within the meaning of section 2169, Revised Statutes?

"2. Does the act of February 5, 1917, (39 Stat. L. 875, section 3) disqualify from naturalization as citizens those Hindus, now barred by that act, who had lawfully entered the United States prior to the passage of said act?"

If the applicant is a white person within the meaning of this section he is entitled to naturalization; otherwise not. In *Ozawa* v. *United States,* 200 U. S. 178, we had occasion to consider the application of these words to the case of a cultivated Japanese and were constrained to hold that he was not within their meaning. As there pointed out, the provision is not that any particular class of persons shall be excluded, but it is, in effect, that only white persons shall be included within the privilege of the statute. "The intention was to confer the privilege of citizenship upon that class of persons whom the fathers knew as white, and to deny it to all who could not be so classified. It is not enough to say that the framers did not have in mind the brown or yellow races of Asia. It is necessary to go farther and be able to say that had these particular races been suggested the language of the act would have been so varied as to include them within its privileges." . . . Following a long line of decisions of the lower federal courts, we held that the words imported a racial and not an individual test and were meant to indicate only persons of what is *popularly* known as the Caucasian race. But, as there pointed out, the conclusion that the phrase "white persons" and the word "Caucasian" are synonymous does not end the matter. . . .

In the endeavor to ascertain the meaning of the statute we must not fail to keep in mind that it does not employ the word "Caucasian" but the words "white persons," and these are words of common speech and not of scientific origin. The word "Caucasian" not only was not employed in the law but was probably wholly unfamiliar to the original framers of the statute in 1790. When we employ it we do so as an aid to the ascertainment of the legislative intent and not as an invariable substitute for the statutory words. . . .

They imply, as we have said, a racial test; but the term "race" is one which, for the practical purposes of the statute, must be applied to a group of living persons *now* possessing in common the requisite characteristics, not to groups of persons

---

From *Thind* v. *United States,* 1922.

who are supposed to be or really are descended from some remote, common ancestor, but who, whether they both resemble him to a greater or less extent, have, at any rate, ceased altogether to resemble one another. It may be true that the blond Scandinavian and the brown Hindu have a common ancestor in the dim reaches of antiquity, but the average man knows perfectly well that there are unmistakable and profound differences between them today; and it is not impossible, if that common ancestor could be materialized in the flesh, we should discover that he was himself sufficiently differentiated from both of his descendants to preclude his racial classification with either. . . .

* * * *

The eligibility of this applicant for citizenship is based on the sole fact that he is of high caste Hindu stock, born in Punjab, one of the extreme northwestern districts of India, and classified by certain scientific authorities as of the Caucasian or Aryan race. . . .

The term "Aryan" has to do with linguistic and not at all with physical characteristics, and it would seem reasonably clear that mere resemblance in language, indicating a common linguistic root buried in remotely ancient soil, is altogether inadequate to prove common racial origin. There is, and can be, no assurance that the so-called Aryan language was not spoken by a variety of races living in proximity to one another. Our own history has witnessed the adoption of the English tongue by millions of Negroes, whose descendants can never be classified racially with the descendants of white persons notwithstanding both may speak a common root language.

The word "Caucasian" is in scarcely better repute. It is at best a conventional term. . . . it includes not only the Hindu but some of the Polynesians, (that is the Maori, Tahitians, Samoans, Hawaiians and others), the Hamites of Africa, upon the ground of the Caucasic cast of their features, though in color they range from brown to black. We venture to think that the average well informed white American would learn with some degree of astonishment that the race to which he belongs is made up of such heterogeneous elements.

* * * *

It does not seem necessary to pursue the matter of scientific classification further. We are unable to agree with the District Court, or with other lower federal courts, in the conclusion that a native Hindu is eligible for naturalization under §2169. The words of familiar speech, which were used by the original framers of the law, were intended to include only the type of man whom they knew as white. The immigration of that day was almost exclusively from the British Isles and Northwestern Europe, whence they and their forbears had come. When they extended the privilege of American citizenship to "any alien, being a free white person," it was these immigrants—bone of their bone and flesh of their flesh—and their kind whom they must have had affirmatively in mind. The succeeding years brought immigrants from Eastern, Southern and Middle Europe, among them the Slavs and the dark-eyed, swarthy people of

Alpine and Mediterranean stock, and these were received as unquestionably akin to those already here and readily amalgamated with them. It was the descendants of these, and other immigrants of like origin, who constituted the white population of the country when §2169, reënacting the naturalization test of 1790, was adopted; and there is no reason to doubt, with like intent and meaning.

* * * *

What we now hold is that the words "free white persons" are words of common speech, to be interpreted in accordance with the understanding of the common man, synonymous with the word "Caucasian" only as that word is popularly understood. As so understood and used, whatever may be the speculations of the ethnologist, it does not include the body of people to whom the appellee belongs. It is a matter of familiar observation and knowledge that the physical group characteristics of the Hindus render them readily distinguishable from the various groups of persons in this country commonly recognized as white. The children of English, French, German, Italian, Scandinavian, and other European parentage, quickly merge into the mass of our population and lose the distinctive hallmarks of their European origin. On the other hand, it cannot be doubted that the children born in this country of Hindu parents would retain indefinitely the clear evidence of their ancestry. It is very far from our thought to suggest the slightest question of racial superiority or inferiority. What we suggest is merely racial difference, and it is of such character and extent that the great body of our people instinctively recognize it and reject the thought of assimilation.

ESSAYS

The following two essays illustrate how the scientific and legal questions regarding "race" and "whiteness" became increasingly tangled in the early twentieth century. John Higham, of Johns Hopkins University, traces the ideological developments regarding the definition of *race*. He shows how categorizations of race became increasingly influential and how they were fused with judgments about the morality of the categorized peoples. Higham explains how some Americans, using new ideas about heredity and racial categories, were able to develop a powerful variant of nativism that wedded contemporary immigrants to their purported racial inferiority. In contrast, legal historian Ian F. Haney-Lopez, who teaches law at the University of California at Berkeley, analyzes the thinking of the Supreme Court regarding definitions of "whiteness" in its *Ozawa* and *Thind* decisions in the early 1920s. Both Takao Ozawa and Bhagat Singh Thind, who argued that they could become naturalized citizens because they were "white," took their claims to the Supreme Court. Whereas the Court could rule that Japanese-born Ozawa was not white because he was "Mongolian," how would it rule in the case of Indian-born Thind, who was technically "Caucasian"? Haney-Lopez shows how the Court, in the face of the increasingly complex scientific theories of race discussed by Higham, argued that "whiteness" could be interpreted according to common-understood ideas of what a "white" person was.

The Evolution of Thought on Race and the Development of Scientific Racism

JOHN HIGHAM

. . . in one major respect the pattern of nativist thought changed fundamentally. Gradually and progressively it veered toward racism. Absent from the strictures of the eighteenth century nationalist, notions of racial superiority and exclusiveness appeared in the mid-nineteenth, but they were to undergo a long process of revision and expansion before emerging in the early twentieth century as the most important nativist ideology. Several generations of intellectuals took part in transforming the vague and somewhat benign racial concepts of romantic nationalism into doctrines that were precise, malicious, and plausibly applicable to European immigration. The task was far from simple; at every point the race-thinkers confronted the liberal and cosmopolitan barriers of Christianity and American democracy. Ironically and significantly, it was not until the beginning of the present century, when public opinion recovered much of its accustomed confidence, that racial nativism reached intellectual maturity.

Of course racial nativism forms only a segment, though a critical and illuminating segment, of the larger evolution of race consciousness in modern times. The greater part of the complex phenomenon which is now fashionably called "race prejudice" lies beyond the scope of this [article]; its history is tangled and still largely unwritten. What concerns us is the intersection of racial attitudes with nationalistic ones—in other words, the extension to European nationalities of that sense of absolute difference which already divided white Americans from people of other colors. When sentiments analogous to those already discharged against Negroes, Indians, and Orientals spilled over into anti-European channels, a force of tremendous intensity entered the stream of American nativism.

The whole story of modern racial ferment, nativist and otherwise, has two levels, one involving popular emotions, the other concerning more or less systematic ideas. Most of the emotions flow from a reservoir of habitual suspicion and distrust accumulated over the span of American history toward human groups stamped by obvious differences of color. The ideas, on the other hand, depend on the speculations of intellectuals on the nature of races. The distinction is partly artificial, for the spirit of white supremacy—or what may be labeled race-feeling—has interlocked with race-thinking at many points. Indeed, their convergence has given the problem of race its modern significance. But at least the distinction has the merit of reminding us that race-feelings and explicit concerns about races have not always accompanied one another. The Anglo-Saxon idea in its early form did not entail the biological taboos of race-feeling.

From John Higham, *Strangers in the Land: Patterns of American Nativism* by John Higham. Copyright © 1967. Reprinted by permission of Rutgers Unversity Press.

Nor did the pattern of white supremacy, in all likelihood, depend at the outset on formal race-thinking. Traditional religious beliefs, often hardly articulated at all, served the pragmatic purposes of the English colonists who enslaved Negroes and who scourged Indians as Satanic agents "having little of Humanitie but shape." However, the evolution of white supremacy into a comprehensive philosophy of life, grounding human values in the innate constitution of nature, required a major theoretical effort. It was the task of the race-thinkers to organize specific antipathies toward dark-hued peoples into a generalized, ideological structure.

To the development of racial nativism, the thinkers have made a special contribution. Sharp physical differences between native Americans and European immigrants were not readily apparent; to a large extent they had to be manufactured. A rather elaborate, well-entrenched set of racial ideas was essential before the newcomers from Europe could seem a fundamentally different order of men. Accordingly, a number of race-conscious intellectuals blazed the way for ordinary nativists, and it will be useful to tell their story . . . .

From Romanticism to Naturalism

Two general types of race-thinking, derived from very different origins, circulated throughout the nineteenth century. One came from political and literary sources and assumed, under the impact of the romantic movement, a nationalistic form. Its characteristic manifestation in England and America was the Anglo-Saxon tradition. Largely exempt through most of the century from the passions of either the nativist or the white supremacist, this politico-literary concept of race lacked a clearly defined physiological basis. Its vague identification of culture with ancestry served mainly to emphasize the antiquity, the uniqueness, and the permanence of a nationality. It suggested the inner vitality of one's own culture, rather than the menace of another race. Whereas some of the early racial nationalists attributed America's greatness (and above all its capacity for self-government) to its Anglo-Saxon derivation, others thought America was creating a new mixed race; and, such was the temper of the age, many accepted both ideas at the same time. But whether exclusive or cosmopolitan in tendency, these romantics almost always discussed race as an ill-defined blessing; hardly ever as a sharply etched problem. During the age of confidence, as Anglo-Saxonism spread among an eastern social elite well removed from the fierce race conflicts of other regions, it retained a complacent, self-congratulatory air.

Meanwhile a second kind of race-thinking was developing from the inquiries of naturalists. Stimulated by the discovery of new worlds overseas, men with a scientific bent began in the seventeenth and eighteenth centuries to study human types systematically in order to catalogue and explain them. While Anglo-Saxonists consulted history and literature to identify national races, the naturalists concentrated on the great "primary" groupings of *Homo sapiens* and used physiological characteristics such as skin color, stature, head shape, and so on, to distinguish them one from the other. Quite commonly this school associated physical with cultural differences and displayed, in doing so, a feeling of white superiority over the colored races. On the whole, however, the leading scientific thinkers did not regard race differences as permanent, pure, and unalterable. A minority insisted that races were immutable, separately created species; but the influence of this polygenist argument suffered from its obvious violation of the Christian doctrine of the unity of mankind. For the most part, early anthropologists stressed the molding force of environmental conditions in differentiating the human family.

In the course of the nineteenth and early twentieth centuries, the separation between the two streams of race-thinking gradually and partially broke down. Racial science increasingly intermingled with racial nationalism. Under the pressure of a growing national consciousness, a number of European naturalists began to subdivide the European white man into biological types, often using linguistic similarity as evidence of hereditary connection. For their part, the nationalists slowly absorbed biological assumptions about the nature of race, until every national trait seemed wholly dependent on hereditary transmission. This interchange forms the intellectual background for the conversion of the vague Anglo-Saxon tradition into a sharp-cutting nativist weapon and, ultimately, into a completely racist philosophy.

Behind the fusion—and confusion—of natural history with national history, of "scientific" with social ideas, lay a massive trend in the intellectual history of the late nineteenth and twentieth centuries. Hopes and fears alike received scientific credentials; and men looked on the human universe in increasingly naturalistic terms. In religion, literature, philosophy, and social theory ancient dualisms dissolved. Human affairs and values were seen more and more as products of vast, impersonal processes operating throughout nature. The Darwinian theory represented a decisive step in this direction; in the eyes of many, it subsumed mankind wholly under the grim physical laws of the animal kingdom.

Enter the Natural Scientists

In the 1890's nativist intellectuals had barely begun to think of European races as a biological threat or to associate national survival with racial purity. Even Walker's birth-rate theory offered no logical reason to suppose that the country would suffer from the replacement of old stock by new. Perhaps the most serious intellectual handicap of American race-thinkers before the twentieth century was the lack of a general scientific principle from which to argue the prepotency of heredity in human affairs. But at the turn of the century, when social science and history came increasingly under the sway of environmental assumptions, biologists advanced dramatic claims for heredity and even helped to translate them into a political and social creed.

The new science of heredity came out of Europe about 1900 and formed the first substantial contribution of European thought to American nativism after the time of Darwin. The study of inheritance suddenly leaped into prominence and assumed a meaningful pattern from the discovery of the long-unnoticed work of

Gregor Mendel and its convergence with August Weismann's theory of germinal continuity. Together, these hypotheses demonstrated the transmission from generation to generation of characteristics that obeyed their own fixed laws without regard to the external life of the organism.

Amid the excitement caused in English scientific circles by these continental discoveries, Sir Francis Galton launched the eugenics movement. Galton, who was England's leading Darwinian scientist, had long been producing statistical studies on the inheritance of all sorts of human abilities and deficiencies. But it was only in the favorable climate of the early twentieth century that he started active propaganda for uplifting humanity by breeding from the best and restricting the offspring of the worst. To Galton, eugenics was both a science and a kind of secular religion. It certified that the betterment of society depends largely on improvement of the "inborn qualities" of "the human breed," and Galton preached this message with evangelical fervor. Thus he provided biologists and physicians, excited over the new genetic theories, with a way of converting their scientific interests into a program of social salvation—a program based wholly on manipulation of the supposedly omnipotent forces of heredity.

In the latter part of the 1900's the eugenics movement got under way in the United States, where it struck several responsive chords. Its emphasis on unalterable human inequalities confirmed the patricians' sense of superiority; its warnings over the multiplication of the unfit and the sterility of the best people synchronized with the discussion of race suicide. Yet the eugenicists' dedication to a positive program of "race improvement" through education and state action gave the movement an air of reform, enabling it to attract the support of many progressives while still ministering to conservative sensibilities. By 1910, therefore, eugenicists were catching the public ear. From then through 1914, according to one tabulation, the general magazines carried more articles on eugenics than on the three questions of slums, tenements, and living standards, combined.

The leading eugenicist in America was Charles B. Davenport, a zoologist of tremendous ambition and drive who established the country's first research center in genetics at Cold Spring Harbor, Long Island. Davenport's father, a descendant of one of the Puritan founders of New England, was a genealogist who traced his ancestry back to 1086, and Davenport himself often mourned "that the best of that grand old New England stock is dying out through failure to reproduce." His early experiments at Cold Spring Harbor were devoted to testing the Mendelian principles in animal breeding; by 1907 he was beginning to apply them to the study of human heredity. In 1910 he persuaded Mrs. E. H. Harriman to finance a Eugenics Record Office adjacent to his laboratory with the aim of compiling an index of the American population and advising individuals and local societies on eugenical problems. Over a course of years she poured more than half a million dollars into the agency, while Davenport—already one of America's leading biologists—gave the rest of his life to studying the inheritance of human traits and spreading the gospel of eugenics. An indefatigable organizer, Davenport was also one of the leaders of the American Breeders' Association, where the eugenics agitation first centered. Established in 1903 by practical plant and animal breeders who wanted to keep in touch with the new theoretical advances, the association enlarged its field in 1907 to embrace eugenics.

The racial and nativistic implications of eugenics soon became apparent. From the eugenicists' point of view, the immigration question was at heart a biological one, and to them admitting "degenerate breeding stock" seemed one of the worst sins the nation could commit against itself. It was axiomatic to these naïve Mendelians that environment could never modify an immigrant's germ plasm and that only a rigid selection of the best immigrant stock could improve rather than pollute endless generations to come. Since their hereditarian convictions made virtually every symptom of social disorganization look like an inherited trait, the recent immigration could not fail to alarm them. Under the influence of eugenic thinking, the burgeoning mental hygiene movement picked up the cry. Disturbed at the number of hereditary mental defectives supposedly pouring into the country, the psychiatrists who organized the National Committee for Mental Hygiene succeeded in adding to the immigration bill of 1914 an odd provision excluding cases of "constitutional psychopathic inferiority." By that time many critics of immigration were echoing the pleas in scientific periodicals for a "rational" policy "based upon a noble culture of racial purity."

None were quicker or more influential in relating eugenics to racial nativism than the haughty Bostonians who ran the Immigration Restriction League. Prescott F. Hall had always had a hypochondriac's fascination with medicine and biology, and his associate, Robert DeCourcy Ward, was a professional scientist. They had shied away from racial arguments in the nineties, but in the less favorable atmosphere of the new century their propaganda very much needed a fresh impulse. As early as 1906 the league leaders pointed to the new genetic principles in emphasizing the opportunity that immigration regulation offered to control America's future racial development. Two years later they learned of the eugenics sentiment developing in the American Breeders' Association. They descended upon it, and soon they were dominating its immigration activities. The association organized a permanent committee on immigration, of which Hall became chairman and Ward secretary. Ward proceeded to read papers on immigration legislation before meetings of eugenicists, and for a time the two considered changing the name of their own organization to the "Eugenic Immigration League." Meanwhile they seized every occasion to publicize the dogma that science decrees restrictions on the new immigration for the conservation of the "American race."

Obviously the eugenics movement had crucial importance for race-thinking at a time when racial presuppositions were seriously threatened in the intellectual world. But basically the importance of eugenics was transitional and preparatory. It vindicated the hereditarian assumptions of the Anglo-Saxon tradition; it protected and indeed encouraged loose talk about race in reputable circles; and in putting race-thinking on scientific rather than romantic premises it went well beyond the vague Darwinian analogies of the nineteenth century. On the other hand, eugenics failed utterly to supply a racial typology. In their scientific capacity, the eugenicists—like their master Galton—studied individual traits and reached conclusions on individual differences. When they generalized the defects of individual immigrants into those of whole ethnic groups, their science deserted them and their phrases became darkly equivocal. Indeed, the more logical and consistent eugenicists maintained that America could improve its "race" by selecting immigrants on the ground of their individual family histories regardless of their national origins.

In the end the race-thinkers had to look to anthropology to round out a naturalistic nativism. Anthropology alone could classify the peoples of Europe into hereditary types that would distinguish the new immigration from older Americans; it alone might arrange these races in a hierarchy of merit and thereby prove the irremediable inferiority of the newcomers; and anthropology would have to collaborate with eugenics to show wherein a mixture of races physically weakens the stronger.

American anthropology remained cautiously circumspect on these points. The influence of the foreign-born progressive, Franz Boas, was already great; in 1911 he published the classic indictment of race-thinking, *The Mind of Primitive Man.* In the absence of interest on the part of American anthropologists, a perfected racism depended on amateur handling of imported ideas. In a climate of opinion conditioned by the vogues of race suicide and eugenics, however, it is not surprising that scientifically minded nativists found the categories and concepts they needed without assistance from American anthropologists.

Again the inspiration came from Europe. There, chiefly in France and Germany, during the latter half of the nineteenth century anthropologists furnished the scientific credentials and speculative thinkers the general ideas out of which a philosophy of race took shape. The first of the thoroughgoing racists, Count J. A. de Gobineau, reached a limited audience of proslavery thinkers in America on the eve of the Civil War and then was forgotten. His successors were even less effective. Once in a while an immigrant writer tried to translate some of this literature into terms that might appeal to an American public, but the stuff simply was not read. Not until the beginning of the twentieth century did the invidious anthropological theories which had been accumulating in Europe for over thirty years reach a significant American audience. And when they did, they were delivered in a characteristically American package.

William Z. Ripley was a brilliant young economist who had the kind of mind that refuses to stay put. In the mid-nineties, before he was thirty years old, Ripley was teaching economics at the Massachusetts Institute of Technology, while simultaneously developing a unique course of lectures at Columbia University on the role of geography in human affairs. In its conception this course reflected Ripley's conviction of the basic importance of environmental conditions in molding the life of man; but he quickly came up against the problem of race. The question led him to the controversies among continental scholars on the anthropological traits of European peoples, and he chose the locale of Europe as a crucial test of the interplay of race and environment. In *The Races of Europe,* a big, scholarly volume appearing in 1899, he anatomized the populations of the continent, pointing temperately but persistently to ways in which physiological traits seemed to reflect geographical and social conditions.

This was cold comfort to nativists, but the book had another significance apart from the author's well-hedged thesis. Ripley organized into an impressive synthesis a tripartite classification of white men which European ethnologists had recently developed. For the first time, American readers learned that Europe was not a land of "Aryans" or Goths subdivided into vaguely national races such as the Anglo-Saxon, but rather the seat of three races discernible by physical measurements: a northern race of tall, blond longheads which Ripley called Teutonic; a central race of stocky roundheads which he called Alpine; and a southern race of slender, dark longheads which he called Mediterranean. Here was a powerful weapon for nativists bent on distinguishing absolutely between old and new immigrations, but to make it serviceable Ripley's data would have to be untangled from his environmentalist assumptions.

It is ironical that Ripley himself did some of the untangling. For all of his scholarly caution he could not entirely suppress an attachment to the Teutonic race that reflected very mildly the rampant Teutonism of many of the authorities on which he relied. In the early twentieth century the new genetic hypotheses and a growing alarm over the new immigration turned his attention from environmental to inherited influences. He began to talk about race suicide and to wonder about the hereditary consequences of the mixture of European races occurring in America.

Before abandoning anthropology completely to concentrate in economics, Ripley delivered in 1908 a widely publicized address in which he suggested an answer to the old problem of how the crossing of superior and inferior races can drag down the former. His roving eye had come upon the experiments that some of the Mendelian geneticists were making on plant and animal hybrids. Hugo De Vries and others were demonstrating how hybridization sometimes caused a reassertion of latent characters inherited from a remote ancestor. The concept of reversion was an old one, discussed by Darwin himself, but the rise of genetics brought it into new prominence. Ripley fastened on the idea and raised the question whether the racial intermixture under way in America might produce a reversion to a primitive type. In contrast to the theory of race suicide, this doctrine—torn from the context of genetics and applied to the typology of European races—provided a thoroughly biological explanation of the foreign peril. Presumably race suicide might be arrested by legislation and by education raising the immigrant's standard of living; but reversion seemed remorseless. All of the pieces from which a sweeping statement of racial nativism might be constructed were now on hand.

The man who put the pieces together was Madison Grant, intellectually the most important nativist in recent American history. All of the trends in race-thinking converged upon him. A Park Avenue bachelor, he was the most lordly of patricians. His family had adorned the social life of Manhattan since colonial times, and he was both an expert genealogist and a charter member of the Society of Colonial Wars. Always he resisted doggedly any intrusion of the hoi polloi. On his deathbed he was still battling to keep the public from bringing cameras into the zoo over which he had long presided.

In addition to a razor-sharp set of patrician values, Grant also had an extensive acquaintance with the natural sciences and a thoroughly naturalistic temper of mind. Beginning as a wealthy sportsman and hunter, he was the founder and later the chairman of the New York Zoological Society, where he associated intimately with leading biologists and eugenicists. In the early years of the twentieth century he published a series of monographs on North American animals—the moose, the caribou, the Rocky Mountain goat. He picked up a smattering of Mendelian concepts and, unlike his eugenicist friends, read a good deal of physical anthropology too. Ripley's work furnished his main facts about European man, but he also went behind Ripley to many of the more extreme European ethnologists. Thus Grant was well supplied with scientific information yet free from a scientist's scruple in interpreting it.

By 1910 Grant's racial concepts were clearly formed and thoroughly articulated with a passionate hatred of the new immigration. He showed little concern over relations between whites and Negroes or Orientals. His deadliest animus focused on the Jews, whom he saw all about him in New York. More broadly, what upset him was the general mixture of European races under way in America; for this process was irretrievably destroying racial purity, the foundation of every national and cultural value.

Grant's philippic appeared finally in 1916. It bore the somber title, *The Passing of the Great Race,* summing up the aristocratic pessimism that had troubled nativist intellectuals since the 1890's. Everywhere Grant saw the ruling race of the western world on the wane yet heedless of its fate because of a "fatuous belief" in the power of environment to alter heredity. In the United States he observed the deterioration going on along two parallel lines: race suicide and reversion. As a result of Mendelian laws, Grant pontificated, we know that different races do not really blend. The mixing of two races "gives us a race reverting to the more ancient, generalized and lower type." Thus "the cross between any of the three European races and a Jew is a Jew." In short, a crude interpretation of Mendelian genetics provided the rationale for championing racial purity.

After arguing the issue of race versus physical environment, Grant assumed a racial determination of culture. Much of the book rested on this assumption, for the volume consisted essentially of a loose-knit sketch of the racial history of Europe. The Alpines have always been a race of peasants. The Mediterraneans have at least shown artistic and intellectual proclivities. But the blond conquerors of the North constitute "the white man par excellence." Following the French scientist Joseph Deniker, Grant designated this great race Nordic. To it belongs the political and military genius of the world, the daring and pride that make explorers, fighters, rulers, organizers, and aristocrats. In the early days, the American population was purely Nordic, but now the swarms of Alpine, Mediterranean, and Jewish hybrids threaten to extinguish the old stock unless it reasserts its class and racial pride by shutting them out.

So the book turned ultimately into a defense of both class and racial consciousness, the former being dependent on the latter. The argument broadened from nativism to an appeal for aristocracy as a necessary correlative in maintaining racial purity. Democracy, Grant maintained, violates the scientific facts of heredity; and he was obviously proud to attribute feudalism to the Nordics. Furthermore, Grant assaulted Christianity for its humanitarian bias in favor of the weak and its consequent tendency to break down racial pride. Even national consciousness ranked second to race consciousness in Grant's scale of values.

This boldness and sweep gave *The Passing of the Great Race* particular significance. Its reception and its impact on public opinion belong to a later stage in the history of American nativism, but its appearance before America's entry into the First World War indicates that the old Anglo-Saxon tradition had finally emerged in at least one mind as a systematic, comprehensive world view. Race-thinking was basically at odds with the values of democracy and Christianity, but earlier nativists had always tried either to ignore the conflict or to mediate between racial pride and the humanistic assumptions of America's major traditions. Grant, relying on what he thought was scientific truth, made race the supreme value and repudiated all others inconsistent with it.

This, at last, was racism.

The Evolution of Legal Constructions of Race and "Whiteness"

IAN F. HANEY-LOPEZ

When the Supreme Court first addressed the racial prerequisite issue, it came down squarely in the muddled middle. In *Ozawa v. United States,* the Court wrote that the term "white persons" included "only persons of what is *popularly* known as the Caucasian race." It thereby ran together the rationales of common knowledge, evident in the reference to what was "popularly known," and scientific evidence, exemplified in the Court's reliance on the term "Caucasian." Within three months, however, the Court established a contrasting position in *United States v. Thind,* retreating from the term "Caucasian" and making the test of Whiteness solely one of common knowledge. Comparing the rationales put forth in *Ozawa* and *Thind* suggests that the Supreme Court abandoned scientific explanations of race in favor of those rooted in common knowledge when science failed to reinforce popular beliefs about racial differences. The Court's eventual embrace of common knowledge confirms the falsity of natural notions of race, exposing race instead as a social product measurable only in terms of what people believe.

Ozawa

Takao Ozawa was born in Japan in 1875, and moved to California as a young man in 1894. Educated at the University of California at Berkeley, he eventually settled in the territory of Hawaii and, in 1914, applied for naturalization. Ozawa began the case backed only by a few close friends, but with a fervent belief in his suitability for citizenship. In a legal brief he himself penned, Ozawa wrote:

From Ian F. Haney-Lopez, *White by Law: The Legal Construction of Race,* copyright © 1996. Reprinted by permission of New York University Press.

In name, General Benedict Arnold was an American, but at heart he was a traitor. In name, I am not an American, but at heart I am a true American. I set forth the following facts which will sufficiently prove this. (1) I did not report my name, my marriage, or the names of my children to the Japanese Consulate in Honolulu; notwithstanding all Japanese subjects are requested to do so. These matters were reported to the American government. (2) I do not have any connection with any Japanese churches or schools, or any Japanese organizations here or elsewhere. (3) I am sending my children to an American church and American school in place of a Japanese one. (4) Most of the time I use the American (English) language at home, so that my children cannot speak the Japanese language. (5) I educated myself in American schools for nearly eleven years by supporting myself. (6) I have lived continuously within the United States for over twenty-eight years. (7) I chose as my wife one educated in American schools . . . instead of one educated in Japan. (8) I have steadily prepared to return the kindness which our Uncle Sam has extended me . . . so it is my honest hope to do something good to the United States before I bid a farewell to this world. . . .

The U.S. District Attorney for the District of Hawaii opposed Ozawa's application on the ground that he was of the "Japanese race" and therefore not a "white person." Though defeated at each successive stage, Ozawa persisted in his pursuit of citizenship for eight years, eventually reaching the Supreme Court. After Ozawa's petition for citizenship captured the attention of the country's highest court, his case quickly became an important test for the Japanese community. With the help of the Pacific Coast Japanese Association Deliberative Council, an immigrant civic association, Ozawa retained a former U.S. Attorney General, George Wickersham, to represent him before the Supreme Court.

Ozawa based his case for naturalization on several arguments. The most interesting, however, was his assertion regarding skin color. Ozawa acknowledged he was of Japanese descent, but nonetheless asserted that his skin made him "white." Taking the "white person" requirement literally, Ozawa argued that to reject his petition would be "to exclude a Japanese who is 'white' in color." In support of this proposition, Ozawa quoted in his brief to the Court the following from different anthropological observers: "in Japan the uncovered parts of the body are also white"; "the Japanese are of lighter color than other Eastern Asiatics, not rarely showing the transparent pink tint which whites assume as their own privilege"; and "in the typical Japanese city of Kyoto, those not exposed to the heat of summer are particularly white-skinned. They are whiter than the average Italian, Spaniard or Portuguese." . . .

* * * *

. . . In response to Ozawa's emphasis on skin color, the Court said: "Manifestly, the test [of race] afforded by the mere color of the skin of each individual is impracticable as that differs greatly among persons of the same race, even among Anglo-Saxons, ranging by imperceptible gradations from the fair blond to the swarthy brunette, the latter being darker than many of the lighter hued persons of the brown or yellow races." The Court in *Ozawa* stated a simple fact: skin color does not correlate well with racial identity. This had become quite evident to scientists by the close of the nineteenth century, prompting raciologists to downplay the importance of integument in racial classifications. This is also what led the district court in *Najour* to suggest that dark skin need not foreclose the possibility that one is White. In *Ozawa,* the Supreme Court used the imprecise relationship between race and skin color to state the converse: light skin does not foreclose the possibility that one is non-White. These statements are the flip sides of the proposition that pigmentation alone does not denote race.

By the close of the nineteenth century, scientists increasingly understood that morphological attributes, chief among them skin color, varied gradually rather than by the sharp, clearly demarcated disjunctions fundamental to the myth that races can be readily differentiated. The physical features that code as race do not change abruptly between those who are White and those who are Black or Yellow. Instead, these features permute gradually, permitting no easy divisions. As one moves up the African continent and then across the Eurasian land mass, where exactly does one find the lines between Black, White, and Yellow? Neat divisions do not exist; instead of lines one sees only clines, a numberless series of subtly different features among different population groups stemming from heredity, environment, and relative isolation. . . .

The Court in *Ozawa* recognized this, writing that "to adopt the color test alone would result in a confused overlapping of races and a gradual merging of one into the other, without any practical line of separation." Intent on avoiding this "confused overlapping of races," the Supreme Court rejected a racial test based solely on skin color. But the Court did not go as far as it might have in rejecting physical definitions of race.

Ozawa sought to turn skin color to his advantage, attempting to establish a White identity on the basis of his fair skin. By implication, his argument drew into question the credibility of all physical taxonomies of race, for if skin color could not be relied upon to indicate race, then perhaps no physical features could serve this purpose. This was exactly the dilemma facing the contemporary science of race. By the end of the nineteenth century anthropologists had tried and failed to fashion practical physical typologies along various axes besides skin color, including facial angle, jaw size, cranial capacity, and hair texture. None of these physical indices could support the division of humankind into the races people already knew to exist. . . . Ozawa's argument undermined the basic division of humans into races, or at least into the scientific and thus supposedly physical groupings of "Caucasians," "Negroids," "Amerinds," and "Mongolians."

The Supreme Court ignored the implications of Ozawa's argument. Because Ozawa was Japanese, the justices could reject a skin color test without having to question the validity of the scientific divisions of race. Science defined Ozawa as a Mongolian, and thus the Court could continue to rely on science without considering the obvious challenge to such taxonomies posed by Ozawa's argument.

As the Solicitor General of the United States argued in opposition to Ozawa's petition:

> The ethnological discussions have covered a wide range of most interesting subjects, particularly in the border-line cases, the Syrian case and the Armenian case. But the present case cannot be regarded as a doubtful case. . . . While the views of ethnologists have changed in details from time to time, it is safe to say that the classification of the Japanese as members of the yellow race is practically the unanimous view.

The Solicitor's argument appealed to the Court. Regardless of the ethnological questions surrounding the status of those from western and southern Asia, the vast majority of experts consistently placed the Japanese wholly outside of the Caucasian race. Relying on this, a unanimous Court held that "the words 'white person' are synonymous with the words 'a person of the Caucasian race.' " The Court then held that "the appellant . . . is clearly of a race which is not Caucasian," alluding to "numerous scientific authorities, which we do not deem it necessary to review." On this basis, the Court upheld the denial of Takao Ozawa's application for citizenship, establishing as the supreme law of the land first that "white" and "Caucasian" were synonyms and second that Japanese persons were not White.

The ruling in *Ozawa* allowed anti-Japanese racial animosity to continue unchecked. More, it blessed such animosity with the weight of enlightened opinion, confirming Japanese racial difference at law. In the Japanese immigrant press, one journal lauded the decision with intentional irony. "Since this newspaper did 'not believe whites are the superior race,' it was 'delighted' the high tribunal 'did not find the Japanese to be free white persons.' " Most newspapers, however, took a more direct route in criticizing the Court and its decision, forthrightly "deplor[ing] the decision as an expression of 'racial prejudice' at odds with the 'original founding spirit of the nation.' "

* * * *

Thind

Three months after holding that Japanese persons were not Caucasian and therefore not White, the Supreme Court in *United States v. Thind* rejected its equation in *Ozawa* of "white" with Caucasian. Bhagat Singh Thind was twenty-one years old when he arrived in the United States on the Fourth of July, 1913. Born in India and a graduate of Punjab University, Thind was part of a new wave of Asian immigrants, one of approximately 6,400 Asian Indians in the United States by 1920, when he sought naturalization. This latest group from Asia, however, differed in an important respect from other Asian immigrants: anthropologists classified Asian Indians not as "Mongolians," but as "Caucasians." This classification provided the springboard for Thind's naturalization petition. Drawing on the syllogism advanced in *Najour,* Thind argued he was "Caucasian," therefore "white," and therefore eligible for citizenship.

On October 18, 1920, the district court agreed with Thind and granted his petition for naturalization. The court cited as precedent three cases that followed reasoning similar to that of *Najour.* The federal government appealed Thind's naturalization to the Ninth Circuit Court of Appeals, which in turn requested instruction from the Supreme Court on the following question: "Is a high caste Hindu of full Indian blood, born at Amrit Sar, Punjab, India, a white person?" The thick language of the question typifies the confusion in the courts concerning issues of racial identity. The language betrays entrenched beliefs about the racial significance of class and caste, blood and birthplace, and even religion in establishing racial identity. Consider, for example, the elision between race and religion evident in the question. The reference to Thind as a Hindu followed prevalent social nomenclature, and seems to have been more racial than religious, as few Asian Indian immigrants to the United States early in this century practiced the Hindu religion. As Ronald Takaki remarks, "Called 'Hindus' in America, only a small fraction of the Asian-Indian immigrants were actually believers of Hinduism. One third were Muslim, and the majority were Sikhs." In the United States, "Hindu" served as a racial appellation of difference, its use of obscure but certain origin in the Western colonial discourse of race, culture, civilization, and empire. The inclusion of questions of religion, caste, nationality, descent, and geography as part of an assessment of whether Thind was "a white person" confirms the intricate sociohistorical embeddedness of racial categorization. Whatever its complexities, inaccuracies, and implications, however, the question stood: Was Bhagat Singh Thind a White person?

Oral argument before the Supreme Court was scheduled for January 11, 1923. In the winter leading up to his court date, Thind must have felt especially confident. The opinion in *Ozawa* adopting the equation of "white" and "Caucasian" came down on November 13, 1922, almost exactly two months before oral argument was to proceed in *Thind.* It must have seemed to Thind that he could not lose, for the Supreme Court itself had made Caucasian status the test for whether one was White, and every major anthropological study classified Asian Indians as Caucasians. In addition to the apparent precedential value of *Ozawa,* four lower courts had specifically ruled that Asian Indians were White, while only one had held to the contrary. Moreover, Thind was a veteran of the U.S. Army, and though he had served only six months, he perhaps thought that his service to the country, as well as the congressional decision to make citizenship available to those who had served in the military for three years, might favorably affect his case. All of these hopes and rationalizations, however, would have been mistaken.

Addressing Thind's two-part argument, the Court did not dispute his first assertion, that, as an Asian Indian, he was a "Caucasian." The Court conceded this point, albeit tangentially and without grace, writing: "It may be true that the blond Scandinavian and the brown Hindu have a common ancestor in the dim reaches of antiquity, but the average man knows perfectly well that there are unmistakable and profound differences between them today." In other words, the Court was willing to admit a technical link between Europeans and South Asians, even while insisting on their separation in the popular imagination. This insistence, encapsulated in the reference to what "the average man knows perfectly well," signaled the Court's position in the conflict over rationales that had been dividing the prerequisite courts since *Najour.* The Court made this position explicit when it turned its attention to Thind's second argument, that Caucasians were "white persons."

The Court in *Thind* repudiated its earlier equation in *Ozawa* of Caucasian with White, rejecting as well the science of race more generally. . . .

* * * *

Thind ended the reign of the term "Caucasian." With this decision, the use of scientific evidence as an arbiter of race ceased in the racial prerequisite cases. In its place, the Court elevated common knowledge, ruling as follows: "What we now hold is that the words 'free white persons' are words of common speech, to be interpreted in accordance with the understanding of the common man, synonymous with the word 'Caucasian' only as that word is popularly understood." The words of the statute, the Court wrote, were "written in the words of common speech, for common understanding, by unscientific men." The Court adopted the "understanding of the common man" as the exclusive interpretive principle for creating legal taxonomies of race, rejecting any role for science. Applying this common man's understanding to Thind, the court concluded: "As so understood and used, whatever may be the speculations of the ethnologist, it does not include the body of people to whom the appellee belongs. It is a matter of familiar observation and knowledge that the physical group characteristics of the Hindus render them readily distinguishable from the various groups of persons in this country commonly recognized as white." The Court ignored the weight of precedent and science, reversing Thind's naturalization on the authority of "familiar observation and knowledge." On matters of race, *Thind* crowned ignorance king; as a contemporary commentator remarked, now "the most ignorant man would believe that he could infallibly say who belonged to the white race."

After *Thind,* the naturalization of Asian Indians became legally impossible: Asian Indians were, by law, no longer "white persons." Even worse, many Asian Indians, like Thind himself, lost the citizenship they believed secure. In the wake of *Thind,* the federal government began a campaign to strip naturalized Asian Indians of their citizenship, denaturalizing at least sixty-five people between 1923 and 1927. One former citizen committed suicide following his denaturalization. Vaisho Das Bagai arrived in the United States with his family in 1915, and subsequently naturalized. Dispossessed of his citizenship, Bagai took his own life in 1928. In his suicide note, he wrote: "But now they come to me and say, I am no longer an American citizen. . . . What have I made of myself and my children? We cannot exercise our rights, we cannot leave this country. Humility and insults, who are responsible for all of this? . . . Obstacles this way, blockades that way, and the bridges burnt behind." For Bagai, his family, and Asian Indians generally, *Thind* was a tragedy. However, not all or even most Americans were disheartened by the Supreme Court's decision. In fact, many rejoiced, as the holding resonated with the antipathy toward foreigners in general, and toward those perceived as non-White in particular, which has in advancing and receding waves long swept over our country. Always outspoken on racial matters, the *San Francisco Chronicle* welcomed the decision in *Thind* on the ground that "Hindus are degraded" and unfit for citizenship. Seizing on the Court's pronouncement, the *Chronicle* demanded that the state do something to end "the menacing spread of Hindus holding our lands." California obliged, vigorously enforcing its legal prohibitions on the ownership of land by those racially barred from citizenship against this newest group of permanent "aliens." In *Thind,* the Supreme Court once again signed its assent to racial injustice, allowing others to use its words to perpetrate further harm.

The Social Construction of Race

Despite the Court's belief in the naturalness of racial categories, many of its decisions concerning race, *Ozawa* and *Thind* in particular, demonstrate that race is not a measured fact, but a preserved fiction. The celebration of common knowledge and the repudiation of scientific evidence show that race is a matter not of physical difference, but of what people believe about physical difference. To be sure, physiological differences distinguish persons from around the world. Yet, the common knowledge about race is never a naked, untainted assessment of such differences. Rather, as Barbara Fields argues, "physical impressions are always mediated by a larger context, which assigns them their meaning, whether or not the individuals concerned are aware that this is so. It follows that the notion of race, in its popular manifestation, is an ideological construct and thus, above all, a historical product." Herein lies the significance of the judicial debate about skin color that *Najour* and *Ozawa* explored from opposite directions. It is not pigmentation, but rather the social understandings of integument that denote race. Thus, some dark-skinned people are identified as White, and some light-skinned individuals are denied similar status. While not entirely irrelevant to races, the role of nature is limited to providing the morphological raw materials society uses to build systems of racial meaning. Recognizing this frees us to consider the many ways in which skin color has come to connote racial difference—frees us, that is, to examine the way in which race has been constructed socially and legally. Despite a natural component, race is entirely social. Race is nothing more than what society and law say it is.

 F U R T H E R   R E A D I N G

David H. Bennett, *The Party of Fear: From Nativist Movements to the New Right in American History* (1988).

Roger Daniels, *The Politics of Prejudice: The Anti-Japanese Movement in CA and the Struggle of Japanese Exclusion* (1962).

Arnoldo De Leon, *They Called Them Greasers: Anglo American Attitudes Toward Mexicans in Texas, 1821–1900* (1983).

Leonard Dinnerstein, *Anti-Semitism in the United States* (1991).

Leonard Dinnerstein, *Uneasy at Home: Anti-Semitism and the American Jewish Experience* (1987).

David Gerber, ed., *Anti-Semitism in American History* (1986).

Ian Haney-Lopez, *White by Law: The Legal Construction of Race* (1996).

John Higham, *Strangers in the Land* (1963).

Donald Kinzer, *An Episode in Anti-Catholicism: The American Protective Association* (1963).

Dale T. Knobel, *America for the Americans: The Nativist Movement in the United States* (1996).

Alan Kraut, *Silent Travelers: Germs, Genes, and the "Immigrant Menace"* (1994).

Stuart Creighton Miller, *The Unwelcome Immigrant: The American Image of the Chinese, 1785–1882* (1969).

Robert K. Murray, *Red Scare: A Study in National Hysteria, 1919–1920* (1955).

Alexander Saxton, *The Indispensable Enemy: Labor and the Anti-Chinese Movement in California* (1971).

Barbara Soloman, *Ancestors and Immigrants* (1965).

CHAPTER
10

Responses to Immigration: Exclusion, Restriction, and Americanization, 1880–1924

As rates of immigration to the United States swelled in the decades straddling the turn of the century, Americans pondered how immigrants and "ethnics" could best be integrated into the American republic. Their answers varied widely. Some voices continued to celebrate the idea of the melting pot, where immigrants would combine the positive qualities they brought to the country with new patterns of behavior made possible by life in the United States. The melting pot metaphorically created an alloy of the "American," an improvement over its constituent elements. Others posited a cultural pluralist model of American life wherein national subgroups would live amicably together as Americans. The richness of the variety of people maintaining cultural pasts would enliven life in the United States and prohibit the blandness that resulted from attempts to make all Americans conform to a single American ideal. Some immigrants themselves chided the American-born for their behavior and suggested that, by maintaining patterns of religion and life that they carried to the United States, they were better Americans than the American-born.

A combination of historical forces in the early twentieth century, however, coalesced to advance still more powerfully a sentiment of Americanism and Americanization. Proponents of this view argued that immigrants should cast off their cultural pasts and conform as quickly as possible to an American ideal. The first force was a series of movements—fueled, in part, by the racialization of immigrants discussed in the last chapter—that focused on the danger of the immigrant and the need for immigration to be restricted and for immigrants to be transformed, if possible, into Americans. Second, the Progressive movement in the early twentieth century contributed to the conviction that a variety of institutions, such as the school, should and could be used to teach immigrants proper behavior and thought and to transform them into Americans. Third, a vigilant nationalism leading up to World War I, that became almost xenophobic during the war, *fostered a campaign of total loyalty to the United States, its institutions, even its English language.*

This three-pronged offensive created a climate of opinion that fostered movements of Americanism and Americanization at the expense of beliefs in the melting pot or cultural pluralism. Critics repeatedly warned against "hyphenism," the notion that one who was, say, an Italian-American could be both Italian and American. In fact, they contended that one was either Italian or American. In hopes that immigrants would choose the latter, they advocated the "100 percent Americanism" that affirmed that all residents of the United States should be entirely loyal to American institutions. In order to foster Americanism, many Americans advanced an Americanization movement that was explicitly aimed at transforming immigrants into Americans using such institutions as the schools, the workplace, and even the home. Certain aspects of these movements, such as Jane Addams's work with the immigrants (see Chapter 8), were essentially tolerant attempts simultaneously hoping to understand the immigrants and to encourage them to accept conditions of American life. Others, however, reflected a fanaticism that often accompanies a nation at war. Indeed, whereas certain aspects of the Americanization movement expressed a hope to remake the immigrant into an American, the less tolerant voices began to call for increasingly powerful restrictive laws, an outcry that came to fruition in the restriction laws of 1921 and 1924.

DOCUMENTS

The following documents illustrate the many conceptions of integrating immigrants into American society in the late nineteenth and early twentieth centuries. The first four documents from the late nineteenth century show a variety of beliefs about immigrants in American society. A Protestant clergyman (1885) portrays what he calls the "perils" of immigration for American society—immigrants' tendency to have "low" morals and be affiliated with the Catholic or Mormon Church. Likewise, members of the Immigration Restriction League (1894) focus on the relationship between criminality, illiteracy, and underemployment of immigrants. At about the same time (1883), however, Emma Lazarus, wrote her sonnet "The New Colossus" (reproduced as the third document), which welcomes the "huddled masses yearning to breathe free." Likewise, only some years later (1889), a German Catholic priest castigates the "American nationality" for *its* immorality, its "mammon-worship" and "hypocritical spirit." The next four documents illustrate various models to integrate immigrants into American society in the early twentieth century. Israel Zangwill (1909), a Jewish American playwright, celebrates the melting pot that fuses the "races" into an American, perhaps a "superman." In contrast, Theodore Roosevelt (1915) argues that there is no room for "hyphenated" Americans and that the only good American is someone with absolute loyalty to the United States. Randolph Bourne (1916) argues against both Americanism and the melting pot. For him, the United States should exhibit a transnationalism where many nationalities are woven into a cosmopolitan fabric. World War I furthered Roosevelt's vision, as exemplified in the final document: the governor of Iowa's 1917 proclamation that only English could be spoken in public, over the telephone, and in church.

Josiah Strong, a Protestant Clergyman, Considers the "Perils" of Immigration, 1885

Consider briefly the moral and political influence of immigration.   1. Influence on morals. Let me hasten to recognize the high worth of many of our citizens of foreign birth, not a few of whom are eminent in the pulpit and in all the learned professions. Many come to us in full sympathy with our free institutions, and desiring to aid us in promoting a Christian civilization. But no one knows better than these same intelligent and Christian foreigners that they do not represent the mass of immigrants. The typical immigrant is a European peasant, whose horizon has been narrow, whose moral and religious training has been meager or false, and whose ideas of life are low. Not a few belong to the pauper and criminal classes. . . . Moreover, immigration is demoralizing. No man is held upright simply by the strength of his own roots; his branches interlock with those of other men, and thus society is formed, with all its laws and customs and force of public opinion. Few men appreciate the extent to which they are indebted to their surroundings for the strength with which they resist, or do, or suffer. All this strength the emigrant leaves behind him. He is isolated in a strange land, perhaps doubly so by reason of a strange speech. He is transplanted from a forest to an open prairie, where, before he is rooted, he is smitten with the blasts of temptation.

. . . Is it strange, then, that those who come from other lands, whose old associations are all broken and whose reputations are left behind, should sink to a lower moral level? Across the sea they suffered many restraints which are here removed. Better wages afford larger means of self-indulgence; often the back is not strong enough to bear prosperity, and liberty too often lapses into license. Our population of foreign extraction is sadly conspicuous in our criminal records. This element constituted in 1870 twenty per cent. of the population of New England, and furnished seventy-five per cent. of the crime. That is, it was twelve times as much disposed to crime as the native stock. The hoodlums and roughs of our cities are, most of them, American-born of foreign parentage. . . .

Moreover, immigration not only furnishes the greater portion of our criminals, it is also seriously affecting the morals of the native population. It is disease and not health which is contagious. Most foreigners bring with them continental ideas of the Sabbath, and the result is sadly manifest in all our cities, where it is being transformed from a holy day into a holiday. But by far the most effective

From Josiah Strong, *Our Country: Its Possible Future and Its Present Crisis* (New York: The Baker & Taylor Co., 1885).

instrumentality for debauching popular morals is the liquor traffic, and this is chiefly carried on by foreigners. . . .

2. We can only glance at the political aspects of immigration. As we have already seen, it is immigration which has fed fat the liquor power; and there is a liquor vote. Immigration furnishes most of the victims of Mormonism; and there is a Mormon vote. Immigration is the strength of the Catholic church; and there is a Catholic vote. Immigration is the mother and nurse of American socialism; and there is to be a socialist vote. Immigration tends strongly to the cities, and gives to them their political complexion. And there is no more serious menace to our civilization than our rabble-ruled cities. These several perils, all of which are enhanced by immigration, will be considered in succeeding chapters.

Many American citizens are not Americanized. It is as unfortunate as it is natural, that foreigners in this country should cherish their own language and peculiar customs, and carry their nationality, as a distinct factor, into our politics. Immigration has created the "German vote" and the "Irish vote," for which politicians bid, and which have already been decisive of state elections, and might easily determine national. A mass of men but little acquainted with our institutions, who will act in concert and who are controlled largely by their appetites and prejudices, constitute a very paradise for demagogues.

. . . There is among our population of alien birth an unhappy tendency toward aggregation, which concentrates the strain upon portions of our social and political fabric. Certain quarters of many of the cities are, in language, customs and costumes, essentially foreign. Many colonies have bought up lands and so set themselves apart from Americanizing influences.

* * * *

. . . A strong centralized government, like that of Rome under the Cæsars, can control heterogeneous populations, but local self-government implies close relations between man and man, a measure of sympathy, and, to a certain extent, community of ideas. Our safety demands the assimilation of these strange populations, and the process of assimilation will become slower and more difficult as the proportion of foreigners increases.

The Immigration Restriction League Outlines the "Immigration Problem," 1894

There is no subject of national importance about which so much has been written and of which so little is generally known as the immigration question. In view of

From "The Present Aspect of the Immigration Problem," by the Immigration Restriction League, 1894.

the fact that attention has again been turned to this subject by reason of the formation of the "Immigration Restriction League" of Boston, an account of our immigration laws, of their working, and of the changes that should be made in them,
seems particularly opportune at the present time.

* * * *

. . . We do not speak of the millions of thrifty immigrants who have settled
here, have built up our country and have become patriotic American citizens. It is
with the lower and criminal classes that we have to deal. The evils resulting from
this kind of immigration are very numerous. One of the greatest is the enormous
increase in the number of criminals in this country, which can be traced directly to
the growth of the lower foreign elements in our midst. According to the census of
1880, the foreign-born element, although constituting less than one-seventh of the
population, furnished more than one-third of the paupers.

The census of 1890 shows that persons of foreign birth and parentage make up 38
per cent, or somewhat over one-third of our total white population. THIS ONE-THIRD
FURNISHES MORE THAN ONE HALF OF OUR CRIMINALS, NEARLY TWO-THIRDS OF THE IN-
MATES OF OUR REFORMATORIES, AND NEARLY TWO THIRDS OF THE PAUPERS IN OUR
ALMSHOUSES.

Illiteracy of Immigrants

The illiteracy of the immigrants we are now receiving in great numbers is a source
of imminent danger to the country. In every hundred foreigners over sixteen years
of age, who came here from February 1 to October 31, 1892, there were the following number of illiterates, according to the countries from which the immigrants
came: England, ten; Ireland, eight; Wales, six; Germany, two; Scandinavian countries and Denmark, less than one; Poland, fifty-six; Italy, sixty-six; Hungary,
twenty-eight; Russia proper, twenty.

Of the 440,793 immigrants who came to this country in the year ending June
30, 1893, 57,897 OVER 16 YEARS OF AGE COULD NOT READ; 59,582 COULD NOT WRITE,
AND 61,038 COULD NEITHER READ NOR WRITE.

This danger from illiteracy is still further aggravated by the fact that many of
our recent immigrants do not try to assimilate with us or become Americanized,
but live in colonies by themselves, speaking their own language and keeping all
their own customs, unaffected by the higher civilization around them. The safety of
this country depends upon our assimilating and Americanizing all these heterogeneous elements, but the process of assimilation must become slower and more difficult as the foreign element increases, and as it thus tends to keep more and more
by itself. Time fails to do more than mention the harm done by the foreign ideas
and customs, imported into this country from the slums of Europe, in the morals
and in the sanitary conditions of our larger cities, and in such distinctly un-American and in the highest degree dangerous occurrences as the Haymarket massacre at
Chicago, and the Mafia incident at New Orleans.

The serious riots that have taken place among the miners in Pennsylvania during the past winter were instigated and carried out by foreigners, principally Slavs,
Huns, Italians and Poles. In such disturbances as these the Anglo-Saxon element

has been almost unanimously on the side of law and order. Such evils may be directly traced to the influence of the lower classes of immigrants.

Immigration and the Unemployed

The evils of unrestricted immigration are perhaps best seen and most fully realized at such a period of financial depression as that through which we have been passing. It seems almost unnecessary to point out the connection that their immigration problem has with the question of the "unemployed." Although we have far more unemployed here than we can take care of, our gates are still wide open, and the stream of immigration, partly checked, it is true, by the temporary financial depression, but still of no mean size, has continued to flow on. There can be no need of stating, what everyone must see at once, that every shipload of immigrants landed on our shores from day to day increases the number of the unemployed, the competition for work and the burden which our philanthropic citizens have to bear.

Emma Lazarus's Poem at the Foot of the Statue of Liberty, 1883

Not like the brazen giant of Greek fame,
With conquering limbs astride from land to land
Here at our sea-washed, sunset gates shall stand
A mighty woman with a torch, whose flame
Is the imprisoned lightening, and her name
Mother of Exiles. From her beacon-handed
Glows world-wide welcome; her mild eyes command
The air-bridged harbor that twin cities frame
"Keep, ancient lands, your storied pomp!" cries she
With silent lips. "Give me your tired, your poor,
Your huddled masses yearning to breathe free,
The wretched refuse of your teeming shore.
Send these, the homeless, tempest-tost to me,
I lift my lamp beside the golden door!"

A German American Attacks "False Americanism," 1889

With regard to Americanism we make a distinction. There is a true and a false Americanism. True Americanism consists in the promotion of the peace, the happiness, and the prosperity of the people, and in the advancement of the public good and the general welfare of the country. . . .

. . . And, since the Catholic religion promotes virtue, piety, and morality, true Americanism must desire the growth and spread of the Catholic Church.

_____

From Emma Lazarus, "The New Colossus."

From Rev. A. H. Walburg, *The Question of Nationality in Its Relations to the Catholic Church in the United States*, 1889.

False Americanism is a spirit of pride and self-conceit, and looks with contempt upon other nationalities. It is a boasting, arrogant spirit. It glories in the biggest rivers, the tallest trees, the grandest scenery, and considers this country superior to every other country on the face of the globe. It is a pharisaical, hypocritical spirit, putting on the garb of virtue when all is hollowness and rottenness within. It is a spirit of infidelity and materialism. False Americanism is mammon worship. It adores the golden calf and is directed to the accumulation of wealth with an ardor which is unquenchable and with an energy which never tires. The eagerness for wealth is paramount and controls every other feeling. The ideal set before every American youth is money. Money is not only needful, but is the one thing needful. Money is a power everywhere, but here it is the supreme power. Abroad, there is the nobility, the pride of ancestry. This is vanity artificial and empty, yet it is not so degrading as money. Abroad, eminent worth counts for something. But here, we acknowledge only one god, and his name is Mammon.

* * * *

. . . This is the great evil of false Americanism, the curse of our society. It is demoralizing us. The hunger and the thirst after money consume like a raging fire all warmer sympathies, all better feelings of our nature. It dwarfs all higher aspirations. What are moral excellence, culture, character, manhood, when money-bags outweigh them all? How can better sentiments be impressed upon the children, when all about them teach them that these are of no value without money? Hence the startling dishonesty in the race for riches. Hence the bribery of officers, the purchase of office, the corruption and jobbery, the general demoralization, that threaten our institutions.

And with its vaunted independence, this spurious Americanism, in its ostentatious display of wealth, stoops to Foreignism, copies European fashions, imports a Parisian cook, and considers itself fortunate to exchange its wealth for the musty title of some needy descendant of the nobility.

In Europe, a man enjoys his competence; but here, no one has enough. No laborer is satisfied with his wages; no millionaire, however colossal his fortune, ceases in his greed for more. From the first dawn of manhood to the evening of old age, the gold fever continues to increase in strength and violence, till death puts an end to the raging malady.

The American nationality, properly so-called, is the Anglo-Saxon or the Anglo-American nationality, the descendants of early settlers who came from England. These can justly claim the honorable distinction of being called the American nationality. We were, in the beginning, substantially an English people. The first settlers in this country, the Pilgrim Fathers, were English. They had a long and bloody struggle to maintain against the Indians and suffered untold privations and hardships in effecting a firm and permanent foothold in this country. Notwithstanding all obstacles, the first colonies improved, and by dint of perseverance, courage, and industry, became very prosperous. They resisted British tyranny and oppression. . . .

* * * *

Notwithstanding this pre-eminence, and the fact that whatever is honorable in our history and worthy of esteem in our institutions, is owing chiefly to our forefathers, who, it is often said, built better than they knew, nevertheless the American nationality, when tried by the test of true Americanism will in many respects be found wanting. It is often the hotbed of fanaticism, intolerance, and radical, ultra views on matters of politics and religion. All the vagaries of spiritualism, Mormonism, free-loveism, prohibition, infidelity, and materialism, generally breed in the American nationality. Here, also, we find dissimulation and hypocrisy. While the Irishman will get drunk and engage in an open street fight, and the German drink his beer in a public beer-garden, the American, pretending to be a total abstainer, takes his strong drink secretly and sleeps it off on a sofa or in a club-room. Who are the trusted employes, the public officers, that enjoyed the unlimited confidence of the people, and turned out to be hypocrites, impostors, and betrayers of trusts? As a rule they are not Irish or Germans, but Americans. Who are the devotees at the shrine of mammon? Who compose the syndicates, trusts, corporations, pools, and those huge monopolies that reach their tentacles over the nation, grinding down the poor and fattening in immense wealth? They are not Germans or Irish, but Americans. Who are the wild and reckless bank speculators, the forgers, the gamblers, and the defaulting officials? They are not Irish or German, but Americans. Read the list of the refugees to Canada and you will find it made up of American names. We meet here also all species of refined wickedness. The educated villain, the expert burglar, the cool, calculating, deliberate criminal, generally belongs to the American nationality. Where the foreigners are corrupt they have in a great measure been corrupted by the example of Americans. A republic that is not based upon morality and religion, where virtue is depressed, is ripe for an ignoble grave.

The Anglo-Saxon nationality has always been in England and in this country the bulwark of Protestantism and the main-stay of the enemies of the faith. It is so puffed up with spiritual pride, so steeped in materialism, that it is callous, and impervious to the spirit and the doctrines of the Catholic religion. It is true there are eminent converts in England and a few in this country; but they have no followers; the bulk of the people are as remote as ever from entering the Church.

A Jewish American Playwright Celebrates the American "Melting Pot," 1909

DAVID A fee! I'd pay a fee to see all those happy immigrants you gather together—Dutchmen and Greeks, Poles and Norwegians, Welsh and Armenians. If you only had Jews, it would be as good as going to Ellis Island.

VERA [*Smiling*] What a strange taste! Who on earth wants to go to Ellis Island?

DAVID Oh, I love going to Ellis Island to watch the ships coming in from Europe, and to think that all those weary, sea-tossed wanderers are feeling what *I* felt when America first stretched out her great motherhand to *me!*

VERA [*Softly*] Were you very happy?

DAVID It was heaven. You must remember that all my life I had heard of America—everybody in our town had friends there or was going there or got money orders from there. The earliest game I played at was selling off my toy furniture and

---

From Israel Zangwill, *The Melting-Pot* (New York: Macmillan, 1920).

setting up in America. All my life America was waiting, beckoning, shining—the place where God would wipe away tears from off all faces.

[*He ends in a half-sob.*]

MENDEL [*Rises, as in terror*] Now, now, David, don't get excited.

[*Approaches him.*]

DAVID To think that the same great torch of liberty which threw its light across all the broad seas and lands into my little garret in Russia, is shining also for all those other weeping millions of Europe, shining wherever men hunger and are oppressed—

DAVID Oh, Miss Revendal, when I look at our Statue of Liberty, I just seem to hear the voice of America crying: "Come unto me all ye that labour and are heavy laden and I will give you rest—rest—"

[*He is now almost sobbing.*]

MENDEL Don't talk any more—you know it is bad for you.

DAVID But Miss Revendal asked—and I want to explain to her what America means to me.

MENDEL You can explain it in your American symphony.

VERA [*Eagerly—to* DAVID] You compose?

DAVID [*Embarrassed*] Oh, uncle, why did you talk of—? Uncle always—my music is so thin and tinkling. When I am *writing* my American symphony, it seems like thunder crashing through a forest full of bird songs. But next day—oh, next day!

[*He laughs dolefully and turns away.*]

VERA So your music finds inspiration in America?

DAVID Yes—in the seething of the Crucible.

VERA The Crucible? I don't understand!

DAVID Not understand! You, the Spirit of the Settlement!

[*He rises and crosses to her and leans over the table, facing her.*]

Not understand that America is God's Crucible, the great Melting-Pot where all the races of Europe are melting and re-forming! Here you stand, good folk, think I, when I see them at Ellis Island, here you stand

[*Graphically illustrating it on the table*]

in your fifty groups, with your fifty languages and histories, and your fifty blood hatreds and rivalries. But you won't be long like that, brothers, for these are the fires of God you've come to—these are the fires of God. A fig for your feuds and vendettas! Germans and Frenchmen, Irishmen and Englishmen, Jews and Russians—into the Crucible with you all! God is making the American.

MENDEL I should have thought the American was made already—eighty millions of him.

DAVID Eighty millions!

[*He smiles toward* VERA *in good-humoured derision.*]

Eighty millions! Over a continent! Why, that cockleshell of a Britain has forty millions! No, uncle, the real American has not yet arrived. He is only in the Crucible, I tell you—he will be the fusion of all races, perhaps the coming superman. Ah, what a glorious Finale for my symphony—if I can only write it.

Theodore Roosevelt Advocates "Americanism," 1915

. . . There is no room in this country for hyphenated Americanism. When I refer to hyphenated Americans, I do not refer to naturalized Americans. Some of the very best Americans I have ever known were naturalized Americans, Americans born abroad. But a hyphenated American is not an American at all. This is just as true of the man who puts "native" before the hyphen as of the man who puts German or Irish or English or French before the hyphen. Americanism is a matter of the spirit and of the soul. Our allegiance must be purely to the United States. We must unsparingly condemn any man who holds any other allegiance. But if he is heartily and singly loyal to this Republic, then no matter where he was born, he is just as good an American as any one else.

The one absolutely certain way of bringing this nation to ruin, of preventing all possibility of its continuing to be a nation at all, would be to permit it to become a tangle of squabbling nationalities, an intricate knot of German-Americans, Irish-Americans, English-Americans, French-Americans, Scandinavian-Americans or Italian-Americans, each preserving its separate nationality, each at heart feeling more sympathy with Europeans of that nationality, than with the other citizens of the American Republic. The men who do not become Americans and nothing else are hyphenated Americans; and there ought to be no room for them in this country. The man who calls himself an American citizen and who yet shows by his actions that he is primarily the citizen of a foreign land, plays a thoroughly mischievous part in the life of our body politic. He has no place here; and the sooner he returns to the land to which he feels his real heart-allegiance, the better it will be for every good American. There is no such thing as a hyphenated American who is a good American. The only man who is a good American is the man who is an American and nothing else.

For an American citizen to vote as a German-American, an Irish-American, or an English-American, is to be a traitor to American institutions; and those hyphenated Americans who terrorize American politicians by threats of the foreign vote are engaged in treason to the American Republic.

Americanization

The foreign-born population of this country must be an Americanized population—no other kind can fight the battles of America either in war or peace. It must talk the language of its native-born fellow-citizens, it must possess American citizenship and American ideals. It must stand firm by its oath of allegiance in word and deed and must show that in very fact it has renounced allegiance to every

From Philip Davis (ed.), *Immigration and Americanization* (Boston: Ginn and Company, 1920).

prince, potentate, or foreign government. It must be maintained on an American standard of living so as to prevent labor disturbances in important plants and at critical times. None of these objects can be secured as long as we have immigrant colonies, ghettos, and immigrant sections, and above all they cannot be assured so long as we consider the immigrant only as an industrial asset. The immigrant must not be allowed to drift or to be put at the mercy of the exploiter. Our object is to not to imitate one of the older racial types, but to maintain a new American type and then to secure loyalty to this type. We cannot secure such loyalty unless we make this a country where men shall feel that they have justice and also where they shall feel that they are required to perform the duties imposed upon them. The policy of "Let alone" which we have hitherto pursued is thoroughly vicious from two standpoints. By this policy we have permitted the immigrants, and too often the native-born laborers as well, to suffer injustice. Moreover, by this policy we have failed to impress upon the immigrant and upon the native-born as well that they are expected to do justice as well as to receive justice, that they are expected to be heartily and actively and single-mindedly loyal to the flag no less than to benefit by living under it.

We cannot afford to continue to use hundreds of thousands of immigrants merely as industrial assets while they remain social outcasts and menaces any more than fifty years ago we could afford to keep the black man merely as an industrial asset and not as a human being. We cannot afford to build a big industrial plant and herd men and women about it without care for their welfare. We cannot afford to permit squalid overcrowding or the kind of living system which makes impossible the decencies and necessities of life. We cannot afford the low wage rates and the merely seasonal industries which mean the sacrifice of both individual and family life and morals to the industrial machinery. We cannot afford to leave American mines, munitions plants, and general resources in the hands of alien workmen, alien to America and even likely to be made hostile to America by machinations such as have recently been provided in the case of the two foreign embassies in Washington. We cannot afford to run the risk of having in time of war men working on our railways or working in our munition plants who would in the name of duty to their own foreign countries bring destruction to us. Recent events have shown us that incitements to sabotage and strikes are in the view of at least two of the great foreign powers of Europe within their definition of neutral practices. What would be done to us in the name of war if these things are done to us in the name of neutrality?

✳ ✳ ✳ ✳

One America

All of us, no matter from what land our parents came, no matter in what way we may severally worship our Creator, must stand shoulder to shoulder in a united America for the elimination of race and religious prejudice. We must stand for a reign of equal justice to both big and small. We must insist on the maintenance of the American standard of living. We must stand for an adequate national control which shall secure a better training of our young men in time of peace, both for the work of peace and for the work of war. We must direct every national resource, material and spiritual, to the task not of shirking difficulties, but of training our people to overcome difficulties. Our aim must be, not to make life easy and soft, not to soften soul and body, but to fit us in virile fashion to do a great work for all mankind. This great work can only be done by a mighty democracy, with these qualities of soul, guided by those qualities of mind, which will both make it refuse to do injustice to any other nation, and also enable it to hold its own against aggression by any other nation. In our relations with the outside world, we must abhor wrongdoing, and disdain to commit it, and we must no less disdain the baseness of spirit which lamely submits to wrongdoing. Finally and most important of all, we must strive for the establishment within our own borders of that stern and lofty standard of personal and public neutrality which shall guarantee to each man his rights, and which shall insist in return upon the full performance by each man of his duties both to his neighbor and to the great nation whose flag must symbolize in the future as it has symbolized in the past the highest hopes of all mankind.

Randolph Bourne Promotes Cultural Pluralism, 1916

The failure of the melting-pot, far from closing the great American democratic experiment, means that it has only just begun. Whatever American nationalism turns out to be, we see already that it will have a color richer and more exciting than our ideal has hitherto encompassed. In a world which has dreamed of internationalism, we find that we have all unawares been building up the first international nation. The voices which have cried for a tight and jealous nationalism of the European pattern are failing. From that ideal, however valiantly and disinterestedly it has been set for us, time and tendency have moved us further and further away. What we have achieved has been rather a cosmopolitan federation of national colonies, of foreign cultures, from whom the sting of devastating competition has been removed. America is already the world-federation in miniature, the continent where for the first time in history has been achieved that miracle of hope, the peaceful living side by side, with character substantially preserved, of the most heterogeneous peoples under the sun. Nowhere else has such contiguity been anything but the breeder of misery. Here, notwithstanding our tragic failures of adjustment, the outlines are already too clear not to give us a new vision and a new orientation of the American mind in the world.

It is for the American of the younger generation to accept this cosmopolitanism, and carry it along with self-conscious and fruitful purpose. . . . If he is still a colonial, he is no longer the colonial of one partial culture, but of many. He is a colonial of the world. Colonialism has grown into cosmopolitanism, and his motherland is no one nation, but all who have anything life-enhancing to offer

From Randolph Bourne, *War and the Intellectuals*, 1916.

to the spirit. .... If the American is parochial, it is in sheer wantonness or cow-ardice. His provincialism is the measure of his fear of bogies or the defect of his imagination.

Indeed, it is not uncommon for the eager Anglo-Saxon who goes to a vivid American university to-day to find his true friends not among his own race but among the acclimatized German or Austrian, the acclimatized Jew, the acclima-tized Scandinavian or Italian. In them he finds the cosmopolitan note. In these youths, foreign-born or the children of foreign-born parents, he is likely to find many of his old inbred morbid problems washed away. These friends are oblivious to the repressions of that tight little society in which he so provincially grew up. He has a pleasurable sense of liberation from the stale and familiar attitudes of those whose ingrowing culture has scarcely created anything vital for his America of to-day. He breathes a larger air. In his new enthusiasms for continental literature, for unplumbed Russian depths, for French clarity of thought, for Teuton philosophies of power, he feels himself citizen of a larger world. He may be absurdly superfi-cial, his outward-reaching wonder may ignore all the stiller and homelier virtues of his Anglo-Saxon home, but he has at least found the clue to that international mind which will be essential to all men and women of good-will if they are ever to save this Western world of ours from suicide. His new friends have gone through a sim-ilar evolution. America has burned most of the baser metal also from them. Meet-ing now with this common American background, all of them may yet retain that distinctiveness of their native culture and their national spiritual slants. They are more valuable and interesting to each other for being different, yet that difference could not be creative were it not for this new cosmopolitan outlook which America has given them and which they all equally possess.

A college where such a spirit is possible even to the smallest degree, has within itself already the seeds of this international intellectual world of the future. It suggests that the contribution of America will be an intellectual internationalism which goes far beyond the mere exchange of scientific ideas and discoveries and the cold recording of facts. It will be an intellectual sympathy which is not satisfied until it has got at the heart of the different cultural expressions, and felt as they feel. It may have immense preferences, but it will make understanding and not in-dignation its end. Such a sympathy will unite and not divide.

Against the thinly disguised panic which calls itself 'patriotism' and the thinly disguised militarism which calls itself 'preparedness' the cosmopolitan ideal is set. This does not mean that those who hold it are for a policy of drift. They, too, long passionately for an integrated and disciplined America. But they do not want one which is integrated only for domestic economic exploitation of the workers or for predatory economic imperialism among the weaker peoples. They do not want one that is integrated by coercion or militarism, or for the truculent assertion of a mediæval code of honor and of doubtful rights. . . .

* * * *

Only America, by reason of the unique liberty of opportunity and traditional isolation for which she seems to stand, can lead in this cosmopolitan enterprise. Only the American—and in this category I include the migratory alien who has lived with us and caught the pioneer spirit and a sense of new social vistas—has the chance to become that citizen of the world America is coming to be, not a nationality but a trans-nationality, a weaving back and forth, with the other lands, of many threads of all sizes and colors. Any movement which attempts to thwart this weaving, or to dye the fabric any one color, or disentangle the threads of the strands, is false to this cosmopolitan vision. . . . How are we likely to get the more creative America—by confining our imaginations to the ideal of the melting-pot, or broadening them to some such cosmopolitan conception as I have been vaguely sketching?

The war has shown America to be unable, though isolated geographically and politically from a European world-situation, to remain aloof and irresponsible. She is a wandering star in a sky dominated by two colossal constellations of states. Can she not work out some position of her own, some life of being in, yet not quite of, this seething and embroiled European world? This is her only hope and promise. A trans-nationality of all the nations, it is spiritually impossible for her to pass into the orbit of any one. It will be folly to hurry herself into a premature and sentimental nationalism, or to emulate Europe and play fast and loose with the forces that drag into war. No Americanization will fulfill this vision which does not recognize the uniqueness of this trans-nationalism of ours. The Anglo-Saxon attempt to fuse will only create enmity and distrust. The crusade against 'hyphenates' will only inflame the partial patriotism of trans-nationals, and cause them to assert their European traditions in strident and unwholesome ways. But the attempt to weave a wholly novel international nation out of our chaotic America will liberate and harmonize the creative power of all these peoples and give them the new spiritual citizenship, as so many individuals have already been given, of a world.

* * * *

. . . Let us face realistically the America we have around us. Let us work with the forces that are at work. Let us make something of this trans-national spirit instead of outlawing it. Already we are living this cosmopolitan America. What we need is everywhere a vivid consciousness of the new ideal. Deliberate headway must be made against the survivals of the melting-pot ideal for the promise of American life.

We cannot Americanize America worthily by sentimentalizing and moralizing history. When the best schools are expressly renouncing the questionable duty of teaching patriotism by means of history, it is not the time to force shibboleth upon the immigrant. This form of Americanization has been heard because it appealed to the vestiges of our old sentimentalized and moralized patriotism. This has so far held the field as the expression of the new American's new devotion. The inflections of other voices have been drowned. They must be heard. We must see if the lesson of the war has not been for hundreds of these later Americans a vivid realization of their trans-nationality, a new consciousness of what America meant to them as a citizenship in the world. It is the vague historic idealisms which have provided the fuel for the European flame. Our American ideal can make no progress until we do away with this romantic gilding of the past.

All our idealisms must be those of future social goals in which all can participate, the good life of personality lived in the environment of the Beloved Community. No mere doubtful triumphs of the past, which redound to the glory of only one of our trans-nationalities, can satisfy us. It must be a future America, on which all can unite, which pulls us irresistibly toward it, as we understand each other more warmly.

To make real this striving amid dangers and apathies is work for a younger *intelligentsia* of America. Here is an enterprise of integration into which we can all pour ourselves, of a spiritual welding which should make us, if the final menace ever came, not weaker, but infinitely strong.

* * * *

The Governor of Iowa Proclaims English the State's Official Language

A Proclamation

To the people of Iowa:

Whereas, our country is engaged in war with foreign powers; and

Whereas, controversy has arisen in parts of this state concerning the use of foreign languages;

Therefore, for the purpose of ending the controversy and to bring about peace, quiet and harmony among our people, attention is directed to the following, and all are requested to govern themselves accordingly.

The official language of the United States and the state of Iowa is the English language. Freedom of speech is guaranteed by federal and state constitutions, but this is not a guaranty of the right to use a language other than the language of the country—the English language. Both federal and state constitutions also provide that "no laws shall be made respecting an establishment of religion or prohibiting the free exercise thereof." Each person is guaranteed freedom to worship God according to the dictates of his own conscience, but this guaranty does not protect him in the use of a foreign language when he can as well express his thought in English, nor entitle the person who cannot speak or understand the English language to employ a foreign language, when to do so tends, in time of national peril, to create discord among neighbors and citizens, or to disturb the peace and quiet of the community.

Every person should appreciate and observe his duty to refrain from all acts or conversation which may excite suspicion or produce strife among the people, but in his relation to the public should so demean himself that every word and act will manifest his loyalty to his country and his solemn purpose to aid in achieving victory for our army and navy and the permanent peace of the world.

If there must be disagreement, let adjustment be made by those in official authority rather than by the participants in the disagreement. Voluntary or self-constituted committees or associations undertaking the settlement of such disputes, instead of promoting peace and harmony, are a menace to society and a fruitful cause of violence. The great aim and object of all should be unity of purpose and a

---

From Governor Harding's proclamation about language in Iowa, 1917.

solidarity of all the people under the flag for victory. This much we owe to ourselves, to posterity, to our country, and to the world.

Therefore, the following rules should obtain in Iowa during the war:

First. English should and must be the only medium of instruction in public, private, denominational or other similar schools.

Second. Conversation in public places, on trains and over the telephone should be in the English language.

Third. All public addresses should be in the English language.

Fourth. Let those who cannot speak or understand the English language conduct their religious worship in their homes.

This course carried out in the spirit of patriotism, though inconvenient to some, will not interfere with their guaranteed constitutional rights and will result in peace and tranquility at home and greatly strengthen the country in battle. The blessings of the United States are so great that any inconvenience or sacrifice should willingly be made for their perpetuity.

Therefore, by virtue of authority in me vested, I, W. L. Harding, governor of the State of Iowa, commend the spirit of tolerance and urge that henceforward the within outlined rules be adhered to by all, that petty differences be avoided and forgotten, and that, united as one people with one purpose and one language, we fight shoulder to shoulder for the good of mankind.

In testimony whereof I have hereunto set my hand and caused to be affixed the great seal of the State of Iowa.

Done at Des Moines, this twenty-third day of May, 1918.

(Seal)   W. L. HARDING.

By the Governor:

W. S. Allen, Secretary of State.

ESSAYS

The following two essays illustrate different models for integrating immigrants in the United States from perspectives of social and intellectual history. In the first essay, Stephen Meyer, a historian at University of Wisconsin, Parkside, shows how Americanization came to be an explicit policy in adapting the immigrant worker to the industrial workplace. Meyer focuses on the Americanization campaign instituted by Henry Ford in his automotive plant. In an attempt to temper absenteeism and labor turnover and to diminish unionization, Ford instituted the "Five Dollar Day," which offered relatively high wages and a profit-sharing plan to workers. Employees could profit from the Five Dollar Day, however, only if they met "American" standards at home and in the workplace. In this way, Ford linked work discipline and economy opportunity to "American" behavior of its largely immigrant workforce. If Americanization and Americanism were powerful ideologies in the early twentieth century, so too was ethnic pluralism, as argued by historian John Higham, professor at Johns Hopkins University. Viewing the ideas of a variety of intellectuals, Higham argues that pluralism was embedded in the assimilation process and that fundamental to pluralist theory was the assumption that the continuation of ethnic minorities was essential to democracy. Ironically, cultural pluralism, Higham states, was most attractive to those already assimilated; it was one of the products of the melting pot.

Efforts at Americanization in the Industrial Workplace, 1914–1921

STEPHEN MEYER

Americanization involved the social and cultural assimilation of immigrants into the mainstream of American life. However, the process also constituted a unique, and distinctly American, method for the resolution of a key industrial problem—the problem of work-discipline and of the adjustment of new workers to the factory environment. In the early twentieth century, the Ford Motor Company established an Americanization program in order to adapt immigrant workers to its new system of mass production. This [article] will examine the Americanization policies and practices of the Ford Sociological Department, a novel experiment in welfare capitalism, and the Ford English School, an institution which taught immigrant workers the English language. It will treat both institutions in relation to the problem of the adaptation of an immigrant workforce to new conditions of production.

For the most part, Americanization has not usually been the concern of labor or industrial historians. Historians of Americanization have generally emphasized the differences between American and immigrant cultures. Edward G. Hartmann, the movement's principal historian, examined the early Americanization campaign from this perspective. . . . He concluded that:

> the Americanization effort stressed the desirability of the rapid assimilation of the millions of immigrants who had come to America during the pre-war decades, through the attendance of the newcomers at special classes, lectures, and mass meetings, where they might be instructed in the language, the ideals, and on the life which had come to be accepted as the American way of life.

In this form, the Americanization campaign was voluntary, benevolent, and educational. Nevertheless, when the programs emanated from within factory gates, they had their darker side. The issue was not simply different national or ethnic cultures, but also pre-industrial and industrial cultures, and even class cultures. Americanization was an important movement for the adjustment of immigrant workers to a new industrial environment and to American urban and industrial conditions, not just to American society in the abstract.

* * * *

Even before the development of the modern system of mass production, Ford officials and managers proposed their industrial ethos to a predominantly German and American workforce. For example, in 1908, the *Ford Times* provided a model New Year's resolution for Ford employees. "Of my own free will and accord, I sincerely covenant with myself," the resolution began. It later continued:

From Stephen Meyer, "Adapting the immigrant to the line: Americanization in the Ford factory, 1914–1921," *Journal of Social History*, Vol. 14, No. 1, Fall 1980. Copyright © 1980. Reprinted by permission of Carnegie Mellon University.

> To exalt the Gospel of Work, and get action here and now. To keep head, heart, and
> hand so busy that I won't have time to think about my troubles.
> Because idleness is a disgrace, low aim is criminal, and work minus its spiritual quality
> becomes drudgery.

Over and over again, in anecdotes, homilies, and stories, Ford literature for workers reiterated similar outlines of the American work ethic with the prospect of upward mobility as a reward for patience, self-denial, and hard work. Later, as more
and more immigrants streamed into the newly mechanized Highland Park factory,
the Ford Americanization program propounded similar socio-cultural themes for
the new workers.

Modern mass production profoundly altered the character of the Ford factory
and the Ford workforce. Developed from 1910 to 1914, the new methods and techniques of production drastically diluted the skills necessary for factory operations.
Consequently, as the physical plant expanded to meet the growing demand for the
Model T Ford, thousands of unskilled Southern and Eastern European immigrants
swarmed into the Highland Park factory. By 1914, the Ford Motor Company employed 12,880 workers and the overwhelming majority (9,109) were foreign-born.
The five largest nationality groups—Poles, Russians, Romanians, Italians and Sicilians, and Austro-Hungarians—constituted a majority of the workforce and came
from the least industrialized areas of Europe. Generally, American industrial leaders
and factory managers rated these nationalities low in their "racial efficiency," as they
defined industrial skill and efficiency in terms of work-habits and work-discipline. In
addition, the immigrant workers' non-American styles and standards of living com-
pounded the problems of their preindustrial origins and preindustrial attitudes and
habits. In their homes, their neighborhoods, and their separate networks of economic, social, and cultural interaction, immigrant workers maintained residues of
their former cultures and remained in isolation from the broader American society.
Finally, middle-class and other Americans believed that the isolation and autonomy
of immigrant communities generated alien and radical social philosophies. . . .

Ford officials, managers, and engineers expressed the most concern about the
immigrants' poor and inefficient habits of work. These men . . . found that productivity under actual factory conditions fell far short of anticipated levels derived
from ideal laboratory conditions. . . .

* * * *

In the new Ford factory, the rates of absenteeism and labor turnover steadily rose
with the completion of the new productive system. In 1913, "daily absences"
amounted to a staggering ten per cent of the entire workforce. This meant that an
average of from 1,300 to 1,400 workers were absent from their work stations each
day. For the same year, the rate of labor turnover reached a phenomenal 370 per
cent. In order to maintain a workforce of about 13,600 workers, the company hired
over 52,000 workers in the course of a year. The numbers indicated a complete
lack of work-discipline. Yet the new methods and techniques of production required new and more severe forms of work discipline. It needed workers more
closely attuned to the coordinated regimen of the machines and assembly lines.
The predindustrial culture of immigrant workers had to be restructured to meet the
requirements of new and more sophisticated industrial operations.

At this point, Ford inaugurated his grand experiment in welfare capitalism. Announced in January 1914 and popularly known as the Five Dollar Day, it was an ingenious profit-sharing scheme to induce Ford workers to alter their attitudes and habits to meet the rigorous requirements of mass production. Under the Ford Profit Sharing Plan, the company divided an unskilled worker's income into two approximately equal parts—his wages and his profits. Each worker received his wages for work done in the factory. But he received his profits, and, hence, the Five Dollar Day, only when he met specific standards of productive efficiency and specific standards and conditions of domestic life. The "work standard" for a particular job and the pace of the assembly line determined the standard of efficiency.

In addition a new institution, the Ford Sociological Department, later named the Ford Educational Department, examined the Ford worker's domestic life and attempted to elevate him and his family to a proper "American" standard of living. Ford and his managers held the progressive notion that environment shaped and molded men's attitudes, values, and habits. Their new institution sought to improve the worker's home and neighborhood environment in order to improve his ideas and behavior toward the factory. The Sociological Department investigated each worker and interviewed his family, friends, and neighbors. If the worker met specified requirements—"thrift, honesty, sobriety, better housing, and better living generally"—he received the Five Dollar Day. If not, the company withheld his profits and a Ford advisor periodically counselled on how to mend his ways. If after six months, the worker did not raise himself to Ford standards, the company discharged him.

The Ford Profit Sharing Plan was deeply paternalistic. In this feature, it captured the Progressive Era's contradictory attitude toward the unskilled immigrant worker. On the one hand, it attempted to assist the worker and to elevate him to a better standard of life. On the other hand, it sought to manipulate or to coerce the worker to match a preconceived ideal of that better life. John R. Commons, the progressive labor historian, noted the double edged character of the Ford program. The Ford plan, he reported, "is just old fashioned industrial autocracy tempered by faith in human nature." A benevolent end—the uplift of the unskilled and unschooled immigrant worker—justified a manipulative and coercive means.

From the very beginning, the Ford Profit Sharing Plan attempted to fit the immigrant worker into its preconceived mold of the ideal American. An early memorandum clarified the objectives of the Ford plan to a branch manager. "It is our aim and object," the Home Office noted, "to make better men and better American citizens and to bring about a larger degree of comforts, habits, and a higher plane of living among our employees. . . ." Henry Ford expressed his concern about non-American workers to an interviewer: "These men of many nations must be taught the American ways, the English language, and the right way to live." He then elaborated on the "right" life for the foreign-born worker. Married men "should not sacrifice family rights, pleasure, and comfort by filling their homes with roomers and boarders." Single men should live "comfortably and under conditions that make for good manhood and good citizenship." A company report on progress among immigrant workers noted that the Ford ideal was to create "a comfortable and cozy domesticity."

In its literature for workers, the Ford Motor Company repeatedly advised them where and how to live. A pamphlet pointed toward "right" living conditions:

> Employees should live in clean, well conducted homes, in rooms that are well lighted and ventilated. Avoid congested parts of the city. . . .

Ford and his managers deeply believed that tenement life in the immigrant neighborhoods of the city polluted body and soul. They also considered physical and moral cleanliness important attributes for work in modern industrial society. A clean home reduced the chances for illness and absenteeism. A clean mind provided the sound foundation for the construction of good work habits.

The Ford Sociological Department even extended its interest and attention to the children of immigrant workers. It prescribed a strong dose of Victorian morality for them in order to promote and develop good bodies and souls. "Choose a home," a pamphlet advised:

> where ample room, good wholesome surroundings, will enable the children to get the greatest benefit possible from play, under conditions that will tend to clean helpful ideas, rather than those likely to be formed in the streets and alleys of the city.

Particularly in adolescence, young men and women "should be guarded well, and not allowed to contract habits and vices injurious to their welfare and health."

S. S. Marquis, who headed the Ford Sociological Department, recalled Ford's own reason for this concern about the morality of children. "By underpaying men," Ford told the Episcopalian minister:

> we are bringing up a generation of children undernourished and underdeveloped morally as well as physically; we are breeding a generation of workingmen weak in body and mind, and for that reason bound to prove inefficient when they come to take their places in industry.

The good worker was both physically fit to perform his tasks in the factory and morally fit to perform these tasks diligently.

Often, Ford's paternalistic advice on the care of the home and family contained overt manifestations of middle-class arrogance towards the new immigrant workers. In one instance, a Ford pamphlet advised:

> Employees should use plenty of soap and water in the home, and upon their children, bathing frequently. Nothing makes for right living and health so much as cleanliness. Notice that the most advanced people are the cleanest.

Again, the advice cut in two directions. On the one hand, health and cleanliness were important for immigrant workers. On the other hand, the assumption was that lower classes were generally unclean. Indeed, these sentiments typified upper- and middle-class American attitudes towards Southern and Eastern European immigrants.

* * * *

In 1915, several Ford investigators wrote a number of "Human Interest" stories and other reports to describe the Sociological Department's welfare work among Ford workers. . . . Horatio Alger style stories told how Southern and Eastern European immigrant workers met their good fortune in the form of the Five Dollar Day. One story involved a Russian immigrant and his family. . . .

F. W. Andrews, a Ford investigator, wrote his story on Joe, a former peasant, his wife, and their six children. Three years earlier, they left Russia for the United States. "Life was an uphill struggle for Joe since landing in America," Andrews reported. However, he had a positive trait—his willingness to work hard. "He was a willing worker and not particular about the kind of employment he secured." In the recent past, he dug sewers and worked as an agricultural laborer. When work ran out, he moved to Detroit with his family. "And here," Andrews noted, "for five long months he tramped with the 'Army of the Unemployed'—always handicapped by his meager knowledge of the English language, and was unable to find anything to do." As a result, his wife bore the "burden of supporting the family." She "worked at the washtub or with the scrubbing brush when such work could be found."

Fortunately, the tale continued, Joe applied for and received a job at the Ford factory. After the company hired him, Andrews went to Joe's home to determine his eligibility for the Ford Five Dollar Day. The scene could have been from a Dickens novel. He discovered "an old, tumbled down, one and a half story frame house." The family's apartment, Andrews related, "was one half of the attic consisting of three rooms, which were so low that a person of medium height could not stand erect—a filthy, foul-smelling hole." It had virtually no furniture, only "two dirty beds . . . , a ragged filthy rug, a rickety table, and two bottomless chairs (the five children standing up at the table to eat)." The family led a precarious hand-to-mouth existence and ate only when the wife earned enough to purchase food for the evening meal. They owed money to the landlord, the grocer, and the butcher. The oldest daughter went to a charity hospital a few days earlier. The wife and the other five children "were half clad, pale, and hungry looking."

This scene of poverty and misery set the Sociological Department's paternalistic programs into motion. Through special arrangements, the pay office issued Joe's wages each day instead of every two weeks. The company provided him with an immediate loan from its charity fund for "the family's immediate start toward right living." However, the investigator, and not Joe, took the fifty-dollar loan and paid the bills and rented a cottage. He also purchased inexpensive furniture and kitchen utensils, provisions, and cheap clothes for the wife and children. (Andrews reported that he bought "a liberal amount of soap" and gave the family "instructions to use freely.")

After Andrews arranged for this initial assistance for Joe and his family, a remarkable ritual followed. The Ford investigator:

> . . . had their dirty, old, junk furniture loaded on a dray and under the cover of night moved them to their new home. This load of rubbish was heaped in a pile in the back yard, and a torch was applied and it went up in smoke.
>
> There upon the ashes of what had been their earthly possessions, this Russian peasant and his wife, with tears streaming down their faces, expressed their gratitude to Henry Ford, the FORD MOTOR COMPANY, and all those who had been instrumental in bringing about this marvelous change in their lives.

In this ritual of fire, an old life went up in smoke as Joe and his family testified to their loyalty to Henry Ford.

In time, the children were well dressed and clean. They attended public school. The wife wore "a smile that 'won't come off.'" Joe soon repaid his loan and expected "to soon have a saving for the inevitable 'rainy day.'"

* * * *

Against [this uplifting case], a single and revealing incident demonstrated the motives of the company's concern for the ways in which immigrant traditions affected industrial efficiency. In January 1914, a few days after its impressive gesture—the announcement of the Five Dollar Day—the Ford Motor Company dismissed "between eight and nine hundred Greeks and Russians, who remained from work on a holiday celebration." The holiday happened to be Christmas. Using the Julian calendar, the Greek and Russian Orthodox Christian workers celebrated Christmas thirteen days later than the rest of the Ford workforce. As justification for this large-scale dismissal, which amounted to about six per cent of the Ford workforce, a Ford official stated that "if these men are to make their home in America they should observe American holidays." The absence of this many workers disrupted production in the mechanized Highland Park plant. "It causes too much confusion in the plant," the official concluded, ". . . when nearly a thousand men fail to appear for work."

The Ford English School extended the Ford Americanization program into the classroom. Its exclusive concern was the Americanization of the immigrant worker and his adaptation to the Ford factory and to urban and industrial society. In the English School, as adult immigrant workmen struggled to learn and to comprehend the strange sounds of a new language, they also received the rudiments of American culture. In particular, they learned those habits of life which resulted in good habits of work. In 1916, S. S. Marquis defended the objectives of the Ford educational program before an audience of American educators. The Ford English School, he noted, "was established especially for the immigrants in our employ." It was one part of a total program to adapt men to the new factory system. "The Ford School," he reported:

> provides five compulsory courses. There is a course in industry and efficiency, a course in thrift and economy, a course in domestic relations, one in community relations, and one in industrial relations.

Later, using the Ford factory as a metaphor for the entire educational program, he added:

> This is the human product we seek to turn out, and as we adapt the machinery in the shop to turning out the kind of automobile we have in mind, so we have constructed our educational system with a view to producing the human product in mind.

The Ford managers and engineers devised a system wherein men were the raw materials which were molded, hammered, and shaped into products which had the proper attitudes and habits for work in the factory.

In April 1914, the Ford Motor Company called upon Peter Roberts, a Young Men's Christian Association educator, to develop a program of English language instructor for immigrant workers in the Highland Park factory. In 1909, as the result of his activities among immigrant coal miners in Pennsylvania, Roberts published a preparatory course of English language instruction, *English for Coming Americans.* This course provided a complete package of materials to teach the basic elements of the English language. The core of the program centered around a Domestic, a Commercial, and an Industrial Series of lessons. Each series applied the English language to different aspects of the immigrant worker's life. . . .

The Domestic Series provided specific English lessons for the immigrant worker in his role as the head of an "American" family unit. This series, Roberts explained, identified "the experiences common to all peoples reared in the customs of western civilization." The ten lessons included such topics as "Getting Up in the Morning," "Table Utensils," "The Man Washing," and "Welcoming a Visitor."

The Commercial Series supplied the immigrant worker with the vocabulary to serve in his role as a consumer. In particular, it attempted to break the economic power of immigrant bosses, who sold goods and services, who served as employment, travel, and shipping agents, and who functioned as bankers in the immigrant neighborhoods. Moreover, the lessons emphasized and encouraged the virtues of thrift and property ownership, which created stable and reliable citizens. . . .

* * * *

The lessons intended to make the immigrant worker a consumer of American goods and services from American merchants. In this series, the subject matter included "Buying and Using Stamps," "Pay Day," "Going to the Bank," "Buying a Lot," "Building a House."

Finally, the Industrial Series provided flexible lessons to meet the immigrant worker's needs as a producer in the factory. The aim of this series was "to meet the need of thousands who have common experience in industrial life." Here, the lessons included "Beginning the Day's Work," "Shining Shoes," "A Man Looking for Work," and "Finishing the Day's Work."

The lessons in each series had characteristically prosaic titles. And, indeed, the lessons provided helpful and useful information for the immigrant worker. Nevertheless, each lesson contained specific social and cultural norms for life in urban and industrial America. Ford workers learned the value of time in their personal and working lives. They learned the importance of cleanliness and health. They learned self-discipline through regular habits of saving and work. They learned to invest in and to purchase property and to become responsible citizens. These positive virtues—timeliness, cleanliness, thrift, self-discipline, regularity, and citizenship—represented the Ford, and generally the American middle-class, ideal for remaking former European peasants into reliable and efficient factory workers. The English language was an important means for the adaptation of immigrant workers to the regimen and the discipline of the mechanized factory.

As part of its instructional program, the Ford English School also taught immigrant workers not to offend their social betters in their manner and their behavior. For this reason, table manners and etiquette were important parts of the curriculum. "Last, but not least," S. S. Marquis reported, "must be mentioned our professor of table manners who with great dramatic art teaches the use of napkins, knife and fork and spoon." The Ford instructor taught the immigrant worker "the art of eating a meal in a manner that will not interfere with the appetite of the other fellow." In addition, Marquis continued: "We also have a professor of etiquette, such as is required for the ordinary station in life." Moreover, Ford English instructors expected their students to dress properly for the classes. "A by-product of the classes," a report noted, "was a rise in the 'standard of living' by making men conscious of their personal appearance." Instead of going directly from work to school, the instructors required that "class members first go home, wash, and change clothes."

In 1919, Clinton C. DeWitt, the Director of the Ford English School, defended the Ford system of industrial Americanization with its practical teachers from the shop floor before an unfriendly audience of American educators. He argued that "a real live American born man, who is a leader among the fellows of his department" would make "in a short time out of Europe's downtrodden and outcasts, good Americans." He also catalogued the advantages of the industrial teacher:

> . . . both teacher and student have so many things in common. He works for the same employer, he works the same hours, he has the same pay day, he has the same environment, he has the same legal holidays, he refers to the same head office, the same pay office, the same superintendent's office, the same safety department, the same Americanization school. The main doorway, the different buildings, and all the printed signs are thoroughly common to teacher and student.

From DeWitt's perspective, the factory hierarchy facilitated instruction. The foreman, the natural leader in his shop, instructed his subordinates in the English language, American values and customs, and Ford shop practices.

In 1915, Oliver J. Abell, an industrialist journalist, praised Ford's "benevolent paternalism" in industry. He maintained that the "greater must care for the less." Furthermore, he continued:

> We provide schools for the child. Instruction and discipline are compulsory, and it is well. But we forget that measured in the great scale of knowledge, there are always children and grownups, pupils and teachers, and age is nothing.

Here, Abell captured the essence of Ford paternalism and of the relationship between dominant and subordinate groups in American society. Superiors considered their inferiors—Blacks, servants, women, and even workers—as no more than children. Indeed, the Ford immigrant worker was no more than a child to be socialized, in this case, Americanized, to the reigning social and cultural norms of American society.

S. S. Marquis, the liberal clergyman, explained how the company coerced workers into attending their English lessons. "Attendance," he reported:

> is virtually compulsory. If a man declines to go, the advantages of the training are carefully explained to him. If he still hesitates, he is laid off and given uninterrupted meditation and reconsideration. When it comes to promotion, naturally preference is given to the men who have cooperated with us in our work. This, also, has its effect.

In the early twentieth century, Ford officials duplicated the disciplinary patterns which early industrialists utilized in eighteenth-century England. The carrot and the stick rewarded or punished the worker as though he were an errant child.

Gregory Mason, a strong advocate of Americanization programs, questioned "the grotesquely exaggerated patriotism in the Ford plant." In the course of the

English lessons, "the pupils are told to 'walk to an American blackboard, taken a piece of American chalk, and explain how the American workman walks to his American home and sits down with his American family to their good American dinner.' " "The first thing we teach them to say," Marquis related, "is 'I am a good American,' and then we try to get them to live up to that statement." "It is a very common thing," DeWitt noted, "to have a fellow born in Austria yell to a teacher passing by, 'We are all good Americans!' " In this period, Ford and other employers began to give good citizenship and Americanism their own definition. A Ford pamphlet noted:

> Automatically, upon graduation, the English school alumni become members of the American Club. At weekly meetings they practice speaking, reading, debating, and discuss points of history, civil government, and national problems of current interest.

By the end of the First World War, Americanism countered those social and economic philosophies which threatened managerial prerogatives of production, namely Bolshevism, socialism, and even trade unionism.

The mass ritual of graduation was the most spectacular aspect of Americanization in the Ford factory. Ford English School graduates underwent a symbolic ritual which marked the transformation from immigrant to American. DeWitt describes the ceremony as:

> a pageant in the form of a melting pot, where all men descend from a boat scene representing the vessel on which they came over; down the gangway . . . into a pot 15 feet in diameter and 7-1/2 feet high, which represents the Ford English School. Six teachers, three on either side, stir the pot with ten foot ladles representing nine months of teaching in the school. Into the pot 52 nationalities with their foreign clothes and baggage go and out of the pot after vigorous stirring by the teachers comes one nationality, viz, American.

Marquis enriched this image and emphasized the conformity of the one nationality: "Presently the pot began to boil over and out came the men dressed in their best American clothes and waving American flags."

Following this pageant, teachers and community leaders gave speeches which praised the virtues of American citizenship. When the graduation ceremony ended, all went on "a trip to some park, where American games are played by teachers and students for the rest of the day." In the evening, the company rewarded its volunteer teachers for their time and their efforts. It held "an entertainment and banquet for the volunteer instructors and their wives. The expense, of course, being paid by the company." At this celebration, DeWitt reported, "the teachers meet with Mr. Ford and other high officials of the company, and a great spirit of one for all and all for one predominates the entire evening."

Americanization in the Ford factory was important for a number of reasons. First, the Ford programs touched the lives of tens of thousands of Ford workers in its effort to influence those institutions which shaped working-class culture—the home, the neighborhood, and the factory. From 1914 to 1917, Ford statistics, derived from the reports of sociological investigators, revealed that bank accounts, home and property ownership, neighborhoods, home conditions, and habits of Ford workers either increased or improved. In addition, from 1915 to 1920, the company reported that some 16,000 workers graduated from the Ford English

School. Moreover, statistics indicated that while 35.5 per cent of the workforce did not speak English in 1914, only 11.7 per cent did not speak the language in 1917. Second, the Ford Americanization programs indirectly captured the American imagination in the prewar years. They served as the model for a city-wide Americanization campaign in Detroit. And, in 1915, Detroit in turn became the model for the National Americanization Day Committee and its national campaign for the assimilation of immigrants into American society.

Finally, Ford was neither alone nor entirely unique in its attempt to adapt immigrant workers to factory and industrial life. In fact, American industrial leaders and managers developed a new and different strategy for the management of an immigrant workforce in this period. Whereas the traditional managerial practice divided ethnic groups and played their national and cultural rivalries against one another, the new one emphasized conformity with American social, cultural, and industrial values. During the First World War, as manufacturers and managers became increasingly apprehensive about aliens in their midst, they viewed Americanization as a means to remake immigrant workers into their image of efficient and productive American workers. Through cooperative efforts with industry, Peter Roberts and other Y.M.C.A. educators established programs which employed thousands of instructors and taught tens of thousands of foreign workers. And, in the postwar labor upsurge, industrial leaders considered Americanization as the cure for the ills of industrial society. In 1919, George F. Quimby, the keynote speaker of the National Conference on Americanization in Industries, emphasized that the conference should be "based on the fundamental principles of American life—a sound social order." In 1920, Peter Roberts gave citizenship a broad social and economic definition. "Good citizenship," he noted, "means each one in his sphere keeping busy, doing honest work, and contributing to the sum total of wealth for the support of the nation."

In the end, Ford paternalism failed, and, perhaps, even proved irrelevant. Its success rested on the monetary incentive of the Five Dollar Day. Even for unschooled immigrants, money, and not patronizing benevolence, talked in the industrial age. Wartime economic conditions undermined the Ford high income policy. As the new methods of production rapidly diffused to Detroit's other automobile and machine shops, Ford lost the technological and financial advantage over its competitors. In addition, a severe war-induced inflation eroded the incentive of the Five Dollar Day. Gradually, the company shifted the differential between wages and profits.

The Varieties of Ethnic Pluralism in American Thought

JOHN HIGHAM

For many years writers on American ethnic problems have invoked a vision of pluralism as an ideal all men of goodwill should cherish. Pluralism, we are told, will

From John Higham, *Send These to Me,* pp. 196, 198–201. Copyright © 1975 Johns Hopkins University Press. Reprinted by permission.

save us from a foolish belief in assimilation. But what pluralism means in a positive sense—even the extent to which it runs against an assimilationist philosophy—seldom appears. This chapter is a preliminary effort to examine the chronic indistinctness of the pluralist idea in ethnic relations. . . .

The history of pluralist theories will, therefore, have to be examined in a wider context of ideas and values. We will have to take note especially of the interplay between pluralism and opposing theories of assimilation. It is customary today to denounce the melting-pot ideal as a false and even bigoted antithesis to the pluralist vision; and it is true that ethnic pluralism arose as a protest against the losses some minorities were suffering under the stresses of assimilation. Pluralism could become a persuasive alternative only when general doubts developed that assimilation was the democratic way. Nevertheless, as we shall see, the relation between assimilation and pluralism was not a simple dialectic of opposition. From the outset the belief that a democratic society should preserve the integrity of its constituent groups has unconsciously relied on the assimilative process which it seemed to repudiate; and now that assimilation has lost momentum, pluralism has lost its sense of direction.

Finally, we will discover that much of the disorientation in the present discussion of pluralism stems from increasing uncertainty about a cardinal assumption of pluralist theory, namely that the persistence and solidarity of ethnic minorities is essential to democracy. The general appeal of pluralism has inhered in its promise of extending democracy. In recent years, however, the most searching inquiries into pluralistic conditions have shown how extensively they serve to perpetuate inequalities. How much pluralism, and what kinds, a good society should have is a question no one has clearly addressed.

Pluralism in all its forms is a philosophy of minority rights. It arises when minorities become conscious of having a stake in the maintenance of their position within a larger society. A pluralist generally identifies himself with a social minority and writes in its behalf. But he also accepts minority status as a legitimate and perhaps even desirable way of participating in the larger society. Thus pluralism posits a situation in which minorities retain their solidarity and effectiveness; but it does not welcome all such situations. A pluralist wants to develop a mutually tolerable relationship between discrete groups and the social system in which they reside. Specifically, he seeks a relationship that will allow the individual groups both autonomy and unimpeded influence. He opposes assimilation on the one hand, because that threatens group survival; but he also opposes separatism, because that will exclude him from the larger society. Accordingly, pluralism addresses itself to the character and viability of an aggregate that has several components, and its special challenge arises from the attempt to define the aggregate in terms that none of its principal components need find unacceptable.

The belief that a well-ordered society should sustain the diversity of its component groups has, of course, deep roots in early American experience, but it became subordinated during the nineteenth century to the quest for unity. The building of a national republic gave central importance to the process of convergence, to the making of a homogeneous future from a heterogeneous past. The dominant American legend—what was later symbolized in the image of a melting pot—said that a continuous fusion of originally disparate elements was forming a single American people. In the attainment of oneness, rather than the persistence of separate identities, lay the promise of American life. After the Civil War, especially, a drive for national integration took priority over other group loyalties. American business and professional leaders built unifying networks of communications and social control. Intellectuals elaborated monistic schemes of thought, which enclosed the processes of nature and the achievements of man within an all-embracing, rational synthesis. If, as Henry Adams charged, his generation was mortgaged to the railways, it also gave its mind to a larger quest for unity, which Adams himself pursued through the eighties and nineties.

Thus the pluralist ideology which emerged in the early twentieth century, though grounded experientially in the earliest facts of American life, represented a significant departure from conventional wisdom. Pluralism was, in fact, part of a profound intellectual upheaval, which Morton White has described as "the revolt against formalism." Conceptually, it was a revolt against the monistic systems that prevailed in the late nineteenth century. It rejected their rationalistic spirit and their inclination toward a stratified view of society. The antiformalists denied a privileged status to any fixed point of view or any social category. They accepted the multiformity of experience and the relativity of values. Their refusal of any single, all-embracing scheme of things acquired a pluralistic bent when it became a positive celebration of irreducible diversity.

Here the modern pluralist has echoed romanticism. The formalistic pluralism of the early republic, as expressed by James Madison, commended the instrumental value of *multiplicity*. Modern pluralism also champions *variety*. It rests on the romantic premise that differences are intrinsically valuable and should take precedence over conformity to a universal standard. In casting off the constraints of late-Victorian America, antiformalists sounded again the rallying cry of their romantic forebears: *"Vive la différence!"* It is significant that pluralism received its philosophical credentials from William James, the American philosopher who, more than any other, incarnated a romantic love of diversity, particularity, and uniqueness. James's late book, *A Pluralistic Universe* (1909), made the most careful statement of the case, though he had already, in *The Will to Believe* (1897), given wide currency to the term.

For modern pluralism diversity has performed a special function, which was often missing in the romantic tradition. It has consistently worked against authoritarian claims to exclusive or preeminent wisdom. Since the democratic aspirations of the Progressive Era colored and shaped the entire revolt against formalism, modern pluralism was initially harnessed to an egalitarian ethic. Pluralists appealed for an appreciation of differences in order to rectify inequalities.

But there was always in pluralist thought an unrecognized tension between means and ends. Logically, an accentuation of differences should breed more inequality, rather than less. It should drive men apart, instead of bringing them together. The conditions under which the pluralist program could work were more special than its advocates realized. The optimism of the early pluralists seems to have depended on an unstated assumption that a natural harmony underlies the conflicts and discords of life. Pluralists dispensed with any overall design, they renounced the struggle for an inclusive unity, because of an implicit faith that in some deep, unspecified sense it already existed. In an essentially friendly universe the parts can be true to their separate characters. Purposes can clash without rending.

These basic features of a pluralist philosophy—its celebration of differences, its hostility to existing inequalities, its implicit reliance on an underlying harmony—made it especially suitable to the defense of minority rights. Applied to society, pluralism provided minorities with a means of resisting absorption; they could now claim to constitute the very structure of the social order. From the point of view of the integrationist or the tender of the melting pot, minorities must appear subordinate and declining elements. Pluralism, on the other hand, defined the minorities as primary. The unity of the whole resided in their relations with one another. This was the pluralist's thesis, regardless of how he identified America's minorities. They might be regional or ethnic or—much later—religious groups.

For Frederick Jackson Turner the pluralist pattern inhered in regional (i.e., sectional) diversity. On ethnic issues the leading American historian of the early twentieth century was an assimilationist. He looked upon the West as a great melting pot of European peoples, and his whole approach to American history can be understood partly as a way of asserting the primacy of geography over race and culture. Turner's pluralism was an affirmation of sectional diversity as the dynamic principle in American life.

Other historians at the beginning of the twentieth century construed the main theme of American history as the gradual triumph of national unity over states rights and sectional differences. Sectionalism, in the conventional view, meant discord, disruption, even treason. Turner, on the other hand, looked on sectional differences as a continuing source of vitality for a democratic society. Born in a Wisconsin town in 1861, he never felt the scars of the Civil War deeply. For him national unity was an accomplished fact. But it posed new problems in the twentieth century. Under the imperatives of industrialization, unity might become a deadening uniformity. Would it perhaps obliterate the distinctiveness of his own beloved Middle West? Turner could not accept that prospect. Diversity would survive, he believed, through the socioeconomic contrasts and rivalries grounded in the principal regions of the country. To this vision Turner gave historical substantiation by showing that sectionalism was not ordinarily antithetical to nationalism but rather its matrix. American politics functioned through a complex, balanced interplay of at least three sections—North, South, and West—in which the characteristic strategies were bargaining and compromise. Turner first explored this theme in *Rise of the New West, 1819–1829* (1906). He carried it forward, but with ever-increasing difficulty, in a posthumous work he was never able to complete, *The United States, 1830–1850: The Nation and Its Sections* (1935). Turner's story broke off, let us note, just at the point in American history when the sectional struggle was turning into a rigid dualism, for which his pluralistic theory did not allow.

Turner spoke for the Middle West at a time when homogenizing forces of national integration threatened its distinctive character. Similarly, the early advocates of pluralism in ethnic relations were defending self-conscious minorities whose survival seemed endangered by the pressures of assimilation. Just as Turner thought that American democracy depended on the persistence of sections, ethnic pluralists maintained that its enduring basis lay in ancestral cultures. Whereas Turner described the United States as a federation of sections, proponents of "cultural pluralism" called it a federation of nationalities. Turner tried to show that sectional differences could and should endure, since he identified with a section that might otherwise be submerged. His counterpart, Horace Kallen, argued for the indestructibility of ethnic cultures in an effort to resist the disintegration of his own.

No immigrant group brought to the United States an older, prouder heritage than did the Jews, and none seemed in early-twentieth-century America more exposed to an erosion of group identity. The great exodus from the *shtetls* of eastern Europe had already torn hundreds of thousands of Jews loose from traditional roots, and the very real prospect of a wider life in a more receptive milieu intensified the urge to cast off the burden of a distinctive heritage. Those who tried to do so encountered a rising anti-Semitism, often expressed in the belief that they were incorrigibly alien to American life. Nevertheless, there were enormous opportunities in America for Jews, particularly for those who could escape the anti-Semitic slurs. It was a Jewish playwright, Israel Zangwill, whose enormously popular melodrama, *The Melting Pot* (1908), offered the most ringing apostrophe to the glories of assimilation, though the play also revealed (through a veil of sentimental clichés) the searing conflicts that process created between generations. Wracked with internal divisions and assailed from without, the Jewish community in the early twentieth century might well have questioned its future in America.

In this situation the Zionist movement worked to rally Jewish group consciousness. In calling for the rebirth of a Jewish nation, Zionism affirmed a commonality of all Jews transcending religious, social, and political differences. In America it made its strongest appeal as an antidote to assimilation. By awakening the rising generation to the value of its ethnic heritage, Zionism proposed to save American Jewry from disappearance. As early as 1909 the outstanding American spokesman for cultural Zionism, Judah L. Magnes, was criticizing the melting-pot idea that national groups in America were destined to lose their special character.

The chief author of the theory of cultural pluralism, Horace Kallen, was an early and active Zionist, deeply stirred by the hope of a Jewish national revival. As a graduate student at Harvard University in 1906, he had a leading part in founding the Harvard Menorah Society. This was the beginning of an intercollegiate movement designed to overcome a "shameful ignorance of things Jewish" among Jewish students and thus to combat their impulse to forget or to hide their origins. In an early address to the Intercollegiate Menorah Association, Kallen propounded what would become a cornerstone of his thesis: people cannot successfully change their ethnic identity. Mixing occurs only in external relations, not in a man's inner life. "An Irishman is always an Irishman, a Jew always a Jew. Irishman or Jew is born; citizen, lawyer, or church-member is made."

An antiassimilationist attitude would not alone have made Kallen a genuine pluralist, however. He also posited an intimate connection between ethnic separateness and national unity. Like Turner and like James, Kallen embraced the whole as well as its parts. An American nationalist as well as a Zionist, he believed that all the varied groups in America could coexist, each conserving and perfecting its selfhood, in a kind of natural harmony.

This belief did not come easily. Kallen arrived at it through a deep inner struggle between Jewish and American allegiances. Born in Silesia, he was brought to the United States at the age of five. He was raised in Boston, he recalled, on "the Hebrew Bible with its Judaist commentaries and the difficult and heroic economy of the orthodox Jewish home." But in the Boston public schools, visiting Bunker Hill and listening to teachers recite the precepts of Ralph Waldo Emerson, Kallen underwent during the 1890's the common second-generation experience: loss of religion and an uncritical enthusiasm for America. "It seemed to me that the identity of every human being with every other was the important thing and that the term 'American' should nullify the meaning of every other term in one's personal make-up. . . . Everything Jewish could be absorbed and dissolved in something quite non-Jewish and identical with the Yankee being as I knew it in Boston."

Eager for that consummation, the youthful idealist was drawn to the inner sanctum of the Yankee world. There, in Harvard College, his simple Americanism received a series of shocks. A nearby social settlement, where Kallen worked for room and board, exposed him to socialist and anarchist ideas and to a maelstrom of ethnic aspirations. He began to participate in the romantic spirit of liberation, which affected so many of the younger intellectuals in the early twentieth century and reached a crest on the eve of the First World War. Kallen's thinking matured in that effervescent context.

Meanwhile, a more orthodox but no less exciting intellectual experience occurred in the classroom of Barrett Wendell, whose course on American literature yielded a startling new perception of the link Kallen was seeking between himself and America. Wendell, the very incarnation of genteel New England culture, was himself a conservative assimilationist, for whom English—and more specifically Puritan—traits constituted the American character. But the Puritans in turn, Wendell emphasized, modeled themselves on the Old Testament prophets. America began as another Israel. Wendell even entertained a curious theory that the early American Puritans were largely Jewish in blood. Kallen thought he had escaped from a Hebraic past. Here what he was running away from suddenly became central to what he was pursuing. The stimulus of Wendell's course led him to a renewed study of Jewish culture and thus to Zionism. It suggested that one could remain an unreconstructed Jew while belonging to the core of America.

The other major influence came from William James. Kallen's studies under the great Harvard pragmatist, begun as an undergraduate, continued through a Ph.D. in 1908. The young man then became a colleague during James's last years; he remained always a devoted disciple. By translating James's philosophy into social terms, Kallen gave a general reference to the newly discovered relationship between his Jewish and his American self. James intended pluralism to overcome an either/or choice between rival absolutes. Applied to the problem of national identity, it legitimized the intersection of comparatively independent loyalties. Kallen was especially struck by James's use of a powerful American metaphor. Echoing the aboriginal pluralism of American political institutions, James had described the universe as "more like a federal republic than like an empire or a kingdom." Could not the same image apply to an American union of ethnic collectivities, in which each enjoys both the irreducible singularity and the full civic partnership Kallen had found in his own special heritage?

For the traditional American faith in assimilation through fusion, the young Jewish social philosopher substituted a federal or polycentric ideal. He summoned every ethnic group to be American by being true to itself, by preserving its own separate culture. His ideas seemed more radical than they actually were, because they crystallized at a time of sharply increasing ethnic tensions, when the melting-pot idea came under attack from those who thought it was too permissive as well as those like Kallen who considered it too exclusive. During the years just before the United States entered the First World War, when Kallen was teaching at the University of Wisconsin and enjoying the ethos of a state rich in minorities, an almost hysterical fear of "hyphenated Americans" seized public opinion. This was accompanied by a more or less racist belief that further assimilation would dilute the purity of an already fixed American type. Kallen was especially stung by demands, from some of his progressive colleagues, for tighter restrictions on immigration. When the prominent Wisconsin sociologist Edward A. Ross published a scathing assessment of the harm the newer foreign groups were doing to the United States, Kallen replied with a famous article in the *Nation* in 1915, "Democracy Versus the Melting Pot." Summing up ideas he had nurtured for more than a decade, Kallen suggested that the current ethnic ferment showed the bankruptcy of the melting-pot theory. America faced more drastic alternatives: a regimentation that would stifle all minorities, or a new understanding of democracy as a federation of autonomous, self-realizing nationalities. "Democracy," he wrote a year later, "involves not the elimination of differences but the perfection and conservation of differences."

In effect, Kallen called for an ethnic policy which would not depend on the classic American belief that all men are basically alike. To that extent he concurred with his most implacable adversaries, Anglo-Saxon racists like E. A. Ross. Both sides agreed that fundamental human differences would not dissolve in any melting pot. Both asserted that ethnic character was somehow rooted in the natural order. But Kallen contemplated nature's diversities with the benign gaze of a romantic. Whereas Ross saw everywhere a harsh Darwinian struggle between unequal species, Kallen observed a freely proliferating universe with room for all. "Nature is naturally pluralistic," he wrote; "her unities are eventual, not primary; mutual adjustments, not regimentations of superior force." Kallen lifted his eyes above the strife that swirled around him to an ideal realm where diversity and harmony eternally coexist.

Perhaps even more important in giving the new ethnic pluralism its beneficent, idealistic flavor was Kallen's exclusive concentration on culture as the locus of group identity. Kallen distinguished sharply between "inward" experience, which is essential and irrefragable, and the outer sphere of public policy and economic life. The latter belongs to Caesar, but not the former. The state may intervene in external conditions to promote justice or equality; but the collective consciousness of each ethnic group must remain free and spontaneous. Kallen never admitted that cultural differences might flow from or reinforce social inequities. He took no account of the social barriers between groups.

They belonged to the rigidities of an artificial environment, not to the essence of a people. In the theory of cultural pluralism, culture was primary, and it was innocent.

The incompleteness and the bias of Kallen's pluralism becomes obvious once we ask what role it assigned to the Negro. The answer is: none. The theory that preserving differences promotes democracy surely called for some special attention to the ethnic group whose differentness most Americans were determined to maintain. Kallen carefully evaded the problem. Although he purported to write about the group life of all of the "American Peoples," he drew his examples and arguments exclusively from the experience of European immigrants, particularly Jews. He liked to describe the American ensemble as an orchestra; but there was a fatal elision when he wrote that America could become "an orchestration of mankind" by perfecting "the cooperative harmonies of European civilization." Nothing in Kallen's writings gave away the magnitude of that elision. In the fullest statement of his argument there was only a single, obscure footnote on the point. "I do not discuss the influence of the negro," Kallen confessed in fine print. "This is at once too considerable and too recondite in its processes for casual mention. It requires separate analysis." The pluralist thesis from the outset was encapsulated in white ethnocentrism.

Possibly that was inevitable. Could anyone have designed a pluralism that would have suited blacks as well as Jews, the minorities that were left behind as well as those that were thriving? Could anyone, for that matter, have built a pluralist philosophy on the black experience? From time to time some American Negroes adopted a separatist (i.e., black nationalist) attitude, but their desire for liberation *from* America should not be confused with the pluralist's goal of liberalizing America. The difficulties black writers confronted in looking at the United States from a pluralist perspective may be judged from the efforts that W. E. B. Du Bois made to do so.

The foremost ideological spokesman for American blacks in the first half of the twentieth century, Du Bois was not a separatist, but neither was he consistently an unambiguous integrationist. Like Kallen, he struggled as a young man to reconcile his racial and his national identity, "two warring ideals in one dark body." "Am I an American or am I a Negro?" Du Bois asked in anguish. "Can I be both? Or is it my duty to cease to be a Negro as soon as possible and be an American?"

In grappling with the problem he drew on some of the same cultural and personal influences that stimulated Kallen. Both men felt a romantic appreciation of the spiritual diversity of mankind. Both regarded culture in an exalted way, as the finest flower of group life; and in the tradition of Herder and other romantic nationalists, they interpreted each race or nationality as the custodian of some great idea or artistic gift. Moreover, as a student at Harvard, Du Bois took encouragement from the same teachers who also served Kallen so well. Although Du Bois received his Ph.D. in history in 1895, he remembered William James as his favorite teacher, closest friend on the faculty, and "guide to clear thinking." Du Bois studied with Barrett Wendell too, and basked in his praise. "God was good," Du Bois remembered, "to let me sit awhile at their feet and see the fair vision of a commonwealth of culture open to all creeds and races and colors." Kallen could well have uttered the same thanksgiving.

In 1897, when he was twenty-nine years old, Du Bois published a little-known essay, "The Conservation of Races." As fresh and striking in its way as Kallen's paper of 1915, it anticipated much of the latter's argument. Like Kallen, Du Bois was fighting against the kind of assimilation that breeds contempt for one's origins. In reviving ethnic pride, both men emphasized the priority of the organic group over the individual. Whereas whites had always advised blacks to gain acceptance and respect by conforming as individuals to the values of the larger community, Du Bois argued that that was not enough. Individuals do not make history. The great changes in human affairs come about through the collective action of races. Blacks should take advantage of that fact by organizing, asserting, and developing themselves as a distinct race, destined to make a special contribution to the future of the world. Replying to the fear that such moves toward racial solidarity would only sharpen the existing cleavage in society, the young militant asserted that the pursuit of separate "race ideals" could be compatible with equal participation in the polity and economy of a common country. Thus far Du Bois adumbrated positions Kallen would take. He too was groping toward a compromise between diversity and equality. Nevertheless, to describe Du Bois as a cultural pluralist blurs a crucial distinction.

Du Bois never visualized America as a genuinely multiethnic complex, in which a variety of groups could enjoy an equal status and maintain their cultural autonomy indefinitely. The situation of black Americans was too special to be relativized and too severe to be equated with that of other groups. The reality confronting Du Bois must have seemed not many-sided, but starkly dualistic: everything was either black or white. The cleavage might be lived with, even turned to advantage; it could not be accepted as a permanent good. Looking far into the future, Du Bois projected an ultimate fusion—a city of man, not a federation of peoples. "Some day on American soil," he prophesied, "two world-races may give each to each those characteristics both so sadly lack." He called for the maintenance of racial identity only "until this mission of the Negro people is accomplished, and the ideal of human brotherhood has become a practical possibility." Here, in attenuated form, was the old ideal of assimilation.

Du Bois had little reason, either theoretical or practical, to see the United States as a nation of minorities. Although William James evidently made a strong impression on him in college, Du Bois was no pragmatic relativist. Fundamentally he had a dogmatic, absolutistic cast of mind. Truth was singular for Du Bois, not plural. If this reflected his own temperament, it may also have expressed the special need of the American Negro to rely on nothing less than the universal premises of the Enlightenment for a viable connection with America. Certainly Du Bois did not have the opportunity, which Harvard gave to Kallen, of finding his own people enshrined within the self-image of New England's founding fathers.

Du Bois, in urging group effort and racial pride, was not offering a general philosophy of minority rights. He was speaking specifically to his own ethnic group with the overriding objective of combating a paralyzing sense of inadequacy and inferiority. Kallen, on the other hand, addressed a general audience, using his own ethnic past as a model for other groups in the conviction that assimilation threatened them in much the same way. Kallen wanted to save a special tradition; Du Bois was trying to build or to discover one. Before American blacks could adopt a pluralistic ideology, they would need a stronger group life and a firmer cultural identity. Du Bois contributed to those ends, and during the 1920's other Negro artists and intellectuals overcame some important constraints; but they still remained overwhelmingly preoccupied with problems of self-definition.

We may anticipate, then, that cultural pluralism would appeal to people who were already strongly enough positioned to imagine that permanent minority status might be advantageous. It was congenial to minority spokesmen confident enough to visualize themselves at the center rather than the periphery of American experience. Accordingly, cultural pluralism proved most attractive to people who were already largely assimilated. It was itself one of the products of the American melting pot.

Perhaps that is the principal reason why the theory did not prosper until the late 1930's. Ethnic hatred reached an all-time high in the riots, hysterias, and proscriptions that accompanied and immediately followed the First World War. This 100 per cent Americanism—an indiscriminate rejection of all deviant groups—would have to subside before a pluralist America could seem a real possibility. The great leap forward in assimilation, which followed the enactment in 1924 of a permanent immigration restriction law, would have to get well under way before the desirability of complete assimilation could be widely questioned.

 F U R T H E R   R E A D I N G

Marion T. Bennet, *American Immigration Policies: A History* (1962).
Stephan Brumberg, *Going to America, Going to School: The Jewish Immigrant — Public School Encounter in Turn of the Century New York* (1984).
Mina Carson, *Settlement Folk: Social Thought and the American Settlement Movement* (1989).
Sucheng Chan, *Entry Denied: Exclusion and the Chinese Community in America, 1882–1943* (1991).
Roger Daniels, *The Politics of Prejudice: The Anti-Japanese Movement in California and the Struggle for Japanese Exclusion* (1962).
Roger Daniels, *Racism and Immigration Restriction* (1974).
Robert Divine, *American Immigration Policy, 1924–1952* (1957).
John Higham, "Integrating America: The Problem of Assimilation in the Nineteenth Century," *Journal of American Ethnic History* 1 (1981), 7–25.
Edward P. Hutchinson, *Legislative History of American Immigration Policy, 1798–1965* (1981).
Matthew Frye Jacobson, *Special Sorrows: The Diasporic Imagination of Irish, Polish, and Jewish Immigrants in the United States* (1995).
Rivka Shpak Lissak, *Pluralism and Progressives: Hull House and the New Immigrants* (1988).
Frederick C. Luebke, *Bonds of Loyalty: German-Americans and World War I* (1974).
Gwendolyn Mink, *Old Labor and New Immigrants in American Political Development* (1990).
Charles J. McClain, Jr., *In Search of Equality: The Chinese Struggle Against Discrimination in Nineteenth-Century America* (1994).
Delber L. McKee, *Chinese Exclusion versus the Open Door Policy* (1977).
Gary Okihiro, *Cane Fires: The Anti-Japanese Movement in Hawaii, 1865–1945* (1991).
Joel Perlmann, *Ethnic Differences: Schooling and Social Structure Among the Irish, Italians, Jews, and Blacks in an American City, 1880–1935* (1989).

Lucy Salyer, *Laws Harsh as Tigers: Chinese Immigration and the Shaping of Modern Immigration Law* (1995).

George Sánchez, " 'Go After the Women': Americanization and the Mexican Immigrant Woman, 1915–1929," in Ellen Carol DuBois and Vicki L. Ruiz, ed. *Unequal Sisters: A Multicultural Reader in U.S. Women's History* (1990).

Kathryn Kish Sklar, "Hull House in the 1890s: A Community of Women Reformers," in Ellen Carol DuBois and Vicki L. Ruiz, eds., *Unequal Sisters: A Multicultural Reader in U.S. Women's History* (1990).

Eileen H. Tamura, *Americanization, Acculturation and Ethnic Identity: The Nisei Generation in Hawaii* (1994).

David Tyack, *The One Best System: A History of American Urban Education* (1974).

CHAPTER
11

Immigrant and Ethnic Life in Twentieth-Century America, 1924–1965

Although the passage of the National Origins Act of 1924 profoundly altered patterns of immigration, it affected different nationalities in dissimilar ways. From one perspective, the act powerfully reduced the immigration from many nations. The quotas, which finally went into effect in 1929, were based on an annual immigration of 2 percent of the number of each nationality that had resided in the country in 1890. An immigration flow that had been 805,228 in 1921 was reduced to a ceiling of 164,000 per year. Because the benchmark for the quotas was set for 1890, the quotas for nationalities that immigrated in large numbers after that year were reduced to a trickle. The quota for Italy, for example, was 4,000; for Poland, 6,000; for Greece, 100. Moreover, the immigration of persons who "were ineligible for citizenship"—which had become shorthand for Asians—was forbidden. The legal restrictions that had disadvantaged Asians for decades, then, were only made worse. This restriction of immigration altered patterns of immigration and had profound consequences for ethnic communities themselves. European ethnic communities, because they were not replenished by immigrants, were put at risk—especially following the unadulterated Americanism of the World War I era. Many members of Asian American ethnic communities continued to be victimized by detention when they entered the United States. Although the most discriminatory aspects of the quotas for Asians were modified during and after World II, the national quotas remained in force until 1965.

In contrast, the national origins quotas did not apply for nations in the Western Hemisphere, nor did protectorates of the United States, such as the Philippines, receive quotas. As a result, immigration from Mexico, especially after the Mexican Revolution, beginning in 1910, and the Philippines surged. Responding, in part, to the dearth of labor created by the implementation of national quotas and in part to the further development of the western United States, this immigration filled a growing need for agricultural labor that was often poorly paid by American standards.

As ethnic communities were affected in varying ways because of immigration law, immigrants and their descendants were also influenced by cultural and political change in the United States. The radio, the movies, and the automobile are three examples of technological advancements that challenged and changed all ethnic communities. Political change that followed from the stock market crash in 1929 and the Great Depression that followed, however, had a differential impact on ethnic communities. On the one hand, as many European ethnic and racial minority institutions proved unable to deal adequately with the challenges of economic collapse, the national state stepped in. White ethnic and African American families received relief from national agencies and workers were able to organize unions under the auspices of the New Deal legislation. Historians have suggested that the magnitude of the economic crisis challenged ethnic and other minority communities and increasingly folded their membership into American institutional life. On the other hand, the depression encouraged Congress to restrict the migration from the Philippines and Mexico. First, the Tydings-McDuffie Act of 1934 connected the independence of the Philippines that would occur ten years later with restriction of Filipino immigrants. Next, federal and local officials dealt harshly with Mexican immigrants forcing a repatriation to Mexico of some half million people between 1929 and 1937 (discussed in Chapter 12). Whereas European ethnic groups were powerfully integrated into American society as a result of the depression and the New Deal, many members of the Mexican community were forcefully removed from it. Because of these different experiences, we are forced to see the multifaceted effects of depression and governmental efforts to address it. For some Americans, it was a godsend; for others, it meant deportation.

DOCUMENTS

The documents in this chapter explore the experiences of immigrants in the period between the passage of the National Origins Acts of 1924 and the Immigration and Nationality Act of 1965. The first four documents focus on Asian and Latin American immigrants who were filling occupational niches in the American West and whose experiences differed from European immigrants, who came mainly to the eastern United States. A Korean American woman discusses her encounters with prejudice in southern California in 1921 and her concern during the relocation of Japanese Americans early in World War II (1941). Carey McWilliams (1939) explores the work performed by Asian and Latin American immigrants in the fields of large California agricultural firms in the early decades of this century. A Mexican American (1927) recounts his migration within Mexico and ultimately to the United States. He tells of his happiness upon returning home to Mexico. Carlos Bulosan (1937), a Filipino immigrant, describes the travails of working in the agricultural fields yet expresses a hope that the ideals of America might be made to conform to reality. The fifth document (1934) explores one aspect of the twentieth-century European American experience in its depiction of the efforts at unionization by an Italian American near Pittsburgh in the 1930s. The final two documents portray the inconveniences engendered by the migration laws for some of those attempting to settle in the United States. A Chinese American describes how he migrated to America as a "paper son" in 1920, labored in a variety of occupations, and traveled back and forth between China and the United States until he was finally able to settle down with his wife, who joined him with some difficulty in 1931. Some years later (ca. 1945), another Chinese American remembers his entry into the United States—an experience that was marred by detention upon arrival.

Mary Paik Lee, a Korean American, Confronts Racism in Los Angeles, 1921, 1941

... in 1921, we left Willows with only our bedding and a few cooking utensils in our car. We stopped in Los Angeles to visit friends. There were no Korean churches then, but we heard that services were being held at Philip Ahn's house. . . .

Los Angeles then was not the huge metropolis it is today; I remember there were not many automobiles. We went on to Anaheim, where H.M. [her husband] had rented a house on Oak Street, next door to an old friend. The house had five rooms, a bathroom and a real bathtub and toilet, and a gas stove in the kitchen with a hot water tank on the back porch. We had a real house at last, with a big backyard and a fig tree. It was the first time we ever had everything just like the white people did. It really felt good.

The residents of Anaheim were mostly German Americans, and they did not think much of Orientals. When I first moved there, I was surprised to see the "For Whites Only" signs everywhere in town. One afternoon as I was preparing to close up, a young man came in, obviously very drunk. He slapped me hard on the back and said, "Hi Mary!" in a loud voice. I was so surprised and annoyed that I turned around and hit him as hard as I could on his back and said, "Hi Charlie!" He replied angrily, "My name's not Charlie!" Then he staggered over to the lunch counter in the middle of the market, saying what he thought of the "so and sos."

Two days later, he came in, apologized, and said, "Something bothers me. Why did you call me Charlie?" I replied, "Why did you call me Mary?" He said, "I thought all you Jap women were Mary." That really got to me. "How stupid can you be?" I asked. "Do you mean to tell me that all the women in Japan have the same name? Even animals have a different grunt for each other and birds have different chirps and songs. Why should humans who can talk have the same names? The reason I called you Charlie is because people like you always call all Oriental men by that name. Isn't that true?" He nodded yes. "Also, you call all black men 'boy'—young and old. White people always say 'Hey boy!' " He had to admit that was also true, and that he hadn't thought about it and had just gone along with whatever others were doing. He was nice enough to admit he was wrong and stupid. We became good friends after that. Every time he came in, he wanted to know more about Oriental people and Asian countries.

From Mary Paik Lee, *Quiet Odyssey*. Copyright © 1990. Reprinted by permission of the University of Washington Press.

One beautiful Sunday afternoon all the flowers in the park were in bloom, so H.M. and I went for a walk. As we passed a group of people, I said hello to a lady who was a good customer of ours. She turned and pretended not to know me. I didn't care; it had happened so often I didn't give it a thought. The following day she rushed into the store, obviously very angry, and said, "How dare you speak to me in public! You humiliated me in front of my friends. Don't you dare do that again!" I didn't say anything in reply; just turned around and went on with my work. I thought she would never come in again, but she did. But I never spoke to her after that.

* * * *

When the tragedy of Pearl Harbor struck, all the Japanese were forced to leave their homes and property and were taken to concentration camps. Our neighbors asked if we would look after their farms; they told us to take anything we wanted from their homes. They were our friends, so we couldn't do that, but we said we would look after their things as much as possible.

One friend asked us to live on his property, rent-free, to keep out strangers who might be coming around to take whatever they could. We told all of them that we would do our best. . . . After the Japanese left, however, many white people came in trucks, intending to take away all kinds of belongings. But when they saw us watching, they left. Many prominent Japanese were taken away quickly. We heard that many Japanese homes were looted, especially in the cities, but no one protested such actions. Another Japanese neighbor asked us to watch his land and live in his house when he was taken away. I said, "I won't live in your house, but I'll live in one of the shacks you built for your workers." So, we moved again, from one chicken shack into another. That address was 12933 S. Saint Gertrude's Road, Whittier.

The day of Pearl Harbor, we had left home very early and had worked all day in the field. We had no way of knowing what had occurred. After taking the workers home, around 7 P.M., I stopped by the [name deleted] grocery store to buy something. . . . I was surprised to see the room full of people who stared at me with hateful expressions. One man said, "There's one of them damned Japs now. What's she doing here?" Mrs. Hannah Nixon came over to me and said to her friends, "Shame on you, all of you. You have known Mrs. Lee for years. You know she's not Japanese, and even if she were, she is not to blame for what happened at Pearl Harbor! This is the time to remember your religion and practice it." What a wonderful, courageous woman to take such an unpopular stand for me, an Oriental, upon whom every white person was looking with hatred. Later, whenever I heard President Nixon refer to his mother as an angel, my thoughts went back to that sad day in her grocery store.

. . . They [whites] just assumed that all Orientals were Japanese; they didn't even bother to find out before committing violence. Even after all the Japanese were taken away to concentration camps, other Orientals were subjected to all kinds of violence. They were afraid to go out at night; many were beaten even during the day. Their cars were wrecked. The tires were slashed, the radios and batteries removed. Some friends driving on the highways were stopped and their cars were overturned. It was a bad time for all of us.

Carey McWilliams Describes South Asian and Mexican Agricultural Laborers, 1939

"Rag Heads"

Boasting vociferously at all times of their intense Americanism, the farm industrialists of California have always been indifferent as to the sources they have tapped for cheap labor. Any labor will do, providing only that it is cheap and docile. In the years 1907, 1908, 1909, and 1910, "the tide of turbans" began, as Hindustani workers appeared in the fields. Entering the United States for the most part by way of Canada, they gradually drifted south to the great farm valleys of California. For a time they worked as railroad section hands, but it was not long before they became an important source of farm labor. Most of them were trained agricultural workers, with experience in the cultivation of corn, sugar cane, cotton and melons. . . .

From the growers' point of view, the Hindus fitted nicely into the pattern of farm labor in California. Not only were they good workers, but they could be used as one additional racial group in competition with other racial groups, and thereby wages could be lowered. A notable fact about farm labor in California is the practice of employers to pay wage scales on the basis of race, i.e. to establish different wage rates for each racial group, thus fostering racial antagonism and, incidentally, keeping wages at the lowest possible point. As part of this general strategy, "it is a common custom of the ranches to entrust a particular work to a group of laborers of the same nationality." In this manner, of course, the races are kept segregated and are pitted one against the other. Because of their difference in custom, language, and appearance, the Hindus were a particularly valuable intermediary group. They were used, and still are to some extent, as a wedge to separate the Mexican and Oriental groups. . . .

Regarded as excellent farm laborers, the Hindus no longer figure as an important racial group in California. Like the Japanese, they moved rapidly into the landownership class. By 1918, they operated, as owners or lessees, some 45,000 acres of rice land in California. The census of 1930 gives the number of Hindu residents in the State as 1873, and the number of residents seems to be decreasing. The number of Hindu workers in the State, however, is in excess of this figure.

From *Factories in the Field: The Story of Migratory Farm Labor in California* by Carey McWilliams. Copyright © 1939 by Carey McWilliams.

Prior to the war [World War I], there were approximately 10,000 Hindu workers in the fields. As California farmers, they soon faced the same restrictions that were imposed against the Japanese. By the Immigration Act of 1917, which excluded immigration from certain "barred zones," further Hindu immigration was prohibited. Since further immigration has been prohibited and since most of the Hindus in California are men, many of them have returned to India in quest of wives. It should also be pointed out that the Alien Land Act operates against Hindus as well as Japanese, and its enactment naturally tended to discourage further Hindu immigration.

* * * *

The Mexicans

Mexican labor, to some extent, was used in California agriculture prior to the World War. It was during the war, however, that the great influx of Mexican labor began. The newspapers and farm journals in 1917 contain many references to large groups of Mexicans, in units of 1500 and 2500, being brought into Imperial Valley by truck from San Felipe and Guaymas "to relieve the labor situation." The Immigration Law of 1924, which practically stopped immigration from Europe, gave an added impetus to Mexican immigration. . . .

* * * *

During this decade, 1920 to 1930, the farm industrialists were enchanted with the Mexican. The Mexicans were available in large numbers (at least 150,000 worked in the fields during these years); they were good workers; unorganized; and, at the end of the season, "hibernated." Time and again, in their deliberations, the growers have emphasized the fact that the Mexican, unlike the Filipino, can be deported. It has been estimated, for example, that 80 per cent of the Mexicans in California have entered illegally, due to technical violations, and are subject to deportation. The Mexican, moreover, is easily exploited not only by the growers, but by the small merchants in the rural towns. "The Mexican," writes Ralph H. Taylor, dean of the California farm-capitalist publicists, "has no political ambitions; he does not aspire to dominate the political affairs of the community in which he lives." "The Mexican," writes A. C. Hardison, a California building-and-loan-company official, "gives less trouble with collections than the whites." . . . The general attitude of the growers towards the Mexicans is summarized in a remark made by a ranch foreman to a Mexican: "When we want you, we'll call you; when we don't—git."

* * * *

Throughout the years from 1914 to 1930 the large farms used Mexican labor as their main source of cheap, easily exploitable farm labor in the State, beating down wage rates and forcing the cities to assume the burden of supporting the Mexicans during the period of "hibernation." . . .

* * * *

. . . during the depression, the cities began to rebel. The burden of the Mexican in the winter months became oppressive, and thousands of Mexicans were "repatriated." Beginning in February, 1931, thousands of Mexicans, many of whom were citizens of the United States, were herded together by the authorities and shipped back to Mexico, to get them off the relief rolls. The last figures which I had on the "repatriations" indicated that in excess of 75,000 Mexicans had been shipped out of Los Angeles alone, at the expense, not of the growers, but of the taxpayers of the city of Los Angeles; but, when the harvest season once again came around, the growers dispatched their "emissaries" to Mexico, and again recruited thousands of Mexicans. Many Mexicans have been "repatriated" two and three times, going through this same curious cycle of entry, work, repatriation. The threat which the authorities held over the Mexicans was, of course, that either they must "agree" to repatriation or relief allotments would cease. The net result of these developments—the agitation for a limitation on Mexican immigration and the repatriation shipments—has been a marked curtailment in the use of Mexican labor.

Carlos Almazán, a Mexican American, Recounts Life in the United States and His Desire to Leave, [1927]

. . . "My brothers and I, therefore, occupied ourselves with farm work, planting corn and other grains although not as we do here in the United States. There we had to use the old plows which weren't good for anything. After a struggle we managed to make a comfortable place for our mother, and then, tired of living in the country, I decided to go to Mexico City to seek my fortune. When I got to the capital I got a job in a butcher-shop. . . . When the revolution came the meat and lard business began to suffer. I didn't want to go on in that business anyway, for it didn't even leave me time to rest. With the little money that I had, I began to buy fruits and grains in Veracruz, and brought them to the capital to sell. . . . The business was going well, but as the paper money which was being used at that time was declared worthless, I went bankrupt.

"On account of this failure I went to [town] to visit an older brother of mine in order to ask his advice. My brother told me to come to the United States and that perhaps here I could again make my fortune. That was what I did. I fixed everything so that my wife and children were left with some means, and then I left for Ciudad Juarez, Chihuahua. On arriving there I began to look for a way in which to get into this country. That was just four years and some months ago. I saw a group of workmen who were fixing the street-car line which goes to El Paso. I asked one of them to ask the foreman if he had any work for me. The foreman said that he did and I began to work right there. My work consisted of

From Manuel Gamio, *The Mexican Immigrant: His Life Story,* copyright © 1971. Reprinted by permission of the University of Chicago Press.

carrying rails and digging ditches with a pick and shovel. It was all hard work; they offered to pay me $1.80 a day. I worked all day and in the evening the fore- man told me to go with them to El Paso. I went with the gang on an electric flat- car without knowing that I was crossing over illegally but as I was going with all the workmen no one said anything. . . . as I brought a letter from Mexico for a friend who worked in a packing-house I took advantage of it, and this friend got me a job in that packing plant where they paid me $1.25 for nine hours work and that was because I knew the work. When they saw that I could dress hogs and make sausages they put me to doing that work, but the foreman told me that they weren't going to give me a raise. I kept on working there and was thinking of go- ing back to Mexico when I was advised from the Capital that my wife and chil- dren had started for the United States. I then left the hotel, for almost all of what I was earning had been spent there, and I rented a little cottage so that I could at least receive my family. When they got to El Paso and I told them at what I was working, we were all very discouraged on account of the situation. We decided to come to California and did so. In Los Angeles I found a friend of mine at the em- ployment office who had been in El Paso, and he advised me to go to the brick- yard at Simons, Laguna, . . . and that I would find work there. I went to that place and got a job there. They paid me $4.00 for working eight hours, but what eight hours! I was left almost dead, especially the first days. I had to buy my groceries from the commissary store of the same brick factory, so that very little of my pay was left. After about six months of this I began to think of some way of earning more or of having some other job and I then found a friend of mine who pro- posed to me that we plant a number of acres of land together. We planted lettuce, tomatoes and chicory, and I kept on at the same time working in the brick-yard so that I was working day and night. I got up at four in the morning and began to work on the field, then at about seven after break-fast I would go to the brick- yard and work there until five or six in the afternoon whenever the shift was over. I would then leave and go directly to the little farm and keep on working until eight or nine at night when I went to get my supper and to rest. After the first crop, which came out well, I was encouraged to rent some land on my own account and work for myself, so that I left working in the brick-yard where I had been for a year and nine months. . . .

* * * *

I don't believe that I will ever return to this country for I have here spent the hardest days of my life; it is here where I have worked the hardest and earned the least. Besides the people here don't like us, for even the Japanese treat the Mexi- cans without considerations of any kind. They think that we aren't as good as they and as we are submissive they do whatever they want to with our labor which they often steal with impunity.

As I have always been with one foot in the stirrup, ready to go back to Mexico, I don't even have a decent little house to which to invite you. I have built this little hut on the land which I have been renting. I built it myself. At first I had a carpen- ter, but I saw that he had spent two days taking measurements and making esti- mates so that I sent him away and I myself built the cottage.

Carlos Bulosan, a Filipino American, Depicts His Ambivalence About America's Kindness and Cruelty, 1937

Some weeks after our work had begun rumors of trouble reached our camp. Then, on the other side of town, a Filipino labor camp was burned. My fellow workers could not explain it to me. I understood it to be a racial issue, because everywhere I went I saw white men attacking Filipinos. It was but natural for me to hate and fear the white man.

I was nailing some boards on a broken crate when Frank came running into the vineyard.

"Our camp is attacked by white men!" he said. "Let's run for our lives!"

We ran to the freight yards, only to discover that all the boxcars were loaded. I climbed to the top of a car that was full of crates and my companions followed me. The train was already moving when I saw four detectives with blackjacks climbing up the cars. I shouted to my companions to hide. I ran to the trap door of an icebox, watching where the detectives were going.

José was running when they spotted him. He jumped to the other car and hid behind a trap door, but two more detectives came from the other end and grabbed him. José struggled violently and freed himself, rolling on his stomach away from his captors. On his feet again, he tried to jump to the car ahead, but his feet slipped and he fell, shouting to us for help. I saw his hands clawing frantically in the air before he disappeared.

I jumped out first. Frank followed me, falling upon the cinders almost simultaneously. Then we were running to José. I thought at first he was dead. One foot was cut off cleanly, but half of the other was still hanging. Frank lifted José and told him to tie my handkerchief around his foot. We carried him to the ditch.

José jerked and moaned, then passed out. Frank chewed some tobacco and spread it on the stump to keep the blood from flowing. Then we ran to the highway and tried to hail a car, but the motorists looked at us with scorn and spat into the wind. Then an old man came along in a Ford truck and drove us to the county hospital, where a kind doctor and two nurses assured us that they would do their best for him.

Walking down the marble stairway of the hospital, I began to wonder at the paradox of America. José's tragedy was brought about by railroad detectives, yet he had done no harm of any consequence to the company. On the highway, again, motorists had refused to take a dying man. And yet in this hospital, among white

From Carlos Bulosan, *America Is in the Heart*. Copyright © 1973. Reprinted by permission of Harcourt Brace and Company.

people—Americans like those who had denied us—we had found refuge and tolerance. Why was America so kind and yet so cruel? Was there no way to simplifying
things in this continent so that suffering would be minimized? Was there no common denominator on which we could all meet? I was angry and confused, and
wondered if I would ever understand this paradox.

I was becoming aware of the dynamic social struggle in America. We talked
all night in my brother's room, planning how to spread progressive ideas among
the Filipinos in California. [My brother] had become more serious. When he
talked, I noticed his old gentleness and the kind voice that . . . rung with sincerity.
. . . His words seized my imagination, so that years afterward I am able to write
them almost word for word:

"It has fallen upon us to inspire a united front among our people," he said. "We
must win the backward elements over to our camp; but we must also destroy that
which is corrupt among ourselves. These are the fundamentals of our time; but
these are also the realities that we must grasp in full.

"We must achieve articulation of social ideas, not only for some kind of economic security but also to help culture bloom as it should in our time. We are ap-
proaching what will be the greatest achievement of our generation: the discovery
of a new vista of literature, that is, to speak to the people and to be understood by
them.

"We must look for the mainspring of democracy, but we must also destroy
false ideals. We must discover the origin of our freedom and write of it in broad national terms. We must interpret history in terms of liberty. We must advocate democratic ideas, and fight all forces that would abort our culture.

"This is the greatest responsibility of literature: to find in our struggle that
which has a future. Literature is a living and growing thing. We must destroy that
which is dying, because it does not die by itself.

"We in America understand the many imperfections of democracy and the
malignant disease corroding its very heart. We must be united in the effort to
make an America in which our people can find happiness. It is a great wrong that
anyone in America, whether he be brown or white, should be illiterate or hungry or
miserable.

"We must live in America where there is freedom for all regardless of color,
station and beliefs. Great Americans worked with unselfish devotion toward one
goal, that is, to use the power of the myriad peoples in the service of America's
freedom. They made it their guiding principle. In this we are the same; we must
also fight for an America where a man should be given unconditional opportunities
to cultivate his potentialities and to restore him to his rightful dignity.

"It is but fair to say that America is not a land of one race or one class of men.
We are all Americans that have toiled and suffered and known oppression and defeat, from the first Indian that offered peace in Manhattan to the last Filipino pea
pickers. America is not bound by geographical latitudes. America is not merely a
land or an institution. America is in the hearts of men that died for freedom; it is
also in the eyes of men that are building a new world. America is a prophecy of a

new society of men: of a system that knows no sorrow or strife or suffering. America is a warning to those who would try to falsify the ideals of freemen.

"America is also the nameless foreigner, the homeless refugee, the hungry boy begging for a job and the black body dangling on a tree. America is the illiterate immigrant who is ashamed that the world of books and intellectual opportunities is closed to him. We are all that nameless foreigner, that homeless refugee, that hungry boy, that illiterate immigrant and that lynched black body. All of us, from the first Adams to the last Filipino, native born or alien, educated or illiterate—*We are America!*

"The old world is dying, but a new world is being born. It generates inspiration from the chaos that beats upon us all. The false grandeur and security, the unfulfilled promises and illusory power, the number of the dead and those about to die, will charge the forces of our courage and determination. The old world will die so that the new world will be born with less sacrifice and agony on the living. . . ."

Dominic Del Turco, an Italian American Laborer, Remembers Union Organizing, 1934

I returned to Aliquippa in 1924 and went to J & L and applied for a job. I was two, three months from being eighteen. So they hired me. I got hired in the welded-tube, same place my dad worked.

I was sent to welded-tube because they needed younger people there. It was [a] type of work that the younger man was more adept at. They could learn faster, and when you're young, you get around faster too. The reason for that was because you had to be fast in doing this work, because when the pipe came out of the mill, then it came down on the floor, and you had to sort it out. So you was under continuous operation, all the time.

No, we didn't have any union at all then. But they brought Negroes from the South to put them against whites and keep us from organizing. They could get them for cheap labor. Of course, even the whites were getting cheap labor. There's no secret about that. We got no vacations. I was hired in 1924, and from 1924 to '29, five consecutive years, I worked six, seven days a week, ten hours in the day, ten and a half at night, no vacations. Nobody got the same rate. They had what they called the 'fair-haired boys'; they paid them a certain rate. And the rest got a lesser rate. One would be getting a higher rate and one would be getting a lower rate. Well, that's because that was a company policy. They figured it all depends whether you were sympathetic toward the company.

In one case, they fired a foreman after it was exposed that this guy was making a lot of his employees kick back. When they finally started protesting, they got rid

From John Bodnar, *Worker's World,* copyright © 1983. Reprinted by permission of The Johns Hopkins University Press.

of him. I don't know where they sent him, but I think they might have sent him somewhere else.

They didn't have no company union then either. The company union came in J & L in 1934. As a matter of fact, it became prevalent in all the steel industries in 1934.

If accidentally [a] guy shot his mouth off and said, 'How much you making on your job, boy?' that's how we used to find out. We got to checking and found out that some of the boys who were considered company people—when I say company people, that [means] they were leaning towards management more than they were towards the people that worked in there—were making more. And there was no secret that a lot of people were getting higher rates than other people who did the same type of work.

They spied on you. Sure, that's the idea of giving them a higher rate. Certainly there was nothing new about that.

. . . When we first started working on organizing the union, we had a man named Mike Keller. I don't mind mentioning his name because he died for the cause. He was a Serbian man from Aliquippa. A 'fair-haired boy' for the company—I don't want to mention his name because his people are still living there—attacked him. When we were first organizing the union in Aliquippa, the police department was against us, the fire department, every governmental group was against us. That's why they call Aliquippa the 'Little Siberia.' You couldn't even breathe in there without somebody stooging on you. While we was just out organizing the union, Mike Keller was one of these aggressive little Serbian men. In 1935 Keller was standing right in front of the police, in the middle of the street. I was not too far from him. Now this guy was a little fella; Mike Keller was little fella. He was about five feet, two inches. And this guy walked up to him [and] without any reason at all started beating him up. Now this man was big, he was about six one or two, weighed about two hundred thirty or forty pounds. And he beat this man up so bad, five or six years later he dies from the effects of the beatings. He busted his ear drums, kicked him in the head, kicked him in the stomach so bad; he was beat up so bad. And the police were standing right there and they wouldn't move, because they had orders not to interfere. That's how J & L [the steel mill company] was trying to control the people. But it didn't work, because guys were so incensed about this thing that we were more determined to organize the union.

You had to be a 'fair-haired boy.' Everything in town was controlled. You could not get a loan unless it was O.K.'d. You couldn't do anything in that town unless it was O.K.'d by higher powers to be. The banks were controlled by the corporation.

* * * *

In the 1930s, before the union, we would work a few days a week. They tried to enlist me in the Communist Party, and I told them that communism and unionism doesn't mix. 'I'm a union man [Amalgamated Association of Iron and Tin Workers at this time], and I'm going to stay a union man. I don't want no part of communism.'

An organizer came down, and I was going to work. I heard him call my name. I turned around and he gave me a false name. He told me his name was Ben Gold.

But I found out later on it wasn't. And he says, 'I came down purposely to see you. You're a very aggressive young man. You're an educated boy and you have a good vocabulary, and you are a forceful speaker.' And he said, 'We can use people like you.' And I said, 'Are you representing a union?' He says, 'No.' 'Well,' I says, 'you're talking to the wrong man, because I am already committed to the union. And I am organizing the union [Amalgamated] in this community and this valley.'

This was 1934. And he says to me, 'Well, we still could use you.' I said, 'If you're talking about any party, you're talking about the Communist Party.' Of course, I was aware that there was a couple of organizers sent down talking to the people. He said, 'Yes.' That's when I told him. I said, 'The Communist Party and unionism doesn't mix. I'm a labor man and I'll stay that way. And I'm a Christian. I don't believe in communism.'

* * * *

. . . We had quite a few people then. We already had a large group, about forty or fifty, somewhere around there. Then we went up to as high as six thousand members, which is a heck of [a] lot of members, considering that the people we were affiliated with wasn't doing anything for us. We found that out later.

Jones & Laughlin Steel Corporation hired Pinkertons, and the Burnses, believe it or not. And one of the Burnses or Pinkertons, whatever he was, became vice-president of our union when he came down here. He joined the union. The company asked him to join our union just to spy on us. And this guy was trained for this. He was an ex-boxer. He was a lightweight, but boy was he good!

. . . the two plants that really were strong [for the union] was the welded-tube and the seamless. The strongest group of people that were for the union [Amalgamated] and really held to it was, like I told you, Mike Keller and the Serbians, the Croats, the Ukrainians, the Italians, and the Irish. Of course, the Irish wasn't as large a group as the rest of them. But those five groups were very aggressive groups.

The organizing part of it, I like [that] the best. The strength that we would have. It was emphasized by one man. He said if we organize, we have strength. You got the power to fight power.

During the Amalgamated days, the organization didn't have any power to convince the company that we wanted recognition. And I recognized that, and I knew that if we didn't have a powerful body behind us, we would never get nowhere, because at that time J & L already had started their espionage system, their beatings. People who were out trying to organize, to get people to sign up to join the union, were beaten. I escaped a beating one night while I was out signing cards.

Later on, there was division in the local union itself. We were dissatisfied with what the Amalgamated was doing, and so a more aggressive group—you can call us radical if you want to as far as the union is concerned—decided things didn't look so good. So we decided that we wanted to send somebody down to see John L. Lewis in Washington and see what he could do about it.

. . . So they went down. We couldn't do it because the officers left; good Lord knows what the company would do to the members. Lewis talked to them and all. He says, 'I promise you that we will organize the steelworkers in the very near future.' And Philip Murray, who was then with Lewis for the miners, was appointed by Lewis to organize the steelworkers. And then when we were successful we had a three-day strike down in J & L to convince J & L we meant business. That was 1936, when the SWOC [Steel Workers Organizing Committee] came in.

Eventually Philip Murray met with these corporations and told them, 'We want you to recognize the union.' They wouldn't, so there was a strike called in the steel mills in 1937.

In the meantime, a committee was set up to negotiate with the Jones & Laughlin Steel Corporation. . . . After three days J & L agreed to recognize us as the bargaining unit for the employees. And that's how it began. Then we had an election on the premise that they would hold the election and the union would lose the election, that they wouldn't recognize them. So what happened is we took it and got 7,000 for and 1,000 against."

Yuen Tim Gong, a Chinese American "Paper Son," Recalls His Life in California, 1920–1931

Coming to Gold Mountain

When I was eight years old [1913], our paternal uncle Chaap Kuen sponsored Older Brother Yik Hau to come to Gold Mountain. After that, we received remittances from America and I was able to attend school for eight years. In the ninth year of the Republic [1920], when I was fifteen years old, Older Brother Yik Hau had me come to Gold Mountain [the United States] under the "paper son" practice [as a United States citizen]. . . .

Economy was bad when I landed; I couldn't find any work. It was not until April that year that I finally found work ironing clothes at Hop Lee Laundry. There was a rule at the laundry; a newcomer must apprentice for twenty weeks. When you were an apprentice, the laundry fed you, but you didn't get paid. After that you would become a regular worker. I endured those 140 days before I began to earn ten dollars a week.

In 1923 the Hop Lee partners, all ten of them, saw that I had been a hard worker. Besides that, I was the only person at Hop Lee with a driver's license. Hence they made me a partner; I was in charge of pick-up and delivery. We kept our books on the laundry this way: Each Saturday evening we tabulated the income and expenses. We would divide whatever amount we made into eleven shares. Our earnings varied weekly—sometimes each of us cleared twenty or thirty dollars;

From *Chinese America: History and Perspectives*, Vol. 6, 1992. Chinese Historical Society of America. Reprinted by permission.

sometimes only a few dimes! At any rate, I calculated my total 1923 earnings to be less than five hundred dollars.

A Home-Bound Gamsaan Haak

By 1928 I was twenty-three years old and had been in America for eight years. I wanted to return home to China for a visit. . . . I had saved, including the coins in my pants pockets, only $450. I spent $85 on a boat ticket and, through a lawyer, over $10 for an exit permit. In addition, I made out a money order for $1,000 in Hong Kong dollars so that I would have money for my return fare from Hong Kong. At that time, the exchange rate was U.S. $1 to $5.70 in Hong Kong currency. . . . I also bought a Western suit for $30, and a pair of leather shoes for $3. After all these expenditures, I only had a little over $100 left in my pocket. Yet I went home "triumphantly" with that much cash on hand!

I reached home on the fifteenth day of the eighth lunar month in 1928. Two weeks later I had a benediction banquet and invited all my friends and relatives for a feast. While everyone was having a wonderful time, I was counting how much money I had left—less than one hundred dollars! . . .

A Homesteading Gamsaan Haak

I returned to Gold Mountain in [month] 1930 and had to work like a mule all over again. . . .

. . . I went back to Hop Lee Laundry with only a nickel in my pocket! Lucky for me I started work the next morning. Otherwise, I couldn't imagine what would have happened to me.

I had planned to return to the States with my wife. However, the immigration laws disallowed the wife of a [Chinese] American citizen to immigrate. In 1931, the Chinese American Citizens' Alliance spent five thousand dollars on an attorney to file a lawsuit against United States Immigration. They won, and the law against the immigration of wives of [Chinese] American citizens was lifted. I immediately applied for a visa to visit China again. However, I was flat broke. So I borrowed four hundred dollars from Uncle Wah Fong and commissioned a lawyer to file a petition for me to return to China to bring my wife over. I quickly prepared a "coaching book" and sent it to my wife, telling her to memorize the contents well. On the sixteenth day of the fifth lunar month of that year [1931], I was back in China again. I went to the American consulate in Hong Kong as soon as possible and filed all the necessary papers. . . . On the sixteenth day of the tenth lunar month, I took my wife to Hong Kong. A week later we set sail for the United States.

We arrived in First City on the fifteenth day of the eleventh lunar month. My wife was detained at the Angel Island Immigration Station for processing. She made several mistakes and was denied entry by the immigration office. She was about to be deported, but fortunately she was into the sixth month of her pregnancy. The deportation was delayed. What actually happened was that the immigration official was corrupt. Immediately I talked to my lawyer and spent three hundred dollars on bribes. . . . Finally, my wife was released. . . . We settled down at last.

A Chinese American Describes His Detention Upon Arrival in San Francisco, ca. 1945

Oh, So-and-so's going to Gold Mountain! Gold Mountain! It sounds so beautiful, as if it is a place full of gold. You could just "pick up the gold" once you get there. Well, that was what the villagers thought of America. Never would they imagine that we in Gold Mountain only had an iron in our hand, ironing clothes day in and day out! Or that we, soaked in sweat, were just stir-frying noodles in a kitchen! Never would they know that foreigners called us "Chinaman" and "Chink!" Not in their wildest dreams would they realize that the so-called "gold" was really earned with our blood and sweat—working in hardship for over ten hours a day.

When I received my visa, my friends and relatives sent me all sorts of gifts. However, I was apprehensive—I knew it wouldn't be easy to just "pick up the gold" in a faraway place without friends. Other than the English alphabet, I knew only a few simple words. I could tell I would have it tough in a foreign country. . . . It was tough, just as the proverb says: "Life's most painful moment is either separation or death." I believe many fellow countrymen shared that heavy-hearted feeling of leaving one's motherland, a feeling beyond any written description!

For two days I was ten thousand feet above the Pacific Ocean, passing through the Philippines, Guam, and Hawaii. Finally, as the plane approached the Golden Gate, I could see the world famous Golden Gate Bridge. From above, it was like a tiny snake across the ends of two pieces of land. A short distance away I saw the more impressive "Oakland Bridge." So this is Gold Mountain, I told myself.

The plane descended for landing, dashing above huge buildings like a strong wind. A gust of excitement burst inside me. A rumbling sound disrupted my thought. The plane had landed. I left the cabin and saw a middle-aged man waving at me with a big smile. He was my father, whom I hadn't seen for over ten years. Other than the white hair, he looked just like his photograph. We were chatting for about ten minutes, when a foreigner came over and said to me, "*Ready to go, boy?*" I stared at him, not knowing that I had to go through immigration.

. . . I was led up to the ninth floor. First I was frisked, then issued a blanket and bedding. Afterwards, someone took me through a steel door and directed me inside. As I walked in, a group of young Chinese cheered and welcomed me: "Well! Here comes a newcomer!" They shook my hand and helped me with my luggage. They led me to a vacant bed and started asking me all sorts of things about Hong Kong and Canton. I answered them all and told them that after settling down, I would chitchat more. I sat down and looked around. The dormitory occupied about half the floor space. The door was of reinforced steel; all the windows were embedded with two sets of iron bars. There was also a wired fence out-

From "The Most Memorable Event of My Stay in the United States," *Chinese America: History and Perspectives,* 1991. Chinese Historical Society of America, San Francisco, CA.

side the window. Really tight security! These young Chinese here were all about twelve to twenty years old. Their beds were messy as dog houses, with their wash hanging alongside. Some sat on their beds quietly; some joked around, making loud noises; some played mahjong and domino. The bathroom was to the back of the dormitory.

* * * *

There were about forty to fifty of us, mostly from the Four Districts [Taishan, Xinhui, Kaiping, Enping] or from the Jungsaan [Zhongshan] district. Not too many of them could speak the Canton City dialect. Nevertheless, I could understand their local dialects. There was one exception, a young man who was about five beds away from me. He was a northerner who only could speak either Putonghua or the Shanghai dialect. He had come with a Kuomintang government passport and had been stranded here for one year, without knowing why his entry was denied. He wrote repeatedly to the Chinese Consulate for help and even requested to be deported to either Hong Kong or Taiwan. However, there was no response, as if his requests were like rocks sunk into the bottom of a sea. Luckily he was a happy-go-lucky person. . . .

Meanwhile a young man came by and asked me in the Toisaan [Taishan] dialect, "Brother, where are you from?" . . . He had been detained there for two whole years. Thrice he tried to commit suicide but was rescued in the nick of time. He could have died and a good young life would have been wasted.

* * * *

One morning an immigration official called my name. I was apprehensive, not knowing what was going on. . . . He led me to a small reception area and told me to wait there. I knew it was interrogation time. . . . The interrogator asked me all sorts of questions, covering everything from my ancestral lineage to the chopsticks, pots, and pans at home. Finally he asked me what was my wish. I said I hoped to get entry to America as soon as possible. He smiled and said, "Your father is outside. When he's finished with the paper work, you may go with him." I was overjoyed. I thanked him and left the room quickly. I felt so relieved, so free, like a swallow gliding in the open sky. Another immigration official led me back to the detention quarters.

* * * *

Father was waiting by the door. I claimed my luggage, and with big steps, left the immigration building. As I walked across the street, I turned to look back up at the twelve-storied building. I saw the windows crowded with heads peeking out and with hands waving at me. I waved back. We might not be able to hear each other, yet we understood the words of silence.

Father's car was parked across the street. He came over to help me with my luggage. After we got into the car, he started the motor and we headed straight for Chinatown. I turned back to look for my friends—they were still by the window. We made a turn and I lost sight of them.

Many years have passed, but that experience is still vivid in my mind.

E S S A Y S

These two essays explore how the great changes in American society between the two world wars affected immigrants and ethnics as well. Lizabeth Cohen, a historian at New York University, focusing on Chicago—mainly on its European and African American communities—argues that the Great Depression and the New Deal transformed life in the ethnic neighborhoods. When economic troubles descended on the community, members of immigrant and ethnic groups, as in the past, looked to ethnic institutions, such as ethnic and church relief agencies, fraternal organizations, and ethnic banks. The depression, however, was of such magnitude that these traditional institutions proved unable to address the crises stemming from it. Immigrants and ethnics, Cohen argues, increasingly relied on institutions beyond the community and eventually turned to the national state, which intervened in a variety of ways to contend with economic crisis. For George Sánchez, historian at the University of Southern California, the growth of mass culture in the 1920s was pivotal for the Mexican American community in Los Angeles. As Mexican Americans enjoyed motion pictures, radio, and the increased availability of consumer goods, they redefined the nature of Mexican culture in the American city. For Sánchez, this is best exemplified in music. As Mexican American musicians utilized new entertainment media, such as the radio and phonographs, the music they created was supported almost entirely by the Mexican American community.

The Impact of the Great Depression on Local Ethnic Institutions in Chicago

LIZABETH COHEN

. . . Industrial workers had faced economic downturns before. Many remembered vividly the hard times that followed World War I and the periodic unemployment that became almost a way of life during the 1920s. The Great Depression, however, took place on an unprecedented scale. Hardly a working family escaped its grasp. Workers routinely found their working hours and their pay cut when they were lucky and lost their jobs when they were not. Only half the people employed in Chicago manufacturing industries in 1927 were still working in 1933, whereas company payrolls had shrunk to an astounding one-quarter of what they had been five years before. . . . With a cataclysm of such magnitude overtaking Chicago, the nation, and even the world, people began to doubt that their lives would ever return to normal.

But to understand the impact of the Great Depression on working-class families in Chicago, it is important to do more than measure the magnitude of their hardships. It is necessary to ask how the very structure of people's lives, particularly their relationship to basic institutions and authority figures in their ethnic communities, workplaces, and families, was transformed during the crisis. . . . during the twenties, workers in Chicago manufacturing looked to their ethnic

From Lizabeth Cohen, *Making a New Deal: Industrial Workers in Chicago, 1919–1939.* Copyright © 1990. Reprinted by permission of Cambridge University Press.

communities for security. They accepted as well whatever assistance they could get from their welfare capitalist employers, though it was frequently less reliable. . . .

The Ethnic Community in Crisis

Understandably, people first tried to handle the new crises that were engulfing their lives in familiar ways. When chief breadwinners lost their jobs early in the depression, other family members went looking for work, much as they had done in the 1920s. If the immediate family could not cope on its own, it turned to established networks of relatives and friends within the ethnic community.

But the magnitude of the city's economic crisis severely limited the help that family and friends could give intimates who were in trouble. These informal networks had worked before because people suffered their ups and downs at different times. In the 1920s, if a man was laid off during a slack season in one industry, chances were his wife or daughter or brother could find employment in an industry at more peak operation. When one family faced an emergency like illness or death, neighbors and other close associates could usually afford to help. But the effects of the Great Depression were so pervasive that people could no longer count on much assistance from these old networks. In the 1930s, spouses and children had a much harder time finding work when chief breadwinners lost their jobs. . . . Workers' relatives and friends helped when they could, but more often than not they were already pushed to the limit coping with their own problems. A study of one hundred applicants for relief in the winter of 1933 documented that relatives and friends had been willing to assist many of the needy at first, in some cases to avoid the "disgrace" of having the family on charity. But as the circle of unemployment widened, intimates became less able to help, engrossed as they were in their own difficulties. . . . As time went on, Chicago's industrial workers could hardly manage their own problems. Despite their concern for those outside their immediate families, they could offer little material help.

As their troubles increased and they exhausted the informal networks available to them, Chicago workers looked, as was their habit, to the ethnic- and religious-affiliated community institutions that had long supported them in good and bad times. When the Great Depression made it harder for workers to hold jobs, to pay bills, rents, amd mortgages, and to cope emotionally, they looked for salvation to their old protectors.

As workers reeled from one bewildering crisis, such as losing a job or a home, to another, the welfare agencies that had served their ethnic group or religious faith in the past seemed the obvious place to seek help. Even those who had managed without much assistance in the 1920s now turned to these organizations to cope with their troubles. "We had a number of people come to us, for assistance and advice, who for years have not identified themselves with the Polish-American group," acknowledged Mary Midura, a staff member of the Polish Welfare Association. "When they found themselves in financial distress, they sought contact with people of the nationality group from which they themselves emanated." In search of money, jobs, food, and clothing, needy workers and their families called upon the Slovenian Relief Organization, the Polish National Alliance Benevolent Association, the Bohemian Charitable Association, the Jewish Charities, the Catholic Charities, and other sectarian welfare organizations. Local churches were particularly swamped by appeals for charity. The parish priest of a Catholic Church in Back of the Yards found himself bombarded night and day with calls from the needy of his congregation, including many of his thriftiest families. They came, he said, "often bathed in tears—and [they] pleaded inability to help themselves any longer."

Ethnic and religious welfare institutions were committed to delivering the services that their constituents expected. Just as they had aimed to keep "their own kind" from being a public burden during the twenties, so they struggled to care for them now, even in the midst of a severe depression. "Let's have pride enough *not* to sponge upon public support when Catholic charity is still able to care for its own interests," one priest urged his flock. The depression in fact impelled the Chicago Archdiocese to establish a comprehensive relief structure that rivaled the widely acclaimed Jewish Charities of Chicago. The Catholic Charities' Central Charity Bureau coordinated a decentralized operation that at its peak in the 1930s oversaw six thousand volunteers working in 325 St. Vincent de Paul Conferences organized on the parish level. Catholics were proud of their volunteer-staffed relief organization for minimizing overhead costs and blessing the souls of the saviors while sustaining the needy.

* * * *

For the Catholic Church hierarchy quite blatantly, and for other groups more subtly, the Great Depression presented a challenge to their authority. Legitimacy rested on continuing to meet their constituents' needs and on protecting their group's good name in the larger community. Mayor Kelly, addressing the Catholic Slavic Day Fundraiser at Pilsen Park, congratulated the Slovaks for "taking care of their own hungry and destitute," in other words keeping them off the county rolls. Less successful groups felt the sting of public condemnation. Mexican leaders, for example, urged their community to take more responsibility for the suffering of Mexican immigrants in Chicago: "Due to our own negligence, either willingly or forcibly we are compelled to join the public charities. Therefore, we say that only through a strong organization we can, to a certain extent, overthrow the hostile propaganda voiced in some of the newspapers who accuse us of being a burden to the Relief institutions, a menace to the public health, and a hindrance to the stability and advancement of the life of the native worker."

Yet despite the commitment of ethnic- and religious-affiliated agencies to serve their own people, these private charities could not handle the enormous demand for assistance. Church soup kitchens, ethnic fund-raising bazaars, and used clothing drives went only a small way toward meeting the huge demand. Observers repeatedly noted the inadequacy of private relief, claiming that organizations like the St. Vincent de Paul Conferences were less effective in practice than in theory.

* * * *

It did not take long for clients, agencies, and civic leaders alike to recognize that the traditional voluntary approach to relief was floundering in an economic crisis of unprecedented magnitude. Still, the depth of popular commitment to a system of private welfare serving particular populations of needy was evident in the emergency measures cities like Chicago embraced. Rather than calling for an alternative system of state-supported relief to bail out beleaguered private charities, business and community leaders followed the advice of President Hoover's Emergency Committee for Employment. Much as they had done on a smaller scale during the depression of 1921–2, they collaborated to raise special funds to replenish the depleted treasuries of existing social agencies. Prominent Chicagoans orchestrated two drives for emergency money. . . .

Chicago's private charities hoped that this system of subsidy would help them serve the clients they felt were rightfully theirs without interference by other agencies or the state. No one else, they felt, was better prepared to meet the material and emotional needs of Chicagoans in distress. The only people who repeatedly criticized this approach were professional social workers who argued that review of program quality should accompany funding. Although Cardinal Mundelein applauded the subsidy approach for sparing Catholics "fear of any discrimination" by non-Catholic relief agencies, United Charities' social workers despaired that Catholics were left to their parishes "where we feel that they will probably not receive the attention they should have." The territoriality of existing agencies, not the highest standards of social service, drove the welfare system of the early 1930s, critics pointed out. Increasingly, professional social workers advocated a system of relief that had public funding and universal standards.

The public relief that existed in these early depression years was organized on the county level and offered few alternatives to private agencies. Although the Cook County Bureau of Public Welfare spent millions between 1929 and 1931, the money went not for general relief but to pay for Mothers' Pensions, Blind Pensions, Aid to Ex-Service Men, and commodity orders of food, milk, shoes, and coal intended to supplement the contributions of private agencies. Moreover, an extremely high rate of tax delinquency in Cook County further limited the funds available for relief. . . . Those Chicagoans who did not receive adequate relief from the welfare organizations of their cultural communities were far more likely to go to the private, nonsectarian United Charities than to the county.

To the frustration of Chicago's supporters of local, private welfare, even the emergency fund drives failed to solve the relief crisis. Within months of the completion of both drives, the money was exhausted, causing relief stations to close, monthly allowances to be cut, "no-rent" policies to go into effect, and most crucially, client disillusionment with existing agencies to grow. By trying to keep their claim on their communities amidst the upheavals of severe depression, sectarian social agencies inadvertently invited rejection when they failed to provide adequately for their clients.

The dissatisfaction that Chicago's Catholics displayed with the church's efforts to help them cope with the depression illustrates this development. Many needy church members criticized the way the Catholic Charities handled their applications. . . .

Some unemployed Catholics mistrusted not only the Central Charity Bureau but also their local St. Vincent de Paul Societies and their parish priests. By early 1932, the pastor at St. Augustine's parish in Back of the Yards felt obligated to defend the reputation of his St. Vincent de Paul Society volunteers from community attack. Acknowledging that cuts in the weekly allowance had been necessary, he added, "The people of St. Augustine's have no reason to complain. In fact our St. Vincent de Paul men are deserving of the highest praise. They are working and slaving incessantly to aid our families. It has been said that some of our men are being paid. This is a mean lie."

Catholics' resentment over the church's inadequate relief soon spread to other aspects of church policy. Parishioners expressed anger that the church still expected them to pay parochial school tuition, and many moved their children to local public schools. People also resented the fees that the church charged for performing ritual acts. In working-class neighborhoods of the city, baptisms, first holy communions, confirmations, church marriages, and burials declined noticeably during the depression. . . .

* * * *

. . . The Catholic Church, by taking responsibility for the worldly needs of its parishioners, could no longer get by with just offering spiritual solace to its suffering. Needy Catholics were increasingly judging it as a social institution.

The Catholic Church was not the only religious institution in Chicago to lose favor through its failure to provide members with adequate relief. Black Protestant churches had long played an important welfare role in black communities. Prior to 1929, for example, St. Marks Methodist Episcopal Church, a large established congregation at Wabash and 50th Street, kept its doors open every day and six nights a week for worship, socializing, and welfare activities. A staff of five social workers assisted parishioners with their problems. By 1934, however, the church's income had dropped 40 percent; the building was closed four days and four nights a week, three of the social workers had left, and the number of active church members had greatly declined. According to the Reverend J. B. Redmond, "As the church became less able to render financial support to its members, they turned more and more to the relief agencies. ". . .

St Clair Drake and Horace Cayton, in their investigation of the "black metropolis" during the depression, . . . found that throughout the Black Belt people were accusing the old-line churches of being "rackets," constantly demanding money without delivering much in return. In contrast, the churches that flourished in black neighborhoods during the depression were Holiness and Spiritualist storefront congregations, which offered worshippers an intense, emotional experience and took little responsibility for anything but their souls. The Reverend Mary Evans, pastor of the revivalist Cosmopolitan Community Church, for instance, reported an increase in attendance of 40 percent from 1929 to 1934. Observers noted that by the mid-1930s there was hardly a block of the Black Belt without a Holiness or Spiritualist church. For relief help, blacks increasingly turned to the United Charities, the county, and whatever other agencies on which they could prevail. . . . the overwhelming poverty in the community meant that indigenous welfare institutions, particularly the established churches, had an even harder time than their white counterparts relieving community distress.

By the time desperation drove Chicago's Joint Emergency Relief Service to demand help from the Illinois state legislature in the winter of 1932 and the State of Illinois in turn to request federal assistance the following July, there was much less opposition in the city to the notion of public-supported relief. The failure of private welfare agencies to meet Chicago's needs ensured that. Even Edward Ryerson, the steel industrialist and important Chicago philanthropist who had long defended private welfare, finally recognized that a new era had arrived. In February, he went to Springfield and demanded $12 million to help the needy. When that ran out, he called on Hoover himself. "I got for the State of Illinois, the first federal money for relief ever granted," he reported. "It was a curious thing for me to do. I was bitterly opposed to federal funds at that time. But I realized the problem was beyond the scope of local government." . . .

Private welfare was not the only pillar of ethnic life to collapse under the pressure of the depression. Other institutions that ethnic workers had depended on during the 1920s failed them as well, most importantly ethnic benefit societies, ethnic banks and building and loan associations, and ethnic neighborhood stores. The fraternal insurance policies, bank accounts, mortgages, and credit arrangements that had once symbolized security or even success had less and less to offer workers.

The mutual benefit and fraternal insurance societies that had served as anchors of ethnic community life through the 1920s encountered rough seas during the Great Depression. Begun as self-help organizations by immigrants from the same region of the Old World or a common corner of America, those societies had assured members a proper burial. During the 1920s, small local societies had consolidated into national ones and new state regulations had mandated more stringent and less cooperative-style operations. But even as their societies changed, ethnic Chicagoans remained loyal, retaining memberships despite their group policies at work or supplementary industrial-type insurance purchased from commercial companies. Those other policies might come and go with a job or a fortune, but fraternal insurance could always be counted on. Under the pressure of the depression, however, many workers began to have trouble keeping up insurance payments, which in no time threatened the stability of fraternal associations. For instance, when many members of the Unione Veneziana found themselves unemployed and thus no longer able to make monthly payments, the organization could not keep up its mortgage payments and lost its hall. Shortly after, the Unione itself disbanded.

* * * *

To make matters worse, many fraternal associations had invested a large percentage of their assets in real estate, either by lending money directly to members or by purchasing mortgages from banks and building associations. For example, the Polish Women's Alliance in 1927 had tied up $1,350,000 of its total assets of $1,540,000 in mortgages. In the same year, the Polish National Alliance had $14,207,000 in assets, with $12,545,000 invested in mortgages, the bulk of which were properties in the Chicago area. When the housing market collapsed with the Great Depression, the fundamental weakness in the investment policy of the fraternals was revealed. Many societies were left holding foreclosed property, now reduced in value and yielding little return.

The crisis among fraternal associations had severe implications. Losing assets and members could jeopardize an ethnic society and, some even felt, an ethnic community itself. As one of the largest ethnic fraternals, the Polish National Alliance, argued in its weekly newspaper in January 1931, "the insurance scheme has been introduced into our Polish organizations as a necessary cement with which to sustain the unity and coherence of the first thousands, and then the tens of thousands of the members and groups of these organizations. Experience and practice have proved that without such cement, without such financial constraint to pay, there could not exist and prosper among the Polish immigrants any organization." As that cement weakened, many began to wonder what would happen to the strength of the ethnic community it had once bonded together.

Most people went to great lengths to keep their policies active. They made other sacrifices before they were forced to borrow on their insurance, to take the cash surrender value if there was any, or in the worst cases, to just let the policy expire because there was no monetary compensation. . . .

But even with scrimping and saving and letting other debts accumulate, it was often impossible to keep up insurance payments. Every study of unemployed families in Chicago during the early years of the depression recorded that large percentages, usually around 75 percent, had been forced to let some or all insurance policies lapse. Not only was insurance a burdensome expense, but also many welfare agencies would not give relief to clients who still held insurance. People in need often had no choice but to give up their long-cherished protection for tomorrow in order to survive today.

Not all the lapsed policies, of course, were fraternal ones. But when they were, the shock to the holder was particularly severe. If a commercial or employer's insurance policy failed them, workers considered it all the more proof that the capitalists had let them down. But when forced to abandon an investment in their own community organization, the betrayal hit closer to home. One investigator noted in the understated, unemotional language of official reporting that nonetheless betrayed the disillusionment of six families who had lost fraternal insurance: "their insurance had failed to provide the present and future security which they had been led to believe it would furnish them in emergency." Workers who could not keep up their insurance payments often felt as if they had been let down by an old friend.

Chicago's industrial workers did not depend on their ethnic communities only in times of trouble. At more prosperous moments, as when saving money at the bank or buying a home, they looked to ethnic banks and building and loan associations. . . . ethnic banks popped up all over Chicago during the 1920s, most of them small, state-chartered institutions located in the new, outlying shopping districts that boomed during the twenties. Because Illinois law prohibited branch banking, what in other major cities were outposts of downtown banks were in Chicago small, often ethnically owned financial institutions that somehow had scraped together enough capital to meet the state's minimum requirements. As a result, by 1928 Chicago could claim 231 incorporated banking institutions, more than any other American city, with 106 others spread throughout suburban Cook County.

Almost every ethnic community in Chicago had a least one bank where people could transact business in their native language.

These small outlying banks were more numerous than stable, however. Illinois prohibition of branch banking and lax requirements for state banking charters had permitted many minimally capitalized and poorly managed banks to operate. In the bank failures that swept the city from 1929 to 1933 and were particularly intense after June 1931, these outlying banks were the first to collapse. By the time of the national bank holiday in March 1933, 163 of the 199 Chicago banks located outside the Loop had closed their doors. Only 16 percent, or 33 outlying banks, weathered the Great Depression. Far more than depositors' lack of confidence caused these bank failures. Chicago's ethnic banks not only suffered from low capitalization; most of them also invested heavily in local real estate. The collapse of that boom brought a sudden depreciation in the value of banks' assets.

Within a few years, disbelieving Chicagoans watched the downfall of such prestigious neighborhood landmarks as the Binga State Bank in the Black Belt, the First Italian State Bank, the Slovak Papanek-Kovac State Bank, the Czech Novak and Stieskal State Bank, the Lithuanian Universal State Bank, the Jewish Noel State Bank, and the largest Polish bank, the Northwestern Trust and Savings Bank, known familiarly in the Polish community as "Smulski's Bank." The *Chicago Defender's* description of the scene outside Binga's Bank in the Black Belt captured the community tragedy of a bank closing: "Crowds of depositors gathered in front of the bank. Two uniformed policemen were out on guard for several days. There were no disorders. Instead, there was a deathlike pall that hung over those who had entrusted their life savings to Binga. . . . It was pride—that pride of seeing their own race behind the cages, that led them to 35th and State Street to do their banking. For years, the Binga Bank was pointed out to visitors as something accomplished by our group."

When these banks failed, even more than when ethnic welfare agencies and ethnic benefit societies faltered, working-class people felt let down by the elites of their communities. Ethnic bank owners and managers had been local heroes, helping individual customers with mortgages and loans and providing leadership and financial assistance to the community. To ethnic workers, it was a scandal that bankers abandoned those who depended on them in a time of crisis. . . .

The managers of an Italian bank in another Chicago neighborhood tried to ward off a run on the bank by calling on someone with even more stature in the community, Father Pavero, the local priest, to calm depositors down. The bankers gave Father their word that nothing was wrong and put him on a soap box to assure those who had assembled in the bank lobby that their money was safe, along with the church's. Most people went home convinced there was no danger. But when the bank closed the next day, Father Pavero found himself "cursed all over the place" along with the once esteemed bankers. . . . The National Urban League concurred that disillusionment from bank failures would have far-reaching ramifications for communities, as the closing of the Binga State Bank was bringing a "tremendous loss of confidence in Negro business enterprise and Negro financial institutions" in its wake.

Ethnic building and loan associations, like banks, had facilitated workers' economic advances during the 1920s only to preside over their downfall in the

1930s. . . . Many societies, like the Italo–American Building and Loan Association, the Lithuanian Dollar Savings, Building and Loan Association, and the Polish
Nasza Chata Building and Loan Association, actually collapsed in the depression.
But even when they did not close, like their close cousins the ethnic benefit societies, building and loan associations failed members . . . who could not keep up
payments. No building and loan association enjoyed abandoning its members;
many tried to extend deadlines and bend rules for a time. But before too long, they
had to foreclose on unpaid mortgages in order to stay afloat. Even then, the damage from the depression remained. As late as 1940, a study by the federal government's Home Owners' Loan Corporation found only a fraction of Chicago's prede-
pression building and loans in business, and very few of these still healthy.
According to S. C. Mazankowski, a director of the Polish–American Building and
Loan Association League of Illinois, irresponsible directors were most at fault. Selected for their wealth and prestige in the ethnic community rather than their brains
and experience, and notorious for their unprofessional banking practices, they deserved, and got, the brunt of the public's blame.

Even when owners did not face foreclosure and managed to hold onto their
property, owning a home did not offer the kind of security during the depression
that it had in the 1920s. Many welfare agencies barred homeowners from receiving
relief. At the same time, moreover, homeowners who were landlords had a difficult
time collecting rents from their tenants. Mary Rupcinski and her husband had unemployed tenants who went for long periods, once as long as eighteen months,
without paying any rent. "They cheated me till I could not pay my interest on my
mortgage and lost my house," she recalled bitterly. Because relief agencies refused
to contribute to clients' rent payments until tenants were faced with eviction, small
landlords, who were often workers trying to make a little extra money, had to
choose between letting renters stay on free or paying the city to initiate eviction.
They lost money either way. . . . all the things that had seemed wise in the twenties,
like buying a home, keeping up fraternal insurance, and saving at the neighborhood bank or building and loan association, only caused trouble in the thirties.

Not even the faithful neighborhood merchant whose credit had sustained
many an ethnic working-class family through bouts of unemployment during the
1920s could be counted on, to the dismay of customer and shopkeeper alike. Many
tradesmen tried to keep up their old patterns of extending credit despite the depression. After all, they knew that credit was one of the main reasons customers patronized their stores over the cheaper chains. But as more customers were unemployed
and not paying up, giving too much credit could bankrupt a store. "People would
come to the store with little books and they would charge everything," Theresa Giannetti remembered angrily. "We'd keep track of what they would buy and if they
had the money at the end of the month, they'd give us some; if they didn't, we just
extended the credit. It got to the point where my Dad gave so much credit that he
lost everything he had for giving the credit. . . . The people who owed us the
money never bothered to pay it."

Ethic merchants like Mrs. Giannetti's father who had managed to survive the
onslaught of the chains during the late 1920s were going broke meeting the traditional expectations of their customers. Some customers ran up more credit than
they could possibly pay back. Still, if a storekeeper refused credit to a family with

a large bill, he risked losing the entire sum owed. Then, too, merchants had to beware of what was known as "grocery cheating," getting all the credit you could from nearby grocers and then moving where people did not know you. Worst of all, when customers had money, small shopkeepers often watched them turn to the cash-and-carry chain store where their money-in-hand bought more. Many independent store owners, fearing bankruptcy, resorted to limiting credit, requiring customers to pay off the previous week's account if they wanted credit the following week. But in doing so, they minimized all the more what distinguished the small store from the chain and further drove customers away.

Independent shopkeepers also fell victim to aggressive chain expansion during the depression. After some initial faltering in the early thirties, many chains figured out how they could make the depression work for them, often taking advantage of their size in ways that were not possible for the small store. . . .

The relief system contributed as well to the difficulty independent stores had competing with chains during the 1930s. Relief agencies run by the private United Charities, Cook County, and eventually, the state of Illinois and the federal government preferred recipients to buy food at chain stores where prices were lower. . . . Not only had grocery chains like National Tea used the relief system to take dollars out of the small grocer's pocket, but they also had then spent the money to modernize and diversify chain operations in ways that hurt independents all the more.

Even after the policy of relief agencies was changed to allow all merchants to compete for the business of relief clients, the independent merchant still felt at a severe disadvantage. Many customers stayed with the chains. "We have lost about twenty-five customers through charity slips on the chain stores. When a customer owes you money, he does not like to come in when he cannot pay you," complained one grocer who after twenty-nine years in business found himself $3,500 in debt. Furthermore, although he or she could now legally fill recipients' grocery orders, the small shopkeeper felt burdened by the relief bureaucracy in ways that the chains, with their professional bookkeeping, did not. . . .

By the mid-1930s, working-class people were finding more chain stores near their homes and patronizing them more frequently. Even when the corner store survived, ethnic workers could less afford to indulge their preference for its familiar food products and comfortable atmosphere. People who may have opposed the chain store in principle found economic realities changing their buying habits. As early as 1931, the major trade journal of chain store executives predicted that "one of the most constructive features of the depression, so far as the chains are concerned, lies in the fact that it operates to make more people chain store conscious, a fact that will undoubtedly work to the advantage of the chains when better conditions return and consumer buying power increases. Thousands of people throughout the country have patronized chain stores this past year who never before felt it necessary to test the economies they claimed to offer." By the end of the 1930s in Chicago, that prediction had come true. In the winter of 1936, when a DePaul University marketing professor conducted an extensive survey of the attitudes of Chicago housewives toward chain food stores, he found that chain stores had become much more popular in recent years, particularly among factory workers. By 1939, a survey by the A. C. Neilsen Company confirmed that 93 percent of what were labeled "lower middle" and 91 percent of "lower" income buyers now paid by cash, not credit, an indication that they were patronizing chain stores.

As the corner grocer offered less credit than usual or closed down entirely, customers were forced to turn elsewhere. Loyalty to the local storekeeper of one's ethnicity had once been greatly valued, but now people felt that he or she had let them down, just when they needed help most. One more aspect of the "safety net" that their ethnic group had previously provided had collapsed with the Great Depression.

Workers' feeling that they could no longer depend on their neighborhood merchants or on other ethnic leaders like the mutual benefit society director and banker suggests that the depression threatened the class harmony of ethnic communities. Through the 1920s, when working-class Poles or Bohemians or Italians felt protected by successful businessmen and civic leaders of their own ethnicity, ethnic communities had remained integrated across class. But as the upheavals of the depression undermined ethnic institutions, particularly the credibility of their leaders, class tensions grew within Chicago's ethnic communities. The local businessman who once had supported ethnic welfare agencies or provided mortgage money was now perceived as only watching out for himself. As workers became more aware of class differences within their own ethnic groups, they were on their way to becoming more sensitive to them in the larger world and more likely to recognize their common fate with workers of other ethnicities.

The Role of Popular Culture in Changing the Mexican American Community in Los Angeles Between 1920 and 1935

GEORGE SÁNCHEZ

Just south of Los Angeles' central Plaza lay the area known throughout the city as the main arena for activities of leisure in the Mexican community of the 1920s. Sundays were not only a big day for religious practice; they also were big business days for the area's movie theatres, gambling dens, and pool halls—all of which dominated the streets to the south. The constant sound of Mexican music—music that ranged from traditional Mexican ballads to newly recorded *corridos* depicting life in Los Angeles—was everywhere. A burgeoning Mexican music industry flourished in the central and eastern sections of the city during the 1920s, largely hidden from the Anglo majority.

From *Becoming Mexican American: Ethnicity, Culture, and Identity in Chicano Los Angeles, 1900–1945* by George J. Sánchez. Copyright © 1995 by George J. Sánchez. Used by permission of Oxford University Press, Inc.

The diminished role of organized religion in the day-to-day life of Mexican immigrants was coupled with increased participation in secular activities. In Mexico, most public events in rural villages were organized by the Catholic Church, with few other opportunities outside the family for diversion. Los Angeles, however, offered abundant entertainment of all sorts. These amusements were generally part of a rapidly growing market in leisure which targeted working-class families during the 1920s. Money spent on leisure-time activities easily outstripped donations to the Church, revealing much about the cultural changes occurring in the Mexican immigrant community. Chicano entrepreneurs responded to the emerging ethnic mass market in cultural forms, even though that market was often dominated by outside advertising and controlled primarily by non-Mexicans. Still, the presence of a growing ethnic market in Los Angeles provided room for many traditional practices to continue, some flourishing in the new environment, but most being transformed in the process.

A description of a dancing club frequented by single males during this period indicates the extent of the intermingling between sexes and nationalities in the Plaza, a situation which concerned reformers. Located on Main Street, the club "Latino" was open every night except Sunday from 7:30 p.m. to 1 a.m., although it did most of its business on Saturday night. Inside and out, the hall was illuminated by red, white, and green lights, the colors of the Mexican flag. Entrance to the club cost 25 cents, and tickets were 10 cents apiece to dance with women. The female employees were mostly immigrant Mexicans or Mexican Americans, although Anglo American, Italian, Filipino, Chinese, and Japanese women also were available. The band, however, was made up of black musicians and played only American pieces. Mexican immigrant men, dressed in working-class garb, danced "Mexican style" to the American songs; a ticket was required for every dance; and the women partners earned 5 cents per dance. In one corner of the dance floor a Mexican woman sold sandwiches, tacos, pastries, and coffee.

As Los Angeles Mexicans moved away from the Plaza and the community became more familial in structure, different diversions predominated. Some customs were carried over to marriage from single life. For example, a federal survey reported that three-quarters of Mexican families in Los Angeles continued to spend an average of $14 a year for tobacco. Almost two-thirds read the newspaper on a regular basis. Increasingly Mexican families began to purchase other forms of entertainment which could be enjoyed by all ages and in the confines of one's home. Over one-third of the families in the Los Angeles study owned radios, often buying the equipment "on time" for an average of $27 a year. A smaller number (3%) owned phonographs, and only 4 percent owned musical instruments. Expenditures for vacations, social entertainment (other than movies), and hobbies were rare.

During the 1920s, many American manufacturers and retailers discovered a fairly lucrative market in the local Mexican immigrant community. Despite the clamor for Mexican immigration restrictions, these producers understood that Los Angeles contained a large and growing population of Spanish-speaking immigrants. By 1930, some national products were advertised in the Spanish-language press, and increasingly large distributors sponsored programs in Spanish on the radio. . . .

Many of the mass-produced consumer goods in the 1920s were specifically marketed with an appeal to youth. This appeal had profound consequences for Mexican immigrant families. Older children who entered the work force often earned enough to become more autonomous. Adolescents and young adults were often the first to introduce a Mexican family to certain foods, clothing, or activities that were incompatible with traditional Mexican customs. For example, younger Mexican women began to use cosmetics and wear nylon stockings. Young men were more likely to seek out new leisure-time activities, such as American sports or the movie houses. Second-generation youth were often the first in their families to see a motion picture. At times, experimentation led to intergenerational conflict, with much tension revolving around consumer purchases and the control of earned income.

Despite some initial reservations, most Mexican parents joined other Americans in the 1920s in a love affair with motion pictures. Ninety percent of all families in the Los Angeles survey spent money on the movies, averaging $22 a year per family. In San Diego, a government committee investigating local economic conditions observed that "as in American families, movie tickets were an essential feature of these Mexican families' spending ways except under pressure of a special need for economy." In addition, the committee presumed that some working children retained a portion of their wages to spend on movie tickets.

The movie industry in Los Angeles aided Mexicans in retaining old values, but also played a role in cultural change. On the one hand, films produced in Mexico made their way into the many theatres in the downtown area in the late 1920s catering to the Mexican immigrant population. These supplemented American- and European-made silent films which were aimed by their promoters at an often illiterate immigrant population. Sound was not introduced until 1929, so that throughout the decade of the 1920s, movies stressed visual images and presented few language barriers for the non-English speaker.

Since their inception in the nickelodeons of eastern seaboard cities, American film consistently contained storylines intentionally made for the immigrant masses. Messages tended to be largely populist and democratic in tone. Plots stressed the commonality of all Americans. The children of Mexican immigrants were especially intrigued by the open sexuality depicted on the screen. The experience of sitting alone in a darkened theatre and identifying with screen characters, as Lary May has argued, could feel quite liberating.

What made American-made films even more appealing was the appearance of actors and actresses who were Mexican by nationality. although Ramón Navarro and Lupe Vélez were introduced to audiences in the early twenties, the arrival of Dolores del Río in 1925 brought Mexican immigrants flocking to the box office. The attraction was not simply the desire to support a compatriot; it was also generated by the close proximity of the movie industry. *La Opinión,* for example, the city's leading Spanish-language periodical, regularly followed the Hollywood scene, paying particular attention to the city's rising Latin stars. As citizens of Mexico themselves, the newspaper's editors were quick to condemn stars who distanced themselves from their national origins, while praising others, like del Río, who showed interest in preserving their Mexican identity.

While the motion-picture industry displayed one aspect of the impact of consumerism on immigrant cultural adaptation, opportunities for other entrepreneurs to make an ethnic appeal emerged during this period. Ethnic marketing, usually considered a recent phenomena, in fact has long-standing roots in this era. . . .

* * * *

. . . El Progreso Restaurant on North Main Street, for example, claimed that it cooked food in the "truly Mexican style." Similar restaurants were frequented by the large Mexican male population around the Plaza. Other businesses attempted to bring Mexican products into the Los Angeles market directly. La Tienda Mexicana, on San Fernando Street, carried herbs and cooking supplies which were generally unavailable elsewhere. Down the street, a clothing store, the Sastrería Mexicana, was less successful in its appeal to ethnic taste in dress. It was one thing to continue to put Mexican food in your stomach and quite another to continue to dress in "traditional" Mexican garb on the streets of Los Angeles.

* * * *

Mexican entrepreneurs, however, were not the only individuals in Los Angeles who appealed to the Mexican consumer; non-Mexicans also tried to capitalize on the growing ethnic clientele. Leading this effort was the medical profession, particularly women doctors and physicians from other ethnic groups not likely to develop a following within a highly male-dominated, Anglo Protestant profession. Most of these physicians were located near the Plaza area, particularly along Main Street, an area which provided direct access to the immigrant population. Female physicians held special appeal as specialists for women, capitalizing on the sense of propriety among immigrant women. "Doctora" Augusta Stone, for example, advertised as a specialist for "las señoras," and was among the first to use the phrase "Habla Español" in her advertisements. Dr. Luigi Gardini, an Italian American physician, also advertised in Spanish-language newspapers in 1916. Asian American physicians, however, were the largest group of non-Mexican professionals to appeal to Mexican immigrants, largely stressing their training in herbal medicine, an area not unfamiliar to rural Mexicans. Among them was Dr. Chee, who characterized himself as "Doctor Chino" in 1920, and Dr. Y. Kim, who boasted the combination of a Yale degree and a speciality in Oriental herbal treatments.

The growth and increasing economic stability of the Mexican immigrant community in Los Angeles made these appeals profitable. While the Mexican middle class remained small and relatively insignificant, the large working-class community was quickly developing east of the Los Angeles River. Lack of capital and professional training in the Mexican community made it difficult for most Mexicans to take direct economic advantage of this growth. Yet their cumulative purchasing power did allow for the growth of certain enterprises which catered to the unique backgrounds of Mexican immigrants, while creating new modes of ethnic expression.

One of the most important of these enterprises was music. Although the musical legacies of different regions in Mexico were significant, traditions were both reinforced and transformed in the environment of Los Angeles. As a diverse collection of immigrant musicians arrived from central and northern Mexico, often via south Texas, they stimulated the growth of a recording industry and burgeoning radio network that offered fertile ground for musical innovation.

Of 1,746 Mexican immigrants who began the naturalization procedure, 110 were musicians (6.3% of the total), making them the second largest occupational group in the sample, well behind the category of "common laborer." . . .

Compared with the larger sample of Mexican immigrants, musicians were more likely to have been born in the larger cities of the central plateau in Mexico, particularly Guadalajara and Mexico City. Over 25 percent of Mexican musicians in Los Angeles came from these two cities alone, compared with 10 percent of the entire sample. . . .

The musical traditions brought to the United States from these locales were varied. The mobility within Mexico caused by economic upheaval and violence related to the revolution had pushed many rural residents, including folk musicians, to seek shelter in towns and cities. There, previously isolated folk music traditions from various locations were brought together, and musicians also encountered the more European musical tastes of the urban upper classes. One study of street musicians in Mexico City during the 1920s, for example, found twelve different regional styles performing simultaneously on the corners and in the marketplaces of the capital. One could hear mariachis from Jalisco, *canciones norteñas* from Chihuahua, troubadors from Yucatán, *bandas jarochas* from Veracruz, and marimba groups from Chiapas and Oaxaca.

If there was one particular musical style which stood out from the rest in popularity during this period, it was certainly the *corrido*. A prominent student of this genre has called the *corrido* "an integral part of Mexican life" and the creative period after 1910 its "most glorious epoch." During the Mexican Revolution, almost every important event, and most political leaders and rebels, became the subjects of one or more *corridos*. Pedro J. González, who later emerged as the most well-known Mexican musician in Los Angeles, remembered composing *corridos* with seven other soldiers fighting with Pancho Villa in secluded mountain hideouts during lulls between battles. None was a trained musician, but each used the opportunity to criticize each other jokingly for past misfortunes or to immortalize some heroic deed through song. As these *corridos* made their way into Mexico's urban centers, they were codified and transformed from folk expression to popular songs.

The *corrido*'s continued popularity during the 1920s in areas far away from its folk origins can be explained by particular characteristics of its style which made it appealing as an urban art form. First, the urban *corrido,* like the *canción ranchera,* embodied what was a traditional music style from the countryside, while adapting it to a more commercially oriented atmosphere. It reminded those who had migrated from rural areas of their provincial roots, and gave urban dwellers a connection to the agrarian ideal which was seen as typically Mexican. Second, most *corridos* appealed to a Mexican's nationalist fervor at a time when the pride of Mexican people, places, and events was flourishing. Several observers have identified the period between 1910 and 1940 as one of "national romanticism" in Mexican cultural affairs, extending beyond music to literature and mural painting. *Corridos* produced in the United States often exalted "Mexicanism" at the expense of American culture, but even those composed within Mexico paid inordinate attention to promoting Mexican cultural identity.

Finally, the *corrido* was an exceptionally flexible musical genre which encouraged adapting composition to new situations and surroundings. Melodies, for the most part, were standardized or based on traditional patterns, while text was expected to be continuously improvised. A vehicle for narration, the *corrido* always intended to tell a story to its listeners, one that would not necessarily be news but rather would "interpret, celebrate, and ultimately dignify events already thoroughly familiar to the *corrido* audience." As such, *corrido* musicians were expected to decipher the new surroundings in which Mexican immigrants found themselves while living in Los Angeles. Its relation to the working-class Mexican immigrant audience in Los Angeles was therefore critical to its continued popularity. As one L.A.-based composer explained, "The *corrido* is a narrative viewed through the eyes of the people—its subject almost always follows the truth." This adaptive style was particularly well suited for the rapidly expanding Los Angeles Mexican community in the 1920s and the ever-complex nature of intercultural exchange in the city.

Los Angeles during the 1920s . . ., presented more possibilities for earning a livelihood as a musician than any other location outside of Mexico City, or perhaps San Antonio. To begin with, the Los Angeles metropolitan area contained a huge Spanish-speaking population, second only to Mexico City itself. By 1930 the Chicano population in the city of Los Angeles was larger than any other in the United States. . . . Since most of these residents were recent migrants from Mexico, they often longed for tunes from their homeland. Others had come from south Texas, where the Spanish-language musical tradition was strong and widespread. In fact, one writer claimed in 1932 that more Mexican music had been composed in the United States than in Mexico.

One stimulus to the Mexican music industry was the explosion of Chicano theatre in Los Angeles during the 1920s. Over thirty Chicano playwrights moved to the city during the decade, producing shows ranging from melodrama to vaudeville. The Spanish-speaking population of the region was able to support five major theatre houses from 1918 until the early 1930s: Teatro Hidalgo, Teatro México, Teatro Capitol, Teatro Zendejas (later Novel), and Teatro Principal. In addition to these five which featured programs that changed daily, at least seventeen other theatres housed Spanish-speaking professional companies on a more irregular basis.

Many of these theatres alternated vaudevillian-style shows with Mexican- or Hollywood-made silent films (three shows a day, four on weekends) during the 1920s. Both live performances and silent movies required musical accompaniment. Theatres, therefore, provided relatively stable employment to a diverse collection of musicians throughout the 1920s. The lack of formal training among many of the musicians did not necessarily hamper them, since playing on the streets often helped them prepare for the spontaneity and improvisation required for this type of performance.

A more disparate, yet still lucrative market for Mexican musicians existed among the streets and informal gatherings of Los Angeles. During Mexican patriotic festivals and the Christmas season, musicians had larger audiences, more exposure, and greater potential for earnings. From these "auditions," Mexican groups were often recruited to play for weddings and other ethnic festivities. Moreover, a market for "traditional" Mexican music also existed among some Anglo residents of Los Angeles, often to provide a nostalgic backdrop to the distinctive "Spanish" past of the city. . . .

The emergence of Hollywood as the leading movie-making capital in the United States during the 1920s stimulated a flourishing recording industry in the city that began to rival New York's. Both these developments boded well for Mexican musicians in Los Angeles, although prejudice, union discrimination, and the lack of formal training kept many out of regular employment in the entertainment industries in the western part of town. Still, by providing the music in English-speaking theatres or working as studio musicians, some were able to break into the larger music business in Los Angeles. Even the possibility of such employment—"the dream of a life in Hollywood"—was enough to attract some performers from south of the border.

Thus musicians from Mexico flocked to Los Angeles during the 1920s, becoming a significant segment of the Mexican cultural renaissance of that decade. Unlike the Harlem Renaissance, where black writers and entertainers were often sponsored by white patrons, this Chicano/Mexicano renaissance was largely supported by Mexican immigrants themselves and existed far out of the sight of the majority of Angelinos. The presence of large numbers of Mexican musicians in the city not only preserved the sights and sounds familiar to Mexican immigrants; it also created an environment of cultural experimentation where traditional music was blended with new methods. In short, musicians often served as social interpreters who translated and reflected the cultural adaptations that were taking place among the Mexican immigrant population as a whole. In fact, one astute observer of *corridos* in Los Angeles recognized that this music often served to "sing what they cannot say":

> Mexicans are so intimidated by the government officials, even by social workers, and so timid on account of the language difficulty that it is almost unheard of for a Mexican to express his opinion to an American. Here, however, he is speaking to his own group and an emotional outlet is offered in the writing of *corridos* on the subject so well known to every Mexican. He is reasonably sure that only Mexicans will ever hear his *corrido*.

* * * *

Local ethnic middlemen played an important role in identifying talented musicians and putting them in contact with recording companies. . . . Not only did Calderon [and others] make money by serving as a go-between between American companies and the Mexican artists, but he [and others] also held a monopoly on the area-wide distribution of these recordings through his store[s]. A standard practice of the time for such businesses was to sell phonographs as well as records, and stores . . . profited as well from these items. . . . A small group of men regularly stood in front of the store, listening intently and enjoying the music. Another popular promotion tactic was to give away records with the purchase of a Victrola.

American laws prohibited the importation of records from Mexico, a fact which greatly stimulated the recording industry in Los Angeles. In addition, Mexican companies were not allowed to record in the United States. These restrictions severely crippled the music industry in Mexico, while creating a vast economic opportunity for American companies and ethnic entrepreneurs. When Mexican recordings were finally admitted during the 1950s, interest in immigrant and native-born Spanish-language talent evaporated quickly, and many Chicano musicians were left without an outlet in the recording world. In fact, some labels which had showcased Mexican artists, such as Imperial, began concentrating on black rhythm and blues artists such as Fats Domino and T-Bone Walker.

During the 1920s and 1930s, however, a vibrant environment for Mexican music existed in Los Angeles. Another factor in creating this cultural explosion was the advent of the radio. During the 1920s, commercial radio was still in an experimental era where corporate sponsors and station managers tried to discover how best to make radio broadcasting profitable and enlightening. For most of the decade, the radio was seen as a way of uplifting the masses, of bringing elite American culture into the homes of common laborers. By the end of the decade, however, advertising and corporate economic interests dominated the airwaves. This transformation created a market for Spanish-language broadcasts. Although many Anglo Americans continued to believe that only English should be heard on the nation's airwaves, the goal of reaching Spanish-speaking consumers silenced their opposition.

American radio programmers scheduled Spanish-language broadcasts during "dead" airtime—early morning, late night, or weekend periods which had proven to be unprofitable for English programs. . . . While Anglo Americans were rarely listening at this hour, many Mexican immigrants tuned into . . . broadcasts while they prepared for early morning work shifts. . . .

Corporate radio sponsors in the mid-1920s were quick to understand the profitability of ethnic programs. Large advertisers such as Folgers Coffee used airtime to push their product in the Spanish-speaking market. More often, local businesses appealed to Mexican immigrants to frequent their establishments. In Los Angeles, radio broadcasting soon became a highly competitive industry. By selling blocks of airtime to foreign-language brokers, marginally profitable stations could capture a ready-made market. During the late 1920s, the hours dedicated to Spanish-language broadcasts multiplied. González's program was expanded until 7 a.m., and additional hours were added at lunchtime and in the early evening. Chicano brokers such as Mauricio Calderón profited handsomely as they negotiated with stations, paying them a flat rate during cheap broadcasting time, which they then sold to businesses advertisements.

Key to the success of Spanish-language broadcasting was its appeal to the thousands of working-class Mexican immigrants within the reach of a station's radio signal. Radio, unlike *La Opinión* and other periodicals, reached Mexican immigrants whether or not they could read. In addition, the content of radio programming focused less on the tastes of the expatriate middle class and more on those of the masses. A 1941 analysis of Spanish-language programming found that over 88 percent of on-air time (outside of advertisements) was dedicated to music, with only 4 percent used for news. Programming was dominated by "traditional" music from the Mexican countryside, rather than the orchestral, more "refined" sounds of the Mexican capital and other large urban centers. "The corrido, the shouts, and all that stuff was popular" with working people, remembered González. Although some bemoaned the commercialization of the *corrido* tradition and its removal from its "folk tradition," most Mexican immigrants found this transformation to their liking because it fit well with their own adaptations to urban living.

* * * *

The economic crisis of the 1930s curtailed much of Mexican cultural activity in Los Angeles. First, deportation and repatriation campaigns pushed almost one-third of the Mexican community back to Mexico, effectively restricting the market for Spanish-language advertising campaigns. Second, the enthusiasm of American companies for investing in "experimental" markets that did not insure a steady flow of income understandably cooled. The Mexican immigrant community itself had fewer resources to support cultural activities, given its precarious economic situation. Since expenditures on leisure-time activities were the first to be reduced during times of need, many families cut back drastically on attendance at musical events or the purchase of radios and phonographs. Many theatres in the community shut down during the Great Depression.

Movies and other forms of cheap, cross-cultural entertainment continued to thrive in Depression-era Los Angeles. Simply because of the economics of scale, Hollywood was able to continue to produce entertainment accessible to families at every economic level. In addition, the introduction of sound to motion pictures made it more difficult to sustain a steady Spanish-language audience with Mexican imports, since the Mexican film industry had difficulty throughout the transition of the 1930s. English talking-pictures, on the other hand, had a wider, and therefore more secure audience. The advent of sound coincided with the rise of the second generation of Mexicans in this country, more likely to be as fluent in English as in Spanish. Increasingly, changing demographics and limited economic resources stunted the growth of the ethnic market. A new era in Mexican/Chicano cultural activity began.

Although commercial activity was slowed during the Depression, Mexican cultural life did not die out in Los Angeles. Indeed, aspects of cultural life were altered dramatically, reflecting the changing composition and nature of the Mexican/Chicano community. Musical activity, for example, became less dependent on *corrido* story-telling (which required the ability to understand Spanish lyrics) and more concentrated in dance clubs. La Bamba night club, at Macy and Spring streets, and La Casa Olvera, adjacent to Olvera Street, were only two of many small clubs which opened during the decade. Dancing, of course, did not require a working knowledge of Spanish, and had appeal well beyond the Mexican immigrant population.

Second-generation youth, in particular, flooded the dance clubs during the 1930s. Social commentators of the period commented on the "dance craze" that had seemingly overtaken adolescents and young adults in Mexican American families. One such nineteen-year-old, known only as Alfredo to his interviewer, boastfully explained this "craze":

I love to dance better than anything else in the world. It is something that gets in your blood. Lots of boys are that way. I go to five dances a week. I can't wait for Saturday night because all the time I am thinking of the dance. It is in my system. I could get a job playing my trumpet in an orchestra but then I couldn't dance. I quit school because I got plenty of everything they teach, but dancing.

This new "dance craze" did not often sit well with Mexican immigrant parents. Even when participation was closely chaperoned in school clubs and community centers, public dancing seemed to offend the sensibilities of decency among older Mexicans. Increasingly, however, it became difficult for parents to withstand the effect of peer pressure on their children, as evidenced by the words of one mother in the early 1930s:

Juanita has joined a club and now she wants to learn to dance. That is what comes of these clubs. It is wrong to dance and my Juanita wants to do it because the others do. Because everybody does it does not make it right. I know the things I was taught as a girl and right and wrong cannot change.

* * * *

Appeal to the tastes of youth also created subtle power shifts within the Chicano community. In Mexico, few outlets were available to young people for influencing cultural practices in an individual village or even one's own family. The American metropolis, on the other hand, gave Mexican youth an opportunity to exercise more cultural prerogatives merely by purchasing certain products or going to the movies. Rebellion against family often went hand in hand with a shift toward more American habits. This pattern was stimulated by the extent to which adolescents and unmarried sons and daughters worked and retained some of their own income. As the second generation came to dominate the Chicano population by the late 1930s, their tastes redefined the community's cultural practices and future directions of cultural adaptation.

Behind the vast American commercial network lay an enterprising group of ethnic entrepreneurs who served as conduits between the Mexican immigrant population and the corporate world. These individuals were often the first to recognize cultural changes and spending patterns among the immigrant population. . . . Although they found tangible financial rewards in their efforts, they also served an important role in redefining Mexican culture in an American urban environment.

FURTHER READING

Rodolfo Acuna, *Occupied America: A History of Chicanos* (1981).

Thomas Archdeacon, *Becoming American: An Ethnic History* (1983).

Ronald Bayor, *Neighbors in Conflict: The Irish, Germans, Jews, and Italians of New York City, 1929–1941* (1978).

John Bodnar, Roger Simon, and Michael P. Weber, *Lives of Our Own: Blacks, Italians, and Poles in Pittsburgh, 1900–1960* (1982).

Al Camarillo, *Chicanos in a Changing Society: From Mexican Pueblos to American Barrios in Santa Barbara and Southern California, 1848–1930* (1979).

Lawrence Cardoso, *Mexican Emigration to the United States* (1980).

Sucheng Chan, *Asian Americans: An Interpretive History* (1990).

Richard B. Craig, *The Bracero Program* (1971).

Roger Daniels, *Asian America: The Chinese and Japanese in the US Since 1950* (1988).

Chris Friday, *Organizing Asian American Labor: The Pacific Coast Canned Salmon Industry, 1870–1942* (1994).

Manuel Gamio, *Life Story of the Mexican Immigrant* (1931).

Juan Ramon Garcia, *Operation Wetback: The Mass Deportation of Mexican Undocumented Workers in 1954* (1980).

Mario T. Garcia, *Desert Immigrants: The Mexicans of El Paso* (1981).

Gilbert G. Gonzalez, *Labor and Community: Mexican Citrus Worker Villages in a Southern California County, 1900–1950* (1994).

Marilyn Halter, *Between Race and Ethnicity: Cape Verdean American Immigrants, 1860–1965* (1993).

Brian Masaru Hayashi, *For the Sake of Our Japanese Brethren: Assimilation, Nationalism, and Protestantism Among the Japanese of Los Angeles* (1995).

Henry Kitano, *Japanese Americans* (1969).

Carey McWilliams, *Factories in the Fields: The Story of Migratory Farm Labor in California* (1939).

Carey McWilliams, *North from Mexico: The Spanish Speaking People in the United States* (1949).

John Modell, *The Economics and Politics of Racial Accommodation: The Japanese of Los Angeles, 1900–1942* (1977).

David Montejano, *Anglos and Mexicans in the Making of Texas, 1836–1986* (1987).

Alixi Naff, *Becoming American: The Early Arab Immigrant Experience* (1985).

June Namias, *First Generation: In the Words of Twentieth Century American Immigrants* (1978).

Victor Nee and Bret de Bary, *Longtime Californ': A Documentary History of an American Chinatown* (1973).

Mark Reisler, *By the Sweat of Their Brow: Mexican Immigrant Labor in the US, 1900–1940* (1976).

George Sánchez, *Becoming Mexican American: Ethnicity and Acculturation in Chicano Los Angeles, 1900–1943* (1989).

Paul C. P. Siu, *The Chinese Laundryman: A Study of Social Isolation* (edited by John Tchen) (1953).

Shin-Shan Henry Tsai, *The Chinese Experience in America* (1986).

Zaragosa Vargas, *Proletarians of the North: A History of Mexican Industrial Workers in Detroit and the Midwest, 1917–1933* (1993).

Renqiu Yu, *To Save China, To Save Ourselves: The Chinese Hand Laundry Alliance of New York* (1992).

CHAPTER
12

Immigrants and Ethnics Amid Depression and War, 1929–1965

The Great Depression, World War II, and the Cold War that ensued following the war's conclusion were powerful forces that altered American life. It is not surprising, then, that they also profoundly influenced the nature of immigration and the debates in the United States about immigrants. The levels of immigration were significantly reduced early in this era as a result of economic dearth and the restrictive clauses of the National Origins Act of 1924. But the traumas of world depression followed world war, and the specter of nuclear holocaust in this period introduced new issues, new classes of immigrants, and new approaches to the meaning of immigration that would have powerful repercussions in the periods to follow. In all of these areas, the role of the national state, for better or worse, was enlarged.

In reacting to these national and international pressures, the American policy toward immigration was a curious combination of explicit humanitarianism and seemingly cruel national policy. The economic shock of the Great Depression resulted not only in the programs to redress its difficulties embodied in the New Deal, but in the forced repatriation to Mexico between 1929 and 1937 of some 500,000 Mexicans then living in the United States. As relief agencies found it increasingly difficult to dispense aid to people suffering from the depression, they gave many Mexicans living in the United States the unenviable choice of accepting train tickets to be repatriated or being denied any further assistance if they remained. Illegal immigrants were denied assistance as a matter of policy and often threatened with deportation if they did not leave voluntarily. As much of the world was going to war in the 1930s, the question of creating opportunities for refugees fleeing persecution arose. Upwards of 250,000 refugees fled to the United States between 1934 and 1941, but the journey was often difficult, and the United States was often not as welcoming as it might have been: All refugees arrived under existing quota laws. The most poignant example perhaps was the congressional joint resolutions that proposed admitting 10,000 German refugee orphans, many of them Jewish, above the German national quota in 1939, when state-sanctioned anti-Semitic violence in Nazi Germany was accelerating. Congress failed to pass the resolutions, and it was left to President Roosevelt to

*use his executive power to admit refugees. Once the United States entered World
War II, the nation forced Japanese Americans into relocation camps beginning
in 1942 and repealed the Chinese Exclusion Act a year later. Because China was
an ally of the United States and Japan was its enemy, the American government
sought to assuage its embarrassment at discriminatory policies aimed at China
while it forced Japanese Americans, many of whom were American citizens, into
detention camps in the alleged interest of American security. Although some
German Americans and Italian Americans were detained in the interest of the
war effort, in such cases the detentions were not so widespread nor were they
group-based. The era following the war was marked by another episode of
refugee crisis, as millions of people throughout the world had been displaced.
The U.S. government responded with legislation to enable "displaced persons"
to immigrate to the United States, thereby increasing the importance of the category of the refugee in immigration policy. In the aftermath of Nazism and the
rise of the Soviet Union, many Americans reexamined the gap between the reality and the rhetoric in opportunity and equality in the United States generally
and in American race relations in particular. Hoping to distance themselves
from Nazism and Communism, Americans celebrated the possibilities of the
"American way of life" as they called for greater activism in the institutions of
the society and the state to redress the realities of inequality and lack of equitable economic opportunity.*

D O C U M E N T S

The following five documents illustrate the dramatic changes for immigrants and
members of many ethnic groups between 1929 and 1965 in response to world events
and federal immigration policy. They show how new categories of "refugee" and "illegal immigrant" became increasingly important in the nomenclature of immigration as
the world became embroiled in war and as the U.S. government became increasingly
activist in addressing immigration issues. The first selection is a series of accounts
from official and personal perspectives documenting the repatriation of Mexicans in
the 1930s. The second document is part of the testimony before the House Committee
on Immigration and Naturalization in 1939; it describes the condition of Jews in Germany and pleads for the admission of 10,000 German orphan children. Next, a Japanese American woman remembers the outbreak of World War II in the United States
and the circumstances leading up to the Japanese relocation in 1942. Fourth, a Greek
American (1949) recounts grisly incidents of life under, and his escape from, Communist regimes in Greece following World War II. The final document (1956) exemplifies
one intellectual approach of the period. Will Herberg, an eminent sociologist, describes the "American way of life," an artifact from the post–World War II era that celebrates an overarching sense of unity for many of the constituent religious groups in
the United States.

Documents and Reminiscences Recall the Mexican Repatriation in the 1930s

[seal of the Mexican Consulate in San Diego, Cal.]

Re: Repatriation of Mexicans Aboard Transport "Progreso."

San Diego, California

August 11, 1932

Sir

The Government of Mexico, with the cooperation and aid of the Welfare Committee of this Country, will effect the repatriation of all Mexicans who currently reside in this County and who might wish to return to their country. . . .

Those persons who are repatriated will be able to choose among the States of Sonora, Sinaloa, Nayarit, Jalisco, Michoacán, and Guanajuato as the place of their final destination, with the understanding that the Government of Mexico will provide them with lands for agricultural cultivation . . . and will aid them in the best manner possible so that they might settle in the country.

Those persons who take part in this movement of repatriation may count on free transportation from San Diego to the place where they are going to settle, and they will be permitted to bring with them their furniture, household utensils, agricultural implements, and whatever other objects for personal use they might possess.

Since the organization and execution of a movement of repatriation of this nature implies great expenditures, this Consulate encourages you . . . to take advantage of this special opportunity being offered to you for returning to Mexico at no cost whatever and so that . . . you might dedicate all your energies to your personal improvement, that of your family, and that of our country.

If you wish to take advantage of this opportunity, please return this letter . . . with the understanding that, barring notice to the contrary from this Consulate, you should present yourself with your family and your luggage on the municipal dock of this port on the 23rd of this month before noon.

★ ★ ★ ★

Effective Suffrage. No Reelection.
Consul.
Armando C. Amador.

As found in Francisco Balderrama and Raymond Rodríguez, *Decade of Betrayal: Mexican Repatriation in the 1930s* (Albuquerque: University of New Mexico Press, 1995).

Repatriation Train Trip. Lucas Lucio.

Source: Interview with Lucas Lucio. Courtesy of Lucas Lucio.

At the station in Santa Ana, hundreds of Mexicans came and there was quite a lot of crying. The men were pensive and the majority of the children and mothers were crying.

When they arrived at Los Angeles, the repatriates were calmed a bit because they were in Los Angeles . . . from Los Angeles to El Paso, some sang with guitars trying to forget their sadness and others cried. [Consul] Hill spoke very little, was very sad . . . the crying and singing. No one had any desire to speak. Varela [Orange County Department of Charities employee] tried to lift spirits and tried to converse.

The train did not arrive at the station in El Paso but rather at the border. There was a terrible cry . . . many did not want to cross the border because many had daughters and sons who had stayed . . . married to others here who did not want to return to Mexico. A disaster because the majority of the families were separated. There was no way for anyone to try [to] leave the train or run or complete their desire to return to the United States.

* * * *

Voluntary
Repatriation in Chihuahua

From Vice Consul
[signature]
Robert K. Peyton
Chihuahua, Mexico.
Date of Completion: March 19, 1939.
Date of Mailing: March 19, 1939

APPROVED:
[signature]
Lee R. Blohm
American Consul

. . . Up to this time only a few scattering families have returned to this district to live and many of these have been unable to locate themselves happily; in fact a certain percentage of them has [*sic*] even attempted to return to the United States to take up residence there again. . . .

While sympathetic with the idea in a general way, the Mexican citizens, particularly big ranchers, do not believe that there is sufficient land available in the State to bring in a large body of migrant farmers. Employers of labor in the various mining centers likewise do not believe that their industries can absorb more labor just at this time, their businesses being somewhat discouraged by the unfriendly attitude of the national administration toward capital and investment.

* * * *

Trying to Survive in Mexico. Teresa Martínez Southard.

Source: Christine Valenciana Interview with Teresa Martínez Southard.
Courtesy of Teresa Martínez Southard.

So we stayed with my aunt. . . . we just had one bedroom for all of us. Since it was still summer time when we arrived that of having only one bedroom didn't bother us too much. So with the warm weather and we couldn't fit in that one bedroom, we slept outdoors.

While we were living with my aunt she would make those corn tortillas. They looked good, but I didn't like them. . . .

Everything was so different. I wasn't used to this life. It was so tough on me.

I used to play baseball with my high heels on. I wore them when I carried water . . . . The people didn't like the way I dressed. They didn't like for us to wear lipstick, rouge, or anything.

I would always say, oh what if I could go back to my country, again . . . I always had intentions of going back home.

Congressional Testimony Advocating Resolutions to Admit German Refugee Children, 1939

The proposal before you is a very simple one. It is a grant of authority under specified conditions—and nothing more. Under its terms authority is granted to admit into the United States not more than 10,000 German children, in excess of the present quota, during each of the calendar years 1939 and 1940. No child shall be eligible for admission who is over 14 years of age, and no child may be admitted unless satisfactory assurance shall have been given by responsible private individuals or by responsible private organizations that the child will not become a public charge. This is the whole proposal—a grant of authority, to the extent that satisfactory assurances are given, permitting, as an emergency matter, the rescue from Germany of a limited number of children of tender years.

The need for this measure is overwhelming. A catastrophe has occurred. Unlike such catastrophes as fire or earthquake or tidal wave, which have commanded the help of America to unfortunates abroad so often in the past, this catastrophe threatens not only death, but a living death, to thousands and thousands of children.

During my stay in Germany there was brough[t] home to me, . . . the appalling extent of this catastrophe and the unbelievable consequences to the innocent child victims. . . .

. . . its intensity and reality can be visualized only if you compare the normal life of a normal child with the life of a rejected child in Germany today. Let us look at that life as it goes on from day to day at this very time. The child cannot go

As found in "Admission of German Refugee Children," *Hearings Before the Committee on Immigration and Naturalization, House of Representatives*, 1939.

to the State schools. Lacking a school, he also lacks all of the legitimate outlets for play. The parks are closed to him. He walks on the street only at the risk of being taunted or spat on by other children or perhaps beaten by his elders. Even in his home the tension and pressure of the environment are upon him. There is the ever present menace of the concentration camp for his father or his older brother. The child's father, a hunted man, sleeps first in one secret place, and then another, but rarely at home. There is the crashing of glass at any time of the day or night when the neighboring rowdies choose to throw stones through the windows. There is terror at a mere knock on the door. And over and around the child and ever present to him is the shattering anxiety of his parents, upon whom he has been accustomed to rely and whose present insecurity invades his life at every point and threatens to destroy the essential security which must be his. And beyond all this terror and insult, his parents have lost their means of livelihood, his family has been put out of their home and crowded into a small, unheated room, wondering how they will eat when the last bit of furniture is sold. This is the daily life of those children in Germany whom the present regime has elected to disinherit.

. . . At the time of the November 10 excesses, masses of men were thrown into concentration camps; estimates have run as high as 35,000 during that period alone. Furthermore, the extreme German laws have led to hundreds and hundreds of divorces where Aryans and non-Aryans have been married. In addition, there is the terrible fact of suicide. An undertaker in Vienna told me after the annexation of Austria that while before that time his average rate of burials was 5 a week, after the annexation the rate increased to 140 per week. The children of families, thus rent asunder by concentration camp, divorce, and suicide, are dependent in many instances upon crumbs from the neighbors' tables, surreptitiously given.

This is the situation as it exists in Germany today. The need is almost beyond description. If you would measure that need, I would request you only to visualize your own children in the situation which I have described and to ask yourself whether you too would not be willing, even eager, to have your children go elsewhere for a haven.

* * * *

The purpose underlying the proposal has a fundamental and universal appeal. At a time when age-old standards have been called into question, it is the children who still represent the essential human hope. That hope, a universal expression of the human spirit, transcends national and group lines. In the deepest sense, we affirm and reaffirm our faith in the future so long as we are willing to assume responsibility for, and to give of ourselves for the benefit of, the children of our time. The proposal, however, is something more. It is, I maintain, especially appropriate that the United States should play its part in the work of rescuing these children. It was here that public education was first viewed as a public necessity. It was here that principles of toleration were early adopted as the law of the land. It is, therefore, fitting and proper that the great democracy should evince particular interest in extending hospitality to the children who have been cast out and have been made wanderers on the face of the earth. I say, then, that the purpose of this bill is first to symbolize our hopes by aiding these children and second, to permit us to live out, in kindness and generosity, the principles which we have always regarded as basic to our society.

* * * *

That there is every likelihood that most of the children can be placed in excellent free homes is already apparent to us. There will be presented to your committee hundreds of offers to receive these children, constituting a part of the offers which have already been received without solicitation by various organizations. These offers, I understand, have come from more than 40 States, and from Jewish, Protestant, and Catholic homes. It thus becomes apparent that a very large proportion of these children can be place[d] in splendid homes among people sufficiently eager to receive them so that they have not even waited for the passage of the bill to make their desires known. . . .

Yoshiko Uchida, a Japanese American Woman, Remembers Her Family's Relocation During World War II, 1942

By the end of February my father's letters and telegrams began to reflect his growing concern [about mass evacuation].

. . . None of us could believe such an unthinkable event would actually take place. Gradually, however, we began to prepare for its possibility. One night a friend came to see us as we were packing our books in a large wood crate.

"What on earth are you doing?" he asked incredulously. "There won't be any evacuation. How could the United States government intern its own citizens? It would be unconstitutional."

But only a few weeks later, we were to discover how wrong he was. . . . On the nineteenth of [February 1942], President Roosevelt issued Executive Order 9066, authorizing the secretary of war and his military commanders to prescribe areas from which "any or all persons may be excluded." Although use of the word "Japanese" was avoided in this order, it was directed solely at people of Japanese ancestry. The fact that there was no mass removal of persons of German or Italian descent, even though our country was also at war with Germany and Italy, affirmed the racial bias of this directive.

By the middle of March, Lieutenant General John L. DeWitt began to execute the order and set in motion the removal from Military Area Number One, along the entire West Coast, of over 120,000 men, women, and children of Japanese ancestry, the majority of whom were American citizens. From his later testimony at a House Naval Affairs Sub-committee on Housing (April 13, 1943), it is apparent that he performed this task with undisguised enthusiasm. He is quoted as having said, "It makes no difference whether the Japanese is theoretically

From Yoshiko Uchida, *Desert Exile*. Copyright © 1982 by Yoshiko Uchida. Reprinted by permission of The Bancroft Library, University of California, Berkeley.

a citizen. He is still a Japanese. Giving him a scrap of paper won't change him. I don't care what they do with the Japs so long as they don't send them back here. A Jap is a Jap."

With such a man heading the Western Defense Command, it is not surprising that no time was lost in carrying out the evacuation order.

Both the Fifth and Fourteenth Amendments to the Constitution providing for "due process of law" and "equal protection under the law for all citizens," were flagrantly ignored in the name of military expediency, and the forced eviction was carried out purely on the basis of race.

Stunned by this unprecedented act of our government, we Nisei were faced with the anguishing dilemma of contesting our government's orders and risking imprisonment (as a few courageous Nisei did) or of complying with the government edict.

* * * *

My sister and I were angry that our country could deprive us of our civil rights in so cavalier a manner, but we had been raised to respect and to trust those in authority. To us resistance or confrontation, such as we know them today, was unthinkable and of course would have had no support from the American public. We naively believed at the time that cooperating with the government edict was the best way to help our country.

* * * *

Each day we watched the papers for the evacuation orders covering the Berkeley area. On April 21, the headlines read: "Japs Given Evacuation Orders Here." I felt numb as I read the front page story. "Moving swiftly, without any advance notice, the Western Defense Command today ordered Berkeley's estimated 1,319 Japanese, aliens and citizens alike, evacuated to the Tanforan Assembly Center by noon, May 1." (This gave us exactly ten days' notice.) "Evacuees will report at the Civil Control Station being set up in Pilgrim Hall of the First Congregational Church . . . between the hours of 8:00 A.M. and 5:00 P.M. next Saturday and Sunday."

This was Exclusion Order Number Nineteen, which was to uproot us from our homes and send us into the Tanforan Assembly Center in San Bruno, a hastily converted racetrack.

All Japanese were required to register before the departure date. . . . From that day on we became Family Number 13453.

* * * *

Because our family had always been close, it wasn't too difficult for us to adjust to living at such close quarters. For other families, however, the tensions of one-room living proved more destructive. Many children drifted away from their parents, rarely bothering to spend time in their own barracks, even eating all their meals with friends at other mess halls. The concept of family was rapidly breaking down, adding to the growing misery of life in camp.

* * * *

As time went on, the residents of Topaz [relocation camp] began to release their frustrations on each other in acts that seemed foreign to the Japanese nature. In communities where they had lived prior to the war, most of them had been respectable, hardworking people. . . . but the corrosive nature of life in camp seemed to bring out the worst in many people, provoking them into doing things they probably would not have done outside.

Nicholas Gage, a Greek Refugee, Recounts His Escape from His Homeland, 1949

. . . on March 3, 1949. My three sisters and I had passage on the *Marine Carp,* a converted American troop carrier pressed into service as a passenger liner after World War II. I was traveling with my oldest sister, Olga, twenty, my second sister, Kanta, sixteen, and my fourth sister, Fotini, ten. Our third sister, Glykeria, fifteen, was missing behind the Iron Curtain, perhaps dead. She had been left behind with our mother. After *Mana*'s [his mother] execution, our sister was driven at gunpoint into Albania with the rest of the villagers by the retreating Communist guerrillas. Now we had no idea where she was.

Although I had lost my mother, the only parent I had ever known, we weren't really orphans, because we had a father in America. . . . Now we would set sail for a country that had always seemed as remote and mythological to us as Atlantis.

Mana used to read us letters from this father who sold fruit and vegetables in Worcester, Massachusetts, and was considered an American millionaire by all the village. He had left Greece for America in 1910, a boy of seventeen with $20 in his pocket, and returned to take a bride in 1926. My absentee father's American citizenship and rumored fortune created envy among the villagers, who referred to my mother as the *Amerikana,* although she herself had never traveled more than fifty miles from her birthplace.

There were times during my first nine years when I was secretly proud of my unknown father's wealth and status, but more frequently I resented him because of his absence and the embarrassment his nationality caused me. Being the son of an American "capitalist" often made me the scapegoat of village boys who had absorbed the propaganda of the Communist guerrillas. When blockades and the shortages of World War II brought famine and we were weak from malnutrition and rickets, searching the ground for weeds to eat and surviving on the scant ration of flour that my grandfather, a miller, grudgingly gave us, I blamed my father for not bringing us to America to join him.

In the brief period of peace between the end of the European war and the outbreak of the Greek civil war in late 1946, *Mana* wrote, begging her husband to fin-

Excerpts from *A Place For Us.* Copyright © 1989 by Nicholas Gage. Reprinted by permission of Houghton Mifflin Company. All rights reserved.

ish filing our papers so that we could emigrate at once, but he hesitated, worried about the risks of bringing adolescent daughters to a worldly place like America. "You have no idea how free the girls are here, running with strangers from an early age . . . ," he wrote. He ordered my mother to arrange a match for Olga, my oldest sister, with a man of good name, and then he would bring us.

But then it was too late. In the fall of 1947 Greek Communist guerrillas occupied the northern Greek villages where we lived. All the men, including my grandfather . . . fled the mountains to avoid being conscripted, leaving the women and children behind. *Mana* wrote to her husband for advice, and he counseled her to stay and guard the house and property. She had survived the invasions of the Italians and the Germans, he wrote; certainly she had much less to fear from fellow Greeks, who were only fighting for their rights.

My mother was an obedient peasant woman who never spoke to a man outside her family until she was betrothed at the age of eighteen to a visiting American fourteen years her senior. She had been brought up to follow men's orders. When the guerrillas came, she gave them our food without complaint and went on daily work details to help build fortifications and carry the wounded. She didn't object when they demanded our house for their headquarters and prison, but simply moved us into her parents' hut. Although the guerrillas and her neighbors made her the object of special indignities because she was the rich *Amerikana,* she remained obedient and uncomplaining.

It was when the guerrillas demanded that she hand over her children that Eleni Gatzoyiannis finally chose to defy them.

In the spring of 1948 the guerrillas held a compulsory meeting in our village to announce that all children from three to fourteen would be taken to camps in Eastern Europe, where they would be reared and educated as Communists. They set out a table of food before the starving villagers, saying that any children whose parents volunteered them would immediately be fed. But despite the cries of their famished children, most of the mothers refused.

Then one day, hiding in my grandmother's bean field, I overheard two guerrilla officers say that all the children, volunteered or not, would be taken by force. When I ran to tell my mother, she chose defiance for the first time in her life and began to plan the escape that ended with her imprisonment, torture, and execution.

As I stood on the dock in Piraeus, I blamed my father for contributing to her death; if only he had moved faster, he could have brought us out during the brief peacetime in 1946 and we would be whole, living in America as a family. Now we were torn apart. My mother's bullet-riddled body had been tossed into a shallow mass grave with other victims and found months later by my grandfather, who interred her remains in the churchyard near the ruins of our house. My fifteen-year-old sister Glykeria was lost to us behind the Iron Curtain. My other three sisters and I were still together, thanks to my mother's courage and love, but we were penniless, owning no more than a change of clothes, and we were about to leave our homeland, cross an ocean to a strange country where no one spoke our language, and live with a father whom I had never seen but had always thought of with a mixture of love, longing, and anger.

If he really loved us, I thought, he would have taken us with him to America at the beginning, instead of leaving his young bride in Greece and returning every few years to visit. When he left Greece for the last time in late 1938, as the clouds of war gathered over Europe, neither Christos Gatzoyiannis nor his wife, Eleni, knew that she was carrying the son they both had prayed for while suffering the births of four daughters.

Even when he learned that his wife had been murdered and his children were living in a refugee camp, Father still had vacillated about sending for us. He wrote asking whether we would prefer to make our home in the village with our grandparents, go to Athens to live with our cousins, or join him in America. But our answer was quick and unanimous, because we remembered so clearly what our mother said on the day she told us goodbye, as the Communist guerrillas took her away to thresh wheat. She promised she would try to escape on her own with Glykeria and find us, but, she told Olga fiercely, "If we don't, I want you to telegraph your father and tell him to get you out to America as soon as possible. Your grandfather will try to talk you into staying behind. My parents only want someone to stay in Greece and care for them in their old age. But whether I'm living or dead, I won't rest until you're all in America and safe."

Then came the moment when she said goodbye to me and was led away down the mountain by the guerrillas until she disappeared into the distance, turning once to raise her hand in farewell. Nearly the last thing she told me and my sister Kanta was, "Remember this: anyone who stays in Greece, who doesn't go to America, will have my curse. When you leave the house tonight, I want you to throw a black stone behind you so you'll never come back."

With our mother's parting words vivid in our memory and the threat of her everlasting curse hanging over us, there was no way we would succumb to the pleas and threats of our grandfather to stay behind. "In America the smoke from the factories is so thick it blocks out the sky. You'll never feel the sun on your faces again," he warned. "You'll never eat olive oil, feta cheese, or lamb again. It's a country filled with foreigners. You'll wind up marrying Italians, or worse."

But we refused to listen to him as he escorted us from the refugee camp in northern Greece to Athens, leading us through the formalities at the American Embassy, where we got our passport—issued in the name of Olga, who was the only one over eighteen. And on that day, as the ship's launch drew near, the old man sulked, refusing to join us in our last portrait as Greeks.

An Eminent Sociologist Analyzes the "American Way of Life," 1956

What . . . is the "common religion" of the American people, as it may be inferred not only from their words but also from their behavior?

From *Protestant Catholic Jew* by Will Herberg. Copyright © 1956 by Will Herberg. Used by permission of Doubleday, a division of Bantam Doubleday Dell Publishing Group, Inc.

It seems to me that a realistic appraisal of the values, ideas, and behavior of the American people leads to the conclusion that Americans, by and large, do have their "common religion" and that that "religion" is the system familiarly known as the American Way of Life. It is the American Way of Life that supplies American society with an "overarching sense of unity" amid conflict. It is the American Way of Life about which Americans are admittedly and unashamedly "intolerant." It is the American Way of Life that provides the framework in terms of which the crucial values of American existence are couched. By every realistic criterion the American Way of Life is the operative faith of the American people.

* * * *

The American Way of Life is the symbol by which Americans define themselves and establish their unity. German unity, it would seem, is felt to be largely racial-folkish, French unity largely cultural; but neither of these ways is open to the American people, the most diverse in racial and cultural origins of any in the world. As American unity has emerged, it has emerged more and more clearly as a unity embodied in, and symbolized by, the complex structure known as the American Way of Life.

If the American Way of Life had to be defined in one word, "democracy" would undoubtedly be the word, but democracy in a peculiarly American sense. On its political side it means the Constitution; on its economic side, "free enterprise"; on its social side, an equalitarianism which is not only compatible with but indeed actually implies vigorous economic competition and high mobility. Spiritually, the American Way of Life is best expressed in a certain kind of "idealism" which has come to be recognized as characteristically American. It is a faith that has its symbols and its rituals, its holidays and its liturgy, its saints and its sancta; and it is a faith that every American, to the degree that he is an American, knows and understands.

The American Way of Life is individualistic, dynamic, pragmatic. It affirms the supreme value and dignity of the individual; it stresses incessant activity on his part, for he is never to rest but is always to be striving to "get ahead"; it defines an ethic of self-reliance, merit, and character, and judges by achievement: "deeds, not creeds" are what count. The American Way of Life is humanitarian, "forward looking," optimistic. Americans are easily the most generous and philanthropic people in the world, in terms of their ready and unstinting response to suffering anywhere on the globe. The American believes in progress, in self-improvement, and quite fanatically in education. But above all, the American is idealistic. Americans cannot go on making money or achieving worldly success simply on its own merits; such "materialistic" things must, in the American mind, be justified in "higher" terms, in terms of "service" or "stewardship" or "general welfare." Because Americans are so idealistic, they tend to confuse espousing an ideal with fulfilling it and are always tempted to regard themselves as good as the ideals they entertain: hence the amazingly high valuation most Americans quite sincerely place on their own virtue. And because they are so idealistic, Americans tend to be moralistic: they are inclined to see all issues as plain and simple, black and white, issues of morality. Every struggle in which they are seriously engaged becomes a "crusade." . . .

* * * *

The reciprocal action of the American Way of Life in shaping and reshaping the historic faiths of Christianity and Judaism on American soil is perhaps more readily discerned. By and large, we may say that these historic religions have all tended to become "Americanized" under the pervasive influence of the American environment. This "Americanization" has been the product not so much of conscious direction as of a "diffuse convergence" operating spontaneously in the context of the totality of American life. What it has brought, however, is none the less clear: "religious groupings throughout [American] society [have been] stamped with recognizably 'American' qualities" to an extent indeed where foreign observers sometimes find the various American religions more like each other than they are like their European counterparts.

Under the influence of the American environment the historic Jewish and Christian faiths have tended to become secularized in the sense of becoming integrated as parts within a larger whole defined by the American Way of Life. "There is a marked tendency," [Robin M.] Williams writes in his discussion of the relations of religion to other institutions in the United States, "to regard religion as a good because it is useful in furthering other major values—in other words, to reverse the ends-means relation implied in the conception of religion as an ultimate value." In this reversal the Christian and Jewish faiths tend to be prized because they help promote ideals and standards that all Americans are expected to share on a deeper level than merely "official" religion. Insofar as any reference is made to the God in whom all Americans "believe" and of whom the "official" religions speak, it is primarily as sanction and underpinning for the supreme values of the faith embodied in the American Way of Life. Secularization of religion could hardly go further.

Denominational pluralism, as the American idea of the church may be called, obviously implies that no church can look to the state for its members or support. Voluntarism and evangelism are thus the immediate consequences of the American idea: for their maintenance, for their very existence, churches must depend on the voluntary adherence of their members, and they are therefore moved to pursue a vigorous evangelistic work to win people to their ranks. The accommodation of the church to American reality extends even to its inner polity. "As the polity of the Roman church followed the pattern of the Roman empire," H. Richard Niebuhr points out, "so the American churches incline to organize themselves [along representative lines] in conformity with the system of state and national legislatures and executives." Even the Roman Catholic Church, with its fixed hierarchical structure, has not been totally immune to American influence of this kind.

The denominational idea is fundamental to American thinking about religion, but it is not the last word. Americans think of their various churches as denominations, but they also feel that somehow the denominations fall into larger wholes which we have called religious communities. This kind of denominational aggregation is, of course, something that pertains primarily to Protestantism and to a lesser degree to Judaism; both have more or less organized denominations which, taken together, form the religious communities. Catholicism, on the other hand, has no such overt inner divisions, but American Catholics readily understand the phenomenon when they see it among Protestants and Jews. Denominations are felt to be somehow a matter of individual preference, and movement between denominations is not uncommon; the religious community, on the other hand, is taken as something more objective and given, something in which, by and large, one is born, lives, and dies, something that (to recall our earlier analysis) identifies and defines one's position in American society. Since the religious community in its present form is a recent social emergent, its relations to the denominations properly so-called are still relatively fluid and undefined but the main lines of development would seem to be fairly clear.

When the plurality of denominations comprehended in religious communities is seen from the standpoint of the "common faith" of American society, what emerges is the conception of the three "communions"—Protestantism, Catholicism, Judaism—as three diverse, but equally legitimate, equally American, expressions of an over-all American religion, standing for essentially the same "moral ideals" and "spiritual values." This conception, whatever may be thought of it theologically, is in fact held, though hardly in explicit form, by many devout and religiously sophisticated Americans. It would seem to be the obvious meaning of the title, *The Religions of Democracy,* given to a recent authoritative statement of the Protestant, Catholic, and Jewish positions. "Democracy" apparently has its religions which fall under it as species fall under the genus of which they are part. And in this usage "democracy" is obviously a synonym for the American Way of Life.

ESSAYS

These two essays illustrate the curiously divergent responses in the United States as the nation dealt with the war and its aftermath. In the first essay, historian Roger Daniels of the University of Cincinnati explores the events leading up to the relocation of Japanese Americans to detention camps in 1942. He describes the panic on the American West Coast that, when combined with a long-standing prejudice against the Japanese, was a dangerous mix for Japanese Americans. Despite protests by the Japanese American community, relocation was ordered in February of 1942. Significantly, Daniels argues that whereas "racial guilt" was not applied to Americans of German or Italian descent, it was employed with regard to Japanese Americans. For Europeans, he writes, guilt was individual, but for Asians it was collective. In contrast, historian Philip Gleason of Notre Dame University argues that World War II forced Americans to grapple with the failings of the United States. As part of what Gleason calls a "great ideological awakening," Americans were compelled not only to revisit the concept of the American identity in relation to their shortcomings as a nation but to contrast their ideological values with Nazism. As a result, they often focused on abstract values of "what America stands for." Because these values were abstract, Gleason argues, they could be attached to [almost] any ethnic group. Thus, as they battled against intolerance, Americans exalted diversity. Ironically, as Americans were verifying their national identity, they were affirming a cultural pluralism.

World War II and the Forced Relocation of Japanese Americans

ROGER DANIELS

As is well known, despite decades of propaganda and apprehension about a Pacific war, the reality, the dawn attack at Pearl Harbor on Sunday, December 7, 1941, came as a stunning surprise to most Americans. Throughout the nation the typical reaction was disbelief, followed by a determination to close ranks and avenge a disastrous defeat. Faced with the fact of attack, the American people entered the war with perhaps more unity than has existed before or since. But if a calm determination to get on with the job typified the national mood, the mood of the Pacific Coast was nervous and trigger-happy, if not hysterical. A thousand movies and stories and reminiscences have recorded the solemnity with which the nation reacted to that "day of infamy" in 1941. Yet, at Gilmore Field, in Los Angeles, 18,000 spectators at a minor league professional football game between the Hollywood Bears and the Columbus Bulldogs "jumped to their feet and cheered wildly when the public address system announced that a state of war existed between Japan and the United States."

The state's leading paper, the Los Angeles *Times* (Dec. 8, 1941), quickly announced that California was "a zone of danger" and invoked the ancient vigilante tradition of the West by calling for

> alert, keen-eyed civilians [who could be] of yeoman service in cooperating with the military authorities against spies, saboteurs and fifth columnists. We have thousands of Japanese here. . . . Some, perhaps many, are . . . good Americans. What the rest may be we do not know, nor can we take a chance in the light of yesterday's demonstration that treachery and double-dealing are major Japanese weapons.

Day after day, throughout December, January, February, and March, almost the entire Pacific Coast press (of which the *Times* was a relatively restrained example) spewed forth racial venom against all Japanese. The term Jap, of course, was standard usage. Japanese, alien and native-born, were also "Nips," "yellow men," "Mad dogs," and "yellow vermin," to name only a few of the choicer epithets. *Times* columnist Ed Ainsworth cautioned his readers "to be careful to differentiate between races. The Chinese and Koreans both hate the Japs more than we do. . . . Be sure of nationality before you are rude to anybody." (*Life* Magazine soon rang some changes on this theme for a national audience with an article—illustrated by comic strip artist Milton Caniff, creator of *Terry and the Pirates* and, later, *Steve Canyon*—which purported to explain how to tell "Japs" from other Asian nationalities.) The sports pages, too, furnished their share of abuse. Just after a series of murderous and sometimes fatal attacks on Japanese residents by

From Roger Daniels, *Concentration Camps USA: Japanese Americans and World War II.* Copyright © 1971 Roger Daniels. Reprinted by permission of Roger Daniels.

Filipinos, one sports page feature was headlined FILIPINO BOXERS NOTED FOR COURAGE, VALOR.

Newspaper columnists, as always, were quick to suggest what public policy should be. Lee Shippey, a Los Angeles writer who often stressed that *some* Japanese were all right, prophetically suggested a solution to California's Japanese problem. He proposed the establishment of "a number of big, closely guarded, closely watched truck farms on which Japanese-Americans could earn a living and assure us a steady supply of vegetables." If a Nazi had suggested doing this with Poles, Shippey, a liberal, undoubtedly would have called it a slave labor camp. But the palm for *shrecklichkeit* must go to Westbrook Pegler, a major outlet of what Oswald Garrison Villard once called "the sewer system of American journalism." Taking time off from his vendettas with Eleanor Roosevelt and the American labor movement, Pegler proposed, on December 9, that every time the Axis murdered hostages, the United States should retaliate by raising them "100 victims selected out of [our] concentration camps," which Pegler assumed would be set up for subversive Germans and Italians and "alien Japanese."

* * * *

. . . Any reading of the wartime Pacific Coast press . . . shows clearly that, although a distinction was continually being made between "good" and "bad" Germans (a welcome change from World War I), few distinctions were ever made between Japanese. The evil deeds of Hitler's Germany were the deeds of bad men; the evil deeds of Tojo and Hirohito's Japan were the deeds of a bad race. While the press was throwing fuel on the fires of racial animosity, other faggots were contributed by politicians, federal officials, and, above all, the military. The governor of California, Culbert L. Olson, a liberal Democrat, had insisted, before Pearl Harbor, that Japanese Americans should enjoy all their rights and privileges even if war with Japan came, and correctly pointed out that equal protection under the law was a "basic tenet" of American government. But Olson's constitutional scruples were a casualty of Pearl Harbor: on December 8, the governor told the press that he was thinking of ordering all Japanese, alien and citizen, to observe house arrest "to avoid riot and disturbance."

The Department of Justice, working through the FBI and calling on local law enforcement officials for assistance and detention, began roundups of what it considered "dangerous" enemy aliens. Throughout the nation this initial roundup involved about 3000 persons, half of whom were Japanese. (All but a handful of these lived on the Pacific Coast.) In other words the federal officials responsible for counterespionage thought that some 1500 persons of Japanese ancestry, slightly more than 1 percent of the nation's Japanese population, constituted some kind of threat to the nation. Those arrested, often in the dead of night, were almost universally of the immigrant, or Issei, generation, and thus, no matter how long they had lived here, "enemy aliens" in law. (It must be kept in mind that American law prohibited the naturalization of Asians.) Those arrested were community leaders, since the government, acting as it so often does on the theory of guilt by association, automatically hauled in the officers and leading lights of a number of Japanese organizations and religious groups. Many of these people were surely "rooting" for the Emperor rather than the President and thus technically subversive, but most of them were rather elderly and inoffensive gentlemen and not a threat to anything. . . . It must be noted that even at this restrained level the government acted much more harshly, in terms of numbers interned, toward Japanese nationals than toward German nationals (most known members of the German-American Bund were left at liberty), and more harshly toward Germans than to Italians. It should also be noted, however, that more than a few young Nisei leaders applauded this early roundup and contrasted their own loyalty to the presumed disloyalty of many of the leaders of the older generation.

In addition to the selective roundup of enemy aliens, the Justice Department almost immediately announced the sealing off of the Mexican and Canadian borders to "all persons of Japanese ancestry, whether citizen or alien." Thus, by December 8, that branch of the federal government particularly charged with protecting the rights of citizens was willing to single out one ethnic group for invidious treatment. Other national civilian officials discriminated in other ways. Fiorello La Guardia . . . pointedly omitted mention of the Japanese in two public statements calling for decent treatment for enemy aliens and suggesting that alien Germans and Italians be presumed loyal until proved otherwise. By implication, at least, Japanese were to be presumed disloyal. . . .

Even more damaging were the mendacious statements of Frank Knox, Roosevelt's Republican Secretary of the Navy. On December 15 Secretary Knox held a press conference in Los Angeles on his return from a quick inspection of the damage at Pearl Harbor. As this was the first detailed report of the damage there, his remarks were front-page news all across the nation. Knox spoke of "treachery" in Hawaii and insisted that much of the disaster was caused by "the most effective fifth column work that's come out of this war, except in Norway." The disaster at Pearl Harbor, as is now generally acknowledged, was caused largely by the unpreparedness and incompetence of the local military commanders, as Knox already knew. (The orders for the relief of Admiral Kimmel were already being drawn up.) But the secretary, who . . . harbored deep-felt anti-Japanese prejudices, probably did not want the people to lose faith in their Navy, so the Japanese population of Hawaii—and indirectly all Japanese Americans—was made the scapegoat on which to hang the big lie. (Knox, it should be remarked, as a Chicago newspaper publisher in civilian life, had a professional understanding of these matters.)

But the truly crucial role was played by the other service, the United States Army. The key individual, initially, at least, was John L. De Witt, in 1941 a lieutenant general and commander of the Western Defense Command and the 4th Army, both headquartered at San Francisco's Presidio. Despite these warlike titles, De Witt, who was sixty-one years old and would be retired before the war's end, was essentially an administrator in uniform, a staff officer who had specialized in supply and had practically nothing to do with combat during his whole Army career. Even before Pearl Harbor, De Witt had shown himself to be prejudiced against Japanese Americans. . . .

✳ ✳ ✳ ✳

It was in this panic-ridden, amateurish Western Defense Command atmosphere that some of the most crucial decisions about the evacuation of the Japanese Americans were made. Before examining them, however, it should be made clear that the nearest Japanese aircraft during most of December were attacking Wake Island, more than 5000 miles west of San Francisco, and any major Japanese surface vessels or troops were even farther away. In fact, elements of the Luftwaffe over the North Atlantic were actually closer to California than any Japanese planes. California and the West Coast of the continental United States were in no way seriously threatened by the Japanese military. . . . Official estimates of Japanese capabilities made late in December concluded correctly that a large-scale invasion was beyond the capacity of the Japanese military but that a hit-and-run raid somewhere along the West Coast was possible.

In the days just after Pearl Harbor there was no concerted plan for mass incarceration. . . . But De Witt and his nervous headquarters staff, ready to believe anything, soon began to pressure Washington for more drastic action against the presumably dangerous enemies in their midst.

The first proposal by the Army for any kind of mass evacuation of Japanese Americans was brought forward at a De Witt staff conference in San Francisco on the evening of December 10. In the language of a staff memo, the meeting considered "certain questions relative to the problem of apprehension, segregation and detention of Japanese in the San Francisco Bay Area." The initial cause of the meeting seems to have been a report from an unidentified Treasury Department official asserting that 20,000 Japanese in the Bay Area were ready for organized action. Apparently plans for a mass roundup were drawn up locally, and approved by General Benedict, the commander of the area, but the whole thing was squelched by Nat Pieper, head of the San Francisco office of the FBI, who laughed it off as "the wild imaginings" of a former FBI man whom he had fired. The imaginings were pretty wild; the figure of 20,000 slightly exceeded the total number of Japanese men, women, and children in the Bay Area. But wild or not, De Witt's subordinate reported the matter to Washington with the recommendation that "plans be made for large-scale internment." Then on December 19 General De Witt officially recommended "that action be initiated at the earliest practicable date to collect all alien subjects fourteen years of age and over, of enemy nations and remove them" to the interior of the United States and hold them "under restraint after removal" to prevent their surreptitious return. (The age limit was apparently derived from the federal statutes on wartime internment, but those statutes, it should be noted, specified males only.)

De Witt was soon in touch with the Army's Provost Marshal General, Allen W. Gullion, who would prove to be a key figure in the decision to relocate the Japanese Americans. Gullion, the Army's top cop, had previously served as Judge Advocate General, the highest legal office within the Army. He was a service intellectual who had once read a paper to an International Congress of Judicial Experts on the "present state of international law regarding the protection of civilians from the new war technics." But, since at least mid-1940, he had been concerned with the problem of legally exercising military control over civilians in wartime. Shortly after the fall of France, Army Intelligence took the position that fifth column activities had been so successful in the European war in creating an internal as well as an external military front that the military "will actually have to control, through their Provost Marshal Generals, local forces, largely police" and that "the

Military would certainly have to provide for the arrest and temporary holding of a large number of suspects," alien and citizen.

Gullion, as Judge Advocate General, gave his official opinion that within the United States, outside any zone of actual combat and where the civil courts were functioning, the "Military . . . does not have jurisdiction to participate in the arrest and temporary holding of civilians who are citizens of the United States." He did indicate, however, that if federal troops were in actual control (he had martial law in mind), jurisdiction over citizen civilians might be exercised. Although martial law was never declared on the Pacific Coast, Chief of Staff George C. Marshall did declare the region a "Theater of Operations" on December 11. This declaration, which was not made with the Japanese Americans in mind, created the legal fiction that the Coast was a war zone and would provide first the Army and then the courts with an excuse for placing entirely blameless civilian citizens under military control.

By December 22 Provost Marshal General Gullion, like any good bureaucrat, began a campaign to enlarge the scope of his own activities, . . . He formally requested the Secretary of War to press for the transfer of responsibility for conduct of the enemy alien program from the Department of Justice to the War Department. This recommendation found no positive response in Stimson's office, and four days later Gullion was on the telephone trying to get General De Witt to recommend a mass roundup of all Japanese, alien and citizen. Gullion told the Western Defense commander that he had just been visited by a representative of the Los Angeles Chamber of Commerce urging that all Japanese in the Los Angeles area be incarcerated. De Witt, who would blow hot and cold, was, on December 26, opposed. . . .

While these discussions and speculations were going on all about them, the West Coast Japanese in general and the citizen Nisei in particular were desperately trying to establish their loyalty. Many Japanese communities on the Coast were so demoralized by the coming of war that little collective action was taken, especially in the first weeks after Pearl Harbor. But in Los Angeles, the major mainland center of Japanese population, frantic and often pitiful activity took place. Most of this activity revolved around the Japanese American Citizens League, an organization, by definition, closed to Issei. . . . Immediately following Pearl Harbor the Japanese American Citizens League (JACL) wired the President, affirming their loyalty; the White House had the State Department, the arm of government usually used to communicate with foreigners, coolly respond by letter that "your desire to cooperate has been carefully noted." On December 9 the JACL Anti-Axis Committee decided to take no contributions, in either time or money, from noncitizens, and later, when special travel regulations inhibited the movement of aliens, it decided not to help Issei "in securing travel permits or [giving] information in that regard." In addition, Nisei leaders repeatedly called on one generation to inform on the other.

Before the end of the week the Los Angeles Nisei had set up a formal Committee on Intelligence and had regular liaison established with the FBI. These patriotic activities never uncovered any real sabotage or espionage, because there was none to uncover. Nor did it provide the protective coloration that the Nisei hoped it would; race, not loyalty or citizenship, was the criterion for evacuation. It did, however, widen the gap between the generations, and would be a major cause of bitterness and violence after the evacuation took place.

* * * *

Although . . . the decision for mass evacuation was made in mid-February, neither the Provost Marshal General's office nor the Western Defense Command, despite their long preoccupation with the idea of a "Jap-free" West Coast, was prepared to act quickly. While they laid and relaid their plans, the Congress of the United States helped prepare and crystallize public opinion. Scattered debates in Congress in mid-February made it clear that no voices of protest would be raised in that body against mass evacuation; in fact, the prevailing sentiment was that the federal authorities were not moving quickly enough. But even more important was a series of hearings held up and down the West Coast by a Congressional committee headed by Representative John H. Tolan of California, which had originally been established to investigate "National Defense Migration." These hearings, held in late February and early March in San Francisco, Portland, Seattle, and Los Angeles, are important, not because of any policy decisions that emanated from them—policy was already largely determined—but because they provide a valuable cross section of West Coast opinion from both the Caucasian and Japanese American communities.

The overwhelming majority of the witnesses supported, unequivocally, the necessity of getting all Japanese, alien and citizen, off the Coast. Some, however, like San Francisco Mayor Angelo J. Rossi, were very much concerned about the rights of aliens, if they were of German or Italian origin. The problems of German and Italian aliens, he insisted, "should be considered separately from those of the Japanese." West Coast civilian leaders were well aware of General De Witt's intention to move all enemy aliens out of California, and most of them resisted the idea. . . .

* * * *

. . . Testimony made it very clear that although West Coast opinion was overwhelmingly in favor of mass incarceration of the Japanese, most of those who discussed the matter insisted that doctrines of "racial guilt" should not be applied to Europeans. For Europeans, guilt was individual; for Asians, it was collective. Ironically, no testimony better demonstrates this dual standard than that of Earl Warren, who would later become a champion of the oppressed. But in 1942 Warren was in the grip of precisely those kinds of conspiratorial notions that would be used to attack him and his works in the 1950s and 60s. Warren, already a declared candidate for the governorship, had local law enforcement officials prepare maps which showed, county by county, property held by Japanese in California. According to the California Attorney General:

An inspection of these maps shows a disturbing situation. It shows that along the coast from Marin County [north of San Francisco] to the Mexican border virtually every important strategic location and installation has one or more Japanese in its immediate vicinity. . . . Undoubtedly, the presence of many of these persons in their present locations is mere coincidence, but it would seem equally beyond doubt that the presence of others is not coincidence. . . . It will interest you to know that some of our airplane factories in this state are entirely surrounded by Japanese. . . .

. . . Warren believed that there was an "Invisible Deadline for Sabotage" that threatened the entire state and the war effort. In a formula that probably came from General De Witt, Warren pushed the conspiracy theory about as far as it would go.

Unfortunately [many] are of the opinion that because we have had no sabotage and no fifth column activities in this State . . . that means that none have been planned for us. . . .

I believe that we are just being lulled into a false sense of security and that the only reason we haven't had disaster in California is because it has been timed for a different date. . . . Our day of reckoning is bound to come in that regard.

[Warren] believed, in 1942, that in wartime "every citizen must give up some of his rights." Japanese who were American citizens, he felt, were more dangerous than the aliens. After all, he pointed out, there were twice as many of them and most of the Issei were over fifty-five years of age. The Attorney General admitted that there were some "loyal ones" among the Nisei, but he insisted that "by and large there is more potential danger" from the Nisei than from the Issei. Questioned about the legality of the proposed evacuation, Warren agreed that it was "absolutely constitutional." Warren also presented a number of statements from California law enforcement officials demonstrating that most of them not only went along with his views, but that some went well beyond them. The District Attorney of San Luis Obispo County, for example, felt that

the best way would be to take every Japanese alien in the United States and in the possessions . . . and send them to Japan or find means of getting them there. . . . We should have as our objective the complete alienation from the United States soil of every single Japanese alien.

Officials in the city of Madera complained that "it is impossible for the police . . . to tell which Japanese are dangerous and which are not. . . . [Therefore] the only safe procedure would be to take up all the Japanese and intern them." The Chief of Police of Culver City argued that the "Nishi be interned along with the Ishi [*sic*]" because as American citizens "they should be pleased to submit to internment rather than place the security of our Nation in jeopardy. It of course stands to reason that if they should object to such treatment, they could not be looked upon as being true and loyal Americans." The Western Growers Protective Association, an organization of white produce farmers, insisted that its members had special knowledge of the situation because of long association with Japanese. They felt that "no individual alien Japanese, or . . . American citizen of Japanese parentage, can be judged as to his loyalty solely by past experience."

* * * *

The County Supervisors Association of California, blunter than most, forwarded a resolution urging that all Japanese and their descendants be placed in a "concentration camp under the supervision of the federal government," a position supported by the city council of Portland, Oregon. The mayor there felt that "50 percent or more of the second generation are loyal: but I do not think anyone is in a position to ferret out the 50 percent." The mayor of Seattle, Washington, had an even higher estimate of the loyalty of Japanese Americans; of 8000 Japanese, he testified, "7,900 probably are above question but the other 100 would burn this town down and let Japanese planes come in and bring on something that would dwarf Pearl Harbor." The Executive Secretary of the left-wing Washington Commonwealth Federation, while denying any prejudice and denouncing "racism," agreed that citizen and noncitizen alike should be moved.

There was some, but not much, dissent from the establishment. Most impressive, perhaps, was the testimony of the conservative Republican mayor of Tacoma, Washington, Harry P. Cain, who insisted that guilt was individual, not collective. He argued that local authorities could differentiate between the loyal and the disloyal. He thought that

> a man's background, regardless of who he is, very generally has much to do with what he is going to do. If born in this country; if a Christian; if employed side by side with others who fill the same classification, for years; if educated in our schools; if a producer now and in the past; if maintained in a position of production—I should think that person could be construed to be a loyal American citizen.

A few other white voices were raised in defense of the Nisei; the most numerous were a group of religious leaders and educators called the Committee on National Security and Fair Play. They, too, argued that guilt was individual and that

> since the Nisei are full-fledged American citizens by virtue of birth and upbringing in this country, certainly they should be given not less consideration than German and Italian aliens, sympathetic as we are with those among them who are thoroughly loyal to democratic ideals.

But by far the strongest statements in support of the Japanese Americans came from A. L. Wirin, counsel for the Southern California Branch of the American Civil Liberties Union, and Louis Goldblatt, Secretary of the State CIO. Wirin insisted that even during wartime,

> there must be a point beyond which there may be no abridgement of civil liberties and we feel that whatever the emergency, that persons must be judged, so long as we have a Bill of Rights, because of what they do as persons. . . . We feel that treating persons, because they are members of a race, constitutes illegal discrimination, which is forbidden by the fourteenth amendment whether we are at war or peace.

Goldblatt, in a position diametrically opposed to most of California's labor leaders, maintained that "the second generation of Japanese in this Nation should not be distinguished from the second generation of any other nationality," and tried, without success, to read to the committee the inscription in the Statue of Liberty. More typical of the left-wing attitude was the line taken by the *People's World,* the West Coast Communist daily. Restrictions upon the liberty of Japanese were "unfortunate, but vital," and by late February General De Witt's plans were termed "a sensible program." These sentiments were echoed by the Los Angeles

Doho, a leftist Japanese newspaper that backed the evacuation in even stronger terms than the Japanese American Citizens League (JACL), saying that "this is no time to holler that our civil liberties and constitutional rights are being denied us," while on the national scene party-lining Congressman Vito Marcantonio of New York gave tacit support to the evacuation by repeating the canard that the disaster at Pearl Harbor was made possible by "the Japanese fifth column." Many liberals, however, perhaps despairing of doing anything much for the Japanese, concentrated their energies on getting fair treatment for refugees, largely German Jews, who were legally German aliens. The distinguished author Thomas Mann, for example, while making an eloquent plea for anti-Nazi refugees, insisted that "it is not my business to talk about the Japanese problem," and even Carey McWilliams, who would later become the chief journalistic champion of the Japanese Americans, devoted most of his prepared testimony to protecting the rights of European-born aliens, who were not really in much danger of mistreatment.

But the confusion among white liberals was nothing compared with the confusion that existed among Japanese American leaders. As a group they had desperately tried to be more American than the Americans, yet most Caucasians viewed them only as Japanese. Either course open to them—resistance to the coming evacuation or acceptance of it—was fraught with peril. Most of the leaders of the Japanese American community and especially those associated with the JACL took the second course. As their national secretary, Mike Masaoka, testified early in the Tolan Committee hearings:

> With any policy of evacuation definitely arising from reasons of military necessity and national safety, we are in complete agreement. As American citizens, we cannot and should not take any other stand. But, also, as American citizens believing in the integrity of our citizenship, we feel that any evacuation enforced on grounds violating that integrity should be opposed.

Masaoka and the other JACL leaders stressed that they wanted federal responsibility for the evacuation. They understood that if they opposed the evacuation, it would merely add to the disloyal stereotype that already existed. It is easier to criticize this accommodationist policy than to construct viable alternatives for a responsible leadership to adopt. Masaoka and the others deliberately chose to cooperate with their oppressors in the obvious hope that by cooperating they would both mitigate the present circumstances and perhaps have a lien on better treatment later. In addition, there was the whole poisonous California climate of opinion which seemed a threat to them all. As Tokie Slocum, a veteran of World War I and a member of both the American Legion and the Veterans of Foreign Wars, put it:

> The very fact and very proof of [the loyalty of the majority of the Japanese Americans] is [that] you don't hear a holler going up when your Commander-in-Chief, through General De Witt says, "Evacuate." Everybody is willing. . . . They want to know where to go and how to go, really. Because when they get there they don't want to be another football, another California problem, and be kicked all over the place again.

Although these views were representative of the majority of the articulate Japanese American community, there were dissenters. James Omura, a worker in the flower industry in San Francisco who published a magazine on the side, felt that the JACL was all wrong.

> . . . I am opposed to mass evacuation of American-born Japanese. It is my honest belief that such an action would not solve the question of Nisei loyalty. If any such action is taken I believe that we would be only procrastinating on the question of loyalty, that we are afraid to deal with it, and at this, our first opportunity, we are trying to strip the Nisei of their opportunity to prove their loyalty.

This, then, was the crux of the Japanese American dilemma: how could they prove their loyalty. For the vast majority of Nisei, at least, loyalty was demonstrated by submissiveness to authority. The government said go, and they went, cooperating, organizing, submitting. This submission, this lack of resistance to oppression, had several consequences. In the long run, perhaps, it proved a viable tactic. In the short run, however, it produced . . . bitterness and fratricide within the Japanese American community.

The Influence of World War II on Changing the American Identity

PHILIP GLEASON

Although it is four decades since the United States entered World War II, some aspects of the nation's wartime experience are still virtually unstudied. Military and diplomatic historians have labored productively for many years, but historians interested in American social and intellectual developments are just beginning to turn their attention to the wartime era. Recent general studies by Richard Polenberg and John M. Blum are especially welcome since, by drawing greater attention to the period, they should stimulate further research. There is much left to be done because the war affected practically every dimension of American life. The present essay deals with one of its less obvious effects—the way in which it shaped the thinking of a whole generation on the subject of American identity.

The expression *American identity* had not yet come into use in World War II. In those days people spoke instead of American nationality or American character. All of these terms are elusive and, in many cases, simply vague. We need not enter into all the semantic complications, but a few preliminary comments are required for the discussion that follows. In the first place, we should note that the underlying question in many contexts where these terms appear is, What does it mean to be an American? Although a straightforward and seemingly simple question, it raises issues of the deepest sort about the values we hold as a people, the goals we should pursue, the loyalties we may legitimately cherish, and the norms of conduct

From Philip Gleason, *Speaking of Diversity.* Copyright © 1992. Reprinted by permission of the Johns Hopkins University Press.

we ought to follow. These issues are not only controversial in that Americans will disagree about the appropriate answers; they are also inherently difficult in that they are subtle, complex, and resistant to perspicuous formulation. In view of these facts it is not surprising that discussions of American identity have historically been marked by a good deal of conceptual unclarity and impassioned misunderstanding.

From the earliest days of our national existence, elements of ideology and ethnicity have figured prominently in these discussions. *Ideology* here refers to the foundational values of freedom, equality, and commitment to self-government under law which served as the justification for the colonies' separation from the mother country, and on which the Founding Fathers erected the constitutional fabric. The ideological element in American identity, in other words, comprises the universalistic political and social principles for which the Republic stands, and through adherence to which individuals identify themselves with the nation. *Ethnicity,* on the other hand, refers to the more particularistic dimensions of group consciousness that have marked the American people, or portions of them, causing them to think of themselves, and to be thought of by others, as belonging to a distinctive community, set apart from others by race, religion, language, national derivation, or some combination of these and other cultural features.

A historical review of the evolution of American thinking on identity shows that ideological and ethnic elements have interacted in complex ways and that their relative salience has varied from one epoch to another. For the revolutionary and immediate postrevolutionary generations, ideological themes predominated strongly. In the years 1830–60, however, religion—specifically the Roman Catholicism of so many immigrants—became the focal point in controversies over what it meant to be an American. In fact, the word *Americanization* was first used to refer to immigrant assimilation in the Know-Nothing debates of the 1850s. Ethnic elements attained their greatest salience in the era that spanned the years from 1890 to the mid 1920s. Religious feeling still ran high, and by then Jews were numerous enough to play a prominent role, especially since they produced writers who helped establish the terms of discourse with respect to national identity. Israel Zangwill, who put the symbol of the melting pot in circulation, and Horace Kallen, who propounded the theory of cultural pluralism, were both Jews. In this era racialism was triumphant, both as scientific doctrine and as popular sentiment. Combining with the chauvinism brought on by the war, and with postwar cultural panic, racialist nativism brought about a reversal of America's century-old tradition of almost completely unrestricted immigration.

In the half-century that has passed since the climax of nativism in the 1920s, there was first an ebbing and then (after the mid 1960s) a resurgence of the ethnic dimension in thinking on national identity. When ethnicity was most recessive (from about 1940 to the early 1960s) the ideological aspect of American identity was given greater emphasis than it had received since the days of the Founding Fathers. In the following pages we will explore some of the factors related to the decline of attention to the ethnic dimension after the mid 1920s and then examine the role played by World War II in accentuating the ideological conception of American identity.

* * * *

. . . [war] in Europe exerted a profound influence on the matters we have been discussing and on the general question of how ethnicity and ideology figured in the national identity. The first notable effect of the war was that, by making the need for national unity more compelling, it intensified the efforts that were already under way to cut down prejudice, improve intergroup relations, and promote greater tolerance of diversity. With the very large exception of the removal of the Japanese-Americans from the West Coast, the government's record was good in this area. Despite uneasiness on the "minorities" issue, German-Americans and Italian-Americans did not become the objects of popular suspicion or official repression. Internal tensions resulting from wartime population shifts, increasing Negro militance, and other social changes did cause serious concern, however, especially after outbursts of racial violence in Los Angeles and Detroit in 1943. Gunnar Myrdal's monumental *American Dilemma,* which came out the following year, underscored the need for action, and by the end of the war no fewer than 123 national organizations were active on the race relations front.

The second and most crucial result of the war was that it stimulated a great ideological reawakening. It was in the context of this revival that activities in the sphere of intergroup relations took place. Myrdal's volume is revealing here, for his principal theme was the contradiction between American racial practice and "the American Creed"—the system of values which Myrdal believed Americans were genuinely committed to. He predicted that the war would hasten the resolution of the dilemma posed by this contradiction because the ideological nature of the conflict made it increasingly glaring and intolerable. He was quite right. But over and above the racial problem, what stands out in retrospect is that the monstrous contrast of Nazism galvanized Americans to a new appreciation of their own ideological values. By 1940, even the detached skeptic Carl Becker was sufficiently aroused to vindicate "Some Generalities That Still Glitter"; and he acknowledged in doing so that Hitlerism was what threw the merits of democracy into bold relief. At about the same time, Max Lerner emphasized the importance of knowing "what we believe in, what America stands for," and the need for "a new tough-mindedness in the service of a set of fervent convictions." The respected newsman Raymond Gram Swing chaired a Council for Democracy organized in the fall of 1940 the purpose of which was "to crystallize and instill in the minds of Americans the meaning, value, and workability of democracy as a dynamic, vital creed—just as Nazism, Fascism, and Communism are to their adherents." Symbolically, Bill of Rights day, marking the 150th anniversary of the ratification of the first ten amendments, fell on the first Sunday after Pearl Harbor and was commemorated by a radio drama written by Norman Corwin and entitled "We Hold These Truths."

The ideological revival had a powerful, but somewhat paradoxical, effect on thinking about intergroup relations, ethnocultural affairs, and national identity. The substance of its message, and its practical effect, was strongly assimilationist in tendency. That is, what was actually being urged—indeed, required—was ideological consensus as the basis for harmonious intergroup relations. Yet the message was couched in the language of pluralism and diversity and gave rise to the confused impression that some sort of particularism either already was or should become the basis of the American identity. We must look into this more closely before turning to a third notable effect of the war, the stimulus it gave to explicit studies of the American character.

The statement of purposes adopted by the Common Council for American Unity illustrates several of these points. This group—the reorganized version of a society long interested in ethnic affairs—stated its first aim in these words: "To help create among the American people the unity and mutual understanding resulting from a common citizenship, a common belief in democracy and the ideals of liberty, the placing of the common good before the interests of any group, and the acceptance, in fact as well as in law, of all citizens, whatever their national or racial origins, as equal partners in American society." The statement went on to call for appreciation of the contributions of each group, for tolerance of diversity, for the creation of an American culture "truly representative" of all the people, for an end to prejudice, and for assistance to immigrants who encountered difficulties in adjusting to American life.

Here ethnicity and pluralism of a sort are prominently featured, but it is clearly ideology—a shared commitment to certain universalistic values—that makes Americans what they are. Acceptance of all groups on an equal basis and tolerance for diversity are not in themselves constitutive of Americanism; rather, they derive as corollaries from "a common belief in democracy and the ideals of liberty." The role of the war in sensitizing the Common Council for American Unity to these matters was made explicit in the first issue of its journal, *Common Ground,* which began publication in the fall of 1940: "Never has it been more important that we become intelligently aware of the ground Americans of various strains have in common . . . that we reawaken the old American Dream, which in its powerful emphasis on the fundamental worth and dignity of every human being, can be a bond of unity no totalitarian attack can break."

But because the "American Dream" was vague, or at least multivalent, and because totalitarianism meant forced uniformity—the barbarous *Gleichschaltung* of the Nazis—it was an easy transition to the view that diversity as such was the essence of the American system. The transition was made almost inevitable by the popularization of the term *cultural pluralism.* Horace Kallen coined this term in 1924, contrasting the ideal for which it stood to assimilation or Americanization. In his original formulation, cultural pluralism prescribed the indefinite perpetuation of immigrant cultures and envisioned the United States as a federation of ethnic nationalities rather than being a country with a nationality of its own. While extreme and unrealistic, this was at least fairly clear. Kallen's concept attracted almost no attention for a number of years. By the time the expression came into general usage in World War II, the original meaning had faded from memory, and the notion of cultural pluralism became hopelessly amorphous. In most cases, it signified merely that the speaker believed diversity was a good thing and always to be prized—unless, of course, it was "divisive," for divisiveness was somehow bad, even though pluralism was good. Yet the term also carried with it some of the portentous freight that the culture concept had accumulated in the thirties, and it seemed to be terribly important since it was often equated with democracy. Kallen himself claimed in 1943 that cultural pluralism defined "both the material and spiritual intent of the four freedoms."

But the real mystification created by this kind of usage was that it effectively concealed the fact that so-called cultural pluralism was predicated upon, and made possible by, a high degree of consensus. Ostensibly it repudiated assimilation; in fact, it embodied assimilation because it assumed that everyone agreed about basic matters that were actually distinctive to the United States, at least in their centrality to the life of the nation, rather than being universally held by the common consent of mankind. Illustrative of such matters are: acceptance of a democratic system of government; respect for the principle of equality before the law; recognition of the dignity of the individual and the rights of minorities; willingness to uphold free speech, freedom of religion, etcetera, and to abide by constitutional guidelines, as interpreted by the courts, in the settlement of disputes. Kallen came close to recognizing the importance of agreement on fundamentals when he wrote in 1956 that cultural pluralism was "grounded on and consummated in the American Idea." But by then the mischief was done. The popularization of the term in the preceding decade created a situation in which we have been unable ever since to talk about ethnicity and national identity without dealing in terminology that confuses the analytical task rather than clarifying it.

The third aspect of wartime influence on thinking about American identity—the boom in national character studies—stands in definite opposition to the pluralism-and-diversity motif just discussed. It is the aspect of wartime influence most explicitly related to our subject because the expression *American identity* came to be used synonymously with *American character.* In contrast to the emphasis on diversity, however, national character studies stressed the presence of common traits—not to say uniformity—among Americans. Even so, we find that immigration and ethnicity figure rather prominently in these studies. What makes the development of American character studies even more interesting is that our friends the cultural anthropologists pioneered in making the kind of scientific investigations that were said to redeem the study of national character from crude racialism and to elevate it above the level of more belletristic speculation.

This all came about, as Margaret Mead later explained, when she and other social scientists such as Ruth Benedict and Erik Erikson were called upon by agencies of the government to apply their skills to such questions as how civilian morale might be maintained, or what kind of propaganda was most likely to influence the enemy. To answer these questions, the social scientists turned to the techniques of the culture-and-personality school of anthropologists, who combined psychological assumptions and ethnographic observation in trying to identify the "basic personality structure" impressed on individuals by the norms of the group to which they belonged. "By the end of the war," Mead wrote, "the term 'national character' was being applied to studies that used anthropological methods from the field of culture and personality, psychiatric models from psychoanalysis, statistical analysis of attitude tests, and experimental models of small-group process."

Mead's *Coming of Age in Samoa* had been one of the earliest culture-and-personality studies; in the 1942 volume *And Keep Your Powder Dry,* she contributed the first of the new national character studies. Despite her claims to the contrary, there was little that was scientific about the book, a loose and rambling affair written in a style of impressionistic omniscience and intended as a contribution to the war effort. Yet the assertion that an American character really did exist carried much weight coming from an anthropologist intimately acquainted with half a dozen exotic cultures. Aside from her emphasis on parent-child relationships, there was nothing terribly novel about the Americans she described—moralistic, ambivalent about aggressiveness, oriented toward the future, and inclined to interpret success or failure as an index of personal merit. A certain ideological interest attaches to her statement that postwar planning would have to eliminate those "social behaviors which automatically preclude the building of a democratic world" and her (unsuccessful) effort to show that such a commitment did not violate the principle that cultural differences were all to be tolerated. But what is more pertinent here is that Mead singled out an aspect of immigrant assimilation as having paradigmatic significance for understanding the American character.

References to immigration recur frequently throughout the book, and its most striking interpretive metaphor is developed in chapter 3, "We Are All Third Generation." Mead's point was not so much that many Americans actually were the grandchildren of immigrants but that nearly all had the kind of "character structure" that resulted from growing up in a family of second-generation parents and third-generation children. She described the outlook produced by this familial setting in these words:

> Father is to be outdistanced and outmoded, but not because he is a strong representative of another culture . . . [and] not because he is a weak and ineffectual attempt to imitate a new culture; he did very well in his way, but he is out of date. He, like us, was moving forwards, moving away from something symbolized by his own ancestors, moving towards something symbolized by other people's ancestors. . . . [We need not rebel against Father. We merely need to pass him.] And to pass him it is only necessary to keep on going and to see that one buys a new model every year. Only if one slackens, loses one's interest in the race towards success, does one slip back.

Mead's colleague in national character work, Geoffrey Gorer, pushed the analysis back a generation further. His book *The American People* (1948), begins with a chapter entitled "Europe and the Rejected Father," depicting the problem of the first-generation immigrant who must abandon much of his past in order to become an American. The immigrant, alas, cannot transform himself completely; the Old World still clings to him, and he becomes an object of scorn to his American-born offspring, who reject their father as role model and authority figure. "It is this break of continuity between the immigrants of the first generation and their children of the second generation which is . . . of major importance in the development of the modern American character," Gorer announced. He then proceeded to elaborate this insight along Freudian lines in explaining Americans' lack of respect for authority, the marginal family role of fathers as compared to mothers, and so on.

For Mead and Gorer, then, the "ethnic"—that is, the immigrant or person of immigrant derivation—is a prototypically American figure, *not* because of any distinctiveness of cultural heritage but for exactly the opposite reason, namely, because he or she exhibits in extreme degree the "character structure" produced by the *American* experience of change, mobility, and loss of contact with the past. This interpretation differed drastically from what the celebration of diversity and cultural pluralism might lead one to anticipate about the American character, but it accorded nicely with the interpretation offered by Oscar Handlin in *The Uprooted*, a work that shaped an entire generation's understanding of the immigrant experience. Published in 1951 when interest in the American character was near its zenith, the book began with the assertion that "the immigrants *were* American history," and the central metaphor of uprootedness was easily transferable to Americans generally. After all, Handlin explained, the "experience of displacement" was the crucial thing; having undergone it, the immigrants "were on the way toward being Americans almost before they stepped off the boat."

Handlin did not fail to note that migration meant liberation and that uprootedness called forth new creative energies, but the tone of the book was elegiac: it was the immigrant's alienation that impressed itself upon the reader. Within a few years, people would be talking about this sort of thing in terms of identity problems and identity crises. Indeed, these terms have become so indispensable that it is almost a shock to note their absence from Handlin's conceptual armamentarium. But *identity* in this sense derives primarily from the work of Erik Erikson, and he was just beginning to put the term in circulation. His book *Childhood and Society,* published only a year before *The Uprooted,* marks its real introduction. It is also a landmark in American character studies since the chapter entitled "Reflections on the American Identity" was the first major publication to equate American character and American identity.

Erikson did not give immigration the same prominence as did Mead and Gorer, but he mentioned it, and what he says is interesting: "We begin to conceptualize matters of identity at the very time in history when they become a problem. For we do so in a country which attempts to make a super-identity out of all the identities imported by its constituent immigrants." In an autobiographical account published twenty years later, Erikson, an immigrant himself, quoted this passage and added that the terms *identity* and *identity crises* seemed to grow out of "the experience of emigration, immigration, and Americanization." Identity problems, he said, "were in the mental baggage of generations of new Americans, who left their motherlands and fatherlands behind to merge their ancestral identities in the common one of the self-made man."

All this put the ethnics right in the middle of things as far as understanding the American character was concerned. It also suggested, however, that they might be particularly prone to the characteristic defects of Americans. Uprooted as they were, alienated, unsure of their identities, were the ethnics also more anxious about status than other Americans? Were they more obsessively conformist? More rigid in their thinking? More intolerant? More ethnocentric?

This was potentially a matter for grave concern, since these qualities of mind and disposition marked "the authoritarian personality." And here we return momentarily to the study of prejudice. Recall that it was beginning to turn toward psychology in the later 1930s and soon became strongly psychoanalytical under the influence of refugee scholars from Europe. But with the key group—the Frankfurt School—psychology was closely interwoven with the critique of modern society, since their so-called dialectical method represented a fusion of Marxist and Freudian elements. This was the orientation within which the study of anti-Semitism was undertaken that resulted in the publication in 1950 of *The Authoritarian Personality.* Given this background, it is understandable that prejudice is implicitly interpreted there not simply as a psychological disorder but as a highly ideological kind of disorder produced by the stresses of an advanced capitalist society. Frustrated by the contradictions of bourgeois civilization, and seeking to "escape from freedom," typical prejudiced individuals were naturally disposed to authoritarianism—in short, they were potential Fascists and the degree of their susceptibility could be measured on the famous F-scale.

No sooner had this diagnosis been offered than the eruption of McCarthyism seemed to confirm it. Here was a political movement exhibiting semihysterical rigidities in thinking and a total incapacity to tolerate ambiguities. It was clearly Fascist in tendency, according to the best qualified observers, and demanded explanation in terms of social psychology. Analysis of this kind was soon forthcoming, and was authoritatively summed up in the volume edited by Daniel Bell under the title *The New American Right* (1955). And who do we find singled out here as the population group most susceptible to the status anxieties and resentments mobilized by McCarthy? Ethnics, of course. The point was made by several of the contributors, most notably by Richard Hofstadter, whose concept of "pseudoconservatism" was taken straight from *The Authoritarian Personality,* and who likewise referred to Margaret Mead's "we-are-all-third-generation" view of the American character.

A decade later, Hofstadter qualified much of his analysis, noting that some of his remarks about immigrant authoritarianism were "gratuitously speculative," and regretting in general his "excessive emphasis" on "the clinical side of the problem." By that time interest in the American character had fallen off sharply, while ethnicity and the American ideology stood on the verge of the seismic transvaluation that would occur in the midst of the Vietnam War, whose effects on thinking about American identity were just the opposite of those of World War II. In the cultural crisis brought on by Vietnam, the racial upheaval, the counterculture, women's liberation, and Watergate, the ideological dimension of the American identity was severely discredited and ethnicity assumed greater positive salience than it had ever had before. But that is another story. What is now in order is a reflective look back at the epoch we have just sketched.

To summarize, then, the argument advanced in this essay is that World War II shaped the self-understanding of Americans, not only with respect to the nation's role in world affairs but also in regard to what we now call the American identity. Following upon a period in which ethnic factors had receded from prominence in discussions of national identity, the war gave unprecedented salience to the ideological dimension. For a whole generation, the question, What does it mean to be an American? was answered primarily by reference to "the values America stands for": democracy, freedom, equality, respect for individual dignity, and so on. Since these values were abstract and universal, American identity could not be linked exclusively with any single ethnic derivation. Persons of any race, color, religion, or national background could be, or become, Americans. Hence, "Americans all . . . Immigrants all!" Historically, however, particularistic ethnic loyalties ("racial," religious, nationality, etc.) had been obscurely, but intimately, interwoven with the commitment to universalistic political and social principles as ingredients in the citizen's sense of Americanness—and this was true of those comprising "old American stock" just as much as it was for the more recently arrived Americans. The war-related emphasis on ideology should therefore be understood as the accentuation of one element—albeit a crucially important one—in a preexisting mix of beliefs, attachments, and loyalties.

One aspect of the ideological revival not mentioned earlier which deserves notice is the remarkable contrast it affords to the situation in the 1920s with respect to the attitudes held by intellectuals concerning American culture. In the twenties intellectuals were alienated. Americanization had assumed forms hateful to liberals such as Horace Kallen; anthropologists such as Sapir, Mead, and Benedict were repelled by the shallowness and discontinuity of American civilization. In World War II, however, intellectuals (including Kallen, Mead, and Benedict) rallied to the nation. Simple patriotism in a time of danger was no doubt a factor; but in the battle against Nazism, America stood for universalistic values dear to the intellectual community. As Carl Becker explained, the rational and humane values that democracy affirmed were "older and more universal than democracy" itself, to say nothing of their being older than the American nation. Yet the United States based itself on these values, and in the war it was their foremost champion. Since intellectuals are the ones who articulate a people's understanding of itself, their identification with the national cause goes far toward accounting for the generally positive and strongly ideological interpretation of national identity that established itself during the wartime era.

But the very generality and abstractness of American values meant that they were subject to divergent interpretations that gave rise to divisive conflicts over whose was the correct understanding of true Americanism. An ironic instance was reported in a 1944 symposium entitled "Approaches to National Unity." The symposium was the fifth sponsored by a group called the Conference on Science, Philosophy, and Religion in Their Relation to the Democratic Way of Life, which had been formed in 1940; after its second meeting, "certain philosophical humanists, positivists, and naturalists" withdrew because they were offended by the religious pronouncements of various participants in the original group. Hence there was by 1943 a rival Conference on the Scientific Spirit and the Democratic Faith, whose members regarded as dangerously undemocratic the views of some of their erstwhile collaborators in the search for unity.

Of the same sort, but more serious and long-lasting, were the issues of loyalty and un-Americanism that reached a climax in the McCarthy era. The nature of the Cold War contest with Communism, both on the world scene and as a potential source of internal subversion, heightened the ideological dimension, but the wartime stress on commitment to American values made it inevitable that fissures in national unity would open up along ideological rather than ethnic fault lines. Hence the national loyalty of Catholics was not called into question, despite the sharp controversies that broke out in the late forties between Catholics and Protestants, Jews, and secular liberals. On the contrary, it was because national identity was defined in ideological rather than ethnic terms that "to be an Irish Catholic became *prima facie* evidence of loyalty. Harvard men were to be checked; Fordham men would do the checking."

There were thus very definite limits to the toleration of diversity in the ideological sphere. In the broader area of intergroup relations, however, tolerance was the touchstone, and to the degree that it was formulated in terms of cultural pluralism it became almost impossible to determine what the limits of tolerance were, if there were any, or, in many cases, even to determine what was being talked about. In battling against totalitarian enemies, it was understandable, as John Higham has written, that Americans should exalt the principle of diversity. But he goes on to say, "The astonishing fact about the emphatic endorsement of cultural pluralism in the postwar years was not its occurrence but rather a general unwillingness or inability to assess critically its relation to the apparently contrary imperative of national integration." As diversity was hailed, even while divisiveness was deplored, the "traditions of pluralism and assimilation blurred into a rosy haze."

To make matters worse, a group of political scientists who analyzed American society in terms of interest groups and crosscutting pressures became known as "pluralists." The relationship of this perspective to that of cultural pluralism was never clarified and possibly not even adverted to at the time. But the growing tendency to speak of pluralism without the modifier *cultural* made the term even more generalized and abstract, as did usages such as *pluralistic,* and *pluralistically.* Also, cultural pluralism itself can be appealed to by persons who have significantly different goals in mind. What might be called a cosmopolitan version of cultural pluralism appeals to persons relatively detached from any specific ethnic tradition as a general vision of a society made up of diverse groups, all interacting harmoniously without losing their distinctiveness. But cultural pluralism can equally well stand for a highly particularistic vision when appealed to by persons who care little about the overall design of American society but are passionately determined to preserve their (often quite "ethnocentric") group traditions.

In short, cultural pluralism in all its ambiguities and complexities is the crucial legacy of World War II with respect to American identity. The frequency with which it is invoked today testifies to its continuing relevance to our present efforts to define what it means to be an American. A great deal more study is needed to clarify the circumstances of its popularization in the wartime era and the vicissitudes of its conceptual evolution since then.

FURTHER READING

Francisco E. Balderrama and Raymond Rodriguez, *Decade of Betrayal: Mexican Repatria-
    tion in the 1930s* (1995).
Richard Breitman and Alan Kraut, *American Refugee Policy and European Jewry* (1987).
Lisbeth Cohen, *Making a New Deal: Industrial Workers in Chicago, 1919–1939* (1990).
Richard B. Craig, *The Bracero Program* (1971).
Roger Daniels, *Japanese Americans: From Relocation to Redress* (1986).
Leonard Dinnerstein, *America and the Survivors of the Holocaust: The Evolution of a U.S.
    Displaced Persons Policy, 1945–1950* (1982).
Juan Ramon Garcia, *Operation Wetback: The Mass Deportation of Mexican Undocumented
    Workers in 1954* (1980).
Deborah Gesenway and Mindy Roseman, *Beyond Words: Images from America's Concen-
    tration Camps* (1988).
Camille Guerin-Gonzales, *Mexican Workers and American Dreams: Immigration, Repatri-
    ation, and California Farm Laborers, 1930–1939* (1994).

Abraham Hoffman, *Unwanted Mexican Americans in the Great Depression: Repatriation Pressures, 1929–1939* (1974).

Jeanne Wakatsuki Houston and James D. Houston, *Farewell to Manzanar: A True Story of Japanese American Experience During and After the World War II Internment* (1973).

Yuji Ichioka, *Voices From Within: The Japanese American Evacuation and Relocation* (1987).

Fred Riggs, *Pressures on Congress: A Study of the Repeal of Chinese Exclusion* (1950).

Yoshiko Uchida, *Desert Exile: The Uprooting of a Japanese American Family* (1982).

Devra Weber, *Dark Sweat, White Gold: California Farm Workers, Cotton, and the New Deal* (1994).

David Wyman, *Paper Walls: America and the Refugee Crisis, 1938–1941* (1968).

David Wyman, *The Abandonment of the Jews: America and the Holocaust, 1941–1945* (1984).

Mark Wyman, *DP: Europe's Displaced Persons, 1945–1951* (1988).

Immigration and Ethnicity in the Post-Industrial World, 1965 to the Present

Both U.S. immigration policy and Americans' understandings about the relationship between nation and ethnic group have been in immense flux in the past three decades. Increasingly strident calls for reducing immigration coexist with explorations of "transnational" convictions that deny the significance of national boundaries. Advocacy of multiculturalism is contested by those who argue for homogeneity in American society. The root of these changes is found in the ferment of the 1960s, when federal immigration policy was revamped while many Americans fundamentally questioned the composition of their nation. First, the Immigration and Nationality Act of 1965 transformed federal immigration policy. It broadened the number of visas available for immigrants to 290,000 per year, created a scheme of preference categories that strongly favored the relatives of residents of the United States, and abolished national quotas. As a result of this act and others that followed, the profile of the immigrant was transformed as the immigrant streams were enlarged. Americans since then have debated the advantages and burdens of immigration in terms of the economy and of governmental entitlements; ultimately, they have debated federal immigration policy itself. Second, the outcome of the civil rights movement in the 1960s forced Americans to reevaluate their views on race relations and the structure of the nation itself in relation to its constituent groups. Subtly but perceptively, the celebration of the "American way of life," which had animated debate in the 1950s, gave way to a more critical assessment of the United States. Whereas many liberal leaders sought to create equality by making racial differences disappear, some civil rights activists, from Dr. Martin Luther King, Jr. to Malcolm X, by the 1960s stressed the fact that racial divisions were so deep-seated that issues of race could not be solved by making race disappear, but by addressing them directly. Moreover, as activists became increasingly impatient with the slowness of change, they became increasingly radical in their critique of the United States. Some gatherings of Native Americans, African Americans, and Chicanos

advocated a racial nationalism that sought separatism from the United States. These sentiments of difference rather than commonality even influenced members of white ethnic groups, who began to speak of a new, white ethnicity. In sum, as a result of political discontent, models of cultural pluralism and multiculturalism supplanted the Americanist paradigm and came to dominate the discussion when Americans considered the relationship between nation and subgroup. More important, however, the new immigration after 1965 changed the complexion of American society, which again altered much of the debate on race and ethnicity in the United States. Because immigrants who came disproportionately from Asia and Latin America were labeled "nonwhite," the race question was broadened from a "black-white" one into a debate that encompassed a variety of racial groups. Racial tensions broadened as well and urban riots, as in Los Angeles in 1992, pitted African Americans and Chicanos against Asian Americans. Furthermore, many of the immigrants were living in a "transnational" world with allegiance both to the country of birth and to the country of residence and with the capability to move between nations. As a result, scholars began to suggest that old model of assimilation no longer operated. In sum, models of immigration, race, nation, and ethnicity were in a state of extraordinary flux as the United States moved toward the millennium.

DOCUMENTS

The following documents address three major themes of immigration and ethnicity in the post-1965 era. The first theme, the creation of an ethnic nationalism by a variety of ethnic and racial groupings, is illustrated in the first two documents. The first is a Chicano manifesto (1969) about Aztlan, the proposed Chicano nation in the southwestern United States. It promotes Chicano separatism from the larger United States. It is followed by a document describing the PIGS (Poles, Italians, Greeks, and Slavs), a white ethnic agglomeration that is, according to the writer, separable from larger, white Anglo-America. The second theme concerns the increasingly contentious questions about race and about immigration. In the third document (1996), Cornel West, a theologian at Harvard University, and Jorge Klor de Alva, an anthropologist at University of California at Berkeley, discuss how race is constructed in the United States from the perspectives of an African American and a Latino scholar, respectively, in a debate moderated by Earl Shorris. The fourth document (1991) explores the question of mixed-race people from the voice of a young American of Japanese and Irish ancestries. The third theme concerns current immigration policy and the contemporary debate on the benefits and costs of immigration for American society. The first document (1994) in this group is the summary of a report from the U.S. Commission on Immigration Reform. It argues that immigration strengthens the country, but that means need to be found to address illegal immigration. The next document (1996) presents the argument of the Federation for American Immigration Reform (FAIR), which considers immigration at its present level to be disadvantageous to the nation and especially to the poorer sectors of society that compete with immigrants. The final selection (1997) offers a more optimistic portrayal of immigration. A study by the National Research Council argues that immigration benefits the U.S. economy overall and has little negative impact on income of and job opportunities for native-born Americans.

A Chicano Conference Advocates the Creation of Atzlan, 1969

The Land of the North: from the Gulf of Mexico on the east, across the state of Texas, through the Llano Estacado to the rich mountain highlands of Colorado. Winding through the Colorado plateaux into the bountiful land of New Mexico, and on west through beautiful Arizona and the Nevada lowlands. Across the burning Sonora and Borrego deserts, into California and over the Sierra Nevadas to the Pacific Ocean and north along the coast, until one sees "the trees of the Gods" . . . this is Aztlan!

This country I speak of is the land of our people. The land that our people fought and died for; the land of the Mestizo. This is the land they meant for us to have; for their children, and ours.

The Toltecs, Aztecs, Mayas, Ahualulcos, Tzendals, Chichimecs, and all of the peoples who spoke to each other through their twenty-three linguistic families, spoke of this land of the north we call Aztlan.

This land of ours has had over it the flags of Spain, France, Mexico, the Lone Star Republic, the California Republic, and the Confederacy. Also, the flag of the United States. But this will all come to pass. We now have our flag, it will be placed where it can be flown high, to catch those gusty winds, sometimes referred to as "The Santa Ana Winds," which will keep it full spread.

Its colors are those of the green crops in the Spring; the liberation we intend to obtain. The white of the innocence in our souls; the peace our people are seeking. The red of the fires of determination in our hearts; the blood of our people spilled upon this earth. In the center—in gold—it bears the three-faced Mestizo Head, symbolizing the Spanish conqueror on the right, the conquered Indian Nation on the left; in the middle is the product of that meeting: us: The Chicano. This center figure is further emblazoned with five sun rays (spears or flames) which are meant to signify the five states that now make up the occupied nation of Aztlan: Arizona, California, Colorado, New Mexico, and Texas.

We want nothing less than freedom for all our people who are suffering oppression under a decaying system ruled by a chosen few.

A "White Ethnic" Differentiates PIGS from WASPs, 1972

Growing up in America has been an assault upon my sense of worthiness. It has also been a kind of liberation and delight.

There must be countless women in America who have known for years that something is peculiarly unfair, yet who only recently have found it possible, because of Women's Liberation, to give tongue to their pain. In recent months I have experienced a similar inner thaw, a gradual relaxation, a willingness to think about feelings heretofore shepherded out of sight.

From Victor Bono, "The Land of the North," *Aztlan,* No. 1, Ano 2, February 21, 1972, p. 9. Issued by prisoners at the Leavenworth Penitentiary.

From Michael Novak, *The Rise of the Unmeltable Ethnics: Politics and Culture in the Seventies,* 1972 Macmillan Publishing Company. Reprinted by permission of the author.

I am born of PIGS—those Poles, Italians, Greeks, and Slavs, those non-English-speaking immigrants numbered so heavily among the workingmen of this nation. Not particularly liberal or radical; born into a history not white Anglo-Saxon and not Jewish; born outside what in America, is considered the intellectual mainstream—and thus privy to neither power nor status nor intellectual voice.

Those Poles of Buffalo and Milwaukee—so notoriously taciturn, sullen, nearly speechless. Who has ever understood them? It is not that Poles do not feel emotion—what is their history if not dark passion, romanticism, betrayal, courage, blood? But where in America is there anywhere a language for voicing what a Christian Pole in this nation feels? He has no Polish culture left him, no Polish tongue. Yet Polish feelings do not go easily into the idiom of happy America, the America of the Anglo-Saxons and yes, in the arts, the Jews. (The Jews have long been a culture of the word, accustomed to exile, skilled in scholarship and in reflection. The Christian Poles are largely of peasant origin, free men for hardly more than a hundred years.) Of what shall the young man of Lackawanna think on his way to work in the mills, departing his relatively dreary home and street? What roots does he have? What language of the heart is available to him?

The PIGS are not silent willingly. The silence burns like hidden coals in the chest.

All four of my grandparents, unknown to one another, arrived in America from the same county in Slovakia. My grandfather had a small farm in Pennsylvania; his wife died in a wagon accident. Meanwhile, Johanna, fifteen, arrived on Ellis Island, dizzy from witnessing births and deaths and illnesses aboard the crowded ship. She had a sign around her neck lettered PASSAIC. There an aunt told her of a man who had lost his wife in Pennsylvania. She went. They were married. She inherited his three children. . . .

Nowhere in my schooling do I recall any attempt to put me in touch with my own history. The strategy was clearly to make an American of me. English literature, American literature, and even the history books, as I recall them, were peopled mainly by Anglo-Saxons from Boston (where most historians seemed to live). Not even my native Pennsylvania, let alone my Slovak forebears, counted for very many paragraphs. (We did have something called "Pennsylvania History" somewhere; I seem to remember its puffs for industry. It could have been written by a Mellon.) I don't remember feeling envy or regret; a feeling, perhaps, of unimportance, of remoteness, of not having heft enough to count.

The fact that I was born a Catholic also complicated life. What is a Catholic but what everybody else is in reaction against? Protestants reformed "the whore of Babylon." Other were "enlightened" from it, and Jews had reason to help Catholicism and the social structure it was rooted in fall apart. The history books and the whole of education hummed in upon that point (for during crucial years I attended a public school): to be modern is decidedly not to be medieval; to be reasonable is not to be dogmatic; to be free is clearly not to live under ecclesiastical authority; to be scientific is not to attend ancient rituals, cherish irrational symbols, indulge in mythic practices. It is hard to grow up Catholic in America without becoming defensive, perhaps a little paranoid, feeling forced to divide the world between "us" and "them."

* * * *

From 1870 until 1941 ethnics were told they were not worthy of America. They are cynical about authority, but they believed the dream.

The flag to [white] ethnic Americans is not a symbol of bureaucracy or system (of which the middle classes know far more than they). It is a symbol of spiritual and moral value. It was held beyond their grasp for generations. The flag invoked asceticism, struggle, a long climb up a bitterly contested mountain. Blood flowed until it was implanted on the peak. Iwo Jima was another Calvary.

To ethnics, America is almost a religion. The flag alone proves that they are not stupid, cloddish, dull, but capable of the greatest act men can make: to die for others. The flag is not a patriotic symbol only. It is the symbol of poor and wretched people who now have jobs and homes and liberties. It is a symbol of transcendence. Many millions proved that they were men, not PIGS, by expressing a willingness to die beneath those colors. When that flag flaps, their dignity is celebrated.

Those who attack the flag attack the chief symbol of transcendence, human dignity, and acceptance available to millions of human beings.

"I AM AN AMERICAN!" How many humiliations were endured until one could say those words and not be laughed at by nativists.

Where has the dream led, in reality? While a young Italian lawyer was working with a civil rights team in Mississippi, his home city was running an expressway through the traditional homes of his family. While a young Pole was in Vietnam, his brother was laid off from work. His parents became so furious at being stereotyped as racists they are wondering why they ever came to America.

A Latino and an African American Debate the Construction of Race, 1996

[Jorge] Klor de Alva: Nobody is born black. People are born with different pigmentation, people are born with different physical characteristics, no question about that. But you have to learn to be black. That's what I mean by constructedness.

[Cornel] West: But are people born human? Is "human" itself constructed, as a category?

Klor de Alva: Certainly as a category, as a social, as a scientific category, of course it's a construct. The species could have been identified in some other fashion. Since Columbus's landfall you had very extensive debates as to whether indigenous people in the Americas were human, like Europeans, or not. The priest Montesinos posed that question to the Spanish colonists in 1511, and Las Casas, a fellow priest, and the theologian Sepúlveda debated the issue at mid-century before Emperor Charles V.

West: You see, this historical process of naming is part of the legacy not just of white supremacy but of class supremacy. Tolstoy didn't believe his peasants were

From "Our Next Race Questions"—Forum. Copyright © 1996 by *Harper's Magazine*. All rights reserved. Reproduction from the April issue by special permission.

actually human until after he underwent conversion. And he realized, "My God, I used to think they were animals, now they're human beings, I have a different life and a new set of lenses with which to view it." So it is with any talk about blackness. It's associated with subhumanness, and therefore when we talk about constructed terms like "black" or "peasant" or "human," it means that the whole thing's up for grabs in terms of constructedness. And if that's so, then all we have left is history.

* * * *

Klor de Alva: . . . We have, in the United States, two mechanisms at play in the construction of collective identities. One is to identify folks from a cultural perspective. The other is to identify them from a racial perspective. Now, with the exception of black-white relations, the racial perspective is not the critical one for most folks. The cultural perspective was, at one time, very sharply drawn, including the religious line between Catholics and Protestants, Jews and Protestants, Jews and Catholics, Jews and Christians. But in the course of the twentieth century, we have seen in the United States a phenomenon that we do not see anyplace else in the world—the capacity to blur the differences between these cultural groups, to construct them in such a way that they became insignificant and to fuse them into a new group called whites, which didn't exist before.

West: Yes, but whiteness was already in place. I mean, part of the tragedy of American civilization is precisely the degree to which the stability and continuity of American democracy has been predicated on a construct of whiteness that includes the subordination of black people, so that European cultural diversity could disappear into American whiteness while black folk remain subordinated.

Klor de Alva: But everything, even whiteness, must be constructed and is therefore subject to change.

* * * *

Shorris: We've just demonstrated one of the tenets of this conversation. That is, we have discussed almost exclusively the question of blacks in this society. But we started out saying we would have a black-brown dialogue. Why does that happen? And not only in the media. Why did it happen here, among us?

Klor de Alva: Part of the answer, as Cornel was pointing out, is that blacks are the central metaphor for otherness and oppression in the United States. Secondly, in part I take your question, when focused on Latinos, to mean, Don't Latinos have their own situation that also needs to be described if not in the same terms, then at least in terms that are supplementary?

I'm not sure. The answer goes to the very core of the difference between Latinos and blacks and between Cornel and myself: I am trying to argue against the utility of the concept of race. Why? Because I don't think that's the dominant construct we need to address in order to resolve the many problems at hand. Cornel wants to construct it in the language of the United States, and I saw we need a different kind of language. Do you know why, Earl? Because we're in the United States and blacks are Americans. They're Anglos.

West: Excuse me?

Klor de Alva: They're Anglos of a different color, but they're Anglos. Why? Because the critical distinction here for Latinos is not race, it's culture.

West: Speaking English and being part of American culture?

Klor de Alva: Blacks are more Anglo than most Anglos because, unlike most Anglos, they can't directly identify themselves with a nation-state outside of the United States. They are trapped in America. However unjust and painful, their experiences are wholly made in America.

West: But that doesn't make me an Anglo. If I'm trapped on the underside of America, that doesn't mean that somehow I'm an Anglo.

Klor de Alva: Poor whites similarly trapped on the underside of America are also Anglos. Latinos are in a totally different situation, unable to be captured by the government in the "five food groups" of racial classification of Americans. The Commerce Department didn't know what to do with Latinos; the census takers didn't know what to do with Latinos; the government didn't know what to do with Latinos, and so they said, "Latinos can be of any race." That puts Latinos in a totally different situation. They are, in fact, homologous with the totality of the United States. That is, like Americans, Latinos can be of any race. What distinguishes them from all other Americans is culture, not race. That's where I'm going when I say that Cornel is an Anglo. You can be a Latino and look like Cornel. You can be a Latino and look like you, Earl, or like me. And so, among Latinos, there's no surprise in my saying that Cornel is an Anglo.

* * * *

Klor de Alva: Do you think of Latinos as white?

West: I think of them as brothers and sisters, as human beings, but in terms of culture, I think of them as a particular group of voluntary immigrants who entered America and had to encounter this thoroughly absurd system of classification of positively charged whiteness, negatively charged blackness. And they don't fit either one: they're not white, they're not black.

Shorris: What are they?

West: I see them primarily as people of color, as brown people who have to deal with their blackness-whiteness.

Shorris: So you see them in racial terms.

West: Well, no, it's more cultural.

Shorris: But you said "brown."

West: No, it's more cultural. Brown, for me, is more associated with culture than race.

Shorris: But you choose a word that describes color.

West: Right. To say "Spanish-speaking" would be a bit too vague, because you've got a lot of brothers and sisters from Guatemala who don't speak Spanish. They speak an indigenous language.

Klor de Alva: You have a lot of Latinos who aren't brown.

West: But they're not treated as whites, and "brown" is simply a signifier of that differential treatment.

A Person of Mixed Race Explores Notions of Race, 1991

My dad is thirteenth generation white, Anglo-Saxon Protestant. My mother is a second generation Japanese American. People say, "Did they meet under the bridge at the River Kwai?" and I say "No, the bridge at 160th and Amsterdam." It's a typical American romance except that one happens to be of Japanese ancestry. My dad is from Massachusetts. He came to New York after the war. My mom is from Seattle. She came to New York via an internment camp in Idaho.

I define myself as a male human being. I think it's society's need to compartmentalize people that makes people call us half this or half that. I think the word white should be abolished because it perpetuates the notion that you can be this pure thing, and when your children are of European ancestry and something else, they are somehow seen as something less. So I never use the word white unless I have to. I define myself as Asian American because that is how I am perceived. The closest I've come to passing for an Asian is to have my middle name legally changed from Douglas to Tajitsu. I was doing a lot of writing for Asian American papers, and people were wondering why a white man was writing about these issues, so I did it for that reason, and partly to honor the spirit of my mom's family. That's the closest I've come to wanting more of an Asian identity, and not having to explain all the time. . . .

A lot of people are quizzical in a nice way. But it's unfortunate that we have to always be defining ourselves. People ask questions like, "Do you know a good Chinese restaurant." I went through a real militant phase where I asked them, "Well, you're French. Do you know a good French restaurant?" You know, the whole attitude that we should suddenly be experts on our cultures. I'm Japanese. Have I seen all of Kurosawa's movies? Well of course not. I like some of his stuff, but I'm not expected to know everything about his work. I was never really angry at myself or my parents. The anger was more towards others for forcing me into situations where I would have to define myself. You look at the Irish European who can say, "Well, I'm a biologist. I'm not a black biologist." Why do we always have to define ourselves? To that extent, I'm still a little bit indignant. I don't take it out on the average person who brings it up, because they just can't be expected to know. I'm at a more mellow place right now where I take it as it comes. I'm trying to define for myself where I want to go. . . .

* * * *

I'm proud of this country, but I'm not proud of all that has happened here. There is national chauvinism, things that are done in the name of this country that are not things I would do. Things are done in Hawaii, like annexation and racism. But I like the people. There is a basic goodness here. I'm not a blind patriot. I've travelled all around the world, and there are some good things here and there are some bad. My favorite quote is from Gandhi. Someone asked him what he thought

From *Asian American Experiences in the United States: Oral Histories of First to Fourth Generation Americans from China, the Philippines, Japan, India, the Pacific Islands, Vietnam, and Cambodia* © 1991 Joan Faung Jean Lee, by permission of McFarland & Company, Inc., Publishers, Jefferson, NC 28640.

of Western civilization, and he said, "I'd love to see it." I see myself as a patriot. I feel I belong here. . . .

I don't think the identity issue is one that will ever be fully resolved. My wife is part Haitian and part Chinese. I sometimes consider what our children will be like. The geneticists will want to see all the variations that could come out of our two gene pools. Haitians by definition are so mixed up genetically that we have cousins who may have black curly hair, with a blonde, blue-eyed sister. That happens with Haitian families, so that literally could happen to us. My wife's father had red hair when he was younger. The recessive gene for blue eyes could happen to one of our kids, and we could have blue-eyed Asians without contact lenses. Or we could have someone who is very black-looking. So I'm personally prepared for whatever happens. I think it will be interesting.

* * * *

I imagine I'm going to be thinking about these issues for the rest of my life. The very knowledge that there is so much to think about has set me free. I know what I don't want to be called, and anything else is fine.

The U.S. Commission on Immigration Reform Assesses Current Immigration Policy, 1994

The Commission believes that legal immigration has strengthened and can continue to strengthen this country. . . . the Commission members agree that immigration presents many opportunities for this nation. Immigrants can contribute to the building of the country. In most cases, they have been actively sought by family members or businesses in the U.S. The tradition of welcoming newcomers has become an important element of how we define ourselves as a nation.

The Commission is mindful of the problems that also emanate from immigration. In particular, we believe that unlawful immigration is unacceptable. Enforcement efforts have not been effective in deterring unlawful immigration. This failure to develop effective strategies to control unlawful immigration has blurred the public perception of the distinction between legal and illegal immigrants.

For the Commission, the principal issue at present is how to manage immigration so that it will continue to be in the national interest.

- How do we ensure that immigration is based on and supports broad national economic, social, and humanitarian interests, rather than the interests of those who would abuse our laws?

- How do we gain effective control over our borders while still encouraging international trade, investment, and tourism?

- How do we maintain a civic culture based on shared values while accommodating the large and diverse population admitted through immigration policy?

As found in "U.S. Immigration Policy: Restoring Credibility," 1944, U.S. Commission on Immigration Reform.

The credibility of immigration policy can be measured by a simple yardstick: people who should get in, do get in; people who should not get in are kept out; and people who are judged deportable are required to leave.

During the decade from 1980 to 1990, three major pieces of legislation were adopted to govern immigration policy—the Refugee Act of 1980, the Immigration Reform and Control Act of 1986, and the Immigration Act of 1990. The Commission supports the broad framework for immigration policy that these laws represent: a legal immigration system that strives to serve the national interest in helping families to reunify and employees to obtain skills not available in the U.S. labor force; a refugee system that reflects both our humanitarian beliefs and international refugee law; and an enforcement system that seeks to deter unlawful immigration through employer sanctions and tighter border control.

The Commission has concluded, however, that more needs to be done to guarantee that the stated goals of our immigration policy are met. The immediate need is more effective prevention and deterrence of unlawful immigration. . . .

In the long term, immigration policies for the 1990s and beyond should anticipate the challenges of the next century. These challenges will be substantially influenced by factors such as the restructuring of our own economy, the establishment of such new trade relationships as the North American Free Trade Agreement [NAFTA], and changing geopolitical relations. No less importantly, immigration policy must carefully take into account social concerns, demographic trends, and the impact of added population on the country's environment.

Finally, current immigration is the first to occur in what economists call a post-industrial economy, just as it is the first to occur after the appearance of the modern welfare state. . . .

Recommendations

Serious problems undermine present immigration policies, their implementation, and their credibility: people who should get in find a cumbersome process that often impedes their entry; people who should not get in find it all too easy to enter; and people who are here without permission remain with impunity.

The Commission is convinced that unlawful immigration can be controlled consistent with our traditions, civil rights, and civil liberties. As a nation with a long history of immigration and commitment to the rule of law, this country must set limits on who can enter and then must credibly enforce our immigration law. Unfortunately, no quick and easy solutions are available. . . .

Border Management   The Commission believes that significant progress has been made during the past several years in identifying and remedying some of the weaknesses in U.S. border management. Nevertheless, we believe that far more can and should be done to meet the twin goals of border management: preventing illegal entries while facilitating legal ones.

* * * *

Worksite Enforcement   The Commission believes that reducing the employment magnet is the linchpin of a comprehensive strategy to reduce illegal immigration.

The ineffectiveness of employer sanctions, prevalence of fraudulent documents, and continued high numbers of unauthorized workers, combined with confusion for employers and reported discrimination against employees, have challenged the credibility of current worksite enforcement efforts.

Benefits Eligibility and Fiscal Impact   The Commission believes a clear and consistent policy on immigrant eligibility for public benefits is needed. The Commission also believes that the federal government has a responsibility to mitigate the impacts of unlawful immigration on states and localities, particularly through renewed efforts to reduce illegal entries.

Eligibility   The U.S. has the sovereign authority to make distinctions as to certain rights and responsibilities of various people subject to its jurisdiction—illegal aliens, legal immigrants, and U.S. citizens. Policies regarding the eligibility of aliens for public benefits should be consistent with the objectives of our immigration policy.

The Commission recommends that illegal aliens should not be eligible for any publicly-funded services or assistance except those made available on an emergency basis or for similar compelling reasons to protect public health and safety (e.g., immunizations and school lunch and other child nutrition programs) or to conform to constitutional requirements. Illegal aliens are now eligible for few benefit programs. The Commission firmly believes that benefits policies should continue to send this message: if aliens enter the U.S. unlawfully, they will not receive aid except in limited instances. Federal legislation should permit states and localities to limit eligibility of illegal aliens on this same basis. Should illegal aliens require other forms of assistance, their only recourse should be return to their countries of origin.

The Disadvantages of Immigration Reform, 1996

Americans have sentimental attachments to immigration as an idea. Flattered by the fact that immigrants want to come to the United States, they are reminded of the frontier days, when . . . America still had virgin areas, vast untamed wilderness, and seeming[ly] endless resources. However, times have changed, and, when polled, two thirds of Americans favor reducing the present level of immigration. A brief look at the results of our current immigration policy explains why they feel that way.

The immigrant population has twenty-four million people, meaning that one out of every eleven people in this country is an immigrant. As large as those numbers seem now, they're going to get larger. That population is slated to grow prodigiously, both from natural growth (the fertility rate of the immigration population is 25 percent higher than natives' rate) and admissions (between 700,000 and 900,000 new people each year). Half of this country's population growth is due to the immigrant population. With immigration at its present level, our nation will be

Reprinted by permission of the Federation for American Immigration Reform.

unable to stabilize its overall population, and the damage we do to our environment will be multiplied by more and more people every year.

* * * *

Immigrants have economic problems. Their median income is about 23 percent less than the national median income. Twenty-three percent of immigrants live below the poverty line; that's 60 percent more than natives. Among immigrants, 20 percent need some kind of public assistance, which is 50 percent more than the national average. Their unemployment rate is one third higher than natives' level of unemployment. The truth is, most immigrants are poor; indeed, that is why they come here. Through present immigration policy, we are admitting 800,000 to 900,000 mostly poor people in our society every year—a society which is already challenged to deal with the poverty of its natives.

The cost of the immigrants to our society is enormous. The most recent estimate places the costs of post-1969 immigrants at $65 billion in 1996 alone ($40.5 billion from legal immigrants and $24.5 billion from illegal immigrants). This is the net cost; that is *after* immigrants' contribution in taxes is counted in their favor.

As high as the cost is now, the rising tide of immigration will lift it even higher in years to come. By 2006, the annual net cost of immigration will be $108 billion—66 percent higher than the cost in 1996. The net national cumulative costs for the decade 1997–2006 for all post-1969 immigrants will be $866 billion, an average of almost $87 billion a year.

* * * *

High-immigration cheerleaders claim that we need immigration for our economy. But they ignore the detrimental effect that importing workers has on American workers, particularly low-skilled natives. In a supply-and-demand economy like ours, the more of something there is, the less value it has. By artificially inflating the number of workers in our country, immigration lowers the value of workers, and wages are depressed. As one expert has noted, "I know business people who tell me they're not interested in hiring Americans because the people who come from outside are cheaper. But . . . if there's an unlimited supply of labor facing this country from outside, from the South or wherever, at five dollars an hour, I don't care how fast this economy grows, the wage rate for such people is going to be five dollars an hour!"

Most of the immigrants being admitted are low-skilled. Only 5 percent of immigrants admitted in 1995 were admitted as skilled workers. Out of all the working-age immigrants admitted in 1995, 47 percent had no profession, occupation, or job at all. The average immigrant has only a ninth-grade education; more than a third of immigrants over 25 are not high school graduates.

* * * *

The effect of immigration on those low-skilled Americans is profound, and your government knows it: "Undoubtedly, access to lower-wage foreign workers has a depressing effect [on wages]." Government research suggests that 50 percent of wage-loss among low-skilled Americans is due to the immigration of low-skilled workers. Some native workers lose not just wages but their jobs through immigrant competition. An estimated 1,880,000 American workers are displaced from their jobs every year by immigration; the cost for providing welfare and assistance to these Americans is over $15 billion a year.

The effects are most pronounced in the cities where immigrants go. High-immigration cities have twice as much unemployment as low-immigration cities. Because too much immigration keeps wages low, wage increases in low-immigration cities have been 48 percent higher than in high-immigration cities. Thus, immigration contributes to the growing disparity between the rich and the poor in this country, and the shrinking of the middle class. But the damage is not confined to high-immigration locales. The harm is carried to other cities when poor Americans whose wages have been depressed or who have been displaced from their jobs by immigration move to low-immigration areas in search of greener pastures.

In short, the mass importation of low-skilled workers through immigration damages the job market for Americans, depresses wages for low-skilled natives, and costs the taxpayer billions a year—all for the benefit of businesses that have become dependent on cheap, foreign labor. An immigration system that admits too many people, without regard to their skill levels or impact on the labor force is to blame. We must reform the immigration laws to lower the level of annual immigration country and to ensure that those immigrants who are admitted complement, not compete, with our native labor force.

National Research Council Stresses the Advantages of Immigration, 1997

Throughout its history, the United States has been a nation of immigrants. The door may not always have been wide open, but it has never been completely shut. The current debate over the wisdom of high rates of immigration is not new; it stretches back even to colonial times. There are concerns about the effect of immigration on the economic prospects of native-born residents, on population growth, and on the ability of immigrants to interweave themselves into the social fabric of the nation.

Responding to these concerns, Congress in 1990 appointed a bipartisan Commission on Immigration Reform to review the nation's policies and laws and to recommend changes. In turn, the commission in 1995 asked the National Research Council to convene a panel of experts to assess the demographic, economic, and fiscal consequences of immigration. . . .

* * * *

[One] charge to the panel concerned the impact of immigration on the U.S. economy. . . .

Reprinted with permission from *The New Americans.* Copyright © 1997 by the National Academy of Sciences. Courtesy of the National Academy Press, Washington.

Using a basic economic model, with plausible assumptions, we show that immigration produces net economic gains for domestic residents, for several reasons. At the most basic level, immigrants increase the supply of labor and help produce new goods and services. But since they are paid less than the total value of these new goods and services, domestic workers as a group must gain.

The gains to the domestic economy come from a number of sources. On the production side, immigration allows domestic workers to be used more productively, specializing in producing goods at which they are relatively more efficient. Specialization in consumption also yields a gain.

Immigration thus breaks the rigid link between domestic consumption and domestic production. From this perspective, the effects of immigration are comparable to those of international trade. That the two processes are so similar suggests that, when trade is relatively free, any change in the number of immigrants will affect the incomes of domestic workers less than it would have without trade.

* * * *

Even when the economy as a whole gains, however, there may be losers as well as gainers among different groups of U.S. residents. Along with immigrants themselves, the gainers are the owners of productive factors that are complementary with the labor of immigrants—that is, domestic, higher-skilled workers, and perhaps owners of capital—whose incomes will rise. Those who buy goods and services produced by immigrant labor also benefit. The losers may be the less-skilled domestic workers who compete with immigrants and whose wages will fall. To the extent that immigrants specialize in activities that otherwise would not have existed domestically, immigration can be beneficial for all domestic residents. In this case, there is little substitution of new immigrant workers for domestic workers, and domestic consumers gain from the lower prices of these services.

* * * *

Overall, in the massive and complex U.S. economy, immigration is unlikely to have a very large effect on relative earnings or on gross domestic product per capita. Among the legions of factors that affect the economy, many are far more critical than immigration, including savings and investment and the human capital of U.S. workers. Immigration over the 1980s increased the labor supply of all workers by about 4 percent. On the basis of evidence from the literature on labor demand, this increase could have reduced the wages of all competing native-born workers by about 1 or 2 percent. Meanwhile, noncompeting native-born workers would have seen their wages increase, and both competing and noncompeting workers may have benefited as consumers.

* * * *

Potentially, immigration may have much larger effects on certain parts of the labor market—workers in geographic areas that receive large numbers of immigrants or those with low levels of education. However, comparisons of geographic areas with different levels of immigration show only a weak relationship between native wages and the number of immigrants in a city or state. Furthermore, in these studies the numerically weak relationship between native wages and immigration is observed across all types of native workers, skilled and unskilled, male and female, minority and nonminority. The one group that appears to suffer substantially from new waves of immigrants are immigrants from earlier waves, for whom the recent immigrants are close substitutes in the labor market.

While some have suspected that blacks suffer disproportionately from the inflow of low-skilled immigrants, none of the available evidence suggests that they have been particularly hard-hit on a national level. Some have lost their jobs, especially in places where immigrants are concentrated. But the majority of blacks live elsewhere, and their economic fortunes are tied largely to other factors.

* * * *

The evidence points to the conclusion that immigration has had a relatively small adverse impact on the wage and employment opportunities of competing native groups. This effect does not appear to be concentrated in the local areas where immigrants live, but instead is dispersed across the United States. This dispersal comes about in part because competing native workers migrate out of the areas to which immigrants move. Over the last two decades, immigration thus played some role in explaining the declining wages of high school dropouts, but little part in the expanding wage inequality for any other group of native workers.

Immigration most directly affects the welfare of the immigrants themselves. Immigrants expect to gain from immigration, or they would not come. Wages are higher in the United States than in less economically developed countries, such as Mexico and the Philippines. In addition, the spread of wages is broader in the United States than in most of the developed sending countries, such as [those of] Western Europe and Canada. Because of these differences, emigration to the United States should be attractive to most workers from less developed countries and to more highly skilled workers from many developed countries.

* * * *

What jobs do immigrants do? A higher proportion of immigrants than of the native-born work in many jobs that call for high levels of education: they are college teachers of foreign languages, medical scientists, economists. But they are even more disproportionately represented in many of the lowest-paying jobs: as waiters and waitresses, agricultural graders and sorters, private household workers. Immigrants also account for a disproportionate number of workers in many occupations that require little education but much skill, such as tailors, dressmakers, and jewelers.

 E S S A Y S

These two selections explore how the shifting contours of immigration and ethnicity came together—and continue to come together—to transform the ways in which Americans think about ethnicity and immigration. In the first essay, historian David G. Gutiérrez from the University of California at San Diego recounts the contemporary debate regarding Mexican immigration among Mexican Americans. Whereas Mexican Americans had been divided on the question of Mexican immigration earlier in this century, they were deeply moved by the Chicano movement in the early 1970s that stressed the inherent relationship between the U.S. attitude toward Mexican immigration and Mexican Americans' perception of their place in the United States. In this essay, Gutiérrez cleverly links the programs of ethnic groups and their construction of an ethnicity with policies regarding immigration. The second essay, by David H. Hollinger, a historian at the University of California at Berkeley, questions modern-day constructions of race and ethnicity and argues that we ought to move into an era of "postethnicity." Noting that a person, in a sense, chooses his or her specific, single identity, Hollinger suggests that a postethnic America, where one can choose to maintain more than a single identity, is a strategy that simultaneously honors historical circumstance and provides Americans with greater individual flexibility.

The Influence of Political Change in the 1960s on Mexican American Attitudes Toward Mexican Immigration

DAVID G. GUTIÉRREZ

The emergence of the Chicano movement in the mid-1960s probably did more than any other series of events to transform Mexican Americans' opinions about the relationship and significance of the immigration issue to their own status in American society. Originating as a series of localized protests erupting in New Mexico, Colorado, Texas, and California early in the decade, by 1968 this militancy had taken on the characteristics of a cohesive social movement. Inspired by the pioneering and widely publicized efforts of César Chávez and the United Farm Workers Union (UFW) in California and by Reies López Tijerina and his irredentist organization in New Mexico, the first stage of this period of accelerating social and political activism helped to lay the foundation for the unprecedented politicization of thousands of Mexican Americans across the country.

By 1966 these initial efforts opened the way for a second phase of Mexican American political activity. At this time young Mexican Americans, particularly high school and college students, began to express increasing dissatisfaction with discrimination, inferior education, and what they perceived as severely limited life opportunities. In many ways these students represented a paradox. Even though their educational and occupational levels continued to lag behind those achieved by other Americans, young Mexican Americans growing up in the late 1950s and early 1960s had significantly outstripped the levels of education and employment their parents had been able to attain. In the context of rising expectations for social reform emanating from the New Frontier and Great Society rhetoric of the Kennedy and Johnson administrations, however, Mexican American students grew increasingly impatient with the pace of social change. As the antiwar and black-power movements intensified in the United States after 1965, young Mexican

From David Gutiérrez, *Walls and Mirrors: Mexican Americans, Mexican Immigrants, and the Politics of Ethnicity.* Copyright © 1995 The Regents of the University of California Press. Reprinted by permission of The University of California Press.

Americans also began to voice their frustrations and protests. To a certain extent emulating the style and rhetoric of these militant movements, in 1967 and 1968 Mexican American students spontaneously walked out of classes in California, Texas, Colorado, and New Mexico, thus signaling the birth of the Chicano student movement.

One of the most important thrusts of this second stage of increasing political activism—and arguably the development that ultimately had the most impact in transforming Mexican American opinion on the immigration issue—was the adoption and promotion among young Mexican Americans of a new, Chicano identity. Long used as a slang or pejorative in-group reference to lower-class persons of Mexican descent, in the 1960s the term *Chicano* was adopted by young Mexican Americans as an act of defiance and self-assertion and as an attempt to redefine themselves by criteria of their own choosing. Similar to the dynamics involved in the shift from *Negro* to *black* as the preferred self-referent of young African Americans that was taking place at about the same time, young Mexican Americans soon adopted the term *Chicano* as a powerful symbolic code. The term implied pride in the Mexican cultural heritage of the Southwest and symbolized solidarity against what Chicano activists argued was a history of racial oppression and discrimination at the hands of Anglo Americans. Chicanismo—the idea of being Chicano—established strong symbolic ethnic boundaries for young Mexican Americans who explicitly and stridently rejected the notion of inherent Anglo-American superiority. Although adopted and used primarily by young Mexican American high school and university students, by 1970 the student movement had attracted sufficient attention that the term had entered fairly general usage as a descriptor of the Mexican American population at large.

This new assertion of ethnic solidarity was carried one step farther in the concept of Aztlán, an idea first articulated and debated in 1969 at the landmark First National Chicano Youth Liberation Conference in Denver, Colorado. Sponsored by the Crusade for Justice, a Colorado community organization founded by Rodolfo "Corky" Gonzales in 1965, the meeting attracted more than two thousand delegates representing Chicano students, community organizers, and political organizations from across the country. The conference marked the first time a large group of Chicano activists had come together to discuss the goals and strategy of a broad-based national Chicano movement.

In the process of refining their new sense of ethnic identity, the participants at the Denver meeting proclaimed the idea of Aztlán in the conference's famous manifesto, "El Plan Espiritual de Aztlán." The Spiritual Plan of Aztlán drew its inspiration from Aztec myths and from the vivid expressions of Chicano cultural pride explored in the writings of Corky Gonzales and the Chicano poet Alurista. Aztlán referred to the presumed ancestral homeland of the Aztecs and thus, by extension, of the Mexican people. Interpreted as the lost territories that Mexico had surrendered to the United States in 1848 after the Mexican War, to Chicano activists Aztlán represented the symbolic territorial base of the Chicano people. The Plan of Aztlán presented an almost millennial vision of the future, painting an image of a separate Chicano culture and nation that ultimately would be reclaimed by the Chicano descendants of the ancient civilization. Proclaiming, "We are a Bronze People with a Bronze Culture," participants at the First National Chicano Youth

Liberation Conference declared, "Before the World, before all of North America, before all our brothers in the Bronze Continent, We are a Nation, We are a Union of free pueblos, we are Aztlán. Por La Raza todo, Fuera de la Raza nada" (For the [Chicano] people everything; for [non-Chicanos] nothing).

The Plan of Aztlán marked an important turning point in young Chicanos' ongoing efforts to refine their conception of a collective Chicano identity and to build a political program based on that identity. In the idea of Aztlán the young activists presented a quasi-nationalist vision of the Chicano people which extolled a pre-Columbian, native ancestry while diminishing or even rejecting their connection with American culture and society. In so doing they also dismissed traditional notions of Americanization and assimilation as nothing more than *gabacho* (a derisive term for Anglo) attempts to maintain hegemony over Chicanos by destroying their culture. Pursuing a logic similar to that followed by black nationalists of the period, the Chicano nationalists at the Denver conference proposed to break Anglo hegemony by demanding community control or local autonomy over schools, elected offices, businesses, and even financial institutions located in areas of high Chicano concentration.

Clearly, much of the ethnic separatism and nationalism expressed in the Plan of Aztlán represented a symbolic act of defiance, rather than a formal declaration of secession from American society. Nevertheless the conference and its ringing manifesto galvanized the student delegates and stimulated a new level of activism and the formation of numerous new student and community groups throughout the Southwest. In addition, after the Denver conference Chicano activists Corky Gonzales and south Texas organizer José Angel Gutiérrez attempted to implement their plans for achieving Chicano community control by building an alternative, ethnically based political party in the Southwest, El Partido de La Raza Unida, or La Raza Unida Party (LRUP).

. . . [E]vents surrounding the 1969 conference contributed to an intensifying debate among Mexican Americans over the wisdom of pursuing the politics of ethnic militancy. Despite Chicano militants' claim that they represented the true interests of the Mexican-descent people of the United States, their tactics and rhetoric often provoked strong, hostile reactions from more moderate, old-line Mexican American political activists, who tended to view the militants' demands as unrealistic, counterproductive, or even racist.

* * * *

One largely unforeseen effect of this internal debate over political ideology, ethnic identity, and the redefinition of the Chicano community was the profound influence it eventually exerted on Mexican Americans' attitudes about the Mexican immigration issue. This development was ironic in that very few Chicano or Mexican American activists had recognized immigration as a significant political issue in the late 1960s. Just when Mexican Americans were becoming embroiled in an escalating debate over such fundamental issues as the appropriate basis for political organization and activism, the sources and salience of ethnic identity in contemporary society, and the very nature of the Mexican American community, however, the immigration issue suddenly reemerged.

After a brief period during which the controversy over Mexican immigration receded, several factors contributed to a renewed movement of immigrants across the international frontier. Among the most important of these were the inability of the Mexican economy to keep pace with population growth and the attraction of the booming American economy of the Vietnam era. Whatever the reason, by the late 1960s a slow but steady increase in the number of undocumented entries was being recorded by the INS. . . .

Americans became aware of the renewal of undocumented immigration when a sharp recession threw Americans out of work in 1970 and 1971, rekindling concern that Mexicans were stealing jobs from American citizens. This impression undoubtedly was reinforced when prominent news publications . . . began to publish stories describing the illegal alien influx as a human flood or a silent invasion. In a series of particularly inflammatory articles and public statements, INS Commissioner Leonard Chapman described the illegal alien issue in alarming terms, warning of dire long-term consequences to the national interest. In one widely publicized article Chapman termed the illegal alien issue a "national disaster," claiming that illegal aliens were "milking the U.S. taxpayer of $13 billion annually by taking away jobs from legal residents and forcing them into unemployment; by acquiring welfare benefits and public services; by avoiding taxes." "Clearly," Chapman asserted, "the nation can no longer afford these enormous, growing costs."

* * * *

The increasingly negative national press coverage of the so-called illegal alien crisis, the policy debate in Congress, and the intensified and highly publicized enforcement efforts of the INS set the stage for renewal of debate among Mexican American civil rights activists over the Mexican immigration issue. Although, as always, Mexican Americans remained divided on the question, recent political developments contributed to the most far-reaching and broad-based reassessment of the immigration issue in Mexican American history. . . .

Over the long run . . . the discussion over Mexican Americans' ethnic and cultural identity provoked by Chicano movement activists probably influenced Mexican Americans' responses to the immigration issue more than any other factor did. Having attempted to redefine the Chicano community by rejecting the assimilationist model and emphasizing the central importance of Mexican culture, history, and language to contemporary Chicano society, Chicano activists had raised some complex questions as to the boundaries of their community. . . .

Initially, few of the early Chicano groups made any connection between their objectives and the immigrant question. The important exception to this was a group known as El Centro de Acción Social Autónoma, Hermandad General de Trabajadores (the Center for Autonomous Social Action, General Brotherhood of Workers, or simply, CASA). Established in 1968 by veteran Mexican American community activists and labor organizers Bert Corona and Soledad "Chole" Alatorre in Los Angeles, CASA was founded as a "voluntary, democratic mutual assistance social welfare organization" to provide needed services to undocumented Mexican workers in the United States. Patterned after the traditional Mexican mutualista, CASA had expanded by 1970 to include autonomous local affiliates in other California cities and in the states of Texas, Colorado, Washington, and Illinois. These locals provided undocumented workers with a variety of direct services, including immigration counseling and notary and legal assistance. Moreover, in 1973 CASA helped to establish the National Coalition for Fair Immigration Laws and Practices, a coalition of a broad range of predominantly Mexican American community and labor groups that played an important role in articulating Mexican American opinion on the immigration controversy throughout the debate in the 1970s.

What most distinguished CASA from other groups was that it was the first Chicano-era organization to explore systematically the significance of the relationship between immigration, Chicano ethnicity, and the status of Mexican Americans in the United States. Basing their political perspective on more than four decades of labor-union organizing and activism in Mexican communities in the Southwest, CASA's founders, particularly Corona and Alatorre, argued that Mexican immigrant laborers historically represented an integral component of the American working class and that, as such, they had legitimate claims to the same rights as other workers in the United States. This assertion represented a significant departure from the views of most other contemporary Mexican American and Chicano organizations, but CASA's organizing slogans, "Somos Un Pueblo Sin Fronteras" (We Are One People without Borders) and "Somos Uno Porque America Es Una" (We Are One Because America Is One), had even more sweeping political connotations. From CASA's point of view the historical and ongoing exploitation of both Mexican American and Mexican immigrant workers in the United States made them virtually indistinguishable.

* * * *

The political demands that stemmed from these assertions were truly revolutionary, in light of the assimilationist assumptions that had informed nearly two hundred years of American immigration policy and had deeply influenced Mexican American political thought in the twentieth century. CASA asserted that naturalization, and surely Americanization, was largely irrelevant in a society that refused to recognize the full rights of citizenship for its ethnic and racial minorities. CASA's spokespersons argued that immigrant workers had for too long suffered as scapegoats for social and economic dislocations in the United States. CASA members consistently argued that the inferior social, economic, and political position of Mexicans in the United States did not derive from their cultural backwardness and refusal to assimilate into American culture and society but, rather, reflected the inherently exploitative nature of American capitalist development.

* * * *

In many ways CASA's views represented an extreme position on the growing controversy in the early 1970s. However, the government's recent actions in immigration policy and enforcement, the tenor of media coverage on immigration, and Mexican Americans' growing impatience with the pace of social change soon led others to join in a spirited critique of American immigration policy. Moreover, CASA's strong advocacy of working-class solidarity with Mexican immigrants held great appeal for Chicano student activists, who by 1972 had begun to explore Marxian class analyses to help explain the subordination of Mexicans in American society. Utilizing these more sophisticated conceptual frameworks to analyze Chicanos historical experience, Chicano students and a small but growing number of Mexican American academicians developed a new understanding of the close correspondence between the historical exploitation of Mexican and of Mexican American workers in the American labor market.

* * * *

Although activists in the Chicano movement led the growing clamor against the government's proposals for immigration reform, some politically moderate and even conservative old-line organizations, such as LULAC [League of United Latin American Citizens] and the American G.I. Forum, began to be pulled toward a new position on the question. During the initial [Peter] Rodino [congressional] hearings in 1971, even LULAC began to express growing ambivalence on the issue. Before then most LULAC spokesmen seemed to support the government's general approach to the issue. Over the course of the hearings, however, some LULAC leaders seemed to be having second thoughts on the question of undocumented Mexican workers. LULAC's growing ambivalence on the immigration controversy was a new permutation of the group's traditional concern about the impact of immigration on Mexican Americans. . . .

As LULAC was advancing this rather startling departure from traditional mainstream Mexican American opinion on the immigration question, other organizations were beginning to make the same kind of arguments. MAPA also revised its position at this time. Established as an organizational offshoot of the CSO in 1959, MAPA (Mexican American Political Association), like LULAC and the G.I. Forum, had been among the strongest critics of the Bracero Program and had lobbied extensively for abolition of the program and for stricter enforcement of laws against undocumented immigration. During the debate . . . in the California assembly, however, MAPA executed a reversal in its position on immigration reform that was every bit as remarkable as LULAC's shift.

In testimony before Arnett's subcommittee in late 1971, MAPA's state president, Armando Rodríguez, detailed the logic behind his organization's change in position. Though MAPA had once supported employer sanctions as an effective means of controlling undocumented immigration, he explained, his organization now intended to oppose the Arnett legislation because it would open the door to discrimination against anyone who looked Latino. Although Mexican Americans had made this argument before (most notably during Operation Wetback in 1954), Rodríguez took the criticism a significant step farther. Reminding the committee that MAPA traditionally had "favored employment for legal aliens and [American] citizens as opposed to employment of illegal aliens," MAPA's president went on to insist that the proposed legislation "should not be used by employers to continue harassing Mexican American people seeking employment, be they legals, illegals, citizens or otherwise."

* * * *

The change in LULAC's and MAPA's positions was significant, but the most dramatic evidence of change was provided by a dispute that developed over the UFW's position on the question. Established in California in 1962 by César Chávez and Dolores Huerta, the UFW undoubtedly had been most instrumental in publicizing the plight of Mexican Americans to a national public. Chávez's farm-workers' movement had begun as a modest struggle merely to gain collective bargaining rights and union recognition for Mexican American and Filipino farmworkers in California. But by skillfully employing nonviolent tactics and utilizing emotionally charged ethnic symbols, such as the union's stylized black Aztec eagle insignia and banners of Mexico's patron saint, the Virgin of Guadalupe, to attract members and garner publicity, Chávez succeeded in capturing the imagination of Mexican Americans across the Southwest. He cultivated the image of a modest, pious man committed to using the powers of civil disobedience on behalf of his downtrodden people. More than any other individual, Chávez gave Mexican Americans a nationally recognized role model and champion. Moreover, by winning the support of priests, nuns, ministers, and a multiethnic horde of idealistic young student volunteers, Chávez imbued his movement with a moral dimension that transcended traditional labor-union politics. His ability to gain mass media attention during the 1960s was also instrumental in eventually garnering the public support of national celebrities, including comedian/musician Steve Allen, writer Peter Matthiessen, labor leader Walter Reuther of the powerful United Autoworkers Union, and such liberal politicians as Robert Kennedy, Eugene McCarthy, and George McGovern.

Chávez was convinced, however, that in order to achieve the UFW's goals, the union's energies needed to be expended exclusively on behalf of American citizens and resident aliens. Consequently, from its inception in 1962 the UFW lobbied for strict control of the Mexican border. Like Ernesto Galarza before him, César Chávez argued that the presence of a large pool of politically powerless noncitizen workers severely hampered efforts to unionize American citizen workers. Moreover, the UFW stressed that American employers had always used undocumented Mexican workers to break strikes by American citizens. Chávez therefore stubbornly argued for the repeal of the Bracero Program and was among the most vocal critics of illegal immigration. . . .

By 1973 it was apparent, however, that Chávez's stated position on the immigration issue was seriously out of line with the public views expressed by other Chicano and Mexican American groups. In the spring of that year CASA and the National Coalition for Fair Immigration Laws and Practices led a growing chorus of criticism against the UFW's apparent continued support of the Arnett and Rodino legislation. Such criticism was remarkable in that it simultaneously marked the erosion of support for an individual leader and a political cause that up to this point had enjoyed the overwhelming support of Mexican American and Chicano activists and the crystallization of opinion on the immigration issue.

The UFW's vacillation on the immigration issue renewed conflict among Chicano groups to such a point that the coalition issued an open letter to the union in July 1974. Incensed over an Associated Press story which quoted UFW officials as stating that aliens were "depriving jobs [from] farm workers and posing a threat to all people," the coalition's letter was the clearest statement yet as to the new position of Mexican American and Chicano activists. The coalition insisted that "all workers have the right to seek work in order to support themselves and their families. When we ask for the deportation of all of the workers who have no visas," the letter stated, "we are attacking many good union brothers and sisters that have no visas but would never break a strike." . . .

Chávez was made painfully aware of the strength of Mexican American and Chicano advocates' position on the immigration issue when the controversy made newspaper headlines again that autumn. It was reignited when Attorney General William B. Saxbe announced the Justice Department's intention of deporting a million illegal aliens from the country. Saxbe's announcement was particularly inflammatory in light of the increasing Mexican American sensitivity to the INS raids of the previous eighteen months, but when Saxbe claimed the full support of the UFW the issue exploded. Within days a coalition of organizations, including CASA, MAPA, the American G.I. Forum, LULAC, and the Los Angeles-based Chicana organization Comisión Feminil, angrily denounced the government's plan and demanded Saxbe's immediate resignation.

Chávez gamely tried to defend his policies by flatly asserting that "most of the [Chicano] left attacking us has no experience in labor matters. They don't know what a strike is." "They don't know," he continued, "because they're not workers." . . . Aware, however, that he desperately needed to maintain his base of support among urban Mexican Americans—particularly Chicano activists and students— Chávez was compelled to reassess his union's position on the increasingly explosive issue. In a letter to the editor of the *San Francisco Examiner* dated November 22, 1974, Chávez detailed the UFW's latest stand on the question. While reiterating the UFW's long-term objections to the use of undocumented workers as strike breakers, he subtly altered his position by pinning primary responsibility for "the mass recruitment of undocumented workers for the specific purpose of breaking our strikes and jeopardizing the rights of all farm workers" on the Justice Department and the INS. Chávez flatly denied supporting Saxbe's proposal and charged that the government's plan for mass deportation was nothing but "a ploy toward the reinstatement of a bracero program, which would give government sanction once more to the abuse of Mexican farm workers and, in turn, of farm workers who are citizens." . . . Concluding with a clear overture to militant Chicano groups, Chávez pledged his support to the undocumented because "the illegals [are] our brothers and sisters."

The UFW's shifting position on the immigration question provided a good barometer of the extent to which Mexican American thinking on immigration had changed by the mid-1970s. The debate between the UFW and Chicano and Mexican American activists over Mexican immigration was seriously affecting support for Chávez's movement—and for what up to that point had been the most successful and unified political effort in Mexican American history. Clearly, many Mexican Americans continued to believe that political efforts on behalf of immigrants must remain secondary to efforts made on behalf of American citizens. But by 1975 Chicano activists and most major Mexican American advocacy organizations, including the UFW, had come to a new understanding of the relationship between the immigration controversy and the ongoing struggle to achieve equal rights for Americans of Mexican descent. . . .

* * * *

If anything, the united front of Chicano and Mexican American advocates became more solid after 1975. . . .

. . . Thus, when President Carter announced his immigration reform package in the summer of 1977, Mexican American and Chicano civil rights advocates were shocked to learn that the administration's plan closely resembled Rodino's . . . in arguing that illegal aliens "had breached [the] Nation's immigration laws, displaced many American citizens from jobs, and placed an increased financial burden on many state and local governments," . . .

Virtually every major Mexican American and Chicano organization immediately protested the Carter Plan. . . .

* * * *

The single most dramatic manifestation of the broad-based agreement on the issue was the landmark First National Chicano/Latino Conference on Immigration and Public Policy, held in San Antonio in October 1977. . . . [T]he conference attracted nearly two thousand participants representing groups and individuals as diverse as LULAC, the American G.I. Forum, MALDEF, the Crusade for Justice, CASA, the Socialist Workers Party, and numerous Latino elected and appointed government officials. In the weeks preceding the conference and during the three-day meeting itself, participants made it clear that the government's proposals would meet with widespread Latino opposition. The conference's "Call for Action" rejected virtually all of the government's stated premises on immigration reform, charging that "the truth of the matter [was] that Latinos are to be made the scapegoat for this administration's ineptness at solving economic problems of inflation, unemployment, wage depression and rising consumer frustration." Voicing their dismay at a president from whom they had expected support, the conference organizers protested that "the very same man our Raza supported for the Presidency now seeks to deport us. The Carter administration is designing a new immigration policy. We are the main target."

* * * *

Acting on this new-found unity, conference delegates passed a series of resolutions demanding full and unconditional amnesty for undocumented workers already in the country and the extension of full constitutional rights to resident aliens. Furthermore, the conference demanded that the government guarantee aliens the right to unionize, to receive unemployment compensation, and to educate their children in the United States. After nearly six years of intense debate, Chicano and Mexican American activists had achieved an unprecedented consensus on the immigration controversy, a consensus that would last well into the debate over the Simpson-Rodino immigration proposals in the 1980s.

Conclusion

In many ways the First National Chicano/Latino Conference on Immigration and Public Policy marked the culmination of nearly a half century of Mexican American debate on Mexican immigration. Though the delegates remained ideologically divided on other issues, the meeting's resolutions demonstrated just how far Mexican American and Chicano activists had come on the complex question of the political, social, and cultural relationships between Mexican Americans and immigrants from Mexico. The conference also demonstrated the degree to which immigration had become a central issue in Mexican American politics.

This state of affairs was the outcome of a complicated historical process in which Chicano and Mexican American activists, in their separate pursuits of equal rights for the Mexican-descent minority in the United States, came to recognize how closely linked their campaigns were to the plight of Mexican immigrants. Forced to confront the recurrent issue of the mass immigration of relatively impoverished Mexican laborers into their communities, Mexican American political activists were also constantly compelled to assess and define their own sense of social and cultural identity vis-à-vis the recent arrivals. In the late 1960s few militant Chicano organizations and activists considered Mexican immigration a pressing concern, but the media's depiction of what it termed the illegal alien crisis and the government's subsequent actions in the immigration arena, combined with their own awakened sense of ethnic identity, soon stimulated a strong response among them. In the context of the ethnic catharsis symbolized by the rise of the Chicano movement, young Chicanos tended to view these reform efforts as yet another attack on the Mexican minority in the United States. By the early 1970s their central concern with exploring the sources of Chicano identity, their attempts to redefine the Chicano community, and a growing recognition that Mexican immigrants were Chicanos in the making led them to adopt a new, empathic stance on the issue. By 1975 most Chicano organizations had come to accept the view, as CASA's San Jose, California, affiliate succinctly put it, that "to learn how to protect the rights of workers without papers is to learn how to protect ourselves."

Mexican American moderates had also come to a new understanding of the immigration dilemma. Indeed, by almost any measure the shift in Mexican American activists' opinion on the immigration issue in the 1970s represented a fundamental realignment on one of the most historically vexing and divisive issues in Mexican American politics. Though initially not nearly as aggressive as their Chicano counterparts, Mexican American moderates responded to what they too had come to perceive as an unwarranted campaign of anti-Mexican hysteria. Once they realized that the proposed immigration policy held potentially grave civil rights implications for American citizens of Mexican descent, organizations spanning the political spectrum began to soften their traditional restrictionist positions. And although few Mexican American advocates would admit it, the rhetoric of Chicano militants on both immigration and ethnic politics contributed to their growing awareness of the close relationships that bound Mexican immigrants to American citizens of Mexican descent.

An Attempt to Move Beyond Multiculturalism to a Postethnic America

DAVID H. HOLLINGER

"If Alex Haley had traced his father's bloodline, he would have traveled twelve generations back to, not Gambia, but *Ireland*," Ishmael Reed has observed of Haley's *Roots*. Haley's choice of roots is an emblem for three points that drive this [essay]: the United States is endowed with a *non*ethnic ideology of the nation; it is possessed by a predominantly *ethnic* history; and it may now be squandering an opportunity to create for itself a *post*ethnic future in which affiliation on the basis of shared descent would be more voluntary than prescribed.

The national ideology is nonethnic by virtue of the universalist commitment—proclaimed in the Constitution and the prevailing political discourse—to provide the benefits of citizenship irrespective of any ascribed or asserted ancestral affiliations. This commitment lies behind our sense that Haley had a real choice, and one that was his to make: individual Americans are to be as free as possible from the consequences of social distinctions visited upon them by others. Yet the decision Haley made was driven by a history predominantly ethnic in the extent to which each American's individual destiny has been determined by ancestrally derived distinctions. These distinctions have been flagged, at one time or another, by such labels as Negro, Jewish, Indian, Caucasian, Hispanic, Indigenous, Oriental, Irish, Italian, Chinese, Polish, white, black, Latino, Euro-American, Native American, Chicano, and African American. That any person now classified as black or African American might see his or her own life as more the product of African roots—however small or large a percentage of one's actual, biological genealogy and cultural experience—than of European roots reflects this history.

Hence Haley's choice is the Hobson's choice of genealogy in America. Haley could choose to identify with Africa, accepting, in effect, the categories of the white oppressors who had determined that the tiniest fraction of African ancestry would confer one identity and erase another. Or, Haley could choose to identify with Ireland, denying, in effect, his solidarity with people who most shared his social destiny. The nature of this choice is further illuminated by an experience reported by Reed, whose ancestry is also African and Irish, and who has flirted with the other option in the structured dilemma I am calling Haley's choice. Reed mentioned his "Irish-American heritage" to a "Professor of Celtic Studies at Dartmouth," who "laughed."

In a postethnic America someone of Reed's color could march in a St. Patrick's Day parade without anyone finding it a joke. A postethnic America would offer Haley a choice more real than the one Hobson gave visitors to his stable when he told them that they could take any horse they wanted as long as it was the one nearest the door. And postethnicity would enable Haley and Reed

Excerpts from *Postethnic America* by David A. Hollinger. Copyright © 1995 by Basic Books, a division of HarperCollins Publishers, Inc. Reprinted by permission of HarperCollins Publishers, Inc.

to be both African American and Irish American without having to choose one to the exclusion of the other. Postethnicity reacts against the nation's invidiously ethnic history, builds upon the current generation's unprecedented appreciation of previously ignored cultures, and supports on the basis of revocable consent those affiliations by shared descent that were previously taken to be primordial.

Although this ideal gains some credibility in the context of the recent efforts of mixed-race Americans to defy traditional classifications, the notion of a postethnic America is deeply alien to many features of American and world history. This notion exists in uneasy tension, moreover, with a contemporary system of entitlements predicated on clear, enduring, and monolithic ethno-racial identities. Hence the exploration of the postethnic ideal needs to begin by underscoring the inequalities that have dominated the historical record and recognizing that these inequalities lend credibility to claims made on behalf of communities defined by descent.

Not every citizen's fortunes have been influenced to the same degree, or in the same direction, by America's notorious failure to act on its universalist aspirations. Being classified as Euro-American, white, or Caucasian has rarely been a basis for being denied adequate employment, housing, education, or protection from violence. One response to the patently unequal consequences of ethno-racial distinctions has been to invoke and sharpen the nation's official, Enlightenment-derived commitment to protect all its citizens from them. What this commitment means has been contested, of course, from the day a committee of the Second Continental Congress deleted from the Declaration of Independence Thomas Jefferson's denunciation of slavery to the most recent decisions of the United States Supreme Court concerning the limits of affirmative action. The commitment is plain enough, however, to make obvious the gap between the theory and the practice of American nationality. Indeed, the magnitude and persistence of this gap have inspired a second, very different response: pressure from the gap's other side, its ethnic side.

This alternative strategy for closing the gap asks public authority to facilitate and actively support affiliation on the basis of ancestry. By promoting the development of communities defined by descent, one might reasonably hope for more equal treatment of every descendant of every tribe. After all, the results produced by the long-preferred method of closing gaps—invoking and sharpening the nonethnic ideological tradition—remain disappointing even to most people who believe progress has been substantial. The nonethnic character of the ideological tradition can be construed as part of the problem rather than part of the solution. That tradition treats as irrelevant to citizenship the very distinctions that, in this newer view, need to be asserted, reinforced, and celebrated. Policies that ignore the distinctions now called "ethnic" or "racial" may place at a disadvantage people whose physical appearance, social behavior, or cultural tastes lead others to classify them ethno-racially, and then to discriminate against them in keeping with prevailing prejudice.

This feeling—that the goal of equality demands for America a future even more ethnic than its past—has encouraged the nation to accept a distinctive system of classification by descent-defined communities. This is the set of categories Americans most often confront when asked to identify themselves by a multitude of public and private agencies. On application forms and questionnaires, individuals are routinely invited to declare themselves to be one of the following: Euro-American (or sometimes white), Asian American, African American, Hispanic (or sometimes Latino), and Indigenous Peoples (or sometimes Native American). To gain a clearer understanding of this five-part demographic structure and of the pressures now being brought against it is the chief concern of this [essay].

The ethno-racial pentagon, as we might call it, is a remarkable historical artifact, distinctive to the contemporary United States. The five specified blocs are not equally populated or empowered, but the five-part structure itself is supposed to embrace us all. This structure might also be called a "quintuple melting pot," replacing the "triple melting pot" made famous by Will Herberg's book of 1955, *Protestant-Catholic-Jew.* The distinctions between white Jews, white Catholics, and white Protestants that Herberg and his contemporaries thought so important have now diminished. The elements in each segment of the new structure do "melt" to some extent, but the old figure of the melting pot does not capture the process by which individuals are assigned space on the basis of their perceived communities of descent. Today's device for classification is not even a guide to lines along which genealogical interaction and merging are taking place; rather, it is a framework for politics and culture in the United States. It is an implicit prescription for the principles on which Americans should maintain communities; it is a statement that certain affiliations matter more than others.

Although this ethno-racial pentagon is now visible in many places, it is not the only demographic blueprint now being used. One competitor is defined by the term *people of color.* In this view, white and nonwhite are the two relevant categories, and all distinctions between various "colored" peoples are less significant than the fact that they are nonwhite. But it is the ethno-racial pentagon, not the color-noncolor dichotomy, that public and private agencies most often ask residents of the United States to locate themselves within. A major difference between the two systems of classification concerns culture. The white-colored dichotomy does not have a strong cultural content, but the ethno-racial pentagon does, and increasingly so, especially for educational purposes. An example is the widely publicized decision made in 1989 by the faculty of the University of California at Berkeley to require undergraduates to take a course involving the comparative study of at least three of five American cultures. The three were to be selected from the five blocs in the ethno-racial pentagon.

The pentagon, in its capacity as guide to the cultural life of the United States, has symbolically erased much of the cultural diversity within the Euro-American bloc. The category of Euro-American, observed a journalist concerned with Irish American identity, has accomplished in short order a task that centuries of British imperial power could not complete: making the Irish indistinguishable from the English. Jewish identity, too, receded in significance when all Americans of predominantly European stock were grouped together. To be sure, a value of the pentagon is its capacity to call attention to a certain range of social and cultural diversity. But as is so often the case when the virtues of difference are contrasted to the vices of sameness, at issue is not really difference in general but the highlighting of certain differences at the expense of others.

Indeed, this diminution of the differences between various groups of Euro-Americans has dramatized the contingent, contextual character of the entire process by which differences and similarities are created, perpetuated, and altered. A New Hampshire resident of French Canadian ethnicity may learn, by moving to Texas, that he or she is actually an Anglo. Many European immigrants of the nineteenth century did not come to see themselves as significantly Italian or German until these identities were thrust upon them by the novel demographic conditions of the United States, which rendered obsolete the local identities into which they had been acculturated in Sicily and Swabia. Distinctions between Protestants, Catholics, and Jews of European extraction were once taken as seriously in the United States as are the distinctions now made between Euro-Americans and Asian Americans. Although the insight that ethno-racial distinctions are socially constructed is rapidly gaining ground, it is still obliged to struggle against popular, deeply entrenched assumptions that ethno-racial groups are primordial in foundation.

The sudden transformation of a great number of distinctive ethnic identities into Euro-America ought to make white Americans more sensitive to the comparable erasures of diversity that attend on the other four, pseudoprimal categories, some of which have been sanctioned by longer use. Tribal and linguistic distinctions among Native American peoples have long been lost on many non-Indian observers. The identity one attributes to Americans whose ancestors were Koreans, Cambodians, Chinese, Vietnamese, and Japanese by calling them all Asian Americans (or, in the older usage, Orientals) is obtained by diminishing the differences between them and other Americans of Asian extraction. The Hispanic, or Latino, bloc has more linguistic cohesion than does the Asian American or the Indigenous Peoples bloc, but it, too, can be broken down into subgroups defined, for example, by such points of origin as Argentina, Cuba, El Salvador, Mexico, and Puerto Rico.

The internal diversity of the African American bloc may be the least obvious, as measured by linguistic distinctions and national origins. Nothing, however, illustrates the selective suppression of diversity and the socially constructed character of these ethno-racial blocs more tellingly than the historic denial, by generations of empowered whites, that they share with black Americans a substantial pool of genes. As historian Barbara Fields has put the point, we still have a convention "that considers a white woman capable of giving birth to a black child but denies that a black woman can give birth to a white child." The persistence of the "one-drop rule" deprives those with any hint of black skin of any choice in their ethno-racial affiliation. It makes a mockery of the idea that the ethno-racial pentagon is simply a realistic response to the facts of genealogical life, a set of five gardens each providing natural and sustaining roots. Hence, Haley's choice.

And it is choice, so highly valued by the postethnic perspective, that is so severely limited by this pentagon. A Cambodian American does not have to remain Cambodian, as far as non–Asian Americans are concerned, but only with great difficulty can this Cambodian American cease to be an Asian American. So, too, the Japanese Americans or Chinese Americans. As was implicitly asked by the white autoworker from Detroit who in 1989 clubbed to death the Chinese American Victor Chin, thinking him Japanese, "What's the difference, anyway?" The same applies to the other blocs: indigenous peoples might care who is a Cherokee and who is a Kwakiutl, but outside that section of the pentagon, an Indian is usually an Indian. Some Jewish Americans might take great pride in their particularity as Jews, but from the viewpoint of many African Americans—returning an old favor—it is the whiteness of the whole lot of them that counts. And so on. Moreover, the Bureau of the Census allows the selection of one ethno-racial category and prohibits the choice of more than one.

The lines between the five unequally inhabited sides of the ethno-racial pentagon mark the limits of individual movement, as set by prevailing convention. The several lines distinguishing one segment of the pentagon from another are not resistant in exactly the same degree to intermarriage and other types of border crossing and category mixing. Yet, all are strong enough to function as "racial" as opposed to "ethnic" boundaries. Two kinds of lines are, in fact, being drawn, and they are widely accepted, at least for now: fainter lines distinguish the ethnicities found *within* each of the five blocs (Swedes, Filipinos, Pawnees, etc.), while bolder, thicker lines render the five blocs themselves into races, or race equivalents.

The ethno-racial pentagon is a highly particular creation of recent American history, although it draws upon traditional races. Some of the blocs owe much more than others do to classical race theory of the nineteenth century. Two "races" included in most of those old, now anachronistic schemas—some of which posited the existence of only three or four races, and other of which listed dozens—were called Mongoloid and Negroid, obviously prefiguring the Asian American and African American blocs. But the American adherence to the one-drop rule renders the African American bloc a distinctive formation, unlike the categories traditionally employed in Brazil, South Africa, and elsewhere to recognize racial mixture. Moreover, Mongoloid was generally taken to encompass only the peoples of east Asia, not those of south Asia now routinely included in the Asian American segment of the pentagon. When Mongoloid was construed by race theorists as a broader category, it embraced not the Hindus of south Asia or the Persians of central Asia but the original population of the Western Hemisphere, who, according to some other schemes, were a separate American race. The latter prefigured the Native American or Indigenous bloc.

The Euro-American bloc is obviously derived from the white category, but the American sense of whiteness was not simply an application of the Caucasian of classical race theory. Immigrants from India were undoubtedly Caucasians according to physical anthropologists in the early twentieth century, but the United States Supreme Court ruled in 1923 that south Asian immigrants and their descendants were sufficiently "nonwhite" to be ineligible for naturalization as whites. Jews from Europe and elsewhere were sometimes said to be a separate race. Even European immigrant groups whose whiteness was not legally contested—those from Ireland, Italy, and Poland, for example—were long considered so different that the significance of their whiteness diminished except in contexts when black-skinned people were present. The category of "white people" was articulated in the modern United States primarily in relation to black people and secondarily in relation to people of other colors. It took on greater significance as more and more European immigrant groups consolidated their political and economic connections with the Anglo-Protestant population so obviously in control of American institutions.

"White" is a dehistoricized and culturally vacant category, while "Euro-American" invokes something at least slightly more specific. When voices representing the nonwhite affiliations placed greater emphasis on the cultural component of each of these groups in keeping with the multiculturalism of the 1980s and 1990s, the notion that whites should be comparably particularized as Euro-Americans made better and better sense. The linguistic move from *white* to *Euro-American,* inspired in part by the increasing popularity of *African American* to replace *black* and even *Afro-American,* symbolically cut down to size the whites who would otherwise continue to be anomalously unhistoricized. Whites, too, were migrants from elsewhere to what is now the United States, and thus deserving of a hyphen indicating their point of origin. The transition from "white" to "Euro-American" thus partakes of the particularizing dynamic that has made the ethno-racial pentagon a more sharply defined feature of American life.

The bloc that owes the least to classical race theory is the Hispanic, or Latino, bloc. The various peoples now grouped in this bloc were usually considered white, or Caucasian, until only the last two decades. Also, they were commonly designated by country of origin—Mexico, Cuba, Puerto Rico, etc.—much the way European ethnics were associated with either Italy or Poland or Denmark. "Brown" remained only a colloquial designation, although it served to mark lines of discrimination in many communities, especially in California and Texas. As late as the 1990 census, more than half of the Mexican American population continued to classify itself as white. This notion of the whiteness of Hispanic ethnics has prevailed despite the recognition that the ancestry of the people of Mexico was heavily indigenous and that the population of Puerto Rico consisted largely of a mixture of white and black ancestry in a combination anomalously exempted from the American one-drop rule. A sign of the consolidation of the ethno-racial pentagon, however, is the increasing frequency with which the people in this Latino bloc are being called a "race" in popular discourse.

This gradual racialization of Latinos completes, in turn, the process by which the blocs of the pentagon, whatever their shifting labels, have come to replicate the popular color-consciousness of the past: black, white, red, yellow, and brown. If the classical race theory of the nineteenth century is not directly behind the pentagon, this structure's architecture has its unmistakable origins in the most gross and invidious of popular images of what makes human beings different from one another.

Yet it was enlightened antiracism that led to the manufacturing of today's ethno-racial pentagon out of old, racist materials. The most immediate force behind the creation of the pentagon has been the antidiscrimination and affirmative action policies of the federal government. Reliable statistics were required to enforce the Voting Rights Act of 1965. It was difficult to protect black people from being disenfranchised without census data revealing the extent and exact location of their exclusion from voting. The same dynamic applied to employment discrimination; pools of candidates identified by ethno-racial category had to be available to facilitate enforcement of Title VII of the Civil Rights Act of 1964. Affirmative action runs on numbers. In this context, the single event most responsible for the lines that separate one bloc from another was the issuing in 1977 of what seemed to be a modest directive by the Office of Management and Budget designed to enable government workers to collect needed information.

Statistical Directive 15 of this office of the federal bureaucracy instructed federal agencies to classify people racially as white, black, American Indian, and Asian or Pacific Islander, and to distinguish within the white race between those of Hispanic and those of non-Hispanic origin. Although the words commonly used to denote these groups have shifted somewhat during the years since 1977, and still vary somewhat from context to context, the five blocs of the pentagon are clearly visible in this administrative directive. That it makes sense to call these blocs race equivalents is borne out by the demand of the National Council of La Raza that the Census Bureau reclassify Hispanics as a race rather than merely an ethnic group for the census to be taken in the year 2000.

* * * *

Hence, the blocs of the pentagon get their integrity not from biology, nor even from culture, but from the dynamics of prejudice and oppression in U.S. history and from the need for political tools to overcome the legacy of that victimization. *Race* may be a word we are stuck with, but there are sound reasons to resist its continued use as an unmodified noun. The notion of race was originally developed to refer to the deeply structural differences between human groups; these differences were understood to be both highly determinative of human character and immutable, as in the old figure of speech, "the leopard cannot change his spots." Yet now, paradoxically, we rely upon the word *race* to mark something virtually antithetical: identities created by patterns in human *conduct* that we take to be *changeable,* indeed, exactly the ones we would *most* like to change, namely, the patterns of unequal treatment according to perceived descent. The word *racism* still works splendidly to indicate this pattern of unequal treatment.

The parties to this interaction that are still commonly called races I prefer to subsume under the more general category ethno-racial blocs. This phrasing better reflects our understanding of the contingent and instrumental character of the categories, acknowledges that the groups traditionally called racial exist on a blurred continuum with those traditionally called ethnic, and more easily admits the renunciation, once and for all, of the unequal treatment in America of human beings on the basis of the marks of descent once called racial. Changing our vocabulary will not do much to diminish unequal treatment, but it might at least keep us aware of the direction in which antiracists want to be heading. Racism is real, but races are not.

Real, too, are differences from bloc to bloc in the degree of freedom individuals have to choose how much or how little emphasis to place on their community of descent. Nowhere within the entire ethno-racial pentagon do individuals have more of this freedom than within the Euro-American bloc. The ease with which American whites can affirm or ignore their ethnic identity as Italians, Norwegians, Irish, and so on has often been noted by sociologists, and was convincingly documented by Mary C. Waters in her 1990 book, *Ethnic Options: Choosing Identities in America.* Many middle-class Americans of third- or fourth-generation immigrant descent get a great deal of satisfaction out of their ethnic affiliations, which, in the current cultural and political environment, cost them little. Waters found that these white ethnics tended to avoid aspects of communal life that imposed obligations and intruded on their privacy and individuality. They affirmed what the sociologist Herbert Gans calls "symbolic ethnicity." They take pleasure in a subjective feeling of ethnic identity, but shy away from the more substantive ethnicity that demands involvement in a concrete community with organizations, mutual commitments, and some elements of constraint.

✳ ✳ ✳ ✳

Uncertain as the future is, there is no doubt that the ethno-racial pentagon is now being placed under severe pressure by the rate of intermarriage and by the greater visibility of mixed-race people. The conventional term *mixed race* perpetuates the anachronism of race I quarreled with above. But here the retention of the word *race* actually serves to convey more dramatically than *bloc* the depth of the challenge presented to the system by people whose proclaimed descent lies in more than one of the segments of the pentagon. Between a quarter and a third of all marriages involving Japanese Americans are now out-group marriages. More indigenous people marry outside the Indigenous bloc than marry within it. Even marriages between African Americans and whites, prohibited in some states as late as the 1960s, have increased by 300 percent since 1970. A society long hostile to racial mixture, and exceptionally skilled at denying its reality, now confronts a rapidly increasing population of avowedly mixed-race families and individuals.

And it is the avowal that matters, even more than the numbers. Organizations advancing the distinctive interests of mixed-race peoples have multiplied in recent years and often lobby the Bureau of the Census to recognize them as a distinctive ethno-racial group of their own. The significance of the increase in cross-bloc mixtures consists also in the specific kinds of mixtures that now demand public acceptance. Asian European mixtures are highly visible because the society does not have a long-standing convention of concealing them by automatically consigning them to the Asian side of the descent, as it consigns black-white mixtures to the black side. Moreover, Asians have been more widely understood to be a race than Latinos have been, with the result that Asian European mixtures are, again, more dramatic challenges to the system than have been Latino European mixtures. Mexican Americans, in particular, have long embodied and taken for granted a mixed ancestry. Yet in the present climate this tradition of mixture, as it is reaffirmed and proclaimed, also contributes to the challenge being mounted against the constraints of the pentagon. "By merely reaffirming their heritage," suggests Carlos Fernandez, Mexican Americans are "uniquely positioned to upset the traditional Anglo-American taboo" against mixing.

The most potent threat to the ethno-racial pentagon is probably the increase in avowed double minorities and multiple minorities. People whose descent is divided between African American and one or more of the other non-Euro-American blocs represent a special challenge to the terms of Haley's choice. The phenomenon of the double minority is not new. But persons of mixed African American and either indigenous or Latino descent were traditionally classified as belonging to any one or another of these three blocs, depending on the immediate social environment. The one-drop rule was sometimes quietly compromised when non-Euro-American people were involved. . . .

Thus the routine, public attribution of cultural significance to the blocs of a pentagon originally designed for the purposes of economic and political equality has brought to a point of tragic contradiction two valuable impulses in contemporary America: the impulse to protect historically disadvantaged populations from the effects of past and continuing discrimination, and the impulse to affirm the variety of cultures that now flourish within the United States and that flourish even within individual Americans. Whatever we as a society decide to do with our ethno-racial pentagon, we will do well to remember both the tragic character and the depth of this contradiction. David Harvey has wisely reminded us that a "politics which seeks to eliminate the processes which give rise" to racism may turn out to look very different from a "politics which merely seeks to give full play to differentiated identities once these have arisen."

Just how prescriptively ethnic American society should be is but one of a legion of questions about affiliation that have intensified during the past generation. A prominent characteristic of our era is a preoccupation with affiliation: when the term "we" is invoked, what community is implied? Affiliation has come to the fore in discussions of scientific knowledge, moral values, nationalism, human rights, and the physical health of the earth. In a multitude of discourses, the claims of particular, historically specific communities have been advanced against claims made on behalf of all humankind. The ethno-racial pentagon is a vivid artifact of a sweeping movement from species to ethnos. Within this larger movement in recent and contemporary intellectual history the multiculturalist debates can be addressed most productively, and a postethnic perspective elaborated most clearly.

FURTHER READING

Richard Alba, *Ethnic Identity: The Transformation of White America* (1990).

Vernon M. Briggs, Jr., *Immigration Policy and the American Labor Force* (1984).

Kathleen Neils Conzen, et al., "The Invention of Ethnicity: A Perspective from the USA," *Journal of American Ethnic History* (1992).

David Gutiérrez, *Walls and Mirrors: Mexican Americans, Mexican Immigrants, and the Politics of Ethnicity* (1995).

Keith Fitzgerald, *The Face of the Nation: Immigration, the State, and the National Identity* (1996).

Michael Fix and Jeffrey S. Passel, *Immigration and Immigrants: Setting the Record Straight* (1994).

Herbert J. Gans, "Symbolic Ethnicity: The Future of Ethnic Groups and Cultures in America," in Herbert J. Gans, et al., eds., *On the Making of Americans — Essays in Honor of David Riesman,* (1979), 193–220.

Milton Gordon, *Assimilation in American Life: The Role of Race, Religion, and National Origins* (1964).

Andrew Greeley, *Why Can't They be Like Us?* (1972).

Nathan Glazer and Daniel Moynihan, *Beyond the Melting Pot: The Negroes, Puerto Ricans, Jews, Italians, and Irish of New York City* (1963).

Philip Gleason, *Speaking of Diversity: Language and Ethnicity in Twentieth Century America* (1992).

Will Herbert, *Protestant-Catholic-Jew* (1955).

David Hollinger, *Postethnic America: Beyond Multiculturalism* (1995).

Gil Loescher and John A. Scanlan, *Calculated Kindness: Refugees and America's Half-Open Door, 1945–Present* (1986).

C. Nelson and M. Tienda, "The Structuring of Hispanic Ethnicity: Historical and Contemporary Perspectives," *Ethnic and Racial Studies,* (1985), 49–74.

Michael Novak, *The Rise of the Unmeltable Ethnics* (1972).

Stephen Steinberg, *The Ethnic Myth* (1981).

Subcommittee on Immigration and Refugee Affairs, *U.S. Immigration Law and Policy, 1952–1986* (1988).

Ronald Takaki, ed., *From a Different Shore: Perspectives on Race and Ethnicity in America* (1987).

Mary Waters, *Ethnic Options: Choosing Identities in America* (1990).

Aristide R. Zolberg, "Reforming the Back Door: The Immigration Reform and Control Act of 1986 in Historical Perspective" in Virginia Yans-McLaughlin, ed., *Immigration Reconsidered,* 315–339.

CHAPTER
14

Immigration Transforms America, 1965 to the Present

The Immigration and Nationality Act of 1965 transformed the profile of immigrants to the United States. By repealing national quotas and enlarging the number of visas available to prospective immigrants, the act ushered in a new era of immigration. A series of legislative acts followed—the Refugee Act of 1980, the Immigration Reform and Control Act of 1986, and the Immigration Act of 1990—that fine-tuned immigration policy or dealt with new concerns. The result was a pattern of immigration modified in a number of ways. Most obviously, more immigrants arrived in the United States after 1965. Between 1966 and 1993, 17.4 million legal—and many illegal—immigrants entered the United States. Second, the origins of the immigrants changed. When discriminatory restrictions on immigrants from Asia were lifted, the immigration from Asian countries grew. Migration from Latin America and the Caribbean likewise increased whereas the proportion of immigrants from Europe decreased. In 1990, for example, 43 percent of immigrants came from Latin America and the Caribbean, 25 percent from Asia, 26 percent from Canada and Europe, and 6 percent from other countries. Third, law and circumstances have combined to enlarge such categories of immigrants as refugees, skilled immigrants, and undocumented aliens. Streams of refugees entered the United States either fleeing Communist states or leaving the ravages of war. Even before the passage of the Immigration and Nationality Act, Hungarian and Cuban refugees in the late 1950s were welcomed by the U.S. government as exemplars of people escaping Communism. Although refugees were written into the Immigration and Nationality Act as a preferred category, illegal immigration endures. Modern immigration to the United States thus encompasses a variety of immigrant pasts. Nonetheless, immigrants from diverse origins can be categorized as refugees, entrepreneurs, skilled immigrants, and undocumented immigrants not only by their experience in the United States, but also by increasingly all-encompassing categories of American immigration law.

D O C U M E N T S

The documents in this section depict the variety of immigrant experiences in the United States following the passage of the Immigration and Nationality Act of 1965. The first document (1971–1976) is the story of an immigrant from the West Indies who moves illegally to New York City and discovers his identity in the United States before moving back home to Barbados. The next document (1994) presents a picture of life on the border between Mexico and the United States from the viewpoint of a Mexican who has worked in agricultural labor on both sides of the border. The next two selections consider the refugee experience. First, a Cuban American (1979) describes how he came to dislike life in Castro's Cuba and fled the island by boat illegally, eventually arriving in Miami. Then, a Hmong immigrant from Laos (1975) describes his people's alliance with the Central Intelligence Agency during the Indochinese War, a collaboration that subsequently forced members of his family to flee their native land and attempt to adjust to life in the United States. The final three documents explore the lives of some of those in America's immigrant communities. A Filipina American (1979) portrays her life as a skilled immigrant who muses over her identity and writes of her struggles to adapt to differences of life in the United States. Next, a Korean American (1984–1992) bitterly recounts his condition in the United States. The owner of a small grocery store, he feels unappreciated, bitter about race relations, and wishes to return home to Korea. Finally, a Vietnamese American woman (1975–1984) who fled her country after the Vietnamese War explains her difficulties. An immigrant who did not want to move, she finds herself in a country where relationships within the family—especially between parents and children—are very different.

A Caribbean American Observes Life in New York City, 1971–1976

When I went [to the United States] in 1971 I said I'd stay away for no more than five years. That way when I'd get back to Barbados I'd still be in my twenties and I could build a house and start things going. My aspirations at the time were a house, a car, lots of money, and good clothes. I looked at the aim of life as being material gain. Art and the things that are important to me now never even ventured into my mind.

I took a plane to New York. Coming out from the airport was beautiful. I thought, I'm going to have a glamorous life. But then we got into Brooklyn, and I am thinking, Gosh, I'll be glad to get out of this area. Then we pulled up to a house, to my girlfriend's relatives, and I couldn't believe it. The neighborhood was worse than anything I'd ever seen in Barbados. Can this be America? Is this the same place the people talk about? That's what I thought to myself. That was Bed-Stuy [Bedford-Stuyevesant], one of the most depressed areas of Brooklyn.

From George Gmelch, *Double Passage: The Lives of Caribbean Migrants Abroad and Back Home.* Copyright © 1993 The University of Michigan Press. Reprinted by permission of The University of Michigan Press.

The first two days were horrifying. My girlfriend's family kept saying to me, "Make sure that you lock the doors." There were three locks on one door. I thought, Nobody needs three locks on one door. I couldn't believe it. In Barbados we kept our front door open, and now in Brooklyn they're telling me that not only must I keep the door closed at all times, but I need three locks.

* * * *

. . . I went and applied for a job in the garment district. I went to Starwood Fabrics; there were two Bajans working there and some Puerto Ricans, and I got the job. . . .

* * * *

The garment district was my education. Here I was in the middle of the garment center, and I'd go into these men's offices, they were so fabulous, so plush. . . . I'd think, If this guy's office is like this, imagine what his home is like. You'd read in the newspaper that some of these guys come in to work from Long Island by helicopter. You are impressed, and you start thinking that you'll work toward that, toward what these guys have.

* * * *

When I first saw those fabulous offices in the garment district I'd think to myself, If I work hard, I can do well too, and I can have these nice things. To improve myself I tried to absorb what I was seeing in New York, to learn from it and apply it in a positive way. Later what I came to want was to see my people develop, not just me as an individual. I realized that none of those bosses I saw in the garment district would be considered great men, because they were out for themselves.

It was meeting Paul Webster that changed my life in New York. He was a young Barbadian, about my age, but he was from a different background than I am. He was from the privileged class; he grew up in . . . an area . . . which was then almost totally white. He grew up as one of the bourgeoise. When I met him I couldn't understand why he'd want to live in New York, in poor conditions, when he didn't have to . . . Through him I learned about other people who were also privileged and who were struggling against the unfairness in their societies . . . Through him I started to take things seriously, and I started to read.

I read James Baldwin's *If Beale Street Could Talk, The Autobiography of Malcolm X, The Muhammed Ali Story,* and books by W. E. B. Du Bois, Marcus Garvey, and Frederick Douglass. I followed the life of Adam Clayton Powell and Harry Belafonte. I read black history, which I wasn't aware of at all because my experience of anything black had come from reading schoolbooks in Barbados, and that was the British interpretation of history. When we went to school in Barbados we were told that we had no history—that our history was just the slave thing and that it wasn't worth knowing. I believed them. When I look back on it now I realize that the reason I didn't know anything about black history was because it was deliberate. I knew Henry VIII. I knew King Charles I. I knew Shakespeare. But I didn't know the history of my own people.

* * * *

I started moving around New York, seeking information. I checked out the Muslims, I checked out the Italians, I checked out the Jews, I checked out other groups, and I found out what they were all about. I stored that information right up here in my head because I knew that one day I would use it, and that's what I'm doing right now. It comes out piece by piece in my music. When I write a song like "Boots" or "Jack" or "Culture" it almost always comes out of my experience.

I loved New York. I loved the sports, the respect that they paid to artists; I loved the beautiful buildings. But there was a lot that I didn't like too. . . .

* * * *

. . . it was the violence that really bothered me. I had an Arab friend who sold newspapers near the entrance to the Saratoga station on the IRT [Interboro Rapid Transit]. I used to say hello to him each morning. One day I talked to him in the morning, and then later in the day, on my way home, I saw the shop closed. I had never seen him closed at that time. I was thinking it might be an Arabic holiday. Then on the evening news I heard that this Arab guy, my friend, was killed. He was killed resisting the robber; the robber got something like $18. . . . This guy I knew; he was no statistic. I knew him not as an Arab, not as a statistic; I knew him as an intelligent human being. I saw him in the morning, and he was dead in the afternoon.

New York is not like Barbados, where people trust other people. I suppose it's the size of the place, the masses of people, that make people fearful. When we moved to Rockway Parkway in Brooklyn there was this white woman living next door. It was snowing one day, and she had these two huge grocery bags in her car. Now, she never knew me, and I never knew her at that point. I said, "Can I help you with the bags?"

She said, real nervous, "No, no, it's fine, I can manage." She thought I was some mugger.

I said, "Look, I am a West Indian, and I am from an island called Barbados, and my name is Tony, and I want to help you. I live right here, next door."

After a pause she said, "Okay."

I carried the groceries, and, as I went to take them into the house, she said, "No, just leave them on the step." She was afraid to let me in the house.

* * * *

When I first lived in New York I was an illegal alien. Not having the proper papers to work was hard on me. When I saw a policeman on the subway, I'd think he could come and arrest me right now. Once I laughed to myself at the thought, and the policeman looked right at me. Being illegal made me feel horrible, like an eighteenth-class citizen, not a second-class citizen but an eighteenth-class citizen—as low as you can go. I didn't want to live like this; I wanted to live as a respected human being. There were times when I packed up everything, saying, "I am going to leave; I'm going back to Barbados." . . .

But in 1976 I finally came home. . . . But when I got home and got in with my friends and other people I wanted to stay. It was really good to be in Barbados, and after awhile I stopped thinking about New York.

Santiago Maldonado, a Mexican American, Details the Lives of Undocumented Immigrants in Texas, 1994

When I was about eight years old, I worked in the cotton fields in the El Paso area. I used to chop weeds and pick chiles and onions. I averaged ten or twelve dollars a day. It all depended on how much I would pick. Even though the child labor laws prohibit kids from working all day long like I was doing, it was common for the parents to take *all* the family to the field. . . . People used to be transported to the fields every day. There was this place *right* across the international bridge coming from Juárez on El Paso Street. Every morning from 4:00 to 5:30 A.M. the buses would leave and go to the farm fields. I would make it a habit to be there on time around 4:00 every morning and get aboard the buses.

The majority who got on the buses were people from Juárez or people from South El Paso. The people from Juárez were Green Carders. I recall one evening when certain Mexican aliens were on the buses and the Immigration and Naturalization Service officials came aboard the buses to inspect to see if anybody was an illegal alien. Somebody behind me got nervous when they saw him. He got all panicky and decided to get out of the bus through the back door. He started running. An officer started running after him. He caught up with him, and what I saw was really something. He beat him up completely. I could hear the Mexican yelling and yelling for the agent to stop beating him up. He was beating him with a club stick, a *macana.* Finally he stopped. The man was put in a van and detained. I guess he was transported back to Mexico. The illegal alien didn't provoke or resist the officer when he was caught. The officer just wanted to make it look like the illegal was really doing all the resisting, and he wasn't. He seemed like a very good man when he was in the bus.

I recall many instances in Dell City and in El Paso when the Immigration raided the fields. The majority of my friends in the fields were illegal aliens. All the time they would talk about being afraid of getting caught by the Border Patrol, which had a habit of checking the fields. Every time we could see they were coming, the Mexicans would run and hide. It was a daily routine, always going on. Some were lucky and some weren't. . . .

In terms of Mexicans crossing illegally, I would say that the main crossing point along the entire boundary would be the area . . . adjacent to the river, two blocks to the west of the El Paso–Juárez bridge. More people cross at that point

Excerpts from an interview with activist and biculturalist Santiago Maldonado from: Oscar J. Martinez, *Border People: Life and Society in the US-Mexico Borderlands.* Reprinted by permission of the University of Arizona Press.

than any other point that I can think of. I've talked to people who have come all the way from South America and from the interior of Mexico, but the majority are usually from Juárez. The reason I'd talk to them is because I live close to the presidios where the aliens used to hide from the Border Patrol, especially in the rest rooms, on the roofs, under cars—you name it, you'll find them everyplace. Sometimes I do my best to help them. I'll tell them, "The Border Patrol is hiding here and there. I would recommend that you cross at this point so you won't be caught." If I have a car, I'll give them a ride. If I can't get transportation, I'll call a taxi to help them. I've done this a lot.

I'm not really afraid because I got used to it. I know all the ways to escape the Border Patrol. I know where to look. I just don't even think about it. My grandfather was caught twice for transporting illegal aliens in the Sierra Blanca area, and he served two jail sentences. The last time he was put on probation. I got a lot of encouragement from him because I really looked up to him, and that's why I started doing it. Plus it was the fun of obtaining money. I don't charge high prices. As a matter of fact, in the majority of the cases I don't even charge. Sometimes if I don't have gasoline in my car, I ask them for a dollar or two. I just do it to help them. When my grandfather was doing this, a lot of illegal aliens were being arrested, rounded up, and transported back to Mexico. The growers were in desperate need of more cheap labor. My grandfather didn't have a job at that time. That was the only avenue he had, and he took it.

People cross at every hour of the day and night. Occasionally Border Patrolmen station themselves in my neighborhood, but because of a lack of manpower and so many people crossing, they have to turn their attention to other locations, so that leaves the opportunity for more people to cross close to my home.

A Cuban Flees to the United States, 1979

I was born in Trinidad, in Las Villas province, in 1956 and worked as an auto mechanic. There were eleven brothers, of whom I am the youngest. My family was humiliated by Fidel's government, although they had fought in the Revolution and supported it in the beginning. My family eventually turned against the system because they saw that what was happening in Cuba was not what they had struggled for.

There were many reasons for their anger and disappointment. In the early 1960s the government went back on its promise to distribute land among the *campesinos*. Instead, even those like my parents who had small farms had to give them up and those farmers who had never owned land just became paid workers of the state.

* * * *

From *Freedom Flights: Cuban Refugees Talk about Life under Castro and How They Fled His Regime* by Lorrin Phillipson and Rafael Llerena. Copyright © 1980 by Lorrin Phillipson and Rafael Llerena. Reprinted by permission of Random House, Inc.

. . . The freedoms that Cubans had fought for were being taken away—with the newspapers and television and radio stations run by the government, and people arrested and sent to prison only because they were suspected of being against the government. Many of them were revolutionaries. They were *not* opposed to the Revolution but to the methods being used to force everyone to agree with whatever Fidel and his followers said. They removed my family to Havana and put my father in jail for nine years, one of my brothers for seven years, and another for six and a half years. They sent me to a reformatory because I was too young to go to prison. . . .

In Cuba the police don't leave you alone. They tell you that you can't be without a shirt; that you can't have long hair. The young people don't receive anything decent for their work. There are endless lines for everything, and even on the beach there is nothing to eat. You have no aspiration for anything. You can't even work to be able to afford a bicycle because there aren't any available. Here, if I want to buy a car, I may have to work for ten years, but I know that at least I will be able to buy one. In Cuba there isn't a future of any kind. Always they talk about tomorrow, but if you don't have a present, you can't have a future. . . .

* * * *

I decided to come here because there is freedom of thought, and expression. Since I did not belong to any of the mass organizations in Cuba, I had trouble. They fired me from jobs and when I tried somewhere else, they would check my political record and not hire me. Then when I went to another place, they would give me the excuse that I could not work there because I had long hair. I would go somewhere else and they would say they had no jobs, but it was because I did not have any friends there. I wanted to become an engineer, but it is very hard for the average person. It is almost always possible, however, if you are the son of a *pincho*. Then you can go to the university and have a career in engineering. . . . In the present system the blacks are often the most rebellious because the government says the blacks deserve everything—and then they give them the worst jobs. From above they say there is equality. Fine. Go see the Politburo in Cuba. There are almost no blacks on it.

* * * *

I had been planning to escape from the time I was in the military service, but I could not find anyone to go with me. People thought the way I did, but they did not have the courage to try. Most of them wanted to go in a motorboat, but to steal one is a big problem. Also, the radar can pick you up right away. The patrols locate where you are, don't tell you to stop and then they shoot at you. Obviously, I did not want to die, so I looked for a way to fight and escape. . . .

Finally five of us got together and made arrangements during the week before we left, September 21, 1979. One guy worked with me, one worked on the railroad, one who was eighteen was in the military service, and the last one was from La Juventud Cubana [The Cuban Youth]. He was known as an excellent young Communist, a fine worker and a good revolutionary. . . .

* * * *

At two o'clock we lowered the boat into the water. It was hard because we had to climb down a cliff. . . . At first the weather was good, but the trip was very bad. Our clothes were dark so that they would not attract attention, but we wore short-sleeved shirts—mine was of gauzelike cotton—and these weren't much protection. I knew how to swim a little, but some of the others did not know how at all. When we started we did not even know how to row. One oar went one way and the other another way. Then the boat kept turning around and tilting. We couldn't go straight! Finally we caught on to the rhythm of rowing. We rowed without stopping, two of us taking the oars while the other three rested. At night we guided ourselves by the moon and the stars, and in the day time by the sun. We rowed all day Tuesday and then all the next day and night. By then we had advanced a long distance.

The following night it began to rain and we had a storm. When we couldn't see the moon, we had no sense of our direction. We had no orientation that night. It was raining so hard—the drops fell with such force that they burned my face. There was such a strong wind that we lost control of the boat. We couldn't row, so we tried to sleep. We could not really manage to because the boat was so small and the water around us was high. Also, if you were not awake, you could tip the boat over. This was the most frightening part of the trip. When we couldn't row we felt helpless, whereas while we were rowing I knew we could make it. . . . When a lot of water poured into our boat, we tried to bail it out with a boot. We had not even brought a can because we did not want the radar to pick it up.

Wednesday morning the weather improved, but the sea was still very rough. The storm had driven us back toward Cuba. But we began rowing again, saying, "To Cuba? Not even dead!" . . . The sun was very strong. All we had was salty water to drink. Some, like me, only wet our lips with the water. Sometimes because we were so hot and sweaty we put our heads over the side of the boat. One time when we did so, big sharks came around us and followed our boat for a few kilometers. In desperation we threw our shoes at them. After that we stopped leaning over the side to splash our faces. While we were rowing we saw boats far away but had nothing to make reflections with. When we tried signaling one, it did not see us. Then another one coming in our direction detoured. Meanwhile two of our friends were very seasick, nauseated and retching but not vomiting, since we had not eaten anything. For a long time they were too ill to row. By the time we reached the United States our hands were all bloody, and so were our behinds. The skin on our legs was peeling off.

. . . On Friday morning at seven we were in sight of Lighthouse #6 in Miami. The arrival was very nice! . . . Two in our group spoke a little English. They told the people we were from Cuba and wanted water. Then we explained that we had escaped. The American picked up the radio and called the police. He gave us some food, and divers in another boat gave us some sandwiches, apples and Coca-Cola. They took us onto their boat and let us sleep there until the police came in the afternoon to take us to the Coast Guard station. There they questioned us, took us in a jeep to the Miami airport, filled out some forms (like provisional passports), and gave us food and clothing, since we had arrived in rags and without shoes. It is so hard to get used to the idea that we are finally free. What remains for us now is to begin working as soon as we can.

A Hmong's Story of Escape from Laos, 1975

During the war in Vietnam in the early 1960s, the American CIA [Central Intelligence Agency] recruited many Hmong men to help them fight against the Communists. The CIA knew that the northeastern region of Laos [which the 1954 Geneva accords gave to the Communist Pathet Lao to control] was occupied mainly by Hmong, so the CIA recruited Hmong to fight there and farther south along the Ho Chi Minh Trail [that ran along the border between North Vietnam and Laos, and between South Vietnam and Cambodia] to prevent the North Vietnamese from transporting weapons, soldiers, and food to their men fighting in South Vietnam. Many American pilots were shot down in Laos, so our job was to rescue them also.

When the Hmong were asked to help, we did so because we knew the United States of America is a powerful country that will help us in return in the future. Though we were uneducated and without skills, we received no military training before we were sent into battle. We fought first, then trained afterwards. We helped fight the Communists from 1960 to 1975. After the Communists came to power, they started bombing our villages. Many Hmong military leaders left on May 14, 1975. For that reason, we also had to seek refuge elsewhere. That is why we are here in the United States.

Before the CIA started its "secret war" in Laos, we Hmong had lived in peace. We had no wars and no worries. We gathered vegetables from our gardens, harvested rice from our fields, and hunted in the jungles for meat. Our cattle, when sold, provided us with money. Life was simple. Anyone who was not lazy and was willing to farm could feed himself and his family. Because there were no roads to the cities, we lived on what we grew ourselves.

* * * *

When the Communists took over Laos and General Vang Pao fled with his family, we, too, decided to leave. Not only my family, but thousands of Hmong tried to flee. I rented a car for thirty thousand Laotian dollars, and it took us to Nasu. There, we met with other relatives to discuss our plans for fleeing to Thailand. We felt compelled to leave because many of us had been connected with the CIA. . . . Thousands of Hmong were traveling on foot. Along the way, many of them were shot and killed by Communist soldiers. We witnessed a bloody massacre of civilians.

* * * *

In late June 1975, . . . we walked through dense jungles, over many mountains, through rice fields and flat land, and ended in a refugee camp at Pakxom on July 30. Shortly afterward, we were moved to another refugee camp . . ., where we lived for three years. My youngest daughter died there. We came to the United

---

From *Hmong Means Free: Life in Laos and America,* edited and with an introduction by Sucheng Chan. Copyright © 1983 by Temple University. Reprinted by permission of Temple University Press.

States on October 2, 1978. We landed in Los Angeles and stayed there with my brother for ten days. We then settled in Isla Vista [a small community contiguous to the campus of the University of California at Santa Barbara].

Since I spoke very little English, it was hard to find a job. We received public assistance for several months. On August 5, 1979, I was hired as an assembler at Joslyn Electronic Systems in Goleta, where I have worked ever since. Today I have nine daughters and one son. Two of my daughters were born in Laos, one in Thailand, and the rest in the United States.

* * * *

The laws in Laos are very different from those in the United States. That is why people of my generation often feel frustrated living in America. One of the reasons that many Hmong are unhappy in the United States is that back in Laos, a man must pay a price for his wife, but she does not have to pay anything for him. Paying a bride price is a ritual we have practiced for hundreds of years— ever since our ancestors lived in China. Because a man must pay so much money for his wife, if she has an affair with another man, the husband may sue the lover for damaging the marriage. The settlement is not reached in a court of law but between the families involved. In fact, when a wife commits adultery, if the husband is angry enough, he can kill her lover, and it would not be considered a crime.

Besides adultery, stealing is also not tolerated in our homeland. If a person is caught stealing, no matter what his age, he is thrown into prison and tortured. He is released only after he has been tortured so much that he pleads for his life and promises never to steal again. As everyone fears torture, there are very few thieves among the Hmong.

A problem that we Hmong parents face today in America is disciplining our children. It is so difficult! Not only are our children not listening to us, but we parents can be thrown in jail for trying to teach them what is right. In Laos, we disciplined our children by a good beating. If a child fights with other children or with his or her brothers and sisters, or talks back to his or her parents, or steals, then he or she receives a beating. After a few such beatings, children learn their lesson and become better persons. But today, here in America, if we hit our children, if they are smart they will tell their teacher or call the police. The children of today have no respect for their elders and do not fear their parents. Americans do not understand our culture, and we do not understand theirs. Therefore, we run into problems when raising our children in the United States.

* * * *

When I first arrived in the United States . . . .

. . . I was homesick. I missed my country. The mountains, trees, flowers, and animals here are all so different. There is nothing here to remind me of my country, and that makes me sad. The sky, the earth, and the mountains in Santa Barbara County are not the same as those in Laos. The people and the social environment are also different. I am sad not knowing whether I will ever see the flowers and bamboo groves in Laos again.

Valerie Corpus, a Skilled Filipina American, Reflects on the Advantages and Disadvantages of Life in the United States, 1979

I don't consider myself Asian. I am Filipino. When I think of Asian I think of Singaporeans or Malaysians. It's culture. Tagalog is the language I speak and was raised on. That's what I speak. That and Spanish.

I didn't like it when I first got here. . . . I didn't like seeing bums on the street, or people kissing in the street or in stairways, or these kids selling dope.

. . . I hated everything. The most shocking thing to me when I came to this country was . . . having to learn to deal with different types of people. I was on the subway one time, sitting down, reading one of my math books. And this white woman came up to me and told me I didn't belong here, and I should go back to where I came from. She said I had no right to be here and that she should be sitting in my seat. I didn't know what to do. I didn't do anything. There was a white man next to me, and he started talking to her about why she shouldn't say those things. . . .

I have a degree in mathematics, and I want to work on a master's degree in health care administration. The pressure is on for me to get another degree. Most of my cousins are getting master's degrees. . . . My aunt's in Berkeley; she is working on her second degree. My father has three degrees in engineering: electrical, mechanical, and nuclear. Everybody has a degree in my family. My uncle says an undergraduate degree will soon be like a high school diploma, and a master's degree will be like a bachelor's, so that's why I am rushing. I want to get it before it is worthless.

Money is why many Filipinos want to come to the U.S. Everybody leaves, everybody works outside the country. There is no future there. Many Filipinos go into nursing because they know they can get work visas to come to this country easier. Usually, when they hire nurses, the nurses look for housing in the area. Like with my aunt, she lives a block from the hospital, and she took three nurses to live with her, so the nurses can be more comfortable in a foreign country. Usually after their contract expires, the employer petitions to have them stay in the country. If not, they go back to the Philippines. I've heard of some cases too, when their visas expire, they might try to hide or maybe go to Canada.

* * * *

I like it a lot better here, because I have a future here. I don't have a future there. Because over there I would have to call up my uncle or my uncle's friend to ask him to help me do this or that, such as get a job.

I just don't vote. I just don't care. As long as everything is fine in my life, I don't feel a need to. I mean, government doesn't seem to touch me, anyway. It doesn't seem to affect my life personally, so I don't worry about it. I read about it, but I won't worry about it. I don't see it as a responsibility. It's one of those things.

From *Asian American Experiences in the United States: Oral Histories of First to Fourth Generation Americans from China, the Philippines, Japan, India, the Pacific Islands, Vietnam and Cambodia* © 1991 Joann Faung Jean Lee, by permission of McFarland & Company, Inc., Publishers, Jefferson, NC 28640.

Things are better now because I've gotten used to it here. I am a citizen. As for going back [to] the Philippines, it's fun to visit, but I would not go back to live again. I went back to the Philippines last year. I lived with my uncle. When I saw my uncle's maid who had raised him—doing the laundry and cooking—I wanted to help her, but my uncle said, "Oh no, she can manage that, just mind your own business." So it feels different, sitting down at the table and having someone serve you. All you have to do is eat and enjoy it.

A Korean American's Bitter Life in the United States, 1984–1992

When I was growing up in Korea in the 1960s, life was very difficult. We were very regimented, forced to have our hair cut short and forced to wear uniforms to school. I faced a lot of economic hardships. We did not always have enough to eat. Sometimes all of my family members had to share one egg.

✳ ✳ ✳ ✳

After I finished my military service and attended college, someone offered to introduce me to a Korean immigrant woman who was living in the U.S. I agreed to the marriage, and that's how I happened to move to America. I landed in Dallas, Texas, in July 1984.

Since I could not speak English, I was very handicapped. But I worked so hard. I tried everything; I was a janitor for the first three and a half years, then I worked as a white shirt presser at a dry cleaners, and then I was a dishwasher and a hamburger cook. I got a job working for a white shopkeeper in a neighborhood where ninety percent of the customers were black. I got into trouble because I started giving away the ends of salami and other meat chubbs to the customers, since the boss was not able to sell them anyway. When he ordered me to stop doing that, I was threatened and cursed by the customers. I was harassed a lot; even though I could not fully understand what people were saying to me, I could tell it was unkind. . . . The white owner had promoted me to a supervisor position, but I took my old janitorial job back to avoid all the hassles.

✳ ✳ ✳ ✳

I wanted to have my own store because when I used to work in the hamburger shop or the sandwich shop, I would hear the customers complaining about the mustard or whether or not the food was cooked the way they liked it. I thought that if I had my own store, I would not have to listen to these kinds of complaints. . . .

I feel very disabled because I am not good in English. I have never had time to get any education in America. Even if school were free I would not have time to go. I work in this shop fourteen hours a day, seven days a week. My wife works here nine hours a day. The only other thing we do is go to church. But even then, we can't even go together; one person has to mind the store. I have two children,

From *East to America: Korean American Life Stories.* Copyright 1996 by Elaine H. Kim and Eui-Young Yu. Reprinted by permission of *The New Press.*

five and six years old. . . . But I only see them in the morning when I drop them off at preschool before opening our store. By the time I get home at 2:00 A.M., they are already asleep. . . . I have to keep this place open late so that we can pay the rent and service our debts.

My wife and I together work twenty-three hours a day, seven days a week. There are no days off. I figure that our hourly wage is less than minimum wage. Even if I died at this moment, I have nothing to leave behind.

Hundreds of people come into my store. I can't satisfy all of them perfectly. Sometimes dozens and dozens of people want change for a $20 bill in one day. They get the bills from the ATM machine next door. When I refuse, they curse me. I can change money twenty or thirty times, but not hundreds of times. People don't understand.

I always work so hard. I eat at the store. There is a little hot plate upstairs. I just wear jeans and a T-shirt to work. I don't spend money on eating out or on clothes. I know that many Korean store owners have been killed. I feel like this is a war zone and that my life has become like a battle. If I close my eyes or relax my vigilance for a second, I might lose my life. I always have to be on my toes.

After the Rodney King verdict, the other stores around here were broken into. The windows were smashed. One market down the street was completely looted of everything of value. People broke down my door and started looting until I showed them I had a gun. At first, they said, "Go ahead and shoot," and kept putting things into their pockets. So I shot one round into the air. They threw down what they had and left. The police didn't even get here until much later. They advised me to carry Mace instead of a gun.

I am scared every day. I have been beaten, cursed, and spat upon. Sometimes young kids demand cigarettes, and if I don't sell to them, they get angry. Once someone threw a bottle at me. If I hadn't blocked it with my arm, I would have been hit in the face. The bottle broke on contact, and I had to go get stitches on my arm. The police only come after everything is over. They ask for descriptions, write a police report, and leave.

Last year about three hundred students tried to break down the door with a battering ram. The window didn't have steel rails, so they broke through the glass. Again the police came when it was too late. Sometimes street people who are drugged out come in here and start harassing me or throwing things around. Once a drunk came in here and threw merchandise on the floor, broke the window, and ran away. I had to chase him several blocks down the street. I handed him over to the police. Later, when he got out on probation, I signed the release on the condition that he not come back to my store. Last summer, I was badly beaten when I tried to block the doorway as a man who had stolen something before was trying to enter the store. I was alone, and several men beat me up so badly that I had to go to the hospital. After that I got health insurance. Life was hard in Korea, but over there I would not have to endure this kind of abuse.

This is war. There's no end to war. It's just continual escalation. I've tried everything: video cameras, Mace. It's a sign of social disease; there's no end, no solution.

* * * *

Now when I compare the dream I had of America with the reality, I know this is not an easy country to live in. When I finish paying off my debts, I hope I can go back to Korea. People are always saying that anyway: "Fucking Chinese, go home!" I hear that every day.

It is very hard to live as an immigrant here. Race discrimination is far too strong. It's impossible to overcome the limitations on first-generation immigrants. There is a real limit to how far a person can go.

In the old days, it was hard to live in Korea, no matter how hard you worked. But during the last ten years, it seems to have become possible to survive there if you try. My parents are in Korea. They have seen how I live here in America, working like a dog in this crowded little space. They say, "Hurry up and come back home."

I am sick and tired. I feel defeated. The prospects for my further growth are very limited. What kind of future is there? American-born Koreans, when they grow up, will face race discrimination, even if they are born here. It's not fair. Will the second, third, or fourth generation born in the U.S. ever be equal? I know one man who doesn't let his two U.S.-born sons work in his store. They speak fluent English and can understand everything people say and do, so they feel worse. They get into fights with the customers.

In my own case, I am a cripple without any American education. There's no way out. I just have to continue to work hard. I have a college degree in architecture from Hong Ik University in Seoul, but look at me now. Look at what happened to me. When people criticize me, why don't they think about my circumstances? I have worked so hard only to have so many shameful things happen to me. I cannot understand; if other people are partially at fault and don't acknowledge it, they aren't human beings.

* * * *

Right now, the American dream is unattainable. I want to sell this store and move back to Korea. But who would buy this place? Once you get into this kind of work, it never ends.

A Vietnamese American Considers Changing Relations Between Parents and Children in the United States, 1978–1984

. . . I didn't want to leave Vietnam, but all of my children were gone; I'm old, and they have to take care of me. So I had to follow them. . . .

The main problem that I have in America is that I don't know how to speak English. Second, if I wanted to go somewhere, I cannot. I would have to use a car, but I cannot drive. If I use the bus, I am afraid that I will become lost.

I have lots of barriers. If I have to fill out papers, I cannot. I also am unable to answer the phone. I know how to take down phone numbers, just a little, not much.

Reprinted from *Hearts of Sorrow: The Vietnamese-American Lives* by James M. Freeman with the permission of Stanford University Press. © 1989 by the Board of Trustees of the Leland Stanford Junior University.

If I'm sick accidentally, I don't know what to do because we are always home by ourselves, my husband and I. In Vietnam, we had relatives nearby, and if something happened, they would get together. I'm kind of sad because over here relatives are too far away from us. If people speak a little, I can understand only a very little, not a lot.

My children take care of me like usual. I have a hot temper; I always yell at them if they do something wrong. I see that children do not obey me as much as when they were in Vietnam. It's sad sometimes; it creates anger. When I lived in Vietnam, it was different. My children were young at that time. We took care of them so they obeyed us more. They were afraid of us and respected us more.

Here we need them more; they don't need us.

* * * *

If it were peaceful, I would live in Vietnam. I would live in the countryside because I have property and fields near the river, also a big garden with lots of fruits such as jackfruit and banana. I'd go back and live there. I'd make my living selling rice paper or chicken and pigs. It's more of a comfortable life.

Over here, for older people, we receive money from the government; if not, we would die of starvation because we are older and don't know what to do. In Vietnam, we have less fear of survival, but over here, I'm afraid that when I get older I'll have to go into a nursing home to stay there, because all of my children are working. My husband and I have to stay home ourselves, all alone. Now I am fine and can stay home, but later what will happen? Old age here is scary.

Children over here don't take care of their parents. In Vietnam, if poor, a person lived with his children; if rich, with only one child, possibly the youngest. Life was much more comfortable if rich because children and grandchildren would take care of you.

In America, every time we want to go somewhere, we have to wait for our children to take us. If we want to visit relatives, we don't know what to do. In Vietnam, we could travel around much more easily.

In Vietnam, a person would build a house. Children would want to remain in that house. Even if they went away for some reason, they would want to be close by at the time of the death of the parent, and they themselves would want to be buried near their ancestors. Rich people preserve a piece of property on which to bury the family members; it's a grave property. From the twenty-third to the thirtieth day of the new year, children must visit the graves of their ancestors.

In Vietnam we had a house. Once in a while our children came back to visit. Our youngest remained in the family, while those who lived close by would see us often. Here in America, that's not so. Two of my sons I never see. I don't even know my grandchildren, how tall they are.

The difference is that over here children do not obey their parents; in Vietnam, they obeyed us more. Over here, whenever we say something, they like to argue about it. My husband and I dislike this. If our children want something and we don't like it, they will not listen to us. Things we consider to be right they consider wrong. Like a wife they select whom we don't like. They argue with us, against it, saying that it's right for them and that they will take the responsibility for it. They claim it's their *right* and that we don't have the right to tell them what to do. It is just like we are strangers; they won't let us interfere. [. . .]

* * * *

No matter what might happen, no matter where we would have landed or stayed, we had to leave Vietnam, not only for America, but for anywhere. If my husband had remained in Vietnam, the Communists would have arrested and killed him. Therefore we had to go. We left everything behind.

 E S S A Y S

The following two essays address issues regarding the post-1965 immigrant. First, Elliott Robert Barkan, a historian at California State University at San Bernardino, provides an overview of the recent immigration. Focusing on the impact of immigration law, Barkan explores the ways in which immigrants have adapted to legal enactments. He also considers a series of issues such as the "feminization" of immigration, the varieties of immigrant experiences, and the effect immigration has had on the United States in general and on locales welcoming particularly large numbers of immigrants. In the second essay, Timothy P. Fong, a political scientist at University of California at Davis, comprehensively explores one such community. Although many scholars have analyzed urban concentrations of immigrants, Fong examines instead the "suburban Chinatown" of Monterey Park, California. He shows how a recent immigration of people from Taiwan, Hong Kong, and mainland China has recast the population of Monterey Park. As they purchased homes and frequented ethnic shopping centers and grocery stores, they simultaneously encountered suspicion and occasional hostility from long-time residents. In an era of globalization of the economy and in the context of an increasingly large Asian immigration, Fong has depicted a community that is an apt example of multiracial, multiethnic suburbs in America in the future.

The Recent Era of Immigration to the United States, 1965 to the Present

ELLIOTT BARKAN

Challenged by dramatic domestic and international developments, the United States embarked upon a series of immigration reforms as profound in their impact as those of the 1920s. First, Congress abandoned the National Origins System in 1965. Second, in response to the fall of Vietnam in 1975 and the exodus of refugees, Congress was compelled by 1980 to define a more coherent refugee policy. Third, after protracted debate, the government confronted its inability (and in

From *And Still They Come: Immigrants and American Society 1920 to the 1990s* by Elliot Robert Barkan, pp. 115–143, copyright © 1996 Harlan Davidson, Inc. Reprinted by permission.

some respects its unwillingness) to control more thoroughly the presence of un-documented aliens and enacted a sweeping amnesty program in 1986. Finally, in an effort to resolve the demands of many pressure groups, and at the same time to place an overall "cap" on admissions, Congress approved an omnibus immigration act in 1990.

Legislative Reforms: 1965–1986

The piecemeal erosion of the National Origins System since the end of World War II rendered obsolete what many Americans had come to feel was no longer neces-sary, namely severe restrictions on the ethnic composition of newcomers. The overhaul of that system was finally achieved by President Lyndon B. Johnson in 1965. However, the reforms were not intended to alter radically the country's for-eign-born population—which had dropped from 14.7 percent of the nation's total in 1910 to merely 5.4 percent in 1960 (9.74 million persons). Indeed, congres-sional leaders of the bill explicitly argued that no such changes were anticipated. Still, what global events had made compelling, the Civil Rights Movement and other political realities had now made more expedient: a significant retreat from the earlier nativism—but not without compromises.

The Immigration and Nationality Act of October 1965 defined the procedures under which 15.53 million immigrants became admitted to the United States dur-ing the twenty-six fiscal years between 1966 and 1991. It was then modified but not fundamentally altered by the Immigration Act of November 1990 (effective October 1, 1991), by which another 1.88 million were admitted in 1992–93. . . .

The preferences were revised and made uniform for all the nations in the East-ern Hemisphere, abolishing the national origins formula and other provisions dis-criminating against Asians and Africans. The new ceiling of 170,000 visas con-tained a 20,000-per-country limit. . . . The 1965 Act emphasized family reunification over job qualifications. In addition, it included a nonpreference op-tion for those without family ties or needed skills and an adjustment of status op-tion for those who entered as nonimmigrants and then applied for permanent resi-dence—such as tourists, students, or temporary workers. With respect to immigrants from within the Western Hemisphere, the law imposed for the first time a maximum of 120,000 persons. In 1978, Congress combined all the provi-sions into one uniform, worldwide system.

Meanwhile, events following the upheavals in Cuba and Southeast Asia starkly revealed the absence of a coherent U.S. refugee policy and the presence of an ad hoc approach that had been almost entirely concerned with those fleeing Communist regimes. The Refugee Act of March 1980 incorporated the United Na-tions' definition of a refugee—any person unable or unwilling to return to his or her native land "because of persecution, or a well-founded fear of persecution"—and provided for a "normal" (but flexible) admission level of fifty thousand refugees per year. Also inserted into the bill was a new provision whereby each year five thousand persons already in the country could apply for political asylum.

A year later, in 1981, the Select Commission on Immigration and Refugee Pol-icy submitted to Congress a series of recommendations that included amnesty for undocumented aliens, along with sanctions against employers who knowingly hired such persons. Five years of intense debates and differing proposals pitted growers, unions, religious groups, African and Latino Americans, and anti-immigration lobbyists in varying alliances. The resulting Immigration Reform and Control Act of November 1986 (IRCA) was an extraordinary piece of compromise legislation. It provided for the legalization (amnesty) of both undocumented aliens continuously resident since January 1, 1982, and seasonal agricultural workers (Special Agricultural Workers, or SAW) employed for at least ninety days during the year preceding May 1986. All such applicants would have to take courses in English and American civics within two years before they could qualify for permanent residence. The act also provided for sanctions against employers who knowingly hired illegal aliens. Unrelated to amnesty was the introduction in the IRCA of a lottery program of five thousand visas for persons from countries "adversely affected" by the 1965 reforms—that is, nations that had been sending fewer than five thousand immigrants annually. Three million undocumented persons applied for amnesty under the IRCA; by October 1993, 88 percent had been granted permanent residence.

An Overview of Immigration, Documented and Undocumented: 1965–1995

From the perspective of nearly three decades, it is quite clear that the composition of the nation's newcomers was unexpectedly altered by the 1965 legislation, and, yet, the motives for migrating remained both somewhat new and classically traditional—and often ambivalent.

* * * *

The magnitude of the changes in American immigration since 1965 (when compared with the prior forty years) call to mind the turn of the century, when a multitude of new faces, in ever greater numbers, from ever more lands, flowed into the country accompanied by a rather sizable outflow of those who had come as sojourners, temporary workers—"birds of passage"—and others returning who had not achieved their goals. While there are clearly some distinctive features in the immigration of the past three decades, parallels with the earlier era of mass immigration are also evident in the developments of five key factors.

First, a most outstanding indicator of the recent immigration revolution can be seen in *the broad array of countries* represented by the nation's newcomers and in *the shift in their regional origins*. In retrospect, the 1965 act had the effect of dramatically intensifying some of the changes that were already observed during the decade prior to the reform: the rising number of Asians and the increasing proportion from the Americas. As former colonies in Asia, Africa, and the Caribbean acquired independence, more and more of their citizens sought opportunities elsewhere, particularly those with more education: physicians, engineers, nurses, and other professionals. America's military presence in many nations also continued to generate immigrants who were the new spouses of U.S. military personnel. The conventional reasons for migration—political stability or civic upheavals, economic desperation or occupational ambition, and family reunification—likewise remained powerful forces exerting pressure on potential migrants. Once these processes were underway, migration networks emerged and reenforced the streams already in motion.

* * * *

Second, *the growth in the average yearly numbers* admitted has been dramatic, although still not at the level of the first decades of the century. On the average between 1951 and 1965, some 264,000 people entered each year. During the decade 1979–88, with the single system in place, an average of 570,000 were admitted. However, in 1990–91, because of the IRCA, more persons were admitted to permanent residence than in any other year in American history (1.54- and 1.83 million, respectively), surpassing the prior peak year of 1907.

Third, along with increasing immigration has been *persistent return (or, out-) migration.* The INS estimates that an annual average of 113,000 foreign-born persons emigrated during the 1960s, and that figure increased to approximately 133,000 per year after 1980. In other words, about 3.47 million immigrants left between 1966 and 1993. That equals one-fifth of the total admitted for that period—less than during the early 1900s but still a significant proportion. This underscores the very dynamic, even circular, quality of contemporary American immigration, as was true for the period before 1924. Many more persons than most Americans would guess have continued to come with no intention of permanently settling. A great many West Indians, for example, assume that return migration is simply part of their whole migration process, and they "shuttle" between island and mainland residences.

Fourth, there has been a sizable *increase in step migration,* whereby migrants use the provision allowing nonimmigrants such as tourists, students, refugees, businesspersons, fiance(e)s, or temporary workers to apply for an adjustment of status to that of permanent resident after having entered the United States. Between 1972 and 1985, to cite one period, 30 percent of "newcomers" were already present in the country, principally, refugees and tourists. By the early 1990s, this group had grown to 36 percent. . . . The process of step migration has also involved those who have resided in other countries before gaining admission to the United States. It has been suggested that those who go through such "indirect migration" tend to acclimate to a new environment and begin the process of acculturation more easily than those who arrive with no prior migration experience.

Fifth . . . there have been important *shifts in terms of the cities or ports through which newcomers have entered* and where they have settled. In the decade prior to 1966, over two-fifths of all immigrants were processed in New York City, and under one-tenth at the various Pacific ports. By the early 1980s, three out of ten were being admitted in Pacific ports of entry and only about one-fifth in New York City. Although New York remains the premier portal to America for new arrivals, Los Angeles has become second. In terms of destination, a comparable shift to California has occurred. By 1982–94, one-third or more were planning to live in California and under 15 percent in New York State. High numbers of immigrants also listed an intended residence in Texas, Florida, Illinois, New Jersey, and Massachusetts. Over three-quarters of the nation's immigrants were heading to just seven states.

* * * *

A problem that appeared to have gone away in the early 1960s, the illegal alien issue reemerged as soon as the *Bracero* program was terminated in December 1964. During that fiscal year, the number of illegal aliens apprehended jumped to 111,000. Over the next twenty-eight years (1966–93), 17.4 million immigrants were legally admitted, but 25.1 million apprehensions of undocumented aliens were made (many, of course, repeated apprehensions of the same persons). During the decade 1983–92, for example, 93 percent were Mexican. For Mexicans, the channels of migration—legal, temporary, and illegal—are carved so deeply over so long a time that they have become commonplace options for millions south of the border.

Thus, it is not surprising that INS apprehension data include many repeaters. In fact, a 1990 study concluded that "all migrants who attempt undocumented entry into the United States eventually get in, and IRCA has not changed this basic fact." There are few other places in the world where a border separates two such economically disparate countries and where the pressures to migrate on one side at least equal the demands for cheap labor on the other—where a high rate of population growth, severe poverty and unemployment drive men and women north, even in the face of growing American resistance. . . .

* * * *

Although the number of undocumented Mexican migrants is large and the media attention to their continuous efforts to cross the border is extensive, such illegals are not alone. The INS now reports an average of over 160 countries of birth represented among those people apprehended each year for being in the United States illegally—from Guatemalan Mayans to Pakistani Muslims. During the spring and summer of 1993, news reports focused on ships hired by Chinese gangs to smuggle in young Chinese men. . . . In September 1993, the *New York Times* reported 490,000 illegal aliens in New York State, 80 percent of them in New York City. Relatively few were Mexicans or Chinese. The largest groups were Ecuadorans, Italians, Poles, Dominicans, Colombians, Haitians, Jamaicans, and Israelis. Scenes of boatloads of illegal Chinese being smuggled into the country in 1993 raised concerns, but, actually, more illegal Italians than Chinese were present.

Public anxieties and the level of political rhetoric rose considerably by mid-1993 in reaction to both the accounts of rusting ships run aground, filled with illegal Chinese aliens, and the images of borders seemingly "out of control." Massive efforts by the Border Patrol to stem the tide in El Paso, Texas, and San Ysidro, California, and to intercept Chinese boat smugglers appear only to have forced smugglers with their cargoes of Latinos, Asians, and others into taking more circuitous routes—and usually charging higher prices for their services. The Chinese were charging their young fares twenty thousand dollars each and more, and other foreigners were willing to pay such prices, too. Meanwhile, thousands of Irish, Pakistanis, Filipinos, and many others continued to enter, overstay their visas, and begin the covert, insecure lives of illegal aliens.

In October 1992, between 3.2 and 3.8 million undocumented aliens were estimated to be in the country, with that number rising by about one-quarter million each year. Only three-tenths of those in 1992 were calculated to be Mexican; half were "overstayers"—people legally admitted (usually as tourists) from any country, who had failed to depart. The illegal alien issue is, therefore, neither entirely a Mexican one nor entirely a border problem.

Female Immigration

That the majority of immigrants since the late 1920s has been female represented a "feminization" of the nation's newcomers following the enactment of restrictive immigration laws. This has indicated, primarily, the emphasis immigrants place on creating or reuniting families and, secondarily, the willingness of more women to use migration to improve their fortunes and/or those of their families. . . . The greater or lesser presence of women directly affects their communities and the roles these women play in America. Besides their obvious importance in fostering family life, it is frequently the women who create the networks binding the ethnic neighborhoods, and it is their increasing economic contributions . . . that have unavoidably compelled many immigrant men to confront the challenges to their traditional preeminence in the family. For example, Vietnamese male refugees liked to say that "In Vietnam the man of the house is king. Below him the children, then the pets of the home, and then the woman. Here [in America], the woman is the king and the man holds a position below the pets." . . .

Three things have become much clearer in recent years with respect to female migration. First, there have persisted distinctive differences among many groups in terms of the proportion of females migrating. . . . [E]conomic and cultural preferences within particular groups have frequently resulted in greater percentages of males arriving (as among Greeks, Iranians, Egyptians, Ghanaians, and especially Mexicans). Other groups were equally likely to have had steady majorities of females (for example, among Chinese, Koreans, Dominicans, Jamaicans, Colombians, and especially Filipinos because so many came as nurses). Others shifted toward a fairly even distribution or fluctuated in their ratio of female to male (as among Canadians, Poles, and those from the former U.S.S.R.).

Second, during the past three decades, within many groups, particularly Asians, men took advantage of the new opportunities created by the legislative reforms, arrived first in great numbers, and thereafter began sponsoring their wives. Then, together, couples have been bringing over parents, many widowed. . . . At the outset, many more Southeast Asian refugees were males, a pattern that began to change by the end of the 1980s. More decisively, the overwhelming numerical dominance of Mexican males largely accounted for those majorities, especially among those legalized under IRCA (1989–92). With that largely completed by 1992 and those men now permitted to petition for their immediate families, a swing occurred, with far more Mexican women entering in 1993. A similar shift had already begun with other groups, notably Indians, Iranians, and Pakistanis.

The third and rather revealing consequence of many women being admitted as wives who then find it necessary to obtain a job (along with single women who came for that purpose, Filipinas being the foremost case) is that they almost uniformly found it to be a liberating experience. They were out of the house more often, and they began to enjoy their freedom and to insist upon a greater say over the family budget. Although frequently burdened with the dual work roles of being wife and mother as well as breadwinner, they have made renegotiation of roles and relationships commonplace. With that enhanced status, many women who had initially come temporarily became ever more reluctant to return home or to those former roles. A Hmong man, Shoua Vang, explained: "Some Hmong women would like to copy American women, who have much more social mobility and independence from their families. Back in the home country, I didn't have to do any cooking or house cleaning. Not only that—my wife had to wash my feet. But now I help do the laundry, cook and do housecleaning because my wife is working in the factory. This is a big adjustment for me, but I understand her situation."

Where their spouses resisted, more women were inclined to go it alone. Some single women saw their income as a means of insuring their sexual independence; others simply refused to get married. . . . Some came to aid their families back home, some to escape them. Not uncommonly, homeland conditions convinced couples to migrate, as have many from the Dominican Republic, in order to preserve their middle-class status at home—even if it often meant that the woman had to do domestic work or take menial jobs, or that both spouses held jobs in the secondary labor market in the United States (manufacturing, services, hotels, restaurants, unskilled jobs). Frequently mentioned, too, is the willingness of women to suffer these jobs, and the low-wage neighborhoods that co-exist with the low-wage industrialization, in order to provide educational opportunities for their children. Networks of friends and kin have played a crucial sustaining part in the process of adaptation for such women. Large numbers of Chinese and Central American women in the west, for example, and Jamaican, Colombian, and Portuguese women (along with Puerto Ricans) in the east, have relied upon their networks to obtain jobs in garment, toy, jewelry, electronic, and other light (or work-bench) industries. They have furnished the cheap labor that has enabled many businesses to survive although drastic declines in the manufacturing sector occurred, especially in New York City during the 1970s and 1980s. . . .

The Immigrant Experience

The variety of patterns involving women's migration, jobs, and family roles illustrates not only the way recent immigration has undergone continual changes but also the strains experienced by those who uproot themselves in quest of new lives—both personal strains and those between recent newcomers, older immigrants, and the American-born generations. . . .

As was the case earlier, recent immigrants have significantly expanded the number of ethnic communities, from Dominicans and Jamaicans in New York City to Koreans and Mexicans in Chicago to Armenians and Iranians in Los Angeles. But it is the refugees of the past thirty-five years who have far exceeded those refugees admitted after World War II in numbers and diversity: Among them, Cubans, Haitians, and Nicaraguans in south Florida, Soviet Jews in Brooklyn and West Hollywood, Vietnamese in Seadrift (Texas) and San Jose and Westminster (California), and Iranians and Salvadorans in Los Angeles. Although they share many patterns with other immigrants, differences have emerged, particularly as a result of the horrific experiences that compelled many of them to flee.

* * * *

The Hmong of Laos, the Eritreans from Ethiopia, the Afghanis, and the Guatemalans are also among those who have fled conditions of great horror, anguish, and fear, though not on the scale of death in Cambodia. Political refugees during the past three decades from America's other Cold War enemies, most notably from Cuba, China, the former Soviet Union, Nicaragua, Vietnam, Poland, and Rumania, have had to escape their own forms of barbarities and oppression. Over nine-tenths of the three million refugees admitted (1946–94) have been those fleeing Communist regimes; the major exception were Iranians in the 1980s. Although the nation's refugees since 1960 have ranged from preliterate Guatemalan Indians and Laotians who had never seen electrical appliances and indoor plumbing to Soviet scientists and Cuban air force pilots, in many instances it has been the elites and middle classes who have most frequently escaped first. They had the resources and socioeconomic background that would facilitate their adaptation in America. So many among the first wave of Cubans had been accustomed to vacationing in Florida prior to 1960 that they were regarded as off-season tourists who were initially viewing their flight to Miami as an extended vacation. Prior to 1979, Iranians who would subsequently escape the Muslim fundamentalist takeover after the ouster of the Shah had already been transferring billions of dollars out of their country. That enabled many of these Sunnis, Zoroastrians, Christians, Baha'is, and Jews to establish a "Golden Exile," especially in California, where a majority of Iranian Americans resided in 1990. They fondly refer to their principal communities as Irangeles and Persian Hills.

* * * *

Refugees and asylees have frequently drawn public attention because of the dramatic episodes involving their efforts to enter or remain in the United States. The incidences involving Cubans, Haitians, and Southeast Asians have been among the most riveting. In April 1980, about 10,000 Cubans stormed the Peruvian embassy in Havana seeking asylum. Castro opened Mariel port and declared that any who wished to could leave. During the next five months the spectacular "Freedom Flotilla," a vast array of boats chartered by prior Cuban exiles, brought nearly 125,000 people to Florida. Nearby, beginning in 1972, following the death of Francois "Papa Doc" Duvalier in 1971 and the succession of his young son, Jean-Claude, Haitians eager to flee their island homeland had also begun the perilous journey in small boats across six- to seven-hundred miles of open sea to Florida. Between 1977 and 1981, approximately 60,000 Haitians survived the crossing (and possibly as many did not), with a peak of nearly 25,000 landing in far more desperate conditions in 1980 than did the *marielitos* arriving at the same time. Most Cubans were immediately processed and taken in by the Cuban community, whereas by then some 45,000 Haitians had been detained on the grounds that they were economic not political refugees. Most were eventually allowed to remain, but, for these Haitian "entrants," acquiring permanent status proved to be a long struggle.

During the next seven years (1981–87), 21,000 Haitians were intercepted at sea and most were returned to Haiti. In 1991, desperately trying to flee grinding, hopeless poverty, 90 percent unemployment, and oppressive military dictatorship, possibly as many as 40,000 Haitians took to the boats again. At first detained at

Guantanamo Naval Base, 23,000 were ordered repatriated by President Bush. President-elect Clinton ordered the Coast Guard to prevent refugee boats from leaving Haitian waters. In May 1994, he reversed policy and, during the early summer, Haitians took to the sea once more, desperately crowding small boats. In a period of two months, hundreds drowned, and over 21,000 were picked up by the U.S. Coast Guard and placed in detention at Guantanamo Bay. With the restoration to power of elected president Jean-Bertrand Aristide in mid-October, most of the Haitians who had not already volunteered to return were brought back to their homeland; few were given asylum.

* * * *

The Cubans' adjustment to life in America had, at the outset, been considerably eased by the skills, experience, education and even financial resources that the first wave of exiles had brought with them in the early 1960s, along with their strong ethnic bonds. They were assisted by an already existing Cuban community in Miami (over 105,000 had immigrated during the prior two decades), by VOLAGs (Voluntary Agencies), and by state and local governments. In addition, rather quickly in 1960, President Eisenhower allocated $1 million to facilitate their resettlement, and in 1962 Congress enacted the Migration and Refugee Assistance Act, which ultimately channeled $1.4 billion by 1980 into programs for Cuban resettlement.

The parole procedure and the generous financial assistance provided to Cubans served as precedents for the American response to events in Southeast Asia. In April 1975, South Vietnam fell to North Vietnam and its Viet Cong allies, and then Cambodia to the Khmer Rouge, and Laos to the Pathet Lao. All were Communist forces. By planes and boats, 130,000 Indochinese were evacuated within two weeks, nearly all of them Vietnamese. Three-fifths had had less than one day to prepare to leave. The Vietnamese evacuees were mostly urban, middle class, educated, and/or had been employees of their government or of the U.S. government. Four tent cities were immediately set up on military bases in the United States, and Congress moved quickly to appropriate assistance funds and, in October 1977, to permit Vietnamese, Laotians, and Cambodians to be paroled into the country and to be given permanent residence after two years (as were the Cubans).

* * * *

The exodus had not ended with the first wave, for the Vietnamese government soon began a campaign against Sino-Vietnamese business families, forcing them to flee. Cambodians were starting to escape into Thailand and Malaysia from the Khmer killing fields, and Laotians, Hmong and Mien peoples were crossing over to the squalid camps in Thailand. The U.S. government found itself paroling in 7,000 refugees per month, and then 14,000 monthly in 1980 and again in 1981. Nearly 548,000 persons arrived within seven years. The plight of the "boat people" captured world media attention. Nations being asked to resettle refugees from the camps in countries of first asylum soon experienced "compassion fatigue." The United States arranged with Vietnam an Orderly Departure Program through which about 50,000 people annually came to the States directly from Vietnam (1982–87). Then, in 1987, arrangements were made between the United States and

Vietnam for Amerasian children of U.S. soldiers to leave Vietnam, enabling 18,600 children to enter the States between 1988 and 1993. Overall, between 1975 and 1993, somewhat over 1 million Indochinese were received by the United States. Moreover, by the early 1980s, hopes of a quick return to their homelands had started to fade, and, as the Vietnamese became eligible for American citizenship beginning in 1981, ever larger numbers applied. More than 251,500 received American citizenship between 1981 and 1993, along with over 31,500 Laotians and 28,000 Cambodians.

By 1973, after about a dozen years, the U.S. government had spent $1 billion assisting Cuban refugees. By 1978, after merely three years, it had already spent $1 billion aiding the resettlement of Southeast Asians. No regular (nonrefugee) immigrant groups benefitted from any comparable programs or such exceptional largesse.

* * * *

[Ties to the Homeland]

The arrival of over 2.5 million more Europeans after 1965 meant that a number of ethnic communities would be rejuvenated by the infusion of new populations with ties to the old homelands. These ties did not necessarily connect them to all aspects of the "traditional" (usually folk) culture. As in the two postwar decades, 1945–65, changing compositions of new immigrant groups produced both intragroup tensions and intragroup support: revitalization but also reformulation. Be they bearers of new issues or founders of new organizations, the presence of the newcomers was a reaffirmation of European American ethnicity. It had by no means all faded before their arrival, nor is it likely to do so in the near future.

At the same time, newer waves of groups either not here previously or present only in small numbers—from Asia, the Caribbean, Central and South America, Africa (particularly Egypt and Nigeria), and even [Oceania]—produced a sweeping array of immigrant communities from coast to coast, from border to border, from New York and Miami to Los Angeles and Honolulu. The newcomers have resuscitated neighborhoods and cities, with Miami being perhaps the most spectacular instance of this. The impact was no less dramatic than it had been with the earlier waves of immigrants at the turn of the century. Inseparable from this rainbow of new immigrants have been the multiracial refugee and asylee populations that have likewise transformed major communities throughout the country. And, too, an inescapable part of this reality in a number of urban, and even rural, milieus has been the steady circulation of undocumented aliens—overstayers and illegal entries—from almost as many nations as come the legal immigrants.

The persistence of homeland ties continues to influence the rate of acculturation, likelihood of remaining, probability (or at least the speed) of acquiring citizenship, and long term integration. Even just the anticipation of a return has affected immigrants' adjustment experiences. Nonetheless, interest in the homeland has encouraged some groups to form active political interest groups in order to influence government policies concerning those homelands. And many people have also used personal or commercial links with the homelands to establish businesses in America that rely upon political and commercial ties between the United States and those homelands. The resumption of some such diplomatic ties with Vietnam beginning in 1994 is the latest such instance. In this manner, adaptation, acculturation, and the retention of ethnicity interweave.

In 1990, 60 percent of residents in Miami consisted of foreign-born persons, and its neighbor, Hialeah, had the highest percentage of any city in America, 70 percent. Past patterns persist: New York City, 28 percent foreign born; San Francisco, 34 percent; Los Angeles, 38 percent; and, now, Santa Ana, 50 percent. In fact, thirty-two of the forty-eight communities with one-fifth or more foreign born in 1990 were in California. From Boston (20 percent) to Honolulu (21 percent), Americans faced the results of a half century of newcomers: over 22.4 million admitted between the summer of 1940 and the autumn of 1993.

New Ethnic Patterns of Residence:
The First Suburban Chinatown

TIMOTHY FONG

On an early morning walk to Barnes Memorial Park, one can see dozens of elderly Chinese performing their daily movement exercises under the guidance of an experienced leader. Other seniors stroll around the perimeter of the park; still others sit on benches watching the activity around them or reading a Chinese-language newspaper.

By now children are making their way to school, their backpacks bulging with books. They talk to each other in both English and Chinese, but mostly English. . . .

When a nearby coin laundry opens its doors for business, all three television sets are turned on: one is tuned to a Spanish novella, another to a cable channel's Chinese newscast, and the third to Bryant Gumbel and the *Today* show.

Up the street from the park a home with a small stone carved Buddha and several stone pagodas in the well-tended front yard is an attractive sight. The large tree that provides afternoon shade for the house has a yellow ribbon tied around its trunk, a symbol of support for American troops fighting in the Persian Gulf. On the porch an American flag is tied to a crudely constructed flagpole. Next to it, taped to the front door, Chinese characters read "Happiness" and "Long Life" to greet visitors.

These sights and sounds are of interest not because they represent the routine of life in an ethnic neighborhood but because they signal the transformation of an entire city. Monterey Park, California, a rapidly growing, rapidly changing community of 60,000 residents, is located just eight miles east of downtown Los Angeles. . . . An influx of immigrants primarily from Taiwan, Hong Kong, and the

---

From Timothy P. Fong, *The First Suburban Chinatown: The Remaking of Monterey Park, California.* Copyright © 1983 Temple University Press. Reprinted by permission of Temple University Press.

People's Republic of China has made Monterey Park the only city in the continental United States the majority of whose residents are of Asian background. According to the 1990 census, Asians make up 56 percent of the city's population, followed by Hispanics with 31 percent, and whites with 12 percent.

In the early 1980s Monterey Park was nationally recognized for its liberal attitude toward newcomers. In fact, on June 13, 1983, *Time* magazine featured a photograph of the city council as representative of a successful suburban melting pot. The caption read, "Middle-class Monterey Park's multiethnic city council: two Hispanics, a Filipino, a Chinese, and, in the rear, an Anglo." Another national public relations coup came in 1985 when the National Municipal League and the newspaper *USA Today* named Monterey Park an "All-American City" for its programs to welcome immigrants to the community. Nicknamed "City with a Heart," it took great pride in being a diverse and harmonious community. But despite these accolades, there were signs that the melting pot was about to boil over.

Tensions had begun to simmer with the arrival in the late 1970s of Chinese immigrants, many of whom were affluent and well educated. New ethnic-oriented businesses sprang up to accommodate them: nearly all the business signs on Atlantic Boulevard, the city's main commercial thoroughfare, conspicuously displayed Chinese characters with only token English translations. In 1985, the same year Monterey Park received its "All-America" award, some three thousand residents signed a petition attempting to get an "Official English" initiative on the municipal ballot; a local newspaper printed an article accusing the Chinese of being bad drivers; and cars displayed bumper stickers asking, "Will the Last American to Leave Monterey Park Please Bring the Flag?"

In April 1986 the two Latinos and the Chinese American on the city council were defeated in their bids for reelection. Voted into office were three white candidates, one a proponent of controlled growth, the other two closely identified with the official-English movement in Monterey Park and the state. In June the new council passed Resolution 9004, which, among other things, called for English to be the official language of the United States of America. Though the resolution was purely symbolic and carried no legal weight, it was immediately branded as a deliberate slap at the city's Chinese and Latino population. Undaunted, the council continued to take controversial actions that critics labeled "anti-Chinese," among them adopting a broad moratorium on new construction and firing the city planning commission that had approved many Chinese-financed developments. But it was rejection of the plans proposed by a Taiwanese group to build a senior housing project that prompted a rare display of public protest by the usually apolitical Chinese community. Four hundred people, mostly elderly Chinese, marched to City Hall carrying American flags and signs reading, "Stop Racism," "We Are Americans Too," and "End Monterey Park Apartheid."

The Immigrant Chinese Period

Beginning in the early 1970s, immigrant Chinese became the predominant newcomers in Monterey Park, though both the city's population and its ethnic diversity continued to grow. The 1980 census recorded for the first time that Monterey Park was a "majority minority" city: Latinos were 39 percent of some 54,000 residents; the Asian population had mushroomed to 35 percent (with Chinese outnumbering Japanese 8,082 to 7,533); whites now represented just 25 percent; African Americans, 1 percent.

Three factors contributed to the influx of immigrant Chinese to Monterey Park: changes in federal immigration policy; changes in international politics; and the work of a man named Frederic Hsieh.

* * * *

. . . the landmark 1965 Immigration [and Nationality] Act, . . . basing admission policy on needed skills and family reunification, allowed as many as 20,000 quota immigrants per sending country per year; in addition, the spouses, unmarried minor children, and parents of U.S. citizens could enter as nonquota immigrants. Between 1961 and 1970 the number of immigrants from China (including Taiwan and Hong Kong) approached 100,000; it more than doubled between 1971 and 1980, and from 1981 to 1989 it jumped to almost 390,000.

These increases were at least partly due to changes in international politics— United Nations recognition of the People's Republic of China and ouster of Taiwan in 1971; talks between the British and the PRC on the return of Hong Kong to China by 1997—which drove many Chinese from their homelands.

When the Communists came to power in China in 1949, the flight of Chiang Kai-shek's Nationalist government to Taiwan brought turmoil to the island, which—after decades of Japanese domination—had been put under Chinese rule following World War II. The native Taiwanese are ethnic Chinese, descendants of those who migrated during the seventeenth and eighteenth centuries, but they regard themselves as culturally distinct. Moreover, the Nationalists considered their stay on Taiwan a "temporary retreat"—yet though they were only 15 percent of the island's population, they dominated the government, the economy, and the military. The martial law they imposed in 1947, following a native rebellion for independence, was not removed until 1988; they shut the Taiwanese out of government affairs; their children made up a disproportionately large number of the university students. Political repression of Taiwanese opposition groups was enforced and censorship of the media asserted.

After President Richard Nixon announced plans to visit the People's Republic of China, a pall of uncertainly fell over the small island nation. Some feared that the country's rapid economic development would suddenly take a nosedive, or that foreign businesses would no longer invest in Taiwan. If the country lost international status, could the Nationalists hold power against twelve million Taiwanese clamoring for self-government without again resorting to brutality (as they had in executing 10,000 dissidents in 1947)? In 1979 President Jimmy Carter formally established U.S. diplomatic relations with Beijing, and the United States severed official ties and terminated a mutual security treaty with Taiwan, bringing fear of a PRC takeover.

* * * *

Changes in U.S. immigration policy and international politics, then, help explain the overall increase of Chinese immigrants to the United States. But one individual accounts in large measure for the influx of Chinese specifically to Monterey Park. In 1977 Frederic Hsieh, then a young realtor, boldly announced to a gathering of the city's Chamber of Commerce the reason he was buying so much property in Monterey Park: the city, he said, was going to be a "modern-day mecca" for the new Chinese who, because of political insecurity in Asia, were looking for a place in the United States to invest their money and their future. For several years Hsieh had not only been buying property but, in Chinese-language newspapers throughout Hong Kong and Taiwan, aggressively promoting Monterey Park as the "Chinese Beverly Hills." . . .

* * * *

Many of the first wave of Chinese immigrants to come to Monterey Park arrived in the United States with education, professional skills, strong political and class ideologies, and, in some cases, capital to help them on their way into the economic mainstream. From personal experience, Hsieh knew that the crowded and unattractive Los Angeles Chinatown would not suit these affluent newcomers. . . .

Throughout the 1980s Monterey Park and adjacent cities continued to be popular destinations for immigrant Chinese. . . . Between 1983 and 1990 Monterey Park ranked third among the top ten communities where Asians chose to live. Only parts of New York's Chinatown and Flushing, Queens, proved to be more popular. More specifically, however, Monterey Park ranks second among the choices of those coming from Hong Kong, the People's Republic of China, and Taiwan. . . .

* * * *

Many of the Chinese who have lived in Monterey Park for a number of years are now beginning to move to other areas, often to more affluent communities away from the first suburban Chinatown. Even the less affluent Chinese who replace them see Monterey Park as a way station. . . .

The Chinese immigrants who have moved into Monterey Park in the early 1970s, though affluent, did not cause much stir because they were mostly young engineers and other professionals. They lived in the best neighborhoods and were high achievers who adjusted quietly to the community. In the mid-1970s, however, Taiwan and Hong Kong businessmen started to arrive. . . . Some of these newer immigrants brought not only considerable wealth but a certain ostentation that aroused a generalized animosity in the community. Residents spoke with disdain of the sudden increase of luxury cars in town, of $100 bills flashed in restaurants, of business people wearing tailor-made suits and sporting expensive jewelry. . . .

These newcomers could afford to pay for homes and commercial property in cash, engage in land speculation, and sometimes even establish businesses or subsidiaries to serve as a base for bringing money out of their home countries into the United States. "Let's say I'm a manufacturer in Taiwan who exports one million dollars of merchandise," hypothesized Monterey Park realtor Gregory Tse in a candid interview with *Forbes.* "I should get one million dollars back to Taiwan, but instead I say: 'I'm the manager here [U.S. branch]. I'd like to pay myself a salary of $100,000 here, my wife $50,000 and my oldest son, he's got a business degree, $50,000.' So I send $800,000 back to Taiwan. There's nothing illegal."

In fact, large profits were not the primary concern; the overriding objective was to gain long-term stability over short-term profits. Some investors were even willing to take a loss for several years in order to secure a place in the United States. Opening a business here allowed the individual and his or her immediate family to obtain visas to reside in the United States. After a while, the business owner could apply for permanent residence. And the automatic American citizenship of a child born here gave the family a firm foothold in the United States.

Historically, the pattern of Chinese immigration was for the men to come alone to work and earn money, while the wife and family stayed behind. But in the late 1970s it was not uncommon to see wives and children living in Monterey Park while the husbands commuted across the Pacific. Sometimes both parents stayed in Asia and the children were sent over as students; they were set up with a home and sometimes a car, if they were old enough. Once the children were established as permanent residents, they could help the parents immigrate. This pattern, though not the case for the majority of Chinese immigrants to Monterey Park, does continue to this day.

That Monterey Park has become a focal point for Pacific Rim investment is also manifested by the rapidity with which new banks open in the city. Former shoe stores, tire stores, veterinary hospitals, and even doughnut shops have been converted into banks. A 1990 report shows that by 1989 the combined deposits in Monterey Park's twenty-six financial institutions, most of which are Chinese-owned and-operated, had swelled to over $1.9 billion . . . —roughly $30,000 for every man, woman, and child in town.

The arrival of entrepreneurs and their new money worked to reinvigorate a previously inactive business area in Monterey Park, create construction and retail job opportunities, and provide the push for the city to economically recreate itself in a fashion not seen since the mid-1920s. . . . few townspeople in the late 1970s were pleased by what they saw.

* * * *

. . . though many white merchants spent the better part of the 1970s and early 1980s trying to deny and fight off the new Chinese presence in town, some capitalized on it. In 1980 Kelly Sands, then in his twenties, took over his family's electrical contracting firm, Bezaire Electronics, and turned the sputtering business into a success story by hiring Chinese-speaking managers and aggressively seeking out the new market. Sands estimates that nearly 80 percent of his customers are Chinese. "Either you adjust your mindset to reality or you'd better get out of the way," he says.

A similar philosophy guides John Weidner, an immigrant from the Netherlands . . . When Weidner's Nutrition Center, opened in 1971, started losing business in the late 1970s, the owner hired and trained Chinese- and Spanish-speaking sales help; he also translated product brochures and started stocking many Chinese herbal and health food products. Since that time Weidner's sales have increased, and in front of his new, larger location he posts a sign on which Chinese and English are equally prominent.

* * * *

Effects of Chinese Immigration

As the influx of Chinese to Monterey Park began, most community leaders and residents . . . Together they welcomed the Chinese as yet another group of hard-working people who would naturally be more than happy to settle into the established wholesome life of the community. But because these Chinese were new immigrants, expectations for their immediate assimilation proved unrealistic, and several areas of friction developed—involving business and social organizations, schools, and even supermarkets.

Divided Organizations   When it became obvious that no one could stop the influx of Chinese immigrants to the community, Eli Isenberg wrote a conciliatory column in December 1977 titled, "A Call for Open Arms," which was later translated into Chinese and republished in the *Progress:*

> Twenty years ago, Monterey Park became a prestige community for Japanese. . . .
> Today we must offer the same hand of friendship to our new Chinese neighbors. They should be invited to join service clubs, serve on advisory boards, become involved in little theater and PTA. . . . To become and stay a good community, there must be a structured effort to assimilate all those who want to become a part of Monterey Park. The city itself should coordinate this effort through the community relations commission and call on all organizations in Monterey Park to play their part in offering a hand of friendship to our new neighbors.

Isenberg may have written partly in response to the formation of an independent Monterey Park Chinese Chamber of Commerce in September 1977—much to the chagrin of the original chamber. A great deal of animosity and criticism were leveled at this separate group for their reluctance to cooperate with established merchants. Shortly after Isenberg's column appeared, a series of meetings between the two groups resulted in the admission of the Chinese organization to the regular city Chamber of Commerce and the formation of a new Chinese American committee. . . .

* * * *

Bilingual Education   The impact of the newcomers on the local schools also generated a great deal of tension. Brightwood Elementary School is located in the heart of one of the most heavily concentrated Asian sections in Monterey Park (census tract 4820.02), and surrounded by well maintained middle-class homes built in the 1950s. In early 1978 a Chinese bilingual education plan initiated at Brightwood School opened what the PTA president called "a bucket of worms."

* * * *

In 1976 the school district of which Brightwood was a part was cited by the Department of Health, Education and Welfare's Office of Civil Rights for having an inadequate English-as-a-second language (ESL) program. The department ruled that affirmative steps should be taken to correct the language deficiency of many minority children, in order to give them equal educational opportunity. The district complied the following year with a Spanish bilingual program in elementary and secondary schools and planned to phase in a Chinese bilingual program in 1978.

The proposal divided the Brightwood School—which was 70 percent Asian at the time—along English- and non-English-speaking lines. The plan called for all students from kindergarten to third grade to be taught in Chinese *and* English. Opposition to the program was led by American-born parents of Japanese and Chinese ancestry who were fearful that implementation would impede their children's educational progress in the future. . . . Supporters of the plan, mostly immigrant parents, welcomed bilingual education because they believed it would help their children maintain their native language and provide them with emotional and psychological support and the acceptance they needed within a new environment. . . .

During meetings to discuss the plan, the debate became intense. "Let them talk English," cried out one angry mother. "Why don't they leave the whole damn school as it is?" Eventually, even supporters of the program asked the school board to delay implementation until the district could provide parents with more information and options. The delay was granted, and the bilingual program at Brightwood School did not start until early the following year. The result of months of meetings by the Brightwood Bilingual Committee turned out to be a much weaker variation of the original plan. Only one second grade class offered Chinese bilingual instruction; other Chinese students were taught English by "traveling teachers" at the parents' request.

Asian Markets The prominence of Chinese-owned and -operated businesses in town became an even greater source of resentment. Non-Asians in Monterey Park commonly complain that Chinese merchants quickly replaced many established businesses and catered almost exclusively to an Asian and Chinese-speaking clientele. . . . Chinese have taken over all but two of the town's major chain supermarkets. Bok choy is more common than lettuce in produce departments, and dim sum and tea more readily available than a hamburger and coffee in the restaurants.

The first Asian grocery in Monterey Park was opened in 1978 by Wu Jin Shen, a former stockbroker from Taiwan. Wu's Diho Market proved to be an immediate success because the owner hired workers who spoke both Cantonese and Mandarin, and sold such popular items as preserved eggs and Taiwan's leading brand of cigarettes. Wu built the Diho Market into a chain of stores with 400 employees and $30 million in sales. . . .

In Monterey Park there are now half a dozen large Asian supermarkets and about a dozen medium-sized stores. Their proprietors also lease out small spaces to immigrant entrepreneurs who offer videos, newspapers, baked goods, tea, ginseng, and herbs. Together, these enterprises attract Chinese and other Asian residents in large numbers to shop for the kinds of groceries unavailable or overpriced in "American" chain stores: fifty-pound sacks of rice, "exotic" fruits and vegetables, pig parts (arranged in piles of ears, snouts, feet, tails, and innards, as well as buckets of fresh pork blood), live fish, black-skinned pigeon, and imported canned products used in Chinese, Vietnamese, Indonesian, Thai, Philippine, and Japanese menus. In these markets, Chinese is the dominant language of commerce, and much of the merchandise is unfamiliar to non-Asian shoppers.

Growth and Resentment

For many residents, the redevelopment and replacement of businesses . . . throughout . . . the city seemed sudden and dramatic. In January 1979, under the headline "Monterey Park Is Due for Big Facelift," the *Monterey Park Progress* reported that a northern portion of Atlantic Boulevard was set to "be transformed so it's unrecognizable." . . .

Between the influx of new Chinese immigrants, the infusion of large amounts of capital, the rapid introduction of Chinese-owned and -operated businesses, and the disruptions caused by construction crews tearing up the city and starting new projects, rumblings of discontent among long-time established residents became quite audible.

"I Don't Feel at Home Anymore!"   At first the new Chinese-owned businesses seemed novel, innocuous, even humorous. "The gag was that if it wasn't a bank, it was going to be a real estate office, or another Chinese restaurant," says Lloyd de Llamas. But as these and other Chinese businesses proliferated rapidly from 1978 on—taking over previously established merchants, displaying large Chinese-language signs, and seeming to cater only to a Chinese-speaking clientele—residents became increasingly hostile.

* * * *

[. . .] Many long-time residents felt they were not welcomed by new businesses because they were not Chinese. Avanelle Fiebelkorn, wife of Harold Fiebelkorn, told the *Los Angeles Times:* "I go to the market and over 65 percent of the people there are Chinese. I feel like I'm in another country. I don't feel at home anymore." Emma Fry, wife of Howard Fry, agreed: "I feel like a stranger in my own town. You can't talk to the newcomers because many of them don't speak English, and their experiences and viewpoints are so different. I don't feel like I belong anymore. I feel like I'm sort of intruding."

* * * *

Others, however, *have* nursed grievances, and white flight has been the most obvious reaction to the changes in the community. While the Asian population in Monterey Park has grown and the Latino population has remained relatively stable, the white population has plummeted. In 1960 the 32,306 white residents made up 85 percent of the population; by 1990 the number of whites had dropped to 16,245, or just 12 percent. When former Monterey Park resident Frank Rizzo moved out, he cited the large condominium complexes on either side of his house and the people in them as reasons he could no longer stay. Prior to the influx of Chinese, Rizzo said, his neighborhood had been a quiet and friendly block of mostly single-family homes with expansive yards. But his new neighbors lived in large extended families in cramped quarters, spoke little English, and seemed unwilling to give up their traditions and settle into an American way of life. Rizzo, who sold his home to a Chinese developer, was emphatic about leaving Monterey Park: "What I might do is hang a little American flag on my truck and drive through town on my way out and wave goodbye to all my old friends. . . . I'm moving far away from here."

Latinos in Monterey Park too were concerned that they were losing the integrated community they thought they'd moved into. David Barron has lived in the city since 1964 and raised his family there. Previously, he attended nearby East Los Angeles Community College and California State University, Los Angeles. He still remembers when Monterey Park was referred to as the "Mexican Beverly Hills." Fluent in Spanish and proud of his heritage, Barron thought he had found the ideal integrated community. He is still involved in many of the city's social and civic activities and has no immediate plans to move, but he misses the diversity he initially found in the town. "I would like to see a balance maintained," he explains. "I cannot live in a mono-ethnic community. I wouldn't want to live in an all-Hispanic . . . or all-Chinese . . . or all-white community. I want to live in a mixed community."

Like the Latinos who had settled in Monterey Park, long-time Asian American residents had lived their entire lives believing in the "American Dream" that proclaimed just rewards for hard work and initiative. It was an affront to their sensibilities to see so many newcomers acquire the fruits of a material society seemingly without having to struggle. The newcomer Chinese were simply not playing by the rules of assimilation: they bought property, started businesses and banks, and built shopping malls as soon as they arrived—and many of them didn't even speak English! . . .

The resentment of the older Latinos and Asian Americans who had experienced racial segregation and witnessed the civil rights struggles of the 1960s also stemmed from a feeling that Monterey Park's new Chinese immigrants were taking for granted the equality won by the struggles of others. Yee says: "I don't mind the people too much, don't get me wrong; I am of Chinese descent. But the thing is, you get these people with this attitude. . . . they think [everything] was like this all the time. It wasn't. I hear people say, 'China got strong and now the United States and the rest of the world has more respect for us.' Maybe so, but . . . if it wasn't for some of these guys [people of color born in the United States] who squawked about it, went into the service, these changes wouldn't happen. You got the blacks and Mexicans, they all helped change the government. . . . That attitude [among new Chinese immigrants] just burns me up."

Backlash

More than anything else, it seemed, the change that long-time Monterey Park residents resented most was the unsettling presence of an unfamiliar language. . . . Business signs display Chinese characters, Chinese is spoken in the streets, and Chinese music is piped through public address systems in many businesses. Manifestations of the animosity aroused by such prominent display of Chinese language and culture can be traced back to the early 1980s.

Vandalism and Harassment . . . Intense feelings exploded shortly after the *Monterey Park Progress,* under its new ownership, announced in September 1980 that it was about to begin printing Chinese-language pages as a regular feature. Vandals splattered paint on the marquee and smashed windows in Frederic Hsieh's movie theater and other Chinese-language theaters in the area. The *Progress* and its sister newspaper, the *Alhambra Post-Advocate,* were also victims of vandalism and hate mail. One letter, flourishing unproven statistics, derogatory language, and outright threats, was signed by the Alhambra Ku Klux Klan:

> American freedom is being violated.   We can't even see American movies in our own city. The problem originates from the boat people. All those damn chinks. . . . Three-fourths of Monterey Park population aren't even American citizens and are here on visas. To top that off, Monterey Park has the second highest Oriental population in America. . . . It is unjust to print an American paper in chink language. . . . There will be trouble with your paper if you continue to kiss their asses. . . . KKK Alhambra aims to kick the ass not kiss ass. So if you continue [to] roll out the Chinese RED carpet, do so at your own risk. The worst is yet to come.

. . . a chill swept through the Chinese community at what they perceived to be an anti-Chinese backlash.

Chinese immigrant children entering the schools in Monterey Park and surrounding areas quickly became targets of harassment and playground pranks. "I remember my daughter sharing with me all the plights she went through," says Loretta Huang. "White boys were tripping her on the school bus, they were hitting her with throwaway paper, pouring chocolate milk over her hair." Huang . . . arrived in this country in 1979 with two young children and no job. Her husband, a history professor, stayed in Taiwan and visits his transplanted family about four times a year. Wanting the best possible opportunities for their children, the Huangs had jointly decided that emigrating to the United States would be the best thing for them. As a working single parent, however, Loretta Huang has found life very difficult. "It is not true that all Asians come to the United States with suitcases . . . full of cash. I came here with very limited resources. Many of us were in education and public service; I was not in business." . . .

As an ESL teacher and a counselor . . ., Huang also saw firsthand the hostility toward other Asian immigrants. In fact, problems there became so great that in 1981 a group of citizens decided to confront the issue head on. Mancha Kurilich, a school board member and Monterey Park resident, and Bill Gay, juvenile division officer for the police department, created the Human Services Task Force, whose first action was to sponsor a "Youth Values Day Workshop" for a group of sixty Latino, Asian, and white sixth and seventh graders from the Alhambra and Garvey school districts. "I feel there are problems all over the community," Kurilich told the *Monterey Park Progress* in August 1981. "There's an undercurrent of hostility toward ethnic groups. I think it's all underground, and nobody really likes to talk about it." The purpose of the workshop was to get young students to identify with their own cultural backgrounds and values, and then help them relate to those with different cultural backgrounds.

* * * *

A New Era of Transition

In 1960 the population of Monterey Park was 85 percent white, 12 percent Hispanic, and only 3 percent Asian American. By the year 2000 the population could easily be 80 percent Asian (mostly immigrant and American-born Chinese) and only 3 percent white. In other words, by the end of the century, Chinese immigrants will likely have completed their shift from marginal to mainstream population in the city.

An obvious sign of this transition came on February 8, 1992, when Monterey Park and neighboring Alhambra jointly sponsored the first Chinese New Year parade ever held in the area. An estimated 35,000 spectators showed up to celebrate the Year of the Monkey—smaller than the number who attended the parade in Los Angeles' Chinatown but far larger than the number who attend the annual "Play Days" parade marking Monterey Park's birthday. Over $60,000 in donations from private businesses throughout the San Gabriel Valley was raised for the festive event, including an $18,000 contribution from the long-distance telephone company AT&T. The celebration was also shown live over a privately owned cable television station with commentary in Mandarin.

Though race and ethnicity issues have clearly been used as political organizing tools and weapons, what sets Monterey Park apart are the new class dynamics and the diversity of the Chinese living there, within a rapidly shifting global economy. In short, the changes in race and ethnic relations in Monterey Park can be explained in terms of shifts in the primary sector of the broader economy. The city demonstrates on a community level that race relations have entered an era of transition. More broadly, this transition can be seen in the fluidity of power relations between and among races and classes. Old theoretical dichotomies of black versus white, minority versus majority, do not adequately address the rising inter- and intra-ethnic differences brought about in part by the infusion of highly affluent Asians from Pacific Rim localities since 1965.

Globalization of the economy and long-term U.S. partnership with Asian people and nations are facts that will not go away. The worst-case scenario would be the triumph of economic and social nativism. The challenge in this era of transition is to develop responsible public policy through a better understanding of the international, multiracial, multicultural, and dynamic class reality exemplified by Monterey Park.

FURTHER READING

Nancy Abelmann and John Lie, *Blue Dreams: Korean Americans and the Los Angeles Riots* (1995).

Sucheng Chan, *Hmong Means Free: Life in Laos and America* (1994).

Ted Conover, *Coyotes: A Journey Through the Secret World of America's Illegal Aliens* (1987).

Carlos Cortés, ed., *Cuban Exiles in the United States* (1980).

Carlos Cortés, ed., *Regional Perspectives of the Puerto Rican Experience* (1980).

Roger Daniels, *Asian America: The Chinese and Japanese in the United States Since 1950* (1988).

Roger Daniels, *A History of Indian Immigration to the United States* (1989).

Virginia R. Dominguez, *From Neighbor to Stranger: The Dilemma of Caribbean Peoples in the United States* (1975).

James T. Fawcett and Benjamin Carino, eds., *Pacific Bridges: The New Immigration and the Pacific Islands* (1987).

Joseph P. Fitzpatrick, *Puerto Rican Americans* (1971).

Timothy Fong, *The First Suburban Chinatown: The Remaking of Monterey Park, California* (1994).

James Freeman, *Hearts of Sorrow: Vietnamese American Lives* (1989).

Lawrence Fuchs, *The American Kaleidoscope: Race, Ethnicity and the Civic Culture* (1990).

Lawrence Fuchs, "The Reaction of Black Americans to Immigration," in Virginia Yans-McLaughlin, ed., *Immigration Reconsidered*, 293–314.

Nathan Glazer, *Clamor at the Gates: The New American Immigration* (1985).

Kim Ilsoo, *New Urban Immigrants: The Korean Community in New York* (1981).

Joan Jensen, *Passage from India: Asian Indian Immigrants in North* (1988).

Philip Kasnitz, *Caribbean New York: Black Immigrants and the Politics of Race* (1992).

Elaine Kim, *East to America: Korean American Life Stories* (1996).

Harry H. L. Kitano and Roger Daniels, *Asian Americans: Emerging Minorities* (1988).

Virginia Sanchez Korrol, *From Colonia to Community: The History of Puerto Ricans in New York City, 1917–1948* (1983).

Peter Kwong, *The New Chinatown* (1987).

Michael Laguerre, *American Odyssey: Haitians in New York City* (1981).

Ivan Light and Edna Bonacich, *Immigrant Entrepreneurs: Koreans in Los Angeles, 1965–82* (1988).

Luciano Mangiafico, *Contemporary American Immigrants: Patterns of Filipino, Korean, and Chinese Settlement in the United States* (1988).

Thomas Muller and Thomas J. Espenshade, *The Fourth Wave: California's Newest Immigrants* (1985).

Paul Ong, Edna Bonacich, and Lucie Cheng, *The New Asian Immigration in Los Angeles and Global Restructuring* (1994).

Alejandro Portes and Ruben G. Rumbaut, *Immigrant America: A Portrait* (1990).

Alejandro Portes and Robert Bach, *Latin Journey: Cuban and Mexican Immigrants in the U.S.* (1985).

David Reimers, *Still the Golden Door: The Third World Comes to America* (1985).

Parmatma Saran, *The Asian Indian Experience in the United States* (1985).

John Tewhula, *Voices from Indochina: The Southeast Asian Refugee Experience in the United States* (1989).

Reed Ueda, *Postwar Immigrant America: A Social History* (1994).